Not often does a man come on the scene such as S. R. Driver. It does seem that often one man is blessed beyond his own need, but we are grateful for such men.

Driver was born in 1846 at Southampton. His education came from Winchester and Oxford. After graduation from Oxford he was invited to teach there, and did so the remainder of his days. His crowning achievement in life was the compilation of the Hebrew Lexicon with fellow scholars Francis Brown and Charles A. Briggs. That project alone was 23 years in the making. All current Hebrew scholars are indebted to them.

The first edition of this book was published in 1889 and the second in 1912. This is an exact reprint of the second edition. Some of the maps have been reduced in size, for the sake of the printers. Virtually all modern Bibles are equipped with a good set of maps, so this should not present a problem.

We hope that this current work will be of use to you in your study of these important books of the Old Testament.

Franklin & Janice Choate
Owners, ALPHA PUBLICATIONS
Dec. 31, 1983

NOTES ON THE HEBREW TEXT

AND THE TOPOGRAPHY

OF THE

BOOKS OF SAMUEL

WITH AN INTRODUCTION ON

HEBREW PALAEOGRAPHY AND THE

ANCIENT VERSIONS

AND FACSIMILES OF INSCRIPTIONS AND MAPS

BY THE

REV. S. R. DRIVER, D.D.

REGIUS PROFESSOR OF HEBREW, AND CANON OF CHRIST CHURCH, OXFORD
HON. D.LITT. CAMBRIDGE AND DUBLIN ; HON. D.D. GLASGOW AND ABERDEEN
FELLOW OF THE BRITISH ACADEMY
CORRESPONDING MEMBER OF THE ROYAL PRUSSIAN ACADEMY OF SCIENCES

SECOND EDITION, REVISED AND ENLARGED

Wipf & Stock
PUBLISHERS
Eugene, Oregon

Wipf and Stock Publishers
199 West 8th Avenue, Suite 3
Eugene, Oregon 97401

Notes on the Hebrew Text of Samuel
By Driver, S.R.
ISBN: 1-59244-470-9
Publication date 1/15/2004
Previously published by Oxford University Press, 1912

FROM THE
PREFACE TO THE FIRST EDITION

THE present volume is designed as a contribution to the philology and textual criticism of the Old Testament. It may, I hope, be found useful as a sequel to Mr. Spurrell's *Notes on Genesis*[1]. The Books of Samuel are not so suitable as a reading book for a beginner in Hebrew as some of the other historical books: for though they contain classical examples of a chaste and beautiful Hebrew prose style, they have suffered unusually from transcriptional corruption, and hence raise frequently questions of text, with which a beginner is evidently not in a position to deal. But for one who has made further progress in the language, they afford an admirable field for study: they familiarize him with many of the most characteristic idioms of the language, and at the same time introduce him to the grounds and principles of the textual criticism of the Old Testament. The idiomatic knowledge of Hebrew is best acquired by an attentive and repeated study of the Hebrew *prose* writers; and I have made it my aim throughout not merely to explain (so far as this was possible[2]) the text of the Books of Samuel, but also to point out and illustrate, as fully as seemed needful, the principal idiomatic usages which they exemplify. In the Introduction I have sought to bring within reach of the student materials—especially relating to Inscriptions — often with difficulty accessible, including matter which, at least to some readers, will probably be new. More space could easily have been

---

[1] Clarendon Press, 1887 ; ed. 2, 1896.

[2] For there are some passages which—from whatever cause—defy, or elude, explanation.

devoted to the subject of the Ancient Versions ; but enough, I hope, will have been said to illustrate their character, and their value to the student of the Old Testament. Historical questions, and questions touching the structure of the Books of Samuel, lying outside the plan of the work, have been noticed only incidentally: I have, however, articulated the two Books in a manner, the utility of which will, I hope, appear to those readers who proceed to the study of the sources of which they are composed.

A portion of the volume was already in type, when the loan of some MS. notes of the late Prof. Duncan H. Weir, extending as far as 2 Sam. 4, 13 [1], was offered to me. Knowing, from the extracts in Prof. Cheyne's *Isaiah* (1884), the value of Dr. Weir's suggestions, I thankfully availed myself of the offer. The notes, I found, were less complete than I had expected ; and though I gladly quoted from them what I could, I did not obtain from them as much assistance as I had hoped.

It remains to speak briefly of the history of the textual criticism of the Books of Samuel. To Otto Thenius [2] belongs the merit of having been the first to point out systematically how the Septuagint frequently supplied materials for the restoration of the Massoretic text. His Commentary is eminently suggestive and stimulating ; and for the manner in which he has recovered, with the help of the Septuagint, the true text and meaning of numerous passages in the two Books, he has earned the lasting gratitude of Hebrew scholars. Thenius' results were largely utilized by Ewald in the first edition of his *History of Israel* (1843) [3]: Fr. Böttcher [4] followed

---

[1] See the *Academy*, 1889, Aug. 24, p. 119.

[2] *Die Bücher Samuelis* in the *Kurzgefasstes exegetisches Handbuch zum A.T.*, ed. 1, 1842 ; ed. 2, 1864.

[3] Without suitable acknowledgement, as Thenius complains (Pref. ed. 2, p. vii).

[4] *Neue exegetisch-kritische Aehrenlese zum A. T.* (1863). Comp. *ib.*, p. viii.

on the same lines, sometimes correcting Thenius, at other times, not always happily, seeking to supplement him. It cannot, however, be denied that Thenius shewed a disposition to adopt readings from the Septuagint without sufficient discrimination ; and his restorations were sometimes deficient in point of Hebrew scholarship. In 1871 appeared an unpretending but epoch-making work on the textual criticism of the Old Testament—the monograph of Julius Wellhausen on 'The Text of the Books of Samuel.' The importance of this book lies in particular in the strictness with which it emphasizes the *discriminating* use of the Ancient Versions for purposes of textual criticism. With rare acumen and sagacity, Wellhausen compares the Massoretic text with the Ancient Versions (specially with the Septuagint), and elicits from the comparison the principles that must have operated, on the one hand in the process of *translation*, on the other in the *transmission* both of the Hebrew text itself and of the corresponding Ancient Version. He thus sets in its true light the crucial distinction between renderings *which presuppose a different Hebrew original,* and those which do not do this, but are due to other causes ; and shews further that both texts, the Massoretic text as well as that of the Septuagint, have received modification (chiefly in the form of harmonistic or other additions), though in unequal degrees, in the process of transmission. Naturally he endorses a large number of Thenius' restorations; but others he subjects to a keen criticism, shewing that they do not rest upon a substantial basis. Wellhausen's scholarship is fine: his judgement is rarely at fault ; and in the critical treatment of the text, I have been strongly sensible of the value of his guidance. But I have uniformly maintained an independent judgement, whether towards Wellhausen or other scholars ; and I have been careful to adopt nothing of importance, from whatever source, without acknowledgement at the time.

The fact that valuable original readings are preserved by the Septuagint or other Versions has been recognized also by Grätz[1], Stade[2], and other scholars: in this country by Mr. (now Professor) Kirkpatrick[3], in his Commentary on the Books of Samuel in the *Cambridge Bible for Schools and Colleges*, and the Rev. F. H. Woods, in an Essay on the subject contributed by him to the *Studia Biblica*[4].

A more recent work than any of these, also dealing largely with the criticism of the text, is Klostermann's Commentary on the Books of Samuel and Kings, forming part of the *Kurzgefasster Commentar zu den Heiligen Schriften Alten und Neuen Testamentes*, edited by Strack and Zöckler (1887). Klostermann is a genuine scholar, an acute and able critic; and his Commentary has evidently had great pains bestowed upon it. But in his treatment of the text, where he adopts an independent line, it is, unhappily, very rarely possible to follow him. Klostermann can make, and has made, clever and probable emendations: but his originality is excessive; he is too ready with an ingenious but recondite combination; he is apt to assume that the text has suffered more than is probable; and his restorations themselves betray sometimes a defective appreciation of Hebrew modes of expression. But it remains his merit to have been the first to perceive distinctly the critical importance of Lucian's recension of the Septuagint, and to have utilized it consistently in his Commentary.

S. R. D.

CHRIST CHURCH, OXFORD,
November, 1889.

---

[1] *Gesch. der Juden*, i. (1874).   [2] *Gesch. des V. Israels*, i. (1887).
[3] [And now (1912), since 1906, Dean of Ely.]
[4] Oxford, 1885, p. 21 ff.

PREFACE TO THE SECOND EDITION

JUST twenty-three years have elapsed since the first edition of the present work appeared. In the interval much has been done for the elucidation of the Old Testament; and the student of it—especially the English student—finds much at hand to help him which in 1890 either did not exist, or, if it did exist, was either unknown, or with difficulty accessible. If the years have not been marked by any such epoch-making work as Wellhausen's *History of Israel* (1878), yet a number of works placing much new and important matter in the hands of students have appeared : for instance—to name only a few— the two series of Commentaries on the Old Testament, edited by Nowack and Marti; the fifteen volumes which have at present (Oct. 1912) appeared of the *International Critical Commentary;* the Hebrew-English Lexicon, edited by Prof. Briggs, Prof. Brown, and the present writer ; Kittel's very useful *Biblia Hebraica ;* Kautzsch's greatly improved editions (dating from 1889) of Gesenius' *Hebrew Grammar*, two of which have been translated into English (1898, 1910) ; the two great repertories of Biblical learning, Hastings' *Dictionary of the Bible* (1898–1904), and the *Encyclopaedia Biblica* (1899–1903) ; G. A. Cooke's *North-Semitic Inscriptions* (1903) ; and the Papyri of Assuan and Elephantine, published respectively by Sayce and Cowley (1906), and Sachau (1911), which have thrown such unexpected light on the social and religious condition of the Jews of Upper Egypt in the fifth century B.C.

The new knowledge, derivable from these and other sources, I have endeavoured, as far as the scope of the work permitted, to make available for students of the Old Testament in the present edition. This edition exceeds the first edition by more than 100 pages. The character of the work remains,

however, unaltered, its object being still, as I said in the
Preface to the First Edition (p. V), not solely to explain the
text of the Books of Samuel, but, while doing this, to teach
the student to understand Hebrew philology, and to appreciate Hebrew idioms. The increase in size is due partly
to the incorporation of new matter of the kind just referred to,
and to the notice that necessarily had to be taken of the many
new suggestions about the text, which had been made in
(especially) the very ably-written Commentaries of Budde,
H. P. Smith, and Nowack; and partly to the fact that I have
enlarged the scope of the book,—and, I hope, increased at the
same time, its usefulness,—by adding fresh notes, not only on
points of philology and idiom, but also on the *topography*
of the Books of Samuel. I was led in the first instance to
deal with the latter subject by the desire to illustrate from
these Books the force of the 'went up' and 'came down,' at
once so characteristic of the historical books of the Old
Testament, and so vividly reflecting the physical features
of the country in which they were written; and then, in view
of the many highly questionable identifications of ancient
sites in the current English maps of Palestine[1] (to which
I have called attention elsewhere[2]), I went further, and added
notes on the sites of places mentioned in the Books of Samuel.
The notes are brief; but they embody often the result of
considerable research. To illustrate further the topography
of the Books, I have added Maps, indicating the elevations
(which are important for following properly the history), and

---

[1] Except those in the *Encyclopaedia Biblica,* which are above reproach.

[2] See the *Expository Times,* xiii (July, 1902), p. 457 ff.; xxi (Aug. and Sept.
1910), 495 ff., 562 ff.; *Expositor,* 1911, Nov., p. 388 f., 1912, Jan., pp. 25 *n.*, 26 *n.*,
32 f., Feb., p. 124 f. Bartholomew, though an admirable chartographer, clearly does
not possess the philological and historical knowledge enabling him to distinguish
between a sound and unsound identification of an ancient site. But G. A. Smith's
Historical Atlas of the Holy Land, which is likely now (Feb., 1913) to appear
shortly, may be confidently expected to satisfy all requirements.

including all such sites as can be reasonably identified, those which are doubtful or conjectural being marked by a query.

I have naturally, in preparing this edition, adjusted references (e.g. those to Gesenius-Kautzsch) to the latest editions of the works referred to, and also referred to more generally accessible books in preference to the less accessible books which in 1889 were often alone available (e.g. to Dr. Cooke's *NSI.*, in preference to the *CIS.*). I have also enlarged the Index, and made it, I hope, more useful to those who wish to study Hebrew idioms. In the transliteration of Hebrew and Arabic names, especially names of places, I am sorry to say, I have not succeeded in attaining uniformity ; but I hope that no serious misunderstanding will arise in consequence.

Conjectural emendation, especially in the prophetical and poetical books of the Old Testament, is at present much in evidence ; and I venture to add a few remarks upon it.

The value of the Ancient Versions for correcting—naturally, with the precautions noted on pp. xxxviii, xlv—the Massoretic text is now generally recognized by Biblical scholars. But it must be evident to a careful student of the Massoretic text that the Versions do not enable us to correct all errors in it ; and hence the necessity of conjectural emendation must be admitted. Passages often occur which strongly excite suspicion ; and the character of the ancient, unpointed script is such as to lend itself readily to corruption. The fact that a clever scholar can indulge his genius for improvement to excess is not evidence that conjecture, in itself, is illegitimate. We must exercise judgement and discrimination. An emendation, to be convincing, must yield a good sense, unmistakeably superior to that of the Massoretic text, be in accordance with idiom, and not differ too widely from the *ductus litterarum* of the existing text,—especially in the older script. It ought also not to presume unduly that, when only limited remains of Hebrew literature have come down to us, we have an absolute knowledge of what might, or might not, have been said in the ancient language. Conjectural emendations, satisfying these conditions, have unquestionably been made, including some which have afterwards been found to be confirmed by the testimony of an Ancient Version. On the other hand, it is impossible not to feel that a large proportion of the conjectural emendations which have been proposed rest upon arbitrary or otherwise insufficient grounds. There are also many of which it is impossible to say more than that they *may* be right, they are such as the author *might* have written, but we can have no assurance that he did write them. Hence they can be adopted only with the qualification 'perhaps.' The conditions under which the writings of the Old Testament have come down to us are such that the legitimacy of conjectural emendation is undoubted ; we must only satisfy ourselves, before definitely accepting a conjectural emendation, that the grounds upon which it rests are sound and sufficient.

For the typographical accuracy of the volume I am greatly indebted to Mr. J. C. Pembrey, Hon. M.A., the octogenarian Oriental 'reader' of the Clarendon Press. Nearly every Oriental work that has been published by the Press during the last fifty years, including, for instance, Max Müller's *Rig-veda*, Payne Smith's *Thesaurus Syriacus*, and Neubauer's *Catalogue of Hebrew MSS. in the Bodleian Library*, has had the benefit of Mr. Pembrey's watchful supervision : but, notwithstanding his years, his eye, as I can testify from experience, is still undimmed, and he is still as able as ever to bestow upon a book passing through his hands that interest, and more than conscientious care, which so many Orientalists have learnt to appreciate.

S. R. D.

CHRIST CHURCH, OXFORD,
October 28, 1912.

CONTENTS

PAGE

LIST OF ABBREVIATIONS XV

ADDENDA XIX

INTRODUCTION :—

§ 1. *The Early History of the Hebrew Alphabet* . . i
§ 2. *Early Hebrew Orthography* xxvii
§ 3. *The Chief Ancient Versions of the Old Testament* . xxxiii
§ 4. *Characteristics of the Chief Ancient Versions of Samuel* lv

APPENDIX :—

The Inscription of Mesha', commonly known as the 'Moabite Stone' lxxxiv

NOTE ON THE MAPS xcv

NOTES ON I SAMUEL 1

NOTES ON II SAMUEL 231

INDEX OF SUBJECTS 381

INDEX OF HEBREW WORDS AND IDIOMS 384

INDEX OF PLACES 389

FACSIMILES.

I. Hebrew Inscribed Tablet from Gezer . . *To face* p. vii
II. The Siloam Inscription . . . . „ p. ix
III. The Carpentras Stele . . . . . „ p. xii
IV. Part of an Egyptian Aramaic Papyrus, of 484 B.C. „ p. xvi
V. Egyptian Aramaic Papyrus . . . . „ p. xvii
VI. Inscription of Tabnith, King of Zidon . . „ p. xxiv

MAPS.

The Pass of Michmās . . . . . *To face* p. 106
Section of Northern Palestine . . . . „ p. 213
Section of Central Palestine . . *At the end of the volume*
Section of Southern Palestine . . . „ „ „

LIST OF ABBREVIATIONS

AJSL. = *American Journal of Semitic Languages.*

al. = alii, aliter.

alt. = alternatively (to denote one of two suggested views).

Aptow. I, II, III = Aptowitzer, V., *Das Schriftwort in der Rabbinischen Literatur:* (I) in the *Sitzungsberichte der Akad. der Wiss. in Wien,* vol. cliii (1906), Abhandl. VI; (II) *ibid.* vol. clx (1908), Abh. VII (on ancient renderings, and citations, of 1 Sam.); (III) in the *XVIII. Jahresbericht der Isr.-Theol. Lehranstalt in Wien,* 1911 (on 2 Sam. and Joshua).

AV. = Authorized Version.

𝕭 = the Rabbinical Bible, edited by Jacob ben Ḥayyim, and published by Daniel Bomberg, Venice, 1524-5.

Baer = *Liber Samuelis.* Textum Masoreticum accuratissime expressit, e fontibus Masorae varie illustravit, notis criticis confirmavit S. Baer (1892).

Bö. = Böttcher, Fr., *Neue exeg.-krit. Aehrenlese zum A. T.* (above, p. VI f.).

Sometimes also the *Ausführliches Lehrbuch der Hebr. Sprache,* 1866,—a gigantic *Thesaurus* of grammatical forms, of great value for occasional reference, but not adapted for general use.

Bu. = Budde, K., *Die Bücher Samuel erklärt,* 1902 (in Marti's *Kurzer Hand-Commentar zum A. T.*).

Buhl = Buhl, F., *Geographie des alten Palästina,* 1896.

CIS. = *Corpus Inscriptionum Semiticarum,* Parisiis, 1881 ff.

Tom. I contains Phoenician Inscriptions; Tom. II Aramaic Inscriptions.

DB. = Hastings' *Dictionary of the Bible.* In five volumes (1898–1904).

Dh. = Dhorme, Le Père P., *Les Livres de Samuel,* 1910.

EB. = *Encyclopaedia Biblica* (1899–1903).

Ehrl. = Ehrlich, A. B., *Randglossen zur Hebr. Bibel,* vol. iii, 1910.

Clever; but apt to be arbitrary, and unconvincing.

EVV. = English Versions (used in quoting passages in which AV. and RV. agree).

Ew. = Ewald, H., *Lehrbuch der Hebräischen Sprache*, ed. 7, 1863 ; ed. 8, 1870.

The *Syntax* has been translated by J. Kennedy, Edinburgh, 1881.

Gi. = Ginsburg, C. D., *Massoretico-critical edition of the Hebrew Bible*, 1894 ; ed. 2, much enlarged, now [1912] appearing.

GK. = Gesenius' *Hebrew Grammar*, as edited and enlarged by E. Kautzsch (ed. 28, 1909), translated by A. E. Cowley, 1910.

H.G. = G. A. Smith, *Historical Geography of the Holy Land*, 1894.

JBLit. = *Journal of Biblical Literature* (Boston, U.S.A.).

Ke. = Keil, C. F., *Commentar über die Bücher Samuelis*, ed. 2, 1875.

Kenn., Kennedy = A. R. S. Kennedy, *Samuel* (in the *Century Bible*), 1905.

Kit., Kitt. = Kittel, *Biblia Hebraica* (with footnotes, containing a selection of various readings from MSS., the Versions, and conjecture), 1905.

Kit. *ap.* Kautzsch = Kittel's translation of Samuel in Kautzsch's *Die Heilige Schrift des A.T.s*, ed. 2, 1910.

Klo. = Klostermann, Aug. (above, p. VIII).

Kön. = König, F. E., *Historisch-kritisches Lehrgebäude der Hebr. Sprache*, i. (Accidence), 1881 ; ii. (Forms of nouns, numerals, adverbs, &c.), 1895 ; iii. (Syntax), 1897.

Exhaustive, with full discussions of alternative views.

Kp. = Kirkpatrick, A. F., Commentary on Samuel in the *Cambridge Bible for Schools and Colleges*, 1880.

Lex. = *Hebrew and English Lexicon*, by F. Brown, S. R. Driver, and C. A. Briggs, 1906.

Lidzb. = Lidzbarski, *Handbuch der Nordsemitischen Epigraphik*, 1898.

Lö. = Löhr, Max, *Die Bücher Samuels*, 1898 (in the *Kurzgefasstes Exegetisches Handbuch*, taking the place of a third edition of Thenius).

LOT.[8] = Driver, S. R., *Introduction to the Literature of the OT.*, ed. 8, 1909.

Luc., Lucian = Lucian's recension of the LXX (see p. xlviii ff.).

MT. = Massoretic text.

NHWB. = J. Levy, *Neuhebräisches und Chaldäisches Wörterbuch*, 1876–1889.

Now. = Nowack, W., *Richter, Ruth und Bücher Samuelis*, 1902 (in Nowack's *Handkommentar zum A.T.*).

NSI. = G. A. Cooke, *A Text-Book of North-Semitic Inscriptions*, 1903.

Ol. = Olshausen, Justus, *Lehrbuch der Hebräischen Sprache*, i. 1861.

> A masterly work, containing, however, only the Laut-, Schrift-, and Formen-Lehre. The author never completed the syntax. The chapter devoted to the formation of Hebrew proper names is valuable.

Onom. = P. de Lagarde, *Onomastica Sacra*, ed. 1, 1870.

OTJC.[2] = W. R. Smith, *The OT. in the Jewish Church*, ed. 2, 1892.

PEFQS. = *Quarterly Statement of the Palestine Exploration Fund.*

Perles = Felix Perles, *Analekten zur Textkritik des A.T.s*, 1895.

PRE.[3] = *Realencyklopädie für Protestantische Theologie und Kirche*, ed. 3 (edited by A. Hauck), 1896–1909.

PS. = Payne Smith, *Thesaurus Syriacus*.

Reinke = Reinke, Laur., *Beiträge zur Erklärung des A.T.s*, vol. vii. Münster, 1866.

> On transcriptional errors in the Massoretic text, or presupposed by the Ancient Versions, with many illustrations. The author is a Roman Catholic, in his attitude towards the Massoretic text entirely free from prejudice, and in fact not sufficiently discriminating in his criticism.

Rob. = Edw. Robinson, *Biblical Researches in Palestine*, ed. 2, 1856.

RV. = Revised Version.

> The University Presses have issued recently, very unfortunately, an edition of the Revised Version without the marginal notes of the Revisers. This is a retrograde step, which is greatly to be deplored. The Revisers' marginal notes contain not only much other information helpful to the reader, but also a large number of renderings unquestionably superior to those of the text, of which it is an injustice to deprive the public, even in a single edition. Readers of the present volume are asked, as occasion offers, to explain to those who desire to make the best use of the Revised Version the paramount importance of reading it in an edition containing the marginal notes. On the character and value of these notes, and on the best way of making profitable use of them, I may refer to pp. xxiv–xxxii of my *Book of Job in the Revised Version* (1906). In the notes to this edition of Job, as also in Woods and Powell's very useful *Hebrew Prophets for English Readers* (4 vols., 1909–1912), attention is regularly called to the marginal renderings preferable to those of the text.

Sm. = Smith, H. P., *The Books of Samuel*, 1899 (in the *International Critical Commentary*).

Stade = Stade, B., *Lehrbuch der Hebräischen Grammatik*, i. 1879.

> On the lines of Olshausen. The most convenient book for those who desire an accidence more comprehensive than that of Gesenius-Kautzsch, and

yet not so minute or elaborate as those of Olshausen or König. The syntax never appeared.

Th. = Thenius, Otto (above, p. VI).

T. W. = Conder, C. R., *Tent Work in Palestine*, ed. 1887.

We. = Wellhausen, Julius (above, p. VII).

ZATW., *ZAW.* = *Zeitschrift für die Alttestamentliche Wissenschaft*, edited by Bernhard Stade, 1881 ff.

ZDMG. = *Zeitschrift der Deutschen Morgenländischen Gesellschaft.*

ZDPV. = *Zeitschrift des Deutschen Palästina-Vereins.*

וגו׳ = וְגוֹמֵר *and the rest* = 'etc.'

The readings of the Septuagint, when not otherwise stated, are those of Cod. B, as given in Dr. Swete's edition (p. xlvii). Lucian's recension (p. xlviii) is denoted by 'LXX (Luc.)' or 'Luc.' The abbreviation 'LXX' is construed with a plural or a singular verb, according as the reference is more particularly to the translators themselves, or to the translation in the form in which we now have it. In words transliterated from the Hebrew, breathings (except sometimes the light breathings) and accents are not inserted: the earliest uncial MSS. have neither[1]; and those inserted in Swete's edition have no authority whatever, being merely added by the editor in accordance with the orthography and accentuation of the Massoretic text[2]. Their introduction is unfortunate; for not only does it suggest an anachronism, but their presence in the text might readily give rise to false inferences. After what has been said, however, it will be obvious that nothing can be inferred from them respecting either the readings of the MSS. upon which the Septuagint is based, or the accentuation of Hebrew words in the age of the translators. The Peshitto and the Targum are cited from the editions of Lee and Lagarde, respectively.

The sign † following a series of references indicates that all occurrences of the word or form in question have been quoted.

The small 'superior' figure (as *OTJC.*[2]) denotes the *edition* of the work referred to.

In case this volume should reach any German readers, may I be allowed to explain that 'no doubt' and 'doubtless' do not affirm as strongly as 'undoubtedly,' and that they correspond to 'wohl' rather than to 'unzweifelhaft'?

---

[1] Swete, *Introd. to the OT. in Greek*, p. 136.

[2] See Swete's *OT. in Greek*, i. pp. xiii-xiv.

P. 45. Guthe (*Mittheil. des Deutschen Pal.-Vereins*, 1912, p. 49 ff.) agrees that the ' Stone of Help' of 7, 12, set up by Samuel, is not the Eben-ezer of 4, 1, that *Beth-ḥoron* is better than *Beth-car* in 7, 11, and that Yeshanah (p. 65), if = 'Ain Sîniyeh, will not suit 7, 11 f. And on Mejdel Yābā, marked on the Map as a possible site for Apheq, see *ib.* 1911, p. 33 ff.

P. 98, note on *v.* 3, l. 2 : *for* 10, 10 (cf. 6) *read* 10, 5.

P. 106 *bottom*. Conder (in the *PEFQS.* 1881, p. 253) objects to W. Abu Ja'd (leading up to Michmās: see the Map (Plate V) at the end of *ZDPV.* xxviii), as the scene of Jonathan's exploit, on the ground that this approach would have been naturally guarded by the Philistines, and that there would have been no occasion for Jonathan to climb up it on his hands and feet ; and considers the cliff el-Ḥöṣn (= Boẓeẓ), which, with difficulty, he climbed himself almost to the top (p. 252 f.), to be the place where Jonathan made his ascent. If the scene of the exploit is ever to be determined definitely, a fresh exploration of the Wādy would seem to be necessary.

P. 112, last line: *for* Jud. 11, 20 *read* Jud. 11, 30.

I 15, 6. The following synopsis of the occurrences of ר in 𝕭, the critical editions of Baer, Ginsburg, and Kittel, and MSS. and editions cited by Ginsburg, may be convenient. It will shew, among other things, how considerably, on Massoretic minutiae, texts and authorities differ. Fortunately, for exegesis, such minutiae have no importance.

Jud. 20, 43   הִרְדִיפֻהוּ   BaG¹ (v. Baer, p. 102);   הִרְדֻ֯ [*not* ר] 𝕭K.

*1 Sam. 1, 6   הַרְעִמָהּ   𝕭BaKG²; ר 6 MSS., 4 Edd.‡

   *10, 24   הֲרָאִיתֶם   𝕭BaKG²; ר 4 MSS., 3 Edd., and 2 Mass. lists cited by Aptow. II, p. 73.

15, 6   סָרוּ רְדוּ   BaG² 1 MS., Yemenite Massoretic list *ap.* Ginsb. *The Massorah*, iii. 73 ; רְדוּ 𝕭K 39 MSS., 10 Edd.

*17, 25   הֲרָאִיתֶם   𝕭BaKG² 25 MSS., 4 Edd. ; ר 2 MSS., 4 Edd.

23, 28   מִרְדֹּף   BaG² 2 MSS.; מְרֹדֹף 𝕭K 25 MSS., 7 Edd.; מֵרְדֹף [*not* מ] Yemenite Mass. list *ap.* Ginsb. *l.c.*

---

* The asterisk denotes cases mentioned by Kimchi, *Michlol*, ed. Lyck, p. 57ª.

‡ In each case, of the MSS. and early Edd. (excluding 𝕭, which is cited here separately) quoted in Ginsburg's second edition (G²). On the passages cited from his first edition, no MSS. or Edd. are quoted by him.

2 Sam. 18, 16 מִדְלֹף Ba 2 MSS.; מְרֹדֹף K; מֹרְדֹף 𝔅G²; מֵרֹדֹף 4 MSS., 2 Edd., Mass. list, *l.c.* p. 74, cf. Aptow. III, p. 56.

23, 28 מְהֻרַי [sic] Mass. list (but in no MS. or old Ed.; G² *ad loc.*).

*2 Ki. 6, 32 הַרְאִיתֶם 𝔅BaKG², Mass. list, *l.c.* p. 73 (on 1 Sam. 10, 24); ר 5 MSS., 4 Edd.

Jer. 22, 22 תִּרְעֶה־רוּחַ Ba (v. Baer, p. 99; GK. § 22⁸); רוּחַ 𝔅KG².

*39, 12 מְאוּמָה רָע 𝔅BaKG² (v. Baer, p. 110; GK. § 22⁸).

*Ez. 16, 4 לֹא־כָרַּת שָׁרֵּךְ 𝔅BaG¹K.

21, 35 אֶל־תַּעְרָהּ Mass. list; ר 𝔅BaG¹K.

*Hab. 3, 13 מָחַצְתָּ רֹאשׁ BaG² 27 MSS., 1 Ed., Yemenite Mass. list, p. 90; רֹאשׁ 𝔅K 15 MSS., 9 Edd.

*Ps. 52, 5 אָהַבְתָּ רָע 𝔅BaG¹K, Yemen list, p. 93.

Prov. 3, 8 רִפְאוּת תְּהִי לְשָׁרֶּךָ 𝔅BaG¹K.

*11, 21 לֹא־יִנָּקֶה רָע 𝔅BaG¹K.

*14, 10 מָרַּת נַפְשׁוֹ 𝔅BaG¹K.

*15, 1 מַעֲנֶה־רַּךְ 𝔅BaK; רַּךְ G¹.

20, 22 אֲשַׁלְּמָה־רָע Ba; רָע 𝔅G¹K.

Job 39, 9 הֲיֹאבֶה רֵּים BaG¹; רֵּים 𝔅K.

*Cant. 5, 2 שֶׁרֹּאשִׁי נִמְלָא־טָל 𝔅BaG¹K.

Ezr. 9, 6 לְמַעְלָה רֹּאשׁ 𝔅BaG¹K.

2 Ch. 26, 10 מִקְנֶה־רַּב Ba; רַב 𝔅G¹K.

I 17, 17. It was objected, by a reviewer of my first edition, to the proposal to read עשׂרה הלחם הזה, that לחם must be the accusative of specialization (comp. Wright, *Arab. Gr.* ii. § 96), and that the Arabic grammarians (Sibawaihi, ed. Derenb. i. p. 251) in this case distinctly forbid the employment of the art. with the subst. But there are in Hebrew several cases of the numeral in the *st. abs.* followed by a subst. determined by the art. (17, 14 שׁלשׁה הנדלים. Jos. 6, 4. 8 (*bis*), 13 (*bis*). 15, 14 = Jud. 1, 20. 1 Ki. 11, 31 את עשׂרה השׁבטים), or a suff. (Zech. 4, 2); and are we certain that the subst. in such cases is not in *apposition* (GK. § 134ᵇ; Kön. iii. § 312ᵈ)? Or, if in all these passages, the *st. c.* (עֲשֶׂרֶת, etc.) is to be restored, in accordance with the alternative Arabic construction (Wright, *l.c.*), then it will be equally legitimate to restore it in 1 Sam. 17, 17 as well.

On I 17, 40, l. 2, *for* בְּיַלְקוּט *read* בַּיַלְקוּט.

P. 253. Guthe (*ib.* 1912, p. 1 ff.) points out objections to the identification of el-Bireh with Bĕ'ērōth, and suggests *el-Laṭṭāṭín*, 1½ m. NW. of Gibeon.

INTRODUCTION

§ 1. *The Early History of the Hebrew Alphabet.*

THE Old Testament—except, possibly, the latest portions—was not written originally in the characters with which we are familiar; and a recollection of the change through which the Hebrew alphabet passed is preserved both in the Talmud and by the Fathers. In the Talmud, *Sanh.* 21[b], we read: 'Originally the law was given to Israel in the *Hebrew* character and in the sacred tongue: it was given again to them, in the days of Ezra, in the "*Assyrian*" character (בכתב אשורי), and in the Aramaic tongue. Israel chose for themselves the "Assyrian" character and the sacred tongue, and left to the ἰδιῶται the Hebrew character and the Aramaic tongue. Who are the ἰδιῶται? R. Ḥasda[1] said, The Cuthites [i.e. the Samaritans: 2 Ki. 17, 24]. What is the Hebrew character? R. Ḥasda said, כתב ליבונאה[2].' The original character is here termed *Hebrew* (כְּתָב עִבְרִי), the new character אשורי[4]. In the Jerus. Talmud, *Megillah* 1, 71[b], two explanations are offered of the latter term: 'And why is it called אשורי? Because it is *straight* (מְאָשָּׁר) in form. R. Levi says, Because the Jews brought it home with them from *Assyria*[5].' The explanation *Assyrian* is

---

[1] A teacher of the school of Sura, d. 309.

[2] בתחלה ניתנה תורה לישראל בכתב עברי ולשון הקודש חזרה וניתנה להם בימי עזרא בכתב אשורית ולשון ארמי וביררו להן לישראל כתב אשורית ולשון הקודש והניחו להדיוטות כתב עברי ולשון ארמית מאן הדיוטות אמר ר' חסדא כותאי. מאי כתב עברית אמר ר' חסדא כתב ליבונאה.

[3] An expression of uncertain meaning: comp. Hoffmann in the *ZATW.* i. 337; Levy *NHWB.* s. v.

[4] The same term is used elsewhere: thus in the Mishnah, *Megillah* 1, 8 אין בין ספרים לתפלין ומזוזות אלא שהספרים נכתבין בכל לשון ותפלין ומזוזות אינן נכתבין אלא אשורית, i.e. the sacred books might be written in any language, but the *Tefillin* and *Mezuzoth* only in the 'Assyrian' character.

[5] ולמה נקרא שמו אשורי שהוא מאושר בכתבו אמר ר' לוי על שם שֶׁעָלָה בְיָדָם מאשור.

b

the more probable, whether it be supposed to be used loosely for
'Babylonian,' or whether—as others have thought—it have the sense
of *Syrian* or *Aramaic* (as occasionally in later times appears to have
been the case[1]), and so embody a true tradition as to the origin of the
new character. The כתב אשורי is that which in later times acquired
the name of כְּתָב מְרֻבָּע or *square* character[2]. Origen, speaking of the
sacred name, says that in accurate MSS. it was written in archaic
characters, unlike those in use in his own day[3]: ἔστι δὲ παρ' αὐτοῖς
καὶ τὸ ἀνεκφώνητον τετραγράμματον ὅπερ ἐπὶ τοῦ χρυσοῦ πετάλου τοῦ
ἀρχιέρεως ἐγέγραπτο· κύριος δὲ καὶ τοῦτο παρ' Ἕλλησι ἐκφωνεῖται. Καὶ
ἐν τοῖς ἀκριβέσι τῶν ἀντιγράφων Ἑβραικοῖς ἀρχαίοις γράμμασι γέγραπται
ἀλλ' οὐχὶ τοῖς νῦν. Φασὶ γὰρ τὸν Ἔσδραν ἑτέροις χρήσασθαι μετὰ τὴν
αἰχμαλωσίαν. In his Commentary on Ez. 9, 4 he adds that a con-
verted Jew, in answer to an enquiry, told him that τὰ ἀρχαῖα στοιχεῖα
ἐμφερὲς ἔχειν τὸ θαῦ τῷ τοῦ σταυροῦ χαρακτῆρι. Jerome, at the
beginning of the 'Prologus Galeatus[4],' after observing that the
Hebrews, Syrians, and Chaldaeans had all an alphabet of twenty-two
characters, continues, ' Samaritani etiam Pentateuchum Moysi totidem
litteris scriptitant, figuris tantum et apicibus discrepantes. Certumque
est Esdram scribam legisque doctorem, post capta Hierosolyma et
instaurationem templi sub Zorobabel, *alias litteras repperisse quibus
nunc utimur*, cum ad illud usque tempus iidem Samaritanorum et
Hebraeorum characteres fuerint.' On Ez. 9, 4 he makes a remark
to the same effect as Origen. In his letter to Marcella, *De decem
nominibus Dei*[5], he writes, ' Nomen τετραγράμματον quod ἀνεκφώνητον
id est ineffabile putaverunt quod his litteris scribitur יהוה: quod quidam
non intelligentes propter elementorum similitudinem cum in Graecis

---

[1] Cf. Jer. 35 (42), 11. Ez. 32, 29 (Ἀσσύριοι for אדם, i. e. ארם) in the LXX.

[2] For other statements made by the Jews respecting the change of script, and
often dependent upon most fanciful exegesis, see Chapman, *Introd. to the Pentateuch*
(uniform with the *Cambridge Bible*), 1911, pp. 279-287).

[3] On ψ. 2, 2 (quoted by Montfaucon, *Hexapla*, i. 86: in a slightly different
form, from other MSS., in ed. Bened. ii. 539=Lommatzsch xi. 396 f.).

[4] Or Preface to the Four Books of Kings (which were the first translated by
Jerome from the Hebrew), designed as a *defence* (galea) against detractors,—
printed at the beginning of ordinary editions of the Vulgate.

[5] Ep. 25 (ed. Bened. i. 705; Vallarsi i. 129).

litteris repererent הוהי legere consueverunt[1].' Epiphanius[2] (d. 403) makes a statement similar to that contained in the extract from *Sanhedrin*, that a change of character was introduced by Ezra, and that the old form was only retained by the Samaritans.

The fact of a change of character, to which these passages bear witness, is correct: the only error is that it is represented as having been introduced by one man. Tradition, as is its wont, has attributed to a single age, and to a single name, what was in reality only accomplished gradually, and certainly was not completed at the time of Ezra (who came to Palestine B.C. 458).

What, then, was that older character of which the Talmud and the Fathers speak, and which they describe as being still retained by the Samaritans? It was the character which, with slight modifications of form, is found upon the Inscription of Mesha' (commonly known as the 'Moabite Stone'), upon early Aramaic and Hebrew gems, upon Phoenician Inscriptions, and upon the few early Hebrew Inscriptions which we at present possess, viz. those found at Samaria, Gezer, and Siloam[3]. It was the common Semitic character, used alike, in ancient times, by the Moabites, Hebrews, Aramaeans, and Phoenicians, and transmitted by the Phoenicians to the Greeks. This character remained longest without substantial alteration in Hebrew proper and Phoenician: in Greek it changed gradually to the character with which we are now familiar: the transition to what is termed above the כתב אשורי was effected first in *Aramaic;* it was only accomplished at a later period in Hebrew, in consequence, no doubt, of the growing influence of the Aramaic language in Palestine, in the period immediately preceding the Christian era.

Tables of the chief ancient Semitic alphabets are to be found in

---

[1] Comp. the Hexapla on ψ. 26 (25), 1; Is. 1, 2 (with Dr. Field's note); Nestle in the *ZDMG.* xxxii. 466-9, 507.

In the palimpsest *Fragments of the Books of Kings* [1 Ki. 20, 7-17; 2 Ki. 23, 11-27] *in Aquila's Translation,* found by Dr. Schechter in the Cairo Genizah, and published by F. C. Burkitt in 1897, and in those from the Psalms, published in C. Taylor's *Cairo Genizah Palimpsests* (1900), the Tetragrammaton is regularly written in the archaic characters here referred to (cf. Burkitt, p. 15 f.; *DB.* iv. 444).

[2] *De xii gemmis*, § 63 (ed. Dindorf, 1863, IV. 213; cited by Hoffmann, *u. s.* p. 334).

[3] See p. vii ff.

most Hebrew grammars of modern times [1], and they need not be here
repeated. It will be more instructive to place before the reader
specimens of Inscriptions themselves in facsimile. The earliest
Inscription of all, that of Mesha' (*c.* B.C. 900), has not been included,
as facsimiles of it with transcriptions in modern Hebrew characters
are readily obtainable [2]. The characters used in this Inscription
are the most ancient of the West-Semitic type that are known [3],
though they differ but slightly from the earliest of those that are
figured below: the differences may be studied in detail with the aid
of the Tables mentioned below.

Here are examples of seals with Aramaic (Figs. 1 and 2) and
Hebrew (Figs. 3 and 4) Inscriptions, the first three of which are

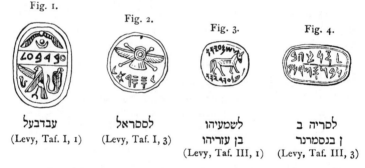

Fig. 1.

Fig. 2.

Fig. 3.

Fig. 4.

עבדבעל

(Levy, Taf. I, 1)

לססראל

(Levy, Taf. I, 3)

לשמעיהו
בן עזריהו

(Levy, Taf. III, 1)

לסריה ב
ז בנסמרנר

(Levy, Taf. III, 3)

assigned by M. A. Levy [4] to the eighth cent. B.C., while the fourth is
somewhat later.

---

[1] There is a good one at the beginning of Gesenius-Kautzsch. More extensive
Tables may be found in Cooke's *North-Semitic Inscriptions* (1903), Plates XII–XIV;
in Plates XLIV–XLVI of the Atlas to Lidzbarski's *Handbuch der nordsemitischen
Epigraphik* (1898); and especially in Chwolson's *Corpus Inscriptionum Hebraicarum enthaltend Grabinschriften aus der Krim*, etc., 1882 (a Table constructed
by the eminent German palaeographer Euting, containing specimens of not less
than 139 alphabets).

[2] See *Die Inschrift des Königs Mesa von Moab für akademische Vorlesungen
herausgegeben von Rudolf Smend und Albert Socin* (Freiburg i. B., 1886); and
Plate I in Lidzbarski's *Handbuch* (above, *n.* 1).

[3] The Inscription on fragments of a bowl dedicated to בעל לבנן, found in
Cyprus in 1872, is, however, considered by some to be of greater antiquity (see
Cooke, *NSI.* No. 11). The characters are very similar (Lidzb. *Atlas*, II. 1).

[4] *Siegel und Gemmen mit aramäischen, phönizischen, althebräischen etc. Inschriften* (Breslau, 1869), pp. 6, 8, 34, 37.

No. 1 was found under the pedestal of a colossal bull at Khorsabad :
Nos. 3 and 4 were obtained by M. Waddington, the former in Aleppo,
the latter in Damascus. The resemblance of some of the characters
to those of the Greek alphabet will be evident : the ר and ס are closely
similar to Δ[1] and Ξ, while the forms of ה and ו become, when turned
round so as to face the right, E and P respectively. The ל and ע
exhibit quite the forms which they still have in modern European
alphabets, L and O, but from which in the later Hebrew alphabet
they both diverged considerably. The characters on old Phoenician
seals and gems are so similar that it has not been deemed necessary
to add illustrations [2]. The following specimens of ancient Inscriptions
from Thera will illustrate the derivation of the Greek alphabet from
the Phoenician [3] : the letters, as is often the case in the most ancient
Greek Inscriptions, are read from right to left :—

Fig. 5.

ΜοΤΑΤΑΝΞ
ΞΖΟΝΞ

'Επάγατος
ἐποίε(ι)

Fig. 6.

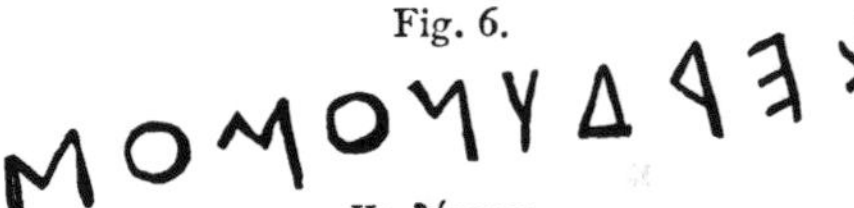

ΜΟΜΟΝΥΔΥΞ

Κερδύνομος

(From Roehl's *Imagines Inscriptionum Graecarum Antiquissimae,*
Berolini, 1883, Nos. 1 and 4.)

The E does not differ materially from the ה in Fig. 3 ; the ת differs
but slightly from the ס of Mesha''s Inscription, and indeed agrees

---

[1] In the Inscription of Mesha', as in that to בעל לבנן, from Cyprus (Cooke,
NSI. No. 11 ; Lidzb., Plate II, A), the ר is a simple triangle, with no elongation
of the right side downwards ; it thus exactly resembles the Greek Δ, and is also
distinct from the ד.

[2] Examples may be seen in Levy, *l. c.* Taf. II ; cf. Cooke, Pl. IX, B 1–7.

[3] For two other rather interesting examples, from the Gortynian Code, and the
Treaty between the Eleans and the Heraeans (*c.* 525 B.C.), see Berger, *Hist. de
l'Écriture dans l'Antiquité*[2] (1892), pp. 132–4 (also in Roberts, *Greek Epigraphy,*
Pt. i. (1887), pp. 42, 288,—with many other facsimiles of archaic Greek inscriptions,
pp. 23 ff., 39 ff., etc.).

substantially with the ן of modern printed texts: the Γ and Κ are quite
the ג and כ of Mesha''s: the ﬧ, which has not yet become a straight
line, retains evident traces of its origin (cf. Fig. 3): the Μ as compared
with the Ν has a double turn at the top, exactly as in Fig. 3, the Ρ and
the Δ are more differentiated, but do not differ in principle from
the forms in Figs. 1 and 2. By turning the letters round so as to face
the right, the later and usual form of the Greek character is (in most
cases) immediately produced. The evidence of Inscriptions thus
confirms the testimony of Herodotus, respecting the origin of the
Greek alphabet from Phoenicia [1].

The most ancient West-Semitic Inscriptions, at present known,
next to that of Mesha', are probably the בעל לבנן Inscription from
Cyprus (p. iv *n.* 3), and the Old Aramaic Inscriptions of Zinjirli, near

---

[1] Hd. 5. 58 Οἱ δὲ Φοίνικες οὗτοι οἱ σὺν Κάδμῳ ἀπικόμενοι ... ἄλλα τε πολλά,
οἰκήσαντες ταύτην τὴν χώρην, ἐσήγαγον διδασκάλια ἐς τοὺς Ἕλληνας, καὶ δὴ καὶ
γράμματα, οὐκ ἐόντα πρὶν τοῖς Ἕλλησι, ὡς ἐμοὶ δοκέειν· πρῶτα μέν, τοῖσι καὶ ἅπαντες
χρέωνται Φοίνικες· μετὰ δέ, χρόνου προβαίνοντος, ἅμα τῇ φωνῇ μετέβαλον καὶ τὸν
ῥυθμὸν (the shape) τῶν γραμμάτων. Περιοίκεον δέ σφεας τὰ πολλὰ τῶν χώρων
τοῦτον τὸν χρόνον Ἑλλήνων Ἴωνες. οἱ παραλαβόντες διδαχῇ παρὰ τῶν Φοινίκων τὰ
γράμματα μεταρρυθμίσαντές σφεων ὀλίγα ἐχρέωντο. Archaic Greek characters are
termed by him accordingly (*ib.* 59) Καδμήϊα γράμματα.

A little consideration will shew generally, how by continued modification in
different directions, the Greek and modern European character on the one hand,
and the Hebrew square character on the other, have been developed from a common
origin. Out of the archaic ב, the Greek Β arose by turning the letter from left to
right, and carrying round the lower part of it so as to form a complete semicircle :
the square ב arose by the opening and ultimate disappearance of the upper part of
the original letter, as explained below (p. xiv f.). Δ and Ρ in Greek preserved
the distinctness of type which these letters shew on Mesha''s Inscription : by the
addition of a tail to the ר, and the gradual degeneration of the upper part of both
letters, they acquired the great similarity of form which they present in most of the
later Hebrew alphabets. Eshmun'azar's ﬨ is almost our Z; by successive shorten-
ing of the strokes, and extension of the angles between them, ז is produced. The
old ﬥ is nearly our L : by the addition of a tail on the right, the square ל is
produced. Mesha''s ﬣ is our O ; the first stage in the derivation of ע will appear
in Plate III. Out of the old ﬡ, the Greek Π arose by the gradual prolongation
downwards of the upper left-hand part of the letter (see the first stage in Fig. 5):
the final ף is nearly the same as the old form; the medial פ merely differs from it
by the turn to the left given to the lower part of the letter, when the end of a word
did not bring the scribe's hand to a pause (cf. p. xix). The crooked ﬧ of the archaic
Greek (Fig. 5; Roberts, 23 ff., 40 ff.) before long becomes straight (*ib.* 30, 61).

PLATE I

HEBREW INSCRIBED TABLET FROM GEZER
(Reproduced by permission of the Palestine Exploration Fund.)

Aleppo (8th cent. B.C.)[1]. For our present purpose, however, these may be passed by; and we may look at what is at present the most ancient Hebrew Inscription known, the Calendar-Inscription discovered in 1908 at Gezer (Plate I)[2]. Its date is uncertain, but in any case it is later than Mesha''s Inscription, and earlier than the Siloam Inscription (p. ix). Those who think that the Siloam Inscription is not earlier than the 3rd cent. B.C., place it in the 6th cent. B.C.[3]; Lidzbarski considers it 'much older than the 6th century[4];' and G. B. Gray assigns it to the 8th century[5].

The Inscription reads (Lidzbarski)—

1 ירחו אסף ירחו ז

2 רע ירחו לקש

3 ירחו עצד פשת

4 ירח קצר שערם

5 ירחו קצרו כל

6 ירחו זמר

7 ירח קץ

I.e. 1 The month of ingathering [Tishri]. The month of (2) sowing. The month of late sowing. 3 The month of cutting (or hoeing up?) flax. 4 The month of barley-harvest. 5 The month of the general harvest. 6 The month of (vine-)pruning. 7 The month of summer-fruits.

1. ירחו. Though ירח ואסף might be read (and similarly in the following lines), ' A month and ingathering' yields a poor sense; and it seems that, in spite of its rarity in the OT. (only once in prose, Gen. 1, 24 חיתו ארץ), the ו is the old case-ending, the 12 occurrences of which in OT. are given in GK. § 90⁰. Was this of more frequent occurrence in the autographs of the OT. than it is in

---

[1] See Cooke, *NSI.* p. 159 ff.; and, for the characters, the Atlas to Lidzbarski's *Handbuch*, Plates XXII–XXIV, XLV, col. 1.

[2] The inscriptions on ostraka, found in 1910 on the site of the ancient Samaria, and belonging to the time of Ahab (*PEFQS.* 1911, p. 79 ff.), are more ancient; but facsimiles of these are not at present (July, 1912) available.

[3] Stanley A. Cook, *PEFQS.* 1909, p. 308 f.

[4] *Ibid.* p. 26; *Ephemeris*, iii. 37.

[5] *PEFQS.* 1909, p. 32.

MT. ? אָסִף, Ex. 23, 16 מִן אֶת־מַעֲשֶׂיךָ בְּאָסְפְּךָ הַשָּׁנָה בְּצֵאת הָאָסִף וְחַג. השדה 34, 22†. 2. לְקֶשׁ (Am. 7, 1†, differently), or (Marti, p. 225) לֶקֶשׁ, here, apparently, the 'late' sowing in Feb. (Dalman, *PEFQS.* 1909, p. 118; cf. Wetzstein, *ap.* Delitzsch on Job 24, 6). 3. עֲצֻר (or עָצֻר), cf. מַעֲצֻר Is. 44, 12. Jer. 10, 3 (an axe for *cutting* trees). In Ethiopic עצר is to *reap.* Flax is usually pulled up; but it may have been anciently cut in Palestine, as it is still about Aleppo (*ibid.* p. 90). Or (Dalm.) it may have been *cut* out of the ground with a מַעֲצֻר, as a קַרְדֹּם was used in time of harvest (*Pē'āh* iv. 4). פֵּשֶׁת, cf. פִּשְׁתִּי Hos. 2, 7. The month meant is March. 4. קְצִר שְׂעֹרִם (2 Sam. 21, 9), in April. The ם is placed below the line for want of space. 5. 'The month of the reaping (or harvest) of all things,' i.e. of the general harvest in May. 6. The pruning (זָמִר Ct. 2, 12) meant will be (Dalm. p. 119), the *second* pruning, in June. 7. קְץ (i.e. קַיִץ) the *late* summer fruits (see on 2 Sam. 16, 1), ripe in July or August. The Calendar is imperfect, containing only 8 months: but this and other difficulties connected with it need not here be considered [1].

The characters are bold and clear, though evidently the work of an unpractised hand. Most of the characters have archaic forms (compare, for instance, the א, ד, ו, ז, ח, ס, צ, ק, שׁ with the earlier forms in the Tables of Cooke, Lidzbarski, or GK.): there are few or none of the curves, or other modifications, which are characteristic of the later forms. The כ in l. 5 is very abnormal; but this may be due to the inexperience of the engraver. The letters at the lower left-hand corner are read by Lidzbarski as . . . . . אב,—perhaps [אֲבִיָּ]דָק [2].

Until the discovery of the Gezer Inscription, the Inscription on the wall of the tunnel of Siloam (Plate II) was considered to be the oldest known Hebrew Inscription. The Pool of Siloam is situated at the extreme S. of the Eastern hill of Jerusalem (on the N. of which the Temple formerly stood), near the entrance to the Tyropoeon valley; and a conduit or tunnel cut through the rock from the Virgin's

---

[1] See further *PEFQS.* 1909, 26 ff. (Lidzbarski), 30 ff. (G. B. Gray), 113 ff. (Daiches, on Babylonian parallels), 118 f. (Dalman), 189 ff. (Gray), 194 f. (Lidzbarski); Lidzbarski's *Ephemeris,* iii. 37 ff. (notice, p. 45, the parallel from *Tosefta,* p. 215, l. 15 ff., ed. Zuckermandel); Marti, *ZAW.* 1909, p. 222 ff.

[2] The *line* above a letter indicates that the reading is not quite certain.

PLATE II

THE SILOAM INSCRIPTION

[Face page ix

Spring ¹—the one natural spring which Jerusalem possesses—situated some distance above it, on the E. side of the same hill, leads down to it, and supplies it with water ². The tunnel is circuitous, measuring 1708 feet (Warren), or 1757 feet (Conder), though the distance in a straight line is considerably less. At a distance of about 19 feet from where the tunnel opens into the Pool of Siloam, and on the right-hand side as one enters it, is an artificial niche or tablet in the rock, the lower part of which is occupied by the Inscription. The Inscription was first observed in 1880, by a pupil of Architect Schick, who, while wading in the Pool with a lighted candle, observed what appeared to be characters engraved on the rock. Ultimately, in 1881, a gypsum cast was obtained by Dr. Guthe, who published a photograph, with accompanying description, in 1882 ³, which has since been often reproduced. A portion of three lines in the Inscription has been destroyed through the wearing away of the rock; but the general sense is quite plain. Here is the Inscription, transliterated into modern Hebrew characters:

1 ‎* * * ‎* * * * * * * * ‎בעוד . הנקבה . דבר . היה , וזה . הַנקבה ‎* * *

2 ‎ק . אש . קל . ע[נשמ ב]הנק[ל , אמת . שלש . ובעוד . רעו . אל . אש . הֻגרזן

3 ‎ה . ובים ‎* * * * ‎. מימן . בצר . זדה . היֺת . כי . רעו . אל . רא

4 ‎וילכו . גרזן . על . נרזן . רעו . לקרת . אש . החצבם . הכו . נקבה

5 ‎ומֺא . אמה . זאלף . במאתיֺ . הברכה . אל . המוצא . מן . המים

6 ‎. החצבם . ראש . על . הצֺר . נבה . היה . אמה . ת

I.e. 1. [Behold] the piercing through! And this was the manner of the piercing through. Whilst yet [the miners were lifting up]

2. the pick, each towards his fellow, and whilst yet there were three cubits to be pierced [through, there was heard] the voice of each call-

3. ing to his fellow, for there was a fissure (?) in the rock on the right-hand . . . . And on the day of the

---

¹ Not the Virgin's *Pool*, as stated incorrectly in the Palaeographical Society's Volume. This is a small artificial reservoir near St. Stephen's Gate, and has no connexion with either the Virgin's *Spring*, or the Pool of Siloam.

² See the Plan in *EB*. ii, facing col. 2419–20, or G. A. Smith, *Jerusalem* (1907), ii, Plan facing p. 39; and comp. i. 87–92.

³ *ZDMG*. 1882, pp. 725–50. See also Lidzbarski, *Ephemeris*, i. 53.

4. piercing through, the miners (lit. hewers) smote each so as to meet his fellow, pick against pick: and there flowed

5. the water from the source to the pool, 1200 cubits; and one hun-

6. dred cubits was the height of the rock over the head of the miners.

The Hebrew is as idiomatic, and flowing, as a passage from the Old Testament. 1. נְקֻבָּה or נָקְבָה does not occur in the OT.: נקב is *to pierce* (2 Ki. 12, 10 al.); نَقْب is *a hole* or *aperture*.—On the use of דבר, comp. p. 192 *note*. 2. רֵעֹ as Jer. 6, 21: usually רֵעֵהוּ.—בעוד as Gen. 48, 7, cf. Am. 4, 7. 3. הית, i.e. probably הָיָת as 2 Ki. 9, 37 Kt.—זדה: the letters are quite clear, but the meaning is altogether uncertain, the word being not otherwise known, and the derivation from זוּד producing no suitable sense. 4. לקרת, vocalize לִקְרֹת, the infin. of קָרָה. 5. The *order* of the numerals in מאתים ואלף (the smaller before the greater), as Nu. 3, 50 שלש מאות ואלף; but the order is rare in OT., except in P, Ez. Chr. (GK. § 134^i), and with אלף *very* rare [1]. 5–6. מְאַת אמה, as מְאַת שנה Gen. 5, 3, and often besides in P (*LOT*. p. 131 (edd. 1–5, p. 124), No. 8; GK. § 134^g). On the *orthography* of the Inscription, see below, pp. xxx, xxxii. The words, as in the Inscription of Mesha', are separated by dots, without spaces [2].

The Inscription has been generally assigned to the time of Hezekiah, who is stated to have 'made the pool, and the conduit, and brought water into the city' (2 Ki. 20, 20) 'to the west side of the city of David' (2 Ch. 32, 30) in terms which appear exactly to describe the function of the tunnel in which the Inscription is [3].

E. J. Pilcher, however (*PSBA.* 1897, p. 165 ff., with a Table of Alphabets; 1898, p. 213 ff.), pointed out the resemblance of several of its characters to those of a later date, and argued that it belonged to the time of Herod. His conclusions were combated by Conder (*PEFQS.* 1897, p. 204 ff.): he replied *ibid.* 1898, p. 56 f. Stanley A. Cook, in his detailed palaeographical study of the Old Hebrew alphabet in the *PEFQS.* 1909, p. 284 ff., though not accepting a date as late as this, agrees (cf. p. 305 *bottom*) that the characters point to a date later than *c.* 700 B.C.: 'if placed early,' he remarks (p. 308), 'it embarrasses, and will always embarrass, Hebrew palaeography;' he cannot, indeed (*ibid. n.* 2), fix the approximate date with any confidence, but thinks a date in the time of Simon, son of Onias (see Ecclus. 50, 3 Heb.),—probably *c.* 220 B.C.,—not impossible. Let us hope that future discoveries will make the date clearer.

---

[1] Add 1 Ki. 5, 12, Ez. 48, 16. 30. 32. 33. 34; and see, for further particulars, Herner, *Syntax der Zahlwörter im AT.*, 1893, pp. 72 f., 74, 79.

[2] See further, *NSI.* No. 2.   [3] Guthe, *l. c.* pp. 745–8; Smith, i. 1c2 f., ii. 151.

For our present purpose it is not necessary to consider this question further. Although some of the Siloam characters do resemble the later, rather than the earlier, examples of the older script (see, in Lidzbarski's Plate XLVI, Table III, the *parallel* cross strokes of the ‏א‎, the ‏ז‎, the curving tail in ‏ב‎, ‏מ‎, ‏נ‎, and ‏פ‎, and the disappearance of the left-hand upright stroke of the ‏צ‎), they are still substantially of the archaic type, and there is no appreciable approximation to the ‘square’ type.

The Samaritan character, as stated in the passages quoted above from the Talmud and the Fathers, preserves in all essential features the old Hebrew type, the modifications being confined to details, and originally, no doubt, being merely calligraphic variations :—

‏ת ש ר ק צ פ ע ס נ מ ל כ י ט ח ז ו ה ד ג ב א‎

In Palestine the old Hebrew character was used regularly on coins, from the earliest Sheqels and half-Sheqels struck by Simon Maccabaeus (B.C. 141–135) to those of the Great Revolt, A.D. 65–68, and of Simon Bar-cochab, A.D. 132–135[1]. The example (Fig. 7) is a Sheqel of the third year (‏ש ג‎ i.e. ‏שנת ג‎) of Simon Maccabaeus :—

Fig. 7.

‏שקל ישראל‎ ‏ש ג‎   ‏ירושלים הקדושה‎

(From Madden's *Coins of the Jews*, p. 68, No. 5.)

As characters that were entirely unknown would evidently not be suitable for use upon coins, it may be inferred that though in the time of Christ the older character had been generally superseded (for the ‏י‎, Matth. 5, 18, is by no means the smallest letter in the old alphabet), it was still known, and could be read without difficulty.

---

[1] Madden, *Coins of the Jews* (ed. 2, 1881), pp. 67 ff., 198 ff., 233 ff.

In the characters represented hitherto, no tendency to modification in the direction of the modern square type has been observable. Such a tendency first manifests itself in the *Aramaic* alphabet, and may be traced most distinctly in Aramaic Inscriptions from Egypt. Plate III is a facsimile of the 'Carpentras stele[1],' a monument carved in limestone, the early history of which is not known, but which is now deposited in the Bibliothèque et Musée d'Inguimbert in the town of Carpentras (dép. Vaucluse) in France. The monument is a funereal one: the representation above the Inscription exhibits the embalmed body of the deceased, a lady named Taba, resting on the lion-shaped bier, and attended by the jackal-headed Anubis at the feet, and by the hawk-headed Horus at the head, with the four customary funereal vases beneath. The figures stationed as mourners at a little distance from the head and feet of the bier are Isis and Nephthys. The first three lines of the Inscription are about $9\frac{1}{2}$ inches long; the height of the letters is $\frac{3}{8}$ of an inch, or a little more.

The Inscription ($=CIS.$ II. i. **141** $= NSI.$ No. **75**), in square characters, is as follows:—

ı	בריכה תבא ברת תחפי	תמנחא זי אוסרי אלהא
2	מנדעם באיש לא עבדת	וכרצי איש לא אמרת תמה
3	קדם אוסרי בריכה הוי	מן קדם אוסרי מין קחי
4	הוי פלחה נמעתי	ובין חסיה . . . . . .

I.e. 1. Blessed be Taba, the daughter of Taḥapi, devoted worshipper of the God Osiris.

2. Aught of evil she did not, and calumny against any man she never uttered.

3. Before Osiris be thou blessed: from Osiris take thou water.

4. Be thou a worshipper (sc. before Osiris), my darling; and among the pious [mayest thou be at peace!].

1. תְּמָנְחָא; *Monḥ* is an Egyptian word, meaning *perfect, pious;* the prefix *ta* (*t'*) is the fem. article. זי = Heb. זה: the demonstrative with the force of a relative, as regularly in Aramaic. But זי (= Arab. ذو) is usually hardened to דִּי in Aram. (Dan. Ezr. passim); the same form,

---

PLATE III

THE CARPENTRAS STELE

Reproduced, by permission, from Plate LXIV of the Facsimiles of Manuscripts and Inscriptions [Oriental Series] published by the Palaeographical Society.

however, recurs in Plate V, lines 1, 3, 5, and, as is now known, is the form all but uniformly found in Egyptian Aramaic[1]. 2. מִנְדַּעַם *something*[2] is the oldest extant form[3] of the word which appears in Mandaic as מינדאם, in the Targums as מָדַּעַם[4], and in Syriac as ܡܶܕܶܡ : comp. *ZDMG.* xxxiv. 568, 766. בְּאִישׁ is the older form of the Syr. ܒܺܝܫ *evil:* comp. באישׁ *to be evil* in the Targums, Gen. 21, 11, and often, בישׁא (emph.) *evil.* עֲבַדת and אֲמַרת are the usual Aram. forms of 3 fem. pf. פַּרְצִי must correspond to what is usually written in Aram. as קרצי (see Dan. 3, 8. 6, 25); in Mandaic, however, the root is written כרץ; and comp. Syr. ܩܽܘܫܛܳܐ=Heb. קָשְׁט, and Mand. כושטא =ܩܽܘܫܬܳܐ=Heb. קְשְׁט. The term will be used here in the *derived* sense of 'calumny' (though this explanation is not free from objection)[5]. תמה cannot mean *perfect* (תַּמָּה) 'because adjectives of this form are very rarely derived from verbs ע"ע (the Aram. form is ܡܟܰܠܶܠ[6]), and because, as the subj. of אמרת, we should expect the emphatic תמתה. If תמה=Syr. ܬܰܡܳܢ=Heb. שָׁם, as in Ezr. 5, 17. 6, 1. 6. 12, it must mean *there, yonder,* the speaker being conceived as in the world beyond the grave, and therefore referring to this earthly life as "yonder." This seems, however, rather forced: and it is perhaps better to adopt Lagarde's suggestion that תמה=Syr. ܬܰܡܽܘܡ (rad. ܬܰܡ) "*ever*"' (Dr. Wright). The word must be allowed

---

[1] See the Glossaries of Sayce-Cowley, *Aramaic Papyri discovered at Assuan* (1906), and Sachau, *Aramäische Papyrus aus . . . Elephantine* (1911). It is also the form found in the old Aramaic of Zinjirli and Nineveh, and in that of Babylon, Têma, and even Cilicia. See the particulars and references given in *LOT.*⁸ 504, 515.

[2] From מָא מִנְדַּע *scibile quid* (cf. מַדַּע, *knowledge,* from יָדַע, Dan. 5, 12); Fleischer, in Levy's *Chald. Wörterb.* ii. 567; Nöldeke, *Mandäische Gramm.,* 186.

[3] Now (1912) attested as early as B.C. 407 and 419 (Sachau, 2, 14; 6, 7), if not as B.C. 510 (Sachau, 52, 11: see p. 185), and also occurring elsewhere in Egyptian Aramaic (see Sachau's Glossary, p. 285), and in Nabataean (Cooke, *NSI.* 94, 5, of the 1st cent. A.D.). Also in the pl. מנדעמתא, Sachau, 2, 12. 3, 11.

[4] So in the Palmyrene Tariff Inscription of A.D. 137, *NSI.* 147, i. 5 מדען; 8, 9 מדעמא; ii. *b* 40 מדעם.

[5] Lagarde, *Symmicta,* ii. p. 61 f.

[6] Comp. ܘܰܐܠܳܠ?, ܚܳܠܳܡ, ܪܝܣܣ, ܡܚܰܠܶܠ, ܡܳܙܝ ܦܣܝ, ܦܡܚ, by the side of רק רך, קר, קל, צח, עז, דל (Lagarde, *Anmerkungen zur griech. Übers. der Proverbien,* 1863, on 4, 3ᵇ).

to be uncertain. 3. מִן קְדָם‎, as Dan. 2, 6, and often. מין‎, i.e. מַיִן‎.
The expression *Receive water* may be illustrated from Greek Inscriptions[1]; and the representation of the bestowal of water upon the
dead is common on Egyptian monuments. 4. נמעתי‎ (which admits
of no explanation) is supposed to be an error of the stone-cutter for
נְעָמָתִי‎ *my pleasant, delightful* one (cf. 2 Sam. 1, 26. Cant. 7, 7).
חַסָיה‎=ﱢﱢﱢ *the pious.* At the end שְׁלִימָה‎ (or הֲוִי וָהֲוִי‎) הֲוִי‎ may be plausibly
supplied: some have thought that traces of these letters are even
discernible on the stone. The language of the Inscription is almost
pure Aramaic: a Hebrew (or Phoenician) element is, however, present
in אִישׁ‎ and קְחִי (לְקַח)‎[2].

The date of this Inscription is not perfectly certain: but it belongs
probably to the fourth cent. B.C. An earlier type of the Egyptian
Aramaic character, dating from B.C. 482, is exhibited on the stele
of Saqqārah (2 miles NW. of Memphis), found in 1877[3]; the stele of
Carpentras has been preferred for reproduction here, as the characters
(in the photograph) are more distinct. Observe that the upper part
of the ב, ד, ר‎, and ע‎ is *open:* this is the first stage in the formation of
the later square character, which is ultimately produced, in the case
of these letters, by the disappearance of the two parallel lines at the
top of ב, ד, ר‎, and by the addition of a tail to the ע‎. (These letters
are formed similarly on the Saqqārah stele.) The stroke at the upper
right-hand corner of the א‎ is almost, if not quite, separated from the
transverse stroke which forms the body of the letter: this is a similar
change in the direction of the later form of the character[4]. The two

---

[1] Boeckh, *Corp. Inscr. Graec.* 6562 : Θ(εοῖς) Κ(αταχθονίοις). Αὐρηλίᾳ Προσόδῳ
Διοσκουρίδης ἀνὴρ τῇ ἑαυτοῦ συνβίῳ χρηστοτάτῃ καὶ γλυκυτάτῃ μνείας χάριν.
εὐψύχει, κυρία, καὶ δοί(η) σοι ὁ Ὄσιρις τὸ ψυχρὸν ὕδωρ. The same wish, *ib.* 6717.

[2] Both now (1912) known to occur frequently in Egyptian Aramaic : see the
Glossaries in Sayce-Cowley and Sachau.

[3] Plate LXIII in the Palaeographical Society's Volume ; Lidzbarski, Plate
XXVIII. 1 (drawn by the author) : cf. the transcription, with notes, in *NSI*.
No. 71. The Inscription is dated the 4th year of Xerxes (= B.C. 482) : the name
Xerxes is written חשיארש‎ *Ḥshiarsh* (Pers. *Khshayârshâ*), as regularly in
Egyptian Aramaic (see the Glossaries in Sayce-Cowley and Sachau).

[4] The form of the א‎ (as of many of the other letters) in Palmyrene is, however,
the one which approaches most closely to the square type : see Fig. 11 below, and
the Tables in Cooke or Lidzbarski.

lower horizontal strokes of the old ה are merged in one, which however is separated from the perpendicular stroke, and hangs down from the upper horizontal stroke, thus anticipating the form ultimately assumed by the letter. ו and ז have both nearly assumed the modern form. ח appears (as on the Saqqārah stele) with only a single horizontal bar: the bar, if a little lowered, produces H, H, if a little raised, ח. On the stone of Mesha‘ (as in the Inscriptions figured above) י appears composed of four distinct strokes (like Z with *two* parallel strokes on the left at the top): here the four strokes are crumpled up so as to form a sort of triangle, which, when reduced in size, becomes the modern י. In the stele of Saqqārah, the י appears still in its old form. The two diverging lines towards the top of the כ, on the left, which still appear on the Saqqārah stele, become a single line, turned up at the end, which in the Papyri becomes in its turn a single thick line. מ exhibits a modification which is difficult to describe, but which, when the tail, as happens afterwards, is curled round to the left, produces an evident approximation to the modern form of the letter [1]. ר scarcely differs from ד except by having a longer tail. ש has been modified, and approaches the modern type: almost the same form appears on the stele of Saqqārah. ת is no longer a complete cross: the horizontal cross-line is confined to the right-hand side of the letter, and is deflected downwards: by the further prolongation of this deflection, and the accompanying reduction of the upper part of the perpendicular stroke, the modern ת is produced. ל, ט, נ, פ, are not materially changed, shewing, as was said, that the transition to the square character was gradual, and not accomplished for all the letters at the same time. The words are separated, not by dots, but by small spaces.

In Papyri, the softer material, written upon by a reed-pen, led naturally to the production of more cursive characters. Here (Plate IV) is part of an Inscription written on a Papyrus discovered in 1907–8, at Elephantine, the ancient Yeb, at the extreme south of Egypt, just below the First Cataract: it is dated in the 2nd year of Xerxes

---

[1] Cf. Lidzbarski, p. 191 ; and see Plates XLV, cols. 6-25, XLVI, 11 a, cols. 2, 6.

(B.C. 484), and is consequently two years older than the Saqqārah stele [1]. Transliterated into square characters, it reads :—

11 כתיבן בספרא זנה אנחנא ננתן די . . . .
12 בית מלכא וקדם ספרי אוצרא ינ . . . .
13 עלידן למובל לנבריא אלה זי כתיבן . . . .
14 לך במנין בבית מלכא וקדם ספרי א[וצרא . . .
15 אנחנא נחוב לך כסף כרשן ז]ד כסף ז . . . . . .
16 אלהא ואנת שלט בפרסן זי בית מלכא . . . . .
17 לן אנת שלט למאחד עד תתמלא בעבורא
18 כתב הושע על פם אחיאב

The Inscription (taking into account the part not here reproduced) is a contract between two Jews of the military colony at Elephantine and a dealer to supply provisions for two ' hundreds ' (companies) of the garrison ; and the passage quoted deals with the payment for what has been supplied : but the words lost at the ends of the lines make it impossible to give a continuous translation. The parts which remain may be rendered as follows :—

11. . . . . . written (i.e. named) in this deed. We will give . . .
12. the house of the king (=the government), and before the scribes of the treasury . . .
13. by our hand (=through us) to bring to these men who are written (named) [in this deed] . . .
14. to thee by number (*or* by mna's) in the house of the king, and before the scribes of the tr[easury] . . .
15. We shall owe thee 100 *karashas* [2] of silver, silver of . . . .
16. the god. And thou hast authority over (a charge upon) our salary, which the house of the king [gives]
17. to us ; thou hast authority to take (it) until thou art fully paid for the corn.
18. Hoshea' has written (this deed) at the mouth (dictation) of Aḥiab.

13. מובל, inf. *Qal* from יבל, which occurs in these Papyri in a trans. sense (l. 9 ; 42, 17. 43 (1), 4 בלני לביתך *bring me to thy house*). In Bibl.

---

[1] Sachau, *Aramäische Papyrus und Ostraka aus einer jüdischen Militär-Kolonie zu Elephantine* (1911), No. 25 (p. 99).

[2] A Persian weight, equal to 10 shekels (Lidzbarski, *Ephemeris*, iii. 76, 130).

PLATE IV

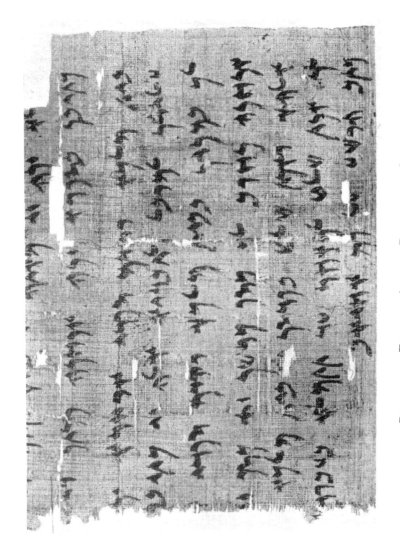

PART OF AN EGYPTIAN ARAMAIC PAPYRUS, OF 484 B.C.

(Reproduced, by permission, from Plate XXV of Sachau's *Aramäische Papyrus und Ostraka*, 1911.)

PLATE V

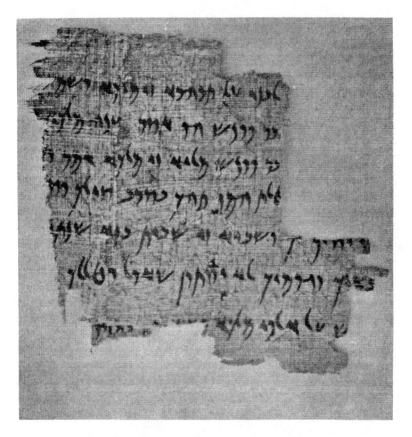

EGYPTIAN ARAMAIC PAPYRUS

Reproduced, by permission, from Plate XXVI of the Facsimiles of Manuscripts
and Inscriptions published by the Palaeographical Society.

Aram., Tgg., and Syr., only the *Aphel*, הֵיבֵל, אוֹבִיל, ܐܘܒܠ. אלה, the form in Egyptian Nabataean and Cappadocian Aramaic, Jer. 10, 11, Ezr. 5, 15 Kt., for the Biblical Aram. and Targumic אִלֵּין: see *Lex.* 1080ᵇ, *LOT.*⁸ 255 *n.*   15. כרשן, כרש¹, as the name of a weight, occurs often besides in these Inscriptions.   16. שלט, i.e. שַׁלִּיט Ezr. 4, 20. 7, 24 al. (*Lex.* 1115ᵇ). פרם, see Sayce-Cowley, L 6, P 3 (=Lidzbarski, *Ephemeris*, ii. 224, 6. 237, 3). The word may mean properly a *portion* or *measure of food* (Sachau, p. 52: cf. فُؤَمَّا = σιτομέτριον Luke 12, 42, PS. col. 3279; and Sachau, Pap. 36 (Taf. 32), 8).   17. תתמלא, see Sachau, Pap. 28 (Taf. 28–9), 11. 17. 18. על פֻּם, so Sayce-Cowley, L 16. Cf. in Heb. Jer. 36, 4 ויכתב ברוך מפי ירמיהו. 6. 17. 18.

As was remarked above, the differences from the Carpentras script are due mainly to the more yielding nature of the material used for producing the characters. Instead of the sharply cut characters incised on the Carpentras stele, the strokes, especially the horizontal and slanting ones, are thick; and those lines which are straight in the stele shew a tendency to curve. And in ב, ד, כ, ר, the part open at the top almost disappears owing to a single thick stroke taking its place: this stroke ultimately becomes the top line of these letters in the square form.

The following (Plate V) is a specimen of the Egyptian Aramaic script on a fragment of Papyrus now in the British Museum, belonging to the late Ptolemaic or Roman period². Here is a transliteration of the Inscription (= *CIS.* II. i. 145 B = *NSI.* No. 76 B):—

1 ... . לבני על תסהדא³ זי מלכא ושמע
2 .... בר פונש הו אחר ענה מלכא
3 .... בר פונש מליא זי מלכא אמר וע
4 .... (ק)טלת המו תהך בחרב חילך וח
5 ..... ה יחלק לך ושביא זי שבית בזא שנתא ...

---

¹ Read incorrectly by Sayce-Cowley (A 7 al.) כבש. See Lidzbarski, *Ephemeris*, iii. 76.

² Plate XXVI in the Palaeographical Society's Volume.

³ So De Vogüé in *CIS.* II. i. 145 B. In the Palaeographical Society's Volume, the word is transliterated תבהבא.

6 .... בָּאלך וגרמיך לא יחתן שאול וטללך . . . . .

7 .... ש על אלפי מלכא . . . . . . במנץ . . . . . .

I.e. 1. . . . for my sons according to the testimony of the king, and he heard . . .

2. . . . the son of Punsh, he delayed (?). The king answered . . . . .

3. . . . the son of Punsh the words which the king had spoken, and . . .

4. . . . thou didst kill them. Mayest thou go with the sword of thy strength, and . . . .

5. . . . . , and the captives which thou hast taken this year . . . . .

6. . . . . in them; and thy bones shall not descend into She'ol, and thy shadow . . . . .

7. . . . . . . on the thousands of the king . . . .

The text, as is evident, is much mutilated. The subject appears to be a tale, 'composed either by a heathen Aramaean, who was hostile to the Egyptian religion[1], or by an Egyptian Jew as a Haggādāh on Ex. 1,—more probably the latter.' The language is Aramaic, tinged (like the Carpentras Inscription) with Hebrew or Phoenician.   2. עָנָה מלכא, cf. Dan. 2, 5. 8. 20 etc.   4. הִמּוֹ *them*, as Ezr. 4, 10. 23 etc. תְּהָךְ, cf. יְהָךְ Ezr. 5, 5.   5. זא (fem.), as Sachau 2, 17 זא באישתא. 6³ זא שנתא, *Répert. d'Épigr. Sém.* i. 247 זא בירתא; = Bibl. Aram. דא (*Lex.* 1086¹): cf. זְ and דְּי, p. xii *bottom*.   6. אִלֵּךְ *those*, as Dan. 3, 12 etc.   יֵחֲתוּן from נְחַת, the common Aram. word for *go down*.

The characters are in general very similar to those of Plate III; but, in so far as there is a difference, they have approached nearer to the square type. The ה assumes a form more resembling the square ה. The tail of the מ shews a tendency to curl round to the left, and the whole letter approximates to the modern form. In the same way the right-hand stroke of the ת is longer, and curls round, so that the letter, especially the one in תהך (l. 4), closely resembles the square ת. The כ (notice ll. 4 תהך, 6 גרמיך) is almost exactly like the square final ך. The square form of ג is produced by the stroke on the left being gradually brought lower down: see

---

[1] There is an allusion to the 'Egyptian gods' in the first column of the Papyrus published as Plate XXV of the same Volume (Cooke, *NSI.* 76 A).

col. 13 in GK. ; the Inscription תחם נזר 'Boundary of Gezer' from Gezer (Lidzbarski, Plate XLVI, II a, col. 3), and the Palmyrene נ (*ibid.* Plate XLV, cols. 10, 13; Cooke, Plate XIV, cols. 6, 7, 9).

The gradual change of script can also be well studied in the Table in Gesenius-Kautzsch (ed. 1910). From this it appears at once that the characters of Mesha''s Inscription (*c.* 840 B.C.) and those of Zinjirli, near Aleppo, of about a century later, are practically identical —only the ב, for instance, being in the latter more curved at the top than in the former. In the Phoen. and Hebrew characters from the ninth to the first cent. B.C. (cols. 2-6) there is not any great change: the marked changes occur in the Aramaic types, from the eighth to the third cent. B.C.; and the earliest examples of the square Hebrew character (col. 14) are developed most immediately, not from the *Hebrew* series (cols. 3-6), but from the *Aramaic* series (cols. 11-13). It further appears from this Table that, of the 'final' characters, ך, ן, ף, ץ are really the older, more original forms of the letters in question: in the middle of a word, in cursive writing, the tail was curved round to the left, producing the medial forms כ, נ, פ, צ; at the end of a word, where there was a natural break, the original long perpendicular line remained. The final ם, on the other hand, is not an original form: it arises from the later form of the מ being closed up on the left (see col. 14; and comp. Lidzbarski, Plate XLVI, II a, cf. XLV, cols. 20-25)[1].

From the immediate neighbourhood of Palestine an early example of the Aramaic transition-alphabet is afforded by an Inscription, consisting of a single word, found at 'Arāq el-Emīr ('Cliff of the Prince'), in the country of the ancient Ammonites, 9 miles NW. of Ḥeshbon[2]. Here (Jos. *Ant.* xii. 4. 11) Hyrcanus, grandson of Tobias, and great-nephew of the High Priest Onias II, being persecuted by his brothers, found himself a retreat among the hills (B.C. 183-176), where he built a stronghold, one feature of which consisted in a series of fifteen

---

[1] See, for further particulars on the gradual evolution of the square characters, Lidzbarski, p. 175 ff. (Phoenician), p. 183 ff. (older Heb.), p. 186 ff. (Aram.), pp. 189-192 (square Hebrew); and the three Tables at the end of his *Atlas.*

[2] See Socin's *Palästina u. Syrien* (in Baedeker's *Handbooks*), Route 10 (end); in more recent editions (revised by Benzinger), Route 17.

caves, in two tiers, hollowed out in the side of the rock [1]. At the right hand of the entrance to two of the caves (Nos. 11 and 13 in the *Memoirs*) in the lower tier, on the smoothed surface of the rock beside No. 13 (Fig. 8), on the unsmoothed surface beside No. 11 (Fig. 9), stands the Inscription, in letters nearly eight inches high.

Fig. 8 (A).

(From No. 383 of the Photographs published by the Palestine Exploration Fund.)

Fig. 9 (B).

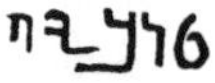

טוביה

(From the Facsimiles attached to Chwolson's *Corp. Inscr. Hebr.*, No. 1.)

From its position, the Inscription cannot well be earlier than the period when the caves were constructed, and may, of course, be later. It must be read טוֹבִיָּה [2]. The transitional character of the alphabet appears in the approximations to the square type: in the ו without the right-hand upper stroke, in the ב open at the top, and in the י and ה approaching the type of Fig. 10. The ט, also, originally a cross

---

[1] See the view of the caves in the *Memoirs of the Survey of Eastern Palestine*, vol. i (1889), opposite p. 72; or in G. A. Smith's *Jerusalem* (1908), ii. 426 (also, p. 428, a photograph of the cave with the Inscription A), cf. p. 427 *n*.

[2] The reading has been disputed. De Vogüé (*Mélanges*, 1868, p. 162 f.), and Clermont-Ganneau (*Researches in Palestine*, 1896, ii. 261), both of whom had seen and copied the Inscription, read it טוביה. On the other hand, the Photograph (Fig. 8), and the reproductions in the *Memoirs*, p. 76 f., and the Plate opposite p. 84, seemed to leave no doubt that the first letter was ע; and so ערביה was adopted in the first edition of the present work, and by Lidzbarski in 1898 (pp. 117, 190). It appears now, however, from the very complete descriptions in the *Publications of the Princeton Archaeological Expedition to Syria in 1904-5* [Division II (Ancient Architecture in Syria), § A (Southern Syria), Part i (Ammonitis), pp. 1–28 ('Arāq el-Amīr); Division III (Inscriptions), § A (Southern Syria), Part i (Ammonitis), pp. 1–7 (Hebrew Inscriptions of 'Arāq el-Amīr), by Enno Littmann], Div. III, § A, Pt. i, p. 2 (Photos. A and B), that (as stated above) there are in fact *two* inscriptions (cf. Smith, 427 *n*.), one (A) agreeing with Fig. 8, the other (B) agreeing with Fig. 9 (except that the circle of the ט should be closed at the top): the second can only be read טוביה, and this determines the reading of the first (in A there are no traces visible, any more than there are in the photograph from which Fig. 8 is taken, of a line, like that in B, drawn upwards from the left-hand upper-corner; but Littmann expresses it distinctly in his sketch of the inscription on the same page). Lidzbarski now accepts טוביה (*Ephem.* iii. 49).

enclosed in a circle, shews (in B) a modification, similar to that in Egyptian Aramaic and Palmyrene, and approximating to the square type.

The next Inscription is that of the Bᵉnê Ḥezir, above the entrance to the so-called Tomb of St. James, situated on the Mount of Olives, immediately opposite to the SE. angle of the Temple-area.

Fig. 10.

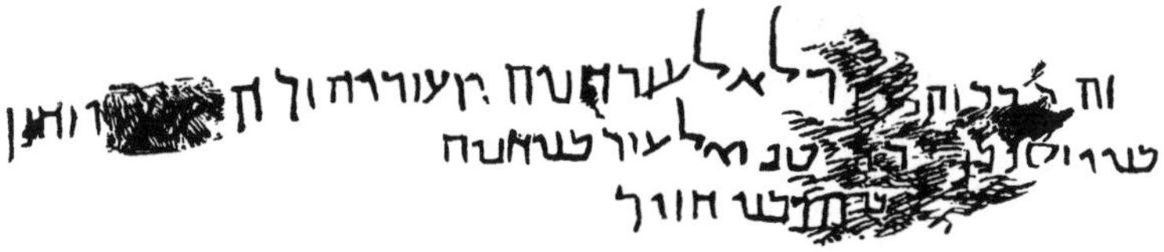

Inscription of the Bᵉnê Ḥezir.

(From Chwolson's *Corpus Inscriptionum Hebraicarum*, No. 6.   Cf. *NSI.* No. 148 A.)

זה [ה]קבר והמש[כ]ב לאלעזר חניה יועזר יהודה שמעון יוחנן

בני יוסף בן . . . ב . . . [וליו]סף ואלעזר בני חניה

. . . . מבני חֵזִיר

I. e. This is the tomb and the resting-place for Eleazar, Ḥanniah, Yo'ezer, Yehudah, Simeon, Yoḥanan,

The sons of Yoseph, the son of . . . . . [and for Yo]seph and Eleazar, the sons of Ḥanniah,

. . . . of the sons (i. e. family) of Ḥezir.

Here we observe *Hebrew* advancing towards the square character. A Ḥezir, ancestor of a priestly family, is mentioned 1 Ch. 24, 15: another Ḥezir, not a priest, but one of the chiefs of the people, is named Neh. 10, 21.   The date of the Inscription is probably shortly before the Christian era.   The advance towards the square character is very marked.   Notice, for instance, the א, the ה, the ל, the ס, the ע, the ר; and the bar of the ח, higher up than in the Egyptian Aramaic. Notice also that by the turn to the left given to the lower part of the נ, when standing in the middle of a word, a *medial* and a *final* form of the letter are distinguished (as in יוחנן at the end of the first line): when י follows, this turn is regularly connected with it, giving rise to a ligature: the same happens with ב followed by נ.   ו and ז are scarcely distinguishable from one another. The first letters of line 3 are uncertain: they may perhaps be read as ביה . . . . .[1]

The ligature just spoken of is peculiarly common in the Palmyrene character. The Palmyrene Inscriptions[2] are written in a dialect of Aramaic[3], and date from B.C. 9 onwards; the character differs from the square type only in calligraphical details. A specimen (Fig. 11) is given (=*NSI.* No. 141), for the sake of illustrating the tendency of Aramaic on the East, as well as on the West, of Palestine to advance in the direction of the square character :—

Fig. 11.

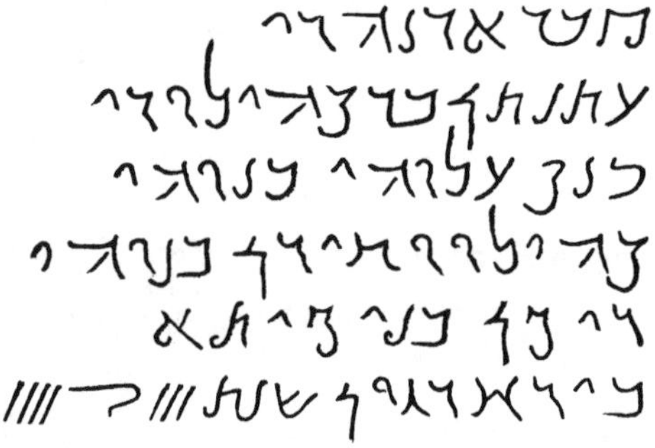

(From De Vogüé's *Syrie Centrale*, 1868, Plate V, No. 30ª.)

קברא דנה די	I.e. This tomb is that of
עתנתן בר כהילו די	'Athinathan, son of Kohilu, which
בנו עלוהי בנוהי	built over him his sons
כהילו וחירן בנוהי	Kohilu and Ḥairan, his sons,
די מן בני מיתא	of (the family of) the children of Maitha,
בירח כנון שנת ‖‖ ‖ כ־‖‖	in the month Kanun, in the year 304
[כנון is *written* דנון]	[Seleuc.=B.C. 9][4].

---

[1] Other Inscriptions (mostly fragmentary) from approximately the same period, may be seen in Chwolson's volume, Nos. 2 (נזר תחם *Boundary* [Aram.] *of Gezer*), 3, 4, 5 (Aram., from the Ḥauran), 7, 8, 9, 10. No. 5 is bilingual, and may be found also in De Vogüé, *Syrie Centrale*, p. 89 : נפשה די חמרת די בנה = 'Οδαίναθος 'Αννήλου ᾠκοδόμησεν τὴν στήλην Χαμράτῃ τῆι αὐτοῦ γυναικί. לה אדינת בעלה

[2] See Cooke, *NSI.* pp. 263-340.

[3] Which exhibits some noticeable affinities with the Aramaic of Ezra and Daniel: see Sachau, *ZDMG.* 1883, pp. 564-7 ; A. A. Bevan, *A Commentary on Daniel* (1892), pp. x, 37, 211 ff.; *LOT.*⁵ 504.

[4] On the *Nabataean* Inscriptions, in which some of the letters, esp. כ, מ, ס,

In the following Inscription (=*NSI.* No. 148 B), from the lintel of
a door, belonging to a ruined Synagogue at Kefr-Bir'im, a village
a few miles NW. of Ṣafed in Galilee, discovered by M. Renan in the
course of his expedition in Palestine in 1863, the transition to the
square character may be said to be accomplished: the date may be
c. 300 A.D. (Renan), or somewhat earlier (Chwolson).

Fig. 12.

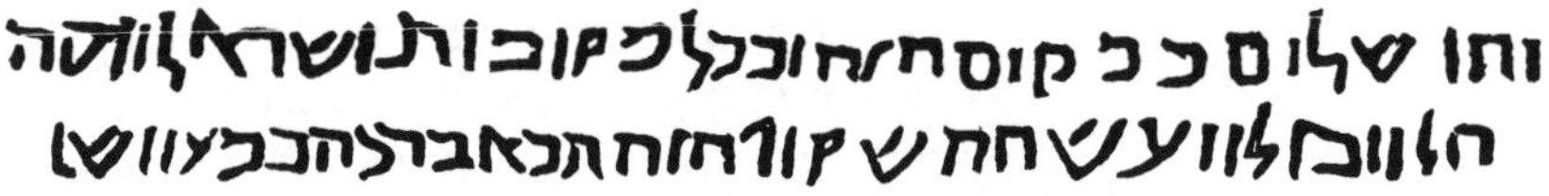

וחו שלוס כ כ קוסחﬨוכלﬤﬡﬢﬦﬢﬡﬤﬢﬡﬦﬥﬤﬢﬡ
הﬥﬦﬦﬥﬧﬨﬦﬦﬥﬦﬦﬢﬦﬦﬧﬥﬢﬡﬦﬦﬢﬦﬦﬦﬦ

(From Chwolson's *Corpus Inscriptionum Hebraicarum* [1], No. 17.)

יהי שלום במקום הזה ובכל מקומות ישראל יוסה
הלוי בן לוי עשה השקוף הזה תבא ברכה במעיוש

I.e. May there be peace in this place, and in all the places of Israel!
Yosah the Levite, son of Levi, made this lintel: may blessing come
upon his works!

מעיוש is evidently an error of the carver for מעשיו: he first omitted
the ש by accident, and then attached it at the end. Notice in this
Inscription the close resemblance between ו and י, which in the
Inscription of the Benê Ḥezir are distinguished by the turn to the left
—a survival of the primitive form of the letter—at the top of the י;
also that between כ and מ (cf. p. lxvii), as well as the *final* ם. Notice
also the regular *plena scriptio.* The resemblance of יהוה to וחו (p. iii)
in a character such as this will be evident.

In conclusion, a specimen is given (Plate VI) of a complete
Phoenician Inscription (=*NSI.* No. 4), which may serve as an
example of the style, as regards character and general appearance,
in which the autographs of the Old Testament must have been written.
The Inscription was found at Ẓidon in 1887, engraved on the base of
a sarcophagus of black basalt, of Egyptian workmanship, and bearing

and ע approach closely to the square characters, see Cooke, *NSI.* p. 214 ff., and, for
the characters, Plate XIV, Lidzb. Plate XLV.

[1] In the original the Inscription is in one line: it is divided here merely for
convenience. See Photograph No. 459 of the Palestine Exploration Fund.

in front a hieroglyphic Inscription, designed no doubt originally for use in Egypt, but diverted from its original purpose and taken to Phoenicia in order to receive the remains of a Phoenician prince. The contents of the hieroglyphic Inscription bear no relation to those of the Phoenician one. Transliterated into square characters, the latter reads as follows:—

1 אנך תבנת כהן עשתרת מלך צדנם בן

2 אשמנעזר כהן עשתרת מלך צדנם שכב בארן

3 ז מי את כל אדם אש תפק אית הארן ז אל אל ת

4 פתח עלתי ואל תרגזן כ אי אדלן כסף אי אדלן

5 חרץ וכל מנם משד בלת אנך שכב בארן ז אל אל תפת

6 ח עלתי ואל תרגזן כ תעבת עשתרת הדבר הא ואם פת

7 ח תפתח עלתי ורגז תרגזן אל י[כ]ן ל[ך] זרע בחים תחת שמ

8 ש ומשכב את רפאם

I. e. 1. I Tabnith, priest of 'Ashtart, king of the Zidonians, son

2. of Eshmun'āzār, priest of 'Ashtart, king of the Zidonians, lie in this coffin:

3. whoever thou art, (even) any man, that bringest forth this coffin, do not

4. open my sepulchral chamber, and disquiet me not; for there is no image of silver, there is no image of

5. gold, nor any jewels of?: only myself am lying in this coffin; do not o-

6. -pen my sepulchral chamber, and disquiet me not; for such an act is an abomination unto 'Ashtart; and if thou at all

7. openest my chamber, or disquietest me at all, mayest thou have no seed among the living under the su-

8. -n, or resting-place with the Shades.

The Tabnith who speaks is the father of the Eshmun'azar (II) whose long and interesting funereal Inscription[1] (22 lines) was found in 1855 on the site of the ancient necropolis of Zidon, and who describes himself (lines 13–15), as son of Tabnith, king of the Zidonians, and of Amm'ashtart, priestess of 'Ashtart, and grandson

---

[1] It may be found in M. A. Levy's *Phönizische Studien*, i. (1856); in Schröder's *Die Phön. Sprache* (1869), p. 224, with Plate I; *CIS.* I. i. No. 3 (with facsimiles); and elsewhere: most recently in Cooke, *NSI.* No. 5 (with facsimile, Plate I).

PLATE VI

INSCRIPTION OF TABNITH, KING OF ZIDON

Reproduced, by permission of M. Ernest Renan, from the *Revue Archéologique*, 1887, juill.-août.

of Eshmun'azar (I), who is mentioned here as Tabnith's father.
From the style of the Egyptian ornamentation displayed both by the
sarcophagus of Tabnith, and also by the related sarcophagus of
Eshmun'azar II, it is concluded that the date of the Inscription is
not earlier than the fourth cent. B.C.; and as upon other grounds
it cannot be much later than this, it may be plausibly assigned to
c. 300 B.C.[1] The Inscription is of value to the Hebrew student, not
only on account of its palaeographical interest, but also on account of
the illustration which it affords of the language and ideas of the Old
Testament.

1. אנך occurs frequently in Phoenician Inscriptions: it was pronounced probably אָנֹךְ (Schröder, *Phön. Spr.*, p. 143): a final vowel
is often not represented in Phoenician orthography: comp. below
תרגמז כ, ז [2]. On the pronunciation *'Ashtart*, see p. 62.

2. אָרֹן of a coffin, or mummy-case, as Gen. 50, 26.

3. ז, i.e. ז (Heb. זֶה). So regularly, as *NSI.* 9, 3 ז השער this gate;
19, 1 ז מצבת this pillar; 42, 3 (the sacrificial table from Marseilles)
ז המשאת this payment; *CIS.* I. i. 88, 4 ז המפקד (cf. Cooke, p. 26).
Observe that ז (unlike the Heb. זה) is without the article, although
the accompanying noun has it: pronounce, therefore, here ז בָּאָרֹן
(not בְּאָרֹן), as line 3 ז הארן.—With 'מי את ונ cf. *NSI.* 64, 5–6. 65, 8:
כל אדם is, however, somewhat awkward. Renan, observing that in
Eshmun'azar's Inscription there occurs twice the similarly worded
phrase, line 4 ז אל יפתח אית משכב, line 20 קנמי את כל ממלכת וכל אדם אל
קנמי את כל ממלכת וכל אדם אל יפתח עלתי, suggests that מי is an error
of the stone-cutter for קנמי, which is supposed, on the strength of
a statement in the Mishnah, *Giṭṭin* 4, 7 (מעשה בצידון באחד שאמר
לאשתו קונם אם איני מגרשך i.e. a man in Zidon said to his wife קונם
'*A curse* (upon me), if I do not divorce thee!'), to have been
a Phoenician formula of imprecation (see further Cooke, p. 34).
Render in this case, then: ' My curse (be) with every man, whosoever

---

[1] Ph. Berger in the *Revue Archéologique*, Juillet 1887, p. 7.

[2] So אל *these* (p. 34 *note*), in accordance with the dissyllabic form found in the
Semitic languages generally, was pronounced in all probability אֵל (in the *Poenulus*
v. 1, 9 written *ily;* in an Inscr. from N. Africa, *ZDMG.* xxix. 240, אלא: Lidzbarski, p. 264[b]). Comp. Cooke, *NSI.* p. 26.

thou art, that bringest forth,' etc.—אש, the Phoenician form of the relative, occurring constantly in the Inscriptions, to be pronounced probably *ish* or *esh*, if not rather as a dissyllable אֶשׁ [1].—תפק prob. תַּפֵּק or תְּפֵק; cf. Aram. נְפַק to *go forth*, אפק to *bring forth*, or Heb. הַפִּיק (Is. 58, 10).—אֵית=Heb. אֵת, the mark of the accus.: for the vocalization, cf. Arab. اِيَّا.

4. עלתי: comp. in Eshmun'azar's Inscription (*NSI.* 5), lines 5–6 ואל יעמסן במשכב ז עלת משכב שני nec superaedificent lecto huic *cameram* lecti alterius, 10, and 20–21 כל אדם אל יפתח עלתי ואל יער עלתי.—תַּרְגִּזֻן, comp. הרגיז used of *disquieting* the spirits of the dead in 1 S. 28, 15. Is. 14, 16.—כ i. e. כְּ (כִּי), as often (Schröd. p. 218 f.; Lidzbarski, p. 295): e.g. *CIS.* 2, 12. 13 כ=אנך אֲנֹךְ כְּ.—אי *not*: cf. p. 49 *note*.—אדלן, probably the Greek εἴδωλον.

5. חָרֵץ, the usual Phoenician word for *gold* (*NSI.* 3, 5; 24, 1 מרקע אז חרץ this plating of gold; 33, 3. 5; *CIS.* 327, 4–5 נסך החרץ the *goldsmith*); in Hebrew confined to poetry.—מָנֵם prob.=Aram. מָאן, pl. מָאנַיָּא.—בלת=בְּלָתִי.

6. כי תעבת עשתרת הדבר הא: comp. the very similar use of תועבת יהוה in Dt. (7, 25 כי תועבת י"י אלהיך הוא 17, 1. 18, 12. 22, 5. 23, 19. 25, 16. 27, 15) and Pr. (3, 32. 11, 20. 12, 22 al.).—הדבר הא, without the art., as ז above: so *CIS.* 2, 22 הא הממלכת that kingdom; 166, *b* 4 הלחם הא. On the orthography of הא, see below, p. xxxi.

7. רָגֹז תַּרְגֵּז, with the inf. *Qal*, according to the scheme noticed on II 20, 18.—יכן, i. e. יָכֵן, impf. from כּוּן (see p. 285 *footnote*; *NSI.* Index, p. 369; and the Glossary in Lidzbarski, p. 294). Cf. *NSI.* 42, 13 יכן לכהנם=Heb.—זֶרַע בַּחַיִּים: comp. the corresponding imprecation in Eshmun'azar's Inscription, lines 8–9 ואל יכן לם בן זרע תחתנם and let him (them) not have son or seed in his (their) stead; 11–12 אל יכן לם שרש למט ופר למעל ותאר בחים תחת שמש (see Is. 37, 31).

8. משכב את רְפָאם: comp. *ib.* line 8 ואל יכן לם משכב את רפאם משכב of a resting-place in the underworld, as Ez. 32, 25: the רפאם as Is. 14, 9. 26, 14. 19. ψ. 88, 11. Pr. 2, 18. 9, 18. 21, 16. Job 26, 5† [2].

---

[1] In the *Poenulus* of Plautus represented by *si* (V. 1, 1. 4. 6. 8), and *ass* (V. 2, 56 *assamar* = אש אָמַר). Comp. Schröder, pp. 162–6.

[2] For further information on the subject of the Phoenician language and Phoenician Inscriptions, the reader is referred to M. A. Levy, *Phönizische Studien* in

§ 2. *Early Hebrew Orthography.*

Having determined the nature of the old Hebrew character, we have next to consider the nature of the old Hebrew orthography. Did this differ from that which we find in modern printed texts? and if so, in what respects?

1. *Division of words.* In the Inscription of Mesha' and in the Siloam Inscription the words are separated by a point, but in Inscriptions on gems and coins and in Phoenician Inscriptions generally (see e.g. Plate VI) separations between words are not marked[1]. Whether they were marked (either by points or spaces) in the autographs of the OT. cannot be determined with certainty: if they were,

---

4 Parts, Breslau, 1856-70; Schröder, *Die Phönizische Sprache*, Halle, 1869; the *Corpus Inscriptionum Semiticarum*, Tom. I (where the Bibliography relating to each Inscription is specified in full); Cooke, *NSI.* pp. 18-158; and Lidzbarski, *Nordsem. Inscr.* pp. 4-83, 493-499 (Bibliography [to 1898]), 204-388, 500-504 (Glossary), 389-412 (synopsis of grammatical forms, etc.). The best treatment of the relation of Phoenician to Hebrew is to be found in the Essay of Stade in the *Morgenländische Forschungen* (Leipzig, 1875), pp. 179-232. All these authorities may, however, in greater or less degree, be supplemented from Inscriptions that have been discovered more recently, and for which search must be made (chiefly) in the *Répertoire d'Épigraphie Sémitique* (from 1900), a supplement, appearing from time to time, to the *CIS.*, and in Lidzbarski's *Ephemeris für Semitische Epigraphik* (from 1902), with Glossaries at the end of each volume.

For further details respecting the history of the West-Semitic alphabets generally, and of the Hebrew alphabet in particular (in addition to the works of Levy, Chwolson, Madden, Berger, and Lidzbarski, mentioned above), reference may be made to Lenormant, *Essai sur la propagation de l'Alph. Phénicien dans l'anc. monde*, 1872-3; Stade's *Lehrbuch*, pp. 23-34; Wellhausen's edition of Bleek's *Einleitung*, ed. 1878, p. 626 ff.; ed. 1886, p. 580 ff.; De Vogüé, *Mélanges d'Archéologie Orientale* (1868), especially pp. 141-178, 'L'Alphabet Araméen et l'Alphabet Hébraïque;' Isaac Taylor's *History of the Alphabet*, Chaps. IV, V; S. A. Cook's study, mentioned above (p. x), in the *PEFQS.* 1909, pp. 284-309; the other Facsimiles of Semitic Inscriptions contained in the Palaeographical Society's Volume; Euting's *Nabatäische Inschriften* (1885); the Plates in the *Corpus Inscriptionum Semiticarum;* and Neubauer's *Facsimiles of Hebrew Manuscripts, with Transcriptions*, Oxford, 1886.

[1] In many of the older Aramaic Inscriptions also the words are separated by a point: in the Papyri they are usually separated by a space. See further Lidzb., p. 202 f. A perpendicular line, seemingly a clause-separator, occurs twice in the Gezer Inscription (ll. 1. 2).

some irregularity and neglect must have been shewn in the observance
of them : for the existing MT. contains instances of almost certainly
incorrect division of words (*a*) ; and the LXX frequently presuppose
a different division from that in MT. (*b*), which (whether right or
wrong) could scarcely have arisen had the separation of words been
marked distinctly. It is probable, however, that before the Massoretic
text was definitely fixed, the division of words had been generally
established, and the distinction made between the medial and final
forms of כ, מ, נ, פ, צ (above, p. xix) : for the Massorites, instead of
altering *in the text* what they view as a wrong division of words, leave
the text as it is, and only direct the *reader* to substitute the correct
division ; this implies that at the time when notes such as those
referred to were added, the division of words found in the כתיב was
regarded as definitely settled (*c*).

(*a*) Gen. 49, 19–20 עָקְבָם׃ מאשר : עקב leg. אָשֵׁר : עֲקֵבָם.

2 S. 21, 1 ואל־בֵּיתָה דמים l. ואל־בֵּית הדמים.

Is. 17, 6 בסעפי הפריה l. בסעפיה פריה.

Jer. 15, 10 כלה מקללוני (a grammatical *monstrum*) l. כֻּלְּהֶם קִלְלוּנִי.

22, 14 וקרע לו חלוני וספון (another grammatical anomaly)
l. וקרע לו חלוניו סָפוּן.

23, 33 אֶת־מַה־מַּשָּׂא l. אַתֶּם הַמַּשָּׂא (so LXX, Vulg.).

Ez. 43, 13 וחיק האמה l. וְחֵיקָה אַמָּה.

Hos. 6, 5 ומשפטיך אור יצא l. וּמִשְׁפָּטַי כָּאוֹר יֵצֵא (so LXX, Pesh.
Targ.).

ψ. 25, 17 הרחיבו והצילני l. הַרְחֵב וְהַצִּילֵנִי (see the Commentators).

42, 6–7 ישועות פניו ואלהי : אלהי l. ישועות פני ואלהי : (so LXX, Pesh. :
comp. *v.* 12. ψ. 43, 5).

73, 4 למותם l. לָמוֹ תָּם (so Ew. Hitz. Del. etc.).

(*b*) Nu. 24, 22 קֵין עַד־מָה : νεοσσιὰ πανουργίας = קֵן עָרְמָה.

1 S. 1, 1 בן־צוף : ἐν Νασειβ = בנציב.

14, 21 סביב וגם המה : ἀνεστράφησαν καὶ αὐτοὶ = סבבו גם המה.

20, 40 לך הביא : πορεύου, εἴσελθε = לְכָה בוֹא.

1 Ch. 17, 10[b] ואגד־לך : καὶ αὐξήσω σε = וַאֲגַדֶּלְךָ.

Jer. 5, 6 זאב ערבות : λύκος ἕως τῶν οἰκιῶν = זאב עד־בית.

9, 4 *end*–5 נלאו : שבתך בתוך מרמה (οὐ) διέλιπον τοῦ ἐπι-
στρέψαι. τόκος ἐπὶ τόκῳ = נלאו שֵׁב : תֹּךְ בְּתוֹךְ.

13, 25 מנת=מנת־מדיך מאתי : μερὶς τοῦ ἀπειθεῖν ὑμᾶς ἐμοί
מֹרֵיכֶם אִתִּי.

17, 11 לא=עשה עשר ולא : ποιῶν πλοῦτον αὐτοῦ οὐ.
עֹשֶׂה עָשְׁרוֹ

31, 8 במועד=בָּם עֻזֵּר : ἐν ἑορτῇ.

46, 15 מדוע=מדוע נסחף : διὰ τί ἔφυγεν (ἀπὸ σοῦ) ὁ Ἆπις;
נָס חַף.

Hos. 11, 2 הֵם=מפניהם : ἐκ προσώπου μου· αὐτοὶ מִפְּנֵי.

Zeph. 3, 19 אִתָּךְ=את־כל־מעניך : ἐν σοὶ ἕνεκεν σοῦ (as though
(לְמַעֲנֵךְ).

Zech. 11, 7 לבנעני=לָכֵן עֲנִיֵּי : εἰς τὴν Χαναανῖτιν.

ψ. 4, 3 כבדי לכלמה : βαρυκάρδιοι; ἵνα τί=כִּבְדֵי לֵב לָמֶה.

44, 5 אלהים צוה : ὁ Θεός μου, ὁ ἐντελλόμενος=אֱלֹהַי מְצַוֶּה.

106, 7 עֹלִים=עַל־יָם : ἀναβαίνοντες.

Pr. 13, 14 ממוקשי מות : ὑπὸ παγίδος θανεῖται=מְמוֹקֵשׁ יָמוּת.

14, 7 ובל־ידעת : ὅπλα δὲ αἰσθήσεως=וּכְלֵי דָעַת.

27, 9 ומתק רעהו מעצת־נפש : καταρρήγνυται δὲ ὑπὸ συμπτω-
μάτων ψυχῆ=וּמִתְקְרָעָה מֵעֲצַת נַפְשׁ.

Job 40, 19 (LXX 14) העשו ינש חרבו : πεποιημένον ἐγκαταπαί-
ζεσθαι=הֶעָשׂוּי לְשַׂחֶק־בּוֹ (ψ. 104, 26).

See also ψ. 76, 7. Jer. 6, 9. 23, cited below, pp. lxv, lxvi ; Gen.
28, 19 Οὐλαμμαυς (for לוז ואולם). Jud. 18, 29 Οὐλαμαις (for ליש ואולם) ;
and the notes on I 1, 24. 2, 13. 21, 7.

(c) a Jer. 6, 29 קרי מאש תם : מאשתם.

ψ. 55, 16 ק׳ יַשִּׁי מָוֶת : ישימות.

Job 38, 1 ק׳ מִן הַסְּעָרָה : מנהסערה.

40, 6 ק׳ מִן סְעָרָה : מנסערה.

Neh. 2, 13 ק׳ הם פרוצים : המפרוצים.

1 Ch. 9, 4 ק׳ בֶּן בָּנִי מִן בני פרץ : בן בנימן בני פרץ.

β La. 4, 3 ק׳ כַּיְעֵנִים : כי ענים.

2 Ch. 34, 6 ק׳ בְּחַרְבֹתֵיהֶם : בחר בתיהם.

γ 2 S. 5, 2 ק׳ היית המוציא והמבי : הייתה מוציא והמבי.

21, 12 ק׳ שָׁמָה פלשתים : שם הפלשתים.

Ez. 42, 9 ק׳ ומתחת הלשכות האלה : ומתחתה לשכות האלה.

Job 38, 12 ק׳ יִדַּעְתָּ הַשַּׁחַר מְקֹמוֹ : ידעתה שחר מקומו.

Ezra 4, 12 ק׳ וְשׁוּרַיָּא שַׁכְלִלוּ : ושורי אשכללו.

However, as the need of a re-division of words is *comparatively* unfrequent, it may perhaps be inferred that in old Hebrew MSS. the divisions between words were not regularly unmarked [1].

2. The *plena scriptio* was rare. Thus in Mesha''s Inscription the י of the plural is regularly not expressed (line 2 שלשן *thirty:* 4 השלכן (p. lxxxix); 5 ימן רבן, i.e. יָמִן רַבִּן *many days;* 16 גברן, i.e. גִּבְרִן *men*): we have also 10. 13. 20 אש, 11 קר for what in MT. would be אִישׁ, קִיר: further (attaching the points, to avoid repetition) 1 מאב, 4 השענ‍ִי *saved me,* 27 בָּנִתִי, הָרֵס: and even 23. 27. 30 בת, 7 בתה, for בַּית, בִּיתה (once 25 בְּבֵיתה); the *duals,* 15 הצהרם (in MT. הַצָּהֳרַים), 20 מאתן *two hundred,* 30 בת דבלתן (Jer. 48, 22 בֵּית דִּבְלָתַים), 31 חורנן (Isa. 15, 5 חֹרֹנָים). Even א is sometimes omitted, not merely in ואחזה 11. 20 (i.e. וָאֶחֱזֶה, וָאֹחֲזֶה), 24 ואמר (וָאֹמַר), where the radical א following the prefix of 1 ps. sg. of the imperfect is dispensed with as in Hebrew, but in רשה 20=ראשה *its chief(s).*

Similarly in the Siloam Inscription we find 2. 4 אש (i.e. אִישׁ), 2 אמת (i.e. אַמֹּת), 3 בצר (בַּצּוּר), 4. 6 מימן (מִיָמִין), החצבם (הַחֹצְבִם), 6 הצר (הַצּוּר); and even (where the ו is radical) 2 קל (so rarely in MT.: usually קוֹל), 3 בים (i.e. בְּיוֹם—never יֹם in MT.). We find, however, beside these 'defective' forms 1. 2 בעור (בְּעוֹד), 5 המוצא, and 6 ראש.

Perhaps the most remarkable case of the *defectiva scriptio* is that of the pron. of 3 *sing.,* which is twice on Mesha''s Inscription (in the masculine) written הא (6 ויאמר נם הא; 27 כי הָרֵס הא). In Phoenician Inscriptions, the same orthography is found regularly with *both* genders [2]: it appears, therefore, that, while הא was all that was written, the context was regarded as a sufficient guide to enable the reader to pronounce it correctly *hu'* or *hi'*, according as the reference was to a masc. or fem. antecedent. (The alternative supposition that *hu'* was used for both genders, is excluded by the fact that *all* other Semitic languages have a feminine with *yod,* which obliges us to

---

[1] Comp. further (with reserve) Perles, *Analekten* (1895), p. 35 ff.

[2] Cooke, *NSI.* 3, 9 הא צדק מלך he was a just king, 13 הא מלאכת that work; 5, 10 הא אדם that man, 11 הא ממלכת that kingdom; 27, 2 (254 B.C.) and *CIS.* I. i. 94, 2 הא שת that year; *NSI.* 44, *b* 4 הא הלחם; and in the Inscription of Tabnith (p. xxiv), line 6. See Lidzbarski, p. 257.

suppose that the double form was already possessed by the ancestors
of the different Semitic nations when they still lived together in a
common home[1].)

It may be inferred that the *plena scriptio* was introduced gradually,
though, so far as א is concerned, the instances of its omission, where
it is required by the etymology, are so exceptional, that it was probably
in use, as a rule, from the beginning. In the case of ו and י there is
abundant evidence that the LXX translated from MSS., in which
it was not yet generally introduced; for in passages where it is found
in MT. they constantly do not recognize it. Thus, to take but a few
examples out of many—

1 S. 12, 7 צדקות יְ᾽ : את כל : τὴν πᾶσαν δικαιοσύνην K.=יְ᾽ צִדְקַת.

8 וישיבום : καὶ κατῴκισεν αὐτοὺς=וַישִׁבֵם.

18, 27 וימלאום : A, Luc. καὶ ἐπλήρωσεν αὐτὰς=וַימַלְאֵם.

19, 5 ראית : (πᾶς 'Ισραηλ) εἶδον=רָאֵת or רָאָת (construction as
17, 21).

20, 26 *end* טהור : κεκαθάρισται=טֹהָר.

21, 14 (13 LXX) ויורד : κατέρρει=וַיֹּרֶד.

23, 25 סלע המחלקות : πέτρα ἡ μερισθεῖσα=סֶלַע הַמַּחְלֶקֶת.

27, 8 הנה ישבות הארץ : ἰδοὺ ἡ γῆ κατῳκεῖτο=הִנֵּה יֹשֶׁבֶת הָאָרֶץ.

2 S. 7, 1 הניח־לו : κατεκληρονόμησεν αὐτὸν=הִנְחִלוֹ.

Jer. 6, 15 יפלו בנפלים : πεσοῦνται ἐν τῇ πτώσει αὐτῶν=יִפְּלוּ בַנֹּפְלִם.

23 כאיש למלחמה : ὡς πῦρ (כְּאֵשׁ) εἰς πόλεμον.

29 ורעים לא נתקו : πονηρία αὐτῶν οὐκ ἐτάκη=וְרָעָם לֹא נִתַּךְ.

12, 15 והשיבתים : καὶ κατοικιῶ αὐτοὺς=וְהֹשַׁבְתִּם.

17, 25 ובסוסים : καὶ ἵπποις αὐτῶν=וּבְסוּסָם.

32 (39), 5 יולך : εἰσελεύσεται=יֵלֵךְ (את being disregarded).

50 (27), 16 זורע : σπέρμα=זֶרַע (in spite of the parallel κατέχοντα
δρέπανον).

51 (28), 59 שר מנוחה : ἄρχων δώρων=שַׂר מִנְחָה.

---

[1] The view formerly held that the epicene הוא was an archaism in Hebrew,
cannot, in the light of these facts, be any longer sustained: Hebrew must have
possessed the double form from the beginning. Cf. Nöldeke, *ZDMG.* 1866,
p. 458 f.; 1878, p. 594; Delitzsch, *Comm. on Genesis* (Engl. Tr.), i. pp. 42 f., 50;
Wright, *Comparative Grammar of the Semitic Languages* (1890), p. 104.

Ezek. 7, 24 נְאוֹן עֻזִּים: τὸ φρύαγμα τῆς ἰσχύος αὐτῶν=נְאוֹן עֻזָּם (comp. 24, 21).

13, 13 רוּחַ סְעָרוֹת: πνοὴν ἐξαίρουσαν=רוּחַ סֹעָרֶת.

42, 16–17 (similarly 17–18) מָדַד סָבִיב: καὶ ἐπέστρεψε . . . καὶ διεμέτρησε i.e. סָבַב מָדַד (so most moderns: comp. *v.* 19 MT.).

ψ. 5 title אֶל־הַנְּחִילוֹת: ὑπὲρ τῆς κληρονομούσης=אֶל־הַנַּחֲלָת.

58, 12 שֹׁפְטִים: ὁ κρίνων αὐτοὺς=שָׁפְטָם.

104, 17 בְּרוֹשִׁים: ἡγεῖται αὐτῶν=בְּרֹאשָׁם.

107, 17 אוֹלִים: ἀντελάβετο αὐτῶν=אוּלָם or אֵילָם[1].

Job 19, 18 עֲוִילִים: εἰς τὸν αἰῶνα=עוֹלָם[2].

3. The suffix of 3 sg. masc. was written ה- instead of ו-, as is normally the case in MT. The original form of this suffix was הו-, as seen still in פִּיהוּ, and in derivatives of ל״ה verbs as מַשְׁקֵהוּ, מְבַהוּ, etc.: also in such verbal forms as שְׁלָחָהוּ, אֲכָלֵהוּ, נְתִיּיהוּ, יַעַבְרֶנְהוּ, תְּנֵהוּ, יְבָרְכֶנְהוּ, אֲהַבְתָּהוּ (Stade, §§ 345, 628), and the form *-hu* is used regularly in Arabic; but in the majority of cases a contraction takes place, the aspirate being rejected, and *a-hu*, for instance, becoming first *au* and ultimately *ó*. At first, however, the orthography was not altered, ה- remained, though it *followed* the *ó*, and in fact was only a sign of the final long vowel: in the end, however, ו- was mostly substituted for it. Mesha' still writes uniformly ה-; e.g. (adding the points) וַיְגָרְשֹׁה, בֹּה, בְּבֵתֹה, בְּנֹה, בְּאַרְצֹה, etc.: on the Siloam Inscription, on the contrary, the examples which occur, viz. רֵעוֹ thrice, have ו-. In MT., though in the vast majority of cases the contracted suffix is written ו-, there occur a number of instances in which ה- has been suffered to remain, testifying (in the light of the cognate dialects) to a previous general prevalence of this form: viz. Gen. 9, 21. 12, 8. 13, 3. 35, 21 אָהֳלֹה; 49, 11 עִירֹה and סוּתֹה; Ex. 22, 4 בְעִירֹה; 26 כְּסוּתֹה; Ex. 32, 17 בְּרֵעֹה; 25 פָּרְעֹה; Lev. 23, 13 נִסְכֹּה; Nu. 10, 36

---

[1] As though from a verb אוּל or אִיל: cf. ψ. 22, 1 אֱיָלוּתִי ἀντίληψις; 20 אֱיָלוּתִי βοήθειά μου; 88, 5 אֵין אֱיָל ἀβοήθητος; Syr. ܐܝܠ help, succour, Ephr. i. 398 al.

[2] Yet in *some* cases the *plena scriptio* must have been in use: Jud. 9, 37 ירדים καταβαίνων κατὰ θάλασσαν (ירד ים); Jer. 22, 20 מַעֲבָרִים εἰς τὸ πέραν τῆς θαλάσσης (מַעֲבָר ים).

וּבְנֹחֹה 23, 8 ;קֻבֹּה; Dt. 34, 7 לְחֹה; Jos. 11, 16 וּשְׁפֶלָתֹה; Jud. 9, 49
שֹׂוכֹה; 2 Ki. 6, 10 הַזֹּהִירֹה; 9, 25 שְׁלִשֹׁה; 19, 23 קָצֹה (Is. 37, 24 קָצֹו);
20, 13 (=Is. 39, 2) נְכֹתֹה; Jer. 2, 3 תְּבֹוּאָתֹה; 17, 24 בֹּה; 22, 18ᵇ הֹלֹה;
Ez. 12, 14 עֶזְרֹה; 31, 18. 32, 31. 32. 39, 11 all הֲמֹונֹה; 48, 8 (so 𝔊,
Kittel, but not Baer and Ginsburg). 15 *end.* 21 *end* תֹּוכֹה; 18 תְּבֹוּאָתֹה;
Hab. 3, 4 עֻזֹה; ψ. 10, 9. 27, 5 בְּסֻכֹּה; 42, 9 שִׁירֹה; Dan. 11, 10 מְעֻזֹה;
and the eighteen (seventeen) cases of כֻּלֹּה quoted on II 2, 9 ¹. The
non-recognition of this form of the suffix has sometimes, as in 1 S.
14, 27 (see note). 2 S. 21, 1 (see note). Is. 30, 33 (rd. מְדֻרָתֹה). Ez.
43, 13 (see p. xxviii), led to error in MT. Comp. also Gen. 49, 10 in
the Versions (שִׁלֹּה). The retention of the form in the instances cited
is probably due to accident : it cannot be said to occur more frequently
in passages that are (presumably) ancient than in others ; thus in
Gen. 49 and Ex. 22 there are numerous cases of the usual form in i-,
in other ancient passages there are no occurrences of ה- whatever ².

§ 3. *The Chief Ancient Versions of the Old Testament.*

It does not lie within the compass of the present work to give
a complete account of the different Ancient Versions of the Old
Testament : it will suffice if enough be said to illustrate their general
character and relation to one another, so far as the Books of Samuel

---

¹ ה- occurs also in שְׁמ[ה] and בה in the Nash Papyrus, containing the Decalogue
and Dt. 6, 4 f. (2 cent. A.D.) : see S. A. Cook, *PSBA.* 1903, 34 ff., or (briefly) my
Exodus, p. 417.

² I do not stop to shew in detail that ancient Hebrew MSS. were *unpointed.*
That they were unpointed is (1) probable, from the analogy of all ancient Semitic
writing, which has come down to us in its original form (Moabitic, Aramaic, Phoenician, Hebrew Inscriptions) ; (2) certain, (*a*) from the *very numerous* renderings
of the Ancient Versions, presupposing a different vocalization from that of the
Massoretic text, which it cannot reasonably be supposed that the translators would
have adopted had they had pointed texts before them ; (*b*) from the silence of the
Talmud and Jerome as regards any system of punctuation, which, when it is considered that passages are frequently *discussed*, and alternative renderings and pro-
nunciations compared, both by the Rabbis and by Jerome, is more than would be
credible, had Hebrew MSS. in their day been provided with points. (On Jerome,
particulars may be found in Nowack's monograph [p. liii *n.* 4], p. 43 ff.) The
system of points must have been introduced during the sixth and seventh cent. A.D.
—a period of which the literary history is unfortunately shrouded in obscurity,
which even the pedigree of Aaron Ben-Asher, brought to light by the Crimean MSS.
(Strack, in the art. cited p. xxxiv *n.* 4, pp. 610–613), does not enable us to pierce.

are concerned, and to establish the principles upon which they may be used for purposes of textual criticism [1].

The special value of the Ancient Versions consists in the fact that they represent MSS. very much earlier than any Hebrew MSS. at present extant, and belonging in some cases to different recensions. The majority of Hebrew MSS. are of the twelfth to the sixteenth centuries [2]. Very few are earlier: the earliest of which the date is known with certainty being the MS. of the Latter Prophets, now at St. Petersburg, which bears a date = A.D. 916 [3]. This MS., though it differs from the great majority of Hebrew MSS. by exhibiting (like others acquired within the last half-century from the East [4]) the super-linear system of points and accents, does not contain a substantially different text. In fact, so soon as we pass beyond the recognized variants known as the *Qrě"s*, the variations exhibited by extant Hebrew MSS. are slight; in other words, *all MSS. belong to the same recension, and are descended from the same imperfect archetype* [5]. Existing MSS. all represent what is termed the *Massoretic* text [6]. That this text,

---

[1] For fuller information on the subject of the following pages, see generally (where special monographs are not referred to) Wellhausen's edition of Bleek's *Einleitung*, ed. 4, 1878, p. 571 ff., or ed. 5, 1886, p. 523 ff., with the references. Comp. Burkitt's art. TEXT AND VERSIONS (OT.) in *EB*. iv, col. 5011 ff.

[2] Comp. Strack's art. TEXT OF THE OT. in *DB*. iv, p. 727 ff.

[3] Published in facsimile with Prolegomena by H. L. Strack, *Codex Babylonicus Petropolitanus* (St. Petersburg, 1876). Another relatively ancient MS. is the Reuchlin Codex of the Prophets at Carlsruhe (A. D. 1105), De Rossi's 154, the facsimile of a page of which may be seen in Stade's *Gesch. Isr.* i. p. 32, or in the Palaeogr. Society's Volume, Pl. LXXVII. Ginsburg (*Introd. to the Heb. Bible*, 1897, p. 475 ff.) describes a MS. (Brit. Mus. Or. 4445), which he assigns to *c.* A.D. 830.

[4] On these MSS. see Strack in the *Zeitschr. für Luth. Theol. u. Kirche*, 1875, p. 605 ff., and Wickes, *Hebrew Prose Accents*, App. ii. p. 142 ff., with the references.

[5] Comp. Olshausen, *Die Psalmen* (1853), p. 17 ff.; Lagarde, *Proverbien*, p. 2; and the note in Stade, *ZATW*. iv. 303.

[6] The variations exhibited by existing MSS. have been most completely collated by Kennicott, *V. T. c. Var. Lect.* 1776, 1780; and De Rossi, *Variae Lectiones V. T.*, 1784–98. But for assistance in recovering the genuine text of the passages—which are not few—in the Hebrew Bible, which bear the marks of corruption upon their face, one consults these monumental works in vain. And how little is to be gained for the same end from the MSS. discovered since De Rossi's day, may be learnt from Cornill's collation of the MS. of A.D. 916, for Ezekiel, *Das Buch des Propheten Ezechiel* (1886), p. 8 f. Baer's editions of the text of different parts of the OT. (the whole, except Ex.-Dt.) are valuable as exhibiting the *Massoretic* text in

however, does not reproduce the autographs of the OT. in their original integrity becomes manifest, as soon as it is examined with sufficient care and minuteness. It is true, since the rise of the school called the *Massorites* in the seventh and eighth centuries, and probably for parts of the Old Testament, especially the Law, from a considerably earlier date, the Jews displayed a scrupulous fidelity in the preservation and correct transmission of their sacred books: but nothing is more certain than that the period during which this care was exercised was preceded by one of no small laxity, in the course of which corruptions of different kinds found their way into the text of the Old Testament. The Jews, when it was too late to repair by this means the mischief that had been done, proceeded to guard their sacred books with extraordinary care, with the result that corrupt readings were simply perpetuated, being placed by them (of course, unconsciously) on precisely the same footing as the genuine text, and invested with a fictitious semblance of originality. Opinions may differ, and, as our data for arriving at a decision are often imperfect, cannot but be expected to differ, as to the *extent* of corruption in the Massoretic text: but of the fact, there can be no question. The proof, as was shewn by Professor Kirkpatrick in a paper read at the Church Congress at Portsmouth, 1885 (*Guardian*, Oct. 7, p. 1478; comp. *The Psalms*, in the *Cambridge Bible*, p. lxvi), is to be found, stated briefly, in the following facts: (1) There are passages in which the text, as it stands, cannot be translated without violence to the laws of grammar, or is irreconcileable with the context or with other passages; (2) parallel passages (especially parallel lists of names) found in more than one

what is deemed by its editor to be its best attested form; but they are naturally of no service to those whose object it is *to get behind the Massoretic tradition*, for the purpose of obtaining a text that is purer and more original. The same may be said of Ginsburg's *Hebrew Bible:* this exhibits the Massoretic text in what its editor considers to be its best attested form: but though variants from the versions, and even conjectural readings, are occasionally mentioned, the great majority of variants collected, especially in the second edition, with indefatigable industry, from a large number of MSS. and early printed editions, relate only to differences of orthography and accentuation, not affecting the sense. The best collection both of variants from the versions and of conjectural emendations is that contained in Kittel's *Biblia Hebraica*. But in the acceptance of both variants and emendations, considerable discrimination must be exercised.

book, differ in such a manner as to make it clear that the variations
are due largely to textual corruption; (3) the Ancient Versions contain
various readings which often bear a strong stamp of probability upon
them, and remove or lessen the difficulties of the Hebrew text.   The
present volume will supply illustrations.   When the nature of the old
character and orthography is considered, the wonder indeed is that the
text of the Old Testament is as relatively free of corruption as appears
to be the case.   If, then, these corruptions are to be removed otherwise
than by conjecture, we must discover, if possible, a text (or texts),
which, unlike the text of all Hebrew MSS. which we possess, is
relatively free from them.   And such texts are afforded by the Ancient
Versions.   These versions were made from MSS. older by many
centuries than those which formed the basis of the Massoretic text;
and when we consult them in crucial passages, where the Massoretic
text has the appearance of being in error, we constantly find that the
readings which they presuppose are intrinsically superior to those
exhibited by the Massoretic text, and have evidently been made from
a MS. (or MSS.) free from the corruption attaching to the latter.

The work of the Massorites, it should be remembered, was essentially
conservative: their aim was not to *form* a text, but by fixing the pronunciation and other means, to *preserve* a text which, in all essentials,
they received, already formed, from others.   The antecedents of the
text which thus became the basis of the Massoretic text can only be
determined approximately by conjecture.   It was already substantially
the same in ii.–v. cent. A.D.; for quotations in the Mishnah and
Gemara exhibit no material variants[1].   The Targums also (see below)

---

[1] This seems to be true, notwithstanding the very large number of variants from
the Talmud, Midrashim, and even later Rabbinical authorities, collected with great
industry by V. Aptowitzer in *Das Schriftwort in der Rabbinischen Literatur* (see
p. XV), from 1–2 Samuel, and (III, 95 ff.) Joshua (cf. Strack, *Proleg. Crit. in Vet.
Test.*, 1873, p. 94 ff.).   These variants, viz., relate mostly to *small* differences, such as
the presence or absence of ו, the article, את, or other unimportant word; על or ל for
אל, or *vice versa;* the sing. for the plural, or *vice versa*, in such a case as I 15, 6 ;
ב for כ with the inf., or *vice versa:* the variants practically never affect the sense
materially, or correct a certainly corrupt passage.   In many cases also the variant
seems to be due to the citation being made from memory, the substance being
recollected correctly, but not the exact wording.   There are, however, cases in
which the number of seemingly independent authorities agreeing in a variant is

presuppose a text which deviates from it but slightly, though the deviations are sufficient to shew that, even in official Jewish circles, absolute uniformity did not exist.   All that can be said is that the text which was adopted by the Jews as a standard, and which, as such, was made by the Massorites the basis of their labours, had in previous stages of its history been exposed to influences, which resulted in the introduction into it of error and corruption.   The MSS. on which the Septuagint is based, and those from which the Massoretic text is descended, must, of course, have had *some* common meeting-point (prior to the second or third century B.C.); and whilst *on the whole* the purer text was undoubtedly preserved by the Jews, in many individual cases the text in their hands underwent corruption, and the purer readings are preserved to us by the Septuagint.   The texts on which the other Ancient Versions are based (which usually deviate less from the Massoretic text, and often accordingly [e.g. Ez. 40 ff.] reproduce corruptions from which the Septuagint is free) will have been derived from the current Jewish text at a later period than the LXX, when the corrupting influences had been longer operative upon it.   Still, these versions also sometimes agree with LXX against MT. in preserving the purer text [1].

----

larger than can be reasonably accounted for by the supposition that the memory was always at fault, and in these cases the variant depends no doubt upon actual MSS.   In some instances this is known to be the case from the MSS. collated by Kennicott and others (e. g. בכל for לכל in I 18, 14 ; הארדוף for ארדוף in I 30, 8); in others, though no MSS. at present known exhibit the variants, there may well have been such,—especially where the variant is supported by the LXX or other ancient version,—extant in Talmudic times, and even later (cf. Aptow. I, p. 3; and, for the distinction of certain, probable, and possible, MS. variants, p. 28, III, p. vi).   But even these variants can hardly be called material or important.   The most noticeable is perhaps האפוד (as LXX) for ארון האלהים in I 14, 18, which seems (Aptow. I, p. 48 ff.) to have been read in MSS. as late as Ibn Ezra's time (A. D. 1104-1165).   On the other hand, there are numerous cases in which the readings of the Talmud agree minutely (e. g. in the *plena* or *defectiva scriptio*) with the Massoretic text (Strack, *op. cit.*, pp. 70-72, 80-94).

[1] No doubt there are passages in the MT., the character of which makes it practically certain that, though neither the LXX nor any other version exhibits any variant, the text is nevertheless corrupt, i. e. the corruption was already present in the MSS. which were the common source *both* of the LXX and other versions, *and* of the MT.   Here, it is evident, the only remedy is critical conjecture (a brilliant

The use of the Ancient Versions is not, however, always such a simple matter as might be inferred from the last paragraph but one. The Ancient Versions are not uniformly word-for-word translations, from which the Hebrew text followed by the translators might be recovered at a glance: sometimes their text, especially that of the LXX, has not been transmitted to us in its primitive integrity; and even where it has been so transmitted, they contain, or are liable to contain, an element of *paraphrase*, the nature and extent of which must be determined as accurately as possible before they are available as safe guides for the correction of the Massoretic text. In determining the character of this element, each Version, and often each book, or group of books, contained in a Version—for the different parts of an Ancient Version were not always the work of one and the same hand, and the different translators were liable to follow different methods in translating—must be examined separately: our standards of comparison must be those parts of the Massoretic text which afford presumptive evidence of being free from corruption; and, in cases where this is matter of doubt, the intrinsic superiority of one text above the other, as estimated by its conformity with the context, its grammatical correctness, its agreement with the general style and manner of the writers of the Old Testament, and similar considerations. In the use of an Ancient Version for the purposes of textual criticism, there are *three* precautions which must always be observed : (1) we must reasonably assure ourselves that we possess the Version itself in its original integrity; (2) we must eliminate such variants as have the appearance of originating merely with the translator; (3) the text represented by the remainder, when we are able to recover it, which will be that of the MS. (or MSS.) used by the translator, we must then compare carefully, in the light of the considerations just stated, with the existing Hebrew text, in order to determine on which side the superiority lies. The second and third of these precautions are not less important than

---

one in Cornill on Ez. 13, 20 : אֹתָן חָפְשִׂים for אֶת־נְפָשִׁים). The dangers of conjectural emendation are obvious; and many such emendations rest upon doubtful theories, or are for other reasons unconvincing : but some, especially such as involve only a slight change in the *ductus litterarum*, are well deserving of acceptance. Cf. G. B. Gray, *Encycl. Brit.*[10] iii. 860 ; F. C. Burkitt, *EB.* iv. 5029-31.

the first : it is necessary to insist upon them, as cases are on record in which they have been unduly neglected[1].

1. *The Septuagint.* The Version that is of greatest importance for purposes of textual criticism is that known as the *Septuagint*[2]. In the case of the Pentateuch, this Version dates, no doubt, from the third century B.C.—according to tradition from the reign of Ptolemy Philadelphus, B.C. 285–247 : the subsequent parts of the OT. were probably completed gradually in the course of the two following centuries, for the differences of style and method exhibited by the different books shew that the whole cannot be the work of a single hand. The characteristics of the LXX are best learnt from actual study of it, though illustrations, so far as the Books of Samuel are concerned, are given below. In some books, the translation is much more literal than in others ; in difficult passages, especially such as are poetical, the translators have evidently been often unable to seize the sense of the original. Except in such passages as Gen. 49. Dt. 32. 33, the Pentateuch is the best translated part of the historical books : the Psalter is tolerably well done, and though few Psalms are wholly free from error, the general sense is fairly well expressed : the translation of Isaiah is poor and paraphrastic ; those of Job and the Minor Prophets are often unintelligible. In the case of Jeremiah the text represented by LXX deviates so considerably from the Massoretic text as to assume the character of a separate recension[3]. There are few books of the OT. in which the Massoretic text may not, more or less frequently, be emended with help of the LXX[4]; but the LXX

---

[1] In Prof. Workman's *Text of Jeremiah* (1889), the neglect to observe the second precaution has led to disastrous consequences : a very large proportion of the examples cited, p. 283 ff., in the 'Conspectus of the Variations' presuppose no difference in the Hebrew text read by the translator, but are due simply to the fact that the translator did not make it his aim to produce a word-for-word version. See a criticism by the present writer in the *Expositor*, May, 1889, pp. 321–337.

[2] See, very fully, on this Dr. Swete's excellent *Introduction to the OT. in Greek* (1900); and St. John Thackeray's *Grammar of the OT. in Greek, acc. to the Sept.*, vol. i (Introduction, Orthography, and Accidence), 1909 ; also Nestle, *DB.* iv. 437 ff.

[3] See *LOT.*[8] 269 f., with the references ; and add L. Köhler, *ZAW.* 1909, 1–39 (on Jer. 1–9).

[4] And naturally, sometimes, of other Ancient Versions as well. A *minimum* of such necessary emendations may be found in the margin of the Revised Version :

Version of Samuel, parts of Kings, and Ezekiel, is of special value, as the MS. (or MSS.) on which the Massoretic text of these books is based, must have suffered more than usually from corrupting influences. *The Versions of Aquila, Symmachus, and Theodotion.* After the destruction of Jerusalem in A.D. 70, a reaction began in Jewish circles against the use of the LXX, partly, as seems probable, originating in opposition to the Christians (who from the times in which the NT. was written had been accustomed to quote the LXX as an authoritative Version of the OT.), partly in a growing sense of the imperfections of the Septuagint translation, and of its inadequacy as a correct representation of the Hebrew original. Hence arose in the second cent. A.D. the three improved Greek Versions of the OT., those of *Aquila, Theodotion,* and *Symmachus.* Aquila and Theodotion are both mentioned by Irenaeus (iii. 21) writing *c.* A.D. 180: Symmachus lived probably somewhat later. Of these translators, Aquila was a Jewish proselyte of Pontus. His method was that of extreme literalness[1], which he carried to such an extent, that he sought to represent words which had acquired derived meanings in accordance with their etymology, and even to reproduce particles for which Greek possessed no proper equivalent[2]. Jerome on Is. 8, 14 mentions a tradition that

a larger selection—the majority, at least as it appears to the present writer, not less necessary—is afforded by the notes in the 'Variorum Bible,' published by Eyre and Spottiswoode. But many more are in fact necessary : see examples in the writer's *Book of Jeremiah*[2] (1906), and *Nah.–Mal.* in the *Century Bible* (1906) ; and compare (with discrimination) any recent critical commentary. A good collection of emendations from the LXX and other Versions, with explanations, will be found in T. K. Abbott, *Essays chiefly on the Original Texts of OT. and NT.* (1891), p. 1 ff.

[1] Δουλεύων τῇ Ἑβραικῇ λέξει, Origen, Ep. ad Africanum, § 2.

[2] Jerome, Ep. 57 ad Pammachium : quia Hebraei non solum habent ἄρθρα sed et πρόαρθρα, ille κακοζήλως et syllabas interpretatur et literas, dicitque ἐν κεφαλαίῳ ἔκτισεν ὁ θεὸς σὺν [אֵת] τὸν οὐρανὸν καὶ σὺν τὴν γῆν. ‏ה‎ *locale* he represented by -δε, as Ὀφείρδε 1 Ki. 22, 49; Κυρήνηνδε 2 Ki. 16, 9. As examples of etymologizing renderings may be quoted στιλπνότης for יִצְהָר, διεδηματίσαντό με for כִּתְּרוּנִי ψ. 22, 13, ἐκλεκτώθητε for הִבָּרוּ Is. 52, 11, τενοντοῦν for עֹרֶף, etc. Sometimes, in genuine Rabbinic fashion (e. g. Gen. 41, 43 Targ.), he treated a word as a compound : thus 1 Sam. 6, 8 בָאַרְגַּז is rendered by him ἐν ὕφει κουρᾶς as though = בְּאֶרֶג גַּז ; ψ. 16, 1 מִכְתָּם ταπεινόφρων καὶ ἁπλοῦς (מָךְ תָּם); 73, 21 אֶשְׁתּוֹנָן πῦρ καπνιζόμενον (אֵשׁ תּוֹנָן): cf. p. lxxxiii. See more in the Prolegomena to Dr. Field's *Hexapla*, p. xxi ff., or in the art. HEXAPLA (by Dr. C. Taylor) in the *Dictionary of Christian Biography*.

Aquila was a pupil of R. Aqiba; and the statement is confirmed by the character of his translation. For R. Aqiba, at the beginning of the second cent. A.D., introduced a new system of interpretation, laying exaggerated stress upon even syllables and letters, quite in the manner followed by Aquila [1].

The Version of Theodotion was rather a revision of the LXX than a new translation, and hence frequently agrees with it. Renderings of Theodotion have often found their way into MSS. of the LXX, sometimes as doublets, sometimes as insertions made with the view of supplying apparent omissions (1 Sam. 17, 12–31 in Cod. A). In the case of Daniel, Theodotion's Version superseded that of the LXX, and occupies its place in ordinary MSS. and editions [2].

Symmachus was an Ebionite (Eus. *Hist. Eccl.* vi. 17). He is praised by Jerome as frequently clever and successful in his renderings: not slavish like Aquila, and yet reproducing, often with happy accommodations to Greek idiom, the sense of the original [3].

Origen's Hexapla. These three translations are not preserved in their entirety: they have been transmitted only in fragments, chiefly through the work of Origen, which is now to be described.

Origen (A.D. 185–254), observing not only the variations between the Septuagint and the Hebrew text current in his day, but also the variations between different MSS. of the Septuagint itself, undertook

---

[1] Illustrations may be found in Dr. Pusey's *What is of Faith as to Everlasting Punishment?* p. 80 ff.; Grätz, *Gesch. der Juden*, iv. 53 ff.

[2] The LXX Version of Daniel was first published from a unique MS. in 1772. In Tisch.'s edition it stands at the end of the second volume; in Swete's it is printed in parallel pages with Theodotion. Renderings agreeing remarkably with Theodotion's Version occur in the NT. (cf. p. 129 *n.*) and writers of the early part of the second century: it has hence been conjectured that his version of this book is based upon an earlier Greek translation independent of the LXX (Salmon, *Introd. to the NT.*, ed. 3, p. 586 ff.).

[3] Illustrations are given in abundance by Dr. Field, *Hexapla*, p. xxxi f.: for instance, in his use of the ptcp., of adverbs, of compounds, 1 Sam. 22, 8 LXX (literally) ἐν τῷ διαθέσθαι τὸν υἱόν μου διαθήκην, Symm. συντιθεμένου τοῦ υἱοῦ μου; Gen. 4, 2 LXX καὶ προσέθηκε τίκτειν, Symm. καὶ πάλιν ἔτεκεν; Pr. 15, 15 טוב לב Symm. ὁ εὔθυμων; Is. 9, 15 פנים נשׂוא αἰδέσιμος; 1 Sam. 25, 3 טובת שׂכל LXX ἀγαθὴ συνέσει, Σ. εὐδιανόητος; *ib.* רע־מעללים LXX πονηρὸς ἐν ἐπιτηδεύμασι, Σ. κακογνώμων; 2 Sam. 12, 8 וכהנה וכהנה LXX κατὰ ταῦτα, Σ. πολλαπλασίονα.

the task of recovering, if possible, the true text of the Septuagint, partly by aid of the Hebrew, partly by aid of the other Greek Versions. For this purpose, he arranged the different texts which he wished to compare in six parallel columns; the work thus formed being known in consequence as the *Hexapla.* In the first column, he placed the Hebrew text; in the second, the Hebrew transcribed in Greek characters; in the third and fourth, Aquila and Symmachus respectively; in the fifth, the Septuagint; in the sixth, Theodotion. In the Septuagint column, additions, to which nothing corresponded in the Hebrew, were marked by an obelus prefixed (÷ ..... ◄)[1]; omissions, where words standing in the Hebrew were not represented in the Greek, were filled in by him, usually from Theodotion, and noted similarly by an asterisk (※ ...... ◄)[2]. In cases where copies of the LXX differed between themselves, it is probable that Origen adopted silently the reading that agreed most closely with the Hebrew. Proper names, also, which the original translators had sometimes transliterated with some freedom, sometimes expressed in accordance with the older pronunciation, or which in other cases had become corrupted by transcription, Origen assimilated to the current Hebrew text. The manuscript of this great work was preserved for long in the Library of Pamphilus in Caesarea; Jerome collated it specially for his own use; but in 638 Caesarea fell into the hands of the Saracens, and from that time the Library and its contents are heard of no more. Copies of the *whole* work were probably never made; but the Septuagint column was edited separately by Eusebius and Pamphilus, and

---

[1] The sign ◄ indicates the *close* of the words to which the obelus or asterisk refers.

[2] The following is the important passage in which Origen himself describes both the motive and the plan of his work: Νυνὶ δὲ δηλονότι πολλὴ γέγονεν ἡ τῶν ἀντι- γράφων διαφορά, εἴτε ἀπὸ ῥᾳθυμίας τινῶν γραφέων εἴτε ἀπὸ τόλμης τινῶν μοχθηρᾶς τῆς διορθώσεως τῶν γραφομένων, εἴτε ἀπὸ τῶν τὰ ἑαυτοῖς δοκοῦντα ἐν τῇ διορθώσει προστι- θέντων ἢ ἀφαιρούντων. Τὴν μὲν οὖν ἐν τῇ διορθώσει τῆς παλαιᾶς διαθήκης διαφωνίαν, θεοῦ διδόντος, εὕρομεν ἰάσασθαι κριτηρίῳ χρησάμενοι ταῖς λοιπαῖς ἐκδόσεσιν . . . καὶ τινὰ μὲν ὠβελίσαμεν ἐν τῷ Ἑβραικῷ μὴ κείμενα οὐ τολμήσαντες αὐτὰ πάντη περιελεῖν, τινὰ δὲ μετ' ἀστερίσκων προσεθήκαμεν, ἵνα δῆλον ᾖ ὅτι μὴ κείμενα παρὰ τοῖς O' ἐκ τῶν λοιπῶν ἐκδόσεων συμφώνως τῷ Ἑβραικῷ προσεθήκαμεν, καὶ ὁ μὲν βουλόμενος πρόσηται αὐτά, ᾧ δὲ προσκόπτει τὸ τοιοῦτον ὃ βούλεται περὶ τῆς παραδοχῆς αὐτῶν, ἢ μή, ποιήσῃ (*Comm. in Matth.* xv. § 14).

was widely used. At the same time, the more important variants from the Versions of Aq. Theod. and Symm., contained in the other columns, were often excerpted; and many of these have thus been preserved to us, partly through citations made by the Fathers, partly from the margins of other MSS. In particular, Origen's text of the LXX (called the *Hexaplar* text), with many such marginal variants, was translated into Syriac by Paul, Bishop of Tella, in A.D. 617-18; and a peculiarly fine MS. of this translation (containing the prophetical and poetical books), preserved in the Ambrosian Library at Milan, has been published in facsimile by Ceriani. The most complete edition of the remains of the Hexapla is that of the late Dr. Field (Oxford, 1875), who has shewn remarkable skill in recovering from the renderings of the Syriac translation the original Greek [1].

Origen's work was projected with the best intentions: and it has been the means of preserving to us much, of priceless value, that would otherwise have perished. But it did not secure the end which he had in view. Origen did not succeed in restoring the genuine translation of the LXX. He *assumed* that the original Septuagint was that which agreed most closely with the *Hebrew text as he knew it*: he was guided partly by this, partly by the other Versions (Aq. Theod. Symm.), which were based substantially upon it: and where the Septuagint text differed from the current Hebrew text, he systematically altered it to bring it into conformity with it. This was a step in the wrong direction. Where a passage appears in two renderings, the one free, the other agreeing with the existent Hebrew text, it is the *former* which has the presumption of being the more original: the latter has the presumption of having been altered subsequently, in order that it might express the Hebrew more closely. Origen, no doubt, freed the text of the LXX from many *minor* faults; but in the main his work tended to obliterate the most original and distinctive features of the Version. To discover the Hebrew text used by the translators we must recover, as far as possible, the text of the Version *as it left the translators' hands;* and Origen's labours, instead of facilitating, rather impeded this process. In addition to this, the practical effect of the

---

[1] See further Swete, *Introd. to the O T. in Greek*, pp. 59-76; *DB*. iv. 442 ff.

method adopted by Origen was not to improve the purity of the LXX MSS. themselves; for not only were the signs which he himself used to indicate additions and omissions often neglected, as the Hexaplar text of the LXX was transcribed, but the Hexapla, from its very nature, encouraged the formation of *mixed* texts or recensions, so that, for instance, MSS. arose exhibiting side by side the genuine LXX and corrections introduced from Theodotion[1].

The original text of the LXX. For the recovery of this, the following canons have been laid down by Lagarde[2]:

1. The MSS. of the Greek translation of the OT. are all either immediately or mediately the result of an eclectic process: it follows that he who aims at recovering the original text must follow an eclectic method likewise. His only standard will be his knowledge of the style of the individual translators: his chief aid will be the faculty possessed by him of referring the readings which come before him to their Semitic original, or else of recognizing them as corruptions originating in the Greek.

2. If a verse or part of a verse appears in both a free and a slavishly literal translation, the former is to be counted the genuine rendering.

3. If two readings co-exist, of which one expresses the Massoretic text, while the other can only be explained from a text deviating from it, the latter is to be regarded as the original.

The first of these canons takes account of the fact that existing Greek MSS. exhibit a more or less *mixed* text, and justifies us in not adhering exclusively to a single MS.: a given MS. may contain on the whole the relatively truest text of the LXX; but other MSS. may also in particular instances, in virtue of the mixed origin of the text which they exhibit, preserve genuine Septuagintal renderings. The second and third canons formulate the principle for estimating double renderings in the same MS., or alternative renderings in different MSS., and derive their justification from the fact that the general method followed by later revisers and correctors was that of assimilating the renderings of the LXX to the Hebrew text (the ' Hebraica veritas ') current in

---

[1] On such ' Hexaplaric' texts, see Swete, *Introd.*, pp. 76–78, 482.
[2] *Anmerkungen zur griech. Übersetzung der Proverbien*, p. 3.

their day. The process, however, of recovering the genuine Septuagintal rendering, from two or more variants, can be successfully
carried on only by the continuous comparison of the existing Hebrew
text : it is this which affords us a *general* idea of what, in a given
passage, is to be expected, and supplies us with a criterion for
estimating the relative originality of the variants that may come before
us. An illustration may be taken from Jud. 5, 8, cited by We. from
Ewald. Cod. A there reads σκεπη νεανιδων σιρομαστων ανηφθη και
σιρομαστης. These words are evidently corrupt ; how are they to be
restored? The Massoretic text is מָגֵן אִם יֵרָאֶה וָרֹמַח. This gave the
clue, which enabled Ewald to explain and restore the words quoted.
The Hebrew shews that they contain a double rendering, which must
be read σκέπην ἐὰν ἴδω καὶ σιρομάστην and σκέπη ἐὰν ὀφθῇ καὶ σιρο-
μάστης, and that the first—either a *freer* rendering of אִם יראה, or
presupposing the variant אִם אראה—is the true reading of the LXX.
But this could hardly have been determined, or at least could not
have been determined with the same assurance, without the guidance
afforded by the Hebrew text itself [1].

Of course, after the application of Lagarde's canons, the two all-
important questions still await the textual critic : whether, viz.,
(1) the reading which deviates from the Massoretic text is actually
based upon a *divergent* text, or is simply a freer rendering of the *same*
text; and whether, further, (2) supposing the former alternative to be
the more probable, the divergent text is superior or not to the
Massoretic text. And these two questions can only be determined
by help of the general considerations alluded to above (p. xxxviii).
Illustrations will be afforded by the notes in the present volume. In
very many cases the answer is apparent at once ; but not unfrequently
more difficult cases arise, in which the answer is by no means

---

[1] Various readings which exist only in the *Greek*, and disappear when the Greek
is translated back into Hebrew, are, of course, only indirectly, and in particular
cases, of importance for the textual critic, who is interested primarily in such
variants alone as presuppose a *different* Hebrew original: thus in Jud. 1, 4. 5. 17
ἔκοψαν (B) and ἐπάταξαν (A) equally express the Hebrew ויכו; in 1 Sam. 5, 4 τὰ
ἐμπρόσθια and τὸ πρόθυρον and αμαφεθ all equally represent the same Hebrew term
המפתן. Variants of this kind are frequent in MSS. of the LXX.

immediately evident, or in which the arguments on both sides may be nearly equally balanced. It is the judgement and acumen displayed in handling the more difficult cases which arise under these two heads, that mark a textual critic of the first order, and distinguish, for example, Wellhausen, in a conspicuous degree, both from Thenius on the one side, and from Keil on the other.

MSS. of the LXX. According to a well-known passage of Jerome, *three* main recensions of the Septuagint prevailed in antiquity, that of *Hesychius* in Egypt, that of *Lucian* in Asia Minor and Constantinople, that of *Origen* in Palestine [1]. The Manuscripts containing the recensions of Hesychius and Origen are not certainly known [2]; though Ceriani with some reason supposes Origen's to be contained in the Syriac version of the Hexaplar text, mentioned above, and in the allied Cod. 88 of Holmes and Parsons, and the Cod. Sarravianus [3]; that of Lucian has been edited (as far as Esther) by Lagarde, and will be spoken of below.

The three principal MSS. of the LXX are the Vatican (B), the Sinaitic (‭א‬ or S), and the Alexandrian (A). The Vatican MS. is complete with the exception of Gen. 1, 1—46, 28. 2 Sam. 2, 5–7. 10–13. ψ. 105, 27—137, 6; the Sinaitic MS. is defective for nearly the whole of Gen.—2 Esdras, in the rest of the OT. the only serious lacuna is Ezekiel; the Alexandrian MS. is complete except for Gen. 14, 14–17. 15, 1–5. 16–19. 16, 6–9. 1 Sam. 12, 18—14, 9. ψ. 49, 20—79, 11. That of all MSS. of LXX, B (with which ‭א‬ frequently agrees), as a rule, exhibits *relatively* the purest and most original

---

[1] Preface to Chronicles (printed at the beginning of the Vulgate): Alexandria et Aegyptus in Septuaginta suis *Hesychium* laudat auctorem ; Constantinopolis usque Antiochiam *Luciani* martyris exemplaria probat; mediae inter has provinciae Palestinos codices legunt quos ab *Origene* elaboratos Eusebius et Pamphilus vulgaverunt : totusque orbis hac inter se trifaria varietate compugnat. The last of these recensions is naturally the source of the *Hexaplar* text spoken of above ; and Jerome states elsewhere (I 635 Vallarsi) that it was read ('decantatur') at Jerusalem and in the churches of the East.

[2] Lagarde, *Mittheilungen*, ii. 52; comp. G. F. Moore, *AJSL.* xxix. 47–50.

[3] *Le recensioni dei LXX e la versione latina detta Itala*, Estratto dai *Rendiconti* del R. istituto Lombardo, Serie II, vol. xix, fasc. IV (Milan, 1886), p. 2. Lagarde, *l. c.* p. 56, says that he knows of one MS. of the Octateuch (in private hands), not yet collated, which 'almost certainly' contains it.

Septuagintal text, is generally allowed[1]: that it contains double renderings, and has otherwise not escaped corruption, will appear presently (p. lv ff.)[2]. The Alexandrian MS. exhibits a text which has been systematically corrected so as to agree more closely with the Hebrew: proof of this is afforded by almost any page: thus 1 Sam. 1, 1 where Cod. B has Ἄνθρωπος ἦν ἐξ Αρμαθαιμ Σειφα, Cod. A has Καὶ ἐγένετο ἄνθρωπος εἰς ἐξ Αρμαθαιμ Σωφιμ=צופים הרמתים מן אחד איש ויהי[3]. The best edition of the LXX for ordinary use is that of Dr. Swete[4], which contains (so far as they are extant) the text of B with the variants of א and other selected uncials on the margin: Lucian must be read in Lagarde's edition[5]. The readings of other MSS. must, however, sometimes be consulted (for they may preserve readings of importance); these, so far as they have been collated, are chiefly to be found in the great work of Holmes and Parsons[6].

---

[1] Its value, however, varies in different books: in some it exhibits more Hexaplaric elements than A. See Procksch, *Studien zur Gesch. der Sept.* (1910), pp. 44–9; Swete, p. 487 f.; and comp. Torrey, *Ezra Studies* (1910), p. 92 ff.

[2] Respecting the recension to which B presumably belongs, its text is of a character which led Dr. Hort to infer (*Academy*, Dec. 24, 1887) that it was copied from a MS. (or MSS.) partially akin to the MS. (or MSS.) which Origen, with the adaptations fitting it to his purpose, made the basis of the LXX text in his Hexapla: comp. Ceriani, *l. c.* p. 7, ' B exhibits the unrevised text of LXX as it was before Origen.' This view was accepted by Cornill (*Gött. gelehrte Nachrichten*, 1888, pp. 194–6, where the view propounded by him in *Ezechiel*, pp. 81, 84, 95, is abandoned); and it has been further confirmed by recent research : see Silberstein, who, in a study on the LXX of 1 Ki. (*ZAW.* 1893, p. 1 f., 1894, p. 1 ff.), agrees (1894, p. 26) with Cornill (p. 196) that ' B cum grano salis is the *Vorlage* of ' Origen's LXX column in the Hexapla; and Rahlfs, *Studien*, i. 85. Rahlfs argues further (*Gött. gel. Nachrichten*, 1899, p. 72 ff.; cf. *Studien*, i. 87), from the order of the books in B agreeing with that given by Athanasius in his 39th Festal Epistle (A. D. 367), that B was written in Egypt, shortly after this date.

[3] See further Swete, *Introd.* p. 125 ff.

[4] *The OT. in Greek according to the Septuagint*, vol. i, 1887 (³ 1901), vol. ii, 1891 (³ 1907), vol. iii (² 1899). This edition supersedes that of Tischendorf. A larger edition (*The OT. in Greek*, edited by A. E. Brooke and N. McLean), containing an extensive *apparatus criticus*, is in course of publication by the Cambridge Press: at present (July, 1912), three Parts (Gen.–Dt.) have appeared.

[5] *Librorum Vet. Test. Canonicorum Pars Prior Graece Pauli de Lagarde studio et sumptibus edita* (1883). This edition is very convenient; but it has no critical apparatus, and the text is not entirely satisfactory (see Moore, *AJSL.* xxix. 56).

[6] *Vetus Testamentum Graecum cum variis lectionibus*, Oxonii, 1798–1827. See Swete, *The OT. in Greek*, i. p. ix; *Introd.* pp. 185–7. But cf. *n.* 3, above.

Lucian's recension of the Septuagint. In the apparatus criticus of Holmes and Parsons four MSS., 19, 82, 93 [1], 108, are cited frequently as agreeing together in exhibiting a text considerably different from that of either B or A. That these MSS. preserved in some cases important readings of superior originality even to those of B was noticed by Wellhausen in 1871 [2], though he did not perceive the full bearing of the fact, or pursue the subject further beyond observing that Vercellone had remarked that the readings of these MSS. often coincided with those of the Itala, or pre-Hieronymian Latin Version of the OT. That these MSS. exhibit in fact the recension of Lucian appears to have been first recognized by Ceriani in 1863 [3]. The same conclusion was arrived at also by Lagarde [4], who pointed to the numerous agreements between the text of these MSS. (to which he adds 118) and the citations of Chrysostom, who, as a priest of Antioch, and Bishop of Constantinople, would presumably, in accordance with Jerome's statement, make use of this recension; and its correctness was further established by Dr. Field [5], who shewed that the text of the same four MSS. corresponded with readings cited in the Syriac Hexaplar text with the letter *L*. Lucian was a priest of the Church of Antioch, who suffered martyrdom at Nicomedia, A.D. 312: according to the passage of Suidas cited below [6], he prepared with great pains a revised edition of the Septuagint, which he sought by comparison with the Hebrew to free from the corruptions which by accident

---

[1] MS. 93 is in the main the basis of Lagarde's text (Rahlfs, iii. 79 f.; Moore, 57).
[2] *Der Text der Bücher Samuelis*, pp. 221-4.
[3] *Monumenta Sacra et Profana*, ii. 2 (1864), pp. 76, 98, 102 (specially Codd. 19, 108, 118, and the Complut. text); also (for the Lamentations) *ib.* i. (1861), on Lam. 2, 22 *end.* 3, 7. 22. 29. 30. 33. 63. 4, 7 etc., where the agreement of Theodoret is also noted. See also Ceriani's opinion as cited in Dr. Field's *Hexapla*, ii. 429 (published originally in 1869).
[4] *Pars Prior* etc. Preface, pp. vii–xiv.
[5] *Hexapla*, p. lxxxvii.
[6] S. v. Λουκιανὸς ὁ μάρτυς· οὗτος τὰς ἱερὰς βίβλους θεασάμενος πολὺ τὸ νοθὸν εἰσδεξαμένας, τοῦ γε χρόνου λυμηναμένου πολλὰ τῶν ἐν αὐταῖς, καὶ τῆς συνεχοῦς ἀφ' ἑτέρων εἰς ἕτερα μεταθέσεως, καὶ μέντοι καί τινων ἀνθρώπων πονηροτάτων, οἳ τοῦ Ἑλληνισμοῦ προειστήκεισαν, παρατρέψαι τὸν ἐν αὐταῖς θελησάντων νοῦν, καὶ πολὺ τὸ κίβδηλον ἐνσκευασαμένων, αὐτὸς ἁπάσας ἀναλαβὼν ἐκ τῆς Ἑβραΐδος ἐπανενεώσατο γλώττης, ἣν καὶ αὐτὴν ἐς τὰ μάλιστα ἦν ἠκριβωκὼς πόνον τῇ ἐπανορθώσει πλεῖστον εἰσενεγκάμενος.

or design had in process of time been introduced into it. One large class of alterations made by Lucian affect, however, only the literary form of the Septuagint: they consist namely in the substitution of synonyms (as παρεγένετο for ἦλθεν, ἐπολέμησε for παρετάξατο, τὸ ἀρεστὸν for τὸ ἀγαθὸν) for the words originally used by the translators. Obviously variants such as these do not point to a different reading of the Hebrew. Double renderings also occur frequently in Lucian's recension, i. e. retaining the normal Septuagintal version of a passage, he placed beside it a rendering expressing more closely the current Hebrew text, either framed by himself, or (more probably) adopted from particular MSS., or other translators. But what imparts to Lucian's work its great importance in the criticism of the OT., is the fact that it embodies renderings, not found in other MSS. of the LXX, which presuppose a Hebrew original self-evidently superior, in the passages concerned, to the existing Massoretic text. Whether these renderings were derived by him from MSS. of the LXX of which all other traces have disappeared, or whether they were based directly upon Hebrew MSS. which had preserved the genuine reading intact, whether in other words they were derived mediately or immediately from the Hebrew, is a matter of subordinate moment: the fact remains that Lucian's recension contains elements resting ultimately upon Hebrew sources, which enable us to correct, with absolute certainty, corrupt passages of the Massoretic text. Several instances will be found in the notes in the present volume. In some of these, it is instructive to notice, a conjectural emendation made by a modern scholar has proved to be afterwards confirmed by the testimony of Lucian[1]. The full gain from this quarter is in all probability not yet exhausted: a number of passages, selected from the Books of Kings, in which the Massoretic text may be emended by the help of Lucian's recension, are noticed by I. Hooykaas[2]. 'Let him who would himself investigate and advance learning, by the side of the other Ancient Versions, accustom himself above all things to

---

[1] So in 2 Ki. 15, 10 Grätz's clever conjecture (*Gesch. der Juden*, ii. 1, p. 99) בִיבְלְעָם for the un-Hebraic קָבְל־עָם is confirmed by Lucian. Cf. on II 24, 5.

[2] *Iets over de Grieksche vertaling van het oude Testament* (Rotterdam, 1888), p. 12 ff. Cf. Burney, *Notes on the Hebrew Text of Kings* (1903), p. xxxi.

the use of Field's *Hexapla*, and Lagarde's edition of the Recension of Lucian [1].'

On Lucian, see now the very thorough discussion of his recension of 1-2 Ki. in Rahlfs, *Septuaginta-Studien*, iii. (1911), with synopses of the various readings (for these books) found in the MSS. (19, 82, 83, 108, 127) of Lucian's recension itself (§§ 9-13), and also of Lucian's readings found in other MSS. of LXX (§§ 4-7), in Josephus (§§ 15-21), or quoted by the Fathers (§§ 25-38). A minute study of Lucian's text of 1 Ki. 1 (pp. 163-191), and a study of all its principal variants in 1-2 Ki. generally (pp. 191-290), lead Rahlfs to the conclusion (pp. 190 f., 192) that while *some* of the variants are corrections introduced by Lucian himself from the Hebrew into the LXX text current at the time, others cannot be so explained, but point to older sources; and (pp. 235, 290 f.) that the foundation of Lucian's text is an old, *pre*-Hexaplaric text, closely allied to (though not identical with) Cod. B, and to the Greek text which formed the basis of the older [2] Ethiopic version [3].

Josephus, though he by no means agrees always with Lucian's readings, affords evidence that readings of Luc. were current in the 1st cent. A. D. Rahlfs (§ 16) cites after Mez, *Die Bibel von Josephus* (1895)—who, however, quotes also many readings not specifically Lucianic—from 1-2 Sam. nine cases of Jos. agreeing with Luc. against Codd. A, B, viz. :—

II   3, 7 הָאִ֫, ⑥ Ιολ : Luc. Σ(ε)ιβα ; Jos. vii. 23 Σιβάτου.

15, 12 גִּילֹנִי, ⑥ Vulg. Γωλαμωναῖος, etc. ; B Θεκωνει ; Luc. Jos. vii. 197 Γελμω-
      ναῖος.

16, 5 בַּחוּרִים, ⑥ Βαουρ(ε)ιμ ; Luc. Χορραμ ; Jos. vii. 207 Χωρανον, Χωραμον.

19, 38. 39 כִּמְהָם (*v.* 41 כִּמְהָן), ⑥ Χαμααμ, Χανααν : Luc. Αχιμααν, Αχινααμ, etc. ;
      Jos. vii. 274 Αχιμανον.

---

[1] Klostermann, *Die Bücher Sam. u. Könige* (1887), p. xl. Of course, this advice must be understood with the needful and obvious qualifications : it is not intended that everything to be found in Lucian is to be indiscriminately preferred to the Massoretic text. There is undoubtedly wheat in Lucian, but there is also much chaff (cf. Torrey, *Ezra Studies*, 1910, 105 ff.); and it is the task of the textual critic to distinguish between them.

The Complutensian Polyglott is based upon the text of Lucian. Holmes' MS. 108 = Vatican 330 is the manuscript which was sent in 1513-14 by Leo X to Spain for the use of the editors of that Polyglott : the minutes relating to the loan and return of the MS. still exist in the Vatican Library (Delitzsch, *Fortgesetzte Studien zur Entstehungsgesch. der Compl. Polygl.*, Leipzig, 1886, p. 2). It does not, however, reproduce MS. 108 exactly. Where the text of the MS. differs materially from the Heb. or the Vulg., it was constantly corrected, sometimes from other Greek MSS., sometimes from the Hebrew (see Rahlfs, p. 18 ff.).

[2] The '*antiqua versio.*' See Cornill, *Ezechiel*, pp. 37-42.

[3] The *antiqua versio* is based upon the LXX, and in particular on the recension represented by B. See Rahlfs, i. 84, 85 ; Raupp in *Z. für Ass.* xvi. (1903), 329 (in a study, p. 296 ff., on the oldest Ethiopic MS. of Sam.-Kings, in the Borgio Museum at Rome; the article contains also a collation of Dillmann's text).

20, 1 בְּכְרִי, ⑤ Boχop(ε)ι = Boχopίoυ of the *Greek* Jos. (vii. 278): Luc. Bεδ-
δaδ(ε)ι, the *Latin* Jos. *Beddadi.*

21, 18 הַחֻשָׁתִי, ⑤ ὁ Aσωθι, ὁ Aσтaтωθει, etc. ; Luc. Jos. vii. 301 ὁ Xεттaîos.

23, 8 '800' [1 Ch. 11, 11 '300'], ⑤ '800' : Luc. (both Sam. and Ch.), Jos.
vii. 308 '900'.

23, 11 אֲנָא, ⑤ Aγa, Aσa, etc.: Luc. Hλa, Jos. vii. 310 'Hλoῦ (genit.).

24, 9 '800,000 + 500,000', so ⑤: Luc. (and Codd. 52, 236, 242, Cat. Nic.), Jos.
vii. 320 ' 900,000 + 400,000 '.[1]

2. The *Targums* are Aramaic Versions made for the use of the
Jews, in Palestine or Babylon, when Hebrew ceased to be generally
spoken.   These are of various and not always certain date.   According to tradition, the Targum that was first committed to writing,
in the first century, was that on Job ; but other of the Targums
undoubtedly embody traditional interpretations that were current
orally before they were definitely fixed in writing.   The Targum was
originally an extemporaneous translation and interpretation of successive verses of Scripture, delivered by the מְתוּרְגְּמָן in the public worship
of the Synagogue.   From the circumstances of its origin it lent itself
readily to expansion : edification, rather than literal translation, was
the aim of the מתורגמן ; and hence the very paraphrastic character
which the Targum—especially that on the Latter Prophets—is apt
to assume.   In the historical books, however, except in poetical
passages (as Gen. 49, Jud. 5, 1 Sam. 2, 1–10, 2 Sam. 23, 1–7), the
Targum is as a rule tolerably literal.   The Targum on the Former
and Latter Prophets is ascribed to Jonathan ben Uzziel[2].

3. The Syriac Version, commonly known as the *Peshiṭṭo* (ܡܰܦܩܳܬܐ
ܦܫܝܛܬܐ *editio simplex*), originated in the needs of the large Syriac-
speaking population N. and NE. of Palestine, whose literary centre
was Edessa.   No historical details respecting its origin have come
down to us : already Theodore of Mopsuestia (fourth cent.) declares
that it is not known who translated the Scriptures into Syriac ; but
it is generally considered to date, at least in the main, from the early
part of the second cent. A. D.   Like the Septuagint, the Peshiṭṭo is

---

[1] On the alleged dependence of Luc. on Theodotion, see Smith, *Comm.*, 402 ff.

[2] For fuller particulars see the art. TARGUM (by E. Deutsch) in Smith's
Dictionary of the Bible ; Bacher in the ZDMG. xxviii, p. 1 ff.; and art. TARGUM
(T. Walker) in DB.

not the work of a single hand; and the style of the different books, or groups of books, varies. Mainly, no doubt, the translators were either Jews or, more probably, Jewish Christians. Thus the translation of the Pentateuch, for instance, often adheres closely to ancient Jewish exegesis[1], traces of which are also discernible in other books, especially in the Chronicles, the translation of which has additions and embellishments, imparting to it quite the character of a Targum[2]. Job, on the other hand, is literal: while the translation of the Psalms is strongly influenced by the Septuagint, with which it often remarkably agrees, where both deviate from the Hebrew.

4. We reach now the Latin Versions. Of these the first is the _Old Latin_ Version, used by early Latin Fathers, as Tertullian (died _c._ 220), Cyprian (d. 257), Lactantius, Lucifer of Cagliari (d. 371), and Augustine[3]. This Version exists only in a more or less fragmentary form, derived partly from MSS., partly from quotations in the Fathers. Of the OT. the part most completely preserved is the Hexateuch, published (to Dt. 11, 4[4]) by Ulysse Robert from a Lyons MS. (1881): in the Books of Samuel only fragments are extant derived from the sources just named. Of these fragments, such as were known at the time were published by Sabatier in 1743 in his great work, _Bibliorum Sacrorum Antiquae Versiones Latinae:_ Vercellone in 1864 in vol. ii of the _Variae Lectiones Vulgatae Latinae Bibliorum editionis_ printed other considerable extracts from the margin of a Gothic MS. at Leon in Spain[5]; three fragments, discovered in the bindings of some books at Magdeburg (II 2, 29—3, 5 [also 1 Ki. 5, 2–9ᵃ]) and Quedlinburg (I 9, 1–8ᵃ; 15, 10–17ᵃ), were edited by Von Mülverstedt in 1874[6]; two other fragments, discovered similarly at Vienna, were published

---

[1] See especially J. Perles, _Meletemata Peschitthoniana_ (Vratislaviae, 1859).

[2] Sig. Fränkel, _Die Syr. Übersetzung zu den BB. der Chronik_ (1879).

[3] See fully, on this Version, H. A. A. Kennedy's comprehensive article, _DB._ iii. 47 ff.: comp. _PRE._[2] viii. 433-443 (Fritzsche); _PRE._[3] iii. 25-31 (Nestle).

[4] On the continuation, see _DB._ iii. 49ᵇ, iv. 446ᵃ.

[5] _Variae Lectiones,_ ii. pp. xxi–xxii, 179, etc.: comp. i. pp. xciii–xcv.

[6] _Zeitschrift des Harzvereins,_ 1874, pp. 251–263. The two Quedlinburg fragments were re-edited by W. Schum in the _Stud. u. Kritiken,_ 1876, p. 123 f. (1 Ki. 5, 9ᵇ—6, 11ᵃ has recently been recovered from the same source: A. Düning, _Ein neues Fragment des Quedlinburger Itala-Codex,_ 1888).

in 1877[1]; in 1885 J. Belsheim edited some longer fragments (of other parts of the OT. as well as 1–2 Sam.) from a palimpsest MS. at Vienna[2]. The Old Latin Version does not, as a rule, possess an independent value for the textual criticism of the OT., for it was not made immediately from the Hebrew, but was formed upon the Greek. As the extant parts of it shew that it existed in different recensions[3], it becomes a matter of importance to inquire how these are related to one another, and upon what MSS., or family of MSS., of the LXX they are based. As will be shewn below (p. lxxvi ff.), in the Books of Samuel the recensions which we possess are based upon a text agreeing with that of Lucian.

More important for our present purpose is the Latin Version of Jerome, commonly known as the *Vulgate*[4]. Jerome began his labours as a translator by merely revising the Old Latin ; but ultimately made a new Version directly from the Hebrew. He had originally learnt Hebrew as a youth[5], and after having dropped the study for a while,

---

[1] *Augustissimae Bibliothecae Caesareae Regiae Palatinae Vindobonensis Praefecto Doctori Ernesto Birk munerum publicorum feliciter peracto XL annorum cyclo gratulantes qui a Bibliotheca sunt Veteris Antehieronymianae Versionis Libri II Regum sive Samuelis Cap. X.* 18—*XI.* 17 *et Cap. XIV.* 17-30 *principem editionem dedicant inlustratam Tabulis Photographicis* (Vindobonae, MDCCCLXXVII). Cited as Vind.[1]

[2] *Palimpsestus Vindobonensis* antiquissimae Vet. Test. Translationis latinae fragmenta e codice rescripto eruit et primum edidit Johannes Belsheim Christianiae, 1885 (1 Sam. 1, 14—2, 15. 3, 10—4, 18. 6, 3-15. 9, 21—10, 7. 10, 16—11, 13. 14, 12-34. 2 Sam. 4, 10—5, 25. 10, 13—11, 18. 13, 13—14, 4. 17, 12—18, 9). Cited as Vind.[2] (One column of this MS., containing II 11, 2-6, had been published previously, as a specimen, by Eichenfeld and Endlicher, *Analecta Grammatica*, Vindob. 1837, p. ix.) For some other recently discovered fragments see *DB.* iii. 50[a].

[3] Regarded by some as independent *versions:* see *PRE.*[2] viii. 434-6; *DB.* iii. 48-9.

[4] On the Vulgate generally, see the elaborate article by Mr. (afterwards Bishop) Westcott in Smith's *Dictionary of the Bible :* on its relation to the Hebrew text of the OT. in particular, the careful monograph of W. Nowack, *Die Bedeutung des Hieronymus für die alttestamentliche Textkritik* (Göttingen, 1875), should by all means be consulted. See also H. J. White's art. VULGATE in *DB.* iv. p. 873 ff.

[5] Preface to Daniel (printed at the beginning of editions of the Vulgate); Ep. 125, § 12 (Migne, i. 1079),—an interesting passage, too long to quote.

resumed it in his later years, after his migration to Bethlehem in 386. The Books of Samuel and Kings were published first (*c.* 393), but the whole work was not completed till 405. For the purpose of perfecting his knowledge of Hebrew, and also subsequently for assistance in the translation of particular books, Jerome engaged the help of Jewish teachers, to whom in his commentaries he more than once alludes[1], and from whom no doubt he derived the Rabbinical interpretations which occur from time to time in the pages of the Vulgate[2]. Though his Version was made afresh from the Hebrew, he did not disdain to avail himself of the labours of his predecessors, and consulted constantly the Greek Versions (both the LXX and Aq. Theod. Symm.), the renderings of which he frequently quotes and discusses. He was especially prone to be guided by Symmachus. Where the Vulgate exhibits a rendering which deviates alike from the Hebrew text and from the LXX, the clue to its origin will generally be found in one of the other Greek translations, especially in that of Symmachus (see pp. lxxxi–lxxxiii).

NOTE.—For the recovery of the original text of the LXX, much yet remains to be done (cf. *EB.* iv. 5021 f.). The first step is the more accurate collation of MSS. for the purpose, if possible, of grouping them in families, or recensions. Upon this field of study Lagarde (d. 1891) stood pre-eminent (comp. Cornill, *Ezech.*, p. 63): but

---

[1] Ep. 84, § 3 : Putabant me homines finem fecisse discendi. Veni rursum Ierosolyma et Bethleem. Quo labore, quo pretio Baraninam nocturnum habui praeceptorem ! Timebat enim Judaeos, et mihi alterum exhibebat Nicodemum. Preface to Chron. : Denique cum a me litteris flagitassetis ut vobis librum Paralipomenon Latino sermone transferrem, de Tiberiade quemdam legis doctorem qui apud Hebraeos admirationi habebatur assumpsi : et contuli cum eo a vertice, ut aiunt, usque ad extremum unguem ; et sic confirmatus ausus sum facere quod iubebatis. Preface to Job : Memini me ob intelligentiam huius voluminis Lyddaeum quemdam praeceptorem, qui apud Hebraeos primus haberi putabatur, non parvis redemisse nummis. On Am. 3, 11 he alludes to the 'Hebraeus qui me in sacris Scripturis erudivit:' similarly on Zeph. 3. 8. Gal. 3, 14 al. On Hab. 2, 15 : Audivi Lyddae quemdam de Hebraeis qui *sapiens* apud illos et δευτερώτης [= נַבָּא] vocabatur narrantem huiuscemodi fabulam, etc. On Zech. 14, 20 : Quod cum ab Hebraeo quaererem quid significaret, ait mihi, etc.

[2] Comment. on Is. 22, 17 on גבר : Hebraeus autem qui nos in Veteris Testamenti lectione erudivit *gallum gallinaceum* transtulit. (See the Comm. of Rashi *ad loc.*) Comp. M. Rahmer, *Die hebräischen Traditionen in den Werken des Hieronymus* (Breslau, 1861) ; continued (with reference to Hosea) in Frankel's *Monatschrift*, 1865, pp. 216, 460 ; 1867, p. 107 ; 1868, p. 419.

the task was greater than any single man, even with Lagarde's extraordinary powers of work, could accomplish ; and he was only able to point the way which others could follow (see Rahlfs, *Sept. Studien*, iii. 3, 23-30). His mantle has fallen upon his pupil and successor at Göttingen, Alfred Rahlfs, who has published exhaustive investigations on the pre-Hexaplar LXX-text of 1-2 Kings, as inferred from Origen's citations ; on the text and MSS. of the Psalms ; and on Lucian's recension of 1-2 Kings (*Septuaginta-studien*, i. 1904, ii. 1907, iii. 1911). See also O. Procksch, *Studien zur Gesch. der Sept.* 1910 (on the text of the Prophets) ; and G. F. Moore's valuable article on the Antiochian Recension of the LXX in *AJSL.* xxix (Oct. 1912), pp. 37-62. And, on the recovery of the Hebrew original of difficult LXX renderings, see Margolis, *ZAW.* 1905, 311 ff., 1906, 85 ff., 1907, 255 ff.; *AJSL.* xxii (Jan. 1906), 110 ff., xxvi (Oct. 1909), 33 ff. ; *Harper Memorial Studies* (1908), i. 133 ff.

§ 4. *Characteristics of the Chief Ancient Versions of Samuel*[1].

1. The Septuagint.

a. Features which presumably are not original elements in the Version, or due to the translators themselves.

(*a*) Examples of double renderings ('doublets') : these are frequently connected by καί :—

I 1, 16 Luc. שיחי מרב=ἐκ πλήθους ἀδολεσχίας μου καὶ ἐκ πλήθους ἀθυμίας μου.

1, 26 עמכה=ἐνώπιόν σου μετά σου.

2, 24 אל בני כי לוא טובה השמעה אשר אנכי שמע=μή, τέκνα, ὅτι οὐκ ἀγαθὴ ἡ ἀκοὴ ἣν ἐγὼ ἀκούω, μὴ ποιεῖτε οὕτως ὅτι οὐκ ἀγαθαὶ αἱ ἀκοαὶ ἃς ἐγὼ ἀκούω.

4, 14-16ᵃ (to אל עלי)=[14 καὶ ἤκουσεν Ἤλει τὴν φωνὴν τῆς βοῆς καὶ εἶπεν Τίς ἡ βοὴ τῆς φωνῆς ταύτης; καὶ ὁ ἄνθρωπος σπεύσας εἰσῆλθεν καὶ ἀπήγγειλεν τῷ Ἤλει· 15 καὶ Ἤλει υἱὸς ἐνενήκοντα ἐτῶν, καὶ οἱ ὀφθαλμοὶ αὐτοῦ ἐπανέστησαν καὶ οὐκ ἔβλεπεν·] καὶ εἶπεν Ἤλει τοῖς ἀνδράσιν τοῖς παρειστηκόσιν αὐτῷ Τίς ἡ φωνὴ τοῦ ἤχους τούτου; 16 καὶ ὁ ἀνὴρ σπεύσας προσῆλθεν Ἤλει καὶ εἶπεν αὐτῷ. In LXX 14 is a doublet to 15ᵇ-16ᵃ : 15ᵇ-16ᵃ represent the original LXX of 14-16ᵃ Heb., 15 Heb. being accidentally omitted; the omission was afterwards supplied, a closer rendering of 14 Heb. being given at the same time.

5, 4 ושתי כפות ידיו כרתות אל-המפתן=καὶ ἀμφότερα τὰ ἴχνη χειρῶν αὐτοῦ ἀφῃρημένα ἐπὶ τὰ ἐμπρόσθια αμαφεθ ἕκαστοι, καὶ ἀμφότεροι οἱ καρποὶ τῶν χειρῶν αὐτοῦ πεπτωκότες ἐπὶ τὸ πρόθυρον.

---

[1] Only the more salient features can be noticed.

6, 7 Luc. אשר לא עלה עליהם עֹל=ἄνευ τῶν τετεγμένων ἐφ᾽ ἃς οὐκ ἐπετέθη ζύγος (ἄνευ τῶν τετ.=עֹל עליהם לא אשר We.).

6, 8 אתו וֹשלחתם=καὶ ἐξαποστελεῖτε αὐτήν, καὶ ἀπελάσατε αὐτήν.

6, 12 Luc. במסלה אחת הלכו הלך וגעו=ἐν τρίβῳ εὐθείᾳ ἐπορεύοντο· ἐκοπίων . . . ἐν ὁδῷ μιᾷ ἐπορεύοντο πορεύουσαι καὶ βοῶσαι (ἐκοπ.= יָגַעוּ for וְנָעוּ).

10, 2 Luc. בצלצח=μεσημβρίας ἁλλομένους μεγάλα (see note).

14, 40 Luc. ויאמר אל כל ישראל אתם תהיו לעבר אחד ואני ויונתן בני נהיה לעבר אחד ויאמרו העם אל שאול הטוב בעיניך עשה=Καὶ εἶπε Σαουλ παντὶ ἀνδρὶ Ἰσραηλ Ὑμεῖς ἔσεσθε εἰς δουλείαν, καὶ ἐγὼ καὶ Ἰωναθαν ὁ υἱός μου ἐσόμεθα εἰς δουλείαν. καὶ εἶπεν ὁ λαὸς πρὸς Σαουλ Τὸ ἀρεστὸν ἐνώπιόν σου ποίει· καὶ εἶπε Σαουλ πρὸς τὸν λαὸν Ὑμεῖς ἔσεσθε εἰς ἓν μέρος, καὶ ἐγὼ καὶ Ἰωναθαν ἐσόμεθα εἰς ἓν μέρος. Here a second translation, correcting the strange mistranslation of LXX, is inserted in the text out of its proper place.

14, 47 לכד המלוכה=ἔλαχεν τοῦ βασιλεύειν, κατακληροῦται ἔργον (המלכה read as הַמְלָאכָה=הַמְּלֶכָה)[1].

15, 3 והחרמתם את כל אשר לו ולא תחמל עליו=καὶ Ιερειμ καὶ πάντα τὰ αὐτοῦ καὶ οὐ περιποιήσῃ ἐξ αὐτοῦ καὶ ἐξολεθρεύσεις αὐτόν· καὶ ἀναθεματιεῖς αὐτὸν καὶ πάντα τὰ αὐτοῦ καὶ οὐ φείσῃ ἀπ᾽ αὐτοῦ. Here each verb is rendered twice (ἐξολεθρ.=החרים as *vv.* 9. 15 al.), והחרמתם being represented moreover a third time by καὶ Ιερειμ.

16, 16 וטוב לך=καὶ ἀγαθόν σοι ἔσται καὶ ἀναπαύσει σε. (The combination of two renderings, though accepted by Th. as the original text, has the effect, as We. remarks, of putting the effect before the cause.)

18, 28 Luc. ומיכל בת־שאול אהבתהו=καὶ [Μελχολ ἡ θυγάτηρ αὐτοῦ καὶ] πᾶς Ἰσραηλ ἠγάπα αὐτόν. Here by the side of the genuine LXX rendering is inserted a second translation expressing the later (and corrupted) Hebrew text: see note.

20, 9 עליך=ἐπί σε . . . εἰς τὰς πόλεις σου (עריך).

---

[1] Lucian combines the two renderings rather cleverly : κατακληροῦται τὸ ἔργον τοῦ βασιλεύειν : cf. 12, 2 (the addition of ἐκ τοῦ νῦν). 16, 20 (p. lviii). 17, 2. 21, 12.

21, 14 (13 LXX) ויתהלל=ויתהלל בידם ויתו על דלתות השער=καὶ προσ-
εποιήσατο ἐν τῇ ἡμέρᾳ ἐκείνῃ, καὶ ἐτυμπάνιζεν (=וַיְתָו) ἐπὶ ταῖς
θύραις τῆς πόλεως καὶ παρεφέρετο ἐν ταῖς χέρσιν αὐτοῦ καὶ ἔπιπτεν
ἐπὶ τὰς θύρας τῆς πόλεως. Each verb is represented in the
Greek twice.

23, 1 והמה שסים את־הגרנות=καὶ αὐτοὶ διαρπάζουσιν καταπατοῦσιν
τοὺς ἅλως. (καταπατέω=שסה 14, 48; =שסם 17, 53.)

II 6, 2 מבעלי יהודה=ἀπὸ τῶν ἀρχόντων Ἰουδα ἐν ἀναβάσει (i.e. במעלה
for מבעלי [see p. lxvii]; Klo.'s view is less probable)[1].

While 'doublets' are thus not infrequent even in Cod. B, they are
peculiarly characteristic of the recension of Lucian[2]. When Lucian
found in his MSS. two divergent renderings of a passage, he systematically *combined* them, producing thereby what would be called in
the terminology of New Testament criticism 'conflate' readings. As
my friend, Prof. Sanday, reminds me, this method of combining
different readings is characteristic of the Syrian school of critics, from
whom the modern 'Textus Receptus' of the NT. is essentially
derived. The application of the same method, at approximately the
same time and place, to the text of both Testaments must be due
to some common influence, even if (as has been conjectured[3]) it be
not Lucian himself to whom the Syrian recension of the NT. is due.

(*b*) Corruptions originating in the Greek text itself in the process
of transmission. Where by the change of one or two letters the
Greek may be brought into conformity with the Hebrew, it is more
probable, as a rule, that the variation originated in the Greek only
(especially if it is one that might be facilitated by the context), than that
it is due to a difference in the Hebrew text used by the translators:—

I 4, 19 ותכרע ἔκλαυσεν from ὤκλασεν (We.): see 1 Ki. 8, 54. 19,
18.—9, 24 וירם ἤψησεν (probably) a corruption of ὕψωσεν (cf. ὑψόω

---

[1] See also the notes on I 20, 30 (Luc.). 27, 8^b. II 13, 16. 14, 6. 15, 17 f. 19,
44. 20, 18–19. 22. 21, 1. 5. For doublets connected by ἤ, see Margolis, *AJSL*.
xxv (July, 1909), p. 259; and cf. II 19, 43 *n*.

[2] Add, from Lucian, I 1, 6. 2, 11. 4, 18. 6, 8. 7, 16. 8, 8. 12. 10, 27^b—11, 1^a.
12, 2. 3. 14, 7. 33. 15, 29. 32. 16, 14. 18. 17, 2 (οὗτοι= אֵלֶּה). 18. 22. 25, 14. 41
end. 26, 17. 27, 8^a. 28, 23. 31, 9 etc.

[3] Westcott and Hort, *The New Testament in the Original Greek*, ii. 138. For
examples of 'conflate' readings, see *ib.*, p. 94 ff.

2 Ki. 2, 13. 6, 7), induced by the context.—10, 2 בגבול בנימין ἐν τῷ ὄρει for ἐν τῷ ὁρίῳ[1].—13, 4 וַיִּצְעֲקוּ ἀνέβησαν corrupted likewise through the influence of the context for ἀνεβόησαν (וַיִּזְעֲקוּ—LXX do not recognize the *Nif.* of this verb: cf. 11, 7). So 14, 20 ἀνέβη for ἀνεβόησε (as in A).—14, 5 (see note).—*ib.* מול *bis*, ἐρχομένῳ 'to one coming . . .,' from ἐχόμενον *close to* (so Luc.), which represents מול Nu. 22, 5. Dt. 11, 30.—14, 45 Luc. ἔλεον (from ὁ λαὸς [עַם read as עַם] to bring the meaning into some relation with the context).— 15, 23 θεράπειαν (from θεραφιν).—16, 20 Luc. γόμον (from γομορ, adapted so as to harmonize with חמור=ὄνον).—17, 40 τελείους (from λείους).—18, 7 ותענינה Luc. ἐξήρχοντο (for ἐξῆρχον).—21 Luc. ἐν ταῖς δυνάμεσιν (for δυσὶν A).—20, 11 ונצא καὶ μένε for καὶ ἴωμεν (We.).— 15 εὑρεθῆναι prob. for ἐξαρθῆναι (as A).—26, 10 παιδεύσῃ (for παίσῃ). —II 17, 9 ΒΟΥΝΩΝ from ΒΟΘΥΝΩΝ.—16 καταπείσῃ (for καταπίῃ).— 23, 8 στρατιώτας (probably for τραυματίας : see *v.* 18).—9 ἀνεβόησεν (for ἀνέβη : cf. the reverse change above)[2]. Cf. II 14, 20 δόλον.

Compare from other books : 2 Ki. 3, 21 ויצעקו מכל חגר חגרה ומעלה καὶ ἀνεβόησαν ἐκ παντὸς περιεζωσμένοι ζώνην καὶ εἶπον 'Ω for καὶ ἐπάνω under the influence of the preceding (incorrect) ἀνεβόησαν; 23, 5. 11 וישב κατέκαυσε for κατέπαυσε ; ψ. 4, 8 מעת ἀπὸ καρποῦ for ἀπὸ καιροῦ; 17, 14 ישבעו בנים ἐχορτάσθησαν ὑείων[3]

---

[1] Luc. ἐν τοῖς ὁρίοις. The same corruption Jud. 2, 9 (Cod. A). ψ. 78, 54ᵃ. Ez. 11, 10. 11 : the converse one Mal. 1, 3.

[2] Comp. in proper names: I 5, 1 Αβεννηρ; 17, 1 Ἰδουμαίας; 21, 2 (see note) Αβειμελεχ; 25, 43 (B). 29, 11 (A, B, Luc.) יורעאל Ἰσραηλ; 25, 44 Luc. τῷ ἐκ Γολιαθ; 30, 14 Γελβουε; II 2, 2 al. Αχινοομ ἡ Ἰσραηλεῖτις; 8, 7 Ἱεροβοαμ; 10, 6. 8 מעכה Αμαληκ; 11, 21. 22 Αβειμελεχ υἱὸν Ἱεροβοαμ; 12, 30 Μελχολ (usually for מיכב); 14, 27 *end* Αβιαθαρ.

Sometimes, also, constantly, as אביניל Αβιγαια (no doubt A for Λ); מיכל Μελχολ; איש־בשת Ἰεβοσθε (but in II 3-4 Μεμφιβοσθε); עבר־אדם Αβεδδαρα (Luc. Ἀβεδδαδαν) ; בת־שבע Βηρσαβεε ; 1 Ki. 1-2 (throughout) אדניה Luc. Ορνια (cf. II 3, 4 B Ορνειλ, A Ορνιας). Comp. נון Ναυη. But where the incorrect form is *constant*, it is probable that it is due generally to the translators, and is not a mere error of transcription.

[3] Whence *saturati sunt porcina* found its way into some copies of the Old Latin Version, and is mentioned by Augustine, e. g. IV. 73 (Bened.) 'ubi dictum est "saturati sunt porcina" non nulla exemplaria "saturati sunt filiis" habent : ex ambiguo enim graeco interpretatio duplex evenit' (quoted by Lagarde in his *Probe einer neuen Ausgabe der lateinischen Übersetzungen des Alten Testaments*, Göttingen, 1885, p. 40).

(swine's flesh!) from υἱῶν; 31, 16 עתתי οἱ κλῆροί μου from οἱ καιροί μου; 39, 6 ספחות παλαιὰs from παλαιστὰs (as A); 44, 13 במחיריהם ἐν τοῖς ἀλαλάγμασιν αὐτῶν from ἀλλάγμασιν[1]; 49,9 וחרל ἐκοπίασεν from ἐκόπασεν (see Amos 7, 5); 69, 27 חלליך τραυμάτων μου from τραυματίων σου; 89, 21 קרשי בשמן ἐν ἐλέει ἁγίῳ from ἐλαίῳ; 139, 9 שחר κατ' ὀρθὸν from κατ' ὄρθρον (A); Jer. 15, 10 לא נשיתי ולא נשו בי ούτε ὠφέλησα, ούτε ὠφέλησέν με οὐδείς, already noted by Origen as a γραφικὸν ἁμάρτημα for ὠφείλησα, ὠφείλησεν; 2 Ch. 18, 2 ἠγάπα from ἠπάτα (so MS. 243: Margolis, *ZAW*. 1907, **226**). Cf. p. 78 *n.*; Thackeray, 36–38; and esp. Margolis, *ib.* 225 ff.

b. Features due presumably to the translators themselves :—

(*a*) The translators are apt to be very literal, representing Hebrew expressions not by idiomatic Greek equivalents, but by word-for-word renderings : thus I 3, 6 προσέθετο καὶ ἐκάλεσεν; 8 al. προσέθετο καλέσαι; II 2, 28 al. προσέθετο τοῦ . . .—3, 10 al. כפעם בפעם ὡς ἅπαξ καὶ ἅπαξ.—4, 7 al. שלשם אתמול ἐχθὲς καὶ τρίτην.—*ib.* (see note) היתה כזאת γέγονε τοιαύτη.—6, 7 ἀπὸ ὄπισθεν αὐτῶν.—7, 8 μὴ παρασιωπήσῃς ἀφ' ἡμῶν τοῦ μὴ βοᾷν.—7, 14. 17, 1 al. ובין . . . בין ἀνὰ μέσον . . . καὶ ἀνὰ μέσον.—18, 22 ב' חפץ θέλειν ἐν; 25 βούλεσθαι ἐν.—20, 21 ממך והנה ἀπὸ σοῦ καὶ ὧδε.—22 והלאה ממך ἀπὸ σοῦ καὶ ἐπέκεινα.—24, 7 μηδαμῶς μοι παρὰ Κυρίου (מיהוה), εἰ ποιήσω . . .—28, 17 λαλεῖν ἐν χειρί τινος.—II 18, 4 אל יד השער ἀνὰ χεῖρα τῆς πύλης.—24, 3 כהם וכהם ὥσπερ αὐτοὺς καὶ ὥσπερ αὐτοὺς (contrast Dt. 1, 11—by a different hand—ככם ὡς ἐστὲ χιλιοπλασίως).

The pron. אנכי (when expressed in the Hebrew) is (after II 7) seven times represented curiously by the *substantive* verb :—

II 11, 5 ἐγώ εἰμι ἐν γαστρὶ ἔχω; 12, 7 καὶ ἐγώ εἰμι ἐρυσάμην σε; 15, 28 ἐγώ εἰμι στρατεύομαι; 18, 12 καὶ ἐγώ εἰμι ἵστημι; 20, 17 Ἀκούω ἐγώ εἰμι; 24, 12 τρία ἐγώ εἰμι αἴρω ἐπὶ σέ; 17 ἰδοὺ ἐγώ εἰμι ἠδίκησα[2]. Comp. 7, 29 ὅτι σὺ εἶ . . . ἐλάλησας[3].

---

[1] Comp. Land, *Anecdota Syriaca*, iv. 190 : and Field's note *ad loc.*

[2] Also Jud. 5, 3. 6, 18. 11, 27. 35. 37. Ru. 4, 4. 1 Ki. 2, 2. 2 Ki. 4, 13. 10, 9. 22, 20. Ez. 36, 36 A (dub.); and occasionally in Aq. and Theod. (Hatch-Redpath, *Concord.*, p. 367). Thackeray (*Journ. of Theol. Stud.* 1907, 272 f.; cf. *Grammar*, p. 55) thinks that the usage is due to an attempt to represent אנכי (as distinguished from אני); but though it does always express אנכי, except 2 Ki. 10, 9. 22, 20. Ez. 36, 36, it by no means stands for אנכי uniformly.

[3] From II 2, 7 (incl.) there is a singular change in the rendering of גם, which is now often represented by καί γε : II 2, 7. 11, 12. 17. 21. 24. 12, 14. 13, 36. 14, 6. 7. 15, 20. 24. 16, 23. 17, 5. 10. 12. 16. 18, 2. 22. 26. 27. 19, 20. 40. 43. 20, 16. 21, 20. (So before in A and Luc. but not in B, as I 1, 6 L. 8, 8 L. 18, 5 A L. 19,

(*b*) They even translate not unfrequently wholly regardless of the sense:—I 1, 26 בִּי אֵל *ἐν ἐμοί.*—5, 6 וישמם *καὶ ἐπήγαγεν αὐτοῖς* (וַיִּשְׁמֵם, the suffix construed as a *dative:* GK. § 117ˣ).—8, 3 אחרי הבצע *ὀπίσω τῆς συντελείας.*—8, 16 תעשה למלאבתו *καὶ ἀποδεκατώσει* (וְעִשֵּׂר) *εἰς τὰ ἔργα αὐτοῦ.*—12, 2 וְשָׁבְתִּי *καὶ καθήσομαι* (יָשַׁבְתִּי).—12, 25 תִּפֶּפוּ *προστεθήσεσθε* (as though תֵּאָסֵף from יָסַף): so 27, 1.—14, 38 *τὰς γωνίας τοῦ* Ἰσραηλ.—14, 40 לְעֹבֵר *εἰς δουλείαν* ([ה]לעבד).—15, 11 *παρακέκλημαι* (so II 24, 26 *παρεκλήθη:* נָחַם = *παρακαλέω*; hence *παρακέκλημαι* derived mechanically to express the *Nifal*).—18, 21 ותהי *καὶ ἦν* (וַתְּהִי) *ἐπὶ Σαουλ* (!) *χεὶρ ἀλλοφύλων.*

(*c*) A Hebrew word not understood, or treated incorrectly as a proper name, or if of a technical character, is often transliterated: I 1, 24 *οιφι, νεβελ* [10, 3 *ἀσκόν*].—2, 18 *εφουδ βαρ.*—28 al. *εφουδ* [in the Pent. regularly *ἐπωμίς*].—32 (Cod. A) *κραταίωμα μουων.*—9, 12. 13 al. *Βαμα.*—10, 5 al. *ναβλα.*—13, 3 *Νασειβ.*—14, 1 *εἰς Μεσσαβ τῶν ἀλλοφύλων* (but 13, 23 *ὑπόστασις*).—6. 11. 12. 15 *Μεσσαφ.*—23 *τὴν Βαμωθ.*—33 *ἐν Γεθθαιμ* (for בְּנֵרְתָּם!).—16, 20 *γομορ* (see note).—17, 18 Luc. *ερουβα.*—20, 19 *παρὰ τὸ εργαβ ἐκεῖνο.*—20 *εἰς τὴν Αρματταρει.* —21 *γοῦζαν.*—41 *ἀπὸ τοῦ αργαβ.*—25, 18 *οιφι, γομορ.*—32. 39 Luc. *Βαρουχ.*—30, 8. 15. 23 *γεδδουρ* (for גְּדוּד).—II 3, 33. 34 *Ναβαλ.*— 12, 31 Luc. במלבן *ἐν Μαδεββα* (no doubt Δ for Λ).—15, 28 and 17, 16 *Αραβωθ.*—15, 32 *ἕως τοῦ Ῥοως* (Luc. Ῥως: so 16, 1); 17, 19 *αραφωθ.*—29 *σαφφωθ.*—21, 20 *Μαδων.*—23, 9 Luc. *ἐν Σερραμ* (for בחרפם).—13 *εἰς Καδων.*—24, 7 *Μαψαρ.* Cf. Thackeray, *Grammar*, i. 32–34 [1].

And so in other books: as Gen. 28, 19 ואולם לוז *καὶ Οὐλαμμαυς* (!). Jos. 7, 24 עמק עכר *Ἐμεκαχωρ.* Jud. 1, 19 כי רכב ברזל להם *ὅτι Ῥηχαβ διεστείλατο αὐτοῖς.* 3, 3 עד לבוא חמת *ἕως Λαβω Εμαθ.* 6, 26 מעון *Μαουεκ.* 8, 7 *αβαρκηνειν.* 9, 27 *καὶ ἐποίησαν ελλουλειμ.* 41 *ἐν* Αρημα. 18, 29 ואולם ליש *καὶ Οὐλαμαις.* 20, 48 מעיר מתם *Μαδβααρ.*

---

24 A. 24, 11 L. II 2, 6 A. 3, 19 A; and in other books sometimes in B, as Jud. 1, 22. 2, 10. 17. 3, 22 al. 1 Ki. 1, 6. 48 al.)

[1] The transliteration of Hebrew words is also characteristic of Theodotion: Field, *Hexapla*, I. xxxix-xlii; Swete, p. 46; C. C. Torrey, *Ezra Studies*, Chicago (1910), pp. 66–81, 339 (who argues from the frequency of such transliterations in the Septuagint of Chr. Ezr. Neh. that the 'LXX' translation of these books is really Theodotion's: a conclusion which is accepted by Moore, *AJSL.* xxix, p. 54, but which, for reasons stated by him, appears doubtful to Rahlfs, *Studien*, iii. 85 f.).

ἀπὸ πόλεως Μεθλα. 2 Ki. 2, 14 הוא אף ἀφφω. 3, 4 נקד νωκηθ. 10, 10 אפוא ἀφφω. 12, 5–7 βεδεκ. 9 [see Stade, *ZATW.* 1885, p. 289 f. = *Akad. Reden u. Abhandl.* 193, 199 ; and Kittel, *ad loc.*]. 23, 4 שדמות σαληημωθ (Λ for Δ). 5 χωμαρειμ, μαζουρωθ, etc.

Sometimes the translation and transliteration are found side by side, giving rise to a species of doublet :—I 5, 4 (p. lv) αμαφεθ.—6, 8 ἐν θέματι βερεχθαν (Α αργοζ).—11. 15 καὶ τὸ θέμα εργαβ (Α αργοζ).—7, 4 τὰ ἄλση Ασταρωθ (העשתרות, as *v.* 3. 12, 10, taken as=האשרות, which is regularly rendered ἄλση).—10, 5 ἀνάστεμα . . . . Νασειβ.—14, 25 Ιααλ (see note).—15, 3 Ιερειμ (p. lvi).—8 Ιερειμ ἀπέκτεινεν (for החרים).—32 Luc. ἐξ Αναθωθ τρέμων.—21, 2 ἐν τῷ τόπῳ τῷ λεγομένῳ Θεοῦ πίστις (as though אל(אֶמְ)מֻנָה) Φελλανει Μαεμωνὶ (for במקום פלני אלמני).—7 συνεχόμενος Νεεσσαραν (נֶעְצָר).—23, 14 ἐν Μασερεμ ἐν τοῖς στενοῖς (for בַּמְצָדות read as במצרות).—19 ἐν Μεσσαρα ἐν τοῖς στενοῖς (for בִּמְצָדות).—24, 23 εἰς τὴν Μεσσαρα στενὴν (for עַל־הַמְצוּדָה).

(*d*) There is a tendency in the version to make slight additions for the purpose of giving an explanation or otherwise filling out the sense : thus I 1, 5 + ὅτι οὐκ ἦν αὐτῇ παιδίον. *ib.* + ὑπὲρ ταύτην. 14 (τὸ παιδάριον) 'Ηλει. *ib.* + καὶ πορεύου ἐκ προσώπου Κυρίου. 21 + ἐν Σηλωμ. 2, 12 'Ηλει (τοῦ ἱέρεως). 28 *end* + εἰς βρῶσιν. 29 (ἀναιδεῖ) ὀφθαλμῷ (see note). 5, 12 οἱ (ζῶντες καὶ) μὴ ἀποθανόντες. 9, 15 + πρὸς αὐτόν. 10, 4 δύο (ἀπαρχὰς) ἄρτων. 11, 10 πρὸς Ναας (τὸν 'Αμμανίτην). 15, 17 + πρὸς Σαουλ. 23^b. 16, 12 ἀγαθὸς ὁράσει (κυρίῳ) ; and afterwards + πρὸς Σαμουηλ and ὅτι οὗτός ἐστιν (ἀγαθός). 17, 36. 43 + καὶ εἶπε Δαυειδ Οὐχὶ ἀλλ' ἢ χείρων κυνός. 19, 8 + πρὸς Σαουλ. 20, 28 εἰς Βηθλεεμ (τὴν πόλιν αὐτοῦ πορευθῆναι). 21, 4 *end* + καὶ φάγεται. 25, 26 τοῦ μὴ ἐλθεῖν εἰς αἷμα (ἀθῶον). 31 *end* + ἀγαθῶσαι αὐτῇ.

(*e*) Hebrew writers are apt to leave something to be supplied by the intelligence of their readers : thus the subject of a verb is often not expressly named, and the object is either not named or indicated merely by a pronoun, the context, intelligently understood, sufficiently fixing the meaning. In such cases, however, there was a temptation sometimes even to a scribe of the Hebrew, but still more to a translator, to facilitate the comprehension of the reader, or to preclude some misapprehension which he contemplated as possible, by inserting explicitly the imperfectly expressed subject or object. Cases in which

MT. and LXX vary in the presence or absence of subject or object are numerous. Thus I 2, 28 אתו τὸν οἶκον τοῦ πατρός σου.—3; 18^b ויאמר καὶ εἶπεν Ἠλει.—6, 20^b καὶ πρὸς τίνα ἀναβήσεται (κιβωτὸς κυρίου) ἀφ᾽ ἡμῶν; 9, 6 τὸ παιδάριον.—24 καὶ εἶπε (Σαμουηλ τῷ Σαουλ).—12, 5 ויאמר אליהם καὶ εἶπε Σαμουηλ πρὸς τὸν λαόν.—15, 27 καὶ ἐκράτησε (Σαουλ).—16, 12 משחהו χρῖσον τὸν Δαυειδ, etc.

Hence Wellhausen lays down the canon that ‘ if LXX and MT. differ in respect of a subject, it is probable that the original text had neither.’

I 2, 20^b והלכו למקומו, LXX καὶ ἀπῆλθεν ὁ ἄνθρωπος εἰς τὸν τόπον αὐτοῦ. The original text was והלך למקומו.—7, 14 ואת גבולן הציל ישראל מיד פלשתים, LXX καὶ τὸ ὅριον Ἰσραηλ ἀφείλαντο κτλ. Both MT. and LXX may be accounted for by the assumption of an original ואת גבולן הציל מיד פלשתים.—10, 22 וישאלו, LXX καὶ ἐπηρώτησεν Σαμουηλ. The original text had וישאל.—11, 9 ויאמרו למלאכים, LXX καὶ εἶπεν τοῖς ἀγγέλοις. Originally ויאמר, here best read as a singular ‘ on account of the definiteness of the message ’ (We.).—15 וימליכו, LXX καὶ ἔχρισε Σαμουηλ.—17, 39^b ויסרם דוד מעליו, LXX καὶ ἀφαιροῦσιν αὐτὰ ἀπ᾽ αὐτοῦ. Originally only ויסרם מעליו, fixed in MT. to a sing. by the addition of דוד, read by LXX as וַיְסִרֵם.—30, 20 ויקח דוד את־כל־הצאן, LXX καὶ ἔλαβεν πάντα τὰ ποίμνια. דוד almost certainly a false ‘ Explicitum : ’ see the note.

c. On the Orthography of the Hebrew Text used by LXX (comp. above, p. xxviii ff.).

(*a*) The number of cases in which LXX and MT. differ in respect of the number of a verb, or in which the MT. itself has one number where the other would be expected, makes it probable that there was a time when the final consonant was not always expressed in writing, and that when the *scriptio plena* was introduced an (apparent) singular was sometimes left, which ought to have become a plural. The omission was in some cases made good by the Massorites in the Qrê, but not always.

Nu. 13, 22 ויאמר בני (read ויבאו). 32, 25 ויעלו בננב ויבא עד חברון. 33, 7. Jud. 8, 6. 1 Sam. 9, 4^b. 19, 20 וירא (of the מלאכים just mentioned), LXX καὶ εἶδαν. 1 Ki. 13, 11 ויבוא בנו ויספר לו (the sequel ויספרום לאביהם shews that ויבֹא בָנו ויספר must ויספר־לו

have been intended: cf. LXX ἔρχονται οἱ υἱοὶ αὐτοῦ καὶ διηγήσαντο).
22, 49 (probably הלך and כי נשבר האניות were intended by the author).
ψ. 79, 7 השמו ... אכל (contrast the *plurals* in Jer. 10, 25ᵇ).

The correction is made in the Qrê (*Ochlah we-Ochlah*, No. 119), Gen. 27, 29
וישתחו; 43, 28 וישתחו ויקדו; Jud. 21, 20. 1 Sam. 12, 10. 13, 19 פלשתים כי אמר.
1 Ki. 9, 9. 12, 7. 2 Ki. 20, 18 יקח (as Is. 39, 7 יקחו; but the sing. may here stand:
LXX λήμψεται). Est. 9, 27 (contrast *v*. 23). Ezr. 3, 3.

Elsewhere the sing. may be explained by the principle noticed on I 16, 4 : Gen.
42, 25 כן להם ויעש sc. העושה (LXX καὶ ἐγενήθη; ויעש would be unnatural).
48, 1 ליוסף ויאמר sc. האומר (LXX καὶ ἀπηγγέλη = ויאמר). 2 ויאמר ... ויגד
(LXX ἀπηγγέλη δὲ ... λέγοντες).

Conversely MT. sometimes has a plural where LXX (not always
rightly) read as a singular: I 7, 13 פלשתים ויכנעו, LXX καὶ ἐταπείνωσεν Κύριος (comp. p. lxii).—10, 23 ויקחהו וירצו, LXX both sing.,
i.e. ויקחהו וירץ.—12, 9ᵇ בם וילחמו, LXX καὶ ἐπολέμησεν.—19, 21
וינדו, LXX καὶ ἀπηγγέλη (וינד—read in MT. as ויגד, by LXX as
ויגד: so 1 Ki. 1, 23).—30, 1ᵇ וישרפו ... ויכו ... פשטו ועמלקי, LXX
all sing. (as MT. itself sometimes in similar cases: 15, 6 קני ויסר,
Nu. 14, 45. Jud. 6, 3).—20ᵇ ויאמרו, LXX καὶ ἐλέγετο (ויאמר, i.e.
either ויאמרו or ויאמר—the latter not idiomatic; cf. p. 258).—21ᵇ וישאל,
LXX καὶ ἠρώτησαν αὐτὸν (the subject is the men left behind). Comp.
Gen. 25, 25 עשו שמו ויקראו, LXX ἐπωνόμασεν: *v*. 26 (in a similar
context) MT. has ויקרא, LXX ἐκάλεσεν.

The correction is made in the Qrê (*Ochlah we-Ochlah*, No. 120): Jos. 6, 7
העם אל (ויאמר קרי) ויאמרו (the subject is Joshua). 9, 7 קרי ויאמר (ויאמרו
ישראל איש (the correction is here unnecessary). 1 Sam. 15, 16. 1 Ki. 12, 3. 21.
2 Ki. 14, 13 ויפרץ ירושלם (ויבא קרי) ובא ... תפש, LXX καὶ ἦλθεν. Ez. 46, 9ᵇ
יצאו (10ᵇ strangely *not* made). Neh. 3, 15 (comp. *v*. 14).

The case is particularly clear in some of the instances in which the
phrase ἀπηγγέλη (or ἀνηγγέλη) λέγοντες occurs. This strange construction κατὰ σύνεσιν[1] might be supposed to have been forced upon
the translators when they found what would only naturally be read
by them as לאמר ויגד I 15, 12. 19, 19. II 6, 12. 15, 31 (MT. הגיד).
19, 1. 1 Ki. 1, 51[2]: but it is scarcely credible that they should have

---

[1] Winer, *Grammar of NT. Greek*, § lix. 11.
[2] So also Gen. 22, 20. 38, 13. 24 (cf. 45, 16. 48, 2). Jos. 10, 17. Jud. 16, 2 (in
MT. ויגד has dropped out). 1 Ki. 2, 29. 41 (without לאמר).

gone out of their way to use it for what in MT. stands as וינידו לאמר
I 14, 33. 23, I. 24, 2 (λεγόντων). II 3, 23. I Ki. 2, 39: in these
instances, therefore, it can hardly be doubted that the original text had
simply ויגד, which was read by LXX as יֻגַּד, but in MT. was resolved
into וַיֻּגְּדוּ.

(*b*) The MSS. used by the LXX translators—except, probably, in
those parts of the OT. which were translated first—must have been
written in an early form of the square character [1]. That it was not
the unmodified archaic character appears clearly from the frequency
with which letters, which have no resemblance to one another in that
character, are interchanged in many parts of the Septuagint. For
the same reason it can hardly have been very similar to the Egyptian
Aramaic alphabet illustrated above. It was no doubt a transitional
alphabet, probably a Palestinian one, of a type not greatly differing
from that of Kefr-Bir'im (p. xxiii). In this alphabet, not only are
ו and י remarkably alike [2], but also ב and כ, and ב and מ (of which
there are many clear instances of confusion in the Septuagint): ה, ח,
and the final ם also approach each other. ד and ר resemble each
other in most Semitic alphabets: so that from their confusion—next
to that of ו and י, the most common in LXX—little can be inferred
respecting the alphabet used [3].

---

[1] So long ago Gesenius, *Gesch. d. Heb. Sprache u. Schrift* (1815), p. 158; for a
more recent opinion, see K. Vollers in the *ZATW.* 1883, p. 230 f.

[2] They are also alike, it may be observed, in the late type of the archaic character in which יהוה is written in the fragments of Aquila mentioned above (p. iii):
see p. 15 in Burkitt's edition.

[3] It is true, the Kefr-Bir'im alphabet is considerably later than the LXX (as the
scriptio plena alone would shew), but the Inscription of Bᵉnê Ḥezir, and those
alluded to p. xxii, *note* 1, appear to shew that an alphabet not differing from it
materially was in popular use in Palestine at least as early as the Christian era:
and if more abundant records had been preserved it would probably be found to
begin at an earlier period still. The confusion of י and ו, and מ and ב (which
cannot be explained from the old character) is in the Pent. so uncommon that it
may be due to accidental causes: the books in which it is frequent can only have
been translated after the change of character had been effected; the Pent., as tradition states, may have been translated earlier. Possibly a large and discriminating
induction of instances (in which *isolated* cases, especially of proper names, should
be used with reserve) might lead to more definite conclusions.

Examples of letters confused in LXX :—

(a) MT. י, LXX ו: II 23, 7 יִמָּלֵא καὶ πλῆρες (=וּמְלֹא): MT. ו, LXX י:
I 2, 29 מָ[עֹון] ὀφθαλμῷ (= עַיִן). 12, 2 (p. lx). 19, 22 בְּשֻׁבוּ ἐν Σεφει
(=בְּשִׁפִי). 24, 16 וִהְיָה γένοιτο (=יִהְיֶה): both changes together, 12, 3
עֵינִי בוּ ἀποκρίθητε κατ' ἐμοῦ (=עֲנוּ בִי).

Very clear examples are afforded by the Psalms: MT. י, LXX ו:—

ψ. 2, 6 נָסַכְתִּי מַלְכִּי κατεστάθην βασιλεὺς ὑπ' αὐτοῦ=נְסַכְתִּי מַלְכּוֹ.

16, 3 כֹל חֲפָצִי πάντα τὰ θελήματα αὐτοῦ=כָּל־חֶפְצוֹ.

20, 10 יַעֲנֵנוּ καὶ ἐπάκουσον ἡμῶν=וַעֲנֵנוּ.

22, 17 כָּאֲרִי ὤρυξαν=כָּאֲרוּ.

32, 4 קַיִץ ἄκανθαν=קוֹץ.

35, 16 לַעֲנִי ἐξεμυκτήρισάν με=לָעֲנוּ.

36, 2 בְּקֶרֶב לִבִּי ἐν ἑαυτῷ=בְּקֶרֶב לִבּוֹ.

38, 12 נֹגְעַי ἤγγισαν=נָגְעוּ (see 32, 6. 88, 4).

45, 12 וְהִשְׁתַּחֲווּ לוֹ καὶ προσκυνήσουσιν αὐτῷ=וְהִשְׁתַּחֲווּ לוֹ.

46, 5 קֹדֶשׁ מִשְׁכְּנֵי ἡγίασε τὸ σκήνωμα αὐτοῦ=קָדֵשׁ מִשְׁכָּנוֹ.

50, 21 הֱיוֹת ἀνομίαν=הַוּוֹת (see 52, 2).

58, 4 דַּבְּרֵי כָזָב ἐλάλησαν ψευδῆ=דִּבְּרוּ כָזָב.

69, 33 דֹּרְשֵׁי אֱלֹהִים ἐκζητήσατε=דִּרְשׁוּ.

73, 7 עֵינֵמוֹ ἀδικία αὐτῶν=עֲוֺנֵמוֹ.

10ᵃ עַמּוֹ ὁ λαός μου=עַמִּי.

76, 12–13 יִבְצֹר : לַמּוֹרָא τῷ φοβερῷ καὶ ἀφαιρουμένῳ=לַנּוֹרָא וּבֹצֵר.

88, 16 נְשֻׂאתִי אָמִיךָ ὑψωθεὶς δὲ ἐταπεινώθην=נִשֵּׂאתִי אָמֻךְ (see Lev.
25, 39, and cf. ψ. 106, 43).

90, 16 יֵרָאֶה καὶ ἴδε=וּרְאֵה.

91, 6 יָשׁוּד καὶ δαιμονίου=וְשֵׁד (see 106, 37).

122, 6 יִשְׁלָיוּ καὶ εὐθηνία=וְשַׁלְוָה (v. 7).

144, 15ᵃ אַשְׁרֵי ἐμακάρισαν=אִשְּׁרוּ,—a passage which shews how
scrupulously the LXX expressed what they found in
their MSS.; for in the parallel clause אַשְׁרֵי=μακάριος.

Add Is. 29, 13 וַתְּהִי יִרְאָתָם אֹתִי וְגֹ' μάτην δὲ σέβονταί με κτλ. (so Mt.
15, 8; Mk. 7, 6)=וַתְּהוּ יְרָאָם אֹתִי.

Jer. 6, 9 עֹולֵל יְעֹולֵל Καλαμᾶσθε καλαμᾶσθε=עֹולְלוּ עֹולֵל.

10, 20 יֹצְאֻנִי καὶ τὰ πρόβατά μου=וְצֹאנִי.

Zech. 5, 6 עֵינָם ἡ ἀδικία αὐτῶν=עֲוֺנָם, etc.

MT. וֹ, LXX י :—

ψ. 17, 11 אשורנו ἐκβαλόντες με= נִי ??? (perhaps Aram. אֲשֻׁרָנִי).

     12 דמינו ὑπέλαβόν με= דִּמּוּנִי.

   22, 25 ממנו ἀπ' ἐμοῦ= מִמֶּנִּי.

     30 ונפשו לא חיה καὶ ἡ ψυχή μου αὐτῷ ζῇ= וְנַפְשִׁי לוֹ חָיָה.

   41, 9 יצוק בו κατέθεντο κατ' ἐμοῦ= בִּי ? .

   56, 8 על און ὑπὲρ τοῦ μηθενὸς= עַל אִין.

   59, 10 עזו τὸ κράτος μου= עֻזִּי (cf. v. 18).

   62, 1 ידותון 'Ιδιθουν [1].

     5 משאתו τὴν τιμήν μου.

   64, 7 וקרב προσελεύσεται= יִקְרַב.

   65, 8 והמון לאמים ταραχθήσονται ἔθνη= לאמים יֶהֱמוּן (or יֶהֱמָיֻן).

   68, 7 שכני צחיחה τοὺς κατοικοῦντας ἐν τάφοις= ? שְׁכֵנֵי.

   73, 10ᵇ ומי מלא καὶ ἡμέραι πλήρεις= ימי מלא (καὶ added).

   76, 7 נרדם ורכב וסום ἐνύσταξαν οἱ ἐπιβεβηκότες τοὺς ἵππους = נרדמו לְכֵי סוס.

   91, 5 וסחרה κυκλώσει σε= יסחרך.

  109, 10 ודרשו ἐκβληθήτωσαν= יֹנֹרְשׁוּ.

     28 קמו οἱ ἐπανιστάμενοί μοι= קָמַי.

  119, 3 לא פעלו עולה οὐ γὰρ οἱ ἐργαζόμενοι τὴν ἀνομίαν= אַף לֹא פעלי עולה.

Add Ez. 48, 10ᵇ יהוה ἔσται= יהיה.

     35 שמו יהוה ἔσται τὸ ὄνομα αὐτῆς= שמו יהיה.

Lam. 3, 22 כי לא תמנו οὐκ ἐξέλιπόν με= לֹא תַמְנוּ (GK. § 117ˣ).

Sometimes both confusions occur in one word or verse:—

ψ. 35, 19 יקרצו עין καὶ διανεύοντες ὀφθαλμοῖς= וְקֹרְצֵי עַיִן.

  145, 5 ודברי λαλήσουσι= ידברו.

Jer. 6, 23 ועל סוסים ירכבו ערוך ἐφ' ἵπποις καὶ ἅρμασι παρατάξεται= על סוסים ורכב יַעֲרֹךְ [2].

---

[1] So in Kt. 39, 1. 77, 1. Neh. 11, 17. 1 Ch. 16, 38 : and in LXX of 1 Ch. 9, 16 etc., where MT. has regularly ידותון.

[2] Instances such as Σειφ for צוף; 'Αγχους for אכיש; ψ. 8 *title* הגתית τῶν ληνῶν = הנתות; 27, 6 ירום ὕψωσε = ירים; 88, 11 אם רפאים יקומו ἢ ἰατροὶ ἀναστήσουσι = אם רפאים יקומו (cf. Is. 26, 14) are not cited, as the difference of pronunciation presupposed by LXX is due probably, not to confusion of ו and י, but to the absence of the *plena scriptio*.

That the MS. (or MSS.) upon which the Massoretic text is founded must also at (β) MT. ר, LXX ד: I 4, 10 and 15, 4 רגלי ταγμάτων (as though רגלי; see Nu. 2, 2, etc.); 10, 24 ירעו ἔγνωσαν; 13, 3 and 14, 21 עברים δοῦλοι; 40 *bis* עבר δουλείαν; 19, 13 כביר ἧπαρ (כבד); 23, 15 בחרשה ἐν τῇ Καινῇ; 24, 3 Luc. צורי τῆς θήρας (ציד); II 19, 18 ועברה העברה καὶ ἐλειτούργησαν τὴν λειτουργίαν; 22, 21. 25 Luc. כְּבֹר δόξαν, δοξασμὸς (כְּבֹד).

MT. ד, LXX ר: I 17, 8 עברים Ἐβραῖοι; 19, 22 נרל ἅλω (נרן); 21, 7, etc. Δωὴκ ὁ Σύρος; 23, 14. 19. 24, 1 מצדות Μασερεμ, Μεσσαρα, ἐν τοῖς στενοῖς; 24, 12 צדה δεσμεύεις (צרר); 30, 8 נדוד γεδδουρ; II 3, 4 אדניה, B Ὀρνειλ, A Ὀρνιας, Luc. Ὀρνια [so 1 Ki. 1—2 Luc., throughout]; 6, 10–12 (so 1 Ch. 13, 13. 14ᵃ, but not 15, 24. 25, etc.) עבד אדם Ἀβεδδαρα (as though עבד־ארה).

And often in other books.

(γ) MT. ב, LXX מ: II 5, 20 בבעל פרצים ἐκ τῶν ἐπάνω διακοπῶν (=ממעל פרצים); 11, 21 f. תבן Θαμασι; 21, 19 נב Ῥομ; and probably (though not certainly) in the following places where ב is rendered by ἀπό, ἐκ: I 4, 3. 25, 14 *end*. II 2, 31. 5, 24. 6, 1. 9, 4ᵇ. 16, 13. 18, 8. 19, 23. 40 Luc. (עמד for עבר; so 2 Ki. 6, 30). Cf. אבינדב Ἀμειναδαβ[1]. Notice the resemblance of ב and מ in the Kefr-Bir'im Inscription (above, p. xxiii, Fig. 12).

MT. מ, LXX ב: I 6, 20 עמד διελθεῖν (עבר); 9, 2 מן ἐν; 26 (see note); 14, 1; II 13, 34ᵃ[2].

one time or other have been written in a character in which י and ו were very similar, is clear from the frequency with which ו occurs with י קרי, and י with ו קרי (*Ochlah we-Ochlah*, Nos. 80, 81, 134–148), the קרי being often, as 1 Sam. 22, 17. 25, 3. 2 Sam. 15, 20 (though not always), indisputably correct.

[1] See also Dt. 1, 44 (משעיר for בשעיר rightly). ψ. 18, 14ᵃ (ἐξ as in ‖ 2 Sam. both LXX and MT.). 32, 3ᵇ. 78, 26ᵃ. 105, 36ᵃ. 119, 84ᵇ. 139, 13ᵇ. Pr. 10, 21 רבים ὑψηλὰ (רמים). 12, 3ᵃ. 24, 5ᵃ. 28, 12. 28 בקום ἐν τόποις (מקום: notice במקומות in the Inscr. of Kefr-Bir'im). 1 Ch. 7, 6 זמרי for זבדי Jos. 7, 1. Hos. 5, 13 and 10, 6 ירב Ἰαρειμ. 13, 9 בי LXX, Pesh. מי (rightly). Jer. 38, 24ᵇ. 46, 10ᵇ. Ez. 16, 6 ἐκ τοῦ αἵματός σου for ברמיך. Ob. 21. Hab. 2, 4 ἐκ πίστεώς μου for באמונתו. Jos. 3, 16ᵇ עברו εἰστήκει (cf. on II 15, 23).

[2] See also ψ. 45, 14ᵇ ἐν. 68, 23ᵇ ἐν in spite of ἐκ 23ᵃ). 36ᵃ. 81, 7ᵇ בדוד תעברנה for (מדוד תעברנה). 104, 15ᵃ. 119, 68ᵇ ומטיב read as (ובטוב): cf. 70, 4 ישובו for ישמו 40, 16. Pr. 17, 10ᵇ. Jer. 21, 1 מעשיה Βασαιον. 46, 25 מנא τὸν υἱὸν αὐτῆς (בנה). Ez. 48, 29 בנחלה for מנחלה rightly (see Jos. 13, 16. 23, 4; מנחלה is untranslateable). Jos. 8, 33 עמדים παρεπορεύοντο. Sometimes, as ψ. 31, 8ᵇ. 135, 21ᵃ. Jer. 9, 18 (19). 20, 17, it may be doubtful whether the variation points to a difference

f 2

Other letters confused in LXX may be noted by the reader for himself. All cannot be reduced to rule: a certain number are due to *accidental* causes, as the partial illegibility of a letter in particular cases [1].

(*c*) According to Lagarde [2], the three letters ה, ם, ח, when occurring at the end of a word, were not written in the MSS. used by LXX, but represented by the mark of abbreviation (´) which already appears on Hebrew coins. This is not improbable: though it may be doubted if it was in use universally. Certainly there are cases in which the difference between LXX and MT. may be readily explained by the supposition that a mark of abbreviation has been differently resolved (or overlooked) in one of the two texts [3]; but they are hardly numerous or certain enough to establish a rule, the differences being frequently capable of explanation in other ways; for instance, from textual imperfection or corruption, or from looseness of rendering on the part of the translators. Thus in the 2 pf., MT. has sometimes a pl. where LXX express a sing., and vice versa: but it is difficult to shew conclusively that such variations can only be explained in this manner; 2 sg. pf. masc. has often ה- in MT. (as נָתַתָּה), and the variation *may* have arisen from confusion between ה and ם; or again, as the variation often occurs in passages where the *number* of the pron. in the Hebrew changes, it may be due to an assimilating tendency on the part of the translators. Change of number is so frequent in Hebrew, according as the speaker or writer thinks of a group or of an individual belonging to, or representing, a group, that the variation may in such cases be original. In the case of numbers, as of persons, the temptation to assimilate to the context, or to define more closely what the Hebrew left undefined, or to adopt a more idiomatic usage in the construction of collective terms, would

---

of reading, as the LXX may have rendered loosely: but in most of the instances quoted, there seems no reason to suppose this. Cf. J. M. P. Smith, *Nahum* (in the *Intern. Crit. Comm.*), 1912, p. 300 f.; and on כ and ט confused, *ibid.* p. 361 (Index).

[1] On graphical errors in MT., comp. (with reserve) Grätz, *Die Psalmen*, pp. 121–144, where they are classified and illustrated.

[2] *Anmerkungen zur griech. Übersetzung der Proverbien*, p. 4.

[3] Consider Lagarde's remarks on Pr. 2, 20ᵃ. 3, 18ᵇ. 7, 17ᵇ. 11, 15ᵇ. 13, 19ᵇ. 14, 10ᵇ. 15, 15ᵃ. 16, 13ᵇ. 16. 21, 23ᵇ.

often be strong: so that, though there are, no doubt, exceptions, it is probable that variations of this kind between MT. and LXX are to be attributed, as a rule, to the translators[1]. At the same time it may well be that abbreviations were in occasional use[2].

2. The Targum. The text deviates but rarely from MT. Only two features need here be noticed: (*a*) the tendency, in this as in other Targums, to soften or remove anthropomorphic expressions with reference to God: (*b*) the tendency to paraphrase.

(*a*) I 1, 3 to worship and sacrifice *before* the Lord of Hosts (so 21); 10 was praying *before* the Lord (so *v.* 26); 11 if the affliction of thine handmaid *is revealed before* Thee (Heb. *if Thou seest*)[3]; 19 *end* and the memory of her entered in before 'י (י קדם דוכרנה ועל); Heb. ויזכרה 'י: so *v.* 11. 2, 21); 28 השאלתיו לי 'י I have delivered him up that he may minister *before* 'י; *ib.* שאול לי he shall minister *before* 'י; 2, 11 ministered *before* 'י; 25ᵇ כי חפץ 'י for it was pleasure (רעוא) *before* 'י to slay them; 35 and I will raise up *before* me; 6, 17 as a guilt offering *before* 'י; 7, 3 and worship *before* Him alone (so *v.* 4. 12, 10ᵇ); 17 and built an altar there *before* 'י; 10, 17 gathered *before* 'י; II 7, 5 shalt thou build *before* me a house? And so frequently.

מן קדם *from before* is employed similarly: I 1, 5 and children were withheld from her *from before* 'י. 20ᵇ for *from before* 'י have I asked

---

[1] So, for instance, 1 Sam. 5, 10ᵇ. 11; 29, 3 אתי ἡμῶν; 30, 22; 2 Sam. 10, 11 *bis*; Ex. 14, 25 אנוסה φύγωμεν; Jud. 11, 19 *end*; 20, 23. 28 etc.

[2] Unless, for instance, the translators found abbreviations in their text, such renderings as the following are difficult to account for: Jud. 19, 18 את בית יהוה εἰς τὸν οἶκόν μου = אל ביתי; Jer. 6, 11 חמת יהוה τὸν θυμόν μου = חמתי; 25, 37 אף יהוה θυμοῦ μου = אפי; and unless they could assume them, as something familiar, they would scarcely have been led to adopt these renderings: Jer. 2, 2ᵇ-3ᵃ אחרי קדש ישראל [repeated by error] λέγει κύριος, ὁ ἅγιος Ἰσραηλ (= 'י קדש see 11, 5); 3, 19 איך γένοιτο κύριε ὅτι = כי אמן יהוה 'א 'י: for γένοιτο = אמן 'א 'כ; Jon. 1, 9 עברי אנכי Δοῦλος κυρίου εἰμὶ ἐγὼ = עבד 'י אנכי. Is. 53, 8 למות (למו) εἰς θάνατον = למו. The supposed 'apocopated plural' in 'י ⎯⎯ (Ew. § 177ᵃ; GK. § 87ᶠ) is also best explained as an error due to the neglect of a mark of abbreviation: comp. Cheyne, critical note on Is. 5, 1; ψ. 45, 9. We. (p. 20) points to 14, 33 בגדתם LXX ἐν Γεθθαιμ, as proof that the abbreviation, though it might be used in some cases, at any rate was not universal. Comp. further (with reserve) Perles, *Analekten zur Textkritik des A.T.s* (1895), pp. 4-35.

[3] So constantly when ראה is used of God: as 9, 16. Gen. 29, 32. 31, 12. Ex. 3, 7. 9 etc.

him. 3, 8[b] that it was called to the child *from before* the Lord [1]. 20 the request which was asked *from before* '. 6, 9 then *from before* him is this great evil done unto us [2]. 9, 9 to seek instruction *from before* ' (Heb. לדרש לאלהים). 15 and it was said to Samuel *from before* ' (so 17). 11, 7 and there fell a terror *from before* ' upon the people. 15, 10 and the word of prophecy was with Samuel *from before* ', saying (so II 7, 4). 26, 19 if *from before* ' thou art stirred up against me, let mine offering be accepted with favour, but if the children of men, let them be accursed *from before* '.

(*b*) Paraphrastic renderings. These are very numerous, and only specimens can be given here: I 1, 12[b] and Eli waited for her till she should cease; 16 Dishonour not thy handmaid before a daughter of wickedness; 2, 11 בחיי עלי in Eli's lifetime (for את־פני עלי); 32[a] and thou shalt observe and shalt behold the affliction that shall come upon the men of thy house for the sins which ye have sinned in my sanctuary; and after that I will bring good upon Israel; 3, 7[a] and Samuel had not yet learnt to know instruction *from before* ', and the prophecy of ' was not yet revealed to him; 19 and Samuel grew, and the Word (מימרא) of ' was his help [3]; 4, 8 who will deliver us from the hand of the 'Memra' of ' whose mighty works these are? 6, 19 and he slew among the men of B., because they rejoiced that they had seen the ark of ' exposed (כד גלי); and he killed among the elders of the people seventy men, and in the congregation 50,000; 7, 6 and poured out their heart in penitence as water before '; 9, 5 they came into the land wherein was a prophet (for ארץ צוף: cf. 1, 1 מתלמידי נביא for צופים; see Hab. 2, 1 Heb.); 9, 12. 14. 25 בית אסחרותא dining-chamber (for הבמה: אסחרותא = הלשכה *v.* 22); 10, 5. 11 ספריא scribes (for נביאים); 15, 29 And if thou sayest, I will turn (repent) from my sin, and it shall be forgiven me in order that I and my sons may hold the kingdom over Israel for ever, already is it decreed upon thee from before the Lord of the victory of Israel,

---

[1] Such impersonal constructions are common in the Targums.

[2] On the ית retained mechanically from the Hebrew, in spite of the construction being varied, see the *Journal of Philology*, xi. 227 f.

[3] So often when Yahweh is said to be 'with' a person: 10, 7. 16, 18. 18, 14. Gen. 39, 2. 3 etc.

before whom is no falsehood, and who turns not from what He has said; for He is not as the sons of men, who say and belie themselves, who decree and confirm not; 25, 29 but may the soul of my lord be hidden in the treasury of eternal life (בגנז חיי עלמא) before '· thy God; 28, 19 (on the margin of the Reuchl. Cod.: Lagarde, p. xviii, l. 10 [1]) and to-morrow thou and thy sons shall be with me in the treasury of eternal life; II 6, 19 אשפר (see note); 20, 18 and she spake, saying, I remember now what is written in the book of the Law to ask peace of a city first [Dt. 20, 10]; so oughtest thou to ask at Abel whether they will make peace; 21, 19 and David the son of Jesse, the weaver of the veils of the sanctuary (Heb. אלחנן בן־יערי ארגים !), of Bethlehem, slew Goliath the Gittite.

3. The Peshitto. The Hebrew text presupposed by the Peshitto deviates less from the Massoretic text than that which underlies the LXX, though it does not approach it so closely as that on which the Targums are based. It is worth observing that passages not unfrequently occur, in which Pesh. agrees with the text of *Lucian*, where both deviate from the Massoretic text [2]. In the translation of the Books of Samuel the Jewish element alluded to above (p. lii) is not so strongly marked as in that of the Pent.; but it is nevertheless present, and may be traced in certain characteristic expressions, which would hardly be met with beyond the reach of Jewish influence. Expressions such as 'to say, speak, worship, pray, sin *before* God,' where the Hebrew has simply *to* God, are, as we have seen, a distinctive feature of the exegesis embodied in the Targums; and they meet us similarly in the Peshitto version of Samuel. Thus I 1, 10 prayed *before* the Lord (so v. 26. 7, 5. 8. 9. 8, 6. 12, 8. 10. 19. 15, 11. II 7, 27). 2, 11 ܡܫܡܫܐ ܗܘܐ ܩܕܡ ܡܪܝܐ ministered *before* the Lord (so 3, 1). 26 in favour *before* God. 8, 21 spake them *before* the Lord (Heb. באזני). 10, 17 gathered *before* the Lord. II 11, 27 *end*

---

[1] Comp. Bacher, *ZDMG.* 1874, p. 23, who also notices the other readings published by Lagarde from the same source, pointing out, where it exists, their agreement with other Jewish Midrashic authorities.

[2] I 12, 11. 13, 5. 14, 49. 15, 7. 17, 12. 30, 15. II 11, 4. 15, 7. 21, 8. 23, 17. 24, 4: for some other cases, in which the agreement is mostly not in text, but in interpretation (as I 4, 15. 10, 2. 17, 18), see Stockmayer, *ZAW.* 1892, p. 220 ff.

(for בעיני). 21, 6. 23, 16 *end.* 24, 10 and 17 (*said* before): in all these passages, except II 11, 27, Targ. also has קדם. Similarly ܡܢ ܩܕܡ *from before:* I 2, 25 ופללו אלהים he shall ask (forgiveness) *from before* the Lord. 16, 14[b] (for מאת: so Targ.). II 3, 28 (for מעם: so Targ.). 6, 9 (so Targ.). 23, 17 ܣܡ ܟܠ ܡܢ ܩܕܡ ܡܪܝܐ (so Targ., as also I 24, 7. 26, 11, where, however, Pesh. has simply ܐ). I 2, 17 י"י נאצו את מנחת is rendered by ܐܪܓܙܘ ܡܢ ܩܕܡ ܐܠܗܐ which is a Jewish paraphrase for *to curse* or *provoke* God: see Lev. 24, 11 al. Onq. (for קלל); 1 Ki. 22, 54. 2 Ki. 17, 11 Targ. Pesh. (for הכעיס: often also besides in Targ. for this word); 2, 22 הצבאות ܘܡܨܠܝܢ *who prayed*, Targ. דאתן לצלאה *who came to pray* (cf. note); 30 לפני יתהלכון *shall minister* before me, Targ. ישמשון קדמי; 17, 49 אל מצחו כמא כסדוהי as Targ.; 21, 3 מקום פלני אלמני לאתר כסי ܐܦ ܘܦܠܢ, cf. Targ. (both here and 2 Ki. 6, 8) וטמיר; 27, 7 ܠܝܡܝ for ימים as Targ.[1]; II 1, 21 תרומות ܘܡܟܬܫܝܢ (cf. the renderings of תרומה and הרים in the Pent., e.g. Ex. 25, 2 Onq. ויפרשון קדמי אפרשותא, Pesh. ܘܢܦܪܫܘܢ ܠܝ, lit. that they *separate* for me a *separation*[2]); 6, 6 נכון מתקנן ܘܡܬܩܢܝܢ 14 מכרכר paraphrased by ܡܫܒܚ *praising*, as in Targ.; 7, 23 נוראות ܣܓܝܐ visions (cf. the rend. of מורא, מוראות by חזוון in Dt. 4, 34. 26, 8. 34, 12 [where Pesh., as here, ܣܓܝ or ܣܓܝܐ]); 8, 18 כהנים ܘܪܘܪܒܢ, Targ. רברבין; 24, 15 עד עת מועד to the sixth hour[3].

As a whole the translation, though not a strictly literal one, represents fairly the general sense of the original. Disregarding variations which depend presumably upon a various reading, the translation deviates from MT. (*a*) by slight and usually unimportant *additions*

---

[1] So 29, 3. II 13, 23 Pesh. (but not Targ.); Gen. 24, 55 Onq. (but not Pesh.); Nu. 9, 22 Onq. and Pesh.

[2] Cf. LXX ἀφαίρεμα. The explanation underlying these renderings is, in all probability, correct: הרים is *to lift off*, תרומה that which is *lifted off*, or separated, from a larger mass for the purpose of being set apart as sacred (cf. p. 236).

[3] 'Syrus in eandem sententiam de verbis עד עת מועד abiit, quam de illis Rabbini statuerunt, *Berach.* 62[b] מהבקר ועד עת מועד מאי עת מועד אמר שמואל סבא התניה דר' חנינא משמיה דר' חנינא משעת שחיטת התמיד עד מן עידן דמתנכיס. שעת זריקתו ר' יוחנן אמר עד חצות ממש Chaldaeus ergo (תמידא ועד דמתמסק) primam, Syrus alteram secutus est sententiam' (Perles, p. 16).

or glosses: (*b*) by *omissions*, due often either to ὁμοιοτέλευτον, or to an inability to understand the sense of the Hebrew: (*c*) by *paraphrases*, due sometimes likewise to an inability to give a literal rendering, and occasionally of a curious character. Specimens of these three classes:

(*a*) Additions: I 2, 13 (and they made themselves a prong of three teeth) and the right of the priests (they took) from the people; 35 a priest faithful (after My own heart); 4, 9 *end*–10 and fight (with them). And the Philistines fought (with Israel); 5, 8 (thrice) + the Lord; 7, 14 to Gath and their borders [את neglected], and (the Lord) delivered Israel, etc.; 8, 6 to judge us (like all the peoples); 12 + and captains of hundreds . . . and captains of tens; 12, 6 the Lord (alone is God,) who, etc.; 24 + and with all your soul; 14, 49 + and Ashboshul (= Ishbosheth[1]); 23, 12 *end* + Arise, go out from the city; 24, 20 and when a man finds his enemy and sends him [ושלחו treated as a continuation of the protasis] on a good way, (the Lord reward him with good); 30, 15 *end* + and David sware unto him (cf. Luc.). II 6, 5 of (cedar and) cypress; 12, 8 and thy master's wives (have I let sleep) in thy bosom; 18, 4 *beginning* + And his servants said to David, We will go out and hasten to fight with them; 8 and (the beasts of) the wood devoured of the people, etc. (so Targ.); 20 Kt. for (thou wilt announce) respecting the king's son that he is dead; 20, 8 *end* and it came out, and (his hand) fell (upon his sword); 24, 7 and they came to the land of Judah (in thirty-eight days) [text disordered]. There are also many instances of the addition of the subj. or obj. of a verb, or of the substitution of a noun for a pron. suffix ('Explicita'), of which it is not worth while to give examples. In 2 Sam. 22 the text has generally been made to conform with that of ψ. 18.

(*b*) Omissions: I 3, 21 ויהי כבוא 5, 10. כי נגלה י״י לשמואל בשלו ². שמעו 13, 4ᵃ אשר עשיתם לפני י״י 17. מתהלך 12, 2. ארון האלהים עקרון לאמר. 14, 1 ויהי היום 34. ואכלתם 35ᵇ from אתו החל 36ᵃ לילה. 16, וילך אליו אנג מערנת 32 ³. אשר שם לו 15, 2. ויאמר 36ᵇ from ויאמר.

---

[1] Pesh. identifies Ishui with Abinadab (see 31, 2).

[2] Probably through ὁμοιοτέλευτον.

[3] Probably not understood.

ܣܘܡܠܬܣ 13 ‏. ‏האלה 17, 11 ‏. ‏אלהים 16^b ‏. ‏. ‏. ‏נא 16^b–15^b. ‏. ‏. ‏אדננו

‏וינדו 31 ‏. ‏שומר 22 14^b. ‏ושם שלשת בניו אשר הלכו במלחמה for

‏ויאמר 12^a–11^b, 23 ‏. ‏והלאה 18, 9^b. ‏2 ‏. ‏אשר 45^b ‏. ‏1ויאמר ‏. ‏. ‏. ‏נסיתי 39

‏שאול1 ‏. ‏. ‏. ‏. 24, 20^b (abbreviated 3). 25, 30 ‏כבל אשר דבר3. 33 *end* 3

[cf. the paraphr. in 26]. II 1, 21 ‏בלי‏. 8, 14 ‏באדום and ‏שם נצבים‏.

13, 12^b. 18 (the whole verse 1). 15, 18 ‏שש מאות איש‏. 20 *end* ܡܐܬ.

‏3 ‏. ‏הרואה אתה 27 ‏. ‏2ברית האלהים ויצקו את ארן 24 ‏. ‏עמך חסד ואמת for

‏ואם ימתו ‏. ‏. ‏. ‏אלינו לב 3 ‏. ‏1 (‏יצא אצא ‏. ‏. ‏. ‏. ‏. ‏. ‏לא תצא כי) 3^a–2^b, 18

‏כי1. 21^b. 26^a (first five words). 19, 18 (first four words). 21. 6

‏בחיר י״י‏. 24, 6^a (6^b follows at the end of *v.* 7). 23 ‏המלך‏.

(*c*) Paraphrases (including some due to a mistranslation or to a faulty text): I 2, 17 (see p. lxxii). 22 ‏ישכבן 24 ‏מעבירים‏. ܡܪܚܡܝܢ. 25. 29 ‏עון *from the wilderness*. 30 ‏יתהלכון לפני should *minister* before me. 32 ‏והבטת צר מעון (31 there shall not be an old man in thy house) or one holding a sceptre in thy dwelling. 3, 13 ‏ותמש 4, 2. ‏ܦܡܪܚܡܝܢ ‏ܦܡܣ ‏ܘܐܟܝ ‏ܚܢܘܘܡܝ ‏ܐܟܡ ‏ܠܚܐܘܐ ‏כי מקללים להם בניו ‏ܠܘܘܗ. 6, 6^b and how *they* mocked them, and did *not* send them away. 10, 22 ‏הבא עוד הלם איש where is this man? 12, 3^a ‏הנני behold, I stand before you. 3^b ‏ܘܐܥܝܠܝܡ ‏ܟܡ ‏ܡܚܘ ‏ܟܝ ‏ܐܥܝܣ ‏ܘܐ‏ܡܝ‏. ‏ܣܘܐܟܝ simply ‏כי צר לו כי ננש העם 6 ‏ܣܡܡ ‏נבאש ‏ܚܠ. 6. 13, 4 and they feared. 7 *end* ‏חרדו אחריו simply ‏ܚܣܘܐ. 12 ‏לא חליתי ‏ܦܠ ‏ܘܐܟܠܚܝ ‏ܚܟܝ ‏כלבבך 14, 7^b ‏ܐܠ ‏ܣܐܠܐ. 24^a And Saul drew near in that day, and said to the people, Cursed, etc. 25^a And they went into all the land, and entered into the woods. 16, 4 ‏ויחרדו ‏ܣ‏ܐܩܡ. ‏ܣܡܡ ‏ܚܠ ‏אשר בצאן. 19 *end* ‏(ܐܘܐܣ ‏ܘܐܡܝܘܐܠ ‏ܟܐܡܣܣܡ ‏אך נגד י״י ‏משיחו 6 20 ‏לחם (and laded it with) bread. 17, 18^b ‏(ܐ‏ܡܐ ‏ܚܠ ‏ܣܘܐܠܝ‏ܐܣܣ‏ (cf. Targ. ‏ית טיבהון חיתי, and the doublet in Luc. καὶ εἰσοίσεις μοι τὴν ἀγγελίαν αὐτῶν). 39 ‏ויאל לכת and would *not* go. 52 ‏ويريעו ‏ܐ‏ܠܚܚܚܐ. 18, 22 ‏השלשית ‏(ܐܘܡ ‏בלט לאמר ‏ܚܐ‏ the son of Jesse (!). 20, 12 ‏בלתי טהור הוא 26 ‏ושלשת. so 19 for ‏ܟܐܐܠܐ ‏ܐܟܡ *at the third hour:* 21, 6 ‏כי לא טהור perhaps he is clean, or perhaps he is not clean. ‏ܚܠ ‏ܣܘ ‏ܚܡܐܟܝ ‏ܡܘܦܟܘܐ (as though ‏אשָׁה עצָרָה לָנו!): see also 21, 14. 22, 19 ‏(ܘܐܬ נב ‏ܣܘܣܡ ‏ܚܠ—the two words read as one and

---

1 Probably through ὁμοιοτέλευτον.　　2 Or perhaps transposed.

3 Probably not understood.

connected with נתן). 23, 22ᵃ. 25, 8. 17ᵇ. 26. 27, 8. 30, 6 מרה
read as מתה). 14ᵃ. II 2, 13 ܟܟ݁ܬܡܐܠ thrice for ברכה). 24 אמה
ܪ̇ܥܐܠ). 27. 29 ܟܠ-הבתרון) ܠܩܠ ܚܡܘܦ (ܠܩܠ). 3, 34. 39ᵃ (רך ומשוח ܠܝܐ
ܠܣܘܠ ܠ/ܠ). 4, 6 (חטים connected with חטאים). 5, 8 (בצנור |ܪܡܒܚܣ.).
6, 16 (מפון ומכרכר |ܣܡܠܠܠܣ |ܪܡܝ). 21ᵇ. 7, 23ᵇ. 8, 13ᵃ. 11, 25
(תאכל it happens in war!). 12, 25 *end*. 13, 4ᵃ. 26. 32 עַל פִּי החרב
ܚܣܟܠܢ in his mind). 14, 7. 17 (מִנְחָה). 20ᵃ (*ut mihi* [פָּנַי] *morem
gereres*: PS. col. 279). 24. 30. 32ᵇ. 15, 19. 32. 34. 16, 1. 2
(מה |ܡܚܡܠ ܡܥ). 4 (השתחויתי ܐ/ܠ ܐܠ ܐܚܝ ܣܡܝ.). 8ᵇ. 21ᵇ. 17, 10
(ܡܚ̈ܡܚܡܠ ܠ ܡܚ̈ܡܚܣܡ will *not* melt). 16ᵇ. 20 (see note). 18, 5ᵃ
(take me the young man Absalom alive). 18. 29. 33 [19, 1 Heb.]
(בְּבִכֹתוֹ for בלכתו). 19, 9ᵇ (10ᵇ). 17 (Heb. 18: וצלחו *they have crossed
and bridged* Jordan). 31 (32) *end*. 35 (36 ܠܩܠܘܣ ܠܩܠܣ, i. e. שרים
וישרות). 20, 8 (בתערה ܠܟܚܠܠ ܝܡ.). 18ᵇ. 19ᵃ. 21, 2ᵇ (in his zeal *to
cause* the Israelites *to sin*). 5. 23, 1 (Saith the man who *set up the yoke
[*הֻקַם עַל*] of his Messiah!*). 8. 11 (הררי ܡܚܡܠ ܠܝܡ ܡܥ *of the mountain
of the king:* so 25 for הררי). 19. 22. 23 (משמעתו אל to go out and
to come in). 33ᵃ (ההררי ܠܚ݂ܠ/ ܠܝܡ ܡܥ.). 24, 13ᵃ. 16. 25 (ויעתר
לארץ י"י ܠܩ̇ܠܢ ܟܠܠ ܚܢ݂ܡ ܚܟ̈ܠܚܠ݁: not so elsewhere).

The Syriac text of Pesh. sometimes (as might indeed be anticipated
from the nature of the character) exhibits corruptions, similar to those
noticed in the case of LXX, p. lvii f. Thus I 1, 21 ܚܣܚܝܣܟ for
ܚܣܚܝܣܟ (so rightly the Cod. Ambr. published in facsimile by
Ceriani[1]: also the Arab. version in the Polyglotts[2], 'to offer'). 2, 8
ܡܢܚ ܠܚܠ for ܠ ܚܢܚܡܠ ܠܟ̈ܡܚ (מ at the beginning has fallen out).
3, 14 ܠܩ̇ܡܠ ... ܐ for ... ܠܩ̇ܡܠ ... (Heb. נשבעתי). 19 ܚܡܘܣ for ܚܡܟܣ
(Heb. וינדל). 9, 4 |ܪܚܡܘܣ for ܠܚ݂ܝܟ݁ܠ (Heb. שלשה[3]). 12, 21 ܠܘܠ
ܘܠܚܡܚܠܣ probably for ܡܚܠܘܠ ܘܠ (Heb. אשר לא יועילו: notice the

---

[1] Cornill, *Ezechiel*, p. 144 f., exaggerates the extent to which this MS. may have
been corrected after MT.: its approximations to MT. (p. 140 ff.) are slight, compared with the cases in which it agrees with other MSS. against it (p. 148 ff.).
Comp. Rahlfs, *ZATW.* 1889, pp. 180-192.

[2] Which, in the Books of Samuel, and in certain parts of Kings, is *based* upon
the Pesh.: see Roediger, *De orig. et indole Arab. libr. V.T. hist. interpr.* (1829).

[3] So Tuch on Gen. 10, 6, and PS. coll. 681-2, 741. Comp. 2 Ki. 4, 42 Pesh.
(שלישה connected similarly with שליש, שלישים, commonly represented in Pesh.
by |ܚܠܚܠ).

following ptcp. for ולא יצילו). 17, 20 ܟܣܝܠܐ for ܟܣܠܐ (so Cod. Ambr.). 40 ܢܡܠ ܡܥ for ܢܡܠ ܡܥ (Heb. מן־הנחל). 28, 6 ܟܬܒܢܐ for ܟܬܒܘܐ (so Arab. ' prophets '). II 12, 8ᵇ ܟܢܐ prob. for ܟܢܝ, though *possibly* a paraphrase. 18, 17 ܣܟܘܝ prob. for ܟܕܟܐ (Heb. ביער). (Several of these instances are noted by Well., p. 8.) The name מרב is represented regularly by ܒܝ.

4. The Latin Versions.

(*a*) The affinity subsisting between the Old Latin Version and the recension of Lucian appears to have been first distinctly perceived (with reference in particular to the Lamentations) by Ceriani[1]. Afterwards, it was noticed, and frequently remarked on, by Vercellone, as characteristic of the excerpts of the Old Latin Version on the margin of the Leon Manuscript (above, p. lii), that, when they diverged from the ordinary Septuagintal text, they constantly agreed with Holmes' four MSS. 19, 82, 93, 108, which, as was clear, represented on their part one and the same recension[2]. A version identical with that represented in the excerpts was also, as Vercellone further pointed out, cited by Ambrose and Claudius of Turin[3]. The conclusion which the facts observed authorize is thus that the Old Latin is a version made, or revised, on the basis of MSS. agreeing closely with those which were followed by Lucian in framing his recension[4]. The Old Latin must date from the second cent. A. D.; hence it cannot be based upon the recension of Lucian as such: its peculiar interest lies in the fact that it affords independent evidence of the existence of MSS. containing Lucian's characteristic readings (or renderings), considerably before the time of Lucian himself[5].

The following comparison of passages from the Old Latin Version of 1 and 2 Sam., derived from one of the sources indicated above (p. lii f.), and all presupposing a text differing from that of the

---

[1] *Monumenta Sacra et Profana*, I. 1 (1861), p. xvi (*Addenda*).

[2] *Variae Lectiones*, ii. 436 (and in other passages).

[3] *Ib.* p. 455 f. (on 3 Reg. 2, 5).

[4] Comp. Ceriani, *Le recensioni dei LXX*, etc., p. 5.

[5] Rahlfs (iii. 159 f.) agrees with Ceriani and S. Berger (*Hist. de la Vulg.*, p. 6) in questioning this conclusion (cf. Moore, *AJSL*. xxix. 60), on the ground that there is no sufficient evidence for the early date assigned to the Leon fragments by Vercellone: he thinks rather that the resemblances shew them to be *later* than Lucian.

normal LXX, but agreeing with that of Lucian, will shew the justice of this conclusion. Although, however, the text upon which the Old Latin is based agrees largely with that of Lucian, it must not be supposed to be *identical* with it: there are passages in which it agrees with B or A, or with other MSS., against Lucian[1]. Sometimes moreover, it is to be observed, other particular MSS. agree with the Old Latin, as well as those which exhibit Lucian's recension. A more detailed inquiry into the sources of the Old Latin Version of the OT. must be reserved for future investigators. (The list is not an exhaustive one. The words printed in heavy type are those in which Lucian's text differs from B. In the passages marked †, the deviation is *confined* to the MSS. which exhibit Lucian's recension, and is not quoted—at least by Holmes and Parsons—for other MSS. The quotations will also illustrate the variations prevailing between different recensions of the Old Latin.)

I 1, 6 Goth. quia ad nihilum reputabat eam.

Luc. **διὰ τὸ ἐξουθενεῖν αὐτὴν** (for בעבור הרעמה). So 55, 158; and similarly (ἐξουθενοῦσα) 44, 74, 106, 120, 134.

---

[1] I 4, 12 Vind.² Et cucurrit.

BA **ἔδραμεν** (Luc. καὶ ἔφυγεν).

16 Vind.² Qui venit homo properans.

B **καὶ ὁ ἀνὴρ σπεύσας προσῆλθεν** (Luc. καὶ ἀπεκρίθη ὁ ἀνὴρ ὁ ἐληλυθώς).

9, 24 Vind.² Ecce reliquum.

BA ἰδοὺ **ὑπόλιμμα** (Luc. μαρτύριον).

10, 2 Goth. et in Selom, in Bacallat salientes magnas fossas.
Vind.² reluctantes hic et salientes magnum.

ἐν Σηλω ἐν Βακαλαθ XI, 44, 64, 74, 106, 120, 129, 134, 144, 236; ἐν Σηλωμ ἐν Βακαλαθ 244; ἐν Σηλωμ Βακαλα 29; ἐσ̄ηλω ἐν Βακαλαθ 242; ἐν Σηλω ἐν Βακαλλαθ 55.—ἀλλομένους μεγάλα BA; Luc. μεσημβρίας ἀλλ. μεγάλα.

10, 17 Vind.² Et praecepit … convenire.

BA **καὶ παρήγγειλεν** (Luc. καὶ συνήγαγε).

12, 25 Goth. apponemini in plaga.

B **προστεθήσεσθε** (Luc. ἀπολεῖσθε).

14, 20 Vind.² Et exclamavit.

A **καὶ ἀνεβόησεν** (B Luc. καὶ ἀνέβη).

17, 1 דמים אספ Goth. Sepherme.

ἐν Σεφερμε 121 (Σαφερμαιμ 29, 119, 143; Σεφερμαειμ 52, 92, 144, 236; Σεφερμαιμ 55, 64; Σαφαρμειν 245).

II 18, 6 Vind.² in silvam Efrē.

B **ἐν τῷ δρύμῳ 'Εφραιμ** (Luc. ἐν τῷ δρ. Μααιναν).

9 Vind.² Et occurrit Absalom.

BA **καὶ συνήντησεν** A. (Luc. καὶ ἦν μέγας A.).

Nor does the Old Latin express Lucian's doublets in I 2, 11. 6, 12. 10, 2 (μεσημβρίας). 27ᵇ. 15, 29. 32. Sometimes, however, his doublets do occur in it, as I 1, 6 G. 16 G. (not V.²). 4, 18 G. 6, 7 G. (not V.²). 16, 14 G. 27, 8 G.

1 2, 10 Vind.² + quia iustus est.

      Luc. δίκαιος ὤν. So other MSS., among them 44, 55, 71, 74, 120, 134, 144, 158, 246.

15 Vind.² + ante Dominum.

      Luc. ἐνώπιον Κυρίου. So other MSS., among them 44, 55, 71, 74, 120, 134, 158.

3, 14 Sab. et nunc sic iuravi.
Vind.² et ideo sic iuravi.

      No Greek MS. is cited with the reading *therefore* for לכן, all having οὐδ' (or οὐχ) οὕτως (see note).

6, 12 Vind.² in viam . . . rectam.

      Luc. ἐν τρίβῳ εὐθείᾳ †.

9, 27 Vind.² in loco summo civitatis.

      Luc. εἰς ἄκρον τῆς πόλεως †.

10, 3 Goth. usque ad arborem glandis electae.
Vind.² ad arborem Thabor alectae (i. e. electae).

      Luc. ἕως τῆς δρυὸς τῆς ἐκλεκτῆς ᵃ.
      246 ἕως τῆς δρυὸς Θαβωρ τῆς ἐκλεκτῆς.

12, 3 Goth. aut calceamentum, et abscondam oculos meos in quo dicitis adversum me, et reddam vobis.
Sab. vel calceamentum, dicite adversus me, et reddam vobis.

      Luc. ἢ ὑπόδημα, καὶ ἀπέκρυψα τοὺς ὀφθαλμούς μου ἐν αὐτῷ; εἴπατε κατ' ἐμοῦ, καὶ ἀποδώσω ὑμῖν †.
      So also (with κἀμοὶ for κατ' ἐμοῦ) Theodoret., *Quaest.* 16 *in* 1 *Reg.*

14, 14 Goth. in bolidis et petrobolis et in saxis campi.
Vind.² in sagittis et in fundibolis et in muculis campi.

      Luc. ἐν βολίσι καὶ ἐν πετροβόλοις καὶ ἐν κόχλαξι τοῦ πεδίου.

14, 15 Goth. et ipsi nolebant esse in laboribus.

      Luc. καὶ αὐτοί, καὶ οὐκ ἤθελον πονεῖν (πονεῖν also in X, 56, 64, 71, 119, 244, 245 : others have πολεμεῖν).

15, 11 Sab. Quedl. verba mea non statuit.

      Luc. οὐκ ἔστησε τοὺς λόγους μου. So A, 123 ᵇ.

17, 39 Goth. et claudicare coepit ambulans sub armis.

      Luc. καὶ ἐχώλαινε Δαυιδ ἐν τῷ βαδίζειν ἐν αὐτοῖς (158 ἀσχολανε).

18, 21 Goth. in virtute eris mihi gener hodie.

      Luc. ἐν ταῖς δυνάμεσιν ἐπιγαμβρεύσεις μοι σήμερον (so 44, 74, 106, 120, 134).

20, 30 Goth. Filius puellarum vagantium, quae se passim coinquinant esca mulierum.

      Luc. υἱὲ κορασίων αὐτομολούντων γυναικοτραφῇ (γυν. added also in 29, 55, 71, 121 marg., 243, 246).

27, 8 Goth. Et apponebant se super omnem appropinquantem, et extendebant se super Gesur.

      Luc. καὶ ἐπετίθεντο ἐπὶ πάντα τὸν ἐγγίζοντα, καὶ ἐξέτεινον ἐπὶ τὸν Γεσσουραῖον. So, except for the difference of one or two letters, 56, 158, 246.

30, 15 *end* (in the current Vulg.) et iuravit ei David.

      Luc. καὶ ὤμοσεν αὐτῷ (121 marg. καὶ ὤ. αὐτῷ Δαυιδ. So Pesh.).

ᵃ תבר being connected with ברר *to choose out*: see II 22, 27.

ᵇ In 9, 4 (per terram Sagalim et non invenerunt) Quedl. agrees also with 123, not with Lucian (who has διὰ τῆς γῆς Γαδδι τῆς πόλεως Σεγαλειμ : cf. 56 Γαδδι τῆς πόλεως alone).

II 1, 19 Goth. Cura te (al. curare), Israel, de interfectis tuis.

Sab. Considera, Israel, pro his qui mortui sunt.

2, 8 Goth. Isbalem.

2, 29 Magd. in castra Madiam [a].

6, 12 Sab. Dixitque David, Ibo et reducam arcam cum benedictione in domum meam.

7, 8 Goth. Accepi te de casa pastorali ex uno grege.

9, 6 Goth. Memphibaal.

10, 19 Vind.[1,2] omnes reges qui convenerunt ad [Vind.[2] cum] Adrazar ... et disposuerunt testamentum coram [Vind.[2] cum] Israel, et servierunt Israhel [Vind.[2] Israeli tribus].

11, 4 Goth. et haec erat dimissa [c] [*Alias* et haec erat abluta] excelso loco.

Vind.[2e] haec autem lota erat post purgationem.

11, 12 Vind.[2e] redi hic.

11, 13 Vind.[1,2] inebriatus est.

11, 16 Vind.[1,2] in locum pessimum ubi sciebat etc.

11, 17 Vind.[2] et caecidit Joab de populo secundum praeceptum Davit.

11, 24 Goth. de servis regis quasi viri XVIII.

13, 21 Vind.[2] et deficit animo valde [h].

13, 32 Vind.[2] in ira enim est ad [? eum] Abessalon.

14, 26 Goth. Vind.[1] centum.

Luc. Ἀκρίβασαι, Ἰσραηλ, ὑπὲρ κτλ. (106 ἀκρίβωσαι στήλωσαι)†. So Theodoret., *Quaest. in* 2 *Reg.*

Cod. 93 (but not 19, 82) Εἰσβααλ.

Luc. εἰς παρεμβολὰς Μαδιαμ. So 158.

Luc. καὶ εἶπε Δαυιδ Ἐπιστρέψω τὴν εὐλογίαν εἰς τὸν οἶκόν μου. So 158.

Luc. ἐκ τῆς μάνδρας ἐξ ἑνὸς τῶν ποιμνίων †.

Luc. Μεμφιβααλ †.

Luc. πάντες οἱ βασιλεῖς οἱ συμπορευόμενοι [so 158] τῷ Ἀδρααζαρ ... καὶ διέθεντο διαθήκην μετὰ Ἰσραηλ καὶ ἐδούλευον τῷ Ἰσραηλ [b] †.

Luc. καὶ αὐτὴ ἦν λελουμένη ἐξ ἀφέδρου αὐτῆς. So the Ethiopic Version [d] and Pesh.

I. e. שַׁב for שׁוּב [f]. Not cited from any Greek MS.

Luc. ἐμεθύσθη †.

Luc. ἐπὶ τὸν τόπον τὸν πονοῦντα [g] [οὗ ἤδει] κτλ.†

Luc. καὶ ἔπεσον ἐκ τοῦ λαοῦ κατὰ τὸν λόγον Δαυιδ.

Luc. ἀπὸ τῶν δούλων τοῦ βασίλεως ὡσεὶ ἄνδρες δέκα καὶ ὀκτώ. So 158.

Luc. καὶ ἠθύμησε σφόδρα †.

Luc. ὅτι ἐν ὀργῇ ἦν αὐτῷ Ἀβεσσαλωμ †.

Luc. ἑκατόν †.

---

[a] But in *v.* 31 Magd. has ab illo = παρ' αὐτοῦ, against Luc.

[b] Καὶ διέθ. διαθ. added to ηὐτομόλησαν on the marg. of B. by an ancient hand.

[c] Based evidently on λελυμένη for λελουμένη. BA ἁγιαζομένη.

[d] Which is based on the LXX; see p. l, *n.* 3.

[e] There are lacunae in these passages in Vind.[1]

[f] Unless indeed *redi* be an error for *sede*: cf. *sedit* in clause *b*.

[g] 'Verba τὸν πονοῦντα eleganter vertunt Hebraeum יָרַע אֲשֶׁר [pro אֲשֶׁר יָדַע]' (Dr. Field).

[h] Goth. *et iratus factus est* agrees here with B καὶ ἐθυμώθη.

II 15, 23 Goth. et omnis terra bene-
dicentes voce magna [*lacuna*] per
viam olivae, quae erat in deserto.

Luc. καὶ πᾶσα ἡ γῆ εὐλογοῦντες φωνῇ
μεγάλῃ καὶ κλαίοντες . . . κατὰ τὴν
ὁδὸν τῆς ἐλαίας τῆς ἐν τῇ ἐρήμῳ †.

17, 8 Goth. sicut ursus qui a bove
[*Alias* ab aestu : *l.* ab oestro]
stimulatur in campo.

Luc. ὥσπερ ἄρκοι παροιστρῶσαι ἐν τῷ
πεδίῳ †.

17, 13 Goth. ut non inveniatur ibi
conversatio.
Vind.² ut non inveniatur tumulus
fundamenti.

Luc. ὅπως μὴ εὑρεθῇ ἐκεῖ συστροφή †.

17, 20 Vind.² festinanter transierunt
prendere aquam ; (et inquisierunt)
etc.

Luc. Διεληλύθασι σπεύδοντες· καὶ ἐζή-
τουν †.

17, 22 Sab. . . . . et antequam denu-
daretur verbum . . .
17, 29 Goth. et lactantes vitulos.
Vind.² et vitulos saginatos.

Luc. ἕως τοῦ μὴ ἀποκαλυφθῆναι τὸν
λόγον, οὕτως διέβησαν τὸν Ἰορδάνην †.
Luc. καὶ γαλαθηνὰ μοσχάρια. So 158.

18, 2 Vind.² Et tripartitum fecit
Davit populum.

Luc. καὶ ἐτρίσσευσε Δαυιδ τὸν λαόν †.

18, 3 Vind.² non stabit in nobis cor
nostrum.

Luc. οὐ στήσεται ἐν ἡμῖν καρδία †.

20, 8 Goth. gladium rudentem (*l.*
bidentem, We.).

Luc. μάχαιραν ἀμφήκη. 158 μάχ. δύ-
στομον (*l.* δίστομον) ἀμφήκη.

20, 23 Goth. Et Baneas filius Joab
desuper lateris et in ponentibus
(*l.* potentibus).

Luc. καὶ Βαναίας υἱὸς Ἰωαδδαι ἐπὶ τοῦ
πλινθίου καὶ ἐπὶ τοὺς δυνάστας †. So
(except δυνατοὺς) Theodoret., *Quaest.*
40 *in* 2 *Reg.*

23, 4 Goth. et non tenebrescet a lu-
mine quasi pluvia, quasi herba de
terra ª.

Luc. καὶ οὐ σκοτάσει [so other MSS.,
among them 44, 56, 158, 246] ἀπὸ
φέγγους ὡς ὑετός, ὡς βοτάνη ἐκ γῆς.

23, 6 Goth. quoniam omnes qui ori-
untur sicut spinae, et reliqui quasi
quod emungit de lucerna.

Luc. ὅτι πάντες οἱ ἀνατέλλοντες ὥσπερ
ἄκανθα, καὶ οἱ λοιποὶ ὡς ἀπόμυγμα
λύχνου πάντες †.

23, 8 Goth. Iesbael filius Thegemani
. . . hic adornavit adornationem
suam super nongentos vulneratos
in semel.

Luc. Ἰεσβααλ υἱὸς Θεκεμανει . . . οὗτος
διεκόσμει τὴν διασκευὴν αὐτῶν ἐπὶ
ἐννακοσίους τραυματίας εἰς ἅπαξ †.

(*b*) On the general characteristics of Jerome's Version of the OT.,
reference must be made to the monograph of Nowack, referred to
above (p. liii). A synopsis of the principal deviations from the
Massoretic text presupposed by it in the Books of Samuel, is given

---

ª But 23, 3 agrees partly with BA : In me locutus est *custos* Israel *parabolam*
Dic hominibus.

ib. pp. 25–27, 35, 37, 38, 50; the most important are also noticed, at their proper place, in the notes in the present volume[1].

The following instances (which could easily be added to) will exemplify the dependence of Jerome in exegesis upon his Greek predecessors, especially Symmachus:—

I 1, 18 עוד לה היו לא Σ. (οὐ) διετράπη (ἔτι), Vulg. non sunt amplius in diversa mutati.

2, 5 חדלו Σ. ἀνενδεεῖς ἐγένοντο, V. saturati sunt.

5, 6 בעפלים Σ. κατὰ τῶν κρυπτῶν[2], V. in secretiori parte.

6, 18 ועד כפר הפרזי Σ. ἕως κώμης ἀτειχίστου, V. usque ad villam quae erat absque muro[3].

9, 24 למועד Σ. ἐπίτηδες, V. de industria.

12, 3 רצותי Ἄλλος· ἐσυκοφάντησα, V. calumniatus sum[4].

22 כי הואיל י״י V. quia iuravit[5] Dominus.

14, 48 ויעש (חיל) Ἄλλος· συστησάμενος, V. congregato (exercitu).

20, 41 עד דוד הגדיל Σ. Δαυιδ δὲ ὑπερέβαλλεν, V. David autem amplius.

22, 6 האשל A. τὸν δενδρῶνα, Σ. τὸ φυτόν, V. (in) nemore. Similarly 31, 13.

---

[1] The current (Clementine) text contains many passages which are no genuine part of Jerome's translation, but are glosses derived from the Old Latin (marked *), or other sources. The following list of such passages (taken from Vercellone, *Variae Lectiones*, ii. pp. ix–xiii) is given for the convenience of students:—

I 4, 1 to *pugnam**; 5, 6 from *et ebullierunt**; 9 from *inierunt**; 8, 18 from *quia**; 9, 25 from *stravit*†; 10, 1 from *et liberabis**; 11, 1 to *mensem**; 13, 15 *et reliqui*... *Benjamin**; 14, 22 from *Et erant**; 41 *Domine Deus Israel* and *quid est ... sanctitatem**; 15, 3 *et non* ... *aliquid**; 12ᵇ–13ᵃ *Saul offerebat* ... *ad Saul**; 32 *et tremens**; 17, 36 *Nunc** ... *incircumcisus*; 19, 21 from *Et iratus**; 20, 15 from *auferat**; 21, 11 *cum vidissent David* ('ex ignoto fonte'); 23, 13–14 *et salvatus* ... *opaco*; 30, 15 *et iuravit ei David**; II 1, 18 from *et ait, Considera**; 26 from *Sicut mater*; 4, 5 from *Et ostiaria*; 5, 23 *Si* ... *meas*; 6, 6 *et declinaverunt eam*; 6, 12 from *et erant*; 10, 19 *expaverunt* ... *Israel. Et*; 13, 21 from *et noluit**; 27 from *Fecerat**; 14, 30 from *Et venientes*; 15, 18 *pugnatores validi*; 20 *et Dominus* ... *veritatem*; 21, 18 *de genere gigantum*.

[2] Comp. Mic. 4, 8 עֹפֶל Σ. ἀπόκρυφος.

[3] Comp. Dt. 3, 5.

[4] Comp. Amos 4, 1 calumniam facitis.

[5] See Ex. 2, 21 ויאל Σ. ὥρκισε δέ, V. iuravit ergo, which shews the source of *iuravit* here.

I 23, 13 ויתהלכו באשר יתהלכו Σ. καὶ ἐρρέμβοντο ὁπουδήποτε [1].

26 עטרים Οἱ λοιποί· περιστεφανοῦντες, V. in modum coronae cingebant.

25, 3 רע מעללים Σ. κακογνώμων, V. (pessimus et) malitiosus.

7 לא הכלמנום Σ. (οὐκ) ἐνωχλήσαμεν (αὐτούς), V. numquam eis molesti fuimus.

18 צמוקים Σ. ἐνδέσμους σταφίδος, V. ligaturas uvae passae. So 30, 12.

29 צרורה Σ. πεφυλαγμένη, V. custodita.

31 לפוקה A. Σ. (εἰς) λυγμόν, V. in singultum.

33 והושע Σ. ἐκδικῆσαι, V. et ulciscerer (me manu mea).

26, 5 במעגל Σ. (ἐν τῇ) σκηνῇ, V. in tentorio.

27, 1 אספה יום אחד Σ. παραπεσοῦμαί ποτε, V. Aliquando incidam una die.

30, 16 נטשים Σ. ἀναπεπτωκότες, V. discumbebant.

II 2, 16 חלקת הצרים A. Σ. κλῆρος τῶν στερεῶν, V. ager robustorum.

8, 2 נשאי מנחה Σ. ὑπὸ φόρον, V. sub tributo.

10, 6 נבאשו בדוד Σ. ἐκακούργησαν πρὸς Δαυίδ, V. quod iniuriam fecissent David.

12, 14 נאץ נאצת Σ. βλασφημῆσαι ἐποίησας (the other versions all differently), V. blasphemare fecisti.

15, 28 מתמהמה Σ. κρυβήσομαι, V. abscondar.

18, 23 דרך הככר Οἱ Γ΄. (κατὰ τὴν ὁδὸν) τὴν διατέμνουσαν, V. per viam compendii.

Three examples, shewing how Jerome followed Aq. or Symm. in dividing artificially a Hebrew word (p. xl *n.* 2), may be added—the last being of peculiar interest, as it explains a familiar rendering of the Authorized Version :—

ψ. 16, 1 מכתם לדוד A. τοῦ ταπεινόφρονος καὶ ἁπλοῦ τοῦ Δαυίδ, Jer.[2] humilis et simplicis David.

---

[1] ' Symmachum ante oculos habuit Hieronymus eleganter vertens : *huc atque illuc vagabantur incerti*' (Field).

[2] Jerome's own translation of the Psalter failed to supersede the older Latin Version that was in general use ; hence it never made its way into the ' Vulgate,'

Ex. 32, 25 לְשִׁמְצָה A. εἰς ὄνομα ῥύπου (לְשֵׁם צָאָה), Jer. propter igno-
miniam sordis.

Lev. 16, 8 לַעֲזָאזֵל Σ. εἰς τράγον ἀπερχόμενον (*v.* 10 ἀφιέμενον), A. εἰς
τράγον ἀπολυόμενον (or ἀπολελυμένον) i.e. לְעֵז אֹזֵל, Jer.
capro *emissario.* Hence the 'Great Bible' (1539–
1541) and AV. *scape-goat*[1].

and must be sought elsewhere (*Opera,* ed. Bened. I. 835 ff.; Vallarsi, IX. 1153 ff.;
Migne, IX. 1123 ff.; Lagarde's *Psalterium Hieronymi,* 1874 [now out of print];
or Tischendorf, Baer, and Franz Delitzsch, *Liber Psalmorum Hebraicus atque
Latinus ab Hieronymo ex Hebraeo conversus,* 1874). The translation of the
Psalter contained in the 'Vulgate' is merely the Old Latin Version, revised by
Jerome with the aid of the LXX.

[1] Comp. Is. 66, 24 לדראון לכל בשר *usque ad satietatem videndi* (as though
לְדֵי רְאוֹן) omni carni. The same interpretation in the Targ.: 'And the wicked
shall be judged in Gehinnom until the righteous shall say concerning them מיסת
חזינא *We have seen enough.*' The renderings of Aq. Symm. are not here preserved; but from their known dependence on Jewish exegesis, there is little doubt
that Jerome's rendering is derived from one of them.

APPENDIX

The Inscription of Mesha', commonly known as the 'Moabite Stone.'

THE Inscription of Mesha' (which has been several times referred to in the preceding pages) is of such importance as an authentic and original monument of the ninth century B. c., remarkably illustrating the Old Testament, that I have inserted here a transcription and translation of it, accompanied by a brief commentary. I have confined myself to the *minimum* of necessary explanation, and have purposely avoided entering upon a discussion of controverted readings or interpretations. The doubtful passages are, fortunately, few in number, being limited chiefly to certain letters at the extreme left of some of the lines, and to two or three ἅπαξ εἰρημένα, and do not interfere with the interpretation of the Inscription as a whole. Palaeographical details must be learnt from the monograph of Smend and Socin, referred to on p. iv, and from Clermont-Ganneau's 'Examen Critique du Texte,' in the *Journ. As.*, Janv. 1887, pp. 72–112[1]. The deviations from the text of Smend and Socin, adopted in the first edition of the present work, were introduced partly on the authority of Clermont-Ganneau, partly on that of E. Renan in the *Journal des Savans*, 1887, pp. 158–164, and of Th. Nöldeke in the *Lit. Centralblatt*, Jan. 8, 1887, coll. 59–61 : in the present edition, a few changes in the uncertain places have been made in consequence of the re-examination of the stone and squeeze by Nordlander (*Die Inschrift des Königs Mesa von Moab*, 1896), and Lidzbarski, *Ephemeris*, i (1902), p. 1 ff.[2] Of the older literature connected with the Inscription, the most important is the monograph of Nöldeke, *Die Inschrift des Königs Mesa von Moab* (Kiel, 1870), to which in parts of my explanatory notes I am indebted. It ought

---

[1] See also the *Revue Critique*, 1875, No. 37, pp. 166–174 (by the same writer).

[2] See also the transcription, with notes, in his *Altsemitische Texte*, Heft i (1907), p. 1 ff.

only to be observed that at the time when this monograph was
published, some of the readings had not been ascertained so accurately
as was afterwards done. On the interpretation of the Inscription,
see also now Cooke, *NSI*. p. 4 ff.; and comp. the present writer's
article MESHA in *EB*. iii.   The line above a letter indicates that the
reading is not quite certain.

אנך . משע . בן . כמש ? ? . מלך . מאב . הד	1
יבני l אבי . מלך . על . מאב . שלשן . שת . ואנך . מלכ	2
תי . אחר . אבי l ואעש . הבמת . זאת . לכמש . בקרחה l ב[מת . י]	3
שע . כי . השעני . מכל . חשלבן . וכי . הראני . בכל . שנאי l עמר	4
י . מלך . ישראל . ויענו . את . מאב . ימן . רבן . כי . יֿאנף . כמש . באר	5
צה l ויחלפה . בנה . ויאמר . גם . הא . אענו . את . מאב l בימי . אמר . בֿ	6
וארא . בה . ובבתה l וישראל . אבד . אבד . עלם . וירש . עמרי . את [אר]	7
ץ . מהדבא l וישב . בה . ימה . וחצי . ימי . בנה . ארבען . שת . ויֿשֿ	8
בה . כמש . בימי l ואבן . את . בעלמען . ואעש . בה . האשוח . ואבֿן	9
את . קריתן l ואש . גד . ישב . בארץ . עטרת . מעלם . ויבן . לה . מלך . יֿ	10
שראל . את . עטרת l ואלתחם . בקר . ואחזה . ואהרג . את . כל . העם . [מ]	11
הקר . רית . לכמש . ולמאב l ואשב . משם . את . אראל . דודה . וא[ס]	12
חבה . לפני . כמש . בקרית l ואשב . בה . את . אש . שרן . ואת . אש	13
מחרת l ויאמר . לי . כמש . לך . אחז . את . נבה . על . ישראל l ואֿ	14
הלך . בללה . ואלתחם . בה . מבקע . השחרת . עד . הצהרם l ואחֿ	15
זה . ואהרג . כלֿה . שבעת . אלפן . ג[ב]רן . וגרן l ונברת . ו[גר]	16
ת . ורחמת l כי . לעשתר . כמש . החרמתה l ואקח . משם . א[ת . כ]	17
לי . יהוה . ואסחב . הם . לפני . כמש l ומלך . ישראל . בנה . אֿת	18
יהץ . וישב . בה . בהלתחמה . בי l וינרשה . כמש . מפנ[י l ו]	19
אקח . ממאב . מאתן . אש . כל . רשה l ואשאה . ביהץ . ואחזה	20
לספת . על . דיבן l ואנך . בנתי . קרחה . חמת . היערן . וחמת	21
העפל l ואנך . בנתי . שעריה . ואנך . בנתי . מגדלתה l וא	22
נך . בנתי . בת . מלך . ואנך . עשתי . כלאי . האש[וח . למ]ין . בקרב	23
הקר l ובר . אן . בקרב . הקר . בקרחה . ואמר . לכל . העם . עשו . ל	24
כם . אש . בר . בביתה l ואנך . כרתי . המכרתת . לקרחה . באסר	25
[י] . ישראל l ואנך . בנתי . ערער . ואנך . עשתי . המסלת . בארנן	26
אנך . בנתי . בת . במת . כי . הרס . הא l אנך . בנתי . בצר . כי . עין . •	27
ש . דיבן . חמשן . כי . כל . דיבן . משמעת l ואנך . מלֿכֿ	28
תֿי מאת . בקרן . אשר . יספתי . על . הארץ l ואנך . בנת	29
י . [את . [מֿהֿדֿ[בֿ]א . ובת . דבלתן l ובת . בעלמען . ואשא . שם . את . נקֿדֿ	30

אש . צאן . הארץ ׀ וחורנן . ישב . בה . בח ה וק	31
ויאמר . לי . כמש . רד . הלתחם · בחורנן ׀ ואֹרֹד	32
[ויש]בה . כמש . בימי . ועל דה . משם . עש	33
שֹת . שדק ׀ ואנ	34

1. I am Mesha' son of Chĕmōsh[kān ?], king of Moab, the Da-

2. -ibonite. My father reigned over Moab for 30 years, and I reign-

3. -ed after my father. And I made this high place for Chĕmōsh in QRḤH, a [high place of sal-]

4. -vation, because he had saved me from all the assailants (?), and because he had let me see my pleasure on all them that hated me. Omr-

5. -i king of Israel afflicted Moab for many days, because Chemosh was angry with his la-

6. -nd. And his son succeeded him ; and he also said, I will afflict Moab. In my days said he th[us ;]

7. but I saw my pleasure on him, and on his house, and Israel perished with an everlasting destruction. And Omri took possession of the [la-]

8. -nd of Mĕhēdeba, and it (i.e. Israel) dwelt therein, during his days, and half his son's days, forty years ; but [resto-]

9. -red it Chemosh in my days. And I built Ba'al-Me'on, and I made in it the reservoir (?) ; and I built

10. Qiryathên. And the men of Gad had dwelt in the land of 'Aṭaroth from of old ; and built for himself the king of I-

11. -srael 'Aṭaroth. And I fought against the city, and took it. And I slew all the people [from]

12. the city, a gazingstock unto Chemosh, and unto Moab. And I brought back (*or*, took captive) thence the altar-hearth of Davdoh (*or* ? דּוְדֹה its (divine) guardian), and I drag-

13. -ged it before Chemosh in Qeriyyoth. And I settled therein the men of SHRN, and the men of

14. MḤRTH. And Chemosh said unto me, Go, take Nebo against Israel. And I

15. went by night, and fought against it from the break of dawn until noon. And I too-

16. -k it, and slew the whole of it, 7,000 men and male sojourners, and women and [female sojourner-]

17. -s, and female slaves: for I had devoted it to 'Ashtor-Chemosh. And I took thence the [ves-]

18. -sels of YAHWEH, and I dragged them before Chemosh. And the king of Israel had built

19. Yahaz, and abode in it, while he fought against me. But Chemosh drave him out from before me; and

20. I took of Moab 200 men, even all its chiefs; and I brought them up against Yahaz, and took it

21. to add it unto Daibon. I built QRḤḤ, the wall of Ye'ārim (*or*, of the Woods), and the wall of

22. the Mound. And I built its gates, and I built its towers. And

23. I built the king's palace, and I made the two reser[voirs(?) for wa]ter in the midst of

24. the city. And there was no cistern in the midst of the city, in QRḤḤ. And I said to all the people, Make

25. you every man a cistern in his house. And I cut out the cutting for QRḤḤ with the help of prisoner-

26. [-s of] Israel. I built 'Aro'er, and I made the highway by the Arnon.

27. I built Beth-Bamoth, for it was pulled down. I built Beẓer, for ruins

28. [had it become. And the chie]fs of Daibon were fifty, for all Daibon was obedient (to me). And I reign-

29. -ed [over] an hundred [chiefs] in the cities which I added to the land. And I buil-

30. -t Mĕhēde[b]a, and Beth-Diblathên, and Beth-Ba'al-Me'on; and I brought thither the *naḳad*(?)-keepers,

31. . . . . sheep of the land. And as for Ḥoronên, there dwelt therein . . . . . . and . . . .

32. . . . . Chemosh said unto me, Go down, fight against Ḥoronên. And I went down . . . .

33. . . . . [and] Chemosh [resto]red it in my days. And . . . . thence . . . .

34. . . . . And I . . . .

The Inscription gives particulars of the revolt of Moab from Israel, noticed briefly in 2 Ki. 1, 1 = 3, 5. The revolt is there stated to have taken place after the death of Ahab; but from line 8 of the Inscription it is evident that this date is too late, and that it must in fact have been completed by the middle of Ahab's reign. The territory N. of the Arnon was claimed by Reuben and (contiguous to it on the N.) Gad; but these tribes were not permanently able to hold it against the Moabites. David reduced the Moabites to the condition of tributaries (2 Sam. 8, 2); but we infer from this Inscription that this relation was not maintained. Omri, however, determined to re-assert the Israelite claim, and gained possession of at least the district around Medeba, which was retained by Israel for forty years, till the middle of Ahab's reign, when Mesha' revolted. How complete the state of subjection was to which Moab had thus been reduced is shewn by the enormous tribute of wool paid annually to Israel (2 Ki. 3, 4). The Inscription names the principal cities which had been occupied by the Israelites, but were now recovered for Moab, and states further how Mesha' was careful to rebuild and fortify them, and to provide them with means for resisting a siege. Most of the places named (1–2, 21, 28 Dibon, 8, 30 Mehēdeba, 9 Ba'al-Me'on, 10 Qiryathên, 10, 11 'Aṭaroth, 13 Qeriyyoth, 14 Nebo, 19 Yahaẓ, 26 'Aro'er, 27 Beth-Bamoth, 30 Beth-Diblathên, Beth-Ba'al-Me'on, 31 Ḥoronên) are mentioned in the OT. in the passages which describe the territory of Reuben (Nu. 32, 37 f. Jos. 13, 15–23) or Gad (Nu. 32, 34–36. Jos. 13, 24–28), or allude to the country held by Moab (Is. 15, 2. 4. 5. Jer. 48, 1. 3. 18. 19. 21. 22. 23. 24. 34. 41. Ez. 25, 9. Am. 2, 2); 27 Beẓer in Dt. 4, 43. Jos. 20, 8: only 3, 21, 24, 25 קרחה, 13 שרן, 14 מחרת, 21 היערן are not known from the Bible. Except, as it seems, Ḥoronaim, all the places named appear to have lain within the controverted territory North of the Arnon.

On the *orthography*, comp. above pp. xxx–xxxii. 1. There seems to be room for only two letters after כמש. Clermont-Ganneau read כמשנד; Lidzb., after a fresh examination of the stone, thinks the letter after ש to be a כ, and suggests, though doubtfully, כמשכן (cf. בְּנָיָהוּ, יְכָנְיָהוּ).—1–2. הדיבני, 21, 28 דיבן, i. e. *Daibon*, not (as pointed in MT.) דִּיבֹן *Dibon*. Had the vowel in the first syllable been merely *i*,

it is not probable that the *scriptio plena* would have been employed.
—2. שֶׁת שְׁלִשָׁן = Heb. שנה שלשים. שֵׁת as in Phoen. (p. 84 *n.*); for
שָׁנָת*, as בַּת for בְּנָת*.—3. הבמת זאת = Heb. הזאת הבמה: notice (1) the
fem in ת-, as in Phoen., and sporadically in the OT.; (2) זאת without
the art., also as in Phoen. (p. xxv). The passage illustrates Is. 15, 2.
16, 12. Jer. 48, 35 (of Moab); comp. 1 Ki. 10, 2 (of Solomon). The
custom of worshipping on 'high-places' was one shared by the
Canaanites and Israelites with their neighbours.—קרחה, perhaps קָרְחֹה
(cf. יָרחֹ, יָרְחוֹ, once in 1 Ki. 16, 34 וִירִחֹה); it is against the apparently
obvious vocalization קָרְחָה, that the *fem.* is regularly represented in the
Inscription by ת.—4. השלכן, i.e. הַשְׁלִכֵן or הַשַּׁלְכִין. השליך in Heb. is
to *fling* or *cast;* possibly it was in use in Moabitic in Qal with the
meaning *throw oneself* against, *attack.* The letter is very indistinct:
המלכן *the kings* was formerly read; but Lidzb. agrees with Cl.-G. and
Nordl. that there is no trace of the shaft of the מ, and says that ' of
all possibilities that of שׁ is the greatest.'—הִרְאַנִי בְּכָל־שֹׂנְאָי ψ. 59, 11.
118, 7.—5. וְיַעַנּוּ (Nöld.) *and afflicted* (Ex. 1, 11), the third radical
being retained. As the text stands, if מלך be read (as seems natural)
מֶלֶךְ, the וֹ can only be explained by *Tenses*, § 117 *a*, GK. § 111ᵇ: this,
however, is harsh; so that probably מלך should be read מָלַךְ, and עַל has
accidentally been omitted before ישראל (cf. l. 2) by the carver of the
Inscription.—יַאֲנַף, impf. *Qal* (1 Ki. 8, 46), in a freq. sense, though a
pf. would rather have been expected. The reading תאנף (i.e. תְּאַנַּף =
the Arab. V conjug.) has been suggested: but Lidzb. says that the וֹ is
clear.—*His land:* cf. Nu. 21, 29. Jer. 48, 46, where the Moabites are
called עַם כְּמֹשׁ.—6. וַיַּחְלְפֹה, cf. خلف, and Is. 9, 9.—בְּנֹה, i.e. Ahab.—
הָא, p. xxx.—גם הא, as Jud. 3, 31. 6, 35 al.—אענו, i.e. אַעַנּוּ.—כ,
probably כָּכָה (1 Ki. 1, 48). כזאת (Jud. 8, 8) would, as Hebrew, be
preferable: but there seems not to be room for more than two
letters[1].—7. וָאֵרֶא בֹה ψ. 118, 7.—עלם as ψ. 89, 2. 3. 38 אָבַד אָבַד עֹלָם.—,
(*poetically* for לעולם). Or possibly אָבַד אָבֵד עֹלָם; cf. Jer. 51, 39.
—וַיִּרַשׁ עמרי, as a plup. sense is required, this by the principles of

---

[1] Smend and Socin imagined that they could read כדבר; but the traces are far
too indistinct to make it probable, in view of the close general similarity of the two
languages, that what is impossible in Hebrew (it should be כדבר הזה or כדברים
האלה) was possible in Moabitic.

Heb. syntax should be עֹמְרִי יָרַשׁ. Or, perhaps, וַיִּרַשׁ should be read.
—8. מֶהְרְבָא, in Heb. מֵידְבָה.—ימה, i. e., if the ה be correct, יָמֶה (for
yamaihu, i. e. יָמָיו): cf. the same rare form in Hebrew (see on
1 Sam. 14, 48; and Wright, *Comp. Gramm.* p. 158). The original ה
(Stade, § 113. 4) is seen (though not heard) in the Aram. ܘܡܝ̈ܗ. The
same phrase occurs Jer. 17, 11.—*Forty years.* On the chronological
difficulty involved, see *EB.* iii. 3047. It is relieved, though not
entirely removed, by reading, with Nordlander and Winckler, בְּנֹה
(like יָמֶה) *his sons'* (i. e. Ahaziah and Jehoram), instead of בְּנֹה *his
son's.*—8–9. וַיְשָׁבֶהָ : the letters supplied were conjectured cleverly by
Nöldeke in 1870, and have been generally accepted.—9. וָאֶבֶן.—
האשוח, prop. *depression* (cf. שׁוּחָה), *pit,* perhaps an excavation used for
the storage either of provisions, arms, etc., or (cf. line 23) of water.
Cf. אשיח Ecclus. 50, 3 Heb., of Simon, son of Onias : אֲשֶׁר בְּדֹרוֹ נִכְרָה
בַּהֲמוֹנוֹ [rd. בַּיָּם] = מִקְוֶה אשיח בם = ἐν ἡμέραις αὐτοῦ ἠλαττώθη [rd.
ἐλατομήθη] ἀποδοχεῖον ὑδάτων, χαλκὸς [rd., with A, λάκκος] ὡσεὶ
θαλάσσης τὸ περίμετρον.—10. קִרְיָתֶן (Nöld.), in Heb. קִרְיָתַיִם.—וָאֶשׁ
(Jud. 20, 17, etc.).—לה, Heb. לוֹ.—11. וָאֶלְתַּחֵם from הלתחם=Arab.
VIII conj.—בַּקֵּר *against the city.*—וָאֹחֲזֹה.—12. רִיַת לכמשׁ *a spectacle
unto Chemosh:* cf. Nah. 3, 6. Ez. 28, 17.—Either וָאֶשַׁב (Jos. 14, 7), or
(Clermont-Ganneau, Renan) וָאֶשַׁב.—אראל, to be explained probably
from Ez. 43, 15. 16 of the *hearth* of the altar, which was prized by the
captors as a kind of 'spolia opima' (Smend and Socin, p. 4). But
this explanation is not certain.—דודה, apparently the name, or title,
of a god: cf. *KAT.*³ 225, 483 ; *EB.* i. 1126, 1127.—12–13. וָאֶסְחָבֶהָ
Jer. 22, 19. 2 Sam. 17, 13.—13. לפני כמשׁ, cf. לפני יהוה 1 Sam. 15, 33.
2 Sam. 21, 9.—וָאֶשַׁב : 2 Ki. 17, 24.—14. *And Chemosh said to me,
Go, take,* etc. ; similarly l. 32: comp. Jos. 8, 1 ; Jud. 7, 9 ; 1 Sam.
23, 4 ; 2 Ki. 18, 25ᵇ.—14–15. וָאֶהֱלֹךְ, cf. Job 16, 22. 23, 8 : in prose
once (in 3 ps.) Ex. 9, 23.—15. בללה=Heb. בַּלַּיְלָה.—מִבְּקַע, cf. Is.
58, 8 : the ordinary Hebrew equivalent would be מֵעֲלוֹת הַשַּׁחַר.—16.
גְּבְרָן, גְּבְרָן, *men, women.* On the גרים, cf. on 2 Sam. 1, 13.—17. רחמת,
Jud. 5, 30 : female slaves are probably meant.—'*Ashtor-Chemosh,* according to Baethgen, *Beiträge,* 254 ff.[1], a compound deity, of a type

---

[1] Cf. pp. 39, 47 f., 84–7; so also G. A. Barton, in an article on ' West-Semitic
Deities with Compound Names,' *JBLit.* 1901, p. 22 ff. ; H. P. Smith in an art. on

of which other examples are cited from Semitic mythology. The *male* 'Ashtor is a South-Semitic deity, *ib.* 117 ff.; cf. *Encycl. of Religion and Ethics*, ii. 115ᵇ.—הֶחֱרַמְתִּהָ: see p. 131.—17-18. א[ת , כ]לּי, others supply א[רא]לּי, cf. l. 12. Renan says that the last two letters of l. 17 are quite ' dans la nuit,' and that את כלי ' garde toute sa probabilité.' Against אראלּי he objects the absence of את (contrast l. 12), and the *plural* (contrast the sing. l. 12).—18. הם (if, as seems to be the case, the reading is correct) must be a case of the independent pron. used as an accus., cf. Aram. הִמּוֹ (Ezr. 4, 10 etc.).—19. וַיֵּשֶׁב־בָּהּ, i. e. he made it a post of occupation during his war with Mesha'.—בהלתחמה, i. e. on the analogy of the inf. of the Arab. VIII, בְּהִלְתְּחֹם: cf. the Heb. place-names אֶשְׁתְּמֹעַ, אֶשְׁתָּאֹל (see on 1 Sam. 30, 28).—וַיְגָרְשֵׁה (provided יהץ be masc.). נרש מפני: Mesha' speaks of כמש in exactly the same terms which the Hebrew used of יהוה, Dt. 33, 27. Jos. 24, 18.—20. מָאתֵן, in Heb. מָאתַיִם.—וָאֶשָׂאה.—21. לָקֶפֶת (Nöld.) from

---

' Theophorous Proper Names in the OT.' in the *Harper Memorial Studies* (1908), i. p. 48. Among the names cited are Milk-'Ashtart (מלכעשתרת: Cooke, *NSI.* 10. 2–3), Eshmun-'Ashtart (אשמנעשתרת: *NSI.* p. 49), אשנמלקרת (*ib.*), אסכנאדר (*CIS.* I. i. 118), מלכבעל and מלכאסר (*NSI.* pp. 49, 103, 104), מלקרתרצף (*NSI.* 150. 5), צדמלקרת and צדתנת (Lidzb. *Nordsem. Epigr.* 356,357); Atargatis (עתרעתה: see *PRE.*³ or *Encycl. of Religion and Ethics*, s. v.); and the Bab. Adar-Malik, and Anu-Malik: in each case, a fusion of the personalities and characters of the deities named being supposed to have taken place. Baudissin, however, argues strongly that in all these cases the second name is in the genitive, so that we should render 'Ashtor of Chemosh, Eshmun of 'Ashtart, etc., the meaning being that 'Ashtor, for instance, was the associate of Chemosh, and worshipped in his temple (*Adonis und Esmun*, 1911, pp. 259–66, 269, 274–9; cf. *PRE.*³ ii. (1897), 157, vii. 293; and Moore in *EB.* i. 737). Ed. Meyer (*Der Papyrusfund von Elephantine*, 1912, p. 62 f.) takes the same view. These Papyri exhibit other remarkable names of deities of the same type, viz. Pap. 18, col. 7. 5 אשמביתאל; *ib.* l. 6 ענתביתאל 'Anāth-Bethel or 'Anath of Bethel [' Bethel ' being the name of a deity: cf. Pap. 34. 5 ביתאלנתן בר יהונתן—the name formed exactly like אלנתן, יהונתן; *CIS.* II. i. 54 ביתאלדלני (cf. דְּלָיָה); and *KAT.*³ 437 f.]; Pap. 27. 7 חרמביתאל חרם another divine name; cf. Pap. 34. 4 חרמנתן [בר ביתאלנתן; and even (Pap. 32. 3) ענתיהו 'Anāth-Yahweh or Yahweh's 'Anāth ('Anāth as belonging to, or associated with, Yahweh). See further Sachau, *Papyri aus . . . Elephantine* (1911), pp. 82–5; Meyer, pp. 57–65; Burney, *Church Quarterly Review*, July 1912, pp. 403–6. It is now clear that in Zech. 7, 2 בית־אל שראצר should be read as one word, ' And Bethelsareẓer sent,' etc.

יָסַף. Pointed irregularly by the Massorites לְסֹפֹת לִסְפּוֹת Nu. 32, 14.
Is. 30, 1.—הַיַּעַר *the woods*,—probably the name of a place.—22.
מִנְדִּלְתָה.—23. בֵּת מֶלֶךְ 1 Ki. 16, 18.—כִּלְאַי either *both* (Nöld.), cf.
كَلَّ, ክልኤ፡, or possibly *the locks* or *dams*, from the root כָּלָא.—לְמֵין
for water.—24. בֹּר *cistern.*—אֵן=Heb. אֵין (Gen. 47, 13 ; cf. on 1 Sam.
21, 2).—25. Probably הַמְכַרְתָת (or הַמְכִרְתֹת) a *cutting* (or *cuttings*)
of some sort : the special application must remain uncertain.—אֵשׁ
בר בביתה ; for the custom of every house having its cistern, cf. 2 Ki.
18, 31, and, in the ancient Leja (see *DB.* i. 146), on the East of
Jordan, Burckhardt, *Travels in Syria* (1822), p. 110 f., cited by
Thomson, *The Land and the Book*, Vol. on Lebanon, Damascus, and
Beyond Jordan, p. 469, and *EB.* i. 88.—25-6. בְּאַפְרִי.—26. המסלת=
Heb. הַמְסִלָּה.—27. בֵּת בָּמֹת, probably the same place as בָּמוֹת Nu.
21, 19 ; בָּמוֹת בַּעַל 22, 41. Jos. 13, 17.—הָרֶם 1 Ki. 18, 30.—עִיֹן Mic.
3, 12.—28. Before שׁ, there is space for four or five letters. After עין,
הָיָה (or ? הָיָה Is. 16, 4) suggests itself naturally as the first word
of l. 28. The conjecture וִ[רֻשׁ] has the support of l. 20, and is the
restoration usually accepted : but Halévy suggests שׁ[בא] for שׁ[בר],
i.e. 'I built Beẓer, for ruins it had become, *with the help of* (cf. l. 25)
fifty *men* of Daibon,' etc.—משמעת, see p. 182 *note.*—29. If מלכתי
28-9 be correct (the כ is not quite certain), the next word must almost
necessarily be עַל : the two letters for which space still remains may be
רשׁ (as exhibited in the translation). Lines 28–29 will then describe
the number of *chiefs*, i.e. either heads of families, or warriors, over
whom Mesha' ruled in Daibon itself (if ורשׁ is right in l. 28), and
in the cities which he recovered.—בַּקִּרֹן *in the cities* (Clermont-Ganneau,
Smend and Socin): with what follows, cf. the expression used of
Yahaẓ ll. 20–21.—30. נֹקֵד, if the reading be correct,—נק is 'possible,'
says Lidzbarski, though the letters seem to him to be מע,—will allude
to the persons engaged in cultivating the breed of sheep, small and
stunted in growth, but prized on account of their wool (see on Am.
1, 1 in the *Cambridge Bible*), for which Moab was famous. It is the
word which is actually used of Mesha' himself in 2 Ki. 3, 4.—32. Cf.
l. 14. With *go down* Clermont-Ganneau pertinently compares Jer.
48, 5 which speaks of the מוֹרַד חוֹרֹנִים or *descent* to Ḥoronaim.—
33. No doubt וַיִּשְׁבֶהָ as ll. 8–9.—Halévy proposes וְעַל יָדָה מַשָׁם ' And

beside it there was set,' supposing the sequel to relate to a guard of twenty men ; but the sing. followed by [שמרן] עש‍[רן is difficult.

The language of Moab is far more closely akin to Hebrew than any other Semitic language at present known (though it may be conjectured that the languages spoken by Ammon and Edom were approximately similar) : in fact, it scarcely differs from it otherwise than dialectically [1]. In syntax, form of sentence, and general mode of expression, it is entirely in the style of the earlier narratives contained in the historical books of the OT. The vocabulary, with two or three exceptions, not more singular than many a ἅπαξ εἰρημένον occurring in the OT., is identical with that of Hebrew. In some respects, the language of the Inscription even shares with Hebrew *distinctive* features, as the *waw* conv. with the impf., הושיע *to save*, עשה *to make*, נם, ראה ב' ירש *to take in possession*, לפני, הרג, the dual צהרם, החרים *to ban*, גרש, בקרב, and especially אֲשֶׁר. It shares אנך with Hebrew and Phoenician, against Aramaic, Arabic, and Ethiopic (اڬ‍, انا, אנא:).

The most noticeable *differences*, as compared with Hebrew, are הבמת זאת (not הזאת as in Hebrew), the ת of the fem. sg., and the ן of the dual (except in צהרם [2] 15) and plural, the ת and ן of the plural both occurring only sporadically in the OT.[3], the conj. הלתחם, קיר *city*, אחז 11, 14 *to take* a city (Heb. לָכַד); and the following words, which, though they occur in the OT., are not the usual prose terms, חלף 6 *to succeed*, בקע 15 of the *break* of dawn, גְּבָרֹת and גְּבָרָן 16 (in a context such as the present, the normal Hebrew expression would be אנשים and נשים), רְחָמֹת 17, נשא 20, 30.

---

[1] By a happy instinct the truth was divined by Mr. (afterwards Sir George) Grove, six years before any Moabite document whatever was known, in his interesting article MOAB, in Smith's *Dictionary of the Bible* (p. 399ᵃ): 'And from the origin of the nation and other considerations we may perhaps conjecture that their language *was more a dialect of Hebrew than a different tongue.*'

[2] If this be really a dual, and not a *nominal* form in D —᷄ : cf. GK. § 88ᵉ (comparing p. 2, below), and on the other side König, ii. p. 437, iii. § 257ᵇ.

[3] The ן 25 times, mostly dialectically, or late (GK. § 87ᵉ [add, as the text stands, 2 S. 21, 20]; Stade, § 323ᵃ), and some doubtful textually, 15 times being in Job, but even there irregularly (מלין 13 times, against מלים 10 times). On the ת of the fem., see GK. § 80ᶠ, ᵍ.

The chief features of historical interest presented by the Inscription
may be summarized as follows: (1) the re-conquest of Moab by
Omri; (2) the fact that Mesha''s revolt took place in the middle of
Ahab's reign, not after his death (as stated, 2 Ki. 1, 1); (3) particulars
of the war by which Moab regained its independence; (4) the extent
of country occupied and fortified by Mesha'; (5) the manner and
terms in which the authority of Chĕmōsh, the national deity of Moab,
is recognized by Mesha'; (6) the existence of a sanctuary of YAHWEH
in Nebo [1]; (7) the state of civilization and culture which had been
reached by Moab at the end of the tenth century B.C. Sir George
Grove, in the article referred to on the last page, writes (p. 396):
'The nation appears' from allusions in the OT.[2] 'as high-spirited,
wealthy, populous, and even, to a certain extent, civilized, enjoying
a wide reputation and popularity. . . . In its cities we discern a " great
multitude" of people living in "glory," and in the enjoyment of
"great treasure," crowding the public squares, the house-tops, and
the ascents and descents of the numerous high-places and sanctuaries,
where the "priests and princes" of Chemosh minister to the anxious
devotees . . . . In this case there can be no doubt that among the
pastoral people of Syria, Moab stood next to Israel in all matters
of material wealth and civilization.' This conclusion is confirmed
by the Inscription. The length, and finished literary form, of the
Inscription shew that the Moabites, in the ninth century B.C., were
not a nation that had recently emerged from barbarism; and Mesha'
reveals himself in it as a monarch capable of organizing and con-
solidating his dominions by means similar to those adopted by
contemporary sovereigns in the kingdoms of Israel and Judah.

---

[1] The reading יהוה is quite certain; the letters can be read distinctly on the
plaster-cast of the stone in the British Museum.

[2] Chiefly Is. 15—16; Jer. 48.

NOTE ON THE MAPS

THE Maps in this volume have been drawn by Mr. B. V. Darbishire, of Oxford. The Map of the Pass of Michmas is reproduced, by permission, from a Map by Gustaf Dalman, the well-known Hebrew and Aramaic scholar, now Director of the German Evangelical Archaeological Institute in Jerusalem, in the *ZDMG.* (see particulars in the note attached to the Map) : and the three Maps of Sections of Palestine are based upon Maps published by the Palestine Exploration Fund, and by Messrs. John Bartholomew & Co., of Edinburgh. In the three last-named Maps the coloured contours, geographical features, and *modern* sites, are reproduced (with permission) from the sources mentioned : the *ancient* sites have been reproduced from them only after a careful examination of the *data* on which the determination of the sites depends, such as rest upon questionable or inconclusive grounds being marked by a query, while those which rest upon clearly insufficient grounds are omitted altogether. The identification of a modern with an ancient site depends mostly, it must be remembered, in cases in which the ancient name itself has not been unambiguously preserved, partly upon historical, but very largely upon philological considerations : and men who are admirable surveyors, and who can write valuable descriptions of the physical features, topography, or antiquities of a country, are not necessarily good philologists. Hence the ⅜ in. to the mile Map of Palestine containing ancient sites, published by the P. E. F., Bartholomew's Maps, and in fact current English Maps of Palestine in general (with the exception of those in the *Encyclopaedia Biblica*), include many highly questionable and uncertain identifications[1]. Maps described as being 'according to the P. E. F. Survey' are not better than others : the description is in fact misleading ; for the 'Survey' relates only to the physical geography, and *modern* topography of the country : the *ancient* sites marked on such a map are an *addition* to what is actually determined by the 'Survey :' the authority attaching to the 'Survey' does not consequently extend to them at all ; and, as a matter of fact, many rest upon a most precarious basis. In the articles and notes referred to above (p. X *n.*), I have taken a number of names, including, for instance, Succoth and Penuel (*Exp. Times*, xiii. 457 ff.), Luhith (Is. 15, 5 ; *ib.* xxi. 495 ff.), and Ja'zer (Is. 16, 8, and elsewhere ; *ib.* xxi. 562 f.), and shewn in detail how very uncertain the proposed identifications are[2].

An example or two may be mentioned here. The compilers of the ⅜ in. to the mile P. E. F. Map, referred to above, mark on the SW. of the Sea of Galilee the

---

[1] On the principles which should regulate the identification of modern Arabic with ancient Hebrew place-names, the scholarly articles of Kampffmeyer, *ZDPV.* xv (1892), 1–33, 65–116, xvi (1893), 1–71, should be consulted.

[2] Guthe's beautiful and very complete *Bibelatlas in 20 Haupt- und 28 Neben-karten* (1911) may be commended to English students as eminently instructive and scholarly. And the forthcoming *Historical Atlas of the Holy Land*, by G. A. Smith, is likely to prove in all respects adequate and trustworthy.

'Plain of Zaanaim:' Bartholomew, in the Map at the beginning of vol. i of Hastings' *Dictionary of the Bible*, does the same, and even goes further; for, both in this and in other maps designed by him, he inserts on the NW. of Hebron—in this case without the support of the P. E. F. Map—the 'Plain of Mamre.' But both these 'plains' are purely imaginary localities; for, as every Hebrew scholar knows, though 'plain' is the rendering of אֵלוֹן and אַלּוֹן in AV., both words really mean a *tree*, most probably a terebinth or an oak, and they are so rendered in the Revised Version (Gen. 12, 6, etc.: Jos. 19, 33; Jud. 4, 11). On the other hand, the P. E. F. authorities, for some inscrutable reason, have never accepted Robinson's identification of Gibeah (= Gibeah of Benjamin and Gibeah of Saul) with Tell el-Fûl, 2¾ miles N. of Jerusalem [1]: it is accordingly, in the ⅜ in. to the mile map, not marked at this spot, but confused with Geba; and Bartholomew, in his maps, including even those edited by G. A. Smith [2], confuses it with Geba likewise. It is true, the two names have sometimes been accidentally interchanged in the Massoretic text [3]: but Is. 10, 29 shews incontrovertibly not only that they were two distinct places, but also, taken in conjunction with Jud. 19, 13, that Gibeah must have lain *between* Ramah and Jerusalem, very near the highway leading from Jerusalem to the North, which is just the position of Tell el-Fûl. Unless, however, the relative positions of Gibeah and Geba are properly apprehended, there are parts of the narratives of Jud. 19—20, and 1 Sam. 13—14, which it is impossible to understand.

In the transliteration of modern Arabic place-names, I have endeavoured to insert the hard breathing (= ع) and the diacritical points in accordance with either Buhl's excellent *Geographie des alten Palästina*, or E. H. Palmer's *Arabic and English Name Lists* published by the P. E. F., though I fear I may not in all cases have secured entire accuracy. Still less, I am afraid, have I attained consistency in marking the long vowels. But I trust that these imperfections will not impair the usefulness of the Maps for those for whom they are primarily designed, viz. students of the history. The frequent *Kh.*, I should add, stands for *Khurbet* (= חָרְבָּה), *ruin, ruined site.*

---

[1] Comp. Grove's art. GIBEAH in Smith's *Dict. of the Bible*, Stenning's art. GIBEAH in *DB.*, and below, p. 69.

[2] Who himself adopts the Tell el-Fûl site (*Jerusalem*, ii. 92 *n.*).

[3] The reader will do well to mark on the margin of his RV. *Gibeah* against *Geba* in Jud. 20, 33 ('on the west of Gibeah:' in *v.* 10 the correction is made already in EVV.; in *v.* 31 put *Gibeon* against *Gibeah*), 1 Sam. 13, 3 (see 10, 5); and *Geba* against *Gibeah* in Jud. 20, 43. 1 Sam. 13, 2 (see *v.* 16). 14, 2 (see 13, 16). 16; also, with a (?), against *Gibeon*, 2 Sam. 2, 24. In 2 Sam. 5, 25, on the other hand, *Gibeon* (LXX; 1 Ch. 14, 16) is better than *Geba;* and in 2 Sam. 21, 6 read probably (see the note; and cf. *v.* 9) ' in *Gibeon*, in the mountain (בהר) of Yahweh ' for ' in *Gibeah* of Saul, the chosen one (בחר) of Yahweh.'

NOTES

ON

THE BOOKS OF SAMUEL

1, 1—4, 1ª. *Birth and youth of Samuel. Announcement of the*
fall of Eli's house.

1, 1. אִישׁ אֶחָד] The same idiomatic use of אֶחָד, especially with אִישׁ,
in the sense of *a certain* (man), *quidam*, as II 18, 10. Jud. 9, 53 אשה
אחת; 13, 2 מנוח ושמו הדני ממשפחת מצרעה אחד איש ויהי. 1 Ki. 13, 11.
20, 13. 2 Ki. 4, 1 al.

הרמתים צופים] Grammatically indefensible. צופים cannot be a ptcp.
in apposition with הרמתים; for this, being fem., would require צוֹפוֹת
(cf. עינים רמות ψ. 18, 28 etc.),—not to say הַצּוֹפוֹת; nor can it, as Keil
supposes, be a *genitive* (!) after הרמתים 'the two heights of the
Zophites[1].' LXX has Σειφα ἐξ ὄρους Ἐφραιμ, pointing to צוּפִי for
צופים[2], the מ of מהר having been in MT. accidentally written twice,
'a certain man of Ramathaim, *a Zuphite* of the hill-country of
Ephraim' (so We. Klo. Bu. etc.; GK. § 125ʰ). The district in which
Ramah lay was called ארץ צוף (*ch.* 9, 5): either therefore Zuph was
actually the name of an ancestor of Elqanah (*v.* 1ᵇ, 1 Ch. 6, 20 Qrê;
ib. v. 11 Zophai [see p. 4]), and the ארץ צוף was so called from its
having been originally settled by the family of Zuph (cf. 27, 10 נגב
הירחמאלי; 30, 14 כלב נגב: see the notes), or, as is more probable
(We. al.), the land is in the genealogy personified as the ancestor
(cf. 'Gilead,' Nu. 26, 29. Jos. 17, 1 al.).

הרמתים] i.e., at least according to the present orthography, 'The
two heights.' It is, however, the opinion of many scholars (see esp.

---

[1] The reference to Ew. § 286ᵉ is inconclusive: the first word in the instances
there cited being in the construct state (on 1 Ki. 4, 12 see on II 20, 15).

[2] ו and י are often interchanged in Hebrew and LXX: cf. 9, 5 Σειφ = צוף.
LXX must have read צוּפִי as צוֹפִי: cf. Ἀβεσσα 26, 6 al., Ῥειβα II 23, 29 (We.).

Philippi, *ZDMG.* 1878, pp. 64–67, Strack, *Genesis*[2], p. 135 f.; GK.
§ 88ᶜ) that in this and many other proper names, if not in all, the dual
form is not original, but is a later artificial expansion of an original
substantival termination in ם֫– (GK. §§ 85ᵇ, 100ᵍ,ʰ). This is based
partly upon the fact that in parallel texts several of these names occur
without the י; partly upon the fact that many of the duals yield
a meaning improbable in itself as the name of a place, or inconsistent
with the character of the places so far as they have been identified; and
and partly on the fact that the most common of these dual forms
יְרוּשָׁלַ֫ם, is shewn by the Tell el-Amarna tablets to have ended originally in -*im* (so נַהֲרַיִם, in אֲרַם־נַהֲרִים, is in the Tell el-Amarna letters
Narima: cf. שְׁמַרָיִן, which must have arisen out of שָׁמְרָן, Aram. form of
the Heb. שֹׁמְרוֹן, 'Samaria'). Thus we have הָעֵינַיִם Gen. 38, 21, but
עֵינָם Jos. 15, 34 (cf. דֹּתַיִן Gen. 37, 17ᵃ, but דֹּתָן *ib.*ᵇ ¹, 2 Ki. 6, 13 ²);
קִרְיָתַיִם 1 Ch. 6, 61³, but קַרְתָּן Jos. 21, 32; קִרְיָתַיִם (Nu. 32, 37. Jos. 13,
19³. Jer. 48, 1. 23³, Ez. 25, 9⁴), בֵּית־דִּבְלָתַיִם (Jer. 48, 22³), חֹרֹנַיִם (Is.
15, 5⁵. Jer. 48, 3³. 5³. 34³), but in Mesha's inscr., l. 10 קְרִיתָן, l. 30
בת דבלתן, ll. 31, 32 חוֹרֹנָן. Other dual forms of nouns cited by Philippi
and Strack are אֶגְלַיִם Is. 15, 8⁶; אֲדוֹרַיִם ⁷ 2 Ch. 11, 9; אֶפְרַיִם ³ 2 S. 13, 23;
גְּדֵרֹתַיִם Jos. 15, 36; פִּתַּיִם 2 S. 4, 3⁸. Neh. 11, 33; חֲפָרַיִם Jos. 19, 19;
מַחֲנַיִם Gen. 32, 3. Jos. 13, 26. 30. 21, 38 (=1 Ch. 6, 65 ⁹). 2 S. 2, 8¹⁰.
12¹¹. 29. 17, 24¹¹. 27¹¹. 19, 33¹¹. 1 Ki. 2, 8¹². 4, 14¹²; עֲדִיתַיִם Jos. 15, 36;
עֵין־עֶגְלַיִם Ez. 47, 10⁶; צָמָרַיִם Jos. 18, 22. 2 Ch. 13, 4¹³; קַבְצִים Jos. 21,
22; שַׁעֲרַיִם Jos. 15, 36 ⁶: cf. עֶפְרַיִן 2 Ch. 13, 19 Qrê (Kt. עֶפְרוֹן)¹⁴. Still
all these do not necessarily fall into the same category, and some may
have been really duals. In several, as the notes will have shewn, the
dual is also expressed in LXX (cod. B). If there were two hills at
Samuel's village, as there are at Gezer, הָרָמָתַ֫יִם would be a very natural
name for it. And we have the corresponding form ܪܡܬ̈ܐ ¹⁵ in the
Syr. version of 1 Macc. 11, 34. Cf. König, ii. 437; and note the forcible
arguments of G. B. Gray, *EB.* iii. 3319.

---

¹ LXX (A) each time Δωθαειμ.   ² LXX (B) Δωθαειμ.   ³ LXX -αιμ.
⁴ LXX πόλεως παραθαλασσίας (= קרית ימה).   ⁵ LXX -ιειμ.   ⁶ LXX
-ειμ.   ⁷ LXX Αδωραι.   ⁸ LXX Γεθθαι.   ⁹ LXX Μααναιθ.   ¹⁰ LXX
-αεμ.   ¹¹ LXX -αειμ.   ¹² LXX Μααναιειον.   ¹³ LXX Σομορων.
¹⁴ LXX Εφρων.   ¹⁵ Codd. AS corruptly 'Ραθαμειν : others 'Ραμαθεμ.

The transition from either הָרָמָתַיִם or הָרָמָתָם to הָרָמָה in *v.* 19 is, however, abrupt and strange. In MT. the form occurs here alone, Samuel's home being elsewhere always הרמה. LXX has Αρμαθαιμ not only here, but also wherever הרמה *occurs accidentally with* ה, in consequence of the ה of motion being attached to it (הרמתה), 1, 19. 2, 11. 7, 17. 8, 4. 15, 34. 16, 13. 19, 18. 22, as well as for ברמה in 25, 1. 28, 3 : in 19, 19. 22. 23. 20, 1 (as in Jud. 4, 5) for ברמה it has ἐν Ῥαμα. In 25, 1. 28, 3 cod. A has Ῥαμα : in this cod. therefore הרמה is consistently Ῥαμα, הרמתים (or הרמתה) and הרמתה are consistently Αρμαθαιμ. Probably, however, this is merely a correction of a kind not unfrequent in cod. A, made with the view of assimilating the Greek text more closely to the Hebrew, and not a part of the original LXX. It is scarcely possible to frame an entirely satisfactory explanation of the variations. It seems clear that in 2, 11 etc. Αρμαθαιμ is due to the presence of the ה in the form of the Hebrew word there read by the translators : but it would be precarious to conclude that this was actually הרמחים (or הרמתם). From the abruptness of the change in *v.* 19 to the sing., We. thinks it probable that the original form of the name was the singular, which in the first instance stood in the Hebrew text everywhere, but that the dual form came into use subsequently, and was introduced as a correction in 1, 1 in MT.; in LXX Ῥαμα was originally the uniform rendering, but in course of time an artificial distinction was drawn between הרמה and הרמתה, and when this was done it was introduced into the text of LXX—in cod. B, however, in 19, 19—20, 1 only, in cod. A uniformly (Ῥαμα = הרמה : Αρμαθαιμ = הרמתה). Klo. ingeniously proposes to punctuate מִן־הָרָמָתִים ' from the Ramathites ' (so Bu. Sm.; not Now.), cf. הרמתי 1 Ch. 27, 27 : but this is not the usual manner in which a person's native place is designated in the OT.

הרמה is the name of several places mentioned in the OT.; and the site of this one is not certain. The best known is the 'Ramah' of Is. 10, 29, which is certainly the modern *er-Rām*, 5 miles N. of Jerusalem. Bu. argues in favour of this; but does not overcome the presumption that the unnamed city, the home of Samuel in *ch.* 9, which was clearly (comp. 10, 2 with 9, 4 f.) *N.* of Benjamin, and consequently not er-Rām, was the Ramathaim of 1, 1 and the Ramah of 1, 19, etc. Eusebius (*Onomastica*[1], ed. Lagarde, 225, 11–14) says that Ramathaim was near Diospolis (Lydda), to which Jerome (*ib.* 96, 18) adds ' in the district of Timnah;' and 1 Macc. 11, 34 speaks of ' Ramathem ' as a toparchy which had belonged to Samaria, but was transferred in B.C. 145 to Jerusalem: Eusebius

(288, 11 f.) and Jerome (146, 23 f.) also identify Arimathaea (= Ramathaim) with 'Ρεμφις or Remfthis, in the territory of Diospolis. These statements would point either (Buhl, *Geogr.*, p. 170; Now.; cf. *H. G.* 254) to *Beit-Rîma*, a village on a hill, 12 miles NW. of Bethel, 13 miles ENE. of Lydda, and 2 miles N. of Timnah, or (Guthe, *Kurzes Bibelwörterb.*, 1903, p. 536; Lagrange) to *Rentis*, a small village 5 miles W. of Beit-Rîma, and 9 miles NE. of Lydda. H. P. Smith and others have thought of *Râm-Allah*, a village standing on a high ridge, 3 miles SW. of Bethel: but either Beit-Rîma or Rentis has better ancient authority in its favour. See further *DB*. iv. 198.

ירחם] LXX 'Ιερεμεηλ, i.e. יְרַחְמְאֵל [1] Yerahme'el, perhaps rightly (the name Yeroham occurs elsewhere). The pedigree of Samuel is given twice besides, with variations similar to those which usually occur in parallel passages in the OT., especially in lists of names:—

1 *Sam.* 1, 1.	1 *Ch.* 6, 13–11 (LXX 28–26).	1 *Ch.* 6, 18–20 (LXX 33–35).
Samuel	13 Samuel	18 Samuel
Elqanah	12 Elqanah	19 Elqanah
Yeroham	Yeroham	Yeroham
Elihu	Eliab	Eliel
Tohu	11 Nahath [2]	Toah [3]
Zuph	Zophai	20 Qrê Zuph [4]

אפרתי] This word appears to represent Elqanah not merely as *resident* in Ephraim (מהר אפרים), but as an *Ephraimite;* in 1 Ch. 6 he is represented as a *Levite*, of the descendants of Qohath (Nu. 3, 27 etc.). The discrepancy is hard to reconcile. Jud. 17, 7 the expression ' of the family of Judah,' applied to a Levite, has been supposed to shew that Levites settled in a particular tribe may have been reckoned as belonging to it; but even if that were the case [5], the addition והוא לוי would

---

[1] Thenius יְרַחְמְאֵל, on which We., *De Gentibus et Familiis Judaeis quae* 1 *Ch.* 2. 4. *numerantur* (Gottingae, 1870), remarks justly (p. 27), ' *Dresdense potius quam Hebraeum.*'

[2] So Vulg. Pesh.; LXX Καιναθ. No doubt the ב is an error for ח, the two letters being somewhat similar in the old character, though which of the three forms is original cannot be definitely determined, probably Tohu. In any case Keil's explanation of the variation is untenable.

[3] LXX (B) Θειε, (A) Θοουε, Vulg. Thohu, i.e. Tohu as in 1, 1. Pesh. ܬܘܚܠ.

[4] So also LXX, Vulg.; Kt. Ziph.

[5] It is more probable that ' Levite' denotes there a *profession*, rather than membership in a tribe: see Moore, *ad loc.*; McNeile, *Exodus*, pp. lxvi f., 26.

there make the double relationship clear; here the addition אפרתי
seems to shew that the narrator has no consciousness of Samuel's
Levitical descent. The explanation that the term designates Elqanah
as an Ephraimite, merely so far as his civil rights and standing were
concerned, makes it express nothing more than what is virtually declared in *v.* [a], and moreover implies a limitation which is not, at least,
sustained by usage. It is a question whether the traditions embodied
in Ch. have been handed down uniformly in their original form, and
whether in some cases the genealogies have not been artificially completed. The supposition that Samuel was really of Ephraimite descent,
and was only in later times reckoned as a Levite, is the simplest
explanation of the divergence.

2. ולו שתי נשים] The *order*, and form of sentence, as 17, 12. 25, 2
(cf. 36), II 14, 30. 17, 18. 23, 18. 22. Jud. 3, 16. Zech. 5, 9. Dan.
8, 3 etc.

אחת] The numeral, being definite in itself, may dispense with the
art.; cf. 13, 17. 18 ; Nu. 28, 4 : Ew. § 290[f]; GK. §§ 126[z], 134[l]. But
in a connexion such as the present האחת would be more classical
(Gen. 2, 11. 4, 19. 10, 25 (all belonging to the Pentateuchal source J);
Dt. 21, 15; II 4, 2), and ought probably to be restored. It is read by
several MSS.

ויהי] *before* the plural ילדים, according to GK. § 145[o]; Ew. § 316[a].
So not unfrequently : e. g. with the same verb Gen. 1, 14. 5, 23. Jud.
20, 46. 1 Ki. 13, 33 ויהי כהני במות that *there might be* (*Tenses,* § 63)
priests of the high places.

3. ועלה] The pf. with *waw* conv. has a frequentative force, *used to
go up;* comp. 4[b]–7[a], where observe that it interchanges, not with the
bare perfect, the tense of simple narrative, but with the *impf.,* which
likewise expresses habituation : see *Tenses,* § 120, GK. § 112[dd]; and
comp. Ex. 17, 11. 18, 26. Jud. 2, 18 f. etc.

מימים ימימה] The same phrase, likewise with reference to the observance of a pilgrimage or sacred season, 2, 19[a]. Ex. 13, 10. Jud. 11, 40.
21, 19†. ימים, lit. *days,* tends by usage to denote the definite period
of a year: cf. *v.* 21. 2, 19[b]; and on 27, 7.

שלה] now *Seilûn,* in a secluded nook, 9½ m. N. of Bethel, and 11 m.
S. of Shechem. See the writer's art. in *DB.* s.v.

וְשָׁם וג׳] LXX καὶ ἐκεῖ Ηλει καὶ οἱ δύο υἱοὶ αὐτοῦ, which has been supposed to point to וְשָׁם עֵלִי וּשְׁנֵי בְנֵי עֵלִי. Some *independent* notice of Eli seems to be presupposed by *v.* 9 : either, therefore (Th. Klo.), וְעֵלִי has dropped out in MT., or (We.) the mention of Eli originally *preceded v.* 3, perhaps in the course of some more comprehensive narrative of the period, of which the life of Samuel which we still possess formed but an episode : in the latter case, the reading of LXX will be a correction, introduced for the purpose of supplying the deficiency which thus arose in the narrative.

4. וַיְהִי הַיּוֹם] The same idiomatic expression recurs 14, 1. 2 Ki. 4, 8. 11. 18. Job 1, 6. 13. 2, 1†. Is it, now, to be construed 'And *there was a day* (Job 1, 6 AV), and . . . ,' or 'And it fell *on a day* (2 Ki. 4, 8 AV.), and . . .'? (GK. § 126ᵃ: We.) Modern authority is in favour of the second of these alternatives : but the fact that הַיּוֹם when used as an adverbial accusative signifies regularly *to-day* may authorize the inference that in this phrase it was conceived as a *nominative*, i.e. as the subject of וַיְהִי (cf. 20, 24 וַיְהִי הַחֹדֶשׁ). In either case the definite article, where we should use the indefinite, is in accordance with the Hebrew manner of thought : in the mind of the Hebrew narrator, the *day* is connected in anticipation with the events about to be described as happening upon it, and is thus regarded as defined. Comp. הַסֵּפֶר Nu. 5, 23, הַחֶבֶל Jos. 2, 15, *the scroll, the cord,* defined in anticipation as those taken for a particular purpose, where our idiom can only employ *a :* see on 6, 8. 10, 25. 19, 13 ; and cf. GK. *l.c.*

וְנָתַן] 4ᵇ–7ᵃ is parenthetical, describing what Elqanah's *habit* was (see on *v.* 3): the narrative of the particular occasion 4ᵃ is resumed in 7ᵇ וַתִּבְכֶּה. Render therefore (for the emendations adopted, see the notes below): '(*v.* 3) And that man *used to go up,* etc. . . . (*v.* 4) And there fell a day, and Elkanah sacrificed : now he *used to give* to Peninnah, etc. . . . : (*v.* 7) and so *used she to do* year by year; as often as they went up to the house of Yahweh, so *used she to vex* her ; and she wept [on the present occasion] and did not eat. (*v.* 8) And Elkanah her husband said to her, etc.'

מָנוֹת] *portions,* viz. of the flesh partaken of at the sacrificial meal: cf. 9, 23.

Notice here the position of the object at the *end,* where it rounds

off the sentence and brings it to its close. The English order, in such
a case, would produce a very weak sentence in Hebrew. For two
striking instances of the same order, see Jer. 13, 13. Am. 6, 14 : cf.
Ex. 8, 17ᵃ; and see further on II 14, 12.

5. אַפַּיִם] Many attempts have been made to find a meaning for this
word, at once defensible philologically, and suited to the context. It
has been rendered (1) 'heavily.' So, for instance, the Vulgate (*tristis*),
several mediaeval authorities (e.g. the 'Great' Bible of 1539: 'a portion
with an heavy cheer'), and amongst moderns, Bö. Th. But for this
sense of אַפַּיִם there is no support in the known usage of the language :
בְּאַפַּיִם occurs with the meaning 'in anger' in Dan. 11, 20; but that
would be unsuitable here, and the expressions נפלו פניך (Gen. 4, 6) and
פניה לא היו לה עוד (below, v. 18) are not sufficient to justify the sense
of a *dejected* countenance being assigned to אפים. It has been rendered
(2) in connexion with מָנָה אַחַת, *one portion of two faces* (=two persons),
i.e. a double portion. So Keil and even Gesenius. It is true that the
Syriac ܐܦ̈ܐ corresponds generally in usage with the Hebrew פנים ;
but, to say nothing of the fact that a Syriasm is unexpected in Samuel,
and that even in late Hebrew אפים does not occur with the *Aramaic*
sense of 'person,' there is nothing in the use of the Syriac word to
suggest that the *dual* would, in Hebrew, denote *two* persons : ܐܦ̈ܐ
(like פנים) is used of *one* person, the singular not occurring. If אַפַּיִם
means *two* persons, it must be implied that the singular אף might
denote *one* person, which the meaning of the word (*nostril*) obviously
does not permit. Secondly, the construction, even if on lexical grounds
this rendering were defensible, would be unexampled. אפים evidently
cannot be a *genitive* after מנה אחת : Ew. § 287ᵇ (cited by Keil) combines together cases of apposition and of the accusative of limitation ;
but the disparity of idea (*one portion* and *two persons*) shews that אפים
cannot be in apposition with מנה אחת : it *might* be an accusative
defining the amount or measure of the מנה אחת (*Tenses*, App. § 194) :
but how unnaturally expressed ! '*one* (emph.) portion,' immediately
defined as a portion suitable for *two* persons, i.e. as a *double* portion,
as in fact not *one* portion at all, but *two !* Upon grammatical grounds,
hardly less decisively than upon lexical grounds, this rendering must
thus be pronounced inadmissible. (3) The rendering of AV. *a worthy*

portion is inherited from the Geneva Version of 1560, and is based ultimately upon the Targum, which has חולק חד בחיר, i.e. 'one *choice* portion.' בְּחִיר *choice* corresponds in the Targum to the Hebrew אפים; but it is clear that it is no translation of it, nor can it be derived from it by any intelligible process. Kimchi, in his *Commentary* and the *Book of Roots*, makes two attempts to account for it—both unsuccessful. Evidently it is a mere conjecture, designed to replace the untranslatable word by something that will more or less harmonize with the context.

The Hebrew text does not admit of a defensible rendering. In the LXX אפים is represented by πλήν, i.e. אֶפֶס. This reading at once relieves the difficulty of the verse, and affords a consistent and grammatical sense. אֶפֶס כִּי restricts or qualifies the preceding clause, precisely as in Nu. 13, 28. 'But unto Ḥannah he used to give one portion:' this, following the *portions* of *v.* 4, might seem to imply that Elqanah felt less affection for her than for Peninnah. To obviate such a misconception, the writer adds: '*Howbeit* he loved Ḥannah; but Yahweh had shut up her womb,' the last clause assigning the reason why Ḥannah received but one portion. This reading is followed by We., Stade (*Gesch. des V. Isr.* i. 199), Now., Kp., Kenn., Dhorme, and is rightly represented on the margin of RV.: the words *because she had no child*, however, though found in LXX, formed probably no part of the text used by the translators, but were added by them as an explanatory comment.

6. וכעסתה . . . גם כעס] 'and . . . *used to vex her even with a vexation*,' i.e. vexed her bitterly. כָּעַס is not (as it is often rendered) to provoke to *anger*, but *to vex*, as כַּעַס is *vexation:* it always denotes the feeling aroused by some unmerited treatment; cf. Job 5, 2. 6, 2; Dt. 32, 19 the vexation caused to Yahweh by the undutiful behaviour of His 'sons and daughters,' 27 'vexation from the enemy,' i.e. the vexation which He would experience from their triumph at Israel's ruin.

כעס] The abstr. subst., in place of the more common inf. abs., as Is. 21, 7 והקשיב קשב; comp. also 22, 17 will hurl thee as a man [*or,* O man] *with a hurling*, i.e. will hurl thee violently, 18 will wind thee up *with a winding;* 24, 16. 22 will be gathered, as captives, *with a gathering* [but read here אָסֹף הָאַסִיר]; Ez. 25, 12. 15; 27, 35; Mic.

4, 9; Hab. 3, 9; Job 16, 14; 27, 12. נֻם occurs in the same position before the inf. abs. Gen. 31, 15. 46, 4. Nu. 16, 13†. Perhaps, indeed (Ehrlich, *Randglossen zur Hebr. Bibel*, iii. (1910), p. 163), we should read here the inf., בַּעַם.

צרתה] 'her *rival-* or *fellow-wife*:' LXX (Luc.) ἡ ἀντίζηλος αὐτῆς, Vulg. *aemula eius*, Pesh. ܚܒܪܬܗ. The meaning is certain. A comparison of Hebrew with the cognate languages, Arabic and Syriac, shews that in old times, when polygamy was prevalent, a common term was in use among the Semitic peoples to denote the idea of a *rival-* or *fellow-wife*, derived from a root צָ̇ר *to injure* or *vex*, viz. Arabic ضَرَّةٌ *ḍarratun* = Syriac ܥܪܬܐ *'arthá* = Hebrew צָרָה. The variation in the initial letter shews that the term was not *borrowed* by one Semitic language from another, within historical times, but that it was already in use at the time when the common ancestors of the Hebrews, Aramaeans, and Arabs dwelt together in a common home: after the three branches separated, the initial consonant in process of time underwent a variation till it appeared finally as צ in Hebrew, as ܥ in Aramaic, and as ض in Arabic [1]. For an example of the Syriac word, see Ephrem Syrus, I. 65 D, where Hagar is spoken of as the ܥܪܬܐ of Sarah: it is also used here in Pesh. to represent צרה. For the Arabic, see Lane's *Arab. Lex.*, p. 1776, and *The 1001 Nights* (Habicht), iii. 276, 8 (cf. Lane's translation, London, 1865, ii. 135), referred to by Lagarde ('Budoor and Ḥayât-en-Nufoos are both wives of Qamar-ez-Zemân, and the one is ضرة = צרה to the other: compare 1 Samuel 1, 6 of the family of Elqanah'); Lane, *Modern Egyptians*, i. 232; S. A. Cook, *The Laws of Moses and The Code of Ḥammurabi*, p. 116 (who cites examples of the working of the system in Syria, and quotes the alliterative proverb, *eḍ-ḍurra murra*, 'A fellow-wife is bitter'): also Saadyah's version of Lev. 18, 18 (in Le Jay's or

---

[1] The variation is in accordance with rule: where Heb. צ corresponds to Arab. ض, its representative in Aramaic is ܥ, ע: e.g. צֹאן = ضَأْنٌ = ܥܢܐ, עָן; אֶרֶץ = أَرْضٌ = ܐܪܥܐ/, עֲרַע (it also, in the Aramaic of Jer. 10, 11 אַרְקָא), of Nineveh and Babylon, Zinjirli, Cappadocia, and Egypt, becomes ק (as עק = אֶע = עֵץ; קמר = עֲמַר = צֶמֶר): see *LOT.*⁸, 1909, pp. 255, 504, 515; Cooke, *NSI.* p. 185). See Lagarde, *Semitica*, I. (1878), pp. 22–27, or the list in the Appendix to the writer's *Hebrew Tenses* (ed. 3), § 178.

Walton's Polyglott, or in Derenbourg's edition of his Works, vol. i,
Paris, 1893) [1]. לְצֹרֵר in Lev. 18, 18 is a 'denominative' (GK. § 38 c)
from צרה, as used here, having the sense of *to take a rival-* or *fellow-
wife* (LXX γυναῖκα ἐπ' ἀδελφῇ αὐτῆς οὐ λήψῃ ἀντίζηλον)[2], just like the
Arab. III قَارَّ. In post-Biblical Hebrew צרה occurs in the same
sense in the Mishnah, *Yebamoth,* ch. i [3].

הִרְעִמָה] On the anomalous ה (with *dagesh dirimens*) see GK. § 22ᵍ
(20ʰ); Ew. § 28ᵇ (*b*); Stade, § 138ᵃ. The root רעם elsewhere in Heb.,
except Ez. 27, 35 (where read probably with LXX, Pesh. דָּמְעוּ פְּנֵיהֶם),
means always *to thunder* (e.g. *ch.* 7, 10); but in Targ. it means in
the Ithpaal *to murmur, complain* (oft. for לון, as Ex. 16, 2 אתרעמו for
וַיִּלּוֹנוּ); and in Syr. (besides meaning *to thunder*) the root, esp. in
Ethpeal and Ethpael, and in its derivatives, is very frequent (see
numerous examples in PS. s.v.) in the sense of *be indignant, complain,*
and also *lament* (e.g. ܠܐ ܬܶܬܪܰܥܡܽܘܢ = μὴ χαλεπαίνετε; ܐܶܬܪܰܥܰܡܘ =
ἠγανάκτησαν; and ܪܽܘܥܳܡܳܐ = μομφή, Col. 3, 13). The Hif. may be
rendered here *to irritate her.*

The Arab. رَغِمَ (which is usually a denom. from رَغَام *earth* or *dust,*
and is used of the nose *cleaving to the dust,* fig. of abasement) has also
the sense of *to anger* (conjj. i and iv; cf. iii and v : Lane, *Arab. Lex.,*
1113 f.). It is possible that, in this sense, it is allied with the Aram.
רעם mentioned above, and with the Heb. הרעים here.

7. יעשה] Difficult. Keil: 'So used he (Elqanah) to do (viz. gave

---

[1] 'And a woman with her sister thou shalt not take لِتَكُونَ ضَرَّتَهَا that she may
be *her fellow-wife.*'
[2] Keil's rendering of לְצֹרֵר, derived from Knobel, is not probable.
[3] See further on this word Lagarde, in his essay *Whether Marriage with a
Deceased Wife's Sister is, or is not, prohibited in the Mosaic Writings,* published
originally in the Göttingen *Nachrichten,* 1882, No. 13, and reprinted in the volume
entitled *Mittheilungen* i. (1884), pp. 125–134. Substantially the word was already
correctly explained by Alb. Schultens in his *Consessus Haririi quartus quintus et
sextus* (Lugd. Bat. 1740), p. 77 : 'Sub ضر regnat speciatim usus *obtrectandi* et
aemulandi, contendendi ex Zelotypia, quae vocatur ضِرَار et ضِرّ. Hinc ضَرَّة צָרָה
est *mulier quae cum alia communem habet maritum.* Sic 1 Sam. 1, 6 :' and he
quotes the phrase نُكِّحَت عَلَى ضِرَّة *ducta fuit super aemulatione,* i.e. *alteri uxori
fuit adiuncta,* and refers also to לְצֹרוֹר in Lev. 18, 18. (Similarly in the
Animadversiones Philologicae et Criticae ad varia loca V. T. (1709), on this
passage : reprinted in the *Opera Minora,* 1769, p. 166.)

her a double portion), . . . ; so used she to vex her,' i.e. the more he
shewed his affection for Ḥannah, the more Peninnah vexed her : but,
even apart from the untenable expl. 'double portion,' there is no
analogy for this sense of the repeated כן : 'the more . . . the more'
is כן . . . כאשר (Ex. 1, 12). Th. We. point יֵעָשֶׂה 'so was it done year
by year . . . , so (namely) did she vex her : ' but this use of the passive
נעשה is hardly a Hebrew idiom.   Probably we should read with Pesh.
(ܘܟܢ ܥܒܕ݂ܐ), Vulg. (implicitly), וכן תַּעֲשֶׂה 'and so *used she* (Peninnah)
to do year by year . . . , so (namely) used she to vex her : ' in this case
the second כן is simply resumptive of the first.

שנה בשנה] year *for* year, i.e. one year like another = yearly.   So
elsewhere, as 1 Ki. 10, 25.   See *Lex.* p. 90ᵃ.

מדֵּי] lit. *out of the sufficiency of,* idiom. for *as often as :* see *Lex.* 191ᵇ.

עלתה] Read probably with Vulg. עֲלֹתָם.

בבית יהוה] After the verb of motion, we expect the accus. בית יהוה,
which is probably to be read with 34 MSS., Kimchi, and three Rabb.
authorities *ap.* Aptowitzer, I (see List of Abbreviations), p. 37.

ותבכה] Instead of continuing, by וּבָכְתָה, to describe what took place
every year, the narrator, by using the hist. tense ותבכה, glides here into
the description of what happened in the *particular* year referred to
in *v.* 4ᵃ.

ולא תאכל] More significant than the normal וְלֹא אָכְלָה : would have
been, and emphasizing the continual condition in which Ḥannah was :
see *Tenses,* §§ 30, 42 β, 85 *Obs.;* GK. § 107ᵉ.   So תבכה *v.* 10ᵇ.

8. לָמֶה] So pointed only in this verse (thrice): GK. § 102ˡ; *Lex.*
554ᵃ.   Comp. the cases in which מָה is pointed anomalously מֶה (Stade,
§ 173 c³); and for the tone *Mil'el* the anomalous לָמֶה Job 7, 20.

ירע לבך] So Dt. 15, 10 : cf. the לב רע (*sad heart*) of Pr. 25, 20, and
the opposite טוב said of the heart *ch.* 25, 36 (where see note): also
פנים רעים (Gen. 40, 7), said in Neh. 2, 2 to be due to רֹע לֵב. LXX
τύπτει σε for רַע, i.e. יֵרַךְ, but unsuitably (see 24, 6. II 24, 10).

9. אכלה] The inf. cstr. with the fem. termination, as regularly with
אהבה, יראה, and with this word in Jer. 12, 9, the Priests' Code, and
Ezekiel; also sporadically with other words [1] (cf. כשמעתו Is. 30, 19;

---

[1] See *Journal of Philology,* XI. (1882), 235 f. ; GK. § 45ᵈ.

לרבקה Dt. 11, 22): and with the suffix omitted, as also takes place exceptionally (e.g. *ch.* 18, 19. Gen. 24, 30. 1 Ki. 20, 12). אָכְלָם (so LXX) is, however, what would be naturally expected—the suffix referring to the party generally, in spite of Hannah's not joining with them. בשלה is, however, in fact superfluous, as the entire incident takes place at Shiloh : perhaps (We.) הַבְּשֵׁלָה *the boiled flesh* (cf. 2, 15), or (Kittel) בַּלִּשְׁכָּה (see on *v.* 18), should be read. Klo., in view of *v.* 18 LXX, for אכלה בשלה אחרי, emends very cleverly וַתַּנַּח אָכְלָה בַּלִּשְׁכָּה, 'and left her food (uneaten) in the (dining-)chamber' (see 9, 22),—followed by (see below), 'and stood before Yahweh.' This emendation is accepted by Bu., but not by Sm. Now.: see further on *v.* 18.

שָׁתֹה] Very anomalous (cf. GK. § 113e *n.*), being the only example of an inf. abs. after a preposition[1]: contrast 1 Ki. 13, 23 אָכְלוֹ אחרי לחם ואחרי שְׁתוֹתוֹ. LXX do not express ואחרי שתה; and it may well be an addition to אחרי אכלה, made on the analogy of other passages in which שתה follows אכל (e.g. Gen. 24, 54). LXX have, however, after בְּשִׁלֹה καὶ κατέστη ἐνώπιον Κυρίου, i.e. וַתִּתְיַצֵּב לִפְנֵי י״י (cf. *v.* 26. 10, 19), which is indeed required for the sequel, and is accepted by Th. We. Klo. etc.

יֹשֵׁב] The ptcp. describes what Eli *was doing* at the time when Hannah appeared where he was.

עַל מזוזת [עַל = *by: Lex.* 756a.

10. מרת נפש] Cf. 2 Ki. 4, 27 מרה לה ונפשה : Job 3, 20. 27, 2 al. The expression implies a state of mental embitterment, i.e. disappointment, dissatisfaction, discontent (Jud. 18, 25. *ch.* 22, 5).

עַל] for the more usual אל, which is read here by several MSS. There is a tendency, however, in these two books to use עַל and אל interchangeably: comp. *v.* 13. 2, 11. II 19, 43 : also 1 Ki. 9, 5b. 20, 43. Is. 22, 15; and see on 13, 13. Cf. *Lex.* 41a.

11. אם ראה תראה] The expression of a condition is often emphasized by the addition of the inf. abs.: see on 20, 6; and exactly as here,

---

[1] The inf. abs. occurs, however, though even then rarely, as the object of another verb (Ew. § 240a; GK. § 113d).—Ewald, in his explanation of this passage (§ 339b), appears to have read אכלה (as some MSS. and Edd. do read [see the note in Michaelis], though against the Massorah). On Ex. 32, 6, which might be thought, perhaps, to afford a parallel to the text, see the note on 22, 13.

Nu. 21, 2. For עָנָי in a similar connexion, cf. Gen. 29, 32; and for זכר (also *v.* 19ᵇ), Gen. 30, 22.

וזכרתני] The pf. with *waw* conv. carrying on the impf. תראה, according to *Tenses*, § 115 s.v. אם. So Ex. 19, 5ᵃ. 23, 22ᵃ etc.

ונתתיו] Here the pf. with *waw* conv. marks the *apodosis: ib.* § 136 *a.* So **20**, 6; Ex. 19, 5ᵇ. 23, 22ᵇ etc.

ונתתיו לי"י כל ימי חייו] LXX has καὶ δώσω αὐτὸν ἐνώπιόν σου δοτὸν ἕως ἡμέρας θανάτου αὐτοῦ· καὶ οἶνον καὶ μέθυσμα οὐ πίεται. This is probably an amplification of the Hebrew text, by means of elements borrowed from Nu. 3, 9. 18, 6. 6, 3 (all P), designed with the view of representing Samuel's dedication as more complete.

12. והיה] As a frequentative sense is here out of place, this must be the perf. with simple *waw*, in place of the normal וַיְהִי, such as is met with occasionally, as 10, 9. 13, 22. 17, 48. 25, 20 (see note). II 6, 16 (see note); and with other verbs 3, 13 (but see note). 4, 19. 17, 38. II 7, 11ᵇ. 13, 18 (ונעל, as Jud. 3, 23). 16, 5. 23, 20 (and more frequently in later Hebrew): see *Tenses*, § 133. We. Bu. and others would correct והיה always to וַיְהִי. This may seem violent: but it is observable that in almost every case *future* tenses precede, so that a scribe might, even more than once, have written והיה by error, supposing inadvertently that the future verbs were to continue. Cf. the discussions in *Tenses*, l.c.; GK. § 112ᴾᴾ⁻ᵘᵘ; Kön. iii. § 370ᶜ⁻ʳ.

הרבתה להתפלל] lit. *did much in respect of* praying, i.e. *prayed long* or *much*: cf. Is. 55, 7 כי יַרְבֶּה לסלוח=for he will *abundantly* pardon, II 14, 11. Ex. 36, 5. ψ. 78, 38. So הקשית לשאול thou hast *done hardly in respect of* asking=thou hast asked a hard thing 2 Ki. 2, 10; יתגנב לבוא=come in stealthily II 19, 4; נחבאת לברח=fled secretly Gen. 31, 27; לא תשוב ללכת=shall not *come back* I Ki. 13, 17; היטבת לראות Jer. 1, 12; קדמתי לברח I *was beforehand in* fleeing=I fled betimes Jon. 4, 2: GK. § 114ⁿ with the footnote.

12–13. ועלי שֹׁמֵר . . . וחנה היא מדברת . . .] Two circumstantial clauses (*Tenses*, § 160), והיה being resumed by ויחשבה in 13ᵇ. שמר has here the sense of *observed*, i.e. *marked*—not a common use of שמר, at least in prose: comp. ψ. 17, 4. Job 39, 1. Zech. 11, 11.

13. היא] For the pron. (which is unusual, as thus joined with the indef. ptcp.) cf. Dt. 31, 3. Jos. 22, 22: *Tenses*, § 199 *note.*

מדברת על לבה] not, of course, as Is. 40, 2 al. in the sense of *consoling*, but, the pron. being *reflexive*, as לדבר אל לבי in Gen. 24, 45 = to speak *to* oneself (where LXX likewise render by ἐν, so that there is no ground for changing here על into ב). Comp. ויאמר אל לבו (followed of course—the verb being אמר—by the words supposed to be said) 27, 1. Gen. 8, 21 (We.). It is another instance of אל=על.

לא ישמע] not לא נשמע, in agreement with the continuance expressed by the preceding ptcp. נָעוֹת.

חשב ל'] as Gen. 38, 15. Job 33, 10 al.

14. תשתכרין] the ן of the 2 fem. sing., retained regularly in Aramaic and Arabic, is found in Hebrew only seven times, viz. here, Jer. 31, 22. Is. 45, 10. Ruth 2, 8. 21. 3, 4. 18 (Stade, § 553; GK. § 47°).

מעליך] *from upon thee*—the wine (in its effects) being conceived as clinging to her, and weighing her down. Comp. for the idiom (applied literally) 17, 39. Gen. 38, 19 al., and (metaphorically) Am. 5, 23: also Jud. 16, 19 ויסר כחו מעליו (in allusion to the hair as the seat of Samson's strength).

15. קשת רוח] The expression occurs only here: upon the analogy of קְשֵׁי לֵב Ez. 3, 7 (cf. Dt. 2, 30) it would denote *hard-spirited*, i.e. obstinate, unyielding. LXX ἡ σκληρὰ ἡμέρα, i.e. קְשַׁת יוֹם, which is supported by Job 30, 25, where קשי יום is used in the sense which is here desiderated, viz. *unfortunate*, lit. *hard of day*, i.e. one upon whom times are hard (cf. δυσημερία). So Th. We. Hitzig (on Job *l.c.*), etc.

אנכִי] *mil'el* (*Tenses*, § 91), the pausal form of אנכִי, here with a *minor* disjunctive accent (*zāqēf*), such as often induces a pausal form (*Tenses*, § 103).

נפשי] i.e. the emotions and desire, of which in Hebrew psychology the 'soul' is the seat: cf. ψ. 42, 5; also 102, 1. 142, 3, which illustrate at the same time שׂיחי *v.* 16. See the synopsis of passages in the writer's *Parallel Psalter*, p. 459 f.

16. לפני בת־בליעל] נתן ל' means *to make into*, נתן כ' *to treat as* (Gen. 42, 30. ψ. 44, 12): נתן לפני means elsewhere *to set before* (1 Ki. 9, 6) or *to give up before* (Dt. 2, 31. 33)—neither sense, however, being suitable here. If the text be correct, לפני must have the force of *like*, which it also appears to possess in Job 3, 24 (parallel with כ). 4, 19 (Ew. Del. Hitz.); but in these passages also the sense is questionable.

LXX express simply לבת־בליעל; but נתן ל׳ never occurs in the sense of
to *represent as.* The best suggestion seems to be to read כְּבַת ב׳...אל־תתן,
treat not . . . as (Gen. 42, 30), throwing out לפני, as having come in by
error from the line above (Sm. Bu.). On בליעל, see *Lex.* s.v.

דברתי] LXX ἐκτέτακα, Targ. אורכית,—both paraphrasing.

17. שְׁלֵתֵךְ] for שְׁאֵלָתֵךְ (unusual), GK. § 23ᶠ. Here begins a series of
plays (1, 17. 20. 27. 28. 2, 20) by which the stem שאל is brought into
connexion with the name Samuel. Cf. Gen. 17, 17. 18, 12. 13. 15.
21, 6 (Isaac); 25, 26. 27, 36 (Jacob).

מעמו] מֵעִם מֵעִם is idiomatic with שאל: *v.* 27. Dt. 10, 12. Is. 7, 11 al.
(*Lex.* 768ᵇ *bottom*). Cf. מֵאֵת 1 Ki. 2, 16 מֵאִתֶּךְ שֹׁאֵל אָנֹכִי אַחַת שְׁאֵלָה.

18. לדרכה] LXX adds καὶ εἰσῆλθεν εἰς τὸ κατάλυμα αὐτῆς, i. e. no
doubt, as We. rightly perceived, וַתָּבֹא הַלִּשְׁכָּתָה (see 9, 22) 'and entered
into the (dining-)chamber'—LXX having incorrectly treated the ה
locale as the suffix of the 3 pers. sing. fem. The לשכה was a chamber
near the היכל יהוה, as in 9, 22 near the במה, in which the sacrificial
meals were held. In later times the word denotes the chambers in the
Temple Court in which the priests lived: Jer. 35, 2. 4. Ez. 40, 17 etc.

ותאכל] LXX for this has an entire sentence, presupposing the Heb.
וַתָּבֹא הַלִּשְׁכָּתָה וַתֹּאכַל עִם אִישָׁהּ וַתֵּשְׁתְּ. If these words are original,—
and they certainly read as if they were,—Hannah leaves the sacred
meal (*v.* 9) *before* it is over, and goes to the temple to pray: she then
returns to the dining-chamber, and finishes her meal with her husband.
Klo.'s emend. of *v.* 9 agrees with this representation. Would the
narrator, however, have said, 'and went her way,' if he had pictured
her merely as returning to the adjoining לשכה (Sm.)? If the additional
words in LXX here are *not* original, then ותאכל will mean 'and ate' in
general; and with this will agree MT. of *v.* 9, according to which
Hannah leaves the לשכה *after* the sacred meal is finished. Klo.'s emend.
of *v.* 9 is brilliant, and attractive: but it is difficult to be as confident that
it is right, as Bu. is. Nowack and Smith do not accept either it, or the
LXX reading here.

ותּאכַל] *milra',* on account of the disjunctive accent, *zāqēf:* out of
pause, we have ותֹאכל (*mil'el*); so e.g. Lev. 10, 2. See GK. § 68ᵈ,ᵉ.

פניה] פנים of a vexed or discontented countenance, as Job 9, 27
אם אמרי אשכחה שיחי אעזבה פני ואבליגה. LXX understood the word

in its ordinary sense, reading (or paraphrasing) וּפְנֶיהָ לֹא נָפְלוּ עוֹד (cf. Gen. 4, 6). Klo. לֹא הַפִּֽילָה (Jer. 3, 12) for לֹא הָיוּ לָהּ.

20. It is doubtful if the text is in its original form. We should expect (cf. Gen. 30, 22 f.) the ‘remembering’ to be followed immediately by the conception, and the date which, in the text as it stands, fixes the time of the conception, to fix rather the time of the birth. Hence Reifmann (*Or Boqer*, Berlin, 1879, p. 28) supposes a transposition to have taken place, and would restore the words וַתַּהַר חנה to the beginning of the verse: ‘And Hannah conceived; and it came to pass, at the close of the year, that she bare a son.’ So in effect LXX (καὶ συνέλαβεν, καὶ ἐγενήθη τῷ καιρῷ τῶν ἡμερῶν καὶ ἔτεκεν υἱόν), but without the retention of חנה, which is desiderated by Hebrew style (וַתַּהַר alone being too light by the side of the long clause following).

לתקופות הימים] Read, with 6 MSS., לִתְקֻפַת (the pl. is strange; and the ו would form no part of the original text: Introd. § 2. 2), *at the* (completed) *circuit of the days*, i. e. not (as Th. We.) at the end of the period of gestation, but like תְּקוּפַת הַשָּׁנָה Ex. 34, 22 (=בְּצֵאת הַשָּׁנָה in the parallel, Ex. 23, 16), of the Feast of Ingathering at the close of the year, which was no doubt the occasion of the pilgrimage alluded to in *v.* 21. Cf. the cogn. נקף in Is. 29, 1 חַגִּים יִנְקֹפוּ ‘ let the feasts *go round,*’ i.e. complete their circuit. ימים as *vv.* 3. 21. לְ of time as II 11, 1. 1 Ki. 20, 22. 26. 2 Ch. 24, 23 לִתְקוּפַת הַשָּׁנָה. תקופה occurs besides only ψ. 19, 7.

שמואל] The current etymologies of this name cannot be accepted. This is evident at once in the case of the old derivation, which still lingers in the margin of AV., ‘ that is, *Asked of God,*’ as if שְׁמוּאֵל were contracted from שָׁאוּל מֵאֵל: for such a contraction would be altogether alien to the genius of the Hebrew language. What the writer means to express must be (as often in the OT.) an *assonance,* not an etymology, i.e. the name שמואל *recalled* to his mind the word שָׁאוּל *asked,* though in no sense derived from it. So קֵין or מֹשֶׁה, for instance, recalled or suggested the verbs קנה *to get,* and משה *to draw out,* though the names do not themselves *signify* either ‘ gotten’ or ‘ drawn out.’ What, however, is the actual meaning of the name שמואל? When the explanation ‘ Asked of God’ was seen to be untenable, an attempt was made to bring the name into some sort of connexion with the text by the suggestion that it was = שְׁמוּעָאֵל, and signified 'heard of God' (so e.g. Keil). Had this, however, been the writer's intention, we should have expected the word *hear* to occur somewhere in the narrative, which is not the case. But there are even more serious objections to this derivation. (1) Had this been the true account of the name, the א rather than the ע would have been naturally the letter elided: an original שְׁמוּעָאֵל would have given rise to שְׁמוּעָאל (on the analogy of וְיִשְׁמָעֵאל) rather than to שְׁמוּאֵל¹. (2) Compound proper names in Hebrew are constructed, for the most part, after particular types or models: thus one large class consists of one of the sacred names followed by a verb in the perfect tense (the last vowel only being lengthened, after the analogy of substantives), as אֱלִידָע, יוֹנָתָן, אֶלְנָתָן, יְהוֹיָדָע, i.e. *El* (or *Yah*) *has given, El* (or *Yah*) *has known*. Another class is similarly compounded, but the verb stands first, as חֲנַנְיָה(וּ), חֲנַנְאֵל, *Yah* (or *El*) *has been gracious*, (וּ)עֲזַרְיָה, עֲזַרְאֵל, *Yah* (or *El*) *has helped*. In a third (less numerous) class the verb still stands first, but is in the imperfect tense, as יְרַחְמְאֵל *El hath mercy* (or, with an optative force, *May El have mercy !*), (וּ)יַאֲזַנְיָה *Yah hearkeneth* (or, *May Yah hearken !*). There are, of course, other types, which need not however be here considered. But numerous as are the proper names compounded of one of the sacred names and a verb, *there are none, or next to none, compounded with a passive participle*. Obvious as such a form as *blessed* or *helped* or *redeemed of Yah* might appear to be, it was uniformly discarded by the Hebrews. In proper names, the passive participle is used only by itself. We have בָּרוּךְ and זָבוּד, for instance, but אֶלְזָבָד, יוֹזָבָד or (וּ)זְבַדְיָה, not זְבוּדְיָה; בְּרֶכְיָה; בְּרוּכְיָה, not יְבֶרֶכְיָהוּ or בֶּרֶכְיָהוּ or בָּרַכְאֵל; we have not only אֶלְנָתָן and יְהוֹנָתָן (or (וּ)יוֹנָתָן), but also (וּ)נְתַנְיָה and נְתַנְאֵל, not however נְתוּנְאֵל; we have (וּ)שְׁמַעְיָה and יִשְׁמָעֵאל (also אֱלִישָׁמָע), but not שְׁמוּעָאל. There is *no* name in the OT. formed analogously to a presumable שְׁמוּעָאֵל *heard of God*²; and the fact that this type of

---

¹ In יְדִיעָאֵל 1 Ch. 7, 6 al. even the א is not elided.

² The only possible exception would be מְחוּיָאֵל Gen. 4, 18, if this mean 'smitten of God,' which, however, is far from certain: following the Qrê, we may vocalize מְחִיָּיאֵל, which would agree with the LXX Μαιήλ, i.e. 'God is a life-giver' (Budde, *Biblische Urgeschichte*, p. 128). But, in any case, an archaic

compound name was studiously avoided by the Hebrews is practically conclusive against the proposed derivation.

The derivation suggested by Gesenius, שְׁמוּאֵל = 'Name of God,' is as obvious as it is natural. It is suitable and appropriate in itself; and the form of compound which it implies is in exact agreement with פְּנוּאֵל 'Face of God,' רְעוּאֵל 'Friend of God,' גְּאוּאֵל 'Majesty of God.' The *ū* is the old termination of the nominative case (see GK. § 90ᵏ), retained as a binding-vowel, both in the instances cited, and also occasionally besides: e.g. in מְתוּשֶׁלַח 'Man of the weapon ¹,' and מְתוּשָׁאֵל ² 'Man who belongs to God.'

The preceding argument, on its negative side, that שְׁמוּאֵל does *not* mean 'Heard of God,' has been generally allowed to be conclusive: but it has been felt by some that 'Name of God' does not yield a good sense for the name of a person; and other explanations of it have been proposed.

1. שְׁמוּאֵל, it has been pointed out, resembles in form certain South Arabian proper names of the type *Sumhu apika*, 'His name is mighty,' *Sumhu-yada'a*, ' His name has determined,' *Sumhu-kariba*, 'His name has blessed,' *Sumhu-watara*, 'His name is pre-eminent' [Heb. יתר], etc.: the names of two of the kings of the first Babylonian dynasty, *c.* 2100 B.C. (of South Arabian origin), *Shumu-abi*, *Shumu-la-ilu*, have been also explained similarly, viz. (*Shumu* being regarded as a contraction of *Shumu-hu*) 'His name is my father,' 'Is not his name God?' Hommel, who first called attention to these resemblances (*Anc. Heb. Trad.*, 1897, 85 f., 99 f.), interpreted these names in a monotheistic sense, and understood 'His name' to be a periphrasis for 'God;' but Giesebrecht, who discussed the subject, and compared many names of similar formation, such as *Ili-kariba*, *Abi-kariba*, (*Die Atliche Schätzung des Gottesnamens*, 1901, pp. 103–113, 140–144), regards it, with much greater probability, as a periphrasis for the name of a god whom the giver of the name for some reason shrinks from mentioning. The same view of the Bab. names is taken by Winckler and Zimmern (see *KAT.*³, pp. 225, 483 f., with the references). And all these scholars regard שְׁמוּאֵל as formed similarly, and as meaning 'His name is God,' i.e. (Giesebrecht, pp. 108 f., 112 f.) the

name such as this has no appreciable bearing upon the usage of the language in historic times. With *active* participles, there occur the compounds מְשֶׁלֶמְיָה(וּ) 1 Ch. 9, 21. 26, 1. 2. 9; and the *Aramaic* מְשֵׁיזַבְאֵל 'God is a deliverer' Neh. 3, 4 al., and מְהֵיטַבְאֵל 'God is a benefactor' Neh. 6, 10 (in Gen. 36, 39 the name borne by the wife of an Edomite king).

¹ Though more probably שׁלח conceals the name of some Babylonian deity: see conjectures in Skinner's *Genesis*, p. 133; and the writer's *Genesis*, p. 81.

² The שׁ marks this word as a *Babylonian* formation: cf. מִישָׁאֵל. מת in the special sense *husband* is common in Ethiopic: in Hebrew, as a living language, it fell out of use, except in the *plural*.

name of the god in question (here יהוה) is itself a Divine manifestation, and possesses a Divine force and power (cf. Ex. 23, 21 כי שמי בקרבו), capable of helping and protecting the child who bears it (cf. the use of שׁם in ψ. 20, 2. 54, 3. Prov. 18, 10: see further on this subject *DB.* v. 640 f.).

2. In Heb., as in other Semitic languages, it seems that long names were in familiar use sometimes abbreviated, and that in this way, 'hypocoristic,' 'carita-tive,' or pet names arose. Thus names of the form חַשּׁוּב (from חֲשַׁבְיָה), יַדּוּעַ (from יְדַעְיָה), שַׁלּוּם (from שֶׁלֶמְיָה), שַׁמּוּעַ (from שְׁמַעְיָה), to judge from modern Arabic names of the same form, and with the same force, are caritatives: there are also other types (Lidzbarski, 'Semitische Kosenamen,' in his *Ephemeris,* ii. 1-23 : see p. 21). Prätorius, now (*ZDMG.* 1903, 773 ff.), considers that these names were originally passive participles (as יָדוּעַ 'known,' short for '[He whom] Yah knows'), though afterwards phonetically modified, when it was felt that they were not really participles, but proper names. And Prätorius would extend this principle to the explanation of שְׁמוּאֵל, and of some other names of the same type : he would regard שְׁמוּאֵל viz. as an abridged caritative of יִשְׁמָעֵאל, formed from the ptcp. שָׁמוּעַ, with loss of the final letter, but with preservation of the Divine name ; and he would explain similarly חַמּוּאֵל (1 Ch. 4, 26) as for חֲמוּלְאֵל, from פְּנוּ אֶל = פְּנוּאֵל ; יִפְתַּח־אֵל from פְּתַח אֶל = פְּתוּאֵל (Joel 1, 1) ; יַחְמְלאֵל from יְפְנֶה־אֵל [cf. וַיִּפְנֶה] ; גְּאוּאֵל = גְּאוּלְאֵל from יְגַאֲלְאֵל (p. 777 ff.). This explanation is, however, purely conjectural : we do not *know* that any of these names were really formed by the process assumed.

3. Jastrow (*JBLit.* 1900, p. 103 f.), observing that in Ass. *shumu,* properly *name,* is often virtually equivalent to *offspring,* esp. in proper names, as *Nabu-shum-ukin,* 'Nabu has established an offspring,' *Bel-shum-uṣur,* 'O Bel, protect the offspring' (cf. שׁם in Heb. in such expressions as *cut off* or *wipe out the name,* Is. 14, 22. Dt. 7, 24, *establish the name,* 2 S. 14, 7—though of course in these expressions שׁם does not *mean* 'offspring'), supposes the meaning of שְׁמוּאֵל to be *son of God,* and that it is the correlative of אֲבִיאֵל 'My father is God.' But would שׁם express this sense, except in a connexion which shewed that the 'name' was thought of as attached to, and perpetuated by, the offspring?

It may be doubted whether the objections to the explanation, 'Name of God,' are cogent. A name, unless there are good reasons for supposing it to have passed through considerable phonetic change, surely *means* what to all appearance it seems to mean. The obvious meaning of שְׁמוּאֵל is 'Name of God.' This may very naturally have been understood to mean 'Bearing the name of God :' cf. Nöldeke, *EB.* NAMES, § 39, who compares Ἀπολλώνυμος, Ἑκατώνυμος = Named after Apollo, Named after Hecate.

כי] For the omission of *saying* cf. Gen. 4, 25. 32, 31. 41, 51. 52 ; Ex. 18, 4.

שְׁאִלְתִּיו] GK. §§ 44ᵈ, 64ᶠ. So *v.* 28 הִשְׁאִלְתִּיהוּ.

21. הָאִישׁ] Used similarly Gen. 19, 9. Ex. 11, 3. Nu. 12, 3. Jud. 17, 5. 1 Ki. 11, 28. Est. 9, 4.

זבח הימים] 'the *yearly* sacrifice;' see on 1, 3. So 2, 19: also 20, 6 of an annual family festival.

22. עד וג'] Cf. Jos. 6, 10. Jud. 16, 2: also II 10, 5 (*Tenses,* § 115 s. v. עד).

את פני] = *in the presence of,* as 2, 11. 17. 18; ψ. 16, 10. 21, 7. 140, 14; Lev. 4, 6. 17 (*in front of* the veil). Perhaps, however, the original reading was רָאָה for נראה, in which case את would be the ordinary sign of the accusative: see the writer's note on Ex. 23, 15, or Dt. 16, 16, Cheyne on Is. 1, 12, Kirkpatrick on ψ. 42, 2 [Heb. 3].

23. את דברו] LXX, Pesh. express the second person אֶת־דְּבָרֶךָ—in all probability, rightly. There has been no mention in the preceding verses of any word or promise on the part of God: and even in so far as it may be supposed to be involved in the *wish* expressed by Eli in *v.* 17, that has been fulfilled already in the birth of the child. 'Establish thy word,' i. e. give it effect, permit it to be carried out. הקים דבר is used especially of a person *carrying out* a command or injunction laid upon him, as 15, 13 Jer. 35, 16; or of Yahweh *giving effect to* His own, or His prophet's, word, as 1 Ki. 12, 15. Is. 44, 26. Jer. 33, 14. LXX, rendering το ἐξελθὸν ἐκ τοῦ στόματός σου, use the more formal expression: see Nu. 30, 13 כל מוצא שפתיה. 32, 24 והיוצא מפיכם תעשו. Dt. 23, 24; also Dt. 8, 3. Jer. 17, 16.

24. בפרים שלשה] LXX ἐν μόσχῳ τριετίζοντι, Pesh. ܟܬܘܪܐ ܬܠܬܐ = בְּפַר מְשֻׁלָּשׁ (see Gen. 15, 9): no doubt correctly, for (1) the *order* פרים שלשה is very unusual[1]: (2) only one פר is spoken of in *v.* 25. The change is really only one in the grouping of letters: for in the older orthography פרים would be written regularly פרמ (without י, and without the distinctive final form of the מ: cf. on the Siloam Inscription הַחֹצְבִים = החצבמ: there are also many indications that the *plena scriptio* was not in use in the MSS. used by the LXX translators. See further in the Introduction). For אחת with *one* term only of the

---

[1] It is, however, doubtful whether this argument should be here pressed: in a list of *different* things, the substantives may stand first for emphasis (GK. § 134ᶜ): cf. Gen. 32, 15 f. (JE), Nu. 7, 17. 23 etc. (P). (In the footnote to GK. § 134ᶜ, l. 5, there is an oversight: 'nearly always *after*' should be 'more often *after*:' Herner, *op. cit.,* pp. 58–59, gives more than three pages of instances in P with the numeral *before* the subst., and hardly half a page of cases with it *after!*)

enumeration cf. 16, 20. LXX add after בפר משלש ולחם = ולחם—
probably (We.) from Ex. 29, 23 f.

קמח] may be either in appos. to איפה אחת, or an accus. of limitation: see *Tenses,* § 194; and cf. GK. § 131ᵈ· ᵖ. So Gen. 18, 6 שְׁלֹשׁ
סְאִים קֶמַח. Ex. 16, 32 מָן הָעֹמֶר מְלֹא, etc.

שלו] The correction בשלו is unnecessary: the *accus.* is under
the influence of ותבאהו: cf. *v.* 19. 10, 26. 15, 34. II 20, 3. Jos. 9, 6.
10, 15. 43. 18, 9ᵇ. Jud. 9, 5. 21, 12ᵇ.

והנער נָעַר:] AV. RV. 'and the child was young.' But this rendering
implies that נער as predicate expresses more than it does as subject,
which cannot be the case. The words can only be rendered 'and the
lad was a lad.' It is just possible that this might be understood—in
accordance with the Semitic usage explained on 23, 13—as meaning
'the lad was what he was—there is no occasion to say more about
him:' but the case is barely parallel to the other examples of the
usage; and this fact about Samuel would be so obvious from the
narrative in general that it would scarcely deserve to be made the
subject of a special remark. It is more probable that the text is in
error. LXX express והנער עָמָם: but this is tautologous, following
24ᵃ MT. It is best to read with Klo. Bu. (LXX εἰσῆλθεν) וַתָּבֹא
בית יהוה]ב[שלו והנער עָמָּה.

25. וישחטו] The subject is not Ḥannah and Elqanah, but הַשֹּׁחֲטִים
(We.): see on 16, 4.

ויביאו] viz. המביאים (see the last note), the attendants of the temple,
perhaps the same as השחטים. Or we might read either with LXX
וַתָּבֹא 'came *with*,' or וַתָּבֵא 'brought.'

26. בי] LXX here and Jud. 6, 13. 15. 13, 8. 1 Ki. 3, 17. 26 render
unintelligibly by Ἐν ἐμοί, elsewhere (Pent. Jos.) correctly by Δέομαι,
Δεόμεθα. On this precative בִּי (Gen. 43, 20 al.), see *Lex.* 106ᵇ.

חֵי נפשך] See on 17, 55.

עמכה] merely an orthographical variation for עִמְּךָ (here only): so
כָּמֹכָה Ex. 15, 11 *bis* †; אֹתְכָה Nu. 22, 33; אֶתְכָה Ex. 29, 35†; בְּכָה Ex.
7, 29. II 22, 30. ψ. 141, 8†; לְכָה Gen. 27, 37. II 18, 22. Is. 3, 6†.

אל] *with reference to, regarding* (not *for*); as Is. 37, 21. 33.

28ᵃ. וגם אנכי] 'et ego vicissim, Job 7, 11' (Th. from Le Clerc), cf.
ch. 28, 22: II 12, 13. The so-called גם *correlativum.' (Lex.* 169ᵇ 4.)

ליהוה . . . היה] The *first* of the two *zāqēfs* always marks the greater break (GK. § 15ᵐ), as indeed the sense frequently shews; comp. 2, 14.

השאיל [השאלתיהו ליהוה is *to let* a person *ask* (viz. successfully), i.e. to grant him his request : lit., therefore, 'let (one) ask him for Y.' = let him be asked for (lent him to) Y. So Ex. 12, 36 (the correlative of *ask* in 3, 22. 11, 2, as of the same word here in *vv.* 17. 27 ; for שאל *ask* in the sense of *borrow*, see also Ex. 22, 13. 2 Ki. 4, 3 ¹). In the cognate languages, however, the word by usage acquires definitely the sense of *lend :* see Luke 11, 5 Pesh., where ܐܘܫܠܢܝ¹ stands for the Greek χρῆσόν μοι ².

כל־הימים וג'] 'all the days for which he shall be (Vulg. *fuerit ;* the fut. perf., as Gen. 48, 6 : *Tenses,* § 17 ; GK. § 106ᵒ), he is granted to (lit. asked for) Yahweh.' It is probable that for היה we should read, with LXX, Pesh. Targ. (though these, as AV., may indeed merely paraphrase), חַי (cf. Gen. 5, 5); but in any case הוא is to be construed with what follows, not (as by LXX) with what precedes.

שאול ליהוה] asked (*borrowed*) *for* (= *lent to*) Yahweh : cf. 2 Ki. 6, 5 שאול והוא (= *borrowed*) ³.

28ᵇ. The last words of *v.* 28 must be dealt with in connexion with 2, 11ᵃ. LXX do not express 1, 28ᵇ; on the other hand they have in 2, 11ᵃ (καὶ κατέλιπεν αὐτὸν ἐκεῖ ἐνώπιον Κυρίου, καὶ ἀπῆλθεν εἰς Αρμαθαιμ) an addition to MT., which looks like a various recension of the words not expressed by them in 1, 28ᵇ. The two texts may be compared, by placing one above the other, as is done by We. :

| MT. | וישתחו שם ליהוה וילך אלקנה הרמתה על־ביתו |
| LXX | וַתַּנִּחֵהוּ שם לִפְנֵי יְהוָֹה וַתֵּלֶךְ הרמתה |

In the light of the context, LXX deserves the preference. For in

---

¹ As Bu. aptly remarks, שאל and השאיל are to *borrow* and *lend*, as a transaction between friends, לוה and הלוה are to *borrow* and *lend* in a *commercial* sense.

² Cf. Sir. 46, 13 Heb. (the clause is not in the Greek text) המשאיל (rd. the Hof. ptcp. המושאל) מבטן אמו : Syr. ܘܐܦܢ ܠܐ ܒܛܢ ܡܢ ܐܡܗ ܘܐܘܫܠ.

³ Jastrow (*JBLit.* xix, 1900, p. 100) supposes השאיל to be a denominative from שְׁאָל *asker* (viz. of the Divine will,—a function of the *priest*), and would render accordingly, 'have made him an *asker (priest)* to Yahweh :' but though שאל ביהוה is often said (e.g. *ch.* 22, 10), שָׁאָל never occurs as a designation of the priest, nor is it throughout this narrative used of Samuel.

MT. Ḥannah alone is mentioned as coming up with Samuel to Shiloh (*vv.* 24–28ᵃ: so *v.* 22 'I,' *v.* 23 'thou'); when the account of the visit is ended, an unnamed ' he ' appears as the subject of וישתחו, who finally (2, 11ᵃ) is resolved into Elqanah. Had Elqanah, according to the conception of the writer, been present at this visit to Shiloh, he would assuredly have been named explicitly at an earlier stage of the narrative. There is the less ground for supposing that LXX altered arbitrarily the genders at the end, as in *their* text Elqanah is already introduced in *v.* 24; so that the masc. in *v.* 28, had the translators had וישתחו before them, would have occasioned no difficulty, and given no occasion for a change. On these grounds there is a strong probability that LXX have here preserved the original text. Pesh. Vulg. render וישתחו by a plural verb (as though the reading were וישתחוו: comp. Gen. **27**, 29. 43, 28ᵇ, where the punctuators direct ישתחו to be read as a plur.); Klo. suggests that שם may be a mutilated fragment of שמואל: but neither of the remedies relieves the real difficulty of MT., that only Ḥannah is mentioned (not allusively merely, but circumstantially) as coming up to Shiloh with Samuel, and only Elqanah is mentioned (2, 11) as returning from Shiloh to Ramah. If it be true that 1, 28ᵇ MT. is but a variant of 2, 11ᵃ LXX, it will follow that Ḥannah's Song is inserted in MT. and LXX in a different place.

2, 1–10. *Ḥannah's Song* [1].

1. רמה קרני] The figure is that of an animal carrying its head high, and proudly conscious of its strength: cf. *ψ.* 92, 11. 112, 9; and (in the Hif'il) *v.* 10. *ψ.* 75, 5. 6. 89, 18 al. On the contrary, Jer. 48, 25, נגדעה קרן מואב.

ביהוה (2)] 27 MSS., and some Rabb. quotations, *ap.* Aptowitzer, I (see List of Abbreviations), p. 37, בֵּאלֹהָי: so LXX, Vulg., and moderns generally. The variation in the parallel clause is an improvement: cf. *ψ.* 3, 8ᵃ. 18, 7ᵃ. Is. 40, 27ᵇ. 49, 5ᵇ.

רחב פי על אויבי כי] For these words LXX seem to have read רחב על אויבי פי, which may be preferable (We. Now. Hpt.): the thought שמחתי בישועתך is rather parallel to clause *c* (cf. *a*), than the ground of it. Bu. Sm. prefer MT. For the figure רחב פי, cf. *ψ.* 35, 21. Is.

---

[1] See on this Song, in addition to the Commentaries, P. Haupt's learned and interesting study, ' The Prototype of the Magnificat,' in *ZDMG.* 1904, pp. 617–632.

57, 4—a gesture of derision and contempt. For the retrocession of the tone (רָחֹב, *mil'el*), cf. 4 אָזְרוּ, 8 מִצְקִי ; and see GK. § 29ᵉˑ ᶠ.

בישׁוּעָתֶךָ] יְשׁוּעָה means here *deliverance, help :* see on 14, 45.

2. כִּי אֵין בִּלְתֶּךָ] The clause gives an insufficient reason for אֵין קָדוֹשׁ כַּיהוה, besides destroying the parallelism, and (by the second person) being out of connexion with 2ᵃ and 2ᶜ; in LXX also it is in a different place, viz. *after* 2ᶜ. Upon these grounds it is probably to be regarded as a gloss (Lö. Now. Dhorme), or, in the form כִּי אֵין קָדוֹשׁ בִּלְתֶּךָ (LXX), as a variant of 2ᵃ (Bu. Hpt.).

צוּר] Cf. Dt. 32, 4. 15. 18. 37 ; Is. 30, 29 ; *ch.* 23, 3 ; and (where the thought also is similar) *ψ.* 18, 32 ; Is. 44, 8.

3. אַל תַּרְבּוּ תְדַבְּרוּ] The two verbs ἀσυνδέτως, the first verb expressing a general relation, for which in English an *adverb* would commonly be used, and the second, expressing the principal idea of the sentence, being subordinated to the first for the purpose of defining and limiting the range of its application : so Jer. 13, 18 הַשְׁפִּילוּ שֵׁבוּ *shew lowliness, sit down = sit down lowly,* and frequently in Hosea : 1, 6 לֹא אוֹסִיף עוֹד אֲרַחֵם ; 5, 11 הוֹאִיל הָלַךְ *hath taken upon himself, hath walked = hath walked willingly ;* 6, 4 = 13, 3 מַשְׁכִּים הֹלֵךְ ; 9, 9 הֶעְמִיקוּ שִׁחֵתוּ ; Is. 7, 11 MT. etc. (GK. § 120ᵍ ; Ew. § 285ᵇ). An idiom more common in Syriac (Nöld. *Syr. Gr.* § 337) than in Hebrew. In Hebrew the construction noticed on 1, 12 is generally preferred.

גְּבֹהָה נְבֹהָה] The reduplication, as Dt. 2, 27 בַּדֶּרֶךְ בַּדֶּרֶךְ ' *in the way, in the way* (and not elsewhere) will I go ;' 16, 20 צֶדֶק צֶדֶק תִּרְדֹּף '*justice, justice* (and this alone) shalt thou follow ;' Qoh. 7, 24 (GK. § 133ᵏ). 'Do not let your words breathe ever (תַּרְבּוּ), and emphatically (נְבֹהָה גְבֹהָה), a spirit of haughtiness.' But the line is unduly long, as compared with 3ᵇ ; and the word may have been accidentally repeated.

יֵצֵא וג'] Clause *b*, though not attached to *a* by וָ, is governed by אַל at the beginning : so *ψ.* 35, 19. 75, 6, and with לֹא *ψ.* 9, 19. Is. 23, 4ᵇ. 38, 18ᵃ, לָמָה לֹא Job 3, 11, פֶּן *ψ.* 13, 5 ; comp. GK. § 152ᶻ.[1] The person of the verb here *changes* in the second clause, and the repetition of אַל (Hpt.) would certainly be an improvement.

---

[1] Comp. similarly after לָמָה *ψ.* 10, 1. 44, 25. 74, 1. 88, 15. Is. 63, 17ᵃ. Hb. 1, 13ᵇ. Job 10, 18 ; עַל מֶה *ψ.* 10, 13 : עַד מֶה 79, 5 (nearly = 89, 47) ; עַד מָתַי 74, 10 ; מִי 62, 4 ; עַד אָנָה 89, 7 (cf. 49). 106, 2. Is. 42, 23.

עתק] ψ. 75, 6: also 31, 19. 94, 4†. See *Lex.* 801ᵃ.

דעות] So Job 36, 4: cf. אמונות Pr. 28, 20; בינות Is. 27, 11; תבונות Is. 40, 14 al.; חכמות ψ. 49, 4 al.; חמות ψ. 76, 11. Pr. 22, 24. Poetic, amplificative plurals (GK. § 124ᵉ).

ולא נתכנו עללות] Read with the Qrê ולו. לא and לו, being pronounced alike, were sometimes in error written one for the other : and in certain cases (though not always) the correction was made by the Massorah (see *Lex.* 520ᵇ). 'And by Him actions are *tested* or *estimated*' (viz. by the application of a measure, תֹּכֶּן, Ex. 5, 18. Ez. 45, 11); for לְ, as introducing the efficient cause with a passive verb, see *Lex.* 514ᵈ, GK. § 121ᶠ. LXX καὶ θεὸς ἑτοιμάζων would correspond no doubt (cf. 4 Ki. 12, 11) to וְאֵל תֹּכֵן: but in all probability the rendering is simply a free one; if ואל תכן had once stood here, it is difficult to understand why it should have been changed to ולו נתכנו. The epithet תֹּכֵן לִבּוֹת *estimater of hearts* is applied to Yahweh in Pr. 21, 2. 24, 12†, and תֹּכֵן רֻחוֹת *ib.* 16, 2†; here it is said that man's *actions* are estimated by Him. The argument is : Do not speak arrogantly : *for* Yahweh has full knowledge of what you do, and your actions are thus all appraised by Him.

4. חַתִּים] in the pl. by attraction to גבורים, because this is the principal idea, and what the poet desires to express is not so much that the bows, as that the warriors themselves, are broken. Cf. Is. 21, 17. Zech. 8, 10; and Ew. § 317ᵈ, GK. § 146ᵃ. Ehrlich, however, suggests cleverly חָתּוּ גברים בְּשִׁ ; the two verbs parallel, as Is. 20, 5. 37, 27 al. האל המאזרני חיל ψ. 18, 33 [אזרו חיל

5. עד וג'] lit. '*even to* the barren—she beareth seven' = even the barren beareth seven. עד recurs in the same sense Job 25, 5 'lo, *even to* the moon, it doth not shine.' For חָדְלוּ עַד (חדל absol. as Dt. 15, 11), Reifm. Klo. Bu. Now. Kitt. would read חָדְלוּ עָבֹד *cease to toil*, probably rightly. The *v.* is evidently related to Jer. 15, 9 אמללה יולדת השבעה : though which is original cannot from a mere comparison of the two passages be determined.

6ᵃ. Dt. 32, 39 אני אמית ואחיה : 6ᵇ. ψ. 30, 4.

ויעל] continuing the ptcp., as ψ. 34, 8. 65, 9 etc.: *Tenses*, §§ 80, 117; GK. §§ 111ᵘ, 116ˣ (*end*).

7. מוריש] To *be poor* is רוּש; so we should expect מֵרִישׁ. ירש (Qal)

means, however, to *impoverish* in Jud. 14, 5 ; and נוֹרָשׁ to *be impoverished*
in Gen. 45, 11 al. (*Lex.* 439ᵇ); so 'contamination of signification
through confusion with רשׁ may be suspected' (Moore, *Judges*, p. 337).

מִשְׁפִּיל אַף מרומם] for this poet. use of אַף, introducing emphatically
a new thought, cf. Dt. 33, 20 קדקד אַף זרוע וטרף. ψ. 65, 14 אַף יתרועעו
יָשִׁירוּ ; and often in II Isaiah, as 42, 13 יצריח אַף יריע. 43, 7 אַף יצרתיו
עשיתיו. Cf. *Lex.* 64ᵇ.

8ᵃ. Hence (with variations) ψ. 113, 7 f. The אשפת (cf. Lam. 4, 5)
is the mound of dung and other rubbish, now called a *mezbele*, or
' place of dung,' which accumulates outside an eastern town or village,
and on which beggars sit, asking alms of passers-by, and, by night,
often sleep. See Wetzstein in Delitzsch's *Hiob* (on 2, 8), quoted in
Davidson's *Job* (in the *Camb. Bible*, p. 14).—In clause *a* the main
division is at אביון (cf. on 1, 28): the two clauses which follow are
parallel, the force of יַנחִלם . . . . . . ו being dependent on, and determined by, להושיב,—'to make them to sit with nobles, *and he will*
(= *and to*) cause them to inherit,' etc. So Is. 10, 2ᵇ. 13, 9ᵇ. 14, 25.
45, 1. ψ. 105, 22. Pr. 5, 2 al.: cf. *Tenses*, § 118; GK. § 114ʳ.

8ᵇ. I. e. because the earth is owned by Yahweh, and He can dispose
of it, as He will. LXX, however, omits 8ᵇ, and in lieu of 9ᵃ reads
διδοὺς εὐχὴν τῷ εὐχομένῳ· καὶ εὐλόγησεν ἔτη δικαίου = נתן לַנֹּדֵר נִדְרוֹ
וּשְׁנוֹת צַדִּיקִים יְבָרֵךְ. Apparently this variation represents an attempt to
accommodate the Song more closely to Ḥannah's position. But, as
We. remarks, it is not in harmony with the general tenor of the Song
(which represents God as granting *more* than the desires or expecta-
tions of His worshippers).

8ᶜ. מצקי] Only here : if correct, from צוּק (Job 28, 2. 29, 6) = יָצַק,
to *pour out, melt, cast,* and so something *cast firm and hard* (cf. יָצוּק,
from יָצַק, Job 41, 15. 16, and מוּצָק Job 38, 38), i. e. a *metal pillar*.

9. רגלי חסידיו ישמר] Ehrlich, cleverly, (Neh. 9, 12) מַעְגְּלֵי חסידיו יָאִיר.
This, it is true, brings the *figure* of 9ᵃ into logical antithesis with that
of 9ᵇ : but the *idea* of 9ᵃ is antithetic to that of 9ᵇ (apart from the
figure by which it is expressed) in MT., and with that the poet may
have been satisfied. On חסידים *godly* (properly, *kind*) see the writer's
Parallel Psalter, p. 443 f.

ידמו] Cf. Jer. 49, 26. 50, 30: also (in Qal) ψ. 31, 18 יִדְּמוּ לִשְׁאֹל.

10. יהוה יחתו מריבו] LXX Κύριος ἀσθενῆ ποιήσει τὸν ἀντίδικον αὐτοῦ, i.e. (cf. 4ᵃ) יָחֵת מְרִיבוֹ (cf. Is. 9, 3) for יְחַתּוּ מְרִיבָיו, which Th. We. Klo. would restore here. But the change is at least not a necessary one; the *casus pendens* (*Tenses*, § 197. 2; GK. § 143ⁿ) is forcible and very idiomatic: see ψ. 10, 5. 11, 4. 46, 5. 89, 3. 90, 10. Is. 34, 3.—The existing text of LXX after this clause exhibits a long insertion borrowed from Jer. 9, 23 f.[1]

עָלָו בשמים ירעם] Cf. ψ. 18, 14. The suffix in עלו (if MT. מְרִיבָיו is retained) is to be referred to individual members of the class מריביו, whom the poet, for the moment, mentally particularizes. There are many such cases in Heb. poetry, e.g. Jer. 9, 7. 10, 4. 16, 6ᵇ. 31, 15 *end* (מֵאָנָה הִנָּחֵם עַל בָּנֶיהָ כִּי אֵינֶנּוּ). Job 18, 5. 21, 19–21. 30. ψ. 7, 3. 17, 11 f. 35, 7 f. 41, 6 f. 84, 8: see further on II 24, 13; GK. § 145ᵐ. Bu. Now. Hpt. would read עֶלְיוֹן בשמים יַרְעֵם *the Most High* in heaven [but משמים *'from* heaven' would be better; on the interchange of ב and מ see Introd. § 4. 1 c *b* γ] will *break them* (ψ. 2, 9).

יְ״י עֹז לעמו יתן] ψ. 29, 11 יִתֵּן עֹז לְ׳.

וְיָרֵם] i.e., as pointed, *that he may exalt*. But the sense is forced: and probably וְיָרָם should be read. Cf. *Tenses*, § 174.

מלכו] So ψ. 18, 51; מלכי ψ. 2, 6.—It is plain that this verse, at any rate, cannot have been spoken by Hannah, even granting that the allusion is to the *ideal* king. The ideal itself, in a case like the present, presupposes the actual (notice especially the expression *His anointed*); and the thoughts of the prophets of Israel can only have risen to the conception of an ideal king after they had witnessed the establishment of the monarchy in their midst. Far more probably, however, the reference is to the actual king. And indeed in style and tone the Song throughout bears the marks of a later age than that of Hannah. Nor do the thoughts appear as the natural expression of one in Hannah's position: observe, for instance, the prominence given to 'the bows of the mighty are broken:' and contrast in this respect the *Magnificat* (Luke 1, 46–55), where though elements are *borrowed* from this Song, they are subordinated to the plan of the whole, and the first thought, after the opening expression of thankfulness, is 'For

---

[1] Comp. the insertion in ψ. 14, 3 LXX from *Romans* 3, 13–18.

He hath regarded *the lowliness of His handmaiden.*' The presence of the Song here does not prove more than that it was *attributed* to Ḥannah at the time when the Books of Samuel were compiled: indeed, as its position in LXX and MT. is not the same, its insertion may even belong to a later period still. A sober criticism, while not asserting categorically that the Song *cannot* be by Ḥannah, will recognize that its specific character and contents point to an occasion of a different kind as that upon which it was composed. The central thought of the Song is the abasement of the lofty and the elevation of the lowly, which the poet illustrates in a series of studied and well-balanced contrasts, *vv.* 4–8. On the ground of some humiliation which, as it seems, has recently befallen his foes, he breaks out *v.* 1 in a tone of triumphant exultation, and bids those whose sole thought was how to magnify their own importance recollect that God's all-seeing eye was ever upon them, *v.* 3. He points *vv.* 4–8 to the instances which experience affords of the proud being abased, and the humble exalted. The poem ends *vv.* 9–10 with an expression of confidence for the future. Human strength is no guarantee of success. Such as set themselves in opposition to Yahweh and seek to thwart His purposes only come to ruin: those devoted to Him are secure. Yahweh *judges* the earth, and in so doing designs the triumph of His own anointed king. From the last words it was inferred by Ewald[1], that the poet is a king, who alludes to himself in the third person. But the tone is national rather than individual; and Smend[2] may be right in supposing it to have been spoken originally in the name of the people, and intended to depict Israel's triumph over the heathen and the ungodly.

11ᵃ. Read with LXX וַתֵּלֶךְ הָרָמָתָה; and connect with 1, 28ᵃ, as shewn on p. 22.

עַל] Several MSS. read אֶל. See, however, on 1, 10.

11ᵇ. היה משרת] *was* ministering (at the time in question, and with which the narrative is about to deal): cf. Gen. 37, 2. Ex. 3, 1. 2 Ki. 6, 8: *Tenses,* § 135. 5. Cf. LXX ἦν λειτουργῶν; Luke 1, 10 ἦν προσευχόμενον. 4, 20. 11, 14. 13, 10. Acts 1, 14. 10, 24. 12, 20 etc.

---

[1] *Die Dichter des Alten Bundes,* I. 1 (1866), p. 157 ff.
[2] *ZATW.* 1888, p. 144.

13–14. Is what is described here an abuse on the part of the priests, or a rightful due ?   *V.* 15 f. clearly describe an abuse ; and גם at the beginning, which expresses a *climax*, shews that *v.* 13 f. must describe an abuse likewise (We.).   משפט, therefore, in MT. will denote merely *custom*, not *right*, and the clause will read, 'And the custom of the priests with the priests (was this)[1] :' since Th., however, practically all Commentators (including even Keil) have followed LXX, Vulg. in joining 13ᵃ to 12ᵇ, and in reading with LXX (παρὰ τοῦ λαοῦ), for הבהנים, מֵאֵת הָעָם את העם הַבֹּהֵן (cf. on 1, 24 : Pesh. Targ. and 9 Heb. MSS. also read מאת, but with the pl. הכהנים): 'they knew not Yahweh, or the right (i.e. the rightful due) of *the priest from* the people :' comp. esp. Dt. 18, 3 וזה יהיה משפט הכהנים מאת העם מאת זבחי הזבח.

It is objected by Ehrlich to this view, that when the first of two or more nouns has את, all must have it, so that ואת משפט וג' would be needed here. It is true, this is the general rule (e.g. Ex. 35, 10–19. Jos. 21, 13–18) : but there are exceptions to it : not only Ex. 24, 12 (where the ו of והתורה והמצוה is explained by Ehrlich as the ו of 'concomitance' [*Lex.* 253ᵃ]), but also Ex. 12, 28 [18 MSS. and Sam. ואת אהרן], 32, 2. 1 S. 7, 3 (text dub.). 8, 14. 18, 4ᵇ [?rd. וממדיו Ehrl.]. II 19, 6. 1 Ki. 1, 10 [10 MSS. ואת]. 44. 10, 4. 15, 15. 2 Ki. 10, 11 ; and in later Hebrew (A. M. Wilson, *Hebraica*, 1890, p. 220), 1 Ch. 1, 32. 2, 13–15. 8, 1. Ezr. 9, 3. Neh. 9, 6. Possibly there are other instances : but these, even disregarding the textually doubtful ones, seem sufficient to shew that the rule, though observed generally, was not absolute.

כל איש וג'] The constr. is unusual.   זֹבֵחַ is to be regarded as a ptcp. absolute (cf. Gen. 4, 15. II 23, 3. Prov. 23, 24. Job 41, 18 MT.), *all men sacrificing = if,* or *whenever, a man sacrificed,* etc. (see GK. §§ 116ʷ, 159ⁱ); the pred. is then introduced by the pf. and *waw* conv. ובא (GK. § 112ᵒᵒ), precisely as, in an analogous case, after אם (Gen. 31, 8 וילדו . . . אם יאמר *if ever* he said . . ., *then* the flock *used* to bear . . . : *Tenses,* § 123 β, GK. § 159ʳ). In other words, כל איש זבח זבח is the syntactical equivalent of איש אם יזבח זבח. The constr. would be more normal, if כל איש were preceded by והיה : see Jud. 19, 30 ; Ex. 33, 7ᵇ.

כבשל] The implicit subject is הַמְבַשֵּׁל : see on 16, 4, and comp. 11, 2.

---

[1] Though we should rather in this case expect וזה משפט . . . : cf. וזה דְּבַר . . . Dt. 15, 2. 19, 4. 1 Ki. 9, 15 ; Nu. 8, 4 . . . וזה מעשׂה. 1 Ki. 7, 28.

So, after a כ of comparison, Jud. 14, 6. 2 S. 3, 24. Is. 10, 14. Zech. 12, 10. 13, 9.

והמזלג שלש השנים] lit. *the prong, the three teeth* [1]—a case of apposition (*Tenses,* § 188; GK. § 131ᵒ). שָׁלֹשׁ (not שלשה), שֵׁן being fem.: cf. שְׁלֹשׁ הֶעָרִים Nu. 35, 14; שְׁלֹשׁ הַשָּׁנִים Lev. 25, 21. To be sure, in 14, 5 שֵׁן in the *metaph.* sense of a *pointed rock* is masc.; whether it was also in that of the *tooth* of a prong, is more than we can say[2]. If it was, we must read either והמזלג שלשה השנים, or (We.) ומזלג שלשה שנים[2].

14 f. Observe how in these verses the tenses are throughout frequentatives (continuing 13 וּבָא).

בו] can only be rendered *therewith:* the Versions express the sense *for himself,* which is more suitable, but requires לו for בו.

שם בשלה] Tautologous. LXX for שם express לִזְבֹּחַ לִיהוה.

15. יְקַטְרוּן] The ן is the original termination of 3 pl. impf. preserved in classical Arabic (in the *indicative* mood), Aramaic (usually), Ethiopic, Phoenician[3].

In the OT. it occurs sporadically (305 times altogether), though the principle regulating its occurrence is difficult to determine. It is not a mark of antiquity, for, though it occurs seldom in the latest books, those in which it occurs with greatest comparative frequency are not (upon any view) the most ancient (56 times in Dt., 37 in Isaiah, 15 in 1–2 Kings, 23 in Job, 12 in Genesis, 7 in Numbers, 15 in a single Psalm, 104). Further, while it sometimes abounds in particular sections (e.g. Gen. 18, 28–32: Joel 2, 4–9), it is absent from others belonging to the same narrative, or of a similar character (e.g. 9 times in the Laws, Ex. 20–23, never in the Laws, Lev. 17–26). From its frequency in Dt., Job, the Book of Isaiah, and some of the Psalms, it may be inferred that it was felt to be a fuller, more emphatic form

---

[1] Cf. the ὀβελὸς τρικώλιος, mentioned in a sacrificial inscription of Cos (*Journ. of Hellenic Studies,* ix. 335 = Paton and Hicks, *Inscriptions of Cos,* 1891, p. 82); and the τριώβολον, which according to Eustathius on *Il.* i. 463 (*ib.* p. 327) was preferred by the Greeks as a sacrificial implement to the πεμπώβολον. (καρπόω in the same inscr., see p. 336, illustrates the use of κάρπωσις, ὁλοκάρπωσις in LXX.)

[2] If Albrecht's explanation (*ZAW.* 1896, p. 76, see p. 60) of שֵׁן in 14, 5 being masc. is correct, it would not follow for שֵׁן here.

[3] Cooke, *NSI.* 5, 22. 33, 6.

than that in ordinary use, and hence was sometimes preferred in an elevated or rhetorical style. In 1 Sam. it occurs 8 times—2, 15. 16. 22 (*bis*). 23. 9, 13 (*bis*). 11, 9 : in 2 Sam. once only, not in the narrative, but in the Psalm 22, 39.

קטר, though rendered conventionally *burn*, does not mean to burn so as to destroy (which is שָׂרַף), but to *cause to become sweet smoke* (קְטֹרֶת: cf. the Greek κνίση): comp. the Arab. *qatara* (of meat), *to exhale odour in roasting*. The word is always used of burning either a sacrificial offering (Lev. 1, 9 etc.) or incense (Ex. 30, 7); and would be better rendered, for distinctness, as in Driver and White's *Leviticus* (in Haupt's *Sacred Books of the OT.*), consume in sweet smoke. In P (always) and Chr. (mostly) the verb is used in the Hif'il; but in the older language the Pi'el is usual (e.g. Amos 4, 5); and probably both here and in *v.* 16 we should vocalize יְקַטְּרוּן (notice in *v.* 16 קַטֵּר יַקְטִרוּן; קַטֵּר יַקְטִרוּן is of a *very* anomalous type; GK. § 113*ᵂ*, second sentence).

וּבָא] LXX rightly ἤρχετο. The pf. with *waw* conv. appears similarly after בטרם, though of reiteration in *present* time, in Ex. 1, 19ᵇ before the midwife comes to them וילדו *they are wont to bear*.

16. ויאמר] This should strictly be וְיָאמֵר, in accordance with the other tenses before and after : but Hebrew is sometimes negligent in such cases to maintain the frequentative tense throughout; see Jud. 12, 5 f.; Jer. 6, 17; and *Tenses*, § 114. However, ויאמר might be a scribal error for ואמר (so GK. § 112ˡˡ; Smith's וַיֹּאמֶר is against the usage of Heb. prose).

קטר יקטירון כיום החלב] 'Let them *burn* (emph.) the fat first, and (then) take,' etc. The inf. abs. strengthens the verb in a manner which may often be represented in our idiom by the use of italics. In כיום, the consciousness of יום is lost, and it is used as a mere adverb of time, especially to express the present time, as contrasted with the future, i. e. (in our idiom) *first of all, first*. So Gen. 25, 31 מכרה כיום את בכרתך לי sell me *first* (before I give thee the pottage) thy birthright, 33. 1 Ki. 22, 5 inquire, I pray, *first* at the word of Yahweh. See Ges. *Thes.* s.v., *Lex.* 409ᵇ h, and We. p. 37 *note*.

כאשר תאוה נפשך] Similarly II 3, 21 בכל אשר תאוה נפשך, Dt. 12, 20. 14, 26. 1 Ki. 11, 37 al. Both אָוָה (in Pi'el), and the subst. אַוָּה (23, 20), are rarely used except in conjunction with נפש.

ואמר לו כי עתה תתן] 'And he would say to him, "Thou shalt give it me now."' With this reading, כי, standing before the direct narration, is like ὅτι *recitativum* (e.g. Luke 4, 21), and ُﻝَ, ﭟ (constantly),

and cannot be represented in English except by inverted commas: so
10, 19 MT. Gen. 29, 33. Jos. 2, 24. 1 Ki. 1, 13. 2 Ki. 8, 13 al. The
Qrê and 17 MSS., however, for לו read לא (so LXX) 'And he would
say, No; for (= but) thou shalt give it now' (cf. 12, 12 : II 16, 18 al.).
The latter is more pointed, and deserves the preference. Targ. here
agrees with MT.; Pesh. Vulg. express *both* readings [1].

לקחתי] The *bare* perf. in the apod. is uncommon and emphatic :
Tenses, § 136 γ : Nu. 32, 23. 'And if not, I take it by force!'

17. כי נאצו וג'] 'for the men (viz. Eli's sons) contemned,' etc. : see
Nu. 16, 30ᵇ י"י את האלה האנשים נאצו כי.   האנשים (with the *art.*)
denotes men who have been in some manner specified (e.g. 6, 10.
Ex. 5, 9), not men in general.

18. נער] accus., *as* a youth, etc.: see GK. § 118ᵠ, and on *v.* 33.

אפור בד] for the constr. in the accus. after חגור, see GK. § 121ᵈ;
and cf. 17, 5. On the 'ephod' see *DB.* (Driver), *EB.* (Moore), and
the writer's *Exodus* (1911), p. 312 f.

19. והעלתה . . . , תעשה] '*used* to make . . . and bring up:' Gen. 2, 6
האדמה פני כל את והשקה יעלה ואד.   הימים זבח, as 1, 21 : cf. on 1, 3.

20. והלכו . . . ואמר . . . וברך] 'and Eli *would* bless . . ., and say
. . ., and they *would* go to his place.'

ישם] LXX ἀποτίσαι, i.e. יְשַׁלֵּם *make good :* cf. Ex. 21, 36 (likewise
followed by תחת). With MT. cf. Gen. 4, 25 (שת). 45, 7.

שאל] Difficult syntactically. As the text stands, the subj. can be
only the implicit הַשֹּׁאֵל (see on 16, 4) 'which he that asked asked' =
which was asked: but the passage is not one in which this impersonal
construction would be naturally in place. Either, with We., we must
point as a ptcp. pass. שָׁאֻל *asked for* = *lent* *to* (see 1, 28: the masc.
ad sensum, the שְׁאֵלָה being Samuel), or we must suppose that שאל
is an error for שְׁאֵלָה ('in lieu of the petition which *she* asked for [2]
Yahweh'). The former gives the better sense, though אשר with a bare
ptcp. is not very common (Dt. 1, 4. 1 Ki. 5, 13). If the latter be right,

---

[1] Similar variations occur in other passages: thus Jos. 5, 14 MT. Vulg. Targ.
לא; LXX, Pesh. לו : 1 Ki. 11, 22 MT. Vulg. Targ. לא; LXX לו; Pesh. both.
Cf. on *v.* 3.

[2] Inadvertently quoted by Jastrow (*JBLit.* 1900, p. 87) 'asked *of.*' Of course
I do not suppose this to be the meaning of שאל ל.

we must suppose the double reference of שָׁאֵל to be played upon: the
'petition' which was asked *of* Yahweh in 1, 17. 27 was also asked *for*
Him. The Versions merely guess: LXX, Pesh. Vulg. 'which thou
didst lend,' unsuitably: Targ. very freely 'which was asked from before
Yahweh.' Bu. Sm. Now. Kit. Dh. read הִשְׁאִלָה, rendering, 'in return
for the *loan* (so EVV.), which *she hath lent* unto Yahweh;' cf. 1, 28.
'Loan' for שְׁאֵלָה may be right: cf. *NHWB.* iv. 491ᵇ; PS. col. 4008.

והלכו למקומו] '*they* would go to *his* place' is not in accordance with
Hebrew style. LXX והלך האיש למקומו: 12 MSS. and Pesh. והלכו
למקומם. Either of these readings *may* be original: but probably We.
is right in concluding והלך למקומו to be the original reading: in MT.
the verb was read as a plur. and so became והלכו, LXX treated it as
a singular, and supplied 'the man.'

21. כי פקד] obviously cannot be right: the fact that Yahweh visited
Ḥannah cannot form the *ground* of what is related in *v.* 20. Read,
with LXX, Pesh. (and AV. implicitly): וַיִּפְקֹד. כ and ו are confused
elsewhere: e.g. Is. 39, 1ᵇ וישמע, for which LXX, Pesh. and the parallel
in 2 Ki. 20, 12 have rightly כי שמע; and Jer. 37, 16 where כי בא is
evidently an error for ויבא (LXX καὶ ἦλθεν).

עם י'] i.e. at His sanctuary: cf. Dt. 22, 2, and *Lex.* 768ᵃ 3.

22. וישמע] as 1, 3: 'and he heard from time to time' (Dr. Weir).

את הנשים וג'] See Ex. 38, 8. The entire clause (from ואת אשר)
is not found in LXX, and is probably not part of the original text (the
context speaks of a היכל with *doors*, not of an אהל: 1, 9. 3, 3. 15).
הצבאות, both here and in Ex., is paraphrased in Targ. Pesh. *who
prayed* (or *who came to pray*): Vulg. renders here *quae observabant*, in
Ex. *quae excubabant.* But צבא is used often peculiarly in the ritual
legislation of the Pent. (the 'Priests' Code') of the service of the
Levites about the Tent of Meeting; and Ex. 38, 8 and here expresses
the performance of menial duties by the women. In the fragments of
a Targum published by Lagarde (*Prophetae Chaldaice,* 1872, p. xiv)
from the margin of the Cod. Reuchl., there appears an endeavour to
palliate the sin of Eli's sons (as described in the existing Hebrew text):
ספ[ר] אח[ר] : וית דמשהן ית קרבני נשיא דמדכירן דאתן לצלאה (*delayed* the
women's offerings). Comp. Bacher, 'On the Targum to the Prophets,'
in the *ZDMG.* 1874, p. 23.

אהל מועד] the Tent of Meeting. The sense in which מועד was understood is explained in Ex. 25, 22. 29, 42.

23. אשר וג'] '*for that, in that* (15, 15. 20, 42) I hear the accounts of you (as) evil, from' etc. רעים, not הרעים, like (דבתם רעה Gen. 37, 2; דבת הארץ רעה Nu. 14, 37; יאכלו לחמם טמא Ezek. 4, 13 (a *tertiary* predicate). But LXX do not express the words; the sense is clear without them; and they may have been originally (Lö. Bu. Now.) a marginal gloss (without את) on כדברים האלה. In this case, of course, אשר will mean simply *which.* Otherwise אֶת־דִּבַּתְכֶם רָעָה (Gen. 37, 2) might well have stood here (Ehrlich), and would yield an excellent sense.

מאת כל העם אלה] 'from all the people, (even) these.' An un-paralleled juxtaposition. Why not מאת כל העם הזה, as uniformly elsewhere? LXX have παντὸς τοῦ λαοῦ Κυρίου, whence We., remarking that in a later time אלהים was apt to be substituted for יהוה (e.g. 2 Ch. 10, 15; 18, 5; 22, 12; 23, 9 compared with 1 Ki. 12, 15. 22, 6; 2 Ki. 11, 3. 10), would restore מאת כל עם יהוה (cf. *v.* 24 *end*). This, however, leaves the article in העם unexplained: and it is simpler to suppose that אלה (once, no doubt, written אל, as still eight times in the Pent., and 1 Ch. 20, 8, and in Phoenician [1]) has arisen by ditto-graphy from the following אל: so Bu. Now. Sm. Ehrl.

מֵאֵת] lit. *from with* = παρὰ with a gen.: so with קנה *to buy*, שאל, לקח (8, 10), etc.; see *Lex.* 86b.

24. אשר וג'] 'which I hear Yahweh's people to be spreading.' So already Rashi, comparing Ex. 36, 6 ויעבירו קול במחנה. Elsewhere, it is true, where this idiom occurs, it is accompanied by an indication of the locality *in* or *through* which the proclamation is 'made to pass' (as Ex. *l. c.;* 2 Ch. 30, 5 בכל ישראל; 36, 22 (=Ezr. 1, 1); Ezr. 10, 7; Neh. 8, 15: Lev. 25, 9 תעביר שופר בכל ארצכם): but the alternative rendering (AV. RV.) '(Ye) *make* the people of Israel *to transgress*' is doubly questionable: (1) אתם is desiderated after מעבירים (see on 6, 3); (2) עבר, when it signifies *to transgress*, is always followed by an accus. of the law or precept 'overpast,' e.g. את פי י"י 15, 24. Nu.

---

[1] Cooke, *NSI.* 5, 22 אלנם הקדשם אל these holy gods; 27, 3 הסמלם האל these images; 45, 2 במקדשים אל; and *CIS.* i. 14, 5 מנחת אל these offerings.

14, 41; תורת Is. 24, 5 (comp. the Commentators on ψ. 17, 3ᵇ), and in the Hif. does not occur in this sense at all. The case is one, however, in which the integrity of the text is reasonably open to suspicion.

25. 'If a man sinneth against a man, God will mediate (for him):
But if a man sin against Yahweh (emph.), who can intercede[1]
for him?'

I.e. For an offence of man against man, God may interpose and arbitrate (viz. through His representative, the judge): for an offence against Yahweh, there is no third party able to do this. For אלהים as signifying, not the judge as such, but the judge *as the mouthpiece of a Divine sentence*, see Ex. 21, 6. 22, 7 f.: and comp. *ib.* 18, 16, where the *judicial* decisions given by Moses are described as the 'statutes and laws of God.' Ideas parallel to this occur among other ancient nations; comp. Sir Henry Maine's *Ancient Law*, ch. i, and the expression applied to judges in Homer: οἵτε θέμιστας Πρὸς Διὸς εἰρύαται (Il. 1. 239). The play between פִּלֵּל *to mediate* (see ψ. 106, 30 ויעמד פינחס ויפלל, where PBV. 'and *prayed*' is quite false), and התפלל *to interpose as mediator*, specially by means of entreaty (Gen. 20, 17), cannot be preserved in English. The idea of mediation or arbitration appears in other derivatives (rare) of פלל; as פלילים Ex. 21, 22. Dt. 32, 31; פלילה Is. 16, 3. In וּפִלְלוֹ the suffix must have the force of a dative, *for him* (GK. § 117ˣ; Ew. § 315ᵇ); but probably, with We., וּפִלְלוּ should be pointed (so Lö. Bu. Now.): the *plur.* would be in accordance with the construction of אלהים, as thus applied, in Ex. 22, 8ᵇ. In אם ליהוה יחטא notice the emph. position of ליהוה. It is the rule with words like אם, לא, למען, פן etc. for the verb to follow immediately; when another word follows immediately, it is because some emphasis attaches to it: see e.g. 6, 9. Lev. 1, 3. 10. Nu. 20, 18.

The general sense is well expounded by We. (after Ew. *Hist.* ii. 581 [Eng. Tr. 412]): For the settlement of ordinary cases arising between man and man, there is a מְפַלֵּל (arbiter), viz. Elohim (speaking through His representative, the judge): if, however, Yahweh is the plaintiff,

---

[1] Or, perhaps (Bu. Now. Sm.), *act the mediator:* but התפלל elsewhere means only to mediate by *entreaty* or *prayer*.

He cannot also (as Elohim) be the מְפַלֵּל. As the priest in point of fact is the judge, this means—the play between 'Yahweh' and 'Elohim' being disregarded: 'the sin of the priest against God cannot be adjusted before the tribunal of the priest, but incurs the direct vengeance of Heaven.'

ולא ישמעו] See on 1, 7.

כי חפץ וג׳] Cf. Jud. 13, 23. Grotius (quoted by Th.) illustrates the thought from Aeschylus (*ap.* Plato, *Rep.* ii. 380 A):

θεὸς μὲν αἰτίαν φύει βροτοῖς
ὅταν κακῶσαι δῶμα παμπήδην θέλῃ.

26. הלך וגדל וטוב]=*continued growing greater and better*: cf. II 3, 1 הולך וחזק . . . הולכים ודלים (which shews that גָּדֵל וָטוֹב are adjectives). 15, 12. Pr. 4, 18. Jon. 1, 11. 13. Est. 9, 4; after ויהי, Ex. 19, 19. 2 Ch. 17, 12: GK. § 113[u] *end.* It is possible, however, that טוב may be used here of bodily physique, and mean *goodly* (i.e. *fine and comely*), as 9, 2. Gen. 6, 2. Ex. 2, 2. 1 Ki. 20, 3 (so Dhorme; cf. Ehrlich).

עם] *in the estimation of*, as II 6, 22. Cf. Luke 2, 52.

27. הנגלה נגליתי] i.e. 'Did I indeed reveal myself to the house of thy father, or not, that ye, his descendants, have thus scorned me?' An impassioned question, expressive of surprise, as though the fact asked about were doubtful (cf. Hitzig on Job 41, 1), not to be weakened by treating הֲ as though it were = הֲלֹא. The inf. abs. adds force to the question: GK. § 113[q]. There is no occasion to treat the ה in הנגלה as dittographed from the ה in יהוה.

בהיותם וג׳] MT. 'when they belonged in Egypt *to* the house of Pharaoh.' But this is unnatural; and it can hardly be doubted that עֲבָדִים has dropped out after במצרים, corresponding to LXX δούλων (cf. Targ. משתעבדין ל). Comp. Lev. 26, 13. Dt. 6, 21.

28. וּבָחֹר] GK. § 113[z]: Ew. § 351[c].

לִי לְכֹהֵן] As Ehrlich observes, the order is correct: see Gen. 12, 19 לי לאשה; 16, 3. 28, 9, and often לו לאשה; 29, 29 לה לשפחה; Jud. 17, 5 ויהי לו לכהן; לי לעם Ex. 6, 7 (cf. Dt. 29, 12. *ch.* 12, 22. II 7, 23. 24, and frequently); ψ. 94, 22 (for cases of the opposite order, induced doubtless by the rhythm, see ψ. 33, 12 [לו לנחלה would here be heavy]. 132, 13. Is. 49, 5. Job 13, 24. 30, 21: *Lex.* 512[b]). The fact, however, that a family, and not an individual, is referred to suggests that we should (with LXX ἱερατεύειν) vocalize לְכַהֵן (Bu.). Ehrlich objects to this that we always have לְכַהֵן לִי (Ex. 28, 41. 29, 1 al.): but might not לִי be prefixed for emphasis? Otherwise the tribe (אתו=*it*, not *him*), as a whole, must be regarded as 'priest' to Yahweh; cf. the sing. numbers in Dt. 31, 16ᵇ–18. Is. 5, 26–30. 17, 13ᵇ–14ᵃ, etc.

לַעֲלוֹת] is naturally Qal (LXX, Pesh. Vulg. Ke. Klo. Bu. Now.), though it *might* be Hif. (Targ. Th.) for לְהַעֲלוֹת (comp. *v.* 33. II 19, 19 לַעֲבִיר; Ex. 13, 21 לַנְחֹתָם; Nu. 5, 22 לַנְפִּל; לַצְבוֹת; Dt. 1, 33 לַרְאֹתְכֶם; 26, 12 לַעְשֹׁר); however, as the contraction is not common (about twenty instances altogether in MT.[1]), and there is nothing here to suggest or require the Hif., the latter is less probable. *To go up* upon the altar, i. e. upon a ledge beside it, as Ex. 20, 26; 1 Ki. 12, 33; 2 Ki. 16, 12 *end;* 23, 9: conversely, ירד is used of *coming down* from it, Lev. 9, 22: cf. 1 Ki. 1, 53.

לִשְׂאֵת אֵפוֹד] 'to *bear*,—not, to *wear*,—the ephod before me.' So always. Cf. *DB.* i. 726ᵇ; Moore in *EB.* ii. 1307; the writer's *Exodus*, 313; and Kennedy's note here. For אִשֵּׁי יהוה, cf. Dt. 18, 1.

29. מָעוֹן] Untranslateable: if מָעוֹן is right, read בִּמְעוֹנִי; מְעוֹנִי (RV., implicitly) is not sufficient[2]. מָעוֹן is a word found mostly in poetry,

---

[1] To those given in the text add II 18, 3 Kt. לְעֹזִיר; 2 Ki. 9, 15 Kt. לַגִּיד; Is. 3, 8 לַמְרוֹת; 23, 11 לַשְׁמֵד; 29, 15 לַסְתֵּר; 33, 1 (corrupt) בַּלּוֹתֵךְ; Jer. 27, 20 בַּגְלוֹתוֹ; 37, 12 לַחְלֵק; 39, 7 לְבִיא; Am. 8, 4 לַשְׁבִּית; *ψ.* 26, 7 לַשְׁמֵעַ; 73, 20 (?) בָּעִיר; 78, 17 לַמְרוֹת. Pr. 31, 3 לַמְחוֹת; Dan. 11, 35 לַלְבֵּן. Qoh. 5, 5 לַחְטִיא. Neh. 10, 39 בַּעְשֵׂר. 2 Ch. 31, 10 לְבִיא. (In some of these instances the text may be doubtful, or the punctuation as Hif. unnecessary.) Comp. in the Nif. לַעֲנֹת Ex. 10, 3. בְּכֻשְׁלוֹ Pr. 24, 17. בַּעֲטֵף Lam. 2, 11. לָאוֹר Job 33, 30; and (as pointed) לֵרָאוֹת Ex. 34, 24. Dt. 31, 11. Is. 1, 12: also בֶּהָרֵג Ez. 26, 15.

[2] בֵּית, or הַבַּיִת (absol.), never means 'in the house:' by custom the use of the accus. to express rest in a place is restricted to cases in which *a noun in the genitive follows*, as בֵּית יְ', בֵּית הַמֶּלֶךְ, בֵּית אָבִיךְ. So פֶּתַח אֹהֶל מוֹעֵד (*v.* 22), פֶּתַח אׇהֳלוֹ (Ex. 33, 10) *at* the entrance of his tent: but *at the entrance* (absolutely) would be בַּפֶּתַח, not הַפֶּתַח simply. So בֵּית־לֶחֶם, בֵּית־אֵל may denote 'in Bethel,' 'in Bethlehem:' but 'in Gibeon,' 'in Dan' must be expressed by בְּדָן, בְּגִבְעוֹן (see 2 Ki. 10, 29ᵇ). Where a word like שִׁלֹה, יְרוּשָׁלַם seems to denote *at* Shiloh, *at* Jerusalem, it will be found that a verb of motion always precedes, of which the subst. expresses the goal: so e.g. II 20, 3; Dt. 3, 1; Jud. 21, 12. Hence קֹדֶשׁ *ψ.* 134, 2 is '*to* the sanctuary.' (Exceptions to what has been here said may be found in MT., but they are very rare: e.g. Is. 16, 2. 2 Ch. 33, 20.)

and the more elevated prose (ψ. 26, 8 מָעוֹן בֵּיתֶךָ, of the Temple; Dt. 20, 15 al. מָעוֹן קָדְשֶׁךָ, of heaven): so it would not be unsuitable. The objections that its *absolute* use is late (מָעוֹנוֹ 2 Ch. 36, 15†), and that it is here superfluous, are not·cogent. LXX (omitting אֲשֶׁר צִוִּיתִי) have ἵνα τί ἐπέβλεψας ... ἀναιδεῖ ὀφθαλμῷ; i.e. הַבֵּטְתָּ (or תַּבִּיט) and (Klo.) מָעֵיֶן, '*Why hast thou looked* (or, *dost thou look*) *upon ... with an evil eye?*' lit. *eyeing* it (18, 9). So Bu. Sm. (not Now.). But מעון is a very doubtful restoration.

להבריאכם] Read probably either the *Nif.* לְהִבָּרַאֲכֶם (Bu.), or לְהַבְרִיאָם (Ehrlich).

לעמי] This again cannot be right. 'We might easily alter ישראל לעמי to ישראל עמי, but the לְ appears also in לִפְנֵי of LXX' (We.). Perhaps לִפְנֵי,—or לְעֵינֵי, though ἔμπροσθεν does not elsewhere represent this,—is the true reading; it is accepted by Hitzig (on Amos 2, 13), Bu. Now.; the meaning will be, *in full view of me*,—aggravating the slight.

30. אָמוֹר אָמַרְתִּי] = '*I said*' (emph.). The intention, which had afterwards to be abandoned, is emphasized by the inf. abs.

יתהלכו לפני] To *walk before* any one is to live and move openly before him (12, 2. 2 Ki. 20, 3); esp. in such a way as (*a*) to *deserve*, and consequently (*b*) to *enjoy*, his approval and favour. The expression is used chiefly of walking before God; and then sometimes one of these ideas is the more prominent, sometimes the other. Thus in Gen. 17, 1, and prob. in 24, 40. 48, 15 the thought of (*a*) predominates (LXX εὐαρεστεῖν ἐναντίον or ἐνώπιον); here, *v.* 35, and ψ. 56, 14. 116, 9 [*shall*, not *will*] the thought of (*b*) predominates. (The expression is not so strong as התהלך אֵת הָאֱלֹהִים Gen. 5, 22. 24. 6, 9.)

31. הנה ימים באים וג'] A formula occurring besides only 2 Ki. 20, 17 (=Is. 39, 6), and in the prophecies of Amos and Jeremiah.

ונדעתי את זרעך] Cf. for the figure Jud. 21, 6 נגרע היום שבט אחד מישראל and Jer. 48, 25 נגדעה קרן מואב וזרעו נשברה. LXX vocalized זַרְעֶךָ; but this by no means agrees so well as MT. וְזְרֹעֲךָ with the *figure* implied in ונדעתי. וְזְרֹעַ metaph. of *strength*, as Job 22, 8 וְאִישׁ; שבר זרע רשע ψ. 10, 15; זרוע לו הארץ 83, 9.

32. צר מעון] Again, if מעון is right (cf. on 29), we must read either מְעוֹנִי (RV.) or בִּמְעוֹנִי (RV. *m.*). Eli, however, whose death is recorded

in 4, 21, did not survive any time when the temple at Shiloh was
unfortunate, and Israel in general prosperous. The clause must
consequently be corrupt. Bö. suggested צֻר מָעוֹז 'and thou shalt look
for *a rock of defence:*' but הביט with an accus. is not to look *for*
something non-existent, or not visible, but to look *at,* or behold,
something actually in view. No satisfactory emendation has been
proposed.

בכל אשר] lit. 'in the whole of (that,) as to which . . .' = 'in all
wherein . . .' בכל אשר is commonly followed by a verb of motion, as
14, 47, in which case it = *wherever.*

ייטיב את] היטיב with a *personal* object is usually construed with ל or
עם (Gen. 12, 16; 32, 10. 13 al.): the construction with an accus. is
chiefly Deuteronomic (Dt. 8, 16. 28, 63. 30, 5; so Jer. 18, 10. 32,
40. 41; also Zech. 8, 15. ψ. 51, 20). A *subject* to ייטיב is desiderated.
We must either suppose that יהוה has fallen out after it (Bu. Now. Kit.:
observe that EVV. supply 'God' in italics), or read איטיב (Sm. Bu.
alt., Dhorme).

33. 'Yet *one* I will not cut off belonging to thee from mine altar,' etc.
לך is the dat. of reference, as often in similar phrases: II 3, 29. 1 Ki.
2, 4. 9, 5. 14, 10 al. (*Lex.* 512ᵇ 5).

מעם] Cf. Ex. 21, 14.

לכלות ונ'] Cf. Lev. 26, 16 (certain diseases) מְכַלּוֹת עינים וּמְדִיבֹת נפש;
Dt. 28, 65 כליון עינים וראבון נפש.

לאדיב] for לְהַאֲדִיב (on *v.* 28), from [אדב] = דאב. ארב, however, is
not substantiated elsewhere, in either Hebrew or the cognate languages:
it is probable therefore that א is merely an error for ה, and that וּלְהָדִיב
(corresponding to מדיבת in Lev. *l.c.*) should be restored. Cf. Jer. 25, 3
השכים for אשכים.

עיניך . . . נפשך] The איש, no doubt, is Abiathar, who escaped the
massacre of the priests *ch.* 22, was David's faithful attendant during
his lifetime, but was removed from the priesthood by Solomon, and
banished by him from Jerusalem, on account of the part taken by him
in the attempt of Adonijah to secure the throne (see 1 Ki. 2, 27). If
MT. be right, the reference must be to the father, supposed to be
conscious of the fortunes of his descendant, and suffering with him.
Such a sense, however, seems to be one which is scarcely likely to

have been in the writer's mind (contrast Job 14, 21). LXX read
נפשׁו . . . עיניו, the pronouns referring to Abiathar himself, the end of
whose life was passed in disappointment and vexation. This is
preferable (so We. Th. Klo. etc.).

מרבית] *the increase* (viz. generally, so far as none are specially
exempted). Or, perhaps, as 1 Ch. 12, 29, *the greater part.*

ימותו אנשׁים] ' will die *as men* ' (= in the flower of their age, AV.),
אנשׁים being an (implicit) accus., defining their condition at the time of
dying. So Is. 65, 20 בן מאה שׁנה ימות will die *as* a man 100 years
old; Lev. 20, 20 (*Tenses,* § 161. 3; GK. § 118q). But, though the
grammatical construction is unexceptionable, אנשׁים does not signify
adults, in contradistinction to men of any other age; and LXX has ἐν
ῥομφαίᾳ ἀνδρῶν; in all probability therefore a word has fallen out in
MT., and בְּחֶרֶב אנשׁים should be restored.

35. כאשׁר וג'] for the expression, cf. 14, 7. II 7, 3. 2 Ki. 10, 30.
The clause is attached to what precedes somewhat abruptly, but a
similar abruptness may be observed sometimes in the Books of
Samuel : e. g. 9, 6ᵃ ; 19, 5 ראית ותשׂמח.

35ᵇ. בית נאמן] Cf. 25, 28 (the hope expressed by Abigail).

משׁיחי] The passage, like 2, 10, presupposes the establishment of
the monarchy (משׁיח י": 16, 6; 24, 7. 11 etc.). The original prophecy must have been re-cast by the narrator, and in its new form
coloured by the associations with which he was himself familiar. The
meaning is that the faithful priest will enjoy the royal favour continually.

36. והיה וג'] lit. ' and it shall be, as regards all that are left
(= whoever is left) in thy father's house, he shall come ' etc. The
construction exactly resembles Dt. 20, 11 ; II 15, 35 : and without
כל, Nu. 17, 20 (cf. 16, 7); 1 Ki. 19, 17 (*Tenses,* § 121, *Obs.* 1). The
force of כל is similar to that in *v.* 13. Instead of יבא the sentence
might with equal propriety have been resumed by the pf. and *waw*
conv. וּבָא: see Nu. 21, 8 ; Jud. 11, 31 : the construction with the
impf. is, however, somewhat more flowing, and less formal.

ספחני] ספח is *to attach :* 26, 19. Is. 14, 1 ונסּפחו על בית יעקב : Job
30, 7 *Pu'al* (= to cling together)†. (In Hab. 2, 15 read מְסַפֵּף.)

The interpretation of the entire passage, from *v.* 31, is difficult. In

MT. two troubles are threatened to Eli, (1) a sudden disaster 31ᵃ [1]. 33ᵇ, from which few will escape of his entire family (בית אביך *v.* 31): (2) a *permanent* weakening of his family (32ᵇ 'no old man in thy house *continually* '). No doubt in 31ᵃ. 33ᵇ the allusion is to the massacre of the priests at Nob (22, 17–20): and Abiathar himself is the one alluded to in 33ᵃ, who escaped the massacre, and so was not ' cut off' from the altar, continuing to hold the office of priest under David, and only superseded by Ẓadoq (the faithful priest of *v.* 35) upon the accession of Solomon. The sign in *v.* 34 is of course the death of Ḥophni and Phineḥas, recorded in *ch.* 4.

But with reference to the passage as a whole, it is difficult to resist We.'s argument. As the text stands, *v.* 32ᵃ expresses a *consequence* of 31 : it deals, however, with something which Eli is to witness himself : hence 31 must refer to something within Eli's own lifetime—which can only be the disaster of *ch.* 4, in which his two sons perished. This implies that the survivor in 33 is Aḥitub (14, 3); and that 35 relates to Samuel (so Th.). But the 'sign' in 34 is also the disaster of *ch.* 4 : consequently, upon this interpretation, the death of Eli's sons is a ' sign,' not of some occurrence in the remoter future, but of itself ! *V.* 31 must thus refer to something *subsequent* to *ch.* 4, and so, subsequent also to Eli's death (the massacre at Nob, as explained above): it follows that the text of 32ᵃ cannot be correct,—as indeed was already surmised above, upon independent grounds. LXX omits both 31ᵇ and 32ᵃ ; and We. supposes that 31ᵇ and 32ᵇ are but two forms of one and the same gloss, due originally to an (incorrect) application of 31ᵃ to the disaster of *ch.* 4. Still, though it is true that 33ᵃ, expressing a *limitation* of 31ᵃ, would form a natural sequel to it, it would follow it somewhat quickly and abruptly ; and the omission in LXX is open to the suspicion of being due to the recurrence of the same words זקן בביתך in both 31ᵇ and 32ᵇ. What is really wanted in lieu of the corrupt words at the beginning of 32 is something which would lead on naturally to the notice of the *permanent* weakening of Eli's family—

---

[1] This sense of the figure seems to be demanded by the *limitation* which follows in 33ᵃ (' Yet one I will not *cut off* to thee from mine altar '). *V.* 33ᵃ cannot be a limitation to 32ᵇ: for the sparing of a single individual, on a particular occasion, forms no exception to the *permanent* weakening of a *family*.

which is the point in which 32ᵇ advances beyond 31ᵇ. Did we possess 32ᵃ in its original form, it would yield, we may suppose, a suitable sequence : 31 would refer to the massacre at Nob, 32 to the after-history of Eli's family (comp. 36 כל הנותר בביתך), and 33 would revert to the subject of 31 in order to follow the fortunes of the survivor, Abiathar (22, 20).

3, 1. יקר] *precious* = rare, as Is. 13, 12 אוקיר אנוש מפז.

נפרץ] *spread abroad* = frequent : 2 Ch. 31, 5 וְכִפְרֹץ הַדָּבָר.

2. 'ועלי שכב וג] From here to the end of *v.* 3 follow a series of circumstantial clauses, describing the conditions which obtained at the time when what is related in *v.* 4 took place.

כֵּהוֹת] fem. pl. from כֵּהֶה, an adj. of the form expressive of bodily defects חֵרֵשׁ, עִוֵּר, פִּסֵּחַ, אִלֵּם (GK. § 84ᵇ. 21). Syntactically the adj. is to be conceived here as an accusative, defining the aspect under which Eli's eyes 'began :' lit., therefore, 'began *as dim ones*' = began to be dim. Cf. Is. 33, 1 כהתימך שודד when thou finishest *as a devastator* = when thou finishest to devastate. See GK. § 120ᵇ ; *Tenses,* § 161. 2, and p. xvi ; and cf. Segal, *Mišnaic Hebrew* (1909), p. 49. But the inf. כְּהוֹת would be more in accordance with the Biblical usage of הֵחֵל (Sm. Bu. Now.): see Dt. 2, 25. 31. Jos. 3, 7 (Sm.).

לא יוכל] expressing his *continued* inability more distinctly than לא יָכֹל would have done : so Gen. 48, 10 ; Jos. 15, 63 Kt.

3ᵇ. Evidently Samuel was sleeping in close proximity to the ark— perhaps, in a chamber contiguous to the היכל in which it was, if not, as the Hebrew taken strictly would imply, actually in the היכל itself.

4. אל שמואל] LXX שמואל שמואל, no doubt rightly : cf. *v.* 10, where we read '*as beforetime,* Samuel, Samuel.' In *v.* 6 LXX repeats the name similarly, not expressing ויקם (which may have come in here as a gloss suggested by *v.* 8). The repetition can hardly have been introduced by LXX on the strength of *v.* 10 ; for there the name (both times) is not expressed by them at all. The only other similar duplications in OT. are Gen. 22, 11. 46, 2. Ex. 3, 4.

5. לי] For the dagesh, see GK. § 20f.

שוב שכב] 'return, lie down' = lie down again : cf. Is. 21, 12 שֻׁבוּ אֵתָיוּ ; and see on 2, 3.

7. טרם] יָדַע followed by a perfect is very rare : *Tenses,* § 27 β *note.*

Here, the parallel יִגְלֶה makes it probable that the narrator himself
would have vocalized יֵרַע: cf. GK. § 107ᶜ.

8. קֹרֵא] *was* calling : Gen. 42, 23 ; EVV. wrongly *had called.*

10. וַיּתיצב] Cf. the description of a nocturnal revelation in Job 4, 16.

כפעם בפעם] So 20, 25. Jud. 16, 20. 20, 30. 31. Nu. 24, 1†; כיום
ביום *ch.* 18, 10†; כשנה בשנה 2 Ki. 17, 4†. פעם בפעם does not occur
alone ; but (on the analogy of שנה בשנה 1, 7) would mean *one time like
another* = generally : hence, with כ prefixed, *as generally*, or, as we may
substitute in a case like the present, 'as at (other) times.'

11. הנה אנכי עשֶׂה] '*Lo, I am doing* = Lo, I am about to do :' the
'futurum instans,' as often in Divine announcements, *v.* 13, Gen. 6, 17.
Ex. 9, 3. Dt. 1, 20 (see *Tenses*, § 135. 3 ; GK. § 116ᵖ). Cf. 10, 8.

11ᵇ. The same figure 2 Ki. 21, 12. Jer. 19, 3†. In both passages,
the form, from צלל, is written תִּצַּלֶנָה (GK. § 67ᵍ). With the form here,
cf. תְּסֻבֶּינָה ; and in explanation of the *ḥireq*, see GK. § 67ᵖ. For the
syntax of כל־שמעו, see *Tenses*, § 121, *Obs.* 1, note ; GK. § 116ʷ.

12. אֶל עלי] LXX ἐπί, Pesh. Targ. עַל, Vulg. *adversum.* אֶל with
the force of עַל : cf. on 1, 12.

אל ביתו] *with reference to* his house : 1, 27. 4, 19.

הָחֵל וְכַלֵּה] 'beginning and ending,' i.e. effecting my purpose completely. The expression occurs only here. Construction as II 8, 2 :
Ew. § 280ᵃ; GK. § 113ʰ.

13. והגדתי] Read, with Klo. Bu. etc., והגדתָּ (with ו consec.): cf. *v.* 15ᵇ.

שפט אני] *Tenses*, § 135. 4. So Jer. 1, 12. 38, 14 al. In Aramaic,
the pronouns of 1 and 2 pers. coalesce with the ptcp. to form a new
tense with the force of a present : but in Hebrew the two parts are
still distinct, and the ptcp. receives some emphasis from its position.

בעון אשר ידע] עָוֹן is in the constr. state, because the following relative
clause is conceived as *defining* and *limiting* its meaning, exactly as
a noun in the genitive would do: GK. § 130ᶜ *footnote;* Ew. § 332ᶜ.
But probably בעון should be omitted (the text then reading, 'Because
(אשר, *Lex.* 83ᵇ c) he knew that his sons did curse God, etc.') : LXX
presupposes בעון בניו; and בעון has probably found its way in here
from a MS. with that reading (We. Lö. al.). Ehrlich regards it as an
old error for יַעַן *because.*

כי מקללים להם בניו] The text hardly admits of being construed : for

קלל does not mean *to bring a curse upon* any one, and is followed not by a *dative*, but by an *accusative*. There can be little doubt that LXX ὅτι κακολογοῦντες Θεόν have preserved the true reading, viz. כי מקללים אֱלֹהִים בניו (cf. Ex. 22, 27 אלהים לא תקלל). If the text be correct, להם can only be construed as a reflexive dative (Ew. § 315ᵃ; *Lex.* 515ᵇ h) ' cursed *for themselves* = at their pleasure :' cf. ψ. 44, 11 *end ;* 80, 7 ילעגו למו ; Job 6, 19 קו למו. But this does not yield a satisfactory sense.

כָהָה] Only here. Apparently (Nöld. *Mand. Gramm.*, p. 72 *n.*) a by-form of Syr. ܟܐܠ to *rebuke* (sq. ܒ 1 Ki. 1, 6 ܟ݀ܐܠ ܒ݁ܗ). In Mand. the form is כהא. Cf. Arab. كلّ *verbis dolore affecit* (Freyt.).

14. לבן] LXX οὐδ᾽ οὕτως (attaching the words to *v.* 13), strangely treating לבן, as though contracted from לא־כן. So elsewhere, as Gen. 4, 15 (also Pesh. Vulg. here); 30, 15 (לָכֵן) in these passages has an idiomatic force : cf. on 28, 2). 1 Ki. 22, 19. 2 Ki. 1, 4. 6. 21, 12. 22, 20 al. With 14ᵇ cf. Is. 21, 14.

אם] On אם after an oath,=*surely not,* see GK. § 149ᵇ,ᶜ; *Lex.* 50ᵃ.

יתכפר] LXX, rightly, ἐξιλασθήσεται. The actual meanings, and usages, of כִּפֶּר can be determined from the OT. itself : see the writer's art. PROPITIATION in *DB.* iv. (1902). Whether, however, as used to be supposed, and is assumed (though not confidently) in this art., the primary meaning of the root was (from Arab. *kafara*) to *cover* is now doubtful. כִּפֶּר corresponds to the Assyr. *kupparu*, which, whether its primary meaning was to *wipe away* (Zimmern, *KAT.*³ 601 f. ; cf. Syr. ܟܦܪ), or to *remove* (Langdon, *Exp. Times*, xxii. (1910–11), pp. 320 ff., 380 f.) [1], in actual use denotes *ritual purgation* (e.g. from disease); and the word seems to have come into Heb. from Assyrian with this sense attaching to it, which was there developed so as to express the related ideas of *to expiate* (or *declare expiated*) sin, *to clear* the offender, and *to appease* the offended person. See the writer's art. EXPIATION in Hastings' *Encycl. of Religion and Ethics.*

15. 'In MT. וַיַּשְׁכֵּם בַּבֹּקֶר (LXX) has been passed over after עד־הבקר ' (We.).

16. את־שמואל] 44 MSS. better, אל שמואל.

17. כה יעשה וג'] A form of imprecation peculiar to Ruth, Samuel,

---

[1] For a third view (that the root meant originally to *brighten*, and so to *purify*), see Burney, *ib.* 325 ff.; Ball, *ib.* 478 f.

and Kings: 14, 44. 20, 13. 25, 22. II 3, 9. 35. 19, 14. Ruth 1, 17.
1 Ki. 2, 23. 2 Ki. 6, 31, and with a *pl.* verb (in the mouth of Jezebel
and Benhadad) 1 Ki. 19, 2 : 20, 10†.

19. ‏ולא הפיל וג׳‏] For the idiom cf. 2 Ki. 10, 10 ‏י״י מִדְּבַר יפל לא כי‏
‏ארצה‏; and, in Qal, and without ‏ארצה‏, in the Deuteronomic passages
Jos. 21, 43 (45). 23, 14. 1 Ki. 8, 56 : also Est. 6, 10. ‏מן‏ has a partitive
force, with a neg. = ‘aught of,’ as Dt. 16, 4 (*Lex.* 580ᵇ **3 a** *c*).

20. ‏נאמן וג׳‏] (was) *one accredited* or *approved* to be a prophet unto
Yahweh. (The ptcp., not the pf.)

‏לנביא‏] as ‏לנגיד‏ 9, 16 ; 13, 14 ; ‏למלך‏ 15, 1 ; II 2, 4 al.

21. ‏להֵרָאה‏] So Jud. 13, 21†, for the normal ‏הֵרָאוֹת‏ : Stade, § 622ᵇ ;
GK. § 75ᶜ.

On the clause at the end of 21 (see Kittel), restored by Klo. from
LXX, Ehrl. remarks rightly (see all the instances on 6, 12) that
wherever the construction ‏וילך הלוך ואכול‏ occurs, the second inf. is
always used absolutely, and is never followed by an object.

4, 1ᵃ. This should stand as the concluding clause of 3, 21.

4, 1ᵇ—7, 1. *Defeat of Israel by the Philistines. Capture and*
restoration of the Ark.

4, 1ᵇ. LXX introduce this section by the words Καὶ ἐγενήθη ἐν ταῖς
ἡμέραις ἐκείναις καὶ συναθροίζονται ἀλλόφυλοι εἰς πόλεμον ἐπὶ Ἰσραηλ =
‏ויהי בימים ההם ויקבצו פלשתים למלחמה על ישראל‏. Something of this
sort is required, if only for the sake of explaining the following ‏לקראת‏,
though the clause (taken with what follows in which the same word
occurs) would be the better for the omission of ‏למלחמה‏.

‏האבן העזר [העזר‏ is in *apposition* with ‏האבן‏ ‘the stone Help’ (*Tenses*,
§ 190). In 5, 1. 7, 12, however, the form used is ‏אבן העזר‏, which is
also best read here. But Eben-ezer here, and 5, 1, in the plain,
somewhere near Lydda (see the next note), can hardly be the Eben-ezer
of 7, 12, near Miẓpah, 18 m. SE. of Lydda, in the hills ; or, if it is,
there will have been different traditions as to its situation.

‏באפק‏] The name *Apheq* has not been preserved : but the Apheq
meant must have been the one in the Sharon (Jos. 12, 18), at some
spot, probably near Lydda or Antipatris, which would form a suitable

starting-point for an expedition either in the direction of Shiloh and Central Palestine, or (*ch.* 29, 1) into the plain of Esdraelon and Gilboa (notice the road leading north from Lydda and Antipatris, through the plain of Dothan, to Jezreel; and also those leading up east into the hill-country of Ephraim). Apheq is mentioned also in 1 Ki. 20, 23. See further W. R. Smith and G. A. Smith in *EB.* s.v. APHEK.

2. ותטש] Perhaps, 'and *spread itself abroad:*' cf. the *Nif.* in II 5, 18. 22. LXX ἔκλινεν, i.e. seemingly וַתֵּט 'and the battle *inclined*' (viz. in a direction adverse to Israel). Smith conjectures plausibly וַתֵּקֶשׁ *and the battle was hard;* cf. II 2, 17 וַתְּהִי הַמִּלְחָמָה קָשָׁה: so Bu.

ויכו] LXX, Pesh. Vulg. וַיִּפּוּ.

3–5. LXX read in *v.* 3 אֶת־אֲרוֹן אֱלֹהֵינוּ, in *v.* 4ª את ארון יהוה (without צבאות), in *v.* 4ᵇ הארון (for ארון ברית האלהים), and in *v.* 5 ארון יהוה, thus omitting ברית each time, in accordance with the general custom of MT. in Samuel (*vv.* 6. 11. 17–22; 3, 3; *ch.* 5–6; II 6 throughout; II 15, 24ᵃᵝ. 25. 29 [on *v.* 24ᵃᵃ see note]). Probably it was introduced here into MT. at a time when the expression was in more general use than it had always been.

4. ושם] LXX, Vulg. omit שם—no doubt, rightly. The point is not that Eli's sons were at Shiloh, but that they came with the ark into the camp (*v.* 11). The word may have been introduced accidentally through a reminiscence of 1, 3 (We.).

5. ותהם הארץ] 1 Ki. 1, 45 ותהם הקריה: Ruth 1, 19 ותהם העיר. On the form וַתֵּהֹם, see GK. § 72ʰ. הוּם (usually הִמֵּם), however, is *to confuse, discomfit,* Dt. 7, 23: what we expect is a form from הָמָה *to be in commotion, stir,* of a *city,* 1 Ki. 1, 41. Is. 22, 2: so Ehrlich may be right in vocalizing וַתֵּהַם.

7. בא אלהים] The Philistines would hardly speak of Yahweh as 'God' absolutely: read probably בָּא אֱלֹהֵיהֶם אֲלֵהֶם (We.).

ויאמרו] Not to be omitted (LXX). Though the speakers are the same as in ª, the remark is of a different character: and in such cases the repetition of ויאמרו is a genuine Hebrew idiom (We.): e.g. 26, 9–10. II 17, 7–8.

כזאת] LXX τοιαύτη—a Hebraism: cf. ψ. 27, 14 μίαν; 102, 19. 119, 50. 56 αὕτη; τὴν μονογενῆ μου=יחידתי ψ. 22, 21 al.; also Jud. 7, 14; ψ. 32, 6; 118, 23 (Matth. 21, 42), notwithstanding the fact that in these cases there is a subst. in the Greek to which the fem. might conceivably be referred.

8. אלהים [האדירים האלה construed as a pl. in the mouth of a heathen (cf. 1 Ki. 19, 2), as also, sometimes, in converse with one, Gen. 20, 13 (Ew. § 318ᵃ *end*). However, this limitation is not universal: see Gen. 35, 7; Jos. 24, 19 כי אלהים קדושים הוא (the plur. of majesty), II 7, 23 (but see note); ψ. 58, 12 (unless אלהים here=divine beings); and in the phrase אלהים חיים Dt. 5, 23 al. (Is. 37, 4. 17 אלהים חי: in poetry also אל חי is used Hos. 2, 1 al.). Cf. GK. §§ 124ᵍ, 132ʰ, 145ⁱ.

אלה הם] Gen. 25, 16 al.: *Tenses*, § 201. 3; *Lex*. 241ᵇ 4.

בכל מכה] 'With every manner of smiting,' Kp., excellently. מכה is not a 'plague,' though it may be a πληγή, but rather denotes slaughter, *v*. 10. 6, 19. 19, 8.

ובמדבר] Probably יֻבַדְּבָר: (We.) should be read.

9. והייתם] carrying on . . . , התחזקו והיו: GK. § 112ʳ. והייתם לאנשים is logically superfluous; but it *resumes* והיו לאנשים after the following clause, in accordance with the principle noticed on 17, 13 and 25, 26.

10. איש לאהליו] The Versions express לאהלו: but in this phrase, except Jud. 20, 8 (which is not altogether parallel), the plural is regularly found.

ויפל] the sing. as Jud. 12, 6ᵇ: cf. on 1, 2.

רגלי] construed with אלף as a collective: so אֶלֶף כִּכָּר, אֶלֶף אִישׁ, etc.

12. איש־בנימן] It is the rule in Heb. (GK. § 127ᵃ),—though there are exceptions (§ 127ᵉ),—that a determinate gen. determines the preceding *nomen regens*: hence We. remarks here that איש ב׳ means only '*the* man of B.,'—either a particular *known* man (Nu. 25, 8. Jud. 7, 14. 10, 1), or, more commonly, 'the *men* of B.' (so איש ישראל, איש יהודה, איש אפרים, etc., constantly): comp. Moore on Jud. 7, 14, p. 207. Accordingly, as איש ב׳ is here not determinate, We. Klo. Bu. Now. would read, with LXX (ἀνὴρ Ἰεμειναῖος), either איש בֶּן־יְמִינִי (cf. 9, 21), or איש יְמִינִי (II 20, 1). Ehrlich, cleverly, בְּנֻסוֹ for בנימן; cf. *v*. 16.

13. דרך מצפה] (Qrê יד) יך] The meaningless יך is corrected by the Massorites to יַד: but though we have . . . , לְיַד 19, 3. ψ. 140, 6 לִיד מעגל; . . . אֶל יַד II 14, 30. על יד דרך השער II 15, 2. Job 1, 14; . . . עַל יַד 18, 4 אל יד השער; . . . , יַד by itself is not used to express position (though such a use of it would not, it is true, be contrary to analogy:

see on 2, 29 *footnote*). The article also (the passage being prose) is desiderated with דרך: so (1) the smallest change would be ליד הדרך ¹ליד מצפה (= Pesh.). (2) LXX παρὰ τὴν πύλην σκοπεύων τὴν ὁδόν = ליד¹ (צִפֵּה דָרֶךְ): so השער מצפה הדרך (cf. Pr. 8, 3 ליד שערים and Nah. 2, 2 We. (cf. *v.* 18). (3) Targ. has על כבש אורח תרעא מסכא exactly as II 15, 2 (and also 18, 4). This rendering agrees with LXX in presupposing 'gate,' and would point to ליד דרך השער מצפה as the original text. The supposition that השער has fallen out would most readily explain the absence of the art. with דרך in MT. But probably the second of the suggested corrections is the best (so Bu. Now.).

15. קמה] עיניו being conceived as a collective is construed with its predicate in the *fem. sing.*: so Dt. 21, 7 ידינו לא שפכה (Qrê needlessly שפכו). ψ. 18, 35. 37, 31 לא תמעד אשוריו 73, 2 Kt. etc.: see Ew. § 317ᵃ; GK. § 145ᵏ. The Arabic 'broken,' or collective, plural is construed constantly in the same way: Wright, *Ar. Gr.*, ii. §§ 144, 146. קם recurs in the same sense 1 Ki. 14, 4 (of Ahijah).

16. אנכי הבא] Not 'I am come,' but 'I am *he that is come*' (ὁ ἥκων LXX): surmising that Eli would expect some one with news, the messenger replies that he is the man. Cf. Dt. 3, 21. 8, 18. Is. 14, 27 (*Tenses*, § 135. 7; GK. § 126ᵏ). Notice the order ואני ו'.

המערכה (first time)] It is an improvement to read, with LXX, Klo. Bu. Kit. Dh., הַמַּחֲנֶה *the camp.*

17. המבשר] The original sense of the word has been forgotten, and it is used for a bearer of tidings generally, even though, as here, the tidings be bad ones.

18. מעל הכסא] We say simply, 'fell *from* the seat:' Heb. in such cases says 'from *upon*:' so מעל המזבח, מעל השלחן, etc. (see *Lex.* 758).

בעד יד] LXX ἐχόμενος (cf. footnote on *v.* 13). We. considers יד and בעד to be different corruptions of an original בְּיַד: and, although ביד in this sense is very rare (Job 15, 23. Zech. 4, 12†²; cf. בידי ψ. 141, 6), the usual idioms being לְיַד, אֶל־יַד, or עַל־יַד (see on *v.* 13), it seems that we must acquiesce in it (so Sm. Bu. Now. Kit.).

---

¹ It is true that elsewhere LXX render compounds of יד by ἀνὰ χεῖρα, or ἐχόμενα: but absolute uniformity is hardly to be expected of them in such a matter as this, even in one and the same book.

² In Jer. 41, 9 בור גדול הוא is clearly to be read, with LXX, for ביד גדליהו הוא.

19. הָרָה fem. from [הָרֶה], of the same form as יָפֶה, יָפָה.

לֶלֶת] An isolated example of a contracted form of the inf. לֶדֶת : the original [לַדְתְּ] becoming exceptionally לַת instead of לֶדֶת, just as [אַחַרְתְּ] the fem. of אֶחָד becomes regularly אַחַת and not [אַחֶרֶת]. The form, however, in the inf. of verbs פ״ו is without parallel; so that in all probability it is a mere transcriptional error for לְלֶדֶת, the usual form (so GK. § 69 m).

אֶל] *with reference to, about,* as *v.* 21. Gen. 20, 2. ψ. 2, 7.

וּמֵת] the finite verb by GK. § 114 r. וַיָּמָת is, however, the tense that would be expected (cf. on 1, 12). But וְאֶל־מוֹת *and about the death of* (Sm., with 6 MSS.) would be better Hebrew.

נהפכו עליה צריה] Dan. 10, 16; צירים also Is. 13, 8. 21, 3 †. *Turned =* came unexpectedly.

20. וכעת מותה וַתְּדַבְּרְנה] The predicate, after a time-determination, being introduced by ·ו, as happens occasionally : 17, 57. Gen. 19, 15. 27, 34. 37, 18 al.: *Tenses,* § 127 β; GK. § 111 b.

עליה] *by* (lit. *over*) her: cf. Gen. 18, 2; and see on II 15, 4.

שתה לבה] Ex. 7, 23. II 13, 20 al., in the same sense of νοῦν προσέχειν, *animum attendere.*

21. אִי כבוד] אִי is frequent as a negative in the Mishnah, and other post-Bibl. Hebrew, and occurs once with the same force in the OT., Job 22, 30 (though the text here is very suspicious)[1]. It may have been current anciently in colloquial Hebrew. It is, however, very doubtful whether 'Inglorious' is the real etym. of Ichabod: more probably it is a popular etymology, like those given for קין, משה, and many other names in the OT. The real meaning of אי כבוד is uncertain; אִיתָמָר and the Ṣidonian אִיזֶבֶל are in appearance of the same formation; but their etym. is equally obscure. איעזר in Nu. 26, 30, if the text be sound, will be a contraction of אביעזר: but more probably it is a textual error for אביעזר (LXX has Ἀχιεζερ).

כי גלה כבוד מישראל] Cf. Hos. 10, 5 כי גלה ממנו (of the כבוד of the calf of Beth-el). גלה is much more than 'departed' AV. (which would represent סָר, as Nu. 14, 9 סר צלם מעליהם. Am. 6, 7 וסר מרזח סרוחים): it is an ominous word in Hebrew, and expresses 'is *gone*

---

[1] It is found also in Phoenician (Cooke, *NSI.* 4, 4. 5, 5 ; *CIS.* 165, 18. 21. 167, 11) : and it is the regular and ordinary negative in Ethiopic.

into exile.' It is probable that this victory of the Philistines was followed by that 'desolation' of Shiloh, of which, though the historical books are silent, the recollection was still far from forgotten in Jeremiah's day (7, 12. 14. 26, 6), and to which a late Psalmist alludes (ψ. 78, 60).

5, 1. אשדודה] Ashdod, now *Esdud*, one of the five principal Philistine cities (6, 1), 33 miles due west of Jerusalem, and about half-way between Joppa and Gaza, 3 miles from the sea-coast.

2. הציג] *to station* or *stand* an object (or person) : Gen. 43, 9. 47, 2. II 6, 17 (likewise of the ark). A more definite word than שים.

3. האשדודים] Read האשדודים.

ממחרת] 'Though in *v.* 4 the purpose for which the Ashdodites arose early is clear from what has preceded, and need not therefore be specified expressly, the case in the present verse is different : and no doubt ויבאו בית דגון must be inserted before והנה with LXX. . . . It will be best also to accept the following וַיִּרְאוּ of LXX at the same time, in order to follow throughout one and the same recension' (We.).

לפניו] to fall *on one's own face,* is always in Heb. either על פניו (17, 49 and often), or else לאפיו (Gen. 48, 12 al.), or על אפיו (II 14, 4 al.); hence We.'s remark : 'For לפניו here and *v.* 4, usage requires either על פניו (LXX¹) or לאפיו.' It is for the purpose of giving a rendering of the existing MT. in accordance with the general usage of the language that RV. *marg.* has the alternative ' before it,' the following לפני ארון יהוה being regarded as an explanation of לפניו. But though such explanatory additions occur (Lev. 6, 8. Nu. 32, 33. 1 Ch. 4, 42. 2 Ch. 26, 14) they are exceptional, and are often under the suspicion of having been introduced as a gloss (Jos. 1, 2 [לבני ישראל not in LXX]. Jud. 21, 7 לנותרים. Jer. 41, 3 [את גדליהו not in LXX]). It is better here to restore על פניו.

ויקחו] LXX καὶ ἤγειραν, i.e. וַיָּקִמוּ ' and *raised up :*' so Sm. Bu. Dh. A more expressive word than 'took.'

4. רק דגון נשאר עליו] 'only Dagon was left upon him' (upon Dagon), which can scarcely be right. LXX πλὴν ἡ ῥάχις Δαγων ὑπελείφθη—

---

¹ It is not, however, certain that LXX read על פניו rather than לאפיו : the latter is rendered by them equally ἐπὶ πρόσωπον αὐτοῦ in 20, 41 and II 18, 28.

according to We., reading probably nothing different from MT., but being led to ῥάχις by the similarity to the Hebrew רק (We. compares δρέπανον for דרבן 13, 21, παρατείνουσα for ברתן (ברתן) II 2, 29, ἐσχαρί-της for אשפר (אשכר), II 6, 19 ; add δορὰ for אדרת Gen. 25, 25 ; πηγαὶ for אפיקים ψ. 42, 2 al., τόκος for תֹּךְ (oppression) 55, 12 al., τροφὴ for טרף 111, 5, τοπάζιον for פז (gold) 119, 127). We. for דגון would read דָּגוֹ (supposing the ן to have arisen by dittography from נשאר) ' only his *fishy part* was left upon him.' This, however, is not very satisfactory ; and, as ῥάχις means ' back,' and πλὴν upon We.'s explanation remains unaccounted for, it is better to insert גַּו *back* before דגון, or (Lagarde) to read גַּוּוֹ *his back* for דגון. So Bu. Now.

5. יָדְרכו] the impf., as II 5, 8. Gen. 10, 9. 22, 14 etc., expressing the custom.

עד היום הזה] LXX add ὅτι ὑπερβαίνοντες ὑπερβαίνουσιν= כִּי אִם־ דָּלֹג יִדְלֹגוּ׃. This *may* be a gloss derived from Zeph. 1, 9 ; but it may also be a genuine part of the text.

6. יד י"] Cf., with כבד, *v.* 11. Jud. 1, 35 ; and with היה *v.* 9. 7, 13. 12, 15. Ex. 9, 3. Dt. 2, 15. Jud. 2, 15 ; also Jos. 4, 24. Ruth 1, 13.

אל] על would be more usual.

וישמם] LXX καὶ ἐπήγαγεν αὐτοῖς, reading וישם (incorrectly) as וַיָּשֶׂם : cf. Ex. 15, 26. Ez. 39, 21 (We.). LXX continue : καὶ ἐξέζεσεν αὐτοῖς εἰς τὰς ναῦς, with a variant (in Lucian's recension) καὶ ἐξέβρασαν εἰς τὰς ναῦς αὐτῶν, on which see We., and Aptowitzer, *ZAW.* 1909, 242 f. וישמם means *and laid them waste* or *desolate,*—usually of places (ψ. 79, 7) or things (Hos. 2, 14, of vines) ; of persons Ez. 20, 26. Job 16, 7. It is a word hardly found elsewhere, except in poetry, and the more elevated prose style (e.g. Lev. 26, 22. 31. 32 ; Ez. 30, 12. 14). ' Destroyed ' (EVV.) is too general. But probably Ehrlich is right in reading וַיְהֻמֵּם (cf. *vv.* 9. 11), which, as Field shews, is also presupposed by Aquila's ἐφαγεδαίνισεν (cf. 7, 10 Aq. ψ. 18, 15 Aq. Dt. 7, 23 Aq.).

בעפלים] To be vocalized בָּעֳפָלִים : the *vowels* of the text refer, of course, to the marginal בַּטְּחֹרִים. The traditional view of עפל was that it denoted either the anus (cf. 5, 12 LXX ἐπλήγησαν εἰς τὰς ἕδρας ; 6, 5 Vulg. *quinque anos aureos*), or an affection of the anus ; and hence, being a coarse word, the Massorites directed טחרים to be read for עפלים wherever it occurs (*vv.* 9. 12. 6, 4. 5. Dt. 28, 27). In fact, however, it is pretty certain that it denotes *plague-boils* (RV. *marg.*), which occur only in the groin, arm-pits, and sides of the neck. See *DB*. iii. 325ᵃ; *EB*. s.v. Emerods; *Exp. Times*, xii. (1900–1), 378 ff., xv. (1903–4), 476 ff.

אֶת־אַשְׁדּוֹד וְאֶת־גְּבוּלֶיהָ] epexeg. of אֹתָם, but attached in a manner unworthy of the best Hebrew style, and probably a marginal gloss. LXX has instead καὶ μέσον τῆς χώρας αὐτῆς ἀνεφύησαν μύες, which may represent an original וַיַּעֲלוּ עַכְבָּרִים בְּתוֹךְ אַרְצָם (cf. Ex. 7, 29). On this, and other additions of LXX in this chapter, see more fully at the end of *ch.* 6.

7. וַאמרו] See on 1, 12. No doubt ויאמרו should be restored.

8. גַּת יֵסֹב] For the *order*, which gives brightness to the style, cf. Ex. 1, 22. Jos. 2, 16 לכו ההרה, Jud. 20, 4. 1 Ki. 2, 26 לך עֲנָתֹת, Is. 23, 12. 52, 4. Jer. 2, 10; also (where the position is emphatic) 1 Ki. 12, 1. Jer. 20, 6. 32, 5. At the end of the *v.* גַּת (LXX εἰς Γέθθα) seems to be desiderated. On the site of Gath, see p. 57.

9. אֲחֲרֵי אֲשֶׁר הֵסֵבּוּ] אֲחֲרֵי אֲשֶׁר occurs frequently: אֲחֲרֵי with a pf. without אֲשֶׁר (GK. § 164ᵈ) only here and Lev. 25, 48. אֲחֲרֵי standing alone is elsewhere construed with an inf. constr.

מְהוּמָה] *confusion, panic, v.* 11. 14, 20. Dt. 7, 23 ('discomfiture').

וַיִּשָּׂתְרוּ] AV. follows the Jewish interpreters (Rashi מכת בית הנסתרים: Kimchi מכת הטחורים במקום סתר מבפנים; cf. LXX καὶ ἐπάταξεν αὐτοὺς εἰς τὰς ἕδρας αὐτῶν, Symm. εἰς τὰ κρυπτὰ αὐτῶν) in treating this as equivalent to וַיֵּחָתְרוּ[1]. There is no difficulty in supposing שׂ to be written for ס: but the meaning assigned to the *Nif.* is not a possible one. In Arabic شتر means *to have inverted* (or *cracked*) *eyelids or lower lips:* if the text, therefore, be correct, it is probable that שׂתר is derived from a root signifying properly *to cleave*, and applied in Hebrew and Arabic to different affections of the skin. Render 'and plague-boils *brake out* to them' (*Anglice* 'upon them')[2].

---

[1] The same explanation is implied elsewhere: the passage is quoted in a Massoretic list of eighteen words written once with שׂ in lieu of the normal ס: *Mass. Magna* on Hos. 2, 8; see also *Ochlah we-Ochlah*, No. 191; and *ib.* p. 42. Amongst the passages cited is Hos. 8, 4 הסירו = השׁירו (RV. *marg.*).

[2] Pesh. has here a doublet: see PS. *Thes.* cols. 2757, 4309. Nestle (*ZAW.* 1909, p. 232), following the second of these, ܘܐܬܟܠܒܬ ܐܢܘܢ (= Aq. περιελύθησαν αἱ ἕδραι), would read וַיִּשָּׂתְרוּ, a Hithp. from שָׂרָה *to loose:* but as עֳפָלִים does not mean ἕδραι, this yields no sense. In illustration of the clause

עֲפֹלִים] i.e. עֳפָלִים : Qrê טְחֹרִים; see on *v.* 6.

10. עקרון] 12 miles NE. of Ashdod, and 12 miles NW. of Beth-shemesh (see on 6, 13).

אלי] *to me*, spoken in the name of the people as a whole. So often : as Ex. 17, 3ᵇ. Nu. 20, 18. 19ᵇ. 21, 22. Jos. 9, 7 ('perhaps *thou* dwell-est in *my* midst,' said by Israel to the ambassadors from Gibeon). 17, 14. Jud. 11, 17. 19 *end;* 12, 3ᵃ. 20, 23ᵇ. Hab. 3, 14 ('to scatter *me*'). Comp. on 30, 22 ; and *LOT.* 366 f. (edd. 6–8, 390).

להמיתני ואת עמי] In the best Hebrew style this would be expressed להמית אתי ואת עמי (as *v.* 11 ; Ex. 17, 3 ; II 14, 16). The same com-bination occurs, however, eleven or twelve times in the course of the OT. : Dt. 11, 6 (contrast Nu. 16, 32). 15, 16. Jos. 10, 30ᵇ. 32. 33. 37. 39. 2 Ki. 20, 6 (=Is. 38, 6). Jer. 32, 29. Ez. 29, 4 (Keil). Zech. 5, 4. Est. 2, 9 ; cf. 2 Ch. 28, 23ᵇ. Comp. Hitzig on Is. 29, 7.

12ᵇ. Ex. 2, 23 ותעל שועתם אל האלהים—the only other passage in which שַׁוְעָה occurs in prose.

6, 1. חדשים] LXX adds καὶ ἐξέζεσεν ἡ γῆ αὐτῶν μύας = וְאַרְצָם שָׁרְצָה עַכְבָּרִים (cf. Ex. 7, 28). See at the end of the chapter.

2. לקסמים] On קסם as well as on the other principal words used by the Hebrews to denote divination and magic, the study of W. Robert-son Smith in the *Journal of Philology*, xiii. p. 273 ff., xiv. p. 113 ff. should be consulted. See also the writer's notes on Dt. 18, 10. 11.

במה] *wherewith ?* as Mic. 6, 6 (Keil).

3. אם משלחים] LXX, Pesh. אם משלחים אַתֶּם. Analogy certainly demands the insertion of the subject; see especially the similarly framed sentences, Jud. 9, 15. 11, 9. Jer. 42, 13 (*Tenses*, § 137): with the ptcp. the subject is omitted only when it is indefinite, or when it has been mentioned just previously (*ib.* § 135. 6 ; cf. GK. § 116ˢ˒ ᵗ).

תשיבו] *return, render as a due* (ἀποδοῦναι): Nu. 5, 7 ; ψ. 72, 10 מנחה ישיבו : 2 Ki. 3, 4 (of Mesha's annual tribute to Israel), etc.

אשם] AV. *trespass-offering*, RV. *guilt-offering* (regularly, except Is. 53, 10, where AV. is not altered, but the correct rendering is given in the margin). On the nature of the אשם see Oehler, *Theol. of O.T.*, § 137, who shews that the cases in which the 'guilt-offering' is

following in LXX and Vulg., see the curious Midrash (*Midr. Sam.* x. 4) cited by Aptowitzer, *ZAW.* 1909, p. 242.

prescribed in the Priests' Code always imply some *infringement* of another's rights,—either a positive injury done, or some right or due withheld. Doubtless אשם is used here in a more popular and general sense; still, the offering of the Philistines is designed as a compensation for the wrong which they conceive has been done to the ark whilst in their territory.

4. מספר וג׳] '*by, according to,* the number of,' an accus. of limitation or definition. Cf. *v.* 18. Ex. 16, 16. Job 1, 5; also II 21, 20; and Ew. §§ 204ᵇ, 300ᶜ; GK. § 118ʰ.

עפלי] i.e. עָפְלֵי. The Massorites mean עָפְלֵי to be *read* טְחֹרֵי; cf. on 5, 6.

לבלם] either לְכֻלְּכֶם (8 Heb. MSS.) or לָכֶם (LXX, Pesh.) must evidently be read.

5. עפליכם] i.e. עָפְלֵיכֶם: Qrê טְחֹרֵיכֶם. *V.* 5ᵃ (We.), or at least the words המשחיתים את הארץ (Dhorme), seems to be a redactional gloss: see p. 61.

ונתחם . . . כבוד] Jos. 7, 19: and, differently, Jer. 13, 16.

יקל . . . מעליכם] הֵקֵל is construed similarly 1 Ki. 12, 10. Jon. 1, 5.

6. תכבדו *make* the heart *heavy,* i.e. *slow to move* or *affect, unimpressionable.* It is the word used by J (*Qal* and *Hif.*) in the narrative of the plagues, Ex. 7, 14. 8, 11. 28. 9, 7. 34. 10, 1. Comp. the writer's *Exodus* in the *Cambr. Bible,* p. 53.

התעלל] So Ex. 10, 2. Not 'wrought wonderfully,' but 'made a toy of' (cf. RV. *marg.*); see on 31, 4.

כאשר . . . וישלחום] So 12, 8: see on 4, 20.

7. אחת] The numeral has here a weaker sense than in 1, 1, and is scarcely more than *a;* cf. Ex. 16, 33; *ch.* 7, 9. 12. 1 Ki. 19, 4. 22, 9. 2 Ki. 7, 8. 8, 6. 12, 10.

עליהם] the *masc.* suff., according to GK. § 135ᵒ; cf. *v.* 10.

8. בָּאַרְגַז] It is possible, of course, that an ארגז may have formed a regular appendage to an עגלה, in which case the art. will be prefixed to it as denoting an object expected, under the circumstances named, to exist (so probably 2, 13 *the* prong: 18, 10ᵇ *the* spear, almost = *his* spear: 25, 23 החמור; II 13, 9 את־המשרת, etc.); but there are many passages to which this explanation will not apply, and the rendering 'a chest' is perfectly in accordance with Hebrew idiom. See more fully on 1, 4 and 19, 13.

9. דֶּרֶךְ גְּבוּלוֹ] the way *to*, etc., as regularly (Gen. 3, 24). On the *position* of דרך גבולו, immediately after אם, see p. 35.

מִקְרֶה הוּא הָיָה לָנוּ:] 'it is an accident (which) hath befallen us' (GK. § 155[d, f])[1].

לֹא יָדוֹ] Notice the unusual order, intended to emphasize יָדוֹ: cf. Gen. 45, 8. Nu. 16, 29 לֹא י׳ שְׁלָחָנִי 'Not Y. hath sent me' (but some one else). ψ. 115, 17. Cf. GK. § 152[e]; *Lex.* 518[b] (*c*).

10. וַיְאַסְרוּם] On the ס-, see GK. § 60[b].

כלו] from כָּלָה with the sense of כָּלָא (GK. § 75[qq]): cf. כְּלָתָנִי 25, 33.

11. 'And they set the ark of Yahweh upon the cart, *and also* the coffer.' The type of sentence is one not uncommon in Hebrew (e.g. Gen. 12, 17. 34, 29. 43, 15. Nu. 13, 23[b]).

Some few of the instances that occur might be explained as due to the com- posite character of the narrative (so Nu. 13, 26[b]) ; but this does not appear to be the case in most : and it must be recognized as a feature of Hebrew style, when two subjects (or objects) have to be combined in one clause, for the clause containing one of the subjects (or objects) to be completed, the other being attached subsequently. See *a.* Gen. 2, 9[b]. 41, 27[a]. Ex. 35, 22. Lev. 22, 4. Nu. 16, 2[a]. 18[b]. 27[b]. Jud. 6, 5[a] כי הם ומקניהם יעלו ואהליהם. 2 Ki. 6, 15: *b.* Gen. 1, 16[b]. 12, 17 וינגע י״י את פרעה נגעים גדלים ואת ביתו. 34, 29. 43, 15. 18. Ex. 29, 3. Jud. 21, 10[b]. 1 Ki. 5, 9. Jer. 27, 7[a]. 32, 29 : *c.* (analogous examples with preposi- tions) Gen. 28, 14[b]. Ex. 34, 27[b] כרתי אתך ברית ואת ישראל. Dt. 7, 14[b]. 28, 46. 54[a]. 56[a]. Jer. 25, 12 MT. 40, 9[a] האיש הרך בך והענג מאד. The word attached cannot, in all such cases, be treated (Ew. § 339[a]) as subordinate.

12. וַיִּשַּׁרְנָה] (*a*) The 3 pl. fem. with the prefix י, as Gen. 30, 38. Dan. 8, 22 †. In Hebrew, except in these three passages, the form of the 3 pl. fem. is always תכתבנה : in Arabic, on the other hand, as also in Aramaic and Ethiopic, it is regularly *yaktubna*, and the form *taktubna* is noted only as a rare dialectical variety (Stade, § 534[2]; GK. § 47[k]). The most original form would seem certainly to be *yaktubna* (2 pl. תכתבנה, תכתבו : 3 pl. יכתבו, יכתבנה): *taktubna* appears to have been produced through the influence of the 3rd fem. sing. תכתב. The latter form, however, came to predominate in Hebrew, while in Arabic it only prevailed dialectically.

---

[1] In illustration of the recourse to the guidance of an animal in cases of doubt, see Wellh. *Reste Arab. Heidentumes* (1887), p. 147, ed. 2 (1897), p. 201.

[2] See Fleischer, *Kleinere Schriften*, i. 1 (1885), p. 99.

(*b*) וַיִשֵּׁרְנָה (with dagesh and short ḥireq) stands for a normal וַיִישַׁרְנָה: cf. וַיִּפֶן 1 Ki. 3, 15 for וַיִיפֶן: Stade, § 121; GK. § 71.

12ª. The main division is at בית שמש, the *first* occurrence of the *zāqēf* (see on 1, 28): what follows is a circumstantial clause, attached ἀσυνδέτως, defining more particularly *how* the kine went along (cf. 1 Ki. 18, 6, and *Tenses*, § 163). On Beth-shemesh, see p. 57.

אחת] is here emphatic: the kine went along *one* highway, without attempting to deviate from it.

הלכו הלך וגעו] Exactly so (except that sometimes there is a ptcp. for the finite verb) Gen. 8, 5 (rd. הָלְכוּ for the wholly irregular הָיוֹ). Jos. 6, 9. 13ᵇ Qrê. Jud. 14, 9. II 3, 16. 2 Ki. 2, 11 ¹†(הֹלְכִים הָלוֹךְ וְדַבֵּר): with the verb at the end, Is. 3, 16 הלוך וטפוף תלכנה. Jer. 50, 4†: with the verb in the middle, ψ. 126, 6 הָלֹךְ יֵלֵךְ וּבָכֹה. And with an impf. with *waw* consec. for the second inf. abs. *ch.* 19, 23. II 16, 13†; with a pf. with *waw* consec. (frequentative) in the same place, II 13, 19 (see note). Jos. 6, 13ª†. Cf. GK. § 113ˢ. Comp. an analogous idiom with an adj. (but see note) on 14, 19. פָּעוֹ for גָּעֹה, GK. § 75ⁿ.

There is another type, occurring twice, viz. Gen. 8, 3 וישובו הלוך וָשֹׁב. 12, 9 ויסע הלוך ונסוע†.

With other verbs we have, of the type וילך הלוך וגעו Gen. 8, 7, וַיֵּצֵא יָצוֹא וָשֹׁב. II 15, 30 וְעָלוּ עָלֹה וּבָכֹה. 1 Ki. 20, 37. 2 Ki. 3, 24 (rd. with Luc. וַיָּבֹאוּ בֹּא וְהַכֵּה). 21, 13ᵇ (rd. מָחֹה וְהָפַךְ). Is. 19, 22 נָגֹף וְרָפוֹא ... וְנָגַף. 31, 5 (rd. וְהַצֵּל and וְהִמְלִיט). Jer. 12, 17. Ez. 1, 14 (rd. וּבֵינוֹת הַחַיּוֹת יָצוֹא יָצֹא וָשֹׁב. Joel 2, 26†.

And of the type וישובו הלוך וָשֹׁב: Jer. 7, 13 הַשְׁכֵּם וְדַבֵּר ... וַאֲדַבֵּר; and similarly, always with הַשְׁכֵּם, 7, 25. 11, 7. 25, 3. 4. 26, 5. 19. 32, 33 (rd. וָאֲלַמֵּד for the first וְלַמֵּד). 35, 14. 15. 44, 4. 2 Ch. 36, 15†.

13. ובית שמש קצרים] GK. § 145ᶜ. Cf. II 15, 23.

בעמק] An עמק, lit. *deepening*, is a 'highlander's term' for a broad depression between hills, especially for a 'wide avenue running up into a mountainous country, like the Vale of Elah [see on 17, 2], the Vale of Hebron, and the Vale of Aijalon' (G. A. Smith, *H. G.*, 384 f., 654 f.; cf. the writer's art. in *DB.* iv. 846 with list of עמקים mentioned in the OT.). Here it denotes (*EB.* s.v. BETH-SHEMESH) 'the broad, and beautiful, and still well-cultivated Wâdy eṣ-Ṣarâr' (*EB.* i. 567), up which the

---

¹ Jer. 41, 6 וַיֵּצֵא ... הָלֹךְ הָלֵךְ וּבָכֹה is anomalous; we should expect ... ויצא הָלֹךְ הָלֵךְ וּבָכֹה. Duhm, Cornill read, after LXX, וְהוּא וְהֵם הֹלְכִים הָלֹךְ וּבָכֹה.

railway now climbs from Jaffa to Jerusalem. Beth-shemesh is now *'Ain Shems*, 917 feet above the sea, on the slope of the hills on the S. of this Wādy, 12 miles SE. of Eqron, and 14 miles W. of Jerusalem. The Wādy opens out on the N. of it, with Zor'āh (Jud. 13, 2 etc.) now *Ṣar'ah*, 2 miles to the N., on the hills on the opposite (N.) side of the Wādy.

לראות] LXX εἰς ἀπάντησιν αὐτῆς = לִקְרָאתוֹ. Though לראות is not ungrammatical, yet the pregnant construction וישמחו לקראתו is so much more forcible and idiomatic (Jud. 19, 3 וישמח לקראתו: also with other verbs, as 14, 5 שָׁאַג לקראתו; *ch.* 16, 4 ויחרדו לקראתו; 21, 2) that it decidedly deserves the preference.

14. בית־השמש] Formed according to the regular custom when the gentile adj. or patronymic of a compound name is defined by the art.: so בית־הלחמי (16, 1), בית־האלי (1 Ki. 16, 34), אבי־העזרי (Jud. 6, 11).

17–18ᵃ. Apparently (on account of the discrepancy between *v.* 18ᵃ and *v.* 4) not part of the original narrative: see p. 61. *V.* 18ᵇ will then continue *v.* 16.

17. עזה] The most south-westerly of the Philistine cities, the last town in Palestine on the route to Egypt. *Ashkelon* was on the sea-coast, 12 miles north of it. The site of *Gath* is not certain (Buhl, 196; G. A. Smith, *H. G.* 196); but it was not improbably *Tell eṣ-Ṣāfiyeh*, the *collis clarus* of William of Tyre, and the fortress *Blanca guarda*, or *Blanchegarde*, of the Crusaders, now a mud village, on the top of a projecting limestone rock, with conspicuous white cliffs, 300 feet high, looking down towards Ashkelon, 12 miles to the WNW. (see view in Conder, *Tent Work in Palestine*, ed. 1887, p. 273: see also p. 275 f.; *H. G.* 196, 226 f.; Cheyne, art. GATH in *EB.*).

18. לחמשת הסרנים] *belonging to* the five lords: ל' as 14, 16.

מעיר וג'] A similar delimitation in 2 Ki. 17, 9 = 18, 8 ממגדל נוצרים עד עיר מבצר. הַפְּרָזִי = *men of the open country, country-folk:* cf. Dt. 3, 5 עָרֵי הַפְּרָזִי cities of the *country-folk:* Zech. 2, 8 פְּרָזוֹת תֵּשֵׁב ירושלם Jerusalem shall sit (metaph. = be inhabited) as *open country districts.*

ועד אבל הגדולה] אבל *meadow* gives no sense here. We must evidently read אבן (see *v.* 15) with LXX, Targ., and for עַד either וְעֵדָה (see Jos. 24, 27. Gen. 31, 52) or (see Jud. 6, 24) וְעוֹד: then, placing a full stop at the end of 18ᵃ, we shall get 'And the great *stone,* upon which they set etc., is a *witness* [or, is *still*] to this day in the field of Joshua the Beth-shemeshite.' The stone on which the ark was set was still shewn in the field of Joshua at Beth-shemesh; and it is appealed to by the narrator as evidence of the facts which he relates.

אבן הגדלה] The use of the art. with the adj. when the subst. is without it, is rare in classical Hebrew, being mostly restricted to cases in which the subst. is a word which may be regarded as defining itself (יום Gen. 1, 31. 2, 3. Ex. 20, 10 al., חצר 1 Ki. 7, 8. 12. Ez. 40, 28; שער Ez. 9, 2. Zech. 14, 10), and even then being exceptional. The instances have been analysed by the present writer in *Tenses,* § 209 ; cf. GK. § 126ʷ, ˣ. Examples of a more exceptional type are *ch.* 12, 23. 16, 23. II 12, 4. 21, 19. Jer. 6, 20. 17, 2.

In *post*-Biblical Hebrew this construction became more common : in the Mishnah there are some forty instances (including some standing ones, as כְּנֶסֶת הַגְּדוֹלָה ‘ the Great Synagogue,’ שׁוֹר הַנִּסְקָל ‘ the ox to be stoned ’), but mostly in cases where (according to Segal, *JQR.* 1908, pp. 665–667 = *Mišnaic Hebrew,* 1909, pp. 19–21) some *emphasis* rests upon the attribute, as contrasted with something different.

Here it is best to restore the art. (וְעֵדָה [or וְעֹד] הָאֶבֶן הַגְּדוֹלָה וג׳).

19. In this verse as it stands in MT. there must be some error, though it is not possible to restore the text with entire certainty. (1) ראה ב׳ does not mean (AV.) *to look into* (which would be rather ראה אל תוך), but *to look on* or *at,* sometimes with satisfaction and pleasure (ψ. 27, 13), at other times with interest and attention (Cant. 6, 11 to *look upon* the green plants of the valley : Ez. 21, 26 he looked *at* the liver : Qoh. 11, 4 ראה בעבים he that looketh *at* the clouds : Gen. 34, 1 : Jud. 16, 27 *end*): if, therefore, the expression be used here in a bad sense, it will signify *to gaze at,* viz. with an unbecoming interest (so We. Kp. Stade, *Gesch.* i. 204). (2) The number of those smitten is incredible in itself ; and the juxtaposition of חמשים without ו is another indication of error[1]. It is true, both numbers are in LXX: but there they are even more out of the question than in MT.; for LXX limits the slaughter to the sons of Jechoniah (בהם for בעם)! Josephus speaks of the number smitten as only *seventy ;* and modern scholars generally (including Keil) reject חמשים אלף איש as a gloss,

---

[1] These are some examples of the repetition of שׁנה, with similar *ascending* numeration, Gen. 5, 8. 10. 13 al., but none without ו.

though how it found its way into the text must remain matter of speculation.

(3) Instead of ויך באנשי בית שמש LXX has the remarkable reading καὶ οὐκ ἠσμένισαν οἱ υἱοὶ Ἰεχονίου ἐν τοῖς ἀνδράσιν Βαιθσαμυς, the originality of which speaks strongly in its favour. Unfortunately ἀσμενίζω does not occur elsewhere in LXX., so that it cannot be ascertained definitely what Hebrew word it may here express. It is not probable that such an unusual word would have been chosen to render a common term like שמח (which indeed in *v.* 13 is represented by the ordinary εὐφραίνεσθαι). We. suggests ולא נקּוּ בני יכניהו, i.e. 'And the sons of Jechoniah *came not off guiltless*, were not unpunished, among the men of Beth-shemesh, because they had gazed at the ark of Yahweh ; and he smote among them (בהם for בעם, as LXX) seventy men ' (so Now.). Klostermann suggests the rare חָדוּ (Ex. 18, 9) for ἠσμένισαν : 'And the sons of Jechoniah *rejoiced not* among the men of Beth-shemesh, when (*or* because) they looked upon the ark of Yahweh[1] ' (so Sm. Bu.). Whatever be the verb to which ἠσμ. corresponds, the adoption of the LXX reading effects a material improvement in the style of the verse : in MT. ויך בעם follows awkwardly upon ויך באנשי בית־שמש, and is in fact tautologous, whereas ויך בהם of LXX refers naturally and consistently to the sons of Jechoniah before mentioned. The first ויך in MT., on the other hand, must be just the mutilated remnant of the clause preserved in LXX[2].

20. מעלינו] more than ממנו,—*from upon us, from off us*, so as to relieve us of its presence: cf. II 13, 17. 20, 21. 22. 1 Ki. 15, 19. 2 Ki. 12, 19ᵇ. 18, 14. Nu. 21, 7.

21. ורדו] The site of Qiryath-ye'arim is not certain, as the name has not been preserved : but it was most probably (Robinson ; *EB.* s.v. ; cf. G. A. Smith, *H. G.* 226) at *Qaryet el-'Enab* (the ' City of grapes '), 9–10 miles NE. of Beth-shemesh, and 7 miles NW. of Jerusalem, among the hills, 2385 ft. above the sea. Beth-shemesh (see on *v.* 13) was much lower: hence 'come down' (notice 'went down,' of the

---

[1] Ew. Then. understand the passage similarly, though they read the less probable ולא שמחו.

[2] Vulg. represents the first איש by *viros*, the second by *plebis :* cf. Targ., and Jerus. *Sanh.* II 4 (20ᵇ 62), as cited by Aptow. *ZAW.* 1909, p. 243.

border from Qiryath-ye'arim to Beth-shemesh, in Josh. 15, 10)[1]. Topographical distinctions are always carefully observed by the Hebrew writers. Let the reader study, with this point of view in his mind, the history of Samson (Jud. 13–16).

7, 1. בנבעה] Read, probably, with 55 MSS., LXX, Pesh., Targ., and II 6, 3 אשר בנבעה.

In *ch.* 6, MT. presents two difficulties: (1) the abrupt mention of the mice in *v.* 4: (2) the disagreement between *vv.* 4 and 18 in the number of images of mice—*v.* 18 speaking of an indefinite number (one for each town and village), *v.* 4 only of five. At first sight, LXX appears to remove these difficulties: for (1) the mention of the mice in *v.* 4 is prepared by two notices describing a plague of mice[2] in the country in 5, 6 (ויעלו עכברים בתוך ארצם) and 6, 1 (וארצם שרצה עכברים); and (2) whereas in MT. 6, 5ᵃ is little more than a repetition of *v.* 4, in LXX *v.* 4 is confined to the עפלים, *v.* 5 to the mice, not, however, limited to five, but an unspecified number (4ᵇ καὶ εἶπαν, Κατ’ ἀριθμὸν τῶν σατραπῶν τῶν ἀλλοφύλων πέντε ἕδρας χρυσᾶς, ὅτι πταῖσμα ἐν ὑμῖν καὶ τοῖς ἄρχουσιν ὑμῶν καὶ τῷ λαῷ, 5ᵃ καὶ μῦς χρυσοῦς ὁμοίωμα τῶν μυῶν τῶν διαφθειρόντων τὴν γῆν). The additions of LXX in 5, 6. 6, 1, and the redistribution of the עפלים and the mice in *vv.* 4–5, are accepted by Thenius.

We. takes a different view. He argues with great force that *vv.* 4–5 MT. is right: the last clause of *v.* 4, 'for one plague was on you all, and on your lords,' he points out, is intended to explain that, although only *three* districts (Ashdod, Gath, and Eqron) were implicated in what had happened to the ark, *all* had suffered through the plague, and *all* must accordingly share in the אשם: the number *five* being thus chosen, as representing Philistia as a whole, it was sufficient for the mice as well as for the עפלים; and the cogency of the argument,

---

[1] Conder's site (*DB.* s.v.) at *'Erma*, 4 miles E. of Beth-shemesh, up the W. Ismain, is much less probable (cf. Buhl, *Geogr.* 167 *n.*). Notice (1) that there is no sufficient reason for supposing 'mount Ye'arim' ('mount of the woods') to have been contiguous to Qiryath-ye'arim; and (2) in so far as the identification rests upon the resemblance of *'Erma* with *Ye'arim,* that the *m* is radical in one word, and merely the mark of the plural in the other.

[2] On the destructiveness of field-mice, see Arist. *Hist. Nat.* vi. 37, p. 580ᵇ, 15–20, who relates how they would sometimes in harvest time appear suddenly in unspeakable numbers, and destroy a crop entirely in a single night.

'for one plague' etc., would be just destroyed, if it were to be applied to the number of the עפלים alone. He concludes that 6, 4–5, as read in LXX, have been corrected for the purpose of agreeing with *v.* 18 ; and accepting *vv.* 4–5 MT., he rejects *v.* 18[a] (to הפרזי), and with it *v.* 17, as inconsistent (in the *number* of golden mice offered) with *v.* 4 [1].

As regards the further point, the abrupt mention of the mice in *v.* 4, he considers the difficulty as apparent merely : the mice, he argues, are mentioned not because there had been a plague of them, but as *emblems of a pestilence* [2] *:* the double אשם, like the double dream in Gen. 41, 25, relates to one and the same object, viz. the plague of עפלים : and *v.* 5[a] is a redactional gloss [3], due to the supposition that *v.* 4 implied that there had been a plague of mice. And accordingly he rejects the additions of LXX in 5, 6. 6, 1, as made merely for the purpose of relieving the apparent difficulty of *vv.* 4–5, on the theory that these verses pre-supposed an actual plague of mice. He admits, however, justly, that if this explanation of the 'mice' in *v.* 4 be not accepted, there is no alternative but to treat the additions in question as a genuine part of the original text.

7, 2–17. *Samuel's judgeship. Defeat of Philistines at Eben-ezer.*

2. 'וירבו הימים וג] *that the days were multiplied* (Gen. 38, 12), *and became twenty years.* Not as EVV.

וינהו] Only here. נהה in Heb. means *to mourn* or *lament* (Ez. 32, 18): so, if the reading be correct, it will be most safely explained as a pregn. constr., *mourned* or *sighed after Yahweh* = went after Him mourning or sighing (for the Nif. cf. נאנח) [4]. It is doubtful if

---

[1] The attempt has been made to reconcile *vv.* 4 and 18 by supposing *v.* 4 to relate the *proposal of the priests*, and *v.* 18 to describe *what was actually done.* But had the proposal not been adopted as it was first made, it is natural to suppose that this would have been in some manner indicated : as it is, the phrase in *v.* 10 is *And the men did so.*

[2] Comp. the form in which the story of the destruction of Sennacherib's army reached Herodotus (2. 141) : *field-mice* gnawing the leathern thongs of the soldiers' bows and shields.

[3] So in his *Composition des Hex. und der hist. Bücher* [2] (1889), p. 241.

[4] So Ewald, *Hist.* ii. 602 (E. T. 427). ܐܢܰܚ is cited by the Syriac lexicographers (PS. col. 2294) with the meaning *ingemuit.* In Eth. the corresponding verb means *recreari, respirare,* in the causative conj. (II. 1) *to console,* in the reflexive (III. 3) *to console oneself* (sc. by confession, as Lev. 16, 21) : Dillm. col. 632.

Ges. is right in rendering *were gathered*. It is true that אתנהי occurs in Targ. in a connexion which implies gathering, but it is always used with reference to some *religious* object, being often followed by לפולחן י״י, or למפלח י״י, so that it is doubtful if it expresses *to be gathered* simply. Thus *ch.* 12, 14 ותתנהון . . . בתר פולחנא די״י אלהכון for 30, 21 ויתנהון למפלח די״י . . . לשמא די״י : היה אחר י״י : Jer. 3, 17 13 ,33 ועמא בית ישראל יתנהון באוריתא: 22ᵇ ,31 ויפלחון לפולחני ויתנהון 17 ,2 .Hos ; (תעברנה על ידי מונה for) יתנהון עמא על ידי משיחא למימרי חמן ,18 ויתנהון לפולחני, similarly 3, 3. 5. The use of נזעק *to be called together* is not parallel: for נהה is not a synonym of זעק. Probably the Targumic usage is merely based upon the Hebrew word occurring in this passage, and the sense which it was there presumed to have, and cannot therefore be regarded as *independent* evidence of its meaning. Whether, however, וינהו is correct, is very doubtful. LXX have ἐπέβλεψε, whence We. conjectured וַיִּפְנוּ (cf. Ez. 29, 16); but perhaps וַיִּטּוּ (Klo. Bu.) is better; cf. 1 Ki. 2, 28; and (with לֵב) Jud. 9, 3. As Ehrlich justly remarks, וינהרו (Is. 2, 2 = Mic. 4, 1; Jer. 31, 12. 51, 44†) *ap.* Kittel is much too poetical for the present context: but his own ויהיו (12, 14) does not read very well after ויהיו just before.

3. הסירו וג׳] The same phrase in Gen. 35, 2. 4; Jos. 24, 23; Jud. 10, 16. אלהי נֵכָר is lit. *gods of foreign-ness* (=*foreign gods*): so בן (בני) נכר = *foreigner(s)*.

הכינו] *make firm, fix*; cf. Job 11, 13. ψ. 78, 8. 1 Ch. 29, 18 (וְהָכֵן לבבם אליך). 2 Ch. 12, 14 al. Comp. נָכוֹן *fixed*, of the heart, ψ. 57, 8. 78, 37, and רוח נכון a *firm*, unwavering, spirit, 51, 12.

עַשְׁתָּרֹת] The pl. of עַשְׁתֹּרֶת, as the name is vocalized by the Massorites: but the Gk. Ἀστάρτη (cf. also the Ass. *Ishtar*) make it practically certain that the real pronunciation was '*Ashtart*, עַשְׁתֹּרֶת (like מֹלֶךְ for *Milk*) having been chosen for the purpose of suggesting בֹּשֶׁת *shame* (cf. on II 4, 4). עשתרת is mentioned frequently in Phoenician inscriptions, often by the side of Baal. Thus Cooke, *NSI.* No. 5 (the Inscription of Eshmun'azar of Ṣidon), l. 14 f. ואמי אמעשתרת כהנת עשתרת רבתן and my mother Am'ashtart, priestess of 'Ashtart our lady; (l. 17 f.) ואנחן אש בנן בתם לאלן צדנם בצדן ארץ ים בת לבעל צדן ובת לעשתרת שם בעל and we are they who have built temples [בָּתִּים] to the gods of the Ṣidonians in Ṣidon, the sea country, a temple [בַּית] to Baʻal of Ṣidon, and a temple to ʻAshtart, the name of Baʻal; 6, 5; 13, 3 (from Kition in Cyprus) an image [סמלת][1] erected by one Yaash לרבתי לעשתרת to her lady, to ʻAshtart; 38, 3 (from Gaulus, i.e. Malta) מקדש בת עשתרת the sanctuary of the temple of ʻAshtart; 45, 1 (from Carthage); *CIS.* I. i. 135, 1; 140, 1 לעשתרת [נח]שת ארך מזבח to ʻAshtart of Eryx[2], an altar of bronze; 255 (from Carthage) עבדמלקרת עבד עשתרת האדרת ʻAbdmelqart, servant of ʻAshtart the glorious; 263 (do.) לרבת לתנת פן בעל ולאדן לבעל חמן אש אמעשתרת אש בעמת אש עשתרת [נדר] to the lady Tanith, the face [probably = revelation] of Baal, and to the lord Baal Ḥamman, which [אֲשֶׁר] Amʻashtart, who was in the congregation of the men [אִישׁ] of ʻAshtart (i.e. among the people attached to her temple), vowed. In Ṣidon ʻAshtart appears to have been the presiding goddess (cf. 1 Ki. 11, 5. 33 עשתרת אלהי צדנם): in Tyre she was subordinated to Melqart (מלקרת). A temple of ʻAshtart in the Philistine town of Ashqelon is mentioned in 31, 10 (see the note). The worship of ʻAshtart was very widely diffused: see particulars in the articles cited on p. 64 *footnote;* and cf. Head, *Hist. Numorum*[2], *Index*, p. 941[b].

העשתרת] *The ʻAshtōreths* will denote either images of ʻAshtart, or (preferably) the goddesses of that name which were worshipped in different localities, just as הבעלים *v.* 4 are the local or other special Baʻals: cf. בעל צדן just cited; בעל לבנן Cooke, No. 54 *a;* בעל צר 36, 1; בעל תרז *Baal of Tarsus* on coins of that city, Gesenius, *Monumenta Phoenicia,* p. 276 f., and Plate 36, VII. VIII. A, B, C, Cooke, pp. 343–346, Head, *Hist. Numorum*, pp. 615, 616[3]; בעל שמם *Baal of heaven,* Cooke, 9, and often: בעל חמן *Baal Ḥamman,* of uncertain meaning (*EB.* i. 402; Paton, as cited, p. 64 *n.,* p. 287 f.), constantly on the Punic votive tablets from N. Africa, Cooke, p. 104; בעל מרפא (apparently) *Baal the Healer, CIS.* I. i. 41 (from Kition); Βαλμαρκὼς or Βαλμάρκωδος, i.e. בעל מרקד *Baal of dances,* in inscriptions from the site of an ancient temple at Deir el Kalʻa in the neighbourhood

---

[1] Heb. סמל (Ez. 8, 3. 5), often (masc. and fem.) in Phoenician inscriptions: e.g. Cooke, 13, 2; 23, 2–5; 25, 1; comp. above, p. 34 *note.*

[2] ʻErycina ridens,' Hor. *Carm.* i. 2. 33.

[3] Ed. 2 (1911), pp. 731 f., 816.

of Beyrout[1]. And in the OT. itself, בעל זבוב, בעל ברית, בעל פעור, and, as preserved in names of places, בעל גד *Baal of Fortune,* בעל מעון, בעל פעור (in Hos. 9, 10), בעל צפון, etc.[2] ; cf. on II 5, 20.

On the *position* of והעשתרות (separated from אלהי הנכר, and after מתוככם), cf. on 6, 11.

ויצל] *that he may,* or (Anglice) *and he will.* On the jussive, see *Tenses,* § 62.

5. המצפתה] with the art., the word being an appellative, meaning the *outlook-point.* The Miẓpah meant is the lofty height now called *Nebi Samwîl* (2935 feet), 5 miles NW. of Jerusalem.

6. לפני יהוה] LXX add ארצה, perhaps rightly: the water was poured out not as a libation (for which וַיִּסְכּוּ would have been said), but probably as a symbolical act implying a complete separation from sin: sin was to be cast away as completely as water poured out upon the earth, II 14, 4 (Ehrlich).

8. אל תחרש ממנו] pregn. ' do not be deaf (turning) from us,' cf. ψ. 28, 1 (GK. § 119ᶠᶠ). מזעק *so as not* to cry (lit. *away from* crying), etc. (§ 119ʸ); cf. Is. 33, 15ᵇ. Gen. 27, 1.

9. אחד] as *v.* 12, and 6, 7.

עולה כליל לי״י] ' as a burnt sacrifice, (even) a whole offering, unto Yahweh.' For כליל cf. Lev. 6, 15 : חק־עולם לי״י כליל תקטר 'a perpetual due, unto Yahweh as a whole offering shall it be burnt,' 16 : Dt. 13, 17. 33, 10. LXX σὺν παντὶ τῷ λαῷ is merely a paraphrase ; cf. Dt. 13, 17, where כליל = πανδημεὶ (We.). כליל occurs as the name of a sacrifice in the Carthaginian Table of Sacrifices and Dues, now at

---

[1] *CIG.* 4536 ; Le Bas and Waddington, *Voyage Archéologique,* vol. iii. pt. 6 (Inscriptions de la Syrie), No. 1855 Εἴλαθί μοι, Βαλμαρκώς, κοίρανε κώμων ; *ib.* 1857 Θεῷ Βαλμαρκῶδι ; Clermont-Ganneau, *Recueil d'Archéologie Orientale* (Paris, 1885 ff.), p. 95 [Κυ]ρίῳ [γ]ε[ν]ναίῳ Βαλμαρκῶδι . . . ; p. 103 Διονύσιος Γοργίου, δευτεροστάτης θεοῦ Βαλμαρκώδου, ἀνέθηκε τὰ δύο. . . . For many other special Ba'als, see Paton (as cited in the next note), p. 285 ff.

[2] The notices of the cult of both Baal and 'Ashtart, as attested by inscriptions and proper names, are collected and discussed by Baethgen, *Beiträge zur Semitischen Religionsgeschichte* (1888), pp. 17-29, 31-37, to be compared with Nöldeke's review in the *ZDMG.* 1888, p. 470 ff. See also the articles ASHTORETH (Driver) and BAAL (Peake) in *DB.,* and by Moore in *EB. ;* and the very full articles, esp. the one on Baal, by L. B. Paton in Hastings' *Encycl. of Rel. and Ethics,* vol. ii. (1909).

Marseilles: Cooke, *NSI.* 42, 3. 5. 7. 9 (so 43, 5), and in the expression שלם כליל 42, 3. 5. 7. 9. 11 (see the notes, pp. 117, 118).

10. ויהי שמואל מעלה] The ptcp. marks the action *in the course of which* the Philistines drew near: so e. g. 2 Ki. 6, 5. 26 (the new subject in the principal clause following standing *first* for emphasis).

11. בית־כר] Not elsewhere mentioned: Targ. בית שרון; Klo. conjectures בֵית־חֹרוֹן (so Dh.). The Beth-ḥorons were about 6 miles NW. of Nebi Samwîl; and the road down to the west from Nebi Samwîl would pass 'under' them, about 1½ mile to the south.

12. השן] We expect some known locality to be specified, corresponding to המצפה, not 'an unnamed crag of rock' (We.). LXX τῆς παλαιᾶς[1] (similarly Pesh. ـمـ) points to such, viz. הַיְשָׁנָה, or יְשָׁנָה (2 Ch. 13, 19). If, however, this was 'Ain Sîniyeh (Buhl, 173; *EB.* s.v.), 3¼ miles N. of Bethel, it was 10 miles from Miẓpah; and not likely to have been named with it in fixing the position of Eben-ezer.

עד הנה] We. Bu. Now. Sm. עֶדָה היא כי; cf. Gen. 24, 30. Jos. 24, 27.

16. והלך וג'] Observe the series of *perfects* with ו conv., descriptive of Samuel's *custom* (see on 1, 3).

מדי שנה בשנה] The same idiom—the idea of recurrency expressed by שנה בשנה (1, 7) being strengthened by the addition of מדי—is found also Zech. 14, 16. 2 Ch. 24, 5† (Is. 66, 23 is to be explained differently: מדי חדש is there made more precise by the addition of בחדשו, on the analogy of דבר יום ביומו Ex. 5, 13 al.).

בית־אל] now *Beitîn*, on a rising hill, 10 miles N. of Jerusalem.

הגלגל] 'The (sacred stone-) circle.' There were several 'Gilgals' in Palestine, the most famous being the one in the Jordan-valley, a little E. of Jericho. The one mentioned here, though in *DB.* ii. 176ᵇ identified with that, is however not likely to have been as distant, and is more probably the village now called *Jiljíliyeh*, 7 miles N. of Bethel. See further *EB.* s.v. On הרמה, see p. 3 f.

את כל המקומות האלה [את is very difficult. Grammatically, the clause is most easily taken as epexeg. of את ישראל 'he judged Israel, even all these places' (Keil): but 'Israel' denotes naturally such a much wider whole than the three places named, that the limitation implied

---

[1] For the *translation* of a n. pr. by LXX, see Jud. 1, 15. 35. 4, 11. 15, 17 al.

in this construction is unnatural.   If such were the sense intended by
the original narrator it would be best to treat את ישראל as a gloss,
introduced on the ground of *v.* 15 by one who conceived Bethel,
Gilgal, and Miẓpah as too narrow a sphere for Samuel's judicial
activity.   The alternative construction is to treat את as the prep. =
near, as in the geographical phrase . . . אשר את : Jud. 3, 19. 4, 11.
1 Ki. 9, 26. 2 Ki. 9, 27: the meaning will then be that the place of
judgement was not *in* but *near* or *beside* the cities mentioned.   It is
doubtful, however, if the passages cited justify this rendering ; for they
are not parallel in form, and את is not construed in them with a *verb.*
AV. *in* is not defensible as a rendering of את : את only (apparently)
signifies *in* or *through,* when it stands to mark the *accusative* after
a verb of motion (Dt. 1, 19; 2, 7).   Ehrlich would read אל, comparing
Dt. 16, 6. 1 Ki. 8, 29ᵇ. 30.

Judgement was regarded as a sacred act (cf. Ex. 18, 15. 16. 22,
7–8, with the writer's notes in the *Camb. Bible*) and administered at
sacred places (cf. Qadesh, 'holy,' also called 'En-Mishpāṭ, 'Spring
of judgement,' Gen. 14, 7 ; and Jud. 4, 6 Deborah judging under
a sacred tree); and from LXX ἐν πᾶσι τοῖς ἡγιασμένοις τούτοις it
might be inferred that the translators read המקדשים (i.e. הַמְּקֻדָּשִׁים,
misread הַמְקֻדָּשִׁים).   Even, however, if this were not the case, מקום
itself (like the Arab. *maqām*) appears to have sometimes the technical
sense of a *sacred* place : cf. Gen. 12, 6, with Skinner's note.

17. שָׁפֵט] Why the pausal form stands here with a *conjunctive*
accent, it seems impossible to explain: cf. Ew. § 138ᵃ *note ;* GK.
§ 29ⁱ *n.*

8. *Introduction to second account* (10, 17–27ᵃ) *of Saul's appointment as
king.   The people ask for a king in consequence of the misconduct
of Samuel's sons, acting as their father's deputies.*

8, 2. הבכור יואל וג׳] A comparison of 1 Ch. 6, 13 is instructive, as
illustrating the manner in which errors have found their way into
MT.,—in this case, by letters having fallen out in the process of
transcription (הבכור [יואל] ו[ה][שני אביה).

בבאר־שבע] in the far south, on the edge of the desert, 50 miles
SSW. of Jerusalem.

3. ויטו אחרי] Cf. Ex. 23, 2 לנטות אחרי רבים; 1 Ki. 2, 28.

ויטו משפט] 'and *turned aside* (i.e. *perverted*) judgement,' Ex. 23, 6. Dt. 16, 19. 24, 17 al.

5ᵃ. אתה זקנת] '*Thou* (emph.) art old.' Notice the separate pronoun.

5ᵇ. Cf. for the phraseology Dt. 17, 14 ואמרת אשימה עלי מלך ככל הגוים אשר סביבתי.

7ᵃ. . . . לבל אשר] *with regard to all that* . . . Cf. 12, 1. Jos. 1, 18. 22, 2ᵇ.

7ᵇ. Notice the emphatic position of אתך and אתי. Cf. Is. 43, 22 ולא אתי קראת יעקב; 57, 11 (*bis*); and see further on 15, 1.

מִמְּלךָ] The מִן as in 7, 8.

8. עשו] LXX adds ἐμοὶ = לִי, which seems indeed to be pre-supposed by גם־לך ('to thee *also*') at the end of the verse (Th. We. Bu. etc.).

9. אך כי] (only here) = 'except *that*' . . .: cf. אפס כי by the side of אפס alone (Nu. 13, 28), אמנם כי (Job 12, 2), הנה כי (ψ. 128, 4), הכי (II 9, 1 al.), הלא כי (II 13, 28), אם לא כי (Dt. 32, 30).

העד תעיד בהם] העיד is properly *to bear witness* in a court of law, then more generally (like *testari*, μαρτύρομαι) *to testify, aver solemnly, protest,*—sq. ב, as usually directed *against* a person,—especially in connexion with a solemn charge or threat: Gen. 43, 3 העד העיד בנו האיש. Ex. 19, 21. 23. 1 Ki. 2, 42. Jer. 11, 7. ψ. 50, 7. 81, 9.

10. מֵאֵתּוֹ] מֵאֵת = παρὰ with a gen. (2, 23): so with שאל Jud. 1, 14 al. (cf. שאל מֵעִם, *ch.* 1, 17), דרש 1 Ki. 22, 7 al. (*Lex.* 86ᵇ).

11. את בניכם יקח] Note how in *vv.* 11–17 the object is in each case placed emphatically *before* the verb.

ושם לו וג'] 'and will place for himself (1 Ki. 20, 34. Jos. 8, 2; cf. *Lex.* 515ᵇ h, *a*) among his chariotry (collectively, as II 15, 1), and among his horsemen.' For ורצו וג', cf. on 22, 17.

12. ולשום] 'and will be for making them,' etc.: an example of the so-called 'periphrastic future,' which occurs now and then in simple prose : see *Tenses,* § 206, GK. § 114ᵖ; and cf. Lev. 10, 10. 11.

13. לרקחות ולטבחות] The form טַבָּח denotes one who possesses an *established character* (as נַגָּח *given to butting*, קַנָּא *jealous*), or *capacity* (as טַבָּח *cook* [lit. *slaughterer*], גַּנָּב *thief*, דַּיָּן *judge*): see GK. § 84 *b*ᵇ, and for a longer list of examples Kön. ii. 89 f., cf. 179 (4). Ehrlich would point לִרְקָחוֹת וּלְטַבָּחוֹת, remarking that 'the later language has indeed

abstract nouns of the form קְטָלָה, but at no time has Hebrew had a *fem.* from the form קְטָל.'

15. 17. יַעֲשֶׂר] Read probably the *Pi'el* (denom.: GK. § 52ʰ) יְעַשֵּׂר: see Neh. 10, 38. And so Dt. 26, 12 (see 14, 22). Neh. 10, 39.

16. בחוריבם] LXX בְּקַרְבֶם (Ehrlich): no doubt, correctly. The 'young men' have been dealt with implicitly already in *v.* 11 f.(בניכם): in this verse the enumeration begins with *slaves*, and continues with *asses.* בקר is a *collective* noun, and may thus be construed with a plur. (II 6, 6 MT. 1 Ki. 5, 3. Job 1, 14). The instances of בקרים are too rare and doubtful (in Neh. 10, 37 unnecessary; in 2 Ch. 4, 3 פקעים must be read with 1 Ki. 7, 24; and in Am. 6, 12 read בבקר ים), for בקריכם (adopted in ed. 1 with We.) to be probable.

ועשה ונ'] 'and use them for his business:' מלאכה as Ez. 15, 5. Ex. 38, 24.

17. ואתם] and *ye yourselves* (opp. to the children and possessions mentioned before).

18. מלפני] a *later* usage, in such a case as this, than מפני (contrast Ex. 3, 7): see *Lex.* 818ᵃ b. Ehrl. would read מפני, supposing מלפני to have arisen from the following מל in מלבכם through a scribe's error.

בחרתם לכם] The reflexive dative in common with בחר: e.g. 13, 2. 17, 40. Gen. 13, 11. Jos. 24, 15. 22.

19. ויאמרו לא] So Gen. 19, 2: cf. לא לו Hab. 1, 6. 2, 6 al. The dagesh in these cases is probably designed for the purpose of securing a distinct articulation of the consonant (Delitzsch on ψ. 94, 12). Comp. Spurrell's note on Gen. *l. c.*; and add to the references there given Baer, Pref. to *Liber Proverbiorum* (rules of Dagesh), p. xiv; GK. § 20ᵍ; and König, *Lehrgebäude der Hebr. Sprache* (1881), i. p. 59 (where the subject is treated at length).

כי אם] = *but* (10, 19. 12, 12 כי alone): so 2, 15. 21, 5 al. See *Lex.* 475ᵃ.

9, 1—10, 16. *First (and oldest) account of Saul's appointment as king. Saul is anointed king by Samuel for the purpose of defending Israel against the Philistines (v. 16), and bidden 'do as his hand may find' when occasion arises.*

9, 1. מבן־ימין] That Kish was of Benjaminite descent is stated in the later part of the verse; and we seem to desiderate here a statement of the *place* to which he belonged (cf. 1, 1 ; Jud. 13, 2). Perhaps, therefore, we should read, with We. Bu. Now. etc., מגבעת בנימן (see 13, 15). 'Gibeah of Benjamin' (13, 15. II 23, 29; cf. Jud. 19, 14 הגבעה אשר לבנימין), or 'of Saul' (11, 4. 15, 34), or הגבעה alone (10, 26. 22, 6. 23, 19. 26, 1), was the modern *Tell el-Fûl*,—or, as there are no ancient remains here, *Ḥawānîl*, 500 yards to the NW. (*ZDPV.* 1909, 2–13),—3 miles N. of Jerusalem (cf. Is. 10, 29).

בן איש ימיני] 'the son of a Benjaminite:' the name of Aphiaḥ's father was either not known or unimportant. There is force, however, in Smith's remark, 'בן איש ימיני is not without analogy, at least איש ימיני is found II 20, 1. Est. 2, 5. But it is unusual to terminate a genealogy by saying "*son of* a Benjaminite." It is probable that בן is the error of a scribe who expected to continue the genealogy.'

ימיני] This occurs elsewhere as the patronymic of בנימן: *v.* 4. 22, 7 בְּנֵי ימיני; II 20, 1 איש ימיני as here.

גבור חיל] Here, probably, as 2 Ki. 15, 20 (Bu.), Ru. 2, 1, a sturdy man of *substance* (not of *valour*, 2 Ki. 5, 1 etc.), a sturdy, honest (cf. on 10, 26), well-to-do country farmer.

3. לקיש] the dative of relation, going with והאבדנה: see *v.* 20 (לך); and cf. Is. 26, 14; *ch.* 13, 22 (נמצא ל׳). But perhaps אתנות לקיש (some) *asses of Kish's* should be read (Nöld. Bu. Ehrl.); cf. 17, 8. 1 Ki. 2, 39 (GK. § 129ᶜ).

אֶת־אַחַד מהנערים] אחד is so closely joined to, and limited by, מהנערים that it lapses into the constr. st. : so frequently, as Gen. 3, 22 כְּאַחַד ממנו, Jud. 17, 11 כְּאַחַד מבניו, etc. (GK. § 130ᵃ). Respecting את with a word not strictly defined see Ew. 277ᵈ, GK. § 117ᵈ; and comp. Ex. 21, 28. Nu. 21, 9. II 4, 11 ; and (with the same word as here) Nu. 16, 15 אֶת־אַחַד מֵהֶם[1].

4. The repeated change of number in this *v.* can hardly be original, though parallels can be found in MT.: Nu. 13, 22 ויבא ; 33, 7 וישב. But it can scarcely be questioned that in all these cases the pl. was designed throughout by the original writers. See the Introduction, § 4. 1 c (*a*). Read therefore, with LXX, ויעברו (thrice).

---

[1] In illustration of a man being led to his destiny through the search for lost animals, Wellh. (*Reste Arab. Heidentumes*, 148, ed. 2, 201) cites *Kitâb al-Aghâni*, i. 133, 4. 8, xix. 3 ff.

ארץ שלישה] presumably the district round בעל שלישה (2 Ki. 4, 42), which, from the context, cannot have been far from the 'Gilgal' of *v.* 38. This 'Gilgal,' from which (2 Ki. 2, 1. 3) Elijah and Elisha 'went down' *to* Bethel, cannot, as the editors of the RV. with marg. references strangely suggest on *v.* 1, be the Gilgal of Jos. 5, 9 in the Jordan valley, between Jericho and the Jordan, some 3000 ft. *below* Bethel, but is, no doubt, the 'Gilgal' of 1 S. 7, 16 (see note), the modern *Jiljîliyeh*, on a high hill (2441 ft.) 7 miles N. of Bethel. This Gilgal is indeed 450 ft. lower than Bethel; but it is separated from it by the great W. ej-Jîb (1746 ft., in some parts 2030 ft.), the descent into which may account for the '*went down* to Bethel' of 2 Ki. 2, 3 (*DB.* ii. 177ᵇ). Βαιθσαρισα (LXX for בעל שלישה in 2 Ki.) is said by Euseb. (*Onom.* 239, 92) to have been 15 Roman miles N. of Diospolis (Lydda), a situation which would just suit the ruined site *Sirîsiā*, 14⅓ Roman miles or 13 Engl. miles N. of Lydda (*EB.* s. v.). Or Ba'al-shalisha itself might very well be the modern *Kefr Thilth*, 4 miles NE. of Sirîsiā (Conder and others): the Arab. *th* corresponds correctly to the Heb. שׁ in שׁלשׁ. Either of these places would be about 25 miles NW. of Gibeah.

שעלים] not mentioned elsewhere. The name has often been supposed to be an error for שעלבים (Josh. 19, 42,—mentioned between Beth-shemesh and Aijalon: Jud. 1, 35; 1 Ki. 4, 9†), a place which, though it was no doubt in the neighbourhood, has been identified very precariously,—for the names do not agree phonetically,—with *Salbît*, 4 miles NW. of Aijalon. Aijalon would be about 20 miles S. of Kefr Thilth (above), and 12 miles W. of Gibeah.

Whether, however, all the places mentioned are rightly identified, must remain an open question : if the map be consulted, a journey in search of the lost asses from Gibeah (Tell el-Fûl) to Kefr Thilth (25 miles to the NW.), then 20 miles to the S., to some place near Aijalon (??), and thence either 13 miles back to Beit-Rîma, or 11 miles to Rentis, or 12 miles ENE. to Rām-Allah (see p. 4), all within 3 days (9, 20),—the land of Zuph (see p. 1) being visited, not because Samuel's home was in it, but accidentally (9, 5. 6),—does not seem very probable.

וָאָיִן] 'and [there was] nought (sc. of them).' In full, וְאֵינָם: but the absolute use of אין in cases such as this is idiomatic, esp. after בקש (Is. 41, 17 וּבִקְשׁוּ שָׁלֹם; Ez. 7, 25 הָעֲנִיִּים וְהָאֶבְיוֹנִים מְבַקְשִׁים מַיִם וָאַיִן; וְאַיִן: cf. *ch.* 10, 14 (כִּי אָיִן), 1 Ki. 18, 10), and קִוֵּה (Job 3, 9 יְקַו לְאוֹר וָאַיִן; Is. 59, 11 נְקַוֶּה לַמִּשְׁפָּט וָאַיִן; ψ. 69, 21). The וּ by GK. § 104ᵉ.

5. המה באו....ושאול אמר] On this graphic and idiomatic manner of expressing a synchronism in place of the more ordinary וַיְהִי כְּבוֹאָם בָּאֶרֶץ צוּף וַיֹּאמֶר שָׁאוּל, see *Tenses*, §§ 165–169 ; and cf. 20, 36 ; II 20, 8 ; Gen. 44, 3. 4; Jud. 15, 14 : also below *v.* 11 (with the ptcp.). 14, 27 ; 17, 23 ; 2 Ki. 2, 23. Ehrlich adds rightly that in this idiom the first sentence must only contain a single verb, with at most the addition of a negative circumst. clause, denoting time or place (as Gen. 44, 4): the Old Lat. ולא מצאו (cited in Kit.) is thus not original.

ארץ צוף] the home of Samuel, in Ephraim (see on 1, 1), which, if the places are rightly identified, Saul must have entered again from the W. end of Benjamin. In 10, 2, when Saul leaves Samuel, he re-enters the territory of Benjamin from the North.

דאג] *to be anxious* or *concerned:* ψ. 38, 19 I am *concerned* on account of my sin: Jos. 22, 24 מדאגה out of *concern.* The pf. and *waw* conv. in continuation of פֶּן יחדל, as Gen. 3, 22. Ex. 34, 15 f., and regularly: see *Tenses,* § 115, s.v., GK. § 112ᴾ.

6. אשר הלכנו עליה] 'on which we *have started.*' דרך is conceived here as including the goal: for of course they would not need to be told the way they had already come. Gen. 24, 42 differently: 'which I *am going* (הֹלֵךְ) upon;' so Jud. 18, 5.

7. והנה] 'And lo, we shall go, and what shall we bring?' etc. =And *if* we go, what . . .? So הֵן, Ex. 8, 22: cf. on 20, 12, and II 18, 11.

אזל] only here in prose, and only altogether five times in Hebrew, mostly in the sense of *going away, departing.* The word is common in Aramaic, being in the Targums the usual representative of הלך (which is not used with the same constancy in Aram. as in Heb.): e.g. in the Targ. of this chapter, *vv.* 3ᵇ. 6. 10.

אין]ותשורה אֵין־לְהָבִיא, as pointed, must, as Ehrlich remarks, belong to the inf. (*Lex.* 34ᵇ 5), and the meaning must be, 'and a present it is impossible to bring.' The sense required is 'and there is no present to bring,' for which we must read either וְאֵין תשורה להביא (Ex. 17, 1), or ותשורה אֵין להביא (Gen. 2, 5. Nu. 20, 5 לשתות ומים אַיִן. 2 Ki. 19, 3: *Lex.* 34ᵇ *top*). The latter is the natural correction to make here.

תשורה] only here: comp. the use of the cognate verb שׁוּר Is. 57, 9. The passage may be illustrated from 2 Ki. 4, 42 (the gifts offered to Elisha).

8. נמצא] *there is found,* idiom. for *there is here* (21, 4), or *there is present* (13, 16); cf. *Lex.* 594ᵃ.

ונתתי] Read וְנָתַתָּה with LXX, Th. We. Kp. etc.: the pf. with *waw* conv. with the force of a precative or mild imperative, as Jud. 11, 8: ch. 20, 25; 25, 27 al. (*Tenses,* § 119 δ).

9. An explanatory gloss, the proper place of which is evidently after *v.* 11, where הראה first occurs in the narrative.

יִקְרָא] *used to be called:* GK. § 107ᵉ.

לְפָנִים] So Ruth 4, 7 (probably a similar gloss); Jud. 1, 23.

11. ... הֵמָּה עֹלִים ... וְהֵמָּה מָצְאוּ] Where, in this idiom (see *v.* 5), the subject of the two verbs is the *same*, the pron. is repeated: as Gen. 38, 25; Jud. 18, 3. Hence 2 Ki. 10, 13 for וַיְהוּא read וְהוּא (connecting 12ᵇ with 13ᵃᵃ. וַיִּמְצָא, suggested in Kittel, would not here be a Heb. construction).

12. יֵשׁ] So, alone, in answer to a question, 2 Ki. 10, 15. Jer. 37, 17 †. Cf. *Lex.* 441ᵇ a.

הִנֵּה לְפָנֶיךָ מַהֵר עַתָּה כִּי הַיּוֹם] LXX ἰδοὺ κατὰ πρόσωπον ὑμῶν· νῦν διὰ τὴν ἡμέραν κτλ., whence We., developing a suggestion of Lagarde[1], restores הִנֵּה לִפְנֵיכֶם עַתָּה בָּא הַיּוֹם 'lo, he is before you: now, just at present, he is come to the city,' etc. In support of this restoration, We. remarks (1) that the *sing.* לְפָנֶיךָ agrees ill with *v.* 12, in which the pl. is used throughout: (2) against MT. מַהֵר, that no reason appears why Saul should *hasten*, if Samuel had just come into the city—not, as has been supposed, from some journey, but—from the neighbouring בָּמָה (where he had recently been, *v.* 23, and given instructions—אֲשֶׁר אָמַרְתִּי אֵלֶיךָ—to the cook). The superfluous הר in MT. We. plausibly explains as a remnant of the 'explicit' subject הָרֹאֶה, which had been inserted by a scribe as a subj. for לִפְנֵיכֶם (though, when the noun to which הנה refers has immediately preceded, the pron., whether הִנֵּה הוּא or (rare) הִנּוֹ, is not unfrequently omitted; cf. 15, 12. 16, 11. 30, 3. 16: *Tenses*, § 135. 6, 2). כַּהַיּוֹם will have the same force as in *v.* 13ᵇ, where it is likewise rendered διὰ τὴν ἡμέραν by LXX. The expression recurs Neh. 5, 11, and means *at once, just now*, the force of יוֹם, as in כְּהַיּוֹם 2, 16, being forgotten.

13. כֵּן] כֵּן often answers to כ in comparisons (*Lex.* 486ᵃ); but to express correspondence in *time*, it is very rare. Cf. Hos. 6, 3, as emended very plausibly by Giesebrecht, כְּשַׁחַר נָכוֹן כֵּן נִמְצָאֵהוּ.

כִּי הוּא] 'for *he* . . .' Notice the emphatic pronoun.

כִּי־אֹתוֹ כְהַיּוֹם תִּמְצְאוּן אֹתוֹ:] 'for *him* just now—you will find him,' the first אתו not being subordinated directly to the verb, but being resumed

---

[1] *Anmerkungen zur Griech. Uebersetzung der Proverbien* (1863), p. iii (לִפְנֵיכֶם לְפָנֶיךָ מַהֵר for הָרֹאֶה).

in אתו at the end, which thus becomes the direct accusative. The case is but an extension of the principle which is exemplified in Gen. 13, 15 כי את כל הארץ . . . לך אתתנה for all the land . . . ., to thee will I give it; 21, 13; *ch.* 25, 29 and often (*Tenses*, 197. 6). The resumption only happens to be rare when the first object is a *pronoun:* but see 2 Ki. 9, 27 גם אתו הכהו Him also, smite him! 'To omit [as Th. would do] one of the two אתו borders on barbarism' (We.). Klo. Bu., however, regard the first אתו as an error for עתה (cf. *v.* 12).

14. ויעלו העיר] The city itself then was on an elevation: and the במה on a still higher elevation outside it (לעלות הבמה: conversely, it is said, *v.* 25 וירדו מהבמה העיר).

בתוך העיר] Probably this is an ancient error for בתוך השער 'in the middle of the *gate:*' this agrees better both with *v.* 18 and with the language of this verse (Saul and his servant were *coming in,* and Samuel was *going out* to meet them).

15. וי״י גלה] An example of the manner in which the pluperfect tense is expressed in Hebrew. By the avoidance of the common descriptive tense ויגל י״י (i.e. lit. 'and Y. *went on to* uncover') the connexion with what precedes is severed, and the mind is left free to throw back the time of גלה to a period prior to the point which the narrative itself has reached. So regularly, as 14, 27. 25, 21. 28, 3; II 18, 18 etc. (*Tenses*, § 76 *Obs.;* GK. §§ 106f, 142b). For גלה את אזן פ׳, cf. 20, 2. 12. 13. 22, 8. 17. II 7, 27.

16. כָּעֵת מחר] 'at the time to-morrow' = when to-morrow has come. So II 20, 12. Ex. 9, 18. 1 Ki. 19, 2. 20, 6. 2 Ki. 7, 1. 18. 10, 6†. Cf. Gen. 18, 10. 14. 2 Ki. 4, 16. 17† כָּעֵת חַיָּה i. e. (probably) 'at the time, (as it is) reviving'=in the returning year. מחר must not in these phrases be regarded as a *genitive,* since כָּעֵת has the art. In full, they would be כְּהָיוֹת העת חיה, כְּהִיוֹת העת מחר (Hitzig on Job 39, 17).

נגיד] 'prince,' lit. *one in front, leader:* used often in the more elevated prose (especially in the prophetic utterances in Sam. and Kings) for the chief ruler of Israel (10, 1. 13, 14. 25, 30. II 5, 2. 6, 21. 7, 8. 1 Ki. 1, 35. 14, 7. 16, 2. 20, 5; cf. Is. 55, 4).

16b. את־עמי] LXX את־עֳנִי עמי (Ex. 3, 7): no doubt, rightly.

כי באה ונ׳] Gen. 18, 21.

17. ענהו] ענה as Jud. 18, 14. Is. 14, 10 al., to *answer,* not something which has been said, but as the situation may require or suggest (*Lex.* 773ᵃ).

אשר אמרתי אליך] ' *as to* whom I said unto thee, This one,' etc.; cf. *v.* 23ᵇ.

יעצר] here only in the sense of *coercere imperio:* cf. עָצַר Jud. 18, 7 (in a passage, however, where the text is very suspicious).

18. את שמואל] ' drew near *to* ' is evidently the sense that is intended, which את *with* will scarcely express. No doubt both here, *ch.* 30, 21, and Nu. 4, 19 (as Jud. 19, 18ᵇ after הלך), את is merely an error for אל.

19. ואכלתם] LXX καὶ φάγε, i.e. וְאָכַלְתָּ (or וְאָכַלְתָּה).

20. היום שלשת הימים] ' to-day, three days' (read with We. Bu., GK. § 134ᵐ, ימים), i.e. *for* three days, (Anglice) *three days ago.* Cf. 30, 13 היום שלשה, where ימים is omitted.

ולאתנות .... להם] להם resumes לאתנות upon exactly the same principle as that explained in the case of the accus. on *v.* 13: cf. Gen. 2, 17 (מן). II 6, 23 (ל). 2 Ki. 22, 18 (אל): *Tenses,* § 197 *Obs.* 1.

אל־תָּשֶׂם וג׳] The tone is drawn back by אל־ (*Tenses,* § 70), as it is (GK. § 72ᵗ) by the *waw* consec.; cf. II 17, 16 אל־תָּלֶן. Ex. 23, 1. The idiom, *set the heart* (mind) *to* (on), as II 13, 20 al. Cf. *Lex.* 523ᵇ (3 c), 524ᵇ (3 c); and on 4, 20.

ולמי וג׳] Rightly rendered by LXX, Vulg. καὶ τίνι τὰ ὡραῖα τοῦ Ἰσραηλ; et cuius erunt optima quaeque Israel? RV. *and for whom is all that is desirable in Israel?* חמדה is used in the same concrete sense as in Hag. 2, 7 ובאו חמדת כל הגוים (where note the *plural* verb) ' and the desirable things (i.e. costly offerings: see Is. 60, 5 *end*) of all nations shall come,' etc. But perhaps both there and here it is better to point חֲמֻדת (ptcp. pass.).

21. אנכי.] *mil'el* (GK. p. 60n.), on account of the pause (see on 1, 15).

מקטני [מִקַּטְנֵי שבטי בנימין should be logically מִקְּטַן, or rather (Ehrlich) מִקְּטֹן¹. The plural may be due to the illogical attraction of שבטי (read as שִׁבְטֵי).

---

¹ So in the one passage in which the *st. c.* of קטן occurs, 2 Ch. 21, 17. Ehrlich maintains that קָטֹן and קָטָן cannot be used promiscuously, but that קָטֹן is the form out of pause, קָטָן the form in pause (cf. GK. § 29ᵘ). It is true, קָטֹן is always found with *athnaḥ* and *soph-pasuq,* and קָטָן is always found with a conj. accent: but with the smaller disj. accents the pointing varies: thus we have קָטֹן

שבטי בנימין] 'Unquestionably an error for 'שֶׁבֶט ב' (Keil). However, curiously enough, the same expression occurs Jud. 20, 12 בכל
שִׁבְטֵי בנימין. We. Stade (p. 204) propose in both cases to point
שִׁבְטֵי, thinking that 'perhaps the archaic form of the *st. c.* (GK. § 90[l])
should be here restored;' but this is hardly probable. With the
passage generally, cf. Jud. 6, 15, where Gideon expresses, or affects,
similar modesty.

הצעירה] = *the smallest:* GK. § 133[g].

22. לשכתה] See on 1, 18. We should expect הלשכתה.

בראש] *at the head* or *top:* 1 Ki. 21, 9. 12. קרואים = those *invited*
to a feast, as 1 Ki. 1, 41. 49 ; cf. קרא *ib.* 9. 10.

23. מנה] See on 1, 4.

24. והעליה] There are three cases in which ה has apparently the
force of the relative[1]; (1) with a verb, (*a*) where the construction
depends upon the consonants. This is well substantiated for *late*
Hebrew (Ch. Ezr.), 1 Ch. 26, 28. 29, 8 al.: but the one example in
middle Hebrew, Jos. 10, 24[2], is so isolated that it rests probably upon
a textual corruption (ההלכים might easily be restored): (*b*) where
the construction depends solely upon the punctuation, chiefly in the
3rd sing. fem. perf. *Qal* (as הבאה Gen. 18, 21 ; 46, 27 השמה Is. 51,
10[b]), or in the 3rd sing. masc. perf. *Nif.* (as in הנולד־לו Gen. 21, 3 ;
הנראה 1 Ki. 11, 9). Whether this punctuation represents a genuine
tradition is extremely questionable : had ה been in use in earlier
Hebrew with the force of a relative, it is strange that it should appear
once only with 3 pl. : its restriction to cases in which a different
accent (הבאה) or punctuation (הנולד, הנראה) would give rise to the
regular construction[3], and the fact that the Massorah itself does not

---

16, 11 al., but קָטֹן 20, 2 al. ; קָטָן II 9, 12†, but קָטֹן *ch.* 5, 9. 20, 35. 22, 15 al. ;
and קָטָן Est. 1, 5†, but קָטֹן *ch.* 25, 36†. If the *normal* form were קָטֹן, it is
strange that we should find always the *fem.* קְמַנָּה, the *pl.* קְמַנִּים, and before a *sf.*
the form קְמַנָּם.

[1] Comp. Ew. § 331[b] (1) and *note:* GK. § 138[i, k].

[2] For Jer. 5, 13 (Hitzig, Graf, Keil) is very uncertain ; either דָּבֵר is a subst.
(Ew. § 156[a]; GK. § 52[o]), or, more probably, הַדָּבָר should be read.

[3] See, e.g. Is. 51, 9 המחצבת; Gen. 48, 5 הנולדים לו. And so in Ez. 26, 17
ההללה, read as ההֻלָּה, may be the ptcp. *Puʻal* without מ, like אֻכָּל Ex. 3, 2 etc.
(Ew. § 169[d]; GK. § 52[s]).

point consistently (see e.g. הבאה Gen. 46, 26 al.; הנראָה Gen. 12, 7. 35, 1), make it highly probable that the anomaly in these cases is not original, and that in fact ה as a relative is unknown to classical Hebrew. (2) Before a preposition—as in the Gk. idiom τὸ ἐπ' αὐτῆς —it occurs here alone in the OT., though combinations of the type אשר עליה are of constant occurrence. The usage here is thus doubly exceptional, and entirely unsupported by precedent or parallel. Under the circumstances it can scarcely be doubted that Geiger (*Urschrift*, p. 380) is right in reading וְהָאַלְיָה and the *fat tail* (Ex. 29, 22 and elsewhere in the ritual laws of P). The אליה is the fat tail of certain breeds of sheep [1] (commonly known as 'Cape sheep'), and is still esteemed a delicacy in the East : when dressed and served at table it much resembles marrow (the writer has seen and tasted it in Syria). The allusion in the *v.* will thus be to certain choice pieces reserved specially (*v.* 23^{b}) for those honoured with a place בראש הקרואים [2].

ויאמר] The subj. is Samuel, not the cook.

כי למועד וג'] 'because unto the appointed time [hath it been] kept for thee, saying, I have invited the people.' לאמר is construed with שמור freely, κατὰ σύνεσιν : cf. Ex. 5, 14 (where the subject of the preceding verb is not that implied in לאמר). The sense thus obtained, however, is not good; and הוא is desiderated after שמור (though see GK. § 116^{a}; שמרו, or (GK. § 144^{d}) שָׁמַר, for שמור would also be an easy emendation). It can thus hardly be doubted that there is some corruption in the text (especially in לאמר העם קראתי). נשאר also does not mean 'reserved' (Ew.), but *left over*. *V.* 13 however suggests that Samuel and Saul did not take their meal after the others had finished, but that the other guests waited to begin their meal until Samuel had arrived : what we expect, therefore, here is a 'polite invitation to Saul, as the guest of honour, to begin the meal;' the others would then begin theirs. Sm. Now. suggest, for הנשאר, הַשְּׁאָר *the flesh* (of

---

[1] Comp. the notice in Hdt. 3. 13; and see in the *Jewish Encycl.* xi. 250 an illustration of such a sheep, with a small cart supporting the long and heavy 'fat tail.'

[2] The shoulder and the 'fat tail' are still the pieces offered by the fellaḥin of Palestine to the guest whom they desire to honour (*ZDPV.* vi. 98, cited by Nestle, *Marginalien*, 1893, p. 13 f.).

flesh prepared for the table, Ex. 21, 10. ψ. 78, 20), and Sm. Bu.
Now., for שמור אחרנו, אָחֲרְנוּ (אָחַרְנוּ) Gen. 32, 5, or אֶחֱרַנוּ Gen. 34, 19)), or
אחרו; Sm. Now. also follow Bu. in reading לֶאֱכֹל עִם הַקְּרֻאִים for לאמר
העם קראתי: we then get, 'Behold, *the flesh* is set before thee! Eat!
for *we* (or *they*) *have tarried* for thee unto the appointed time, *that thou
mayest eat with them that are invited.*' But 'the flesh is set before thee'
is rather a bald and graceless invitation; and אחר always (even in
Gen. 32, 5, where it is opposed to נרתי) has the idea of tarrying *later*
than is usual, or might be expected; though suitable, therefore, with
מן־המועד (II 20, 5), would it be suitable with '*to* the appointed time?'
Nothing preferable to לאכל עם הקראים has been suggested: but in the
earlier part of the verse, it would be a smaller, and perhaps a sufficient,
change to read, for הנשאר, הנשמר 'that which has been *kept* (reserved)'
(see *v.* 23ᵇ), and for שמור, as suggested above, שָׁמְרוּ or שָׁמַר ¹.

25–26. וישכמו : וידבר עם שאול על הגג] LXX καὶ διέστρωσαν τῷ Σαουλ
ἐπὶ τῷ δώματι, καὶ ἐκοιμήθη = : וַיִּשְׁכָּב וַיִּרְבְּדוּ עַל הַגָּג לְשָׁאוּל (Pr. 7, 16).
The sequence in MT. is so bad (וידבר and וישכימו both being pre-
mature, when ויקרא וג' follows) that there can be little doubt that this
is the true reading: 'And *they spread a couch* for Saul on the house-
top, and *he lay down,*' to which Samuel's *calling to* Saul on the
house-top in the morning (*v.* 26 ויהי וג') forms now a natural and
suitable sequel.

27. ביום] = *first of all* (before going on): cf. on 2, 16.

10, 1. את־פך־השמן] Cf. 2 Ki. 9, 1. 3.

הלוא כי] 'Is it not that?'='Hath not?' is shewn by II 13, 28

---

¹ Ew. on the basis of LXX παρὰ τοὺς ἄλλους suggested for לאמר העם, מִשְּׁאָר
הָעָם = '*above the rest* of the people (whom) I have invited,' which We. is disposed
to acquiesce in, though it is true that שאר is not a word found elsewhere in the
best Hebrew *prose* style (Ch. Ezr. Neh. Est., and of course in *Isaiah*); and the
omission of אשר before העם is questionable (on 14, 21). LXX for קראתי have
ἀπόκνιζε *nip off* (= מלק Lev. 1, 15: קצב 2 Ki. 6, 6: קטף Ez. 17, 4. 21), whence
Th. suggests קְרִיְ־נָא *cut off!* (*Anglice* Help yourself!), cf. Job 33, 6 מחמר קֹרַצְתִּי
נם אני. But it is not probable that a word so rare in Heb. as קרץ (and usually
occurring in a different application—יקרצו עין) would have been used in this sense.
It must however be admitted that in post-Bibl. Hebrew קרץ is used of *cutting up*
food into pieces: see Levy, *NHWB.* s. v. LXX εἰς μαρτύριον of course presupposes
nothing different from מועד, which the translators elsewhere connected wrongly
with עוד : cf. σκηνὴ τοῦ μαρτυρίου for אהל מועד.

to be a good Hebrew expression: but the long addition preserved in LXX and Vulg. has every appearance of being original. The insertion would read in Hebrew thus: הֲלוֹא [מְשָׁחֲךָ יְ"י לְנָגִיד עַל־עַמּוֹ עַל־יִשְׂרָאֵל וְאַתָּה תַעְצֹר בְּעַם יְ"י וְאַתָּה תוֹשִׁיעֶנּוּ מִיַּד אֹיְבָיו וְזֶה־לְּךָ הָאוֹת] כִּי מְשָׁחֲךָ יְ"י עַל נַחֲלָתוֹ לְנָגִיד: The circumstantiality of the account is here not out of place: the express mention of the signs at an earlier stage of the instructions to Saul than *v.* 7, is what might be expected: and the omission of the clause in MT. may be readily explained by the supposition that a transcriber's eye passed from the first מָשַׁח יהוה to the second. So Dr. Weir.

2. עִם] = *close to, near:* Gen. 25, 11. 35, 4. II 19, 38 al. As Jer. 31, 15 shews, Rachel's grave must have been very near Ramah, i.e. the Ramah of Is. 10, 29, now *er-Rām.* Er-Rām is 5 miles S. of Bethel, which, according to Jos. 18, 13 (P), was on the N. border of Benjamin: but at this time, it seems, Ephraim extended further to the S. (see esp. Jud. 4, 5). In Gen. 35, 20. 48, 7 הוּא בֵּית לֶחֶם, identifying Ephrath with *Bethlehem,* is either a gloss (so Dillmann and most commentators), or (Delitzsch on Gen. 35, 20) embodies a different tradition.

נְבוּל בִּנְיָמִין] the Northern border: cf. on 9, 5.

בְּצֶלְצַח] The word arouses suspicion. The locality intended seems to be so accurately defined by עִם קְבֻרַת רָחֵל, that we are surprised at a closer definition following, especially in such an obscure form; for, as צֶלְצַח possesses no meaning, it cannot designate any particular spot near Rachel's grave, at which the men were to be met. LXX have ἁλλομένους μεγάλα. Ἀλλομένους = צֹלְחִם (see *v.* 6): but though צלח עַל may be rendered (metaph.) *leap upon,* צלח absolutely cannot express the idea of *leaping.* μεγάλα does not occur elsewhere in LXX in an adverbial sense (We.); so probably here it is nothing but a Hebrew word written in Greek letters, and transformed into something signifi- cant in Greek[1]. Many MSS. after Βενιαμειν insert ἐν Σηλω (= בְּצַלְצָה) ἐν Βακαλαθ; Lucian's recension after Βενιαμιν and before ἀλλ. μεγ.

---

[1] Cf. 1 Ki. 18, 32 θάλασσαν from תְּעָלָה; Am. 3, 12 ἱερεῖς from עָרֶשׂ (as Jerome, cited by Field, points out); Jer. 8, 7 ἀγροῦ; 34, 5 ἕως ᾅδου κλαύσονται. For other examples, see the Introduction, § 4. 1 a *b*; Thackeray, *Gramm. of OT. Greek* (1909), p. 37 f.

adds μεσημβρίας [as though צח בצל = *in umbra sereni:* hence Vulg. *meridie*]. All these are evidently different attempts to render or represent the five consonants which stand now as בצלצח: but they throw no light either upon the word itself or upon the original reading which may underlie it.

את דברי האתנות] = *the matters* = *the concern* of the asses: cf. על דבריכם Dt. 4, 21. Comp. Delitzsch or Cheyne on ψ. 65, 4. But דְּבַר (LXX ῥῆμα) would be more natural.

ודאג] The pf. and ו consec., with a frequentative force (*Tenses*, § 113. 4 *a*; GK. § 112ᵐ), after a bare perfect (GK. § 112ʰ). וְדִאֵג (Bu. al.), following נָטָשׁ, is no improvement: we should need וְדִאֵג הוּא (Jer. 48, 11); the cases noted in GK. § 116ᵍ are different.

3. חלף] To *pass on.* Elsewhere only in poetry, as a poet. syn. of עָבַר, to *come* (or *pass*) *on,* usually with some swiftness or force: of a flood, Is. 8, 8; a tempest 21, 1; a breath, Job 4, 15; of the Chaldaean conqueror compared to a wind, Hab. 1, 11; of God, Job 9, 11. 11, 10; of days passing quickly away like skiffs down a stream, Job 9, 26. The word is hardly one that would be expected here: and Ehrlich would read for it וְהָלַכְתָּ.

עלים] Bethel (2890 ft.) was itself on a hill; and the plateau on which the hill stands is considerably higher than most of the surrounding country. 'To *God,*' Bethel being an ancient sacred place.

שלשת ככרות לחם] כִּכָּר is *fem.* (Ex. 29, 23 al.); and though a fem. numeral is found here and there with a fem. noun (as Gen. 7, 13. Job 1, 4: GK. § 97ᶜ; König, iii. 322), it is probably best to restore with We. שְׁלֹשׁ. Klo. Bu., remarking that two out of three loaves would be a large proportion to give as a present, would read (after LXX ἀγγεῖα) כְּלוּבֵי *baskets* (Am. 8, 1); Sm. would read כְּלֵי (9, 7).

4. ושאלו לך לשלום] *and shall ask thee with regard to welfare,*— a common Heb. expression (17, 22. 25, 5. Gen. 43, 27 al.). Why the direct object is introduced by ל, is not apparent: perhaps (cf. König, iii. § 327ᵏ) from assimilation to לשלום.

שתי לחם] the fem. שתי may be on account of כִּכָּרוֹת understood[1];

---

[1] Which Klo. Bu. Dh. would even insert here, after LXX δύο ἀπαρχὰς ἄρτων, i.e., it is supposed, כִּכָּרוֹת, misread בִּכֻּרוֹת; but בכרות is nowhere else misrendered ἀπαρχαί.

or, as לחם is elsewhere construed as a masc. (עשרה לחם 1 Ki. 14, 3.
חמשה לחם *ch.* 21, 4; cf. שני אנשים, עשרה אנשים: GK. § 97ᵇ), שני should
perhaps be restored.

5. נבעת האלהים] identical, as the נציב פלשתים shews, with the נבע
(rd. נבעה) of 13, 3; and most probably the older name, marking it
as an ancient holy place, of 'Gibeah of Saul.' *Rām-Allah,* 7 miles N.
of Tell el-Fûl (suggested in *H. G.* p. 250), is much too far to the north.
On אחר כן, see GK. § 29ᵍ.

נצבי] LXX, Pesh. Vulg. express a singular; and, as the sing. occurs
also 13, 3. 4, נציב should in all probability be read accordingly here.
The accidental transposition of two contiguous letters is not unfrequent in MT.: in the *Ochlah we-Ochlah,* § 91, there is a list of
sixty-two such transpositions which have been corrected by the
Massorah. Some few of the corrections may be questioned: but
the majority are certainly authorized (e.g. והימשני Jud. 16, 26; שומע
Jer. 17, 23; היאתון Ez. 40, 15; הילכות Pr. 31, 27 cannot be original
readings). As to the meaning, נציב has the sense of *pillar* in Gen.
19, 26, of *prefect* or *deputy* in II 8, 6. 14. 1 Ki. 4, 19; possibly also
it might be used to denote a *post* or *garrison*, like מצב 13, 23.
Which of these senses it has here, it is difficult to say; versions and
commentators are equally divided. (*a*) LXX here (one rendering ¹)
has ἀνάστεμα, i.e. prob. *a pillar* erected as a symbol or trophy of
Philistine domination: so (prob.) Pesh., and amongst moderns Th.
Bö. We. (*b*) Vulg. has *statio,* i.e. a military post, or garrison: so
EVV. Ge. Ke. (*c*) Targ. has אסטרטיני (i.e. στρατηγοὶ) both here and
13, 3. 4 (likewise in the *plur.*): similarly Ew. Gr. Sm. Bu. Now., only
reading as a sing. נציב (*prefect, officer*). On the whole (the sense
statio being not otherwise substantiated), (*c*) is probably to be
preferred.

It appears from this verse that a large area of Central Palestine
was now in the hands of the Philistines.

ויהי וג'] The jussive is unexpected. In II 5, 24 (= 1 Ch. 14, 15),
Ruth 3, 4 it can be explained as expressing a command: but that
is not the case here; and it is better to suppose it to be an error

---

¹ In the other rend. the word is simply transliterated Νασειβ, as in 13, 3. 4.

for וְהָיָה (Sm.). In 1 Ki. 14, 5[b] read וַיְהִי. The explanation in GK. § 112[z] is artificial, and not probable.

והמה מתנבאים] a circumstantial clause, describing the condition in which the prophets would be as they came down from the במה: cf. Jer. 38, 22 והנה אֹמרֹת = *they saying* (*Tenses*, § 160; GK. § 141[e]).

The word, which is in the reflexive conj. and a denominative, denotes *to play* or *act* the prophet, viz. by manifestations of physical excitement —not unlike those exhibited by the dervishes of the present day in the East[1]—such as are more evidently described, on the second occasion when Saul is seized by the contagious frenzy, 19, 20 ff. So 1 Ki. 22, 10 Aḥaz and Jehoshaphat were sitting in the gate of Samaria וכל הנביאים מתנבאים לפניהם: comp. (of the prophets of Baal) *ib.* 18, 29. From this peculiarity, the prophet is sometimes described mockingly as מְשֻׁגָּע 2 Ki. 9, 11. Hos. 9, 7; cf. Jer. 29, 26.

6. וצלחה] the same word *v.* 10; Jud. 14, 6. 19. 15, 14 (of Samson); *ch.* 11, 6; 16, 13 (David); also 18, 10, where the subject is רוח אלהים, but the direction in which the inspired activity displays itself is different.

והתנבית] for והתנבאת; cf. *v.* 13. See GK. § 75[qq].

7. והיה . . . עשה] והיה would be resumed normally by ועשית, or תעשה (the latter less usual in ordinary prose). The uncommon imper. was chosen, no doubt, as more forcible: cf. Dt. 6, 10–12[a].

תבאינה] So Jer. 9, 16. Est. 4, 4. ψ. 45, 16†. The more usual form is תָּבֹאנָה (11 times), or (Gen. 30, 38) תָּבֹאןָ: GK. § 76[g].

אשר תמצא ידך] The same idiom in *ch.* 25, 8. Jud. 9, 33[b]. Qoh. 9, 10.

8. *Introduction to first account of Saul's rejection* (13, 7[b]–15[a]).

'And thou shalt go down before me to Gilgal; and, behold, I am coming down to thee to sacrifice . . .: seven days shalt thou wait, until I come to thee, and declare to thee what thou shalt do.' והנה . . . is a circumstantial clause (cf. Jud. 9, 33) and subordinate to וירדת, הנה throwing the idea which it introduces into relief, and giving it greater prominence than it would otherwise have: then *b* is supplementary to *a*, defining more closely what Saul is to do at Gilgal until Samuel meets him there[2].

[1] Comp. Lane, *Manners and Customs of the Modern Egyptians* (ed. 5, 1871), ii. 151–154, 174 f., 179 f.; W. R. Smith, *Prophets of Israel*, pp. 86, 390 f. ([2]391 f.).

[2] Keil's construction of this verse is illegitimate. The verse refers evidently to

וירדת] The Gilgal here meant is the one in the Jordan-valley (*Jiljul* or *Jiljulîyeh*), near Jericho, 600 ft. below the Medit. Sea, and consequently some 3350 ft. below Gibeah; hence 'go down.'

9. והיה] See on 1, 12. Due probably to a scribe, who judged in error, from the tense of the preceding verses, that another future was still to follow : ויהי is the tense which *ought* to be used, and which ought, no doubt, to be restored.

כהפנתו שכמו] Cf. הפנה ערף (in flight), Jer. 48, 39.

הפך] For the constr., cf. Zeph. 3, 9.

10. שם] redundant before הנבעתה. Read with LXX (ἐκεῖθεν) מִשָּׁם, i. e. either the place where Saul parted from Samuel, or the place mentioned in *v.* 3 f., the account of how the first two signs (*vv.* 1–4) came to pass, having fallen out of the narrative after *v.* 9. The 'Gibeah' will be the 'Gibeah of God' of *v.* 5.

והנה . . . לקראתו] So (without a verb) II 15, 32; 1 Ki. 18, 7 ; Pr. 7, 10.

11. ויראו . . . ויהי כל יודעו] Exactly so, II 2, 23ᵇ ויעמדו . . . ויהי כל הבא; and analogously, with והיה, of *future* time, Nu. 21, 8 al., and of reiteration in the past, Jud. 19, 30. כל יודעו is a ptcp. absol. 'and it came to pass, *as regards* all that knew him, that,' etc.: cf. GK. § 116ʷ; *Tenses,* § 121, *Obs.* 1. For מאתמול, see GK. § 20ʰ.

13, 8–14, whereas, in the Book of Samuel as we have it, Samuel and Saul appear together at Gilgal *earlier,* viz. on the occasion 11, 14 f. Keil therefore, seeking to exclude a reference to this occasion, and to interpret the verse as referring only to the subsequent one, presses the circumstantial clause introduced by והנה, saying that this presupposes that the preceding words ' And thou shalt go down before me ' express merely a *condition,* in view of which, when it is satisfied, Samuel instructs Saul how to act. He construes, therefore : 'And if thou goest down before me to Gilgal, and lo, I come down to thee, etc., then thou shalt wait seven days until I come to thee,' etc. והנה, however, cannot influence the sense of what precedes ; and (what is more important) וירדת followed by תוחל cannot express a *condition.* Had וירדת expressed a (virtual) condition, it must have been followed by וְהוֹחַלְתָּ (so regularly, as 19, 3; Num. 14, 15 etc.: *Tenses,* § 149): שבעת ימים תוחל being attached ἀσυνδέτως, shews that the preceding clause is *complete in itself,* i.e. that וירדת expresses a positive command, and not a condition. The clause וג׳ וירדת expresses what is to be done by Saul not necessarily immediately after 7ᵇ, but as soon after it as is convenient. The collision with 11, 14 f. arises from the fact that this part of the Books of Samuel is composed of sources originally distinct : 10, 8 and 13, 7ᵇ–15ᵃ are thus related to one another, but stand out of connexion with 11, 14 f.

נִבָּא‎] Prob. the ptcp., *was prophesying*, with הוא‎ omitted after הנה‎ (*Tenses*, § 135. 6, 2 ; GK. § 116ˢ).

מהׁ־זה היה‎] *What, now*, has happened to . . .? זה‎ strengthens and gives point to מה‎; so Gen. 27, 20. Jud. 18, 24 al.; similarly in מי זה‎, למה־זה‎. Comp. in Arabic مَا ذَا صَنَعْتَ : and see especially Fleischer, *Kleinere Schriften*, i. 355 f. (who adduces from Arabic usage reasons in support of this explanation of the idiom); Lane, *Arab. Lex.*, s. v. ذا, p. 948. Briefer explanations will be found in GK. § 136ᶜ; Ew. §§ 183ᵃ, 325ᵃ.

12. וּמי אביהם‎] 'But who is *their* father ?' i. e. is *their* father more likely than Qish to have had a son a prophet? Prophetic inspiration is no hereditary possession ; and it is not more remarkable in the case of Saul, than in the case of any other member of the troop of prophets. Against the easier, but weak, reading of LXX, Pesh. אביהו‎, see We.

היתה‎] for the fem. (= *it*), cf. II 3, 37. Jos. 11, 20. 1 Ki. 2, 15: GK. § 144ᵇ.

13. הבמה‎] With הבמה‎ we should have expected ויעל‎ for ויבא‎; the conversation, *vv.* 14–16, is also more likely to have taken place in a private house than on the Bamah. Hence We. and most read: הבַּיְתָה‎ for הבמה‎. Ehrl. objects that אל ביתו‎ or (*v.* 26. 23, 18) לביתו‎, not הביתה‎, is said of a person going to his *own* house. However, in Gen. 43, 26 we have ויבא יוסף הביתה‎; and הביתה‎ here would be not so much *his* house, as *the* house, as opposed to the street (cf. Jud. 19, 15. Jos. 2, 18), where Saul had been playing the prophet. Bu. Dh., after LXX εἰς τὸν βουνόν, read (see *vv.* 5. 10) הגבעה‎ : but that seems to have been reached in *v.* 10.

14. כי אין‎] See on 9, 4.

16. אשר אמר שמואל‎] A misplaced gloss, not expressed by LXX. EVV. conceal the awkward and unnatural position of the words: cf. their rendering of Ex. 14, 9.

10, 17–27ᵃ. *Saul chosen by lot as king (sequel to 8).*

17. המצפה‎] *Nebi Samwîl :* see on 7, 16.

18. אנכי‎] emphatic, as II 12, 7.

הלחצים‎] construed with הממלכות‎ κατὰ σύνεσιν; cf. Jer. 11, 2. 26, 2.

19. ואתם‎] 'And *ye*' (emph.),—in spite of what I have done.

אשר הוא מושיע לכם] 'who is a saviour to you.' הוא after the relative sign, before a ptcp. or adj., as Gen. 9, 3 אשר הוא חי. Nu. 9, 13. 14, 8. 27. 35, 31. Dt. 20, 20 אשר היא עשׂה. Jer. 27, 9. Hag. 1, 9. Ruth 4, 15: similarly Ez. 43, 19. So also in Aramaic, די אנין Dan. 7, 17; and in Targg., as II 20, 19. 24, 17. Is. 42, 18 [1].

ותאמרו לו כי] כי with the direct narration, as 2, 16 MT. (where see note). Several MSS. LXX, Pesh. Vulg. express לא (as 8, 19 MT., 12, 12 MT.), in which case כי will, of course, = *but.* Either reading is admissible, but לא is more pointed and forcible.

התיצבו לפני י"י] *Take your stand, present themselves :* cf. Jos. 24, 1.

אלפיכם] not 'thousands' (EVV.), but tribal subdivisions, *clans ;* cf. 23, 23. Jud. 6, 15. Mic. 5, 2.

20. וילכד] viz. by lot : cf. 14, 14+. Jos. 7, 16–18.

21. המטרי] LXX adds καὶ προσάγουσι τὴν φυλὴν Ματταρι εἰς ἄνδρας i.e. ויקרב את־משׁפחת המטרי לגברים (see Jos. 7, 17), which is required by the sense.

22. הבא עוד הלם איש] 'Is there still (i.e. besides ourselves) any one come hither ?' The people are in despair ; and they inquire whether there is yet any one amongst them, of whom they are not aware. LXX, however, have Εἰ ἔρχεται ὁ ἀνὴρ ἐνταῦθα ; and it is true, as We. remarks, that the answer 'Lo, *he* is hidden,' etc., agrees better with the question, 'Is *the* man come hither (הבא הלם האיש)?' than with 'Is there still *a* man come hither ?' Of course, with האיש, עוד must be omitted. There are several cases in MT. of an article having accidentally dropped out, some (*e.g.* 14, 32) being already noted by the Massorah (*Ochlah we-Ochlah,* No. 165 ; or the Mass. Magna on II 23, 9).

אל הכלים] אל, on account of the motion implied in נחבא : 'he hath hidden himself *in among* the baggage.' Cf. Jer. 4, 3[b].

24. הראיתם] When ראיתם is coupled with the ה *interrog.*, the ר is regularly doubled (as signified by the *dagesh dirimens*): so 17, 25. 2 Ki. 6, 32 : GK. §§ 22[s] (20[h]), 100[l].

יחי המלך] The same formula as II 16, 16. 1 Ki. 1, 25 al.

---

[1] Comp., in Phoenician, Cooke, *NSI.* 27, 2 . . . איש הא שת (= Heb. אֲשֶׁר הִיא . . . , שְׁנַת). And so also in Arabic (Qor. 2, 58. 43, 51) and Ethiopic (Gen. 5, 32. 14, 2 etc.).

25. בַּסֵּפֶר] = 'in a scroll,' in accordance with the principle explained on 1, 4. So, with the same word, Ex. 17, 14; Nu. 5, 23; Jer. 32, 10. Job 19, 23. Comp. GK. § 126ᵃ; and on 19, 13.

34. וְהַנַּח אתו לפני י"י ג'] Ex. 16, 33 וינח

26. החיל] LXX υἱοὶ δυνάμεων i.e. בני החיל = the men of valour (see Jud. 21, 10). בני has accidentally fallen out: חיל means not a mere 'band of men' (AV.), but a military host—a sense that is not here appropriate. בני חיל denotes not merely men of valour, but men morally brave, loyal, and honest (Ex. 18, 21. 25): here the בני חיל and the בני בליעל of v. 27 stand in evident contrast to one another.

27ᵃ. זה] contemptim: cf. 21, 16. 1 Ki. 22, 27.

מנחה] of presents offered to a superior, as Jud. 3, 15. 2 Ki. 8, 8 f.

10, 27ᵇ—11, 13. (14.) 15. Saul 'does as his hand finds' (9, 7), wins a success against the Ammonites, and is made king at Gilgal by the people with acclamation (sequel to **9, 1—10, 16**).

27ᵇ. ויהי כמחריש] MT. may to a certain extent be defended by the use of כ' היה in Gen. 19, 14ᵇ. 27, 12. Nu. 11, 1. II 4, 10, though it is found mostly in connexion with בעיני, which justifies and explains the כ. LXX join the words to 11, 1, rendering καὶ ἐγενήθη ὡς μετὰ μῆνα i.e. וַיְהִי כְּמֵחֹדֶשׁ. This is preferable to MT. The combination of כ with a prep. is most uncommon (see on 14, 14): but it occurs with מן in a phrase so remarkably similar to the present one as fully to justify it here: Gen. 38, 24 ויהי כמשלש חדשים and it came to pass after about three months.

11, 1. יבש גלעד] The name יבש still clings to Wâdy Yabis, which falls into the Jordan from the East, 9 miles S. of Beth-shean: but the site of the ancient town itself is uncertain. Robinson and others have identified it with ed-Deir, on the S. side of Wâdy Yabis, 6 miles E. of the Jordan; but Miryamin, 2 miles NW. of ed-Deir, on the hills on the N. side of the Wâdy seems better to agree with Eusebius' description of it (Onom. 268, 81 f.) as 7 miles from Pella, on the road leading to Gerasa (see DB. and EB. s.v.).

2. בזאת] pointing forwards to בנקור: 'On condition of this will I conclude a covenant with you, on condition of the boring out to you,' etc.; so Gen. 34, 22. 42, 15. 33. Ex. 7, 17. Is. 27, 9. The ל of

reference, as Gen. 17, 10. 34, 22 ; Lev. 26, 5. 26 ; Dt. 23, 3ᵇ. 4ᵇ ;
1 Ki. 14, 13 (comp. on 2, 33) : *Lex.* 512ᵇ (**5** *a*).

אכרות] ברית being understood, as 20, 16. 22, 8.

בנקר] sc. הנוקרים: GK. § 144ᵈˑ ᵉ, and on *ch.* 16, 4 (EVV. of course
paraphrase). The same verb, also of boring out an eye, Pr. 30, 17,
and (Pi.) Jud. 16, 21.

ושמתיה] The fem. suffix = *it:* see GK. § 135ᵖ.

3. הרף לנו] See on 15, 16.

ואם אין מושיע אתנו] The ptcp. in the protasis, as Gen. 24, 42 f.,
Jud. 11, 9 al. (*Tenses*, § 137).

ויצאנו אליך] יצא אל of going out to surrender, as Is. 36, 16 צאו אלי.
2 Ki. 24, 12 (with על = אל). For גבעת שאול, see on 9, 1.

7. Jud. 19, 29 וישלחה בכל גבול ישראל . . . וינתחה לעצמיה. נתח is
to divide by joints, esp. for sacrifice, Lev. 1, 6. 1 Ki. 18, 23.

המלאכים] LXX מלאכים is better.

ואחר] אחרי is far more frequently said in such phrases: yet see
12, 14; and *Lex.* 29ᵇ.

פחד י״י] *the awe* or *terror of Yahweh:* cf. Gen. 35, 5 (חִתַּת אלהים).

ויצאו] LXX ἐβόησαν, a mistranslation of וַיִּצְעֲקוּ: so Jud. 7, 23. 24.
12, 1 ; and even for נזעקת 18, 23 : cf. ἀνεβόησαν 2 Ki. 3, 21 ; ἀνέβησαν
(corrupted from ἀνεβόησαν), *ch.* 13, 4. Jud. 10, 17 ; ἀνέβη (cod. Al.
ἀνεβόησεν) for וַיִּזָּעֵק 14, 20. וַיִּצְעֲקוּ is probably to be restored here,
ויצאו having been suggested (Bu.) by the preceding יצֵא.

כאיש אחד] a frequent expression : II 19, 15. Nu. 14, 15. Jud. 6, 16.
20, 1. 8. 11. Ezr. 3, 1 = Neh. 8, 1†.

8. בזק] now *Ibzik,* 11 miles SW. of Beth-shean, and just opposite to
W. Yabis.

ואיש יהודה] איש construed collectively, as often in this and similar
phrases, e.g. 9ᵃ. 13, 6. 14, 22. 17, 2 etc.

9. ויאמרו] Read with LXX ויאמר.

תשועה] *relief, deliverance:* see on 14, 45 (ישועה).

בחם] Better, with Qrê and 34 MSS., כְּחֹם: cf. Gen. 18, 1. II 4, 5.

11. עמון] LXX, Pesh. express בני עמון, in agreement with the all
but universal custom of the OT. writers [1]. Except once in poetry
(ψ. 83, 8), the Ammonites are always known either as בני עמון, or

---

[1] Nöldeke, *ZDMG.* 1886, p. 171.

(rarely, and mostly late) עמונים. On the other hand, בני מואב[1],
בני עמלק never occur ; בני אָדָם occurs once, ψ. 137, 7.

ויהי הנשארים ויפצו] ‘ And it came to pass, as regards those that
were left, that they were scattered.’ An unusual construction: cf.
however, 10, 11. II 2, 23: *Tenses*, § 78 *note;* GK. § 116ʷ.

12. מי האמר . . . . תנו האנשים] ‘ Who is he that saith, Shall Saul
reign over us? give up the men that we may slay them.’ A particular
case of the idiom which may be most simply illustrated by Jud. 7, 3
מִי יָרֵא וְחָרֵד יָשֹׁב ‘ Who is fearful and trembling? let him return ’ etc. =
‘*Whoso* is fearful and trembling, let him return ’ etc. In this idiom מי
invites attention to a person of a particular character, in order afterwards to prescribe what he is to do (or what is to be done to him), or
to state how he will fare. As in the example quoted, by a slight
change of form in the sentence, מי may be represented by *whoso :* but
it is really a more expressive, less ordinary usage than that of *whoso,
whosoever* in English. Other examples : Ex. 24, 14 ; 32, 33 ; Dt. 20,
5. 6. 7. 8 ; Jud. 10, 18 ; Is. 50, 8 *bis;* Jer. 49, 19 ; and followed by
an imperative, Ex. 32, 24 למי זהב התפרקו ‘ Who has gold? Strip it off
you !’ cf. 26 מי ליהוה אלי ‘ Who is for Yahweh? (Come) to me !’
ψ. 34, 13 f.[2] Comp. *Lex.* 567ᵃ g.

שאול ימלך עלינו] The sense of the words is indicated by the tone in
which they are uttered—either affirmatively, in a tone of irony, or,
more probably, interrogatively. So not unfrequently in Hebrew, as
Gen. 27, 24 אתה זה בני ; אתה עתה תעשה מלוכה 21, 7 ; 1 Ki. 1, 24 ;
על ישראל : *ch.* 21, 16. 22, 7. II 16, 17. Comp. on 16, 4. 25, 11 and
II 11, 11 ; and GK. § 150ᵃ.

13ᵇ. II 19, 23.

15. זבחים שלמים] So Ex. 24, 5. The words are in apposition, the
second having the effect of *specializing* the sense expressed by the
first : *Tenses*, Appendix, § 188. 1; GK. § 131ᵇ.

---

[1] Except once in late Hebrew, 2 Ch. 20, 1.
[2] Not to be confused (as is done by Delitzsch on ψ. 25, 12) with the use of מי in
ψ. 15, 1. 24, 8. 10. Is. 33, 14. 63, 1 where the answer to מי is a *substantive*, not
a verb, and *describes the character* of the person asked about. This usage is a figure
peculiar to poetry, which, as the examples shew, is not the case with that explained
in the text.

12. *Samuel's farewell to the people (sequel to* **7**, 2–17; **8**; 10, 17–27ᵃ).

12, 1. Cf. for the phrases 8, 7. 22. It is evident that two accounts of the appointment of Saul as king, written from different points of view, though fitted together so as to supplement one another, have been combined in our present Book of Samuel. 9, 1—10, 16 (in which nothing is said of the unwillingness of Yahweh to grant a king) is continued by 10, 27ᵇ (LXX). 11, 1–13. 15 (note in particular the connexion between 10, 7 *do that which thine hand shall find* and 11, 5 ff.) and *ch.* 13: the sequel of *ch.* 8 on the other hand is 10, 17–27ᵃ and *ch.* 12. The former narrative, with its greater abundance of details, is the earlier and more original: the latter in its main elements exhibits literary affinities with the Hexateuchal source E [1], but it has probably in parts been expanded by a subsequent writer, whose style and point of view resemble those of the redaction of the Book of Judges, and to whom may be attributed, for instance, parts of *ch.* 12, especially the allusion in *v.* 12 to *ch.* 11 (which is in fact a contradiction, for the attack of Naḥash was not the occasion of the people's asking for a king). The verse 11, 14 in the form in which it now appears seems intended to harmonize the two accounts, by representing the ceremony at Gilgal as a *renewal* of Saul's appointment as king. The differences in style between the two narratives are very noticeable.

2. מתהלך לפניכם] used here in a neutral sense: see on 2, 30.

3. עשקתי . . . רצותי] The two words appear often in parallelism, as Dt. 28, 33. Am. 4, 1. עשק is *to oppress*, in particular by defrauding a labourer or dependent of his due.

כפר . . . בו] כפר is the *price of a life*, the money offered for the life of a murdered man to appease a kinsman's wrath (cf. *DB.* iii. 129). The imposition of a כפר is permitted in the oldest legislation (Ex. 21–23) in a particular case of *homicide* (21, 30); but as compensation for a *murder* (the Gk. ποινή), the payment of it is (in the Priests' Code) strictly prohibited (Nu. 35, 31 ולא תקחו כפר לנפש רוצח אשר

---

[1] Budde, *ZATW.* 1888, pp. 231–236 (= *Richter and Samuel,* 1890, pp. 180–185), who, however (see the last paragraph on p. 248), does not claim to shew that the writer is *identical* with that of E. Comp. *LOT.* 167–168 (edd. 6–8, 177–178).

הוא רשע למות). In the sense of an equivalent for a life conceived as forfeited, it occurs ψ. 49, 8. Is. 43, 3. In Am. 5, 12 the nobles of Samaria are denounced as לקחי כפר. This being the uniform usage of the word, it follows that what Samuel here repudiates is that he has ever as judge taken a money payment on condition of acquitting a murderer brought before him for justice.

ואעלים עיני בו] 'that I might (*Tenses*, § 63) hide my eyes in it.' The sense of the metaphor is obvious: comp. כסות עינים Gen. 20, 16. LXX, however, has ἐξίλασμα καὶ ὑπόδημα; ἀποκρίθητε κατ᾽ ἐμοῦ, καὶ ἀποδώσω ὑμῖν i.e. כֹּפֶר וְנַעֲלַיִם עֲנוּ בִי. The ' pair of sandals' is chosen by Amos (2, 6. 8, 6) as an example of a paltry article, for the sake of which the Israelite of his day would 'sell the poor:' and Sir. 46, 19 (in the praise of Samuel, with plain allusion to this passage), καὶ πρὸ καιροῦ κοιμήσεως αἰῶνος ἐπεμαρτύρατο ἔναντι κυρίου καὶ χριστοῦ Χρήματα καὶ ἕως ὑποδημάτων ἀπὸ πάσης σαρκὸς οὐκ εἴληφα· καὶ οὐκ ἐνεκάλεσεν αὐτῷ ἄνθρωπος, has been held to shew (as the author—see the Prologue—wrote in Hebrew and was conversant with the OT. in Hebrew) that the reading existed in his day not merely in the LXX, but in the Hebrew text of Samuel. The objection to this view is that כפר and נעלים do not agree very well together, and the sense required is '*or even* a pair of sandals' (so Th.: *und* (wären es auch nur) *ein Paar Schuhe?*), which is hardly expressed by the simple copula: it may be questioned also whether a pair of sandals (which is mentioned by Amos as something insignificant) would be a bribe likely to be offered to a judge. The recently recovered Heb. text of Ecclus. (see Strack's *Die Sprüche Jesus', des Sohnes Sirachs*, 1903) has the same reading כופר ונעלם ממ(י לקח)תי וכל אדם לא ענה בו); but neither this nor the LXX is proof that it was the original Heb. reading here. But עֲנוּ בִי is a good antecedent to ואשיב לכם; and Bu. may be right in supposing it to have *fallen out* after עיני בו.

ואשיב לכם] must mean, 'and I will restore it to you;' for 'and I will *answer* you' (We.) the classical expression would be ואשיב אתכם דבר (e.g. Nu. 22, 8), with an *accus.* of the person, and omission of דבר only in poetry (as Job 13, 22), and in the late passage 2 Ch. 10, 16 (דבר of 1 Ki. 12, 16 omitted). In another late book השיב אל occurs in the same sense: Est. 4, 13. 15. Cf. *Lex.* 999ᵇ.

5. ויאמר] sc. האומר (on 16, 4). LXX, Pesh. Tg. Vg. would hardly render otherwise than by a plural, even though they read the verb in the singular: still the sing. is unusual: hence the note ויאמרו סביר, i.e. ויאמרו *is thought* or *supposed* (to be the true reading). ויאמרו is also found in 19 MSS. In the Massoretic apparatus published by Jacob ben Ḥayyim in the large Rabbinical Bible edited by him in 1525, the note סביר occurs on about 190 passages [1]. Dr. Ginsburg in *The Massorah,* ii. (1883), 324–327 (arranged by books), 327–329 (arranged alphabetically), adding the סבירין noted in other MSS., was able to raise the number to about 240; and now, he states [2], he has collected altogether as many as 350. According to the common opinion the note points to a *conjectural* reading [3], which might be expected, from analogy, or from the context, to occur, but does not occur actually in the Massoretic text: but some scholars [4] are of opinion that these notes refer to the readings of actual MSS., not indeed agreeing with the MT., but preferred by the author (or authors) of the notes in question. The two explanations are not inconsistent with each other; but if the latter be true, the value of the notes will be the greater, as many will then embody evidence as to the readings of Codices now no longer extant. Its probability, however, can only be tested by a systematic examination of all the סבירין that occur, and estimate of their value in individual cases. Both Heb. MSS. and Versions not unfrequently (but not always) agree with the reading suggested by a סביר: but this is not proof that manuscript authority is actually referred to by it. Examples: on Ex. 26, 31 יעשה (in the Rabbinical Bibles) occurs the note ב' סבירין תעשה, i.e. twice תעשה

---

[1] Only a section of these are noted in ordinary editions of the Hebrew Bible. The full Massoretic apparatus (on other matters as well as on this) is contained only in the large Rabbinical Bibles. The notes relating to the סבירין, published by Jacob ben Ḥayyim, are collected and explained, and the passages referred to given, in Frensdorff's *Massoretisches Wörterbuch* (1876), pp. 369–373.

[2] *Introduction to the Hebrew Bible,* 1897, pp. 193, 194 f.

[3] See e.g. Elias Levita's *Massoreth ha-Massoreth* (1538), in Dr. Ginsburg's edition (text and translation), London, 1867, pp. 225–227.

[4] Ginsburg in the *Transactions of the Society of Biblical Archaeology,* 1877, p. 138, and *Introd. to the Heb. Bible,* 1897, p. 187 ff.: Grätz, *Die Psalmen* (1882), pp. 115–117; comp. Geiger, *Urschrift* (1857), p. 253 f.

would be expected for עָשָׂה, and a reference is added to Ex. 25, 39.
In both passages, the context would favour the second person; and
this is read in 26, 31 by 6 MSS. LXX, Pesh., and in 25, 39 by 3 MSS.
Sam. and Pesh. (LXX omits). But each case must be examined
upon its own merits: the correction suggested by the note is not
always supported by the Versions, nor is it always in itself necessary[1].
The note in many cases relates to the number of a verb: thus, where
MT. has וַיָּבֹא, the pl. וַיָּבֹאוּ is eight times suggested, where it has יָבֹאוּ,
יָבֹא is fourteen times suggested[2]. וַיֹּאמְרוּ for וַיֹּאמֶר, as here, is suggested eleven times besides (see the Rabb. Bibles on Jud. 11, 15):
viz. Ex. 14, 25. Nu. 32, 25. Jud. 8, 6. 11, 15. *ch.* 16, 4. 19, 22: 1 Ki.
20, 3. 2 Ki. 9, 11. Hos. 12, 9. Zech. 6, 7[3]. The reader may examine
these passages and consider in which of them the correction appears
to him to be necessary[4]. The סְבִיר must be carefully distinguished
from the קְרִי: in no case does it direct the suggested alternative to be
substituted in reading for that which is written in the text. It is true,
however, as Ginsburg shews[5], that a reading which by one School
of Massorites is called a סְבִיר, is by another School sometimes called
a *Qrê* (as בָּם for בָּה in Is. 30, 32), and that it may even be the
recognized 'Oriental' reading (as Nu. 11, 21 לָכֶם for לָהֶם; 1 S. 18, 25
כִּי אִם for כִּי,—in both cases with the support of Western MSS.).

List of סְבִירִין in I-II Sam. as given in Ginsburg's *Hebrew Bible* (ed. 1, 1894):—
I 1, 28 נֻם[6] (for וְנֻם). So 2 Rabbinical quotations (Aptowitzer, II, p. 3).
    2, 13 (ed. 2, 1911, and *The Massorah*, but not in ed. 1) מִן for אֵת [7 MSS.
    De Rossi, 1 Baer (cod. Erf.). Pesh. Targ. read מֵאֵת; see note *ad loc.*].

---

[1] In some cases certainly the correction rests upon a false exegesis, as when בָּהּ
for בּוֹ is suggested in Ex. 4, 17; Dt. 24, 7: in other passages the opinions of
commentators differ; Ez. 2, 9, for instance, Cornill accepts בָּהּ, Hitzig and Smend
defend בּוֹ.

[2] See, on the passages, Frensdorff's note, p. 370 f.

[3] Only eleven passages are cited, though the number (elsewhere, as well as
on Jud. 11, 15) is stated as *twelve*. It is thought that Jud. 11, 19 may be the
omitted passage: see Frensdorff, *l. c.* p. 370. In the lists in Ginsburg's *Massorah*,
ii. pp. 325, 328, the twelfth passage is given as Jos. 24, 21.

[4] Comp. also the notes on many of the סְבִירִין cited above.—On I 27, 6 it is said
אָכֵן סְבִיר in Jer. 5, 2 for לָכֵן: so, probably rightly, 16 MSS., the St. Petersburg
cod. of A.D. 916, and Pesh.

[5] *Introd.*, p. 187 ff.

[6] Not in *The Massorah*.

2, 20 ¹ (ed. 2) למקומם for למקומו. So 10 MSS.²+2 on marg., and Pesh.

12, 5ᵇ ויאמרו. So 18+1 (Appendix, De R.) MSS. LXX, Pesh.

8 מצרימה. So 1 MS. Ginsb., 1 Kennicott, and 1 Rabb. quotation.

16, 4 ויאמרו. So *c.* 30 MSS., and 2 Rabb. quotations.

4 הֲשָׁלֹם ¹. So 1 MS. (Kenn.).

20 וִישַׁלַּח ¹. No MS.

18, 14 בכל (for לבל). So 18 MSS., and many Rabb. quotations.

25 כי אם (for כי). The Oriental reading. Also 9 MSS., and 3 Rabb. quotations.

19, 10 ההוא. 2 MSS. Gi., 3 Kenn.

22 ויאמרו (2°). No MS.

20, 8 עם (for על). 2 MSS. Kenn. (K. 154 = G. ג).

25, 23 ארצה. So 7 MSS.

27 הביאה ¹. So 25+1 (App.) MSS. The Orient. קרי (Baer, 105, 118).

27, 6 על־כן (for לכן). 1 MS. (Gi.).

II 3, 22 באו ¹. 2 MSS. Kenn. (K. 154 = G. ג).

29 ועל ¹. So 10 MSS.

35 ויבא. 2 MSS. Kenn.

6, 11 בבית ¹. No MS.

13, 20 בבית ¹. No MS.

14, 19 יש (for אש). 3 MSS. Kenn.

17, 19 פי (for פני). So 10 MSS.

18, 29 הֲשָׁלוֹם ¹. So 15 MSS. De R. (in 3 the ה deleted)+3 Gi.

19, 8 כי אם (for כי). 1 MS. (Gi.).

9 ויבאו (for ויבא, sc. העם). 1 MS. Gi., 5 Kenn.

22, 44 עמים for עמי (ψ. 18, 44 עם). So 4 MSS.+2 Gi., and LXX.

6. יהוה] LXX Μάρτυς Κύριος = עד י"י, certainly rightly.

עשה] A difficult and anomalous use of עשה. The explanation which is best in accordance with the general use of the verb is that of Keil: *made* Moses and Aaron to be what they were as leaders of men, the word being used not in a physical sense, but morally, of the position taken by them in history. (Ges. rendered *constituit, appointed;* but עשה has this sense only when it is followed by a word implying office or function, as *to make* priests, 1 Ki. 12, 31; *to make* (or *set up*) אוב וידענים 2 Ki. 21, 6: similarly II 15, 1 *to establish* chariots and horses.)

7. אשפטה] The Nif., properly reflexive, as נסתר *to hide oneself,* acquires sometimes a *reciprocal* force, as נשפט *to judge one another,*

---

¹ Not in *The Massorah.*

² MSS. are cited from De Rossi, except where otherwise stated.

i.e. *to plead* or *dispute together in judgement;* so נּוֹכַח *to set right one another,* i.e. *to argue* or *reason together* (Is. 1, 18) : נוֹעַץ *to counsel one another,* i.e. to take counsel together (1 Ki. 12, 6 and often) : cf. GK. § 51ᵈ.

וְאַגִּידָה לָכֶם = ὑμῖν ἀπαγγελῶ καὶ prefix LXX [אֵת כל צדקות 'י. נשפט is construed with an accus. in Ez. 17, 20 וּנשפטתי אִתּוֹ שם מֵעֲלוֹ אשר מֵעַל בי. But the construction is harsh ; and in all probability either במעלו (so 9 MSS.) or עַל מֵעָלוֹ (so 1 MS.) should be read in Ez., and here the words expressed by LXX should be supplied. צדקות 'י is, no doubt, a reminiscence of Jud. 5, 11.

8. כאשר . . . . וַיִּזעקו] as 6, 6ᵇ.

וַיְעַנּוּם מִצְרַיִם = Αἴγυπτος αὐτοὺς ἐταπείνωσεν καὶ add LXX [מצרים (not וַיַּכְנִיעֵם Th. We.: see Ex. 1, 12. Dt. 26, 6. II 7, 10 Hebrew and LXX). The words are needed on account of the following ויזעקו : a copyist's eye passed from the first מצרים to the second.

וישיבום] expresses just what Moses and Aaron did not do. LXX κατῴκισεν, Pesh. ܐܘܬܒ, Vulg. *collocavit* = וַיֹּשִׁיבֵם (the subject being God). The unpointed וישבם has been filled in wrongly in MT.

9. וַיִּמכר] This figure is used first in the 'Song of Moses,' Dt. 32, 30 : and adopted thence by the Deuteronomic redactor of the Book of Judges, who uses it often in the frame-work into which he fits the narratives incorporated by him in his Book (Jud. 2, 14. 3, 8. 4, 2. 10, 7 [rather differently in the *older* narrative 4, 9]). Chapters 7, 8, 12 of 1 Sam. have affinities in style with the redactional elements of the Book of Judges.

שר צבא יבין מלך חצור express LXX [שר צבא חצור, which is more in accordance with Hebrew usage.

10. וַיֹּאמר] Here, where ויזעקו closely precedes, the sing. is corrected by the Massorah into the plural (ויאמרו ק').

11. בדן] No judge or deliverer of this name is elsewhere mentioned. Ewald regarded בדן as an abbreviation of עבדן Jud. 12, 13 ff.: but some better known hero is likely to have been referred to. LXX, Pesh. have ברק. Baraq, it is true, is mentioned in Judges before Gideon ; but between Gideon and Jephthah no suitable name can be suggested : and the order in *v.* 9 is not chronological. Targ. and Jews explain cf Samson, treating בדן fancifully as = בן דן.

ואת שמואל] Pesh. and Lucian ואת שמשון: probably a correction. The passage, of course, does not report the *ipsissima verba* of Samuel: the speech is the work of the narrator, and indeed, in this part, appears to have been expanded by a later editor, who has forgotten that it is Samuel himself who is speaking. The allusion is to the success narrated in *ch.* 7.

בטח] An accus., defining the *state*, '*in* confidence, security:' GK. § 118q. So Dt. 12, 10; and in poetry Dt. 33, 28. Pr. 1, 33 al.: but לָבֶטַח is the usual expression (Lev. 25, 18. 19. Jud. 18, 7. 1 Ki. 5, 5 al.).

12. ותאמרו לי] LXX, Pesh. omit לי. לא כי = *Nay, but* as 2, 16 Qrê; II 16, 18. 24, 24 al.

13. אשר בחרתם אשר שאלתם] Cf. 8, 18: שאל is used of the request for a king in 8, 10. Nevertheless אשר שאלתם appears here to be superfluous, and is probably to be omitted with LXX.

שְׁאֶלְתֶּם] GK. §§ 44d, 64f.

14. The whole verse consists of the protasis, ending with an aposiopesis. (אחר or) היה אחרי = *to follow after*, as Ex. 23, 2. II 2, 10. 1 Ki. 12, 20. 16, 21. Thenius is bold enough to affirm that היה אחר is 'not Hebrew,' and accordingly would insert הולכים before אחר after LXX: not only, however, is this needless in itself, but, as We. remarks, the *position* of πορευόμενοι in the Greek shews that it merely represents a corruption of אלהיכם.

15. והיתה יד י' בכם] Cf. Ex. 9, 3. Dt. 2, 15. Jud. 2, 15.

ובאבותיכם] Since '*and* against your fathers' gives an unsuitable sense, and the passages in which ו means, or appears to mean, *as*[1] are dissimilar, there is no alternative but to accept LXX וּבְמַלְכְּכֶם in place

---

[1] In the formulation of proverbs, where the relation *from which* the comparison is deduced stands in the second place (rare): Job 5, 7 For man is born to trouble *and* sparks fly upwards (i.e. both effects happen similarly); 12, 11. More commonly the opposite order is employed: Pr. 25, 25 Cold waters to a thirsty soul *and* good news from a far country; 26, 3. 9. 14 A door turns upon its hinges *and* a sluggard upon his bed; 27, 21: cf. ψ. 19, 5 MT. (*Lex.* 253a j). Even supposing that the passage could, on other grounds, be treated as an example of the first of these usages, the same verb *will be* must obviously govern both clauses: the substitution of *it was* in the second clause destroys entirely the *parallelism of idea* upon which the idiom itself essentially depends.

of ובאבותיכם: the mention together of 'you' and 'your king' agrees both with *v.* 14 and *v.* 25ᵇ. MT. will be a *lapsus calami*, perhaps due to a reminiscence of *vv.* 6–8.

16. עֹשֶׂה] 'is about to do.' The *fut. instans* (on 3, 11).

17. קלות] 'voices,' viz. of Yahweh, in accordance with the Hebrew conception of a thunderstorm (ψ. 18, 11–14): so Ex. 9, 23. 28 al.: cf. ψ. 29 throughout.

לשאל] *in regard to* asking: in our idiom, '*in* asking' (though בִּשְׁאֹל would never be used in Heb.). So *v.* 19, and often, as 14, 33. Gen. 18, 19. 2 S. 13, 16; cf. GK. § 114ᵒ.

20. אתם] emphatic: '*ye*, indeed, have done this evil: only (אך) do not go further, and turn aside from Yahweh into idolatry.'

21. כי] Intrusive and meaningless: cf. the similar untranslatable כי in 2 Ch. 22, 6 (2 Ki. 8, 29 rightly מן). The word is not represented in LXX. Ehrlich, however, remarks that סור אחרי is nowhere said; and suggests that כי may be a mutilated fragment of לָלֶכֶת,—with סור, as Dt. 11, 28. 28, 14.

התהו] The primary idea of תהו is difficult to seize; but probably the ideas associated with it were those of *formlessness, confusion, unreality, emptiness:* in the Versions it is mostly represented by κενόν, οὐδέν, μάταιον, *inane, vacuum, vanum.* It thus denotes the *formlessness* of the primaeval earth (Gen. 1, 2 'and the earth was *formless* and empty'), and of a land reduced to a formless chaos (Jer. 4, 23: cf. Is. 34, 11),—in each of these passages being parallel to בֹּהוּ *emptiness:* in Job 26, 7 (נֹטֶה צפון על תהו) *empty space;* it then comes to mean *empty, unsubstantial, unreal,* and is used of a *groundless* argument or consideration (Is. 29, 21 וַיַּטּוּ בַתֹּהוּ צַדִּיק), of *moral* unreality, or falsehood (Is. 59, 4 בָּטוֹחַ על תהו), of something *unsubstantial* (Is. 40, 17 שֹׁפְטֵי ארץ כַּתֹּהוּ עשׂה; 23 מֵאֶפֶס וָתֹהוּ נחשבו לו); and so here of *idols;* cf. Is. 41, 29 רוח ותהו נסכיהם 'their molten images are wind and *hollowness,*' 44, 9 יֹצְרֵי פֶסֶל כֻּלָּם תֹּהוּ, with 'profit not' in the following clause, exactly as here. See further *Lex.* s.v.

אשר לא יועילו] Jeremiah's expressions are similar: 2, 8 אחרי לא יועילו (cf. *v.* 11); 16, 19 הבל ואין בם מועיל; cf. also Is. 44, 9. 10. 57, 12—all of false gods or idols.

22. שמו הגדול] Jos. 7, 9: also Jer. 44, 26. Ez. 36, 23.

הוֹאִיל] 'hath *willed:*' see on II 7, 29.

23. אָנֹכִי] A *casus pendens:* cf. Gen. 24, 27. Is. 45, 12ᵇ; GK. § 135ᵍ.

מֵחַטֹא] The inf. after חָלִילָה לִי, expressing the act deprecated, is regularly construed with מִן, Gen. 18, 25. 44, 7. *ch.* 26, 11 : not 'Far be it (lit. *Ad profanum* sit : see *Lex.*) *from* me that I should sin !' but 'Far be it *for* me! so that I should not sin (lit. *away from* sinning).' מֵחֲדֹל is parallel with מֵחָטֹא, and dependent like it upon חָלִילָה לִי.

דרך הטובה] Comp. 2 Ki. 20, 13 שמן הטוב (but Is. 39, 2 השמן הטוב); Jer. 6, 20 קנה הטוב. See above on 6, 18. But there is no reason why here we should not punctuate בַּדֶּרֶךְ (Klo. Bu. Sm. Now.; GK. § 126ˣ).

24. יְרִאוּ] for יִרְאוּ, as Jos. 24, 14. ψ. 34, 10. See GK. § 75ᵒᵒ.

הִגְדִּל] the 'inwardly transitive' or 'internal' Hif'il (GK. § 53ᵈ) hath *shewn* or *exhibited* greatness. With עַם, as ψ. 126, 2. 3.

25. תִּסָּפוּ] shall be *swept away* (not ' consumed,' EVV.): cf. 26, 10. 27, 1. Gen. 19, 15. Nu. 16, 26.

13 ; 14. *The Philistines in the heart of the Israelite country : Saul and Jonathan's successes against them : concluding summary of Saul's other wars, and notice of his family (sequel to* **9,** 1—**10,** 16 ; **10,** 27ᵇ—**11,** 15).

13, 1. בֶּן שָׁנָה שָׁאוּל [בֶּן שָׁנָה in accordance with Hebrew idiom can mean only *a year old* (Ex. 12, 5 and often). And so Lucian's recension of LXX υἱὸς ἐνιαυτοῦ Σαουλ[1]; Symm. (with an explanatory ὡς) υἱὸς ὡς ἐνιαύσιος ; Targ. כבר שנא דלית ביה חובין שאול כד מלך as a child a year old, in whom are no sins, was Saul when he became king (!).

In form, the verse is of the type followed regularly by the compiler of the Book of Kings in stating the age of a king at his accession, and the length of his reign (e.g. 1 Ki. 14, 21. 16, 11. 22, 42, etc.: similarly

---

[1] Explained by Theodoret (quoted in Field's *Hexapla,* ad loc.) in the sense of Symm. and the Targ. : Πῶς νοητέον τό, υἱὸς ἐνιαυτοῦ Σαουλ ἐν τῷ βασιλεύειν αὐτόν; Ὁ Σύμμαχος οὕτως ἐξέδωκεν· υἱὸς ὤν (al. ὡς) ἐνιαύσιος ἐν τῷ βασιλεύειν αὐτόν. Δηλοῖ δὲ τοῦτο τὴν ἁπλότητα τῆς ψυχῆς ἣν εἶχεν ὁ Σαουλ ἡνίκα τῆς βασιλείας τὴν χειροτονίαν ἐδέξατο. Ταύτῃ δὲ οὐκ ἐπὶ πλεῖστον ἐχρήσατο, κτλ. On the version of Symmachus, as exhibiting the influence of current Jewish exegesis, see e pecially Geiger's essay on this translator in the *Jüdische Zeitschrift,* i. (Breslau, 1862), p. 49 ff. ; and cf. HEXAPLA in the *Dict. of Christian Biography,* iii. 20.

II 2, 10. 5, 4): no doubt therefore the number denoting Saul's age was originally intended to have a place between בֶּן and שָׁנָה, although, for some reason, the text as it stands is deficient [1]. In clause *b*, also, שְׁתֵּי שָׁנִים can hardly be correct: to say nothing of the fact that the history seems to require a longer period, שְׁתֵּי שָׁנִים (in spite of שְׁתֵּי נָשִׁים) is not said in Heb. for 'two years:' we have indeed שְׁתַּיִם שָׁנִים II 2, 10. 2 Ki. 21, 19 (= 2 Ch. 33, 21)†; but the regular expression is שְׁנָתַיִם (Gen. 11, 10. II 14, 28. 1 Ki. 15, 25. 16, 8 al.). If with Keil we suppose וְעֶשְׂרִים [2] to have fallen out, the form of שְׁתֵּי שָׁנִים must be supposed to have been altered, and we must restore, in accordance with usage, עֶשְׂרִים וּשְׁתַּיִם שָׁנָה. The entire verse is not represented in LXX, and it is quite possible that it is only a late insertion in the Hebrew text,—originally perhaps a marginal note due to one who desiderated in the case of Saul a record similar to that found in the case of subsequent kings.

2. שְׁלֹשֶׁת אֲלָפִים מִיִּשְׂרָאֵל] 'LXX, Syr. express *men* after 3000.

---

[1] Three or four MSS. of LXX read υἱὸς τριάκοντα ἐτῶν: but in view of the age at which Jonathan, almost immediately after Saul's accession, appears, a higher figure seems to be required.

[2] Not, as Keil writes, כ. There is no ground for supposing (as is sometimes done) that in ancient times numerals were represented in Hebrew MSS. *by the letters of the alphabet*. If the numerals were not written in full, but expressed by symbols, the ancient Hebrews, it is reasonable to suppose, would have adopted a system similar to that in use amongst their neighbours, found equally in Phoenician, Palmyrene, Nabataean, and Old Aramaic inscriptions, and used also in Syriac. This system may be seen exemplified in detail in Euting's *Nabatäische Inschriften aus Arabien* (1885), p. 96 f., in the Table attached to Plate LXXIV of the *Facsimiles of Manuscripts and Inscriptions (Oriental Series)*, published by the Palaeographical Society under the editorship of Professor W. Wright (London, 1875-83), or in Lidzbarski, *Nordsem. Epigraphik* (1898), p. 198 ff., and the Table at the end of his Atlas of Plates. These Tables shew in what manner symbols which at first sight appear distinct, are in reality connected with one another by intermediate links. The first ten numerals in Phoenician are I, II, III, \ III, II III, III III, \ III III, II III III, III III III, ↗; 20 is ⊐ or H; 21 is I⊐ or I H; 30 is ↗H; 40 is HH; 90 is ↗HHHH, etc. The notation by means of letters of the alphabet is found on Phoenician *coins* (but not the earliest), on the coins of Simon Maccabaeus, and since mediaeval times has been in general, though not universal, use (not, for example, in the Epigraph of the St. Petersburg MS. of A.D. 916, or in the Epigraphs of many other MSS.).

H

Perhaps איש has dropped out after אלפים on account of its resemblance to מיש' in מישראל ' (Dr. Weir).

במכמש] Michmas (Is. 10, 28), now *Muḥmās* (1980 ft.), was 2 miles NE. of Geba' (see the next note but one), from which it was separated by the upper part of the valley, which a little lower down begins to have steep rocky sides, called now the *Wâdy eṣ-Ṣuwênîṭ* (see p. 106).

הר בית־אל] *the hill-country* of Bethel, now *Beitîn,* 4½ miles NW. of Michmas. The road from Muḥmās makes an ascent of 900 ft. through Dêr Diwân (2370 ft.) to Beitîn (2890 ft.).

בנבעת בנימין] Read בְּגֶבַע בנימין, as *v.* 16. *Gibeah* (see on 9, 1) was the modern *Tell el-Fûl,* 3 miles N. of Jerusalem : *Geba'* (which Is. 10, 29 shews was distinct) was the modern *Jeba'* (2220 ft.), on the south side of the Pass of Michmas (13, 16. 14, 5), 3 miles NE. of Gibeah ; and the two places, owing to the similarity of their names, are several times confused in MT. נבע בנימין recurs 1 Ki. 15, 22.

3. נציב] See on 10, 5.

ובגבע] Read with LXX, Targ., בַּגִּבְעָה : see 10, 10 (cf. 6).

ישמעו העברים] *Let the Hebrews hear !* viz. the news, and the order, implied in the proclamation, to come and join Saul in the war, which of course must now follow. *V.* 4 then describes how the report spread among the people, and induced them to respond to Saul's invitation. But העברים is strange in *Saul's* mouth : and LXX express לֵאמֹר פָּשְׁעוּ העברים 'saying, The Hebrews *have revolted*' (2 Ki. 1, 1). This, if correct, will of course be in its proper place after וישמעו פלשתים in *a,* and ושאול תקע בשופר בכל הארץ will connect, and connect well, with *v.* 4 (see Jud. 6, 34[b]). So substantially We., who, however, instead of assuming a transposition of the words from clause *a,* regards their incorrect position as indicating that originally they were a marginal gloss. This conclusion, however, is not necessary (Sm. Bu. Now.).

4. נבאש ב'] lit. *made itself malodorous against* (= was in bad odour with) : so II 10, 6 ; sq. את (*with,* i.e. towards) II 16, 21.

5. שלשים] The number of chariots is disproportionately large : no doubt שְׁלֹשִׁים is an error for שְׁלֹשֶׁת (so LXX (Luc.) and Pesh.).

כחול וג'] Jos. 11, 4. Jud. 7, 12.

לרב] *in regard to* muchness : ל, as often, introducing the *tertium comparationis* (*Lex.* 514 e, *b*); cf. Gen. 41, 19. Ex. 24, 10.

וַיַּעֲלוּ] from the low-lying Philistine plain; presumably up the Vale (עֵמֶק) of Aijalon, past the two Beth-ḥorons (on *v.* 18), and across the elevated plateau on which Bethel stands (G. A. Smith, *H. G.* 250; cf. 251, 210 f., 291).

קִדְמַת בֵּית־אָוֶן] Beth-aven was W. (NW.: see the Map) of Michmas, near Ai, E. (SE.) of Bethel (Jos. 7, 2), and the N. border of Judah ran up from it to Bethel (Jos. 18, 12 f.); but its exact site is not known.

6. רָאוּ] the plur. after the collective אִישׁ is in itself unexceptionable (Jud. 9, 55. 15, 10. 20, 17. 20ᵇ. 33. 36ᵇ. 48. 2 S. 20, 2ᵇ: but LXX have the sing. in 9, 55. 20, 33. 36ᵇ. 2 S. 20, 2ᵇ); but LXX εἶδεν presupposes רָאָה, and this is supported by the following צַר לוֹ. The *sing.* after the collective is also very common: Jud. 7, 23. 24ᵇ. 12, 1. 20, 20ᵃ. 41 (*ter*). 21, 1. 1 S. 14, 24. 17, 25 al. (but LXX have the plur. in Jud. 7, 23. 20, 20ᵃ. 41, second and third times).

וּבַחֲוָחִים] *Thistles* (2 Ki. 14, 9) are unsuitable: read with Ewald (*Hist.* iii. 44 [E. T. 31]), Th. We. etc. וּבַחֹרִים, as 14, 11. Caves abound in the rocky sides of the lower part of Wādy eṣ-Ṣuwênît.

צְרִיחִים] Only besides in Jud. 9, 46. 49, of some part of the temple of אֵל בְּרִית, in which the Shechemites took refuge, and which was burnt upon them, though what part precisely is not clear. In Arabic صَرْح means a *tower* or *lofty building* (Qor. 40, 38), قَرِيح (with ض) *a narrow excavation for the body at the bottom of a grave* (Moore, *Judges*, p. 266)[1]: the former suggests an idea which is here not probable; but if צְרִיחַ had some less special sense than قَرِيح, such as *under-ground cavity*, it would suit at least this passage.

7ᵃ. וְעִבְרִים] We.'s objections to עברים are well-founded. The word does not express '*some of the* Hebrews;' and as *v.* 7 carries on the thought of *v.* 6, there is no ground for the *repetition* of the subject עברים, and its emphatic position before the verb: a verb coordinate

---

[1] Also used similarly in the Nabataean Inscriptions (Barth, *AJSL.* July, 97, 273) found at Madâin-Sâliḥ by Mr. Doughty (No. 8, lines 4, 5), and (re-)edited by Euting, *Nabatäische Inschriften* (1885), of a *sepulchral chamber*: see No. 15 (= Cooke, *NSI.* No. 91), line 4 ולארסכסה תלתין תרין מן כפרא וצריחא וחלקה מן גוחיא מדנחא ונוחיא ' and to Arisoxe belong two-thirds of the tomb, and the *sepulchral chamber*; and her share in the niches is the east side, with the niches there,' etc.; with Nöldeke's note, p. 55. See also Cooke, No. 94, 1 (from Petra).

with ויתחבאו *v.* 6 is what would be expected. For ועברים עברו
את־הירדן he conjectures accordingly, with but slight changes, ועברו
מַעְבְּרוֹת הירדן 'and *they passed over the fords of* Jordan.' This is
a decided improvement, except that ועברו should be ויעברו. This,
however, lessens the similarity to ועברים: hence Klo.'s clever suggestion
וְעַם רַב for ועברים is probably best: 'and *much people* passed over
Jordan' (so Bu. Sm.). For the frequent confusion of ב and מ in old
Heb. MSS., see Introd., § 5. 2.

> 7ᵇ–15ᵃ. *First rejection of Saul at Gilgal* (*comp.* 10, 8).

7ᵇ. בגלגל] See 10, 8.

חרדו אחריו] pregnantly (cf. 16, 4, חרד לקראת אל, 'ח Gen. 42, 28)=
followed him trembling. We. conjectured plausibly מֵאַחֲרָיו, which is
also expressed by Luc. (ἀπὸ ὄπισθεν αὐτοῦ): trembled *from* after him =
forsook him trembling: so Now. Dh. Bu., however, prefers MT.,
pointing out that מאחריו is tautologous with 8ᵇ.

8. וייחל] The Kt. is וַיֵּחֶל (*Nif.*) as Gen. 8, 12 (not the *Pi'el* וַיְחַל,
which is confined to poetry). The Qrê is וַיּוֹחֶל (*Hif.*), as 10, 8;
II 18, 14.

ܐܫܪ ܫܡܘܐܠ] ؟ܡܬܕܐ is good Aramaic, but אשר שמואל is not
good Hebrew, in the sense 'of Samuel.' A verb has dropped out.
יָעַד or יְעָדוֹ (see II 20, 5) is suggested by Ges. (*Lg.* p. 851) and Keil:
דִּבֶּר (Gen. 21, 2) or אָמַר (ib. 22, 2ᵇ), the latter of which might easily
fall out after אשר, is expressed by LXX, Targ.: but the word
which might drop out most readily is שָׂם (see Ex. 9, 5) before שמואל
(so 5 MSS.); so also Dr. Weir. Comp. Ew. § 292ᵇ *note.*

ויפץ] The Hif. of פוץ is always *causative,* except here, Ex. 5, 12.
Job 38, 24. Probably Qal should be read each time, i. e. here וַיָּפֶץ.

מעליו] *from beside, from with:* so 2 Ki. 25, 5 with the same verb.
Cf. 28, 14 *footnote; Lex.* 759ᵃ.

11. כי] *recitativum:* see on 2, 16.

נָפֵץ] Nif. from פֵּצַ, which does not occur, but is assumed to be
a parallel form of פּוּץ: GK. § 67ᵈᵈ. But probably נָפֹץ (Nif. from the
ordinary form, פוּץ) should be read. Notice the emph. ואתה.

מכמש] not *at* Michmas (on 1, 24), but *to* Michmas, נאספים implying motion.

12. ירדו] Gilgal (10, 8) being in the Jordan-valley, some 2600 ft. below Michmas (*vv*. 5. 11).

ואתאפַּק] GK. § 54ᵏ.

13. כִּי עתה] כִּי עתה as a rule introduces the apodosis after לֹ (e.g. Nu. 22, 29: *Tenses*, § 144), עתה having the force of *in that case:* and hence Hitzig, We. Bu. etc. would point here לֹא שמעת (so II 18, 12; 19, 7) for לֹא שמעת. This is preferable, though not perhaps *necessary;* for עתה might presumably refer to a condition *implied*, without being actually expressed. Cf. Ex. 9, 15 where, though the context is differently worded, עתה equally refers to a condition which must be inferred from *v*. 14: 'For *in that case* (viz. if such had not been my purpose), I should have put forth my hand, and smitten thee and thy people,' etc.; and Job 3, 13.

אֶל] = עַל, which would be more usual: comp. 2, 34. 3, 12. 5, 4. 6. 6, 15. 14, 34 (contrast 33). 16, 13 (contrast 10, 6). 23 (16 עַל). 17, 3. 51. 18, 10. 19, 9. 16. 20, 25 (by the side of עַל). 22, 13 (8 עַל). 27, 10 (אל after עַל twice). II 2, 9 (thrice אל followed by thrice עַל in the same sentence), 6, 3. 8, 7 etc.: 20, 23ᵃ (23ᵇ and 8, 16 עַל). 24, 4. So sometimes in other books, esp. in Jeremiah. Cf. *Lex*. 41ᵃ.

עַל where אל would be more usual is less common: but see on 1, 10 and add II 14, 1. 17, 11.

14. אִישׁ כלבבו] So Jer. 3, 15†, of the ideal rulers of the future: ונתתי לכם רעים כלבי.

15. ויעל] See on *v*. 12; and cf. Jud. 2, 1. After מִן הגלגל something appears to have dropped out of the narrative. In *v*. 4 Saul is at *Gilgal*, and remains there during the scene 9–14; in *v*. 16 he appears suddenly abiding (יושב) at *Gibeah*. A clause describing his departure from Gilgal and arrival at Gibeah is thus desiderated. LXX has such a clause, continuing, viz. after מִן הגלגל [¹ εἰς ὁδὸν αὐτοῦ¹, καὶ τὸ κατά- λιμμα τοῦ λαοῦ ἀνέβη ὀπίσω Σαουλ εἰς ἀπάντησιν ὀπίσω τοῦ λαοῦ τοῦ πολεμιστοῦ. αὐτῶν παραγενομένων ἐκ Γαλγάλων] εἰς Γαβαα Βενιαμειν, κτλ. This may be accepted in substance, though not quite in the form in which it here appears. (1) לדרכו following, as it would do ויעל,

---

¹ These words do not stand in Tisch.'s text, but they form part of the text of B, and are printed in Dr. Swete's edition. We.'s conjecture, therefore (made in 1871), that ' εἰς ὁδὸν αὐτοῦ has probably fallen out,' is entirely confirmed.

would give rise to a phrase not in use (וילך לדרכו is always said).
(2) εἰς ἀπάντησιν ὀπίσω represents a non-Hebraic combination (though
adopted, without misgiving, by Th.).   (3) αὐτῶν παραγ., if it represents, as it seems to do, הֵם בָּאִים must be followed by פקד וישאול, not
as MT. by ויפקד שאול (so always: see *Tenses*, § 169).   The following
text will satisfy the conditions of Hebrew style: ויקם שמואל ויעל
מז־הגלגל [וַיֵּלֶךְ לְדַרְכּוֹ : וְיֶתֶר הָעָם עָלָה אַחֲרֵי שָׁאוּל לִקְרַאת עַם[1] or] אַנְשֵׁי
הַמִּלְחָמָה וַיָּבֹאוּ מִן הַגִּלְגָּל] גבעת בנימין וג׳.   The omission in MT. is
evidently due to the recurrence of מז־הגלגל.

16. The Philistines had expelled Saul from Michmas (*v.* 5[b]; cf.
v. 2), and he had retired to Geba', where Jonathan already was (*v.* 2).

17. המשחית] So 14, 15.   Probably a technical expression, denoting
(*ZAW.* 1907, 59) the part of an army employed in ravaging and
destruction: cf. esp. Jer. 22, 7 ⟨cutting down trees⟩; also 46, 22.
Ez. 9, 1[b]. 21, 36.   Ew. (*Hist.* iii. 33 *n.*) compared اَلْمُغِيرِ, of a *body of
raiders* (Lane, 2307).

שלשה ראשים] *as* three columns, an accus. defining the manner in
which המשחית issued forth: Ew. § 279[c]; GK. § 118q.   Cf. 2 Ki. 5, 2
וארם יצאו גדודים came out *as* marauding bands.

אחד] the numeral without the art., being definite in itself: see GK.
§§ 126[2], 134[1]; and cf. on 1, 2.   Notice the frequentative יפנה.

עפרה] According to Jerome, 'Ophra was 5 miles E. of Bethel,
whence it has been generally identified with *eṭ-Ṭaiyibeh* (2850 ft.),
4 miles NE. of Bethel (2890 ft.), and 5 miles to the N. of Michmas
(1980 ft.).   Cf. Jos. 18, 23; and on II 13, 23.

ארץ שועל] LXX Σωγαλ.   Unknown.

18. Upper Beth-ḥoron, now *Bêt-'ûr el-fôḳa* (2020 ft.), was 10 miles,
as the crow flies, W. of Michmas.   Lower Beth-ḥoron, now *Bêt-'ûr
el-taḥta* (1310 ft.), was 1¾ miles WNW. of Upper Beth-ḥoron.   The
'way' to Beth-ḥoron from Michmas would be to the NW., past
Dêr Diwān (2370 ft.), up to Bethel (2890 ft.,—900 ft. above
Michmas), and then on to the west.

הגבול] The north border of Benjamin ran up from Jericho to

---

[1] המלחמה (אנשי or) עם is a phrase that occurs in Joshua, but not elsewhere in
I-II Sam.   This, however, is not decisive against its originality here.

near Ramah (on 10, 2); so it would pass, presumably, near Michmas[1].
But דרך 'the way *to*,' suggests a particular place, not a line ; and
הנשקף (*that leans out over :* see Nu. 21, 20. 23, 28) would be more
naturally said of a height than of a border. LXX Γαβεε points to
הַגִּבְעָה 'the hill' (not the place of that name); and this ought probably to be read, with הַנִּשְׁקָפָה for הנשקף. The 'wilderness' meant
will be that consisting of the hills and wādys sloping down eastwards
into the Jordan-valley (see the next note): cf. Jud. 20, 47 'into *the
wilderness*, to the crag of Rimmon' (3½ miles N. of Michmas).

גי הצבעים] the *Ravine of the Hyaenas.* The Wādy eṣ-Ṣuwênît
(see on *v.* 2), at about 5 miles below Michmas, on the SE., runs into
W. Fārah, and 2 or 3 miles below the point of juncture, there is a
valley called *Wādy Abu-Daba'*, running from the SW. into W. Fārah.
This, however, seems an insignificant valley : perhaps (Buhl, *Geogr.* 98)
גי צבעים was the ancient name of W. Fārah itself (which to the east
of this point is now known as W. Kelt). There is a road, about
2 miles north of W. Fārah (see the large PEF. Map), leading straight
down from Michmas into the Jordan-valley, which may be the road
here meant. The גבע (or rather גבעה) may have been a hill near this
road, overlooking W. Fārah or W. Kelt. Cf. *H. G.* p. 291 *n.*

19. ימצא] frequentative, just as (e.g.) Gen. 31, 39.

. . . כי אמר פן] the same idiom, implying always that steps are
taken to prevent what is feared from taking place, 27, 11. Gen. 31, 31
(comp. 26, 7). 42, 4. Ex. 13, 17. ψ. 38, 17 al.

אמר] Qrê אמרו. See *Ochlah we-Ochlah*, No. 119[2], where eighteen
cases of an omitted ו at the end of a word are enumerated, several
(e.g. Jud. 21, 20. 1 Ki. 12, 7) similar to this. See further in the
Introduction, p. lxii f.

20. וַיֵּרְדוּ] Point rather, with Klo., וַיֵּרְדוּ, with a freq. force (on
1, 3), in agreement with ימצא *v.* 19, and והיתה *v.* 21.

הפלשתים] 'LXX εἰς γῆν ἀλλοφύλων. Ought we not to read אל
הפלשתים (from ישראל) or possibly [so Bu. Sm.] אַרְצָה ?' (Dr. Weir.)

---

[1] 2 Ki. 23, 8 'from Geba' to Beer-sheba' implies that Geba' was on the N. border
of the Southern Kingdom ; cf. Zech. 14, 10.

[2] Or, in the Rabbinical Bibles, the Mass. magna on 1 Ki. 1, 1, or the Final
Massorah, letter ו, No. 18.

מַחֲרֵשָׁתוֹ] LXX render this by δρέπανον, Pesh. by ܚܨ̈ܕܐ (ox-goad), both words being used in *v.* 21 to represent הדרבן. Probably, therefore, דרבנו should be read here for מַחֲרֵשָׁתוֹ. The two verses will then agree in the implements enumerated; and the repetition of almost the same word (מַחֲרֵשָׁתוֹ, מַחֲרֵשָׁתוֹ) in one and the same verse will be avoided. Symm. δίκελλα, *mattock* (so EVV.).

21. הַפְּצִירָה פִים] These words are hopelessly corrupt. They are rendered conventionally *bluntness of edges:* but (1) the plur. of פה is elsewhere פִיוֹת; (2) the meaning *bluntness,* viewed in the light of the sense which the root פצר elsewhere expresses, is extremely doubtful[1]; (3) the construction is grammatically inexplicable (הַפְּצִירָה for פְצִירַת). הַפְּצִיר הַפִּים (inf. *Hif.* with the force of a noun—rather הַפְצֵיר, Ew. § 156c), suggested by Keil, would lessen the grammatical anomaly, but does not really remove the difficulty which the words present. LXX ὁ τρυγητὸς for הַפְּצִירָה presupposes almost the same word (הבציר); but their rendering of the clause καὶ ἦν ὁ τρυγητὸς ἕτοιμος τοῦ θερίζειν supplies no basis for a satisfactory restoration of the text. AV. *file* is derived immediately from the Jewish commentators, Rashi, and David Kimchi: its ultimate source is merely the conjectural rendering of Targ. Pesh. (שׁוּפִינָא).

וּלְשַׁלֵּשׁ קִלְּשׁוֹן] Another *crux.* קִלְּשׁוֹן occurs in the Targ. of Qoh. 12, 11 (= Heb. מַשְׂמְרוֹת): but possibly it may be only borrowed from the present passage: it is not cited as occurring elsewhere in Aramaic, or post-Bibl. Hebrew. Still the root (see Levy) has in Aramaic the sense of *being thin* (hence Nu. 7, 13 Ps.-Jon. a silver charger דְּגִילְדָא קְלִישׁ of *thin* plate), so there remains the possibility that קִלְּשׁוֹן may have been in use to denote *a fine point.* In that case שְׁלֹשׁ קִלְּשׁוֹן will be a sort of compound = *tridens.* But such a compound in Hebrew is by no means free of suspicion; and we expect naturally to find a reference to the same implements that are named *v.* 20. LXX saw in the words the high price which the Philistines

---

[1] The combination of פצר with فض *to cleave,* hence as applied to a sword, *to hack,* سَيْفٌ فُطَارٌ *a hacked* i.e. blunted *sword* (Schultens, *Opp. Min.,* p. 168), is altogether questionable, the interchange of consonants being against rule (פצר should correspond to an Arabic فضر, not فطر; see the list of examples in *Tenses,* Appendix, § 178).

exacted for sharpening the tools of the Hebrews: τὰ δὲ σκεύη (= אתים
in *v.* 20) ἦν τρεῖς σίκλοι εἰς τὸν ὀδόντα, i.e. בִּשְׁלֹשָׁה שְׁקָלִים לַשֵּׁן. This
reading will of course presuppose that the corrupt words הפצירה פים
expressed originally the idea of sharpening:—'And sharpening used
to be obtained for the mattocks and for the coulters *at three shekels
a tooth,*' etc. But אתים and מחרשות are not constructed with teeth:
and the price stated appears to be incredibly high.

הַדָּרְבָן: (Baer, with Qimḥi, p. 99). [הַדָּרְבָן: (Bomberg, Ginsb. Kit.)].
The הָ is peculiar; but in spite of the following ב (not בּ), *dor-*, not *dā-rᵉ*,
is intended: GK. § 9ᵛ. On the form, GK. § 85ᵘ; Stade, § 52ᵃ; and
comp. קָרְבָּן *qorbhān* Ez. 40, 43 (Baer, Gi. Kit.); אָבְדָן Est. 8, 6 (*st. c.*).

22. וַיְהִי [והיה would be expected (cf. on 1, 12); and perhaps והיה is
an error for it, due to the preceding והיתה.

מלחמת] the form is cstr. Probably מכמש should follow; so LXX.

23. The garrison of the Philistines moved from Michmas itself
(*v.* 16) to the 'Pass of Michmas,' i.e. to the point on the north edge of
W. eṣ-Ṣuwênît, where the 'pass' across (not *down*) the Wādy began
(see the Map; and cf. on 14, 5).

מצב] LXX ὑπόστασις, attempting, no doubt, to render etymologically.
However, ὑπόστασις was used by Sophocles in the sense of ἐνέδρα
(Hatch, *Essays in Biblical Greek*, 1889, p. 88).

14, 1. ויהי היום] See on 1, 4.

מעבר הלז] '*off*—i.e. *on;* see the note on *v.* 4—*this side-across*
(or *this opposite side*).' הַלָּז *this* recurs 17, 26; 20, 19 LXX; Jud.
6, 20; 2 Ki. 4, 25; 23, 17; Zech. 2, 8; Dan. 8, 16†: cf. הַלָּזֶה Gen.
24, 65; 37, 19†; הַלֵּזוּ Ez. 36, 35†. All are akin to the common
Arabic أَلَّذِى *who, which* (*Lex.* 229ᵇ: Wright, *Arab. Gramm.* i, § 347;
Compar. Gramm., p. 117). Everywhere else, however, the noun to
which הלז is attached has the art.: hence (Bu.) we ought perhaps to
read either מֵהָעֵבֶר הַלָּז (cf. *v.* 4), or מֵעֵבֶר הַמַּעֲבָר הַלָּז 'across this *pass*.'

2. ישב] *was abiding,*—at the time. Notice the ptcp.

בקצה] 'at the *outskirts* (lit. *extremity*) of:' so 9, 27. Nu. 11, 1. 20,
16 al. It is a pity that the obscure archaism 'in the uttermost part
of' has been retained in RV.

הנבעה] Read גבע: see 13, 16; and cf. 14, 5.

4. המעברות] the form is absolute (Jos. 2, 7), not (Sm.) construct.

מהעבר וג' [עבר = *side*, as *v.* 40. Ex. 32, 15 משני עבריהם *on their two sides.* מן, as constantly, in defining position, lit. *off*,—in our idiom, from a different point of view, *on* (*Lex.* 578ᵇ). מזה . . . מזה the repetition has the effect of placing the two identical words in contrast with each other: hence they acquire the sense 'off *here* . . . off *there.*' So often, as 17, 3; 23, 26 מצד ההר מזה . . . מצד ההר מזה. II 2, 13; Nu. 22, 24 גדר מזה וגדר מזה. 32, 19 [1]; and similarly (in Ezek. only) מפֹּה . . . מפֹּה (Ez. 40, 10 al.); and in analogous expressions (e.g. זה . . . זה = *hic . . . ille*). Render, then, 'on the side, off here . . ., on the side, off there' = 'on the one side . . ., on the other side.'

5. LXX ὁδὸς can only be a corruption of ὀδοὺς (cf. in *v.* 4 the second version καὶ ὀδοὺς πέτρας ἐκ τούτου): hence the Gk. text here must have sustained a double corruption; first, ὀδοὺς must have been changed (by accident or design) into ὀδός, and then the *genders* must have been altered designedly to agree with it. With שֵׁן, cf. the Fr. *dent*, of a pointed rock, or mountain top (as in 'Les Dents du Midi,' opposite to Montreux).

On the Pass of Michmas, see especially Dalman's articles, *ZDPV.* xxvii. (1904), 161 ff., xxviii. 161 ff. (with several corrections of the first), containing minute descriptions of the position of Jeba' and Michmas, of the Pass, and other subordinate routes, between them, and of Wādy eṣ-Ṣuwênîṭ [2]. In these articles Dalman places *Bozeẓ* and *Seneh* at *d, c* on the Map, where the sides of the Wādy begin to be steep, but are not yet as precipitous as they become further down the valley. Now, however (*Palästina-Jahrbuch*, 1911, p. 12), he places Boẓeẓ more than a mile further down the Wādy, at *el-Ḥôṣn et-taḥtâni* (see the Map, Plate V at the end of *ZDPV.* xxviii),—i. e. the 'Lower fortress,' a block of hermits' caves with windows in the cliffs,—at the NW. end of a gully running into the Wādy on the N.; and Seneh at the peak *Ḳurnet Challet el-Ḥayy*, on the opposite side of the Wādy, supposing the Philistine post to have been at *el-Merjameh*, nearly a mile SE. of el-Miḳtara. At the mouth of W. Raḥab—seemingly close by el-Ḥôṣn et-taḥtâni—there is (Rawnsley, *PEFQS.* 1879, 122 = *PEF. Memoirs*, iii. 142) 'a tooth of rock that, like a tower on a bracket, hangs in mid air at the angle of the rock cliff;' and Conder (*PEFQS.* 1881, 253; cf. *T. W.* 255 f.) supposes Jonathan to have climbed up the rocks near here. Dalman now agrees with Rawnsley in making him climb up a gully a little further to the S., viz. W. *Abu Ja'd* (= Rawnsley's Sh'ab el-Huti, i. e. *She'b el-Ḥuṭi : ZDPV.* xxviii. 167): but *d, c* would seem to suit the terms of 13, 23. 14, 5 better than either of these suggested sites. See further the *Addenda.*

---

[1] Comp. the writer's *Deuteronomy,* p. xliii *note.*

[2] Properly *es-Suwênîṭ* ('of the little acacias'), but pronounced now (Dalm. *ZDPV.* xxviii. 162, cf. 174) *eṣ-Ṣwênîṭ.* For a fuller description of the Wādy, see *ibid.* 161 ff.

THE PASS OF MICHMAS

a, b. Boẓeẓ and Sêneh, according to Robinson.

c, d. Boẓeẓ and Sêneh, according to Dalman in 1904. (Dalman now places them a mile further down Wâdy eṣ-Suwênîṭ, to the SE.: see above, p. 106.)

e, g, g, g. Present route between Jeba' and Michmâs for passengers with animals.

e, f, e. Shorter route for foot-passengers.

f. Steep descent into Wâdy el-Medîneh (the 'Wâdy of the City,' i.e. leading to Jerusalem).

r. Râs el-Wâdy ('Head of the Wâdy' eṣ-Suwênîṭ).

(Reproduced, by permission, from Plate VI, at the end of ZDMG. xxvii, with slight corrections made in accordance with ZDMG. xxviii. 161 ff. revision.)

מצוק] was *fixed firmly*, or was *a pillar* (2, 8). But the word seems superfluous (contrast clause ᵇ); and it is probably only a corrupt anticipation of מצפון.

מול] *in front of*, on the same side with: Jos. 8, 33 *in front of* the two mountains; Ex. 18, 19 *in front of* God, i.e. representing Him. See W. A. Wright, in the *Journal of Philology*, xiii. 117–120.

6 resumes *v.* 1, after the intervening parenthetical particulars.

ויעשה] עשה is used here absolutely, in the full and pregnant sense which it sometimes has, esp. in poetry: 1 Ki. 8, 32 ועשית *and act*, Jer. 14, 7 עֲשֵׂה למען שמך, ψ. 22, 32 כי עשה, 37, 5 al. (*Lex.* 794ᵃ 4). Jud. 2, 7, which has been compared, is quite different: עשה there has an object, אשר, referring back to כל מעשה יהוה.

מעצור] Not as עצר 9, 17; but in the sense of *constraint, difficulty*: ' There is no difficulty to Yahweh, in regard to saving (either) with many or with few.' Cf. for the thought 2 Ch. 14, 10. 1 Macc. 3, 18 (cited by Th.).

7. נטה לך] The reflexive לך, as elsewhere (e.g. Dt. 1, 7. 40), with verbs of motion. A difficulty in MT. arises however from the use of נטה; for in II 2, 21 נטה לך על ימינך או על שמאלך it preserves its usual force of *incline*, which here seems not to be suitable. LXX express עשה כל אשר לבבך נֹטֶה לו do all *unto which* thine heart (i.e. mind) *inclineth*: cf. נטה with לב Jud. 9, 3. 1 Ki. 11, 9.

כלבבך] Cf. ψ. 20, 5 יתן לך כלבבך. But here also a phrase, which in this connexion is more idiomatic, is suggested by LXX ἰδοὺ ἐγὼ μετὰ σοῦ, ὡς ἡ καρδία σοῦ καρδία μοῦ, i.e. כִּלְבָבְךָ לְבָבִי (so Ew. Th. We. Bu. etc.).

8. הנה אנחנו עברים] Notice the idiom. use of the ptcp., more delicate and expressive than the Engl. 'we will pass over.' Comp. similar sentences in Jud. 6, 37 (also followed by אם); Gen. 24, 13 and 43 (followed by והיה).

9. אם כה יאמרו] The כה, pointing onwards, is idiomatic: see Gen. 31, 8. II 15, 26. דמם and עמד are synonyms, as Jos. 10, 13 וידם השמש וירח עמד (cf. 12ᵇ דּוֹם).

תחתינו] idiomatically = *in our place, where we are*: as Jos. 6, 5 ונפלה חומת העיר תחתיה will fall *in its place*; Jud. 7, 21 ויעמדו איש תחתיו and they stood each *in his place*; Hab. 3, 16 ותחתי ארגז = and I tremble *where I stand*; Is. 25, 10. Cf. *Lex.* 1065ᵇ 2 a.

10. נתנם] *will have* given them : 20, 22 ; II 5, 24.

11. 'הנה עברים וג] 'Behold Hebrews coming out,' etc. הָעִבְרִים (see Kitt.) *the mice*—a term of contempt (cf. Judith 14, 12 Vulg.)— was proposed by Hitzig (*Gesch. Isr.*, p. 135), and is favoured by Bu. ; but it is not probable.

12. המצבה] Read הַמַּצֵּב, as elsewhere in *chs.* 13–14 : LXX Μεσσαφ.

13. ויפלו] LXX ויפנו (cf. Jud. 20, 42). Against this, see We.

ממותת] intensive, as 17, 51. II 1, 9. The Philistines fell down, smitten by Jonathan's sword ; and his armour-bearer, as he went along, *despatched them* after him. The ptcp. represents vividly the armour-bearer's activity on the occasion.

14. 'כבחצי וג] 'as it were within half a furrow, (of) an acre of field.' צמד as Is. 5, 10[1]. If the text be correct, we must imagine the narrator to be thinking of a field, of a size such as the expression צמד שדה would suggest : he says, then, that in a space equal to about half the distance across it, the twenty men were slain. צמד שדה defines in effect the *length* of the מַעֲנָה, and is hence construed in apposition with it (on the principle explained in *Tenses,* § 192 : cf. מָסָךְ עשרים אמה 'a veil, twenty cubits'). Nevertheless the MT. excites suspicion, if only by the combination of כ and ב in כבחצי[2]. LXX has ἐν βολίσι[3] καὶ κόχλαξιν τοῦ πεδίου = השדה וב ? בחצים. However, if the words

---

[1] The area which a צמד of oxen could plough in (presumably) a day.

[2] Which elsewhere occurs *only* in the expression כבראשנה (five times), and in כבתחלה once (Is. 1, 26), in parallelism with כבראשנה. כְּמָן occurs (including 10, 27) three times (the third passage is כמפני חרב Lev. 26, 37). As an ordinary rule, such combinations are avoided in classical Hebrew (GK. § 118[a-w]). Even כעל = *as upon* occurs only in the latest Hebrew, ψ. 119, 14 ; 2 Ch. 32, 19 : and in a different sense, as a strengthened כ, Is. 59, 18 (first time ; the second occurrence must be corrupt) ; 63, 7†.

[3] Tisch.'s text adds καὶ ἐν πετροβόλοις. But on this We.'s acute note, written in 1871, deserves to be transcribed. Comparing LXX with MT., he wrote : ' The first letter of MT. כ is not expressed in LXX, the following five agree, but are combined to form one word (בְּחָצִים) : at the end of the verse LXX agrees also in שדה. It remains to refer, if possible, ענה צמד and καὶ ἐν πετροβόλοις καὶ ἐν κόχλαξι to a common source. When the six letters on the one side and the six words on the other are compared, and when further the meanings of the two principal words in the Greek are taken into account, it is natural to suppose ἐν πετροβόλοις (= אבני קלע Job 41, 20) to be a gloss explanatory of κόχλαξιν *pebbles* (1 Macc. 10, 73), which appear here strangely as a weapon.' We.'s

contain some notice of the *weapons* used, they are certainly out of place at the end of *v.* 14, and (We.) will be a gloss on *v.* 13, intended to explain, in view of 13, 22, what weapons the armour-bearer could have had ; under the circumstances, also, pebbles, at any rate, do not appear likely to have been employed. On מענה, the *furrow* (cf. ψ. 129, 3), at the end of which the ploughman turns, see Dalman, *ZDPV.* 1905, p. 27 ff. Dalm. regards צמד שדה as an explanatory gloss. مَغْنَى still means a *furrow* in Palestine : the average length of one seems to be (p. 31) 20–30 yds., so that half a furrow would be 10–15 yds.

15. 'במחנה וג] ' in the camp, and (so LXX) on the field, and among all the people,' i.e. in the camp (13, 17), among the men posted in the fields around, and among the people generally : even the garrison (13, 23) and the ravaging band (13, 17) trembled as well.

'ותהי וג] 'and it [GK. § 144ᵇ] became a trembling of God,' i.e. the affair resulted in a general panic. חרדת אלהים denotes a terror without adequate apparent cause, and therefore attributed to the direct influence of God. Comp. the later Greek use of πανικὸν (from Πάν : see Liddell and Scott, *s. v.*). Cf. 11, 7 פחד יהוה, Gen. 35, 5 חִתַּת אלהים : also 2 Ki. 7, 6 ; Ez. 38, 21 LXX (לְכָל־חֲרָדָה for לכל הרי חרב). Whether רגז is hyperbolical, or denotes an actual earthquake, is uncertain : רעש is the word regularly used to express the latter idea.

חרדת] from חֲרָדָה : the dagesh is abnormal (GK. § 95ᵍ).

16. הצפים לשאול] GK. § 129ᵇ. Saul's watchmen, or scouts, would follow what was taking place on the other side of the valley.

בנבעת] Read בְּגֶבַע : see 13, 16, and cf. 14, 2. 5.

והנה ההמון נמוג וילך והלם] וְהָלֹם is untranslateable. AV. ' and they went on *beating down* ' connects the word with הָלַם *to hammer* (so Targ.) : but besides the word being unsuitable, and one never used in such a connexion, the construction is an impossible one (the inf. *abs.* would be required : הָלֹךְ וְהָלֹם וַיֵּלֶךְ). LXX has καὶ ἰδοὺ ἡ παρεμβολὴ τεταραγμένη ἔνθεν καὶ ἔνθεν, i.e. והנה המחנה נמוג הָלֹם וָהָלֹם, which yields a thoroughly satisfactory sense. וילך is a corruption of הלם :

and the meaning is that the camp *melted away,* i.e. was disorganized, and dispersed in alarm[1], *hither and thither,* i.e. in every direction.

17. מעמנו] Cf. II 1, 2. Gen. 26, 16 (*Lex.* 87ᵃ, 768ᵇ).

18. הגישה ארון אלהים] We must certainly read, with LXX, הגישה הָאֵפוֹד; cf. *v.* 3, and especially 23, 9 הגישה האפור. 30, 7 הגישה־נא לי האפוד (so also Dr. Weir; and now Bu. Sm. etc.). The ephod, not the ark, was the organ of divination; and, as the passages cited shew, הגיש is the word properly applied to bringing the ephod into use.

ובני ישראל] כי היה ארון האלהים . . . . . ובני ישראל is here untranslateable, ו never having the force of a preposition such as עם, so as to be capable of forming the predicate to היה. Read, after LXX, כי הוא[2] הָיָה נֹשֵׂא הָאֵפוֹר ביום ההוא לִפְנֵי ישראל.

19. עד דַבֵּר] עד דִבֶּר would be in accordance with Ex. 33, 22. Jud. 3, 26. Job 7, 19. Jon. 4, 2 (*Lex.* 724ᵇ b). עד דִּבֶּר (Sta. Bu.) is not possible: with עד we should require either (disregarding the disj. accent on ויהי) ויהי שאול עד דִּבֶּר (cf. 18, 9), or, more idiomatically (without ויהי), עֹדֶנּוּ מְדַבֵּר (or ושאול עדנו מדבר): *Lex.* 729ᵃ.

וילך] וֹ·, the *subject* having preceded, as 17, 24. Gen. 30, 30. Ex. 9, 21 al. (*Tenses,* § 127 a; GK. § 111ʰ). But Klo.'s הָלַךְ is attractive.

וילך הלוך ורב] Exactly so Gen. 26, 13; Jud. 4, 24; II 5, 10 (= 1 Ch. 11, 9); 18, 25.† Cf. GK. § 113ᵘ. But the *adjectives* are peculiar; and analogy (6, 12ᵃ) would strongly support an *inf. abs.* in each case.

20. חרב איש ברעהו] viz. in consequence of the panic: cf. Jud. 7, 22. Ez. 38, 21ᵇ (especially with the reading noticed above, on *v.* 15).

21. סביב וגם המה להיות] On this passage, see *Tenses,* § 206 *Obs.* להיות is in itself defensible grammatically ('Now the Hebrews had been

---

[1] Unless, indeed, as We. suggests, נמוג has here the sense of مَاجَ in Arabic (Lane, 2743; Ex. 15, 15 Saad.; Qor. 18, 99 and we shall leave them on that day بَعْضَهُمْ يَمُوجُ فِى بَعْضٍ part of them *surging* upon the other: 10, 23; 24, 40 al. مَوْج *waves*), viz. *swaying* or *surging* as the waves of the sea. So Bu. Sm. Now.; cf. Moore, *Judges*, p. 141; and it is true, to *shake* (lit.) or *be agitated, perturbed,* would suit nearly all the occurrences of מוג, and is often the sense expressed by LXX.

[2] αὐτὸς LXX. In the *causal* sentence, the subject of the verb is slightly emphatic; and hence the explicit pron. is suitable, if not desiderated: see 9, 13; Gen. 3, 20; Jos. 17, 1; 24, 27; Jud. 14, 3 she (and not another); Jer. 5, 5; 34, 7; ψ. 24, 2; 25, 15; 33, 9; 91, 3; 103, 14; 148, 5; Job 5, 18; 11, 11; 28, 24; Hos. 6, 1; 11, 10; 13, 15 al.

to the Philistines as aforetime, in that they went up with them to the
camp round about; but they also *were for being,*' etc., i.e. they
accompanied the Philistines into the camp, but afterwards prepared
to desert), though this would be the one passage in which the inf.
with ל would be used of *past* time in early Hebrew; and the verse
appears to describe a *fact,* rather than an *intention* (להיות). LXX,
Vulg. for סביב וגם המה have ἐπεστράφησαν καὶ αὐτοί, *reversi sunt ut
essent,* i.e. (Th. We. etc.) סָבְבוּ גַם המה; and, for כאתמול, ἐχθές, *heri,*
i.e. (as Bu. points out; cf. 10, 11) מֵאֶתְמוֹל [1]: 'Now the Hebrews, who
had belonged to the Philistines (viz. as subjects) *aforetime, they also
turned* to be with Israel,' a reading now generally accepted. If,
however, it be adopted, it is almost necessary to suppose that אשר has
fallen out after העברים (so Bu. Sm. Now. Ehrl.): the omission *in prose*
of the relative (except indeed by the Chronicler [2], whose style is peculiar
to himself) is exceedingly rare; and the few passages in which it is
omitted [3] read so strangely that it is questionable if the omission is not
due to textual error (Gen. 39, 4 כל־יש־לו, contrast *vv.* 5. 8; Ex. 9, 4
מכל־לבני ישראל; 13, 8; 18, 20; [4, 13 is different;] Jer. 52, 12
(rd. הָעֹמֵד, or, as 2 Ki. 25, 8, 'עָבֶר מלך ב): Ew. § 333[b]; GK. § 155[d] [4]).

עם ישראל אשר וג'] The restriction makes it probable that Bu. is
right in supposing that איש has fallen out before ישראל.

22. וידבקו] in *Hif.:* GK. § 53[n]. On the syntax of הדביק to *press
close upon,* see on 31, 2. For הדביק אחרי Ehrl. would read דָּלַק אחרי
(as 17, 53) = *go hotly after.* This is plausible here and Jud. 20, 45,
but difficult in 1 Ch. 10, 2: when we find twice וידבקו אחרי for
וידבקו את, is it likely that וידבקו would be twice an error for וידלקו?

23. עברה את־בית־און] *passed over* B.,—עבר with את, as Dt. 2, 18.
Jud. 11, 29: some MSS., however, have עַ. Beth-aven was a little
E. of Bethel (13, 5), 4 miles NW. of Michmas, and 1000 ft. above it.

Luc. reads בית־חֹרֹן. The natural route from Michmas to Aijalon (*v.* 31)

---

[1] כאתמול (19, 7) is rendered ὡσεὶ ἐχθές, *sicut* heri.

[2] See *LOT.*[8], p. 537, No. 30; and add 2 Ch. 1, 4.

[3] Conjunctional phrases such as מֵאָז, על־אשר = על, בְּיוֹם II 22, 1 being
excepted. The relative is also omitted regularly after אי־זה הדרך 1 Ki. 13, 12.
2 Ki. 3, 8. 2 Ch. 18, 23. Job 38, 19. 24†. And comp. below, on *ch.* 25, 15 (ימי).

[4] Comp. also Jud. 8, 1. 20, 15[b]. *ch.* 6, 9. 26, 14.

appears to be first up to Bethel (4 miles), then SW. to Bireh (2 miles); after this, to judge from the map, either due W., by a bridle-path across the mountains (8 miles), straight to Lower Beth-ḥoron (1310 ft.),—or, by a better road, first 4 miles SSW. to el-Jib (Gibeon), then 5 miles WNW. to Upper Beth-ḥoron (2020 ft.), 2 miles to Lower Beth-ḥoron (1310 ft.),—and lastly 6 miles down the valley to the SW. to Aijalon (940 ft.). As both Beth-aven and Beth-ḥoron would thus be passed on the way to Aijalon, either reading would suit.

24. ואיש ישראל נגש ביום ההוא] נגש will mean *had been driven, hard-pressed* by the enemy (as 13, 6): but it is not apparent how this condition would be relieved by Saul's measure וג׳ ויאל. (The rendering of AV. '*had* adjured,' is contrary to Hebrew grammar.) LXX has here a variant, which, at least to *Ephraim*, seems original, and suits the context. For the words quoted it reads : καὶ πᾶς ὁ λαὸς ἦν μετὰ Σαουλ ὡς δέκα χιλιάδες ἀνδρῶν· καὶ ἦν ὁ πόλεμος διεσπαρμένος εἰς ὅλην πόλιν ἐν τῷ ὄρει τῷ Εφραιμ. Καὶ Σαουλ ἠγνόησεν ἄγνοιαν μεγάλην ἐν τῇ ἡμέρᾳ ἐκείνῃ, καὶ ἀρᾶται κτλ., i.e. (as We. rightly restores) וְכָל־הָעָם הָיָה עִם שָׁאוּל בַּעֲשֶׂרֶת אֲלָפִים אִישׁ וַתְּהִי הַמִּלְחָמָה נָפוֹצֶת בְּהַר אֶפְרָיִם: וְשָׁאוּל שָׁגָה שְׁגָנֶה גְדֹלָה בַּיּוֹם הַהוּא. Εἰς ὅλην πόλιν is doubtless a doublet of ἐν τῷ ὄρει : for הר confused with עיר see Jos. 15, 10[1]; 2 Ki. 23, 16; 2 Ch. 21, 11 ; Is. 66, 20 (Trommius): ὅλην is merely amplificatory. נָפוֹצֶת is applied to a battle in II 18, 8 : שגה is found in ch. 26, 21 (LXX ἠγνόηκα).

'Committed a great error,' however, agrees poorly with the context : in the sequel Saul is in no way condemned, and Yahweh is displeased (v. 37) at the curse being unheeded. Klo. conjectured, very cleverly, that ἠγνόησεν ἄγνοιαν was an error for ἥγνισεν ἁγνείαν, which (Bu.) would express הַזִּיר נֵזֶר [2] (cf. Nu. 6, 2 ἀφαγνίσασθαι ἁγνείαν = הַזִּיר לְהַזִּיר ? נָזִיר [לְהַזִּיר נֵזֶר], 3 ἁγνισθήσεται = יַזִּיר) *separated* a great (ceremonial) *separation*, i. e. *imposed* a great *abstinence.* נֵזֶר, and (Nu. 6, 2. 3. 5. 6. 12) הִזִּיר, are chiefly (Nu. 6) used of the vow of separation, or abstinence, made by the נָזִיר (the 'Nazirite'), but at least the Nif. נִזַּר is used more generally (Lev. 22, 2. Ez. 14, 7. Zech. 7, 3 ; Hos. 9, 10†) ; and with this reading the meaning will be that Saul, perceiving by Israel's success that Yahweh was with it, laid upon the people, in accordance with the religious ideas of the time, a 'taboo' of abstinence, hoping thereby to secure His continued assistance. The conjecture is clever, but rests (Now.) upon a precarious basis : הִזִּיר נֵזֶר, also, though it *might* perhaps have borne the meaning supposed, does not actually occur with it.

---

[1] Though here LXX may have paraphrased, treating הר יערים as = קרית יערים.
[2] נָדַר נֶדֶר (Sm. Kenn.) is less probable : this expression is followed, not by a curse, but by a promise dependent on a condition : *ch.* 1, 11. II 15, 8. Gen. 28, 20. Nu. 21, 2. Jud. 11, 20.

וַיֹּאֶל] Hif. of אלה (for וַיַּאַל) *made to swear :* GK. § 76ᵈ; more fully König, i. 578 f.

ונקמתי] in continuation of עד הערב: *Tenses,* § 115, GK. § 112ʷ; similarly Jud. 6, 18; Is. 5, 8.

25. באו] Comp. II 15, 23 וכל הארץ בותים; Gen. 41, 57.

25-26ᵃ. 26ᵃ merely repeats 25ᵃ, though the verses stand too closely together for a resumption to be probable. LXX has καὶ Ἰααλ δρυμὸς ἦν μελισσῶνος κατὰ πρόσωπον τοῦ ἀγροῦ· καὶ εἰσῆλθεν ὁ λαὸς εἰς τὸν μελισσῶνα, καὶ ἰδοὺ ἐπορεύετο λαλῶν. We.'s restoration is remarkably clever: 'Ἰααλ and δρυμὸς are doublets, each corresponding to the Heb. יער. To the same word, however, corresponds in *v.* 26 μελισσῶν, so that we have here in fact a triplet. Through *v.* 26, καὶ ἦν μελισσῶν (or καὶ μελισσῶν ἦν) is confirmed as the genuine rendering of LXX, Ἰααλ was added to μελισσῶν, and was afterwards explained by δρυμός, μελισσῶν being in consequence changed into the genitive, in order to produce a sentence out of the words καὶ Ἰααλ δρυμὸς μελισσῶν. The text of LXX, as thus restored, would read in Hebrew וְיַעַר¹ הָיָה עַל פְּנֵי הַשָּׂדֶה. In *v.* 26ᵃ, LXX agree with MT., except in expressing דבר for דבש. The connexion leads us in דבר to recognize *bees,* and (observing the ו in ואין) to read והנה הלך דברו, vocalizing הֵלְכוּ דְבָרָיו, or more probably הָלַךְ דְּבֹרוֹ [its bees had left it²]. From the text thus presupposed by LXX, MT. arose as follows. יער, which was ambiguous, was first of all explained by דבש *v.* 25; afterwards, however, it was forgotten that דבש was only intended to explain יער, and יער, rendered superfluous by the explanatory דבש, and understood in its common sense as *wood,* was detached from its original connexion, and united with the fragments of the variant of 24 *end,* preserved in LXX [καὶ πᾶσα ἡ γῆ ἠρίστα = וכל הארץ טעם לחם]. In view of the beginning of *v.* 26, the sentence was thus formed which stands now in MT. as *v.* 25ᵃ. דבש for דבר *v.* 26 is no doubt an accidental corruption, though the fact that דבר as a collective term³ does not occur elsewhere in the OT., might con-

---

¹ יער = *honeycomb,* as Ct. 5, 1 יערי עם דבשי.

² The sense *stream* postulated by MT. for הֵלֵךְ is unsupported by analogy.

³ דְּבָרִים in the *plural* (*bees*) occurs Dt. 1, 44 al.

tribute to the mistranscription.' Read, therefore, for *vv.* 25–26ᵃ : ' And there was honeycomb upon the face of the field, and the people came to the honeycomb, and lo, the bees had left it : but no man,' etc.

השיג [ואין משיג ידו אל פיו is *to overtake, reach, obtain ;* with יד as *subject,* it occurs often in the Priests' Code (e. g. Lev. 14, 21) to express the idea of *the means* of a person *sufficing* to meet some expense. Here Klo. is undoubtedly right in restoring השיב : משיב. יד אל פה is the usual Heb. phrase for the sense required : see *v.* 27 and Pr. 19, 24. Dr. Weir makes the same suggestion, remarking ' LXX ἐπιστρέφων as in the next verse :' so also Targ. מתיב. Hitzig (on Am. 9, 10) proposed מַגִּישׁ.

27. אוֹתָהּ] Read אוֹתֹה (on II 21, 1): מטה and קצה are both masc. (Ehrl.).

ותראנה] Kt. נַתִּרְאֶנָה *and his eyes saw :* Qrê וַתָּאֹרְנָה *and his eyes brightened* (as *v.* 29), i. e. he was refreshed, revived ; a metaphor from the eyes brightening after fatigue or faintness : cf. ψ. 13, 4 ; 19, 9 מאירת עינים (i. e. reviving spiritually). The Qrê is here the more forcible reading, and preferable to the Ktib.

28. וַיָּעַף] so *v.* 31, Jud. 4, 21. 2 S. 21, 13, as if from עוף. But the verb is יָעַף : so no doubt the regular form וַיִּיעַף should be restored (GK. § 72ᵗ). ויעף העם, however, here interrupts the connexion, and anticipates unduly *v.* 31ᵇ : either it is a gloss, intended to justify Jonathan's words in *v.* 30, or we should, perhaps, read וַיָּעַד בָּעָם *and he straitly charged the people* (cf. Ex. 19, 21. 23 ; and see on 8, 9).

29. עכר] An ominous word in OT., used of the trouble brought by Achan upon Israel (Jos. 7, 25 מה עכרתנו יעכרך יהוה ביום הזה), and by the daughter of Jephthah upon her father (Jud. 11, 25 ואת היית בעכרי), and retorted by Elijah upon Ahab (1 Ki. 18, 17 f.). ' Troubled ' is not strong enough : the root signifies to *make turbid,* fig. for, *destroy the happiness of, bring disaster on, undo.* Cf. Gen. 34, 30.

הזה [מעט דבש הזה] does not belong to דבש (as accents)—for it could not in that case have the art.—but to the definite מעט דבש ' this little honey :' cf. 15, 14 קול־הצאן הזה (' *this* bleating of the sheep '— צאן is construed as a *plur.,* II 24, 17) ; Dt: 29, 20 ספר התורה הזה *this* book of the law ; 2 Ki. 6, 32 בן־המרצח הזה *this* son of a murderer.

30. אף כי [אף] = *indeed . . . /* with reference to a preceding sentence, *a fortiori,* the more then . . .! (e. g. Job 4, 19). In אף כי,

כי merely strengthens אף, '*tis indeed that . . . !* Here אף כי is prefixed (unusually) to the protasis of a hypothetical sentence: 'The more, then, if the people had eaten, ... [would they have been refreshed likewise]: for now (עתה = *as things are*, as Job 16, 7) the slaughter (read הַמַּכָּה) hath not been great among the Philistines.' In LXX clause *b*, however, agrees with the usual type of sentences introduced by כי עתה (Gen. 31, 42. 43, 10: *Tenses*, § 141), לֹא being omitted, as due to a misunderstanding, as if כי עתה = 'for *now ;*' the sentence will then read: 'The more, then, if the people had eaten . . . , would indeed in that case (עתה = *as things might have been*, as usually in this connexion) the slaughter have been great.'

31. אילנה] Ayyālōn (Aijalon), now *Yālō* (940 ft.), was 6 miles SW. of Lower Beth-ḥoron (*v.* 23), down the Vale (עמק) of Aijalon; so the route would be substantially the same as that by which Joshua drove the Canaanites (Jos. 10); see Stanley, *S. and P.* 207 ff.; *H. G.* 210 f. The entire distance from Michmas to Aijalon would be 20–23 miles (see on *v.* 23).

32. ויעש] Qrê וַיַּעַט, which (or rather וַיָּעַט: see on 15, 19) is evidently correct.

ויאכל העם על הדם] A practice, as the present passage shews, regarded with strong disfavour by the Hebrews: forbidden in the 'Law of Holiness' (Lev. 17–26), Lev. 19, 26 לֹא תאכלו על הדם¹, and censured by Ezekiel (33, 25). על ïn this connexion is idiomatic, and has the force of *together with:* so Ex. 12, 8 על מררים יאכלהו; Nu. 9, 11 על מצות ומררים יאכלהו.

33. בגדתם] seems to be here 'neither the right verb, nor in the right person' (Bu.). Sm., very plausibly, לַמַּגְּדִים; so Bu. Ehrl.

חטאים] *are sinning,*—much more expressive than EVV. 'sin.' The form is for חֹטְאִים, the weak letter א quiescing: GK. §§ 23ᶜ, 75ᵒᵒ.

לאכל] *in respect of eating*, Anglice, '*in* eating.' So above, לשאול 12, 17. 19, and frequently. For היום LXX has הֲלֹם: probably rightly.

34. שֶׂיֵהוּ] GK. § 96. Here only: Dt. 22, 1 שֵׂיוֹ†. From an orig. *say* or *si'ay:* cf. the Arab. pl. (from *shāṭ^{un}*), *shayh^{un}*, *shiyā'^{un}* etc.

אל הדם] a clear example of אל with the force of על.

איש שורו בידו] Some, however, it is natural to suppose, would only

---

¹ Cf. Gen. 9, 4. Lev. 7, 26. 17, 10. Dt. 12, 16. 23.

have a שֹׁה to bring, in accordance with the option permitted by the terms of the invitation: read accordingly with LXX אִישׁ אֲשֶׁר בְּיָדוֹ each *that which was* in his hand, which is altogether preferable. For בידו cf. Gen. 32, 14; 43, 26 המנחה אשר בידם.

הלילה] = '*that* night,'—a questionable usage: הלילה adverbially is elsewhere always either *by night*, or *to-night*, or once (15, 16) *last night*. LXX omits. Klo. Bu. Sm. would read ליהוה (cf. Am. 5, 25).

35. The stone was made into an extemporized altar, and the slain animals being consecrated by presentation at it, their flesh could be eaten. See W. R. Smith, *OTJC.*[2] p. 250. Clause *b* implies that Saul built subsequently *other* altars to Yahweh.

אתו החל . . .] For the position of אתו, cf. on 15, 1: comp. also that of להם Jud. 10, 4. Hos. 13, 2. Job 15, 20; לי II 23, 3; לו Dt. 21, 17; בם Jer. 31, 8.

36. נרדה] from Beth-ḥoron (cf. *v.* 23), or some other place in the hill-country, following the Philistines down the Vale of Aijalon.

וְנָבֹזָה] for וְנָבֹּזָּה GK. § 67[dd]. The ב is partitive (*Lex.* 88[b]), 'plunder *among* them,' like ' smite *among* ' (*v.* 31 al.), אכל ב׳, etc.

ולא נשאר] The jussive is unusual, both in the 1st pers. (*Tenses,* § 46 *n.;* GK. § 48[g] *n.*), and after לֹא (cf. Gen. 24, 8; II 17, 12; 18, 14: *Tenses,* § 50 *a Obs.;* GK. § 109[d]). Read prob. נִשְׁאָר.

37. הארד . . . התתנם] The repeated question, as in the similar inquiries, 23, 11; 30, 8; II 5, 19.

38. גֹּשׁוּ] i. e. *gōshū:* so also, anomalously, out of pause, Jos. 3, 9. 2 Ch. 29, 31† (cf. גֹּשׁוּ Ru. 2, 14†), for the normal גְּשׁוּ Gen. 45, 4 al.: GK. § 65[d].

פנות] *corners*, hence metaph. of princes, the stay and support of their people: so Jud. 20, 2. Is. 19, 13, where Gesenius compares رُكْن *corner-stone* or *corner-pillar* (e. g. Eph. 2, 20), used Qor. 51, 39 of Pharaoh's nobles, and the pr. n. *Rokn-eddin*, 'Pillar of religion.'

במה] *wherein*,—as Mal. 1, 6 '*wherein* have we despised Thy name?' Vulg. expresses במי, which is preferred by Th. We. Bu. etc., and is certainly more pointed. *V.* 39 shews that Saul has a *person* in his mind. In the old character י might easily be corrupted to ה.

39. יֶשְׁנוֹ] thrice besides, but a form contrary to analogy: Stade (§ 370[b]), and GK. (§ 100° *note*) would read יֶשְׁנוּ. As חטאת is fem.,

we ought, however, to have יֵשָׁנָה (or יִשָּׁנָה): cf. LXX ἀποκριθῇ = יענה (with ה). Why, in these and some other forms, as עוֹדֶנִּי, אֵינֶנִּי, the *verbal* suffix should be used, is uncertain: cf. GK. § 100ᴾ.

כי ... כי אם] The first כי introduces the terms of the oath: the second כי is merely resumptive of the first, after the intervening hypothetical clause. So often, as II 3, 9. Gen. 22, 16 f. (*Lex.* 472ᵃ).

41. הבה תמים] AV. 'Give a perfect (lot):' RV. 'Shew the right:' Keil, 'Give innocence' (of disposition, i. e. truth). All these suggested renderings of תמים are without support. תמים is 'perfect,' i. e. in a *physical* sense, of an animal, unblemished; in a *moral* sense, innocent[1], blameless. הבה תמים might mean 'give one who is perfect:' but this is not the sense which is here required: Saul does not ask for one who is perfect to be produced; and though he might ask for the one who is in the right to be declared, this would be expressed by צדיק (Dt. 25, 1; 1 Ki. 8, 32), not by תמים. LXX has for the two words: Τί ὅτι οὐκ ἀπεκρίθης τῷ δούλῳ σου σήμερον; ἢ ἐν ἐμοὶ ἢ ἐν Ἰωναθαν τῷ υἱῷ μου ἡ ἀδικία; Κύριε ὁ Θεὸς Ἰσραηλ, δὸς δήλους· καὶ ἐὰν τάδε εἴπῃ, δὸς δὴ τῷ λαῷ σου Ἰσραηλ, δὸς δὴ ὁσιότητα, whence the following text may be restored: לָמָּה לֹא עָנִיתָ אֶת־עַבְדְּךָ הַיּוֹם אִם יֶשׁ־בִּי אוֹ בִּיהוֹנָתָן בְּנִי הֶעָוֹן הַזֶּה ייי אֱלֹהֵי יִשְׂרָאֵל הָבָה אוּרִים וְאִם יֶשְׁנוֹ בְעַמְּךָ יִשְׂרָאֵל הָבָה תֻּמִּים: The text thus obtained is both satisfactory in itself, and at once removes the obscurity and abruptness attaching to MT. The first clause corresponds with LXX exactly: in the second clause ἐὰν τάδε εἴπῃ δὸς δή cannot be followed; but δὸς δή (omitted in A) seems to be merely a rhetorical anticipation of the δὸς δή following; and considering that LXX render ישנו in v. 39 by a verb (ἀποκριθῇ), there is nothing arbitrary in supposing that τάδε εἴπῃ may represent ישנו here. For אִם יֶשׁ־בִּי cf. 20, 8. Δῆλοι stands for אוּרִים *ch*. 28, 6 and Nu. 27, 21 (as δήλωσις, in Ex. 28, 26. Lev. 8, 8). The cause of the omission in MT. lies evidently in the occurrence of the same word ישראל before both למה לא and הבה תמים. The restored text (which is now generally accepted by scholars) shews (what has often been surmised independently) that the משפט האורים והתמים was a mode of casting lots: cf. הפילו *v.* 42, and note that וַיִּלָּכֵד, which

---

[1] I nnocent, that is, not of a particular offence, but generally.

immediately follows in *v.* 41 (but which in MT. stands unexplained), is the word regularly used of taking by lot, 10, 20 f. Jos. 7, 14. 16.

42. After בני LXX has an addition, which in Heb. would be אשר ילכדנו יהוה ימות ויאמר העם אל שאול לא יהיה הדבר הזה ויחזק שאול מהעם ויפילו בינו ובין יונתן בנו. But although its omission could be readily explained by *homoeoteleuton*, its originality is very doubtful: see We. and Now.

43. טעם טעמתי] ' I *did* taste : ' GK. § 113ⁿ.

הנני אמות] ' Here I am ; I will die,'—Jonathan thus not complaining of the fate to which he has involuntarily rendered himself liable, but declaring his willingness to meet it. For הנני as an expression of resignation, cf. 12, 3, and esp. II 15, 26 ; also Gen. 44, 16. 50, 18. EVV., in ' And lo, I must die,' neglect the suff. in הנני.

44. כה יעשה] LXX adds לי, which at least is a correct explanation of the phrase ; the curse being invoked naturally upon *himself*. Possibly, however, this was understood ; at least, the phrase recurs 1 Ki. 19, 2 without לי (where LXX similarly μοί). The oath followed by כי, as II 3, 9. 35. 1 Ki. 2, 23. 19, 2.

45. ישועה] The passage illustrates the *material* sense of the word : so Ex. 14, 13 ; II 10, 11 ; and תשועה[1] (the more common word in prose), as Jud. 15, 18 ; *ch.* 11, 9. 13. 19, 5 al. The root ישע, as Arabic shews, means properly *to be wide, capacious, ample* (e. g. Qor. 29, 56 إِنَّ أَرْضِى وَاسِعَةٌ behold, My earth is *broad ;* Matt. 7, 13 (Lagarde) وَاسِعٌ = πλατεῖα ; 2 Cor. 6, 11 (Erpenius) اِسَعَ = πεπλάτυνται ; Gen. 26, 22 ; Ex. 34, 24 Saad. وَسَّعَ = הרחיב): hence הושיע is properly *to give width and freedom to* (opp. הֵצַר), and ישועה is ' safety' in the sense of *space to move in, freedom from enemies or constraint* (opp. צַר *narrowness, angustiae*). Etymologically, then, the idea of the root would be best expressed by *deliver, deliverance ;* and in a passage such as 11, 9 מחר תהיה לכם תשועה this sense appears to be clearly distinguishable. By the Prophets and Psalmists, however,

---

[1] Formed as though from a root שׁוּע on the ground, probably, of a false analogy. Similarly תרופה, הְִשָׁאֹות, תקופה as though from [רוּף, שׁוּא, קוּף], though the verbs actually in use are רפא, שׁאה, נקף. Comp. Ol. p. 401 ; Stade, § 266°.

the idea of *deliverance* or *freedom* which ישועה, תשועה connote, is enlarged, so as to include *spiritual* as well as *material* blessings. These words seldom, if ever, express a spiritual state *exclusively:* their common theological sense in Hebrew is that of *a material deliverance attended by spiritual blessings* (e. g. Is. 12, 2 ; 45, 17). In some passages, the temporal element in the deliverance is very evident, e. g. ψ. 3, 9 (RV. *marg.* 'Or, *Victory:*' see *v.* 8); 20, 6 (cf. 7); 28, 8 (note עז and מעוז); 62, 3 (note the parallel figures משגבי, צורי); 74, 12, etc. : cf. תשועה, ψ. 33, 17. 60, 11. The margins in RV. on several of the passages quoted (including those in the historical books) serve as a clue to the manner in which the Hebrew words represented by the English 'salvation' acquired gradually a higher and fuller meaning.

אם יפל משערת ראשו] 'If there shall fall even a single hair of his head to the ground!' שערה is *a single hair*, see Jud. 20, 16 כל זה קלע באבן אל־השערה ולא יחטיא : the fem. being the so-called 'nomen unitatis,' Ew. § 176ᵃ; GK. § 122ᵗ. So אֳנִי *a fleet*, אֳנִיָּה *a ship* (Jon. 1, 3). מן is to be understood here as in מֵאַחַד אַחֶיךָ Dt. 15, 7 : lit. '*starting from* one of thy brethren [1]' = *even* one of thy brethren. This use of מן is elucidated by Arabic: see Ges. *Thes.*, or *Lex.* 581ᵃ (where illustrations are cited); Ew. § 278ᵈ; GK. § 119ʷ (*note*): also Ewald, *Gr. Arab.* § 577; Wright, *Arab. Gr.* ii. § 48 f *b*. Comp. Qor. 6, 59 وَمَا تَسْقُطُ مِنْ وَرَقَةٍ إِلَّا يَعْلَمُهَا *even a single leaf* (nom. unit.) falleth not without His knowing it.—The proverbial expression itself recurs II 14, 11, and with לא for אם 1 Ki. 1, 52.

עם] = *in conjunction with, aided by* (uncommon) : cf. Dan. 11, 39.

ויפדו] *redeemed:* literally, by the substitution of another (Ew. *Hist.* iii. 51 [E. T. 36]; We.), or metaphorically? Had the former been the sense intended, the fact, it is probable, would have been stated more circumstantially, instead of its being left to the reader to infer it from a single word. פדה is the technical word used of the redemption of a life that is forfeit ; but the redemption may be made by the life of an animal, or by a money payment, Ex. 13, 13. 15. 34, 20, cf. 21, 8. 30 (all JE); Nu. 18, 15. 16 (P).

---

[1] Or, according to others, a rhetorical application of the *partitive* sense.

47. ובמלכי] LXX ובמלך, probably rightly: see II 8, 3–12.

הרשיע [ירשיע is *to pronounce* or *treat as wicked,* i. e. *to condemn* (Dt. 25, 1); hence MT. has been supposed to mean *condemned in fact* (Keil), *punished;* and in support of this rendering, the analogy of the Syr. ܚܝܒ prop. *to treat as guilty, to condemn,* but occasionally used in the sense of ἡττᾶν *to put to the worse, overcome* (Ephr. i. 325; ii. 318; *ap.* PS. col. 1213), has been appealed to. But such a usage would be quite isolated in Hebrew: and the absence of a suffix or other object to ירשיע is strongly against it here. LXX has ἐσώζετο = יִוָּשֵׁעַ:—'And wherever he turned *he was victorious,*' a reading in every way satisfactory and suited to the context. For the sense of the *Nif.* cf. Pr. 28, 18 הוֹלֵךְ תָּמִים יִוָּשֵׁעַ; Zech. 9, 9 צַדִּיק וְנוֹשָׁע lit. just and *saved,* i. e. successful and victorious. The impff. denote reiteration or habit in the *past,* just as in Pr. 17, 8 etc. they denote it in *present* time. LXX οὗ ἂν ἐστράφη ἐσώζετο: on οὗ ἂν comp. 17, 34 *footnote.*

48. ויעש חיל] lit. *made might,* i. e. achieved prowess, performed deeds of valour: Nu. 24, 18. ψ. 60, 14. 118, 15. 16.

שסהו] The ptcp. seems intended as a plural: if so, the word affords an example of the very rare form of the suffix 3 masc. הו -ֵ- after a *plural* noun: 30, 26 רֵעֵהוּ, Nah. 2, 4 גְּבוֹרֵיהוּ, Hab. 3, 10 יְדֵיהוּ, Job 24, 23 עֵינֵיהוּ, Pr. 29, 18 אַשְׁרֵהוּ: Stade, p. 20 *note,* § 346ᵃ (2), and p. 355; Ew. § 258ᵃ; GK. § 91¹; Wright, *Compar. Gramm.* p. 158.

49. יִשְׁוִי] in all probability a corruption of אִשְׁיוֹ, or אִשְׁיָהוּ¹, 'man of Yahweh,' an intentional alteration of אשבעל 1 Ch. 8, 33, the real name of 'Ishbosheth,' altered, as We. says, when the title 'Baal' fell into disrepute (see on II 4, 4), 'theils in אִשְׁיוֹ von Vernünftigen, theils in איש־בשת von Unvernünftigen.'

LXX Ἰεσσιουλ (Luc. Ἰεσσιου) presupposes a reading אִשְׁיָהוּ or אִשְׁיוֹ. Not only are a great many pr. names beginning, as pointed by the Massorites, with -ִי represented in LXX by Ἰε- (as Ἰερεμίας for יִרְמְיָהוּ, Ἰεσσαι for יִשַׁי, Ἰεφθαε for יִפְתָּח, etc.), but several pr. names beginning with א are so represented, as Ἰεβοσθε for איש־בשת II 2, 8 al., Ἰεζαβελ regularly for אִיזֶבֶל, Ἰεζειηλ for אשריאל

---

¹ Or of אישיו, אישיהו. יש cannot be derived *phonetically* from אש, only the reverse change from *yi* to 'i being in accordance with analogy (cf. in Syriac, Nöld. *Syr. Gr.* § 40 C). But if י was pronounced softly (*i,* not *yi*: GK. § 47ᵇ and *n.*), יש might be written incorrectly for אש.

Jos. 17, 2, 'Ιεθεβααλ for אתבעל 1 Ki. 16, 31, 'Ιεμηρ for אמֶר Neh. 7, 61, 'Ιεροβααλ
(AQ^a) for ארבאל Hos. 10, 14, 'Ιεσθεμωη (cod. A) for אֶשְׁתְּמֹעַ 1 Ch. 4, 19,
'Ιεσσαι for אִישַׁי (elsewhere יִשַׁי) 1 Ch. 2, 13, comp. 'Ιεσβααλ for אִישׁ־בֹשֶׁת II 3, 8
in Aq. Symm. Theod., and in II 23, 8 Luc.[1]; and for the term. -ιου for יָהוּ cf.
אֵלִיָהוּ Ηλειου or Ηλιου, בְּנָיָהוּ Βαναιου, 1 Ki. 2, 35, עֹבַדְיָהוּ Αβδειου *ib.* 18, 3 ff.

51. בן אביאל] Read בְּנֵי אֲבִיאֵל, though the error is as old as LXX.
But already Josephus says (*Ant.* vi. 6, 6) Νῆρος καὶ Κεῖσος ὁ Σαούλου
πατὴρ ἀδελφοὶ ἦσαν υἱοὶ δὲ 'Αβιήλου.

52. וראה] frequentative: ' *and* Saul *would* see, etc., *and would* take
him to him' = and when Saul saw . . ., he used to take him to him
(*Tenses,* §§ 120; 148. 1: so II 15, 2. 5 etc.). וַיַּאַסְפֵהוּ is irregular for
וַאֲסָפוֹ: see on 2, 16.

15. *Saul and Amaleq. Second rejection of Saul.* (*Introduction to history of David.*)

15, 1. אתי שלח] Position as 14, 35 (see note). Gen. 42, 36
אֹתִי שִׁכַּלְתֶּם. Dt. 1, 38 חַזֵּק אֹתוֹ. 10, 20. ψ. 25, 5 אֹתְךָ קִוִּיתִי. Jer. 4, 22
אֹתִי לֹא יָדָעוּ. 30, 14; also (not at the beginning of a sentence) Gen.
24, 14 אֹתָהּ הֹכַחְתָּ. Jud. 14, 3 קַח לִי אוֹתָהּ. *ch.* 18, 17. Is. 37, 26
אוֹתָהּ עָשִׂיתִי. ψ. 27, 4 אוֹתָהּ אֲבַקֵּשׁ.

For other cases of אתי, אתו, etc. rendered emphatic by being prefixed to a verb,
cp. (*a*) after וְ, Gen. 12, 12 וְהָרְגוּ אֹתִי וְאֹתָךְ יְחַיּוּ . . . Lev. 10, 17 . . . וְאַתָּה נָתַן.
11, 33. Dt. 4, 14. 6, 13 וְאֹתָנוּ תַּעֲבֹד. 13, 5. 20, 19 וְאֹתוֹ לֹא תִכְרֹת. 2 S. 12, 9
11, 37; וְאֹתוֹ צִוִּיתִי לִהְיוֹת נָגִיד עַל . . . 1 Ki. 1, 6^b. 35 וְאֹתוֹ הָרַגְתָּ בְחֶרֶב בְּנֵי עַמּוֹן.
Is. 57, 11 וְאוֹתִי לֹא זָכַרְתְּ and: וְאוֹתִי לֹא תִירָאִי. 58, 2. Jer. 9, 2 וְאֹתִי לֹא יָדָעוּ
16, 11. 46, 28. Ez. 22, 12 וְאֹתִי שָׁכַחַתְּ (cf. 1 Ki. 14, 9). Hos. 2, 15^b; Lev. 26, 33
וְאֶתְכֶם אֱזָרֶה. Dt. 4, 20. 6, 32. Ez. 11, 7; Ez. 12, 13. 23, 10. 33, 31; Job 14, 3:
(*b*) Gen. 41, 13 אֹתִי הֵשִׁיב עַל כַּנִּי וְאֹתוֹ תָלָה. Nu. 22, 33: (*c*) after וְגַם, 2 S. 2, 7
וְלֹא אֹתִי; וְגַם אֹתִי מִשְּׁחוּ וְגֹ'. 2 S. 8, 11: (*d*) after וְלֹא, *ch.* 20, 9. Is. 43, 22
קָרָאת: (*e*) after כִּי, Gen. 7, 1 כִּי אֹתְךָ רָאִיתִי צַדִּיק. 37, 4. כִּי אֹתוֹ אָהֵב
1 Ki. 5, 13. Jer. 4, 17 כִּי אֹתִי מָרָתָה; *ch.* 21, 10; הָ †Jer. 5, 22 הַאוֹתִי לֹא תִירָאוּ
7, 19†. A pronoun in an emph. position should always be noted by the student.

לְמִשְׁחָר] -sho- (not -shā-): GK. § 9^v; and for the metheg § 16^f (δ).
2. פקדתי] 'I will visit,' i. e. punish—the pf. (though unusual in

---

[1] See further examples in the *Supplement*, containing the Proper Names, to
Hatch and Redpath's *Concordance to the Septuagint* (1900), p. 77 ff.

prose, except in נְתַתִּי) as Jud. 15, 3, expressing determination (*Tenses,*
§ 13; GK. § 106ᵐ); and פקד being construed with an accus. of the
sin visited, as Hos. 8, 13 = 9, 9 = Jer. 14, 10.   The sense *mark*
(RV.), *ansehen* (Keil), is not borne out by usage: פקד means to visit
in fact (Ex. 3, 16. 4, 31), not to observe mentally, or to 'direct one's
look at' (Keil).

אשר שם וג'] שם in a military sense, as 1 Ki. 20, 12 ויאמר שימו
וישימו על העיר, and שתו in ψ. 3, 7. Is. 22, 7.   In Dt. 25, 18 (of the
same occurrence) the expression used is אשר קָרְךָ בדרך.

3. והחרמתם] LXX, independently of καὶ Ἰερειμ καί, has two translations of this word, viz. καὶ ἐξολεθρεύσεις αὐτὸν and καὶ ἀναθεματιεῖς
αὐτὸν καί, both pointing to וְהַחֲרַמְתּוֹ וְאֵת כל אשר לו (וּ for ם).   Though
the Hebrew is poor, the combination nevertheless occurs (see on
5, 10), and as the sequel shews that the *nation*, as well as its belongings,
was 'banned,' it is best to adopt it.

3ᵇ. מעולל ועד יונק] 22, 19†.   מאיש ועד אשה *ib.* Jos. 6, 21. 8, 25 al.
מ... ועד] *from ... even unto,* i. e. including both, as often.

4. וישמע] The *Pi'el,* as 23, 8†.   So 1 Ki. 15, 22 al. the Hif'il.

בטלאים] To be pointed probably טְלָאם, and identical with טֶלֶם in
the 'Negeb' of Judah, Jos. 15, 24.

5. וירב] for וַיָּאֶרב, i. e. וַיָּאֶרֶב GK. §§ 68ⁱ, 23ᵈ; Kön. i. 390: cf.
אָזִין for אַאֲזִין Job 32, 11; לְהָכִיל (as generally understood) Ez. 21, 33;
מֵזִין Pr. 17, 4.   The omission of א is somewhat more frequent (though
rare even then) in *Qal:* 28, 24 וַתֹּפֵהוּ; II 6, 1 וַיֹּסֶף (from אסף);
19, 14 תֹּמְרוּ; 20, 9 וַתֹּחֶז; ψ. 104, 29 תֹּסֵף (from אסף); GK. § 68ʰ.

6. On the Qenites, and their former friendly relations with Israel,
see Nu. 10, 29 f. Jud. 1, 16, where Budde (*ZATW.* 1887, p. 101,
and in his Commentary on Judges, *ad loc.*) is certainly right in
reading, after MSS. of LXX, את העמלקי for את העם.

רְדוּ] so 𝔅 (= Bomberg's Rabb. Bible of 1525), Kitt.: Baer and
Ginsb. רְדוּ: cf. Gen. 19, 14 קוּמוּ צְאוּ; and see GK. § 22ˢ (208¹), and
the *Addenda.*

---

¹ Where, in l. 6 of p. 73 of the Engl. translation, insert 'hitherto' (i. e. in
previous editions) after 'When we.'   In l. 2 also 'a question' would be better than
'doubtful;' for, though the note reads somewhat obscurely, Kautzsch does mean
to explain the cases quoted in it by the principle of § 20ᶠ.

עמלקי] Except here and *v.* 15 MT. has throughout the chapter עמלק. As the determined noun is needed, it is better in both these passages to read with Luc. עמלק.

אׂסְפְּךָ] The *metheg*, shewing the ḥireq to be long, appears to indi-cate that the *punctuators* treat the verb as *Hif.* But the Hif. of אסף does not elsewhere occur, and the *metheg* rests, no doubt, upon a false theory as to the nature of the word. Read without metheg, it will be the impf. *Qal* אֹסֵף (as *ψ.* 104, 29), with ◌ֵ shortened to ◌ֶ when the syllable is rendered toneless by the addition of a suffix (so in the *ptcp.* הנני אֹסֵף 2 Ki. 22, 20¹, אֹיִבְךָ *ch.* 24, 5 al.; and in *Pi*''*el* מְאַסְּפְכֶם Is. 52, 12. אֲאַמִּצְכֶם Job 16, 5 etc.). Comp. König, i. 382 f.; GK. § 68ᵇ. אסף, as Jud. 18, 25. *ψ.* 26, 9. Ehrl. suggests אֶסְפְּךָ (Gen. 18, 23. 24).

ואתה] Note the emph. pronoun.

קיני] Read either קין (as Nu. 24, 22. Jud. 4, 11), or (LXX) הקיני (as *v.* 6ᵃ, 27, 10. 30, 29).

7. מחוילה בואך שור] On Shur, see *DB.* s. v. It appears to have denoted the district on the NE. border of Egypt, which gave its name to the מדבר שור Ex. 15, 22. Where חוילה was is uncertain. In Gen. 2, 11. 10, 29. 25, 18 the name most probably denotes a region in the NE. of Arabia, on the W. coast of the Persian Gulf; in Gen. 10, 7 it may denote the Ἀβαλῖται, on the African coast, a little S. of the Straits of Bāb el-Mandeb: but even a region in the NE. of Arabia is too remote to define the starting-point of the defeat inflicted by Saul upon the Amaleqites. Either חוילה is here the name of a place in or near the country of Amaleq, otherwise unknown, or we should simply (with We.) restore מִמֵּלָם (*v.* 4): 'the error may have arisen through a reminiscence of Gen. 25, 18,' where the phrase occurs, closely resembling the one here, מחוילה עד שור אשר על פני מצרים, but where חוילה, as has just been said, appears from the context to denote a place more distant than is suitable here.

על פני] *in front of*, in geographical descriptions, commonly means *to the east of* (*Lex.* 818ᵇ): so Gen. *l. c.* 1 Ki. 11, 7.

9. המשנים] Explained by Kimchi (*Book of Roots*, s. v.) in the sense

---

¹ In the parallel passage, 2 Ch. 34, 28 (Baer and Ginsburg, but not 𝔅, Kittel), in exactly the same phrase, אׂסְפְּךָ is pointed as here, with *metheg*, i. e. as an impf. Hif.!

of שְׁנַיִם מִבֶּטֶן, i.e. young of a second birth, such as had the reputation of being superior to firstlings (see Tanḥum, quoted by Roed. in the *Thes.* p. 1451ᵃ). So Roed. himself (p. 1451ᵇ), and Keil. But the text reads suspiciously, and the position of עַל before הכרים (instead of before the *pair* of similar delicacies המשנים והכרים) suggests error. We. for והמשנים ועל הכרים would read הַשְּׁמֵנִים וְהַכָּרִים 'and the best of the flocks and the herds, (even) the fat ones (comp. Ez. 34, 16), and the lambs,' etc., which undoubtedly forms a better Hebrew sentence, and nearly agrees with the rendering of Pesh. Targ. (ישמיניא ופטימיא), neither of which, at least, appears to have had either משנים, or עַל before הכרים. כרים are mentioned in terms implying that they were a delicacy in Am. 6, 4; Dt. 32, 14.

מלאכה [וכל המלאכה נמבזה ונמס אתה החרימו means *business, occupation* (Gen. 39, 11), and so *property* on which a person is occupied, Ex. 22, 7. 10: here and Gen. 33, 14 specially of property consisting in cattle (cf. מִקְנֶה). נמבזה is a grammatical *monstrum*, originating evidently in the blunder of a scribe. The text had ונמס נבזה: the scribe began by error with the *second* word, wrote the first two letters נמ, then discovered his mistake, but not wishing to make an erasure, simply added the letters בזה. (There are similar *monstra* in Ez. 8, 16. 9, 8.) The words present, however, other difficulties. אֹתָה, resuming כל המלאכה, is indeed defensible by Dt. 13, 1. 14, 6. Ps. 101, 5 al. (*Tenses*, § 197. 1, 2): and for the change of gender there are at least parallels which can be adduced (e. g. 1 Ki. 19, 11: see GK. § 132ᵈ; ψ. 63, 2 בארץ ציה ועיף with Hitzig's note[1]); but the use of נמס is very strange (lit. *melted away* = diseased, consumptive?). The Versions all express a synonym of נבזה—LXX καὶ ἐξουδενωμένον, Pesh. ܘܡܣܠܝܐ, Targ. ובסיר, Vulg. *et reprobum:* and there can in fact be no reasonable doubt that וְנִמְאֶסֶת must be restored, either for ונמס אתה or for ונמס alone (retaining אתה[2]). Indeed, AV. RV. appear both to have adopted implicitly this emendation; for 'refuse' is no rendering of נָמֵס, though it obviously expresses נִמְאָס (Jer. 6, 30 *marg.*) or

---

[1] 'The fem. termination of the adj., once used, can in a way operate forwards, so that the second adj. is left in the simplest, most immediate form.'

[2] Which is expressed by Pesh. Targ. LXX (Luc.), Vulg., and as stated above is fully defensible.

נִמְאֶסֶת. The omission of the art. with the ptcp., after a subst. defined by it, is a further difficulty. The text as it stands expresses the sense 'But all the מלאכה, *being* common [1] (lit. *despised*) and refuse, they banned [2]:' but this contradicts the context; for *some* of the מלאכה was good, and was spared. The sense demanded by the context, viz. 'but *such of* the מלאכה as was common and refuse they banned,' requires either the *presence* of the art. in both cases, or its *absence* in both.

11. מאחרי] *Lex.* 30ᵃ.

12. וישכם . . . לקראת] In thorough analogy with Hebrew usage (see on 6, 13). LXX, Vulg. express וילך, which Th. declares to be a 'necessary' insertion: but the renderings of these versions are merely accommodations to the idiom of a different language. See besides Ct. 7, 13 נשכימה לכרמים; and Ges. *Thes.* p. 1406ᵇ (referred to by We.).

הכרמל] 'The garden-land' (Is. 10, 18 al.),—the word, like other proper names with the art. (as הגבעה), retaining its appellative force. It was a place in the 'hill-country' of Judah (Jos. 15, 55; see *v.* 48), mentioned also in *ch.* 25, 2 ff.; now *el-Kurmul*, 7 miles S. of Hebron.

והנה] without the suffix, as 16, 11. But the ptcp. מציב '*is* setting up' does not agree with the sequel (which states that Saul had *left* Carmel): and doubtless הִצִּיב '*hath* set up' must be read (so LXX ἀνέστακεν).

יד] lit. *hand*, i. e. sign, monument, trophy of the victory: II 18, 18.

וירד הגלגל] Cf. on 10, 8.

14. הזה] See on 14, 29. The correction הַזֶּה (*ZAW.* 1895, p. 317) is unnecessary.

---

[1] 'Vile' (EVV.), unless understood in the old sense of the word (*common, looked down upon*; Lat. *vilis*), is too strong, as it is also in Jer. 15, 19. Lam. 1, 11 EVV., and in AV. of Job 40, 4. Phil. 3, 21. See the writer's *Jeremiah*, p. 362; *Minor Prophets*, vol. ii (Nahum to Malachi), in the *Century Bible*, p. 25.

[2] So ψ. 18, 18; 92, 12 מרעים עלי בַּקָּמִים against those who rise up against me (as) evil doers; 143, 10 רוחך טובה thy spirit (being) good; Jer. 2, 21ᵇ (but rd. נפן); Ez. 24, 13; Hag. 1, 4 (cf. GK. § 126ⁱ). The adj. without the art. forms a species of predicate: cf. on 2, 23. (II 6, 3ᵇ is corrupt: but even were it not so, the grammatical rendering 'drave the cart, being a new one' would be consistent with the context, which, in the case of the phrase here, is just what is not the case.)

15. אשר] אשר is a *link*, bringing the clause which it introduces into relation with what precedes: here the relation is a causal one, *in that, forasmuch as:* 20, 42. 26, 23ᵇ. Gen. 30, 18. 31, 49. 34, 13 (cf. on II 2, 5): elsewhere, אשר may be resolved into the expression of a consequence, *so that,* as Gen. 13, 16; 22, 14; 1 Ki. 3, 12. 13; 2 Ki. 9, 37.

16. הרף] Dr. Weir thus appositely illustrates the usage of this word: 'Dt. 9, 14 הרף ממני ואשמידם. *ch.* 11, 3 הרף לנו שבעת ימים. II 24, 16 הרף ידך. ψ. 37, 8 הרף מאף. 46, 11 הרפו ודעו.'

הלילה] *the* night (that is just past) = *last* night. Elsewhere always of the *coming* night, as Gen. 19, 5; 30, 15 etc.: comp. on 14, 34.

ויאמרו] Qrê ויאמר, a necessary correction. The opposite of the variation noted on 13, 19. See *Ochlah we-Ochlah,* No. 120 (eleven instances of ו at the end of a word כתיב ולא קרי cited: among them Jos. 6, 7; 9, 7; 1 Ki. 12, 3. 21; 2 Ki. 14, 13).

17. 'Though thou art little in thine own eyes, art thou not head of the tribes of Israel? And Yahweh hath anointed thee to be king over Israel' (i. e. thou art in a position of authority, and oughtest to have restrained the people).

18. וְהַחֲרַמְתָּה] but *v.* 20 הַחֲרַמְתִּי. In the pf. Hif. of verbs *primae gutt.,* ◌ַ ◌ַ of 1 and 2 ps. is changed to ◌ֶ ◌ֶ after *waw consec.,* whether the tone is thrown forward by the *waw* or not: so הֶאֱבַדְתָּ Job 14, 19, but וְהַאֲבַדְתִּי Lev. 23, 30 and often; הֶאֱכַלְתִּי Ex. 16, 32, but וְהַאֲכַלְתִּי Is. 49, 26; הֶחֱזַקְתִּי Is. 45, 1, but וְהַחֲזַקְתִּי Ez. 30, 25; הֶעֱלִיתָנוּ Nu. 20, 5, but וְהַעֲלִיתֶם Ex. 13, 19: and, with no change in the place of the tone, הֶעֱבַדְתִּיךָ Is. 43, 23, but וְהַעֲבַדְתִּיךָ Jer. 17, 4; הֶעֱלִיתָ Ex. 33, 1, but וְהַעֲלִיתָ Dt. 27, 6; הֶאֱכַלְתִּיךָ Ez. 16, 19, but וְהַאֲכַלְתִּיךָ Is. 58, 14; הֶעֱמַדְתִּיךָ Ex. 9, 16, but וְהַעֲמַדְתִּיהוּ 1 Ch. 17, 14. And so ofteⁿ elsewhere: cf. Böttcher, ii. 380 f.; GK. § 63°.

עד כלותם אתם] 'Until *they* consume them' cannot be right. Either עַד כַּלּוֹתְךָ אֹתָם (Jer. 9, 15 = 49, 37) must be read (with LXX, Pesh. Targ.), or אֹתָם must be omitted (with the Vulg.), as having arisen by some confusion out of the preceding תם-. עַד־כַּלּוֹתָם 'until (one, people: strictly הַמְכַלֶּה; see on 16, 4) consume them' is the more idiomatic usage: 1 Ki. 22, 11 תִּנַּח אֶת־אֲרָם עַד־כַּלּוֹתָם; ψ. 18, 38.

19. וַתַּעַט] for וַתֵּעַט from עוט: GK. § 72ᶠᶠ; Stade, § 549ᶠ. Cf. 14, 32.

20. אשר] stands as the equivalent of כי, after ראה 18, 15; after ידע Ex. 11, 7. Ez. 20, 26 (unusually in Ezek.; see Hitz.). Qoh. 8, 12; after השביע 1 Ki. 22, 16; and = כי *recitativum* (2, 16), as here, II 1, 4 (cf. 2, 4). Neh. 4, 6 (most probably)[1]. Cf. GK. § 157[c].

22. להקשיב] The inf. cstr. with ל, as the subj., as Is. 10, 7[b]; ψ. 118, 8. 9; Qoh. 7, 2. 5; Pr. 21, 9 טוב לשבת על פנת גג מאשת מדונים ובית חבר (contr. 25, 24).

23. מרי] 'oftenest in Ezek. (2, 5 etc. כי בית מרי המה). Is. 30, 9 עם מרי הוא. Nu. 17, 25 בני מרי. Dt. 31, 27 את־מריך ואת־ערפך הקשה' (Dr. Weir).

אָוֶן] The fundamental idea of אָוֶן is apparently what is *valueless and disappointing:* and it denotes, according to the context, (1) *calamity, misfortune* (as ψ. 55, 4. Am. 5, 5); (2) *naught-y conduct, naughtiness,* a term of disparagement for wickedness, as פעלי און ψ. 5, 6 and often; and (3) *worthlessness, a thing of nought,* esp. an *idol,* as Is. 66, 3 'he that burneth incense is no better than מְבָרֵךְ אָוֶן he that blesseth *an idol;*' cf. Zech. 10, 2 'the teraphim דברו און speak *worthlessness*' (see further *Lex.* 19[b]–20[a]; *Parallel Psalter,* Glossary, p. 449 f.). 'Idols and teraphim,'—the general and the particular,—form, however, an unequal pair; Symm. has ἡ ἀνομία τῶν εἰδώλων, which points to עֲוֹן תרפים; and Klo. Sm. Bu. Now. Ehrl. are probably right in reading this.

תרפים] 19, 13. 16. Gen. 31, 19. 34. 35. Jud. 17, 5. 18, 14. 17. 18. 20. 2 Ki. 23, 24. Ez. 21, 26. Hos. 3, 4. Zech. 10, 2†.

הַפְצַר] in pause for הַפְצֵר, as constantly in verbal forms, as וַיֵּלַךְ, הָשַׁב, הִתַּז: (Is. 18, 5), etc., and occasionally in nouns, as טָבְאַל: Is. 7, 6 for טָבְאֵל (cf. Ezr. 4, 7), שָׁשַׁר Jer. 22, 14, סְפָרַד Ob. 20, אָצַל Zech. 14, 5, אָצַל: 1 Ch. 8, 38 (*v.* 37, out of pause, אָצֵל): Ew. § 93[a], Stade, § 107[a], GK. § 29[q]. הַפְצֵר is the abs. inf. Hif. almost with the force of a subst.: cf. הַשְׁמֵד Is. 14, 23, הַשְׁקֵט 32, 17, הוֹכֵחַ Job 6, 25, הַמְשֵׁל 25, 2 (Ew. § 156[c]). The form, with a substantival force, is rare in Biblical Hebrew; but one nearly the same (הֶבְקֵר) is common in

[1] In late Hebrew אשר appears as = *quod* with greater frequency: Dan. 1, 8 *bis*, Qoh. 5, 4 . . . טוב אשר (contrast Ru. 2, 22 כי). 7, 29. 9, 1; and especially in Est. Neh. (*passim*).

the Mishnah: Siegfried and Strack, *Lehrbuch der Neuhebräischen Sprache* (1884), § 55ᵇ.

The word is, however, a suspicious one. פצר is to *push* or *press upon* (Gen. 19, 9), or to *urge* by persuasion (Gen. 19, 3. 33, 11. 2 Ki. 2, 17. 5, 16); and does not occur elsewhere in the Hif.: if correct, הפצר can mean only to *display pushing* (the 'internal Hif.,' GK. § 53ᵈ), i. e., in the inf., *forwardness, presumption* (not 'stubbornness,' EVV.). Klo. suggests חֵפֶץ רַע *evil desire*, which Bu. adopts; but this is a poor parallel to מרי, and cannot be said to be satisfactory.

וימאסך] 'ֹ in answer to כי, as *v.* 26. Hos. 4, 6 edd. (but Baer, Gi. Kitt. וֹ); cf. Nu. 14, 16. Is. 45, 4. 48, 5 al.: *Tenses*, § 127 γ; GK. § 111ᵇ.

ממלך] 'from king' = 'from being king:' cf. the fuller form in 26ᵇ, and the alternative מִמְּלֹךְ in 8, 7. 16, 1. So וַיִּסְרֵהָ מִגְּבִירָה 1 Ki. 15, 13. יַחַת מֵעָם Is. 7, 8 etc. (*Lex.* 583ᵃ (*b*),—towards the bottom).

28. ממלכות] The usual word is מַמְלָכָה: but the form מַמְלָכוּת (from [מַמְלֶךְ]) occurs besides II 16, 3. Hos. 1, 4. Jer. 26, 1. Jos. 13, 12. 21. 27. 30. 31†. Cf. מלאכות Hag. 1, 13† from מַלְאָךְ: Stade, § 304eᵛ¹. We., observing that the form never occurs in the *absolute* state, questions the originality of the pronunciation expressed by the *plena scriptio*, and would restore everywhere מַמְלֶכֶת.

מעליך] *from off thee:* 1 Ki. 11, 11ᵇ, in the same expression (applied to Solomon). For the figure, cf. עַל Is. 9, 5.

29. נצח ישראל] Probably *the Glory of Israel.* The root נצח appears only in certain derivatives in Hebrew; the manner in which they are related is apparent only in Aramaic. נְצַח in Syriac is properly *splenduit*, hence the adj. ܢܰܨܺܝܚ = λαμπρὸς Apoc. 22, 16; but in the *Pe'al* (= Heb. *Qal*), and more especially in the *Ethpa'el*, it usually appears with the derived sense of *inclaruit, celebris evasit*, and so *victoriam adeptus fuit, triumphavit* (cf. Dan. 6, 4): similarly the subst. ܢܶܨܚܳܐ = *victory* (e. g. Jud. 15, 18 = תשועה), and the corresponding נצחנא in the Targg., as Jud. 7, 18 ונצחנא על ידי גדעון ' and *victory* by the hands of Gideon;' ψ. 35, 23 מרי נצחני 'the lord of my *victory*.' In Heb. נצח has certainly a sense allied to this in the late passages,

---

¹ On forms in תֻ-, see GK. §§ 86ᵏ, 95ᵗ: more fully Kön. ii. 204-6.

Lam. 3, 18; 1 Ch. 29, 11[1]; and the expression here used is doubtless intended to characterize Yahweh as the *Glory* or *Splendour* of Israel. Similarly the Versions, but leaning somewhat unduly to the special (and derived) sense of *victory:* Pesh. ܢܨܚܢܐ ܕܐܝܣܪܐܝܠ the Illustrious *or* Triumphant one of Israel; Targ. מרי נצחניה דישראל the lord of Israel's victory; Vulg. *Triumphator* (no doubt from Aq. or Symm., though their renderings have not been here preserved): so Rashi נצחונו של ישראל. AV. (from Kimchi חזקם וכחם) *strength:* but this sense rests upon no philological foundation, and is merely conjectured from some of the passages in which נצח occurs, and where such a rendering would satisfy a superficial view of the context. Ges. Ke. render *fiducia*, comparing نَصَعَ *purus, sincerus, fidelis fuit* (used of sincerity towards God, Qor. 9, 92, or well-wishing toward men, 28, 11. 19). But it is doubtful if this sense of the Arabic root is sufficiently pronounced and original to justify the definite sense of *confidence* being attached to the Hebrew נצח [2].

כי לא אדם הוא להנחם] Cf. Nu. 23, 19. Contrast here *vv.* 11. 35: as Le Clerc (quoted by Th.) remarked long ago, the *narrative* is expressed ἀνθρωποπαθῶς, the *prophecy* θεοπρεπῶς.

32. מעדנת] An (implicit) accus. defining the *manner* in which Agag advanced, i. e. an adverbial accusative: cf. בטח *in* confidence (12, 11 al.), מישור, מישרים *in* uprightness (poet.): other examples in Ew. § 279ᶜ, GK. § 118 q. The sense, however, is not certain. (*a*) The most obvious rendering is *voluptuously:* cf. עֲדִינָה *voluptuous*, 'given to pleasures,' LXX τρυφερά, Is. 47, 8. שְׁנִי עָם עֲדָנִים II 1, 24. ψ. 36, 9 נחל עדניך LXX χειμάρρους τῆς τρυφῆς σου. Neh. 9, 25 וישמינו ויתעדנו

---

[1] The sense of the root in Aram. explains LXX εἰς νῖκος for נֶצַח(לְ) in II 2, 26. Am. 1, 11. 8, 7. Jer. 3, 5. Lam. 5, 20 (cf. Hab. 1, 4 RV. *m.*), and τοῦ νικῆσαι for לְמְנַצֵּחַ Hab. 3, 19; and the rend. of לַמְנַצֵּחַ in the Psalms (4, 1 etc.) by Aq. τῷ νικοποιῷ, and by Symm. ἐπινίκιος; also of LXX κατέπιεν ὁ θάνατος ἰσχύσας for בלע המות לנצח in Is. 25, 8 (Theod. κατεπόθη ὁ θάνατος εἰς νῖκος, exactly as 1 Cor. 15, 54; Aq. also εἰς νῖκος), and LXX τοῦ ἐνισχῦσαι for לְנַצֵּחַ in 1 Ch. 15, 21, and κατισχύουσίν μου in Jer. 15, 18 for נֶצַח.

[2] נצח in Is. 63, 3. 6 is a different word altogether (though identified by Kimchi, AV.), being connected with the Arab. نَضَحَ *to sprinkle;* see Ges. *Thes.;* Lex. 664.

LXX καὶ ἐτρύφησαν[1]. So Targ.[2] Aq. (ἀπὸ τρυφερίας, i. e. מֵעֲדָנָת),
Symm. (ἁβρός), We. But this is not probable in view of the context.
(*b*) Others compare מַעֲדַנּוֹת in Job 38, 31, which can scarcely be explained
otherwise than by metathesis from מעֲנדות *bands*: hence, here, in
fetters. So Kimchi. (*c*) LXX render τρέμων, whence Lagarde very
cleverly, merely by a change of punctuation, suggests מְעֹרֵנִית (of the
same form as אֲחֹרַנִּית *backwards*, קָדֹרַנִּית *mourningly*), *totteringly* (GK.
§ 100^g). So Sm. Now. Dh. Ehrlich, probably rightly.

אָכֵן [אכן סר מר המות in an exclamation, with asseverative force,
as Gen. 28, 16 אכן יש י״י במקום הזה; Ex. 2, 14 אכן נודע הדבר. It is
a stronger word than אַךְ, which is also used somewhat similarly
(see 16, 6).

מַר] a subst. *bitterness*, as Is. 38, 15 מר נפשי על. סר *is departed,*
gone by, as Am. 6, 7 וסר מרזח סרוחים; and Is. 11, 13 of a state of
feeling (קנאה). LXX, Pesh. omit סר, expressing merely the platitude,
Surely death is bitter![3] (In LXX εἰ οὕτω implies the misreading
of אכן as הֲכֵן.)

33. מנשים] Jud. 5, 24.

וישסף] Only here. Aq. Symm. διέσπασεν, Vulg. *in frusta concidit*,
Targ. Pesh. פשח; LXX more generally ἔσφαξεν. Of the general
sense intended by the narrator there can be no doubt: but whether
the word used by him has been correctly handed down may be
questioned. Etymologically שסף stands isolated: the Syriac שַׁסַּף
fidit (Roed. in *Thes.*) does not correspond phonetically. Should we
read וַיְשַׁסַּע (Jud. 14, 6 al.)?

34. עלה] from Gilgal: cf. *v.* 12 ירד.

The חֵרֶם, referred to in this chapter, is well explained by Ewald in his
Antiquities of Israel, pp. 101-106 [E. T. 75-78][4]. The word itself is derived

---

[1] Comp. מעדנים *dainties* Gen. 49, 20. Lam. 4, 5 האכלים למעדנים.

[2] מפנקא (see Dt. 28, 54 Onq.). *Hilari animo* (Ge. Ew. Ke.) gives the word
a turn which is foreign to the root from which it is derived. Vulg. *pinguissimus*
[*et tremens* of the Clementine text is a doublet, derived from the Old Latin, and
omitted by all the best MSS.] is based probably on Symm. ἁβρός.

[3] Targ. מותא מריר ריבוני בבעו takes it as שר=; cf. Jer. 6, 28 כלם סרי סוררים
כל רברביהון מרדין = (Aptowitzer, II, p. 28).

[4] See also the art. 'Bann' in Riehm's *Handwörterbuch des Bibel. Altertums*[2]
(1893); Dillmann's note on Lev. 27, 28 f.; and *EB.* BAN; *DB.* CURSE.

from a root which in Arabic means *to shut off, separate, prohibit* (حَرَمَ), whence the *ḥaram* or sacred territory of the Temple of Mecca, and the *ḥarîm* (حَرِيم), the secluded apartment of the women, applied also to its occupants, i.e. the 'harem'[1]. In Israel, as in Moab, the term was used of separation or consecration to a deity. Mesha in his Inscription (ll. 14-18[2]) states how, on the occasion of his carrying away the 'vessels of Yahweh' from Nebo, and presenting them before his god Chemosh, he 'devoted' 7000 Israelite prisoners to ''Ashtor-Chemosh.' Among the Hebrews, the usage was utilized so as to harmonize with the principles of their religion, and to satisfy its needs. It became a mode of secluding and rendering harmless anything which peculiarly imperilled the religious life of either an individual or the community, such objects being withdrawn from society at large and presented to the sanctuary, which had power, if needful, to authorize their destruction. The term occurs first in the old collection of laws called ' The Book of the Covenant' (Ex. 20, 23 — *ch.* 23), Ex. 22, 19 with reference to the Israelite who was disloyal to Yahweh (זֹבֵחַ לָאֱלֹהִים יָחֳרָם בִּלְתִּי לַיְיָ לְבַדּוֹ)[3]. More commonly we read of its being put in force against those outside the community of Israel: thus it is repeatedly prescribed in Deuteronomy that the cities and religious symbols of the Canaanites are to be thus 'devoted' to the ban; and the spoil of a heathen city was similarly treated, the whole or a part being 'devoted' or 'banned' according to the gravity of the occasion (Dt. 7, 2. 25 f. 20, 16-18). Instances of the חרם, as exemplified historically, are recorded in Nu. 21, 2 f. (after a *vow*). Dt. 2, 34. 3, 6. Jos. 6, 17-19 (the whole spoil was here made *ḥerem* or 'devoted:' a part of this *ḥerem* was afterwards secreted by Achan, as it was reserved by Saul on the occasion to which the present chapter refers). 8, 2. 26 al. Here, it is put in force, exceptionally, against an *external* political enemy of Israel[4].

וְלֹא יָסַף . . . לִרְאוֹת] But see 19, 24. AV. 'departs from its usual fidelity when it softens this absolute statement, and writes that "Samuel *came* no more to see Saul"' (*OTJC.*[2] 130).

---

[1] Also حَرَم *ḥarâm*, sanctuary (as in the title *Ḥarâm 'es-Sherîf*, or Noble Sanctuary, applied to the area enclosing the 'Dome of the Rock' at Jerusalem, on which the Temple formerly stood); and مُحَرَّم *muḥarram*, the sacred (first) month of the Arabs, in which it was forbidden to carry on war.

[2] Quoted and translated in the Appendix to the Introduction.

[3] Comp. Dt. 13, 13-18 (the idolatrous city in Israel).

[4] In AV. the verb הַחֲרִים is generally rendered *utterly destroy* and the subst. חרם *accursed thing;* but these terms both express secondary ideas, besides having the disadvantage of being apparently unrelated to each other: in RV. by the uniform use of *devote* and *devoted thing*, in the margin, if not in the text (for 'utterly destroy,' with marg. '*Heb.* devote,' has been retained in the text where the reference was to *persons*), the idea attaching to the Hebrew is more clearly expressed, and the connexion between the different passages in which the word occurs is preserved.

16, 1–13. *David anointed by Samuel at Bethlehem.*

16, 1. ואני מאסתיו] a circumst. clause = 'when *I* have rejected him :' *Tenses,* § 160.

בית־הלחמי] like בית־השמשי, etc. ; see on 6, 14.

ראיתי . . . לי] Gen. 22, 8.

2. ושמע שאול והרגני] II 12, 18 would support the construction that treated these words as under the government of אין (*Tenses,* § 115, p. 130), though they might in themselves be construed independently (*ib.* § 149 ; GK. § 159ᵍ : Gen. 44, 22 ועזב את־אביו ומת).

לזבח לי"י באתי] Note the order : Gen. 42, 9. 47, 4. Nu. 22, 20. Jos. 2, 3 ; Jud. 15, 10 ; *ch.* 17, 25. 28ᵇ.

3. בזבח] Read לזבח, as *v.* 5ᵇ.

ואנכי] Note the emph. pronoun.

אמר [אשר אמר אליך = *to name, designate,* as Gen. 22, 2ᵇ. 9. 26, 2 ; 43, 27 ; II 6, 22 ; 2 Ki. 6, 10.

4. ויחרדו . . . לקראתו] See on 6, 13 ; and cf. 21, 4.

ויאמר] sc. הָאֹמֵר.   When the verb appears in Heb. without a subject expressed, the implicit subject is—not *one,* as in English or French— but *the cognate participle* הָאֹמֵר.   The explanation is confirmed by the fact that cases occur in which the cognate participle is actually expressed, Dt. 17, 6 ימות המת. 22, 8 פן יפל הנפל. II 17, 9 ושמע השמע. Is. 28, 4 אשר יראה הראה אתה. Ez. 18, 32 במות המת. 33, 4 ושמע השומע את קול השופר ; cf. Jud. 11, 31 היוצא אשר יצא וג' : with an *indef.* ptcp. Nu. 6, 9 וכי ימות מת עליו. Am. 9, 1.   The idiom is already rightly explained by the mediaeval Jewish grammarians, as Ibn Ezra[1], e. g. on Gen. 48, 1 ויאמר ליוסף (the stock example of the idiom) sc. הָאֹמֵר ; Is. 8, 4 ישא sc. הַנֹּשֵׂא ; Am. 6, 12 אם יחרוש בבקרים sc. הַחֹרֵשׁ, and constantly ; Kimchi on 1 Ki. 22, 38 וישטף השוטף כמו ויאמר ליוסף[2]. Comp. Ew. § 294ᵇ (2) ; Hitzig on Am. 3, 11 והוריד 'namely, הַמּוֹרִיד ; ' GK. § 144ᵈ.   However, some thirty MSS. read here ויאמרו.

---

[1] Who, however, is apt to extend unduly the principle involved.   Comp. Friedländer, *Essays on the Writings of Ibn Ezra,* p. 134 : W. Bacher, *Abraham Ibn Esra als Grammatiker* (Strassburg, 1882), p. 143⁶.

[2] And similarly with the plural, as Is. 2, 20 אשר עשו לו sc. הָעֹשִׂים.

שלם בואך] The interrogation being indicated by the tone of the voice (cf. on 11, 12). So, with the same word, II 18, 29. 2 Ki. 9, 19 (*vv.* 11. 17. 18. 22 הֲשָׁלוֹם). There is no occasion, with Grätz, *Die Psalmen*, p. 116, and H. G. Mitchell (as cited in GK. § 150ᵃ *note*), to restore הֲ. Lit. 'Is thy coming *peace*?' the subst. *peace* being used in preference to the adj. *peaceable*. So often, as 25, 6 ואתה שלום שלום; וביתך שלום; Gen. 43, 27 השלום אביך; 1 Ki. 2, 13 הֲשָׁלוֹם בֹּאֶךָ. On the principle involved see *Tenses*, § 189, GK. § 141ᶜ; and comp. Delitzsch's note on Job 5, 24 (ed. 2).

5. התקדשו] viz. by lustrations (Ex. 19, 14). Cf. Ex. 19, 10. 22. Jos. 3, 5. Job 1, 5.

ובאתם אתי בזבח] LXX express וּשְׂמַחְתֶּם אִתִּי הַיּוֹם. MT. is regarded by We. Bu. Sm. Now., as an explanation of this, which they prefer, as being more original, and less tautologous with the following ויקרא להם לזבח.

6. אך] So often, in an exclamation, to add force to the expression of a conviction (not necessarily a true one): Gen. 44, 28; Jud. 3, 24. 20, 39; *ch.* 25, 21; Jer. 10, 19; ψ. 58, 12. 62, 10 al.

7. גָּבְהַ] Taken usually (GK. § 132ᶜ) as a neuter adj., with the force of a subst.: cf. גָּדֹל Ex. 15, 16. But the *st. c.* of גָּבֹהַ is four times גְּבַהּ; so it is prob. intended as an *inf. c.* (Kön. iii. 578; Ehrl.). No doubt גֹּבַהּ, and in Ex. 15, 16 גֹּדֶל, should be read.

אשר יראה האדם] LXX expresses in addition יראה האלהים, which must have fallen out accidentally. For אשר, כַּאֲשֶׁר must be restored; the passages in which אשר may be rendered *as* (Jer. 48, 8. ψ. 106, 34¹) are not parallel in form to the one here.

לָעֵינַיִם] עַיִן in the *sing.* means *look, appearance*, Lev. 13, 55. Nu. 11, 7; but the dual seems so unsuitable to express this idea that in Lev. 13, 5. 37 בְּעֵינוֹ must almost certainly be read for בעיניו. Klo. לפי עינים; Bu. לְמַרְאֵה עינים according to *that which the eyes behold* (Is. 11, 3. Dt. 28, 34; cf. מראהו אל תבט אל just before). This does seem to be the sense: the contrast between inner and outer is expressed not directly ('*looketh at the appearance*'), but indirectly. For the pathah in לָעֵ, see GK. 35ᵍ.

---

¹ Where אשר is properly *that which*, and may be so rendered. But the writer cannot have intended here to say that 'God seeth not *that which* man seeth!' In Dt. 15, 14 read כאשר for אשר: a כ has dropped out after the preceding כ. In Is. 54, 9. Jer. 33, 22 the construction is doubtful: but the sense *that which*, as the direct object of a verb, is excluded by the following כן (cf. *Lex.* 83ᵇ).

9. שמה] So 17, 13†; שמעה II 13, 3. 32†; שמעא I Ch. 2, 13. 20, 7
= II 21, 21 Qrê†; שמעי II 21, 21 Kt.†

11. הקטן] with a superlative force: GK. § 133ᵍ.

והנה] without the suffix, as the subject referred to immediately
precedes: cf. 15, 12. 30, 3. 16. Gen. 37, 15; and on 10, 11.

נָסֹב] usually explained as meaning to *sit round* the table or divan.
Dr. Weir writes: 'LXX οὐ μὴ κατακλιθῶμεν, Vulg. *non discumbemus*,
Targ. נִסְתַּחַר *surround*, which is used in the Targ. of sitting at meat,
ψ. 1, 1. 26, 4. 5. Gen. 27, 18 = שְׁבָה [and in the Af'el, *ch.* 20, 5.
24. 25]. In all these passages it corresponds to the Heb. ישב. Syr.
ܠ ܐܣܬܚܪ *I will not return.* סבב is nowhere else used in the sense
supposed. Perhaps we might read נֵשֵׁב.' However, סבב is used in
the Hif. (הֵסֵב) in post-Bibl. Heb. (e. g. *Pesaḥim* 10, 1) of sitting (or
reclining) round a table at a meal (cf. also מֵסֵב Ct. 1, 12); and the
word may have been used in this sense much earlier.

12. עם יפה עינים] So 17, 42: but the expression is very remarkable
and anomalous. It is contrary to usage or analogy for עם to be used
with an adverbial force (Ew. § 352ᶜ; Keil; AV. 'withal'): if the
text be sound, יָפֵה must be a neuter adj., like נבה in *v.* 7: 'together
with beauty of eyes.' Grätz suggests עֶלֶם (17, 56) for עם: so also
Max Krenkel in the *ZATW.* 1882, p. 309. Sm. Now. agree.

רֹאִי] in pause for רָאִי: GK. §§ 29ᵐ *end*, 93ᶻ. Elsewhere in this
connexion טוב(ת) מראה is said (Sm.): Gen. 24, 16. 26, 7. II 11, 2.

16, 14–23. *First account of David's introduction to Saul. David is
brought into attendance upon the king for the purpose of soothing
him, during his fits of madness, by his minstrelsy, and is made his
armour-bearer.*

14. ובעתתו] The pf. with *waw* conv. (not simple *waw*) with a freq.
force (cf. 15 *end*, the ptcp.). The word (which is a strong one) occurs
only here and *v.* 15 in prose[1], being elsewhere confined to poetry—
chiefly the Book of Job.

רוח י״י] 'רוח י״י as good spirit is opposed to רוח מאת י״י or
רוח אלהים as evil spirit. This distinction is strictly maintained in

---

[1] Except the Nif., which is found in *late* Hebrew (thrice).

MT.: only 19, 9 would form an exception, but there רוח אלהים
should doubtless be read with LXX for רוח י"י ' (We.).

15. מִבְעָתֶּךָ :] GK. § 80ᵍ.

16. ויאמר ונ'] ' Let our lord, now, command, thy servants are before
thee, let them seek,' etc. There seems to be some disorder in the
sentence. The roughness and abruptness of the Heb. (which is
concealed in RV.) is extreme: LXX, in far better accord with the
usual form of a Hebrew period, express יאמרו־נָא עֲבָדֶיךָ לְפָנֶיךָ וּבִקְשׁוּ
(so We. Sm. Now.). יאמרו was probably originally יאמר (see Introd.
§ 4. 1 c); and אדננו, inserted as an expression of courtesy which was
desiderated, was intended to be taken as a vocative: but יאמר being
ambiguous, it was taken actually as a nom., and so the pronunciation
יאמַר (in lieu of יֹאמַר) became fixed. But as אמר, to *say*, requires to
be followed by the words said, we must, if we adopt this, read ידברו
for יאמרו (cf. II 14, 12). Or, following a suggestion of Ehrlich, we
might read יאמר־נא אדננו ובקשו עבדיך איש ידע מננן בכנור ועמד לפניך
והיה ונ' (cf. 1 Ki. 1, 2).

ידע מננן בכנור] 'knowing, as a player with the harp' (cf. Ew.
§ 285ᵉ). A particular case of the principle by which, in Hebrew
syntax, one verb appears as supplementing or completing the sense
of another (on 2, 3). But perhaps the inf. נַגֵּן should be read, as
v. 18: cf. 1 Ki. 3, 7. Is. 7, 15. For ידע, as denoting technical skill,
cf. 1 Ki. 9, 27 יודעי הים, Am. 5, 16 יודעי נהי, 1 Ch. 12, 32 יודעי בינה
לעתים, Is. 29, 11.

וננן בידו] To specify in detail the instrument or means by which
an action takes place, even though to our mode of thought it may
appear superfluous, is very Hebraic: LXX בכנורו is anything but
an improvement. See *v.* 23. 18, 10. 19, 9; also such phrases as
שרף באש, etc.

17. מיטיב לנגן] Ez. 33, 32 יְמֵטִב נגן; Is. 23, 16 הטיבי נגן.

18. בן לישי] 'a son of Jesse:' see GK. § 129ᶜ.

גבור חיל] See on 9, 1.

נבון דבר] LXX σοφὸς λόγῳ, Vulg. *prudentem in verbis*, i. e. clever,
capable in speech. (*Ready in speech, fluent*, is איש דברים Ex. 4, 10.)
Cf. Is. 3, 3: נְבוֹן לָחַשׁ clever in enchantment.

20. חמור לחם] If the text be correct, this will mean an ass *laden*

with bread. But the expression 'an ass of bread' is peculiar; and as elsewhere לחם is regularly numbered (by loaves), it is quite possible that חמור is a corruption of חמשה or עשרה : LXX γομορ, i. e. עמר [1] favours the latter.

21. עמד לפני] To 'stand before,' said of a single occasion, is equivalent to to 'present oneself before' (Gen. 41, 46. 43, 15. Ex. 9, 10 al.: *Lex.* 763ᵇ bottom): when used of a constant relation, it acquires the force of 'stand before so as to be in attendance on;' see the next note.

22. יעמד נא דוד לפני] עמד לפני is an idiom denoting *to be in attendance upon* one, or, as we should naturally say, to 'wait upon:' 1 Ki. 1, 2; 10, 8 of Solomon's courtiers (cf. 12, 8. Jer. 52, 12): *ib.* 17, 1. 18, 15. 2 Ki. 3, 14. 5, 16 of Elijah and Elisha as the ministers of

---

[1] See Ex. 16, 36 LXX : so Γοθονιηλ = עתניאל, Γοθολια = עתליה, Γαζα = עזה, Γομορρα = עמרה, Ζογορα (Gen. 13, 10), Ζογορ (Jer. 48 [31], 34), or Σηγωρ (Gen. 14, 2 al.) = צוער, Γαι or (Gen. 12, 8) Αγγαι = העי (Ai), ΓαιΒαλ = עיבל, Φογωρ = פעור, Βεελφεγωρ = בעל־פעור, Χοδολλογομορ and Θαλγα = כדרלעמר and תרעל (Gen. 14, 1), 'Ραγαυ (Gen. 11, 18. Luke 3, 35) = רעו, 'Ραγουηλ = רעואל, Γοφερα and Σωγαλ = עפרה and שועל (ch. 13, 17), Γαιδαδ = עירד (Gen. 4, 18), Γεφαρ (Γαφερ, Γαιφα) = עיפה (Gen. 25, 4. 1 Ch. 1, 33 [cf. 2, 46. 47]. Is. 60, 6) : add Gen. 36, 2 Σεβεγων צבעון, 14 'Ιεγλομ יעלם, 23 עלון Γωλων, עיבל ΓαιΒηλ, 35 עיות Γεθθαιμ (so 1 Ch. 1, 46), 40 עלוה Γωλα ; Nu. 1, 8 צוער Σωγαρ ; 33, 35 al. עציון גבר Γεσσιων (Γασιων) ΓαΒερ, 44. 45 עי(ם) Γαι, 46 עלמון Γελμων ; Jos. 15, 59 מערת Μαγαρωθ ; 19, 11 מרעלה Μαραγελδα ; 12 יפיע Φαγγαι, 21, 18 עלמון Γαμαλα [1 Ch. 6, 45 (60) עלמת Γαλεμεθ] ; 1 Ki. 5, 11 (4, 27) איתן Γαιθαν (עיתן or ניתן ?) ; 16, 28 ΓαΒουζα (of Asa's mother עזובה in an addition to MT. ; not with Γ 22, 42. 2 Ch. 20, 31) ; 1 Ch. 1, 9 רעמה 'Ρεγμα ; 2, 47 שעף Σαγαε (Al. Σαγαφ) ; 4, 9 יעבץ 'Ιγαβης (also ὡς γαβης for בעצב) ; 4, 14 עפרה Γοφερα ; 9, 4 עותי Γωθει ; 42 עלמת Γαμελεθ ; *ib.* עזמות Γαζαωθ (but not so 8, 36. 12, 3. 27, 25) ; 11, 32 הערבתי Γαραβαιθθι. In Arabic, the soft and hard sounds of ע are distinguished by a diacritical point (ع, غ) : in Hebrew, though no such sign has been adopted, it is clear, from the transliteration of LXX, that ע had in some words a harder and stronger sound than in others (comp. Stade, § 63ᵒ). See further on this subject the studies of Růžička in *Z. für Ass.* xxi (1908), p. 293 ff., and Flasher in *ZAW.* xxviii (1908), pp. 194 ff., 303 ff. Růžička purports to give lists of *all* proper names in the OT. containing ע, with their LXX transliterations (but his readings are based on the text of Tisch., which sometimes differs from that of Swete², which is based (for cod. B) on the photograph published in 1890) ; Flasher's lists are limited to the names occurring in Genesis. Neither perhaps explains quite satisfactorily how it happens that γ represents ע in many words in which the corresponding word (or root) in Arabic has ع, and not غ (Růžička, p. 302, cf. 339 f.).

Yahweh : elsewhere it is applied technically to the *priest* as in attendance upon *Yahweh*, Dt. 10, 8. 18, 7. Jud. 20, 28. Ez. 44, 15. 2 Ch. 29, 11 ; and to the *Levite* as in attendance upon the *congregation* or the *people*, to discharge menial duties for them (see e. g. 1 Ch. 9, 27–9. 31–2. 2 Ch. 35, 11), Nu. 16, 9. Ez. 44, 11. See more fully the writer's note on Dt. 10, 8 (p. 123)[1]. It is a pity that in passages such as Nu. 16, 9. Dt. 10, 8 to 'wait upon' (with a marg. 'Heb. *stand before*') has not been adopted in EVV.: it may be doubted whether many English readers understand what to 'stand before the congregation' means.

23. Notice the series of perfects with *waw* conv. expressing what happened *habitually*, and represented rightly in the Versions (impff. in LXX, Vulg. ; ptcpp. in Targ. Pesh.[2]). ל חות as Job 32, 20†.

וטוב לו In] טוב ל, טוב is a *verb*, 'to be *good to*' = 'be well with :' Nu. 11, 18. Dt. 5, 30 al.

הרעה [רוח הרעה is an adj. (not a subst. in the gen.) as appears (1) from the analogy of 15ᵇ. 16ᵇ; (2) from the fact that הרעה is not used as a qualifying genitive. Comp. above, on 12, 23. For the conception of the רוח רעה, cf. Jud. 9, 23.

17, 1—18, 5. *Second account of David's introduction to Saul. David, a shepherd youth from Bethlehem, attracts the king's attention by his victory in single combat over Goliath.*

17, 1. שׂוכה] One of the towns in the Shephēlah (Jos. 15, 35), generally identified with *esh-Shuweikeh* (1145 ft.), on the N. slope of a range of low hills running E. and W., 14 miles W. of Bethlehem.

The 'Vale of Elah' (*v.* 2) is immediately below it, on the N. It is (Bu.) strategically important, as it is close to a number of valleys and roads leading up to Hebron, Bethlehem, and elsewhere ; the large PEF. Map marks a Roman road leading up to Bethlehem. LXX have Σοκχωθ. The pl. may be original ;

---

[1] Dr. Orr (*Probl. of the OT.* p. 192) seeks to shew that to 'stand before Yahweh' does not denote distinctively *priestly* functions. But it is idle to argue that to 'stand before Yahweh' means nothing more than to 'stand;' and in 2 Ch. 29, 11 the last word ומקטרים shews that the writer has priests (*v.* 4) in his mind ; for to burn incense was an *exclusively* priestly duty. See the thorough examination of the idiom in McNeile, *Deuteronomy, its Place in Revelation*, 1912, p. 74 ff.

[2] Cf. the same versions in 1, 3. 7, 16. Ex. 33, 8–10 al. (*Tenses*, p. 146).

for (We.) Eus. (*Onom.* 292, 32–4) says that there were *two* villages of this name, an upper and a lower, 9 miles above Eleutheropolis (which agrees fairly with the site of esh-Shuweikeh, 7 miles NE. of Eleutheropolis).

Bliss (*PEFS.* 1900, p. 97 f.) doubts this site, as it shews no signs of pottery earlier than Roman times; and suggests *Tell Zakarîya* (so called from a *wely* dedicated to the father of John the Baptist), 3 miles below esh-Shuweikeh, on the same side of the Wādy, where an Isr. fortress has been excavated (*ib.* 1899, pp. 10–36, 89–98), supposing the old name to have been transferred to esh-Shuweikeh.

אשר ליהודה] Cf. 1 Ki. 19, 3; 2 Ki. 14, 11 (of Beersheba); 1 Ch. 13, 6 (of Qiryath-yeʿarim): also אשר לפלשתים 1 Ki. 15, 27. 16, 15; *ib.* 17, 9: אשר לצידון Jud. 18, 28. 19, 14 הגבעה אשר לבנימין 20, 4.

עזקה] Mentioned next to Sochoh in Jos. 15, 35; an important strong city (Jer. 34, 7. 2 Ch. 11, 9). The site is not known: Tell Zakarîya (confused by Bartholomew in G. A. Smith's Maps with the *village* Zakarîya opposite: see Rob. ii. 21), ʿAskalun (1 mile S. of Tell Zakarîya), and other sites, have been conjecturally suggested.

אפס דמים] A place, not identified, between Sochoh and ʿAzēkah. The name, though peculiar, is supported by 1 Ch. 11, 13 (the parallel to II 23, 9; see note there) פס־דמים. LXX (B) has Εφερμεμ, other MSS. σεφερμαειμ, σαφαρμειν, etc., which, however, lead to nothing. Aq. ἐν πέρατι Δομειμ agrees with MT. (for πέρας = אפס in Aq., see Is. 5, 8. 52, 10 al.). In view of 1 Ch. 11, 13, and of there being no support from Aquila, בעבר המים (Kitt.), of the stream running down the Wādy, is a very doubtful emendation.

2. עמק האלה] The 'Vale of the Terebinth' (*v.* 19. 21, 10†), the 'broad depression between hills' (on 6, 13), formed by the junction of two valleys, from the S. and E., which unite on the E. of esh-Shuweikeh; the valley then narrows to form *W. es-Sanṭ* (the 'Wādy of Acacias'), which afterwards runs down westwards, past the shining white rock of Tell eṣ-Ṣāfiyeh, very probably Gath (on 6, 17), into the Philistine plain (see further Cheyne, *Devout Study of Criticism,* 85 f.; *EB.* s. v. ELAH; and Photograph No. 443 of the Pal. Expl. Fund).

3. והניא ביניהם] 'with *the* ravine between them.' The ravine is probably the deep and narrow gorge cut out by the stream running down the vale on the N. of esh-Shuweikeh, mentioned in the note on *v.* 2 (*H. G.* 227 f.; Conder, *Tent Work,* 279).

The ptcpp. describe the *continuous* position of the parties during the incidents about to be related. The Israelites would be on one of the hills NE. of esh-Shuweikeh, on the opposite side of the עֵמֶק.

4. איש הבנים] i. e. the man of the μεταίχμιον, who came forward as the μεσίτης to bring the warfare to a close. Kimchi: לפי שהיה יוצא יום יום בין שתי המערכות נקרא איש הבנים[1].

גלית] The same fem. termination occurs in other old Semitic (mostly Canaanitish) names: אֲחֻזַּת (m.) Gen. 26, 26 (Philistine); בֵּשְׂמַת (f.), מַחֲלַת (f.), בְּכוֹרַת (ch. 9, 1), וְּנוּבַת (1 Ki. 11, 20—perhaps Edomite), נחת and מנחת Gen. 36, 13. 23; and in Nabataean, Euting, *Nabatäische Inschriften*, pp. 73, 90–2, as חרתת (= 'Αρέτας 2 Cor. 11, 32), בנרת (m.), נזיאת (f.), מנעת (m.), מרת (m.), עבידת (m.), al. (several of these similarly in Arabic)[2].

5. In MT. the giant's weapons of defence are of bronze, those of attack are of iron. Here there is undoubtedly a consistency, which is badly disturbed in LXX (We.).

קשקשׂים] *of scales* (of fish, Lev. 11, 9 al.; of a crocodile, Ez. 29, 4), i. e. scaled armour. For the form, cf. עַפְעַפִּים, וְלַוִּים Is. 18, 5. תַּלְתַּלִּים Cant. 5, 11. חַתְחַתִּים Qoh. 12, 5 (Kön. ii. 91 f., cf. 181, 452 *n.*). 5000 shekels of bronze was probably *c.* 220 lbs. av. (Kennedy, *DB.* iv. 904 ff.).

6. וּמִצְחַת [וּמְצֹחֹת (We.) is preferable.

'וכידון וג] Keil quotes appositely (from Bochart) Il. 2. 45 al. ἀμφὶ δ' ἄρ' ὤμοισιν βάλετο ξίφος ἀργυρόηλον. כידון = *javelin*: see v. 45 and Jos. 8, 18.

7. וחץ] Read, with the Qrê, and the parallel, II 21, 19, וְעֵץ, i. e. *and the shaft*.

מנור ארגים·] LXX in II 21, 19. 1 Ch. 11, 23. 20, 5 ἀντίον; i. e. (Kennedy in his interesting art. WEAVING in *EB.*, iv. 5284 f.) the weaver's 'shaft,' or 'leash-rod' (Lat. *liciatorium*), used for holding

---

[1] Some of the Jews imagined fancifully that the word described Goliath's mixed parentage: Lagarde's *Prophetae Chaldaice*, p. xvi (from the margin of the Cod. Reuchl.): תרגום ירושלמי. נברא פולומרכא (πολέμαρχος) דאיתיליד מבינֵי תרתי גניסן מן שמשון דהוה מן שיבט דן ומן ערפה דהות מן בני מואב גלית שמו. (גניסין pl. of גניס = γένος.) The same tradition evidently underlies the Vulg. *vir spurius*. Cf. Aptowitzer, *ZAW.* 1909, p. 244.

[2] And in many names of *places*. Comp. *Tenses*, § 181 *note*.

the threads of the warp apart, while the shuttle, carrying the weft, was passed between them.

8. ברו לכם] In all probability this is an error for בחרו לכם (as 1 Ki. 18, 25. Jos. 24, 15: and בחר לך II 24, 12 ‖). ברה in Heb. means *to eat food:* and the meaning *select, choose,* is not substantiated for it by either Arabic or Aramaic. (So also Dr. Weir.)

9. 10. אני] Notice the emph. pronoun.

10. חרפתי] חֵרֵף is to *reproach* (sc. with taunts), i.e. to *defy.*

12–31. We here reach the first of the considerable omissions in LXX as compared with MT. These verses are not in cod. B; and though they are supplied in cod. A, they form no part of the original and genuine LXX. This may be inferred from the different style of the translation, which (1) adheres more closely to the existing MT. than is the case in the book generally; (2) deviates in the rendering of particular words, as κοιλὰς τῆς δρυὸς 16 against κοιλὰς ʼΗλα 21, 9; μεσαῖος 23 instead of δύνατος 4 for איש הבנים, Γολιαθ ὁ Φιλιστιαῖος *ib.* against Γολιαθ ὁ ἀλλόφυλος 21, 9. 22, 10; comp. also in the allied passage *vv.* 55–8 ἄρχων τῆς δυνάμεως for שר הצבא against ἀρχιστρατηγὸς 12, 9. 14, 50. 26, 5: ἐστηλώθη 16 against κατέστη (see 3, 10. 10, 19. 23. 12, 7. 16) is of less weight, as it may have been chosen on account of the particular sense of ויתיצב, and recurs in a similar context II 23, 12.

12. הזה] Contrary to grammar, as well as unsuitable. ʻ*This* Ephraimite' would be האיש האפרתי הזה: but the word *this* is out of place,—for the paraphrase (Vulg.) *de quo supra dictum est* (i. e. Jesse, in *ch.* 16) is inadmissible. Still, as the verse, being really superfluous after *ch.* 16, only stands here as introducing a narrative originally unconnected with *ch.* 16, it is possible that הזה is a late and unskilful insertion made with the view of identifying the איש אפרתי here mentioned with the ישי of *ch.* 16. Or it might be an error for הָיָה (Pesh.: so Dr. Weir, comparing II 4, 4), though in point of fact no verb is required (see 25, 2. 1 Ki. 11, 26). Ehrlich thinks it a corruption of הוא, and makes the plausible suggestion that הוא מבית לחם יהודה is a gloss, intended to shew that אפרתי did not mean Ephraimite (1, 1 al.), but *Bethlehemite.*

ולו שמנה בנים] Cf. on 1, 2.

בא באנשים] The text was already the same, when the translation of cod. A was made : but ' and the man in the days of Saul was aged, *entered in among men*'—which is the only rendering that is justifiable—affords no intelligible sense. The most obvious correction is the omission of בא (Hitzig); זקן באנשים will then mean ' aged among men.' Grätz, after Pesh., would read בא בַשָּׁנִים ' entered into years ' (so LXX (Luc.) ἐληλυθὼς ἐν ἔτεσιν). Against the first, We. argues that the parallels היפה בנשים, Am. 2, 16, ἐσθλὸς ἐν ἀνδράσιν etc. are incomplete, זקן not expressing a *distinction* among things in other respects similar, as יפה and ἐσθλὸς do. Against the second proposal is the fact that the phrase in use is always זקן בא בימים (Gen. 18, 11. 24, 1. Jos. 13, 1. 23, 1 (cf. 2). 1 Ki. 1, 1†). In face of this constant usage, it is extremely questionable whether בא בשנים can be regarded as a legitimate and idiomatic alternative for בא בימים. Klo., for וילכו: זקן בא באנשים, conjectured very cleverly זקן מבּא באנשי המלחמה *was too old to enter in among*, etc. (with, naturally, וישׁת for the following שלשׁת); and Bu. accepts this. It may well be right.

13. וילכו ... הלכו] One of the two verbs is superfluous. The theory (Ew. § 346ᶜ n.) that הלכו is annexed for the purpose of giving וילכו the force of a plupf., is artificial and contrary to analogy. No other example of such a usage occurs in OT., cases of resumption, after a *long* intervening clause, being readily intelligible, and resting upon a different footing : e.g. Dt. 4, 42 ונס ; 18, 6 ובא ; Jer. 34, 18–20 ונתתי, etc. (see on 25, 26). Unless the conjecture mentioned in the last note be accepted, הלכו here may be due to a copyist's eye having glanced by error at the following verse, where the word occurs (rightly) between the same words.

14. הוא] Gen. 2, 14 ; 9, 18 etc.: *Tenses*, § 199.

15. הלֵךְ וָשָׁב] ' Speaker's Comm. " was gone," quite arbitrarily ' (Dr. Weir). *Was gone* would be expressed, of course, by ודוד הלַךְ וַיָשָׁב (see 9, 15): the participles can only be meant to describe David's *custom* at the time : RV. rightly, *went to and fro*. The verse is no doubt an addition made by the compiler of the Book for the purpose of accounting for David's absence from the court of Saul, after 16, 21 f. In fact, however, according to the narrative embodied in this chapter, David was still unknown to Saul (*vv.* 55–58). See the note after 18, 5.

מעל] *from attendance on* Saul: see Jud. 3, 19. Gen. 45, 1. Mr. Deane (*David: his Life and Times*, p. 14) has omitted to notice מעל.

17. הקליא] with א *otiosum:* GK. § 23ⁱ. See on II 17, 28.

הזה לחם ועשרה] הזה cannot belong to עשרה (contrast 18 האלה), and לחם הזה is not Hebrew (Jer. 40, 3 דבר הזה is corrected in the Qrê). הלחם הזה must therefore be restored (cf. the *Addenda*): after עשרה, ה might readily have dropped out. הריץ=*take* it *quickly:* Gen. 41, 14.

18. חריצי החלב] lit. *cuts of milk*, i.e. probably (*EB*. iii. 3091), *fresh-milk cheeses.* Luc. τρυφαλίδας, *soft cheeses;* Vg. '*formellas* casei.'

תפקד לשלום] A variation for the usual שאל לפלני לשלום (*v.* 22). Another (uncommon) variation is רְאֵה את שְׁלוֹם אחיך Gen. 37, 14.

ואת ערבתם תקח] 'and take their pledge,' i.e. bring back some token of their welfare. Of the Versions, LXX (Luc.), Targ. Pesh. hit the general sense most nearly: καὶ εἰσοίσεις μοι τὴν ἀγγελίαν αὐτῶν, וית טיבהון תיתי, ܘܐ ܠ ܘܣ¹.

20. על] Cf. *vv.* 22 (על יד). 28; and נתן על Is. 29, 12 (11 אל). Mic. 1, 14.—המעלה (ה *loc.*) to the *round enclosure* (camp: *EB.* i. 636): מעגל as 26, 5. 7†. Some edd. read the *fem.* form המעגלה (*milraʿ*).

וישא] *and lifted up* (viz. the things mentioned in *v.* 17 f. on to the asses: cf. נשא על הגמלים, Gen. 31, 17. 42, 26 al.): but the ellipse is surprising. Bu. suggests the insertion of רגליו after וישא (Gen. 29, 1†): but this seems to suggest a longer and more formal journey than one of 12 miles or so. The same objection may be made to Sm.'s וַיִּסַּע (Gen. 20, 1 al.), which also suggests a journey by *stages.*

והחיל היצא וג'] היצא with the art. must of course be in apposition with החיל: as the text stands, therefore, it can only be rendered 'And the host that went forth to the battle array—they shouted in the war' (והרעו, acc. to *Tenses*, § 123 *a* or 129: RV. implies מֵרִיעַ for והרעו). The construction, however, is very strained; and the fact of the host going forth is surely intended to form part of the information given, and not to be presupposed. No doubt, therefore, יָצָא should be read for היצא: 'And he came to the enclosure, *and* (=*as:* a circum-

---

¹ The later Jews interpreted ערבה oddly of a *deed of divorce;* see Lagarde, p. xvi; cod. 56, Holmes and Parsons (ap. Field) βιβλίον ἀποστασίου; Jerome, *Quaestiones*, ad loc.; and Aptow. *ZAW.* 1909, p. 245.

stantial clause) the host was going forth to the battle array, and (*Tenses*, 113. 4 β ; GK. § 112ᵏ) they were shouting in the war.'

הָרֵעוּ] Read, as elsewhere (e.g. Jud. 15, 14), הָרִיעַ: the verb is רוע, not רעע.

21. וְתֵעֲרָךְ] Cities and countries, regarded as the *mothers* of their inhabitants, are regularly in Heb. construed with a fem. sg.; and occasionally the name, even when it denotes the *people*, is construed similarly (Ew. § 174ᵇ; GK. § 122ʰ, ⁱ): Ex. 12, 33 וַתֶּחֱזַק מִצְרַיִם עַל הָעָם. II 8, 2. 5. 6 (in the parallel 1 Ch. 18, 2. 5. 6 altered to וַיְהִי, וַיָּבֹא, וַיְהִי). 24, 9 וַתְּהִי יִשְׂרָאֵל (in 1 Ch. 21, 5 וַיְהִי). Is. 7, 2. 21, 2. 42, 11. Job 1, 15 וַתִּפֹּל שְׁבָא וַתִּקָּחֵם. By poets the principle is carried further : and they love to *personify* the population of a nation or city, as a woman : e. g. Is. 54, 1 ff. ; and in the frequent בַּת צִיּוֹן, בַּת בָּבֶל, etc., יוֹשֶׁבֶת צִיּוֹן Is. 12, 6 etc.: cf. Mic. 1, 11–13. Jer. 10, 17 etc.

23. וְהוּא מְדַבֵּר ... וְהִנֵּה ...] A special case of the idiom noticed on 9, 5 : 1 Ki. 1, 22. 42. Gen. 29, 9 are closely parallel.

מִמְּעָרוֹת] An error, already noted in the Qrê. LXX, Vulg. Targ. agree with the Qrê in expressing the pl. מִפַּעֲרֹכֹת: Pesh. has the sing. מִמַּעֲרֶכֶת; and one of these must be right.

24. וַיָּנֻסוּ] וָ, as 14, 19ᵇ. Gen. 30, 30 (*Tenses*, § 127 a; GK. § 111ʰ).

25. הִרְאִיתֶם] See on 10, 24.

עָלֹה] without subj., as Gen. 32, 7 ; Is. 33, 5 : *Tenses*, § 135. 6 (2) ; GK. § 116ˢ.

וְהָיָה וְגֹ'] and it shall be, *as regards* the man, etc.: see on 2, 36. For the *Hif.* יַעְשְׁרֶנּוּ, see GK. 53ⁿ; and cf. וִידַבְּקוּ 14, 22.

26. מֵעַל] Cf. Jos. 5, 9. 1 Ki. 2, 31. II 24, 21. 25 (*Lex.* 758ᵇ).

כִּי חֵרֵף] not *that he should reproach* (יֶחֱרַף), but *that he should have reproached* (as a completed fact): ψ. 44, 20 that thou *shouldest have crushed* us in a place of jackals. Gen. 40, 15. יְחָרֵף would no doubt be more usual (18, 18. Ex. 3, 11 : cf. *Lex.* 472ᵇ f): but are we entitled to say (Ehrlich) that the pf. here is 'absolutely un-Hebraic ? '

אֱלֹהִים חַיִּים] the plural of 'majesty:' GK. 132ʰ.

28. הֲהֵנָּה] צֹאן is construed regularly as a *fem. pl.*, e.g. 25, 18 ; Jer. 33, 13 ; Zech. 13, 7·

אָנִי] Note the emph. pronoun : cf. II 7, 8. Jos. 23, 2. 2 Ki. 2, 3.

29. הֲלֹא דָבָר הוּא] ' Was it not a word ? ' i.e. I merely asked a

כתרנומו הלא פתגם הוא דאמרית question : that was all. So Ki. rightly :
כלומר אם דברתי לא עשיתי דבר ואין רצוני לעשות אף על פי שאני מדבר.

30. אֶל מוּל אחר] ' to the front of another.'

וישבהו העם דבר] lit. *turned him back with* (GK. § 117[ff]) *a word*
= *replied to, answered:* see on II 3, 11.

32. לב אדם] LXX, We. לֵב אֲדֹנִי, which is undoubtedly more pointed,
and is recommended by the עבדך which follows: cf. *v.* 11 (which
immediately precedes in LXX). ' It is the custom, when the king
is addressed, to say " my lord " in place of what would be the first
thou ' (We.).

עליו] as ψ. 42, 5. 6. 7. Not ' *within* him ' (=בְּקִרְבּוֹ), which suggests
an incorrect idea, but ' *upon* him.' על in this and similar expressions
is idiomatic: it ' separates the self, as the feeling subject, from the
soul' (Delitzsch). So ψ. 131, 2 as a weaned child is my soul *upon
me.* 142, 4. Lam. 3, 20. Jon. 2, 8. Jer. 8, 18 עלי לבי דוי my heart
upon me is sick. See *Lex.* 753[b] d; *Parallel Psalter,* p. 464.

34. רעה היה וג'] Form of sentence, as 2, 11[b] (see note).

הארי ואת־הדוב] It is strange that here את should be a redundancy,
while in *v.* 36 נם את הארי נם הדוב it is rather desiderated before the
same word for the sake of symmetry. As it is, ואת stands according
to Ew. § 277[d] *end, Lex.* 85[a] 3, to mark a new subj. in a sentence :
but though several instances occur, they are not mostly in passages
belonging to the best style, nor can this use of the particle be counted
an elegancy. Here את is quite superfluous. It would seem as though
a copyist's eye had actually interchanged הדוב here with את הדוב in
v. 36 (so Now.). וְאַף ' and *even* a bear ' (Grätz, Klo. Bu. al.) is
plausible : but was a bear *more* dreaded than a lion ? The poet. וְאָתָה
(Perles) is not probable. The rendering in GK. § 154[a] *n.* (*b*) is very
forced.

שֹה] Many edd. read זה, with the note שה קרי : but the note is not
a Massoretic one; and in fact זה is no part of the Massoretic Text
at all, but is simply an error, first occurring in the Rabbinical Bible
of 1525, edited by Jacob ben Ḥayyim, and perpetuated in subsequent
editions. See De Rossi, *Variae Lectiones,* ad loc., who states that *all*
MSS. known to him (184 of Kennicott's, and 64 of his own, besides
others) read correctly שֶׂה.

34^b–35. The series of *perfects* with ו, instead of the impff. and
waw conv., which is the usual narrative tense, is remarkable. A series
of pff. with *waw*, in an historical book, has the *presumption* of being
designed by the writer in a frequentative sense ; and such is in all
probability the case here, though, as the accentuation shews, the
passage was understood otherwise by the punctuators. If the sense
suggested be adopted, והצלתי must, of course, be read והצלתִּי (see
Jer. 6, 17 ; Am. 4, 7), and והחזקתי—though not quite with the same
absolute necessity ¹—והחזקתִּי. The solitary ויקם is not decisive against
the interpretation proposed (see Jer. *l. c.*, and on 14, 52). In this
case, further, as the allusion will be no longer to a single *particular*
incident, the art. in הארי and הדוב will be generic (GK. § 126^r): 'And
if a lion or bear came, and took a sheep out of the flock, I would go
out after him, and smite him, and rescue it from his mouth : and if
he rose up against me, I would seize hold of his beard, and smite him,
and slay him ².' (So also Dr. Weir.)

35. והצלתי מפיו] Am. 3, 12.

וְהֲמִיתִּיו] ' The dagesh is an indication that וְהֲמִיתִּיו would be the
correct form ; cf. GK. § 72^w ' (Bu.).

37. ויאמר דוד] In accordance with Hebrew idiom, though omitted
in LXX. It is 'a recapitulation of the substance of a preceding
longer speech, entirely in the manner of popular narrative, and of
repeated occurrence in Hebrew ' (We.): cf. *v.* 10.

הוא] resuming the subj. with emph.: *Lex.* 215^b 2.

38. מדיו] [מד] is used chiefly of the outer garment of a warrior :

---

¹ On account of the pashṭa : see Jer. 4, 2 (*Tenses*, § 104).

² So LXX in *v.* 34 ὅταν ἤρχετο καὶ ἐλάμβανεν : in LXX (Luc.) the impff. are
continued, as logically they should be, to the end of *v.* 35. (On the frequentative
force of ὅταν, ἡνίκα ἄν, ἐάν, ὡς ἄν, with the impf. indic., and even with the aorist, in
Hellenistic Greek, see Winer, *Grammar of N. T. Greek*, § xlii. 5 ; Blass, *Gramm. of
N. T. Greek*, § 63. 7 ; Moulton, *Grammar of N. T. Greek*, 1906, p. 168 : and comp.
Gen. 6, 4 [wrongly explained in Winer's note *ib.* ; see the Hebrew : in 27, 30 for ὡς
ἄν Tisch. must be read either ὡς with codd. AD (so Swete) and 10 cursives, or ὅσον
with E and 18 cursives (also Philo) : see Hatch, *Essays in Biblical Greek*, 1889,
p. 163 f.; and Brooke-McLean, *ad loc.*]. Ex. 17, 11. 33, 8 f. 34, 34. 40, 30. Nu. 21, 9.
Jud. 6, 3. II 14, 26 (where Lucian, as here, has also consistently the impf. ἵστα for
ἔστησεν), etc.; and Mark 3, 11 in the Revised Version.)

מַדְוֵיהֶם ; Jud. 3, 16 ;‏ 4. ‏18‏ . וּמַדָּיו קְרֻעִים ‏12‏ ,4 .‏39‏ .*v*‏, as here, מַדָּיו

(from [מַדְוֶה or מָדוּ]; but see note) II 10, 4 = I Ch. 19, 4 ; מְדוּ II 20, 8

[rd. מַדָּי]: Lev. 6, 3 (of a priest), ψ. 109, 18 מַדּוֹ כַּמַּדּוֹ קְלָלָה וַיִּלְבַּשׁ ; מַדּוֹתָיו

ψ. 133, 2 (of Aaron); מִדֵּין (?) Jud. 5, 10†. Cf. *EB.* i. 1137.

קוֹבֵע] So Ez. 23, 24†; *v.* 5 and elsewhere כּוֹבַע.

39. Ehud Jud. 3, 16, for purposes of concealment, girds his sword *under* his מַדִּים (מִתַּחַת לְמַדָּיו). On מֵעַל לְ (chiefly late), v. *Lex.* 759ᵃ ⍬.

וַיֹּאֶל לָלֶכֶת] The words admit of no rendering consistent at once with the meaning of הוֹאִיל, and with the following *causal* clause כִּי לֹא נִסָּה : for *assayed* (AV.), which (as כִּי לֹא נִסָּה shews) must mean 'endeavoured *unsuccessfully*,' is not a sense that is ever possessed by הוֹאִיל. In Targ. Pesh. the difficulty is felt so strongly that the positive clause is transformed into a negative one (וְלֹא אָבָה לְמֵיזַל : ‏(*Jo*)! LXX have ἐκοπίασεν = וַיֵּלֶא 'And he *wearied himself* to go (with them),' i. e. he exerted himself in vain to go with them, which agrees well with the following clause 'for he had not tried them.' Cf. Gen. 19, 11 וַיִּלְאוּ לִמְצֹא הַפָּתַח and they wearied themselves to find the door, i. e. exerted themselves in vain to find it. The reading וילא is accepted by Luzzatto *Il Profeta Isaia* [ed. i. 1855] on 1, 14 (who states that it was first suggested to him by his pupil Abraham Meinster), and Geiger (*Urschrift*, p. 377); it is adopted also (in each case, as it would seem, independently) by We. and Dr. Weir.

וַיִּסְּרֵם דּוד] LXX וַיַּסְרֵם. The original text had no doubt simply ויסרם, which was read by some as a plur., by others as a sing.; by some of the latter דוד was added.

40. חַלְּקֵי אֲבָנִים] *smooth ones of stones* = *smoothest stones:* GK. § 132ᶜ.

וּבִילְקוּט] either read בְּיַלְקוּט (We. Now.), or (Ehrl.) בְּיַלְקוּטוֹ, and delete לוֹ אֲשֶׁר הָרֹעִים כְּלִי, as an explanatory gloss; or (Sm. Bu.; cf. LXX τῷ ὄντι αὐτῷ εἰς συλλογήν) read לְיַלְקוּט לוֹ הָיָה אֲשֶׁר 'his shepherd's bag which served him for a (sling-stone) wallet.'

41. וַיֵּלֶךְ . . . הֹלֵךְ וְקָרֵב] Contrast 14, 19. Cf. II 15, 30ᵃ †.

43. אָנֹכִי] in pause with *zāqēf:* cf. on 1, 15.

בַּמַּקְלוֹת] the plur. is the generic plural. LXX put into David's mouth the singularly vapid reply : καὶ εἶπε Δαυειδ, Οὐχί, ἀλλ' ἢ χείρων κυνός.

46. פגר] collectively, as נבלתי Is. 26, 19. But read probably with
LXX פגרך ופגרי.

וידעו כל הארץ] הארץ construed with a plural, as Gen. 41, 57; and,
more frequently, in late poetical style, as ψ. 66, 1. 96, 1. 9. 100, 1 al.

כי יש אלהים לישראל] 'that Israel *hath* a God.' יש asserts existence
with some emphasis; cf. ψ. 58, 12.

47. יהושיע] The retention of ה of the Hif'il, after the preformative
of the impf., is rare and usually late: Jer. 9, 4; Is. 52, 5; ψ. 28, 7;
45, 18; 116, 6 (as here); Job 13, 9; Neh. 11, 17; Ez. 46, 22 (*Hof.*
ptcp.). These are all the examples of the uncontracted *verb* that
occur in Hebrew: cf. the n. pr. יְהוֹסֵף once ψ. 81, 6; יְהוּכַל Jer. 37, 3
(38, 1 יוּכַל). The form occurs also regularly in Biblical Aramaic, as
Dan. 7, 18. 24. Comp. GK. § 53ᵍ; Stade, § 113. 2; König, i. 294 f.[1]
But Klo.'s הישועה for יהושיע יהוה (so Bu.) both removes the anomalous
יהושיע, and yields a better antithesis to what follows (כי ליהוה ונ').

48. והיה] See on 1, 12.

50. ..., וחרב אֵין] the emph. word before אֵין: 21, 2ᵇ (see note).
II 15, 3. Jud. 14, 6 ומאומה אֵין בידו. 16, 15. 18, 7. 28. 19, 1 al.

51. וימתתהו] See on 14, 13.

52. גיא] The גי in *v.* 3 was the ravine which separated the opposing forces; but this could not also be the goal of their flight:
moreover, if a particular גיא were meant, the article would be required.
The word must thus represent some proper name: LXX have גת
(cf. *b*), which is accepted by both Keil and Commentators generally.

If Gath was Tell eṣ-Ṣāfiyeh, it was about 10 miles W. of Sochoh, down Wādy Sanṭ;
Ekron was 16 miles NW. of Sochoh: Sha'araim is mentioned in Jos. 15, 36, next to
Sochoh and 'Azēqah, as a town in the Shephēlah, so that it was presumably some
place down the valley between Sochoh and Tell eṣ-Ṣāfiyeh. Its actual site can,
however, only be conjectured. Tell Zakarîya has been suggested: but we must
first satisfy ourselves that this is not either Sochoh or 'Azēqah (cf. on *v.* 2). ועד is
preceded naturally by מן: so בְּדֶרֶךְ מִשְׁעַרַיִם (Sm. Kitt.; Bu. alternatively) is a very
probable correction for בדרך שערים.

54. ירושלם] An obvious anachronism. Jerusalem was still a Jebusite stronghold; see II 5, 6–9.

באהלו] Keil (following Th.): 'an archaism for *dwelling*, as 4, 10.

---

[1] So with the art., the non-syncopated form בהשמים ψ. 36, 6 (except in כהיום)
is nearly always late: comp. on II 21, 20.

13, 2 etc.' But אהל has (apparently) this sense only in the phrase
אִישׁ לְאֹהָלָיו, inherited from a time when the nation dwelt actually in
tents. The meaning can only be that David put the armour in the
tent occupied by him, when he was on duty with Saul (18, 2–5 etc.):
afterwards, the sword at any rate was removed to Nob, and placed
behind the ephod (21, 10). Ehrl. בָּאֹהֶל (1 Ki. 1, 39).

55. וּכְרָאוֹת . . . אמר] Not a common type of sentence, in early
Hebrew. 'It is the tendency of the earlier Hebrew, in the case of
temporal or causal clauses, which Greek often places early in a
sentence, either ⟨*a*⟩ to postpone them somewhat, or (*b*) to prefix ויהי:
it is the later Hebrew, that is apt to introduce them at the beginning.
Compare ad (*a*) Gen. 19, 16. 34, 7. 50, 17. Ex. 31, 18. Jud. 8, 3
with 2 Ch. 12, 7. 15, 8. 20, 20. 24, 25. 26, 16. 19[b]. 33, 12. 34, 14.
Dan. 10, 9. 11. 15. 19; and ad (*b*) (וּכְכַלּוֹת(ם 2 Ch. 7, 1. 20, 23[b].
24, 14. 29, 29. 31, 1 against some fourteen times in earlier books
with ויהי prefixed[1],' e. g. *ch.* 18, 1; 1 Ki. 8, 54 (ויהי omitted in the
parallel, 2 Ch. 7, 1). 9, 1.

בֶּן־מִי־זֶה הַנַּעַר] Not as AV. RV. 'Whose son is this youth?' but
'Whose son is the youth?' זה is enclitic, and belongs to מי, as Jer.
49, 19; ψ. 24, 8 etc. (GK. § 136[c]; *Lex.* 261[a] **4 b**). In *v.* 56 EVV.
render correctly.

חֵי נ׳] so always in this expression, and in other oaths not by God
(חֵי פַרְעֹה; II 15, 21; Am. 8, 14): in oaths by God always חַי יהוה,
חַי אָנִי. Either חֵי is the *st. c.* of a subst. חַי, an old sing. of the usual חַיִּים
(*Thes.,* Ke. Kön. ii. 42),=(*By*) *the life of . . . !* (so the Massorites: cf.
Targ. of I 20, 3 al. (קַיָּם הוּא יהוה וְחַיֵּי נַפְשֶׁךָ); or, in spite of the fem. נפשׁ,
we should vocalize חֵי נַפְשֶׁךָ. The explanation of חֵי in GK. § 93[aa] *n.*
as a contracted form of the *st. abs.* חַי is not natural.

56. שָׁאַל אתה] Note both the position and the force of אַתָּה 'Ask
thou:' Ex. 20, 19 דַּבֵּר־אַתָּה עִמָּנוּ speak *thou* with us; Dt. 5, 24;
ch. 20, 8; 22, 18 סֹב אַתָּה; Jud. 8, 21 קוּם אַתָּה וּפְגַע בָּנוּ (*Tenses,* § 202).

הָעֶלֶם] 20, 22†. The masc., of which the corresponding fem. is
עַלְמָה Is. 7, 14 al. For וַיִּקַּח *v.* 57, see on 4, 20.

---

[1] Quoted from a letter of the writer by Prof. Franz Delitzsch in *The Hebrew New Testament of the British and Foreign Bible Society. A contribution to Hebrew Philology.* Leipzig, 1883 [written in English], p. 19.

18, 1. נקשרה וג׳] Gen. 44, 30 ונפשו קשורה בנפשו.

ויאהבו] The Kt. is וַיֶּאֱהָבוֹ (a rare form: Ew. § 249ᵇ; Ol. p. 469; Kön. i. 224, 621; GK. § 60ᵈ: Hos. 8, 3 ירדפו. ψ. 35, 8 תלכדו. Jer. 23, 6 יקראו; Qoh. 4, 12 יתקפו; Jos. 2, 4 [corrupt]; see also on 21, 14 and II 14, 6): the Qrê substitutes the more usual וַיֶּאֱהָבֵהוּ.

2. ולא נתנו לשוב] The same idiom as Gen. 20, 6. 31, 7. *ch.* 24, 8 etc.: and Nu. 20, 21. 21, 23 without ל.

3. ודוד] as יהונתן is the subj. to the end of the verse, Sm. Bu. Now. Kit. read לדוד for ודוד. But כרת ברית ל׳, with the rarest exceptions (2 Ch. 29, 10. Ezr. 10, 3), is used only of a superior, especially a conqueror, prescribing terms to an inferior (11, 1. Jud. 2, 2. Is. 55, 3 al.), so that it would seem here to be unsuitable. Unless, therefore, ן (Ehrl.) is the *waw* of 'concomitance' (Ex. 21, 4: *Lex.* 253ᵃ; above, p. 29), it is better to read את דוד for ודוד.

4ᵇ. ומדיו] = *and also* his (warrior's) garment: cf. on 6, 11. Without the usual מן (before עד: *Lex.* 581ᵇ 5), as Lev. 11, 42. Nu. 8, 4.

5. ישכיל] defines how David fared when he went out: 'And David went forth, wherever Saul sent him he prospered' = prospering wherever Saul sent him. Jer. 15, 6 נטשת אתי אחור תלכי 'Thou didst forsake me, thou wentest ever backward' = going ever backward. Comp. *Tenses*, § 163 with *Obs*. The impff. have of course a frequentative force.

השכיל is *to deal wisely* with the implied consequence of success: in other words, it expresses not success alone, but success as the result of wise provision. No single English word expresses the full idea conveyed by the Hebrew: hence the margins in RV. here, Jos. 1, 8; Is. 52, 13. Success *alone* is denoted in Heb. by הצליח.

The narrative 17, 1—18, 5, precisely as it stands, it appears impossible to harmonize with 16, 14–23. The two narratives are in fact two parallel, and, taken strictly, incompatible accounts of David's introduction to the history. In 16, 14–23 David is of mature age and a 'man of war,' on account of his skill with the harp brought into Saul's service at the time of the king's mental distress, and quickly appointed his armour-bearer (*vv.* 18. 21). In 17, 1—18, 5 he is a shepherd lad, inexperienced in warfare, who first attracts the king's attention by his act of heroism against Goliath; and the inquiry

17, 55–58 comes strangely from one who in 16, 14–23 had not merely been told who his father was, but had manifested a marked affection for David, and had been repeatedly waited on by him (*vv.* 21. 23). The inconsistency arises, not, of course, out of the double character or office ascribed to David (which is perfectly compatible with historical probability), but out of *the different representation of his first introduction to Saul.* In LXX (cod. B), 17, 12–31. 41. 50. 55—18, 5 are not recognised. By the omission of these verses the elements which conflict with 16, 14–23 are greatly reduced (e. g. David is no longer represented as *unknown* to Saul); but they are not removed altogether (comp. 17, 33. 38 ff. with 16, 18. 21ᵇ). It is doubtful therefore whether the text of LXX is here to be preferred to MT.: We. (in Bleek's *Einleitung,* 1878, p. 216 = *Comp. des Hex. u. der hist. Bb.,* 1889, p. 250), Kuenen (*Onderzoek*², 1887, p. 392), Bu. Dh. hold that the translators—or, more probably, perhaps the scribe of the Heb. MS. used by them—omitted the verses in question from harmonistic motives, without, however, entirely securing the end desired[1]. On the other hand, W. R. Smith (*OTJC.*² pp. 120 ff., 431 ff.), Löhr (p. xxxiv), Cornill, *Introd.* § 17. 6, Stade (*EB.* iv. 1276), Sm. Now. Kennedy (p. 121) maintain the superior originality of the shorter LXX text. In either case, however, 17, 1—18, 5 will,

---

[1] And so Kamphausen, *Theol. Arbeiten* (Elberfeld), vii. ' Bemerkungen zur alttest. Textkritik,' pp. 16–18.—Dr. Weir views the Hebrew text similarly, though accounting in a different manner for the omission in LXX : ' " Whose son is this ? " In 16, 21 it is said that Saul loved David, and he became his armour-bearer. To reconcile the two statements, it has been conjectured (*Speaker's Commentary*) that 16, 21 records by anticipation what did not really come to pass till after David's victory over Goliath. But how can this be reconciled with 18, 9. 10, and especially with 18, 13 ? Or, again (Keil), that the question " Whose son is he ? " has relation not to the name, but to the position of David's father (but see *v.* 58) ; or that Saul's madness accounts for his having forgotten David. But all these explanations are insufficient. Are the verses wanting in LXX a later interpolation in the Hebrew text ? This cannot well be : for an interpolation would not insert anything at variance with the narrative interpolated. We seem therefore shut up to the conclusion that the verses omitted in the Vat. MS. belong to an independent narrative, which was in parts incorporated with the older account, but not in all MSS. existing when the LXX translated the book. The Greek translation of the added verses [in cod. A] is very exact and must have proceeded from a later period, when the Hebrew text was fixed as at present.'

more or less, have been derived from a different source from 16, 14–23 (notice how David is introduced in 17, 12 ff. as though his name had not been mentioned before), and embodies a different tradition as to the manner in which Saul first became acquainted with David.

18, 6–30. *Saul's growing jealousy of David*
(*in continuation of* 16, 23).

6. והמחלות (Qrê) [לשיר] The two words correspond in form so imperfectly that the text can scarcely be in its original form. The least change is to read with Bu. בִּמְחֹלוֹת (cf. Ex. 15, 20 ותצאן כל הנשים; אחריה בְּתֻפִּים וּבִמְחֹלֹת; Jud. 11, 34 והנה בתו יֹצֵאת לקראתו בְּתֻפִּים וּבִמְחֹלות; 21, 21 אם יצאו בנות שילה לָחֹגל בַּמְחֹלות). LXX, omitting 6ᵃ (see p. 155) as far as את־הפלשתי, express then ותצאנה הַמְחֹלְלוֹת לקראת דוד מכל ערי ישראל בתפים ונ׳, which is adopted by Sm. Now (though מכל ערי ישראל should *precede* לקראת דוד), at least as the text of what is regarded by them as the main narrative here (LXX, cod. B). במחלות is obviously the right correction of the *Massoretic* text, as we have it: the question of the relation of the Massoretic text of this verse to the LXX is one belonging to 'higher' criticism, which cannot here be considered.

שאול המלך] The order is *late*: see p. 305 *n*.

7. ותעניינה] So Ex. 15, 21 ותען להם מרים.

הנשים המשחקות] 'the women which made merry.' Illustrate from II 6, 5, where David and the Israelites, as they bring the ark up into Zion, are described as מְשַׂחֲקִים לפני י״: also Jer. 30, 19 תודה וקול י״; 31, 4 (in the promise of Israel's restoration) עוד תעדי תֻפַּיִךְ מִשַׂחקים; ויצאת במחול משחקים.—On the omission in LXX, see at the end of the section.

8. רבבות] Read with LXX הָרְבבות, to correspond with הָאלפים (We. Bu. Sm. etc.).

ועוד לו אך המלוכה] 'and there is still only the kingdom (*sc.* to give) to him.' The correction לֹ (Klo. al.) is unnecessary.

9. עון] The Qrê עֹיֵן is right. ויהי with the ptcp. expresses at once origination and continuance—'and . . . came into the condition of one eyeing:' so Gen. 4, 17 ויהי בנה עיר; 21, 20ᵇ; Jud. 16, 21

ויהי טוחן; 2 Ki. 15, 5. The verb is a denom. from עַיִן, 'to eye' (sc. enviously : LXX, cod. A ὑποβλεπόμενος), the ptcp. being perhaps that of Qal, but perhaps also that of Po'el (Ew. § 125ᵃ), with the prefix מ omitted (Stade, § 229; GK. § 55ᶜ), as sometimes in Pu'al (Ew. § 169ᵈ; GK. § 52ˢ). The omission of מ is no doubt irregular : but there is a presumption that for the sense in question, the conjugation which Ew. (§ 125ᵃ) has well characterized by the term 'Conjugation of attack' would be in use. Cf. לֹשֵׁן *to be-tongue,* i. e. to slander, ψ. 101, 4 ¹, and GK. § 55ᵇ˒ ᶜ. The verb, however, does not occur elsewhere ; and Ehrl. would read שַׂנֵּא (the א dropped by haplography, and שׂ then taken as עׂ).

10. וַיִּתְנַבֵּא] *played the prophet,* viz. by gestures and demeanour, as 10, 5.

ודוד מנגן] ' *as* (or *while*) David was playing : ' a circumst. clause.

בידו] See on 16, 16.

כיום ביום] only here. See on 3, 10. יום ביום itself does not occur till the latest Hebrew : Neh. 8, 18. 1 Ch. 12, 22. 2 Ch. 8, 13. 24, 11. 30, 21. Ezr. 3, 4. 6, 9 (Aram.)†.

11. וַיָּטֶל] i. e. *cast,* from טול. But it does not appear that Saul actually cast the javelin on this occasion ; hence Th. We. Kp. al. following LXX (ἦρεν) and Targ. (ארים) would punctuate וַיִּטֹּל *and took up,* from נָטַל, Is. 40, 15.

אכה בדוד ובקיר] ' I will smite David and the wall,' i. e. I will smite them together, I will pin David to the wall : so 19, 10. Cf. Dt. 15, 17.

12. מלפני] elsewhere, to express the source or cause of an act or feeling, mostly late (for the earlier מפני) : see *Lex.* 818ᵃ : and cf. *ch.* 8, 18.

13. I. e. Saul removed him from his circle of immediate attendants, and gave him duties with the army. מעם as 14, 17.

14. לכל־דרכו] '*with regard to* (7, 7) all his ways.' But בכל־דרכו is better ; so 18 MSS., and many Rabb. quotations *ap.* Aptow. I.

---

¹ So מִשְׁפְּטִי Job 9, 15 not *my judge,* but he that would *assail me in* judgement, i. e. my *opponent* in judgement. The conjugation is in more regular use in Arabic, where its signification is also distinctly seen (Wright, *Ar. Gr.* i. § 43) : thus قتل *to kill,* قاتل *to try to kill* = to fight with : سبق *to outrun,* سابق *to try to outrun* = to run a race with.

15. אשר] for the usual כי (*Lex.* 83ᵃ **8 a** β). Cf. on 15, 20.

ויגר מפניו] *and stood in awe* (Kp.) of him. A stronger expression than ויֹרא in *v.* 12: Nu. 22, 3.

16. . . . . כי הוא] Notice the emph. pron. in a causal sentence (p. 110 *n.*); and also the participles in this verse.

17. אתה אתן לך] Note the emphatic position of אתה. Cf. Jud. 14, 3 אותה קח לי; and see on 15, 1.

†.(ספר מלחמת י״י) Nu. 21, 14 .25, 28 [מלחמות י״י

אמר] *said mentally* = *thought*: so *v.* 21. 25, 21. 2 Ki. 5, 11, and frequently (*Lex.* 56ᵃ **2**).

18. חַיָּי] Punctuate חַיִּי 'my folk' (Kirkpatrick). The word is the same as the Arabic حَيّ (so We. Keil, etc.; cf. *Thes.* 471ᵃ), explained at length by W. R. Smith in his *Kinship and Marriage in Early Arabia*, pp. 36–40 (² 41–46), and denoting 'a group of families united by blood-ties,' moving and acting together, and forming a unity smaller than the tribe, but larger than that of a single family. The word is in frequent use in Arabic; but was rare—perhaps only dialectical—in Hebrew, and is hence explained here by the gloss משפחת אבי. The punctuation as a pl. ('my *life*') shews that the meaning of the word had been forgotten. מי (not מה) is used with reference to the *persons* of whom the חַי consists: cf. II 7, 18 מי ביתי, Gen. 33, 8 מי לך כל־המחנה הזה.

19. תת] *of giving*,—though the action is (and, in the present case, remains) incomplete: cf. 2 Ki. 2, 1. Hos. 7, 1. For the omission of the suff., sometimes, as here, indefinite, sometimes definite, cf. Gen. 19, 29. 24, 30. Ex. 13, 21. Jer. 41, 6; and GK. § 115ᵉ *n.*

21. למוקש] מוקש is some kind of *fowling-implement*,—certainly not a 'snare' (i. e. a noose; Germ. *Schnur*, a 'string'), but probably the trigger of a trap with a bait laid upon it (see the illustration in the writer's *Joel and Amos*, p. 157, and p. 158). Hence it is often used metaphorically of that which *allures* a person to destruction, as here, Ex. 23, 33. Dt. 7, 16.

בשתים] The expression recurs Job 33, 14; lit. *with two*, i. e. a second time (RV.)—not, however, excluding the first, but (as the literal rendering shews) together with it. Hence the phrase, as used here, 'must contain an ironical allusion to David's loss of Merab. Still, the

expression remains strange. Ehrlich conjectures ויאמר שאול אל עבדיו
בְּ[פל]שתים יתחתן לי היום 'with the help of the Philistines (*v.* 25ᵃ) shall
he make himself to-day my son-in-law.'

AV. 'with (one of) the twain,' is derived from Rashi, Kimchi, and ultimately
from the Targ. (בחדא מתרין). A rendering which has to supply the most crucial
word in a sentence, it might have been supposed, could have found no defenders:
the Jews, however, discover a parallel for it in the OT.—Jud. 12, 7 and he was
buried בערי הגלעד in (one of) the cities of Gilead !

23. הנקלה] the inf. abs. construed as a fem., as Jer. 2, 17. The הֲ
is of course the interrogative.

נִקְלֶה] Cf. Is. 3, 5 where this word is opposed to נכבד (cf. 16, 14.
Hos. 4, 7. Pr. 3, 35).

25. מהר] The technical word denoting the price paid, according to
ancient custom, by the suitor to the father or family of the bride[1].
See Gen. 34, 12 ; Ex. 22, 15. 16 (which speaks of the מהר בתולת,
i. e. the sum usually paid for a wife). Cf. the Homeric ἕδνα or ἔεδνα,
Il. 16. 178 (of a suitor) πορὼν ἀπερείσια ἕδνα ; Od. 21. 160–2 Ἄλλην
δή τιν' ἔπειτα Ἀχαιιάδων εὐπέπλων Μνάσθω ἐέδνοισιν διζήμενος· ἧ δέ κ'
ἔπειτα Γήμαιθ' ὅς κε πλεῖστα πόροι καὶ μόρσιμος ἔλθοι: also as an
interesting *material* parallel, Il. 9. 141–8 (Nestle, *Marginalien*, p. 14).

כי] 9 MSS. have כי אם, the more usual expression ; so LXX,
3 Rabb. authorities *ap.* Aptowitzer, I ; it is also a סביר (on 12, 5).

26. ולא מלאו הימים] Obscure : perhaps (Ke.) alluding to the time
within which David's exploit was to be performed. The clause is not
in the LXX.

27. מאתים] LXX μέᾱ, which both agrees with the express statement, II 3, 14, and also (as We. observes) is alone consistent with the
following וימלאום (or better, as LXX[2], Aq. Theod. Vulg. וַיְמַלְאֵם),
i. e. *completed* the tale of them to the king. The change was no doubt
made for the purpose of magnifying David's exploit. The clause 26ᵇ
may have been added with the same object: David accomplished in
shorter time than was fixed more than was required of him.

---

[1] Comp. W. R. Smith, *Kinship and Marriage in Early Arabia*, p. 78 (ed. 2,
1903, p. 96) ; Nöldeke, *ZDMG*. 1886, p. 154.

[2] Cod. A and Luc.: in Cod. B וימלאם למלך is not represented.

28[b]. ‏ומיכל בת שאול אהבתהו‏] LXX καὶ πᾶς Ἰσραηλ ἠγάπα αὐτὸν i. e. ‏וְכִי כָל־יִשְׂרָאֵל אֹהֵב אֹתוֹ‏: certainly original. The clause in this form states the *ground* for Saul's greater dread, expressed in *v.* 29: MT. merely repeats without need what has been said before in its proper place, in *v.* 20.

29. ‏ויאסף‏] Written incorrectly, as from ‏אסף‏ : so Ex. 5, 7 (GK. § 68[h]).

‏לֵרֹא‏] Read ‏לִירֹא‏: cf. ‏יְרֹא‏ Jos. 22, 25 (Kön. i. 639 f.; GK. § 69[n]).

In 18, 6–30 there are again considerable omissions in LXX (cod. B), the text of LXX reading as follows:—6[b] (And the dancing women came forth to meet David out of all the cities of Israel, with timbrels, and with joy, etc.). 7. 8[a] (to *but thousands*). 9. 12[a] (And Saul was afraid of David). 13–16. 20–21[a] (to *against him*). 22–26[a] (to *son-in-law*). 27–29[a] (reading in 28[b] 'and *that all Israel* loved him '). In this instance, it is generally admitted that the LXX text deserves the preference above MT.: the sequence of events is clearer; and the gradual growth of Saul's enmity towards David—in accordance with psychological truth—is distinctly marked,—observe the three stages, (*a*) 12[a] 'And Saul was afraid of David:' (*b*) 15 'he stood in awe of him,' and endeavoured indirectly to get rid of him, 20–21[a]: (*c*) 29 'he was yet more afraid of David,' and (19, 1) gave direct orders for his murder. The additions in MT. emphasize unduly, and *prematurely*, the intensity of Saul's enmity. They also harmonize badly with the account of David's betrothal to Michal: if, for instance, he had *already* been betrothed to Merab (*vv.* 17. 19), it is difficult to understand how he could reject as absurd the idea of his becoming the king's son-in-law as he does in *v.* 23 [1].

19—22. *David obliged to flee from Saul. He visits Samuel at Ramah* (19, 18–24), *finds through Jonathan that Saul's enmity is confirmed towards him* (ch. 20), *repairs accordingly first to Ahimelech at Nob, then to Achish at Gath* (ch. 21), *and finally takes refuge in the cave (or stronghold) of 'Adullam* (ch. 22).

19, 1. ‏וידבר . . . להמית‏] Cf. 2 Ki. 14, 27.

---

[1] Comp. Wellh., in Bleek's *Einleitung* (1878), p. 218 (= *Die Composition des Hexateuchs u. der hist. Bücher*[2], 1889, p. 251 f.); Stade, *Gesch.* i. 37–40; Kirkpatrick, on 1 Samuel, p. 242; Kamphausen, *l.c.* pp. 18–23; Kennedy, p. 131.

3. ואני] Notice the emph. pron. (twice).

ב [אדבר בך = *about*, as *v.* 4. Dt. 6, 7. ψ. 87, 3. Respecting another, more special sense of דבר ב', see on 25, 39.

וראיתי מה והגדתי לך] 'And I shall see somewhat, and I will tell thee' = and *if* I see aught, I will tell thee : construction like that of ועזב אביו ומת Gen. 44, 22 : *Tenses*, § 149 ; GK. § 159ᵍ. מה = τι (not τί ;), as II 18, 22. 23 ; Pr. 9, 13 ; 25, 8 al. Comp. Nu. 23, 3ᵇ וּדְבַר מַה־יַּרְאֵנִי והגדתי לך, lit. 'and he will shew me the matter of aught, and I will tell thee' = and *if* he shews me . . . ., I will tell thee.

4. מעשיו] Sing. not plural, the י being due to the fact that מעשה is originally מעשי. Cf. משתיו Dan. 1, 5 ; מחניך Dt. 23, 15 ; מקניך Is. 30, 23 : Ew. § 256ᵇ ; Stade, § 345ᵃ ; GK. § 93ᵃᵃ.

5. וישם וג'] 28, 21 ; Jud. 12, 3 ; Job 13, 14 : cf. ψ. 119, 109.

להמית] '*in* slaying :' cf. 12, 17.

9. רוח י"י] LXX רוח אלהים : see on 16, 14.

והוא בביתו יושב] The position of the ptcp. as 24, 4. 25, 9. II 11, 11. The circumst. clause, as Gen. 18, 1. 8. Jud. 3, 20. 1 Ki. 19, 19, etc. (*Tenses*, § 160 ; GK. § 141ᵉ).

ביד] Read בְּיָדוֹ (16, 16. 23), noting the following ו,—unless, indeed, ביד were purposely chosen, for the sake of avoiding the assonance with the preceding בידו (comp. on 26, 23).

10. בדוד ובקיר] Cf. on 18, 11.

ויפטר] Only here in the sense of *depart, escape*. In post-Biblical Hebrew, the *Nif.* occurs frequently (e. g. *Yoma* 1, 5), particularly in the sense of departing from life : cf. Phil. 1, 23 in Delitzsch's Hebrew N. T. (published by the British and Foreign Bible Society), where לְהִפָּטֵר = εἰς τὸ ἀναλῦσαι.

בלילה הוא] A rare variation for the normal בלילה ההוא, which should probably be restored: Gen. 19, 33. 30, 16. 32, 23†; on this and the other passages quoted, ההוא is a סביר (on 12, 5). On the words themselves, We. remarks, 'As David no doubt fled immediately after Saul's attempt, and there is no ground for supposing that this was made *at night*, it is better to connect the definition of time with *v.* 11, where it is required [cf. the following בבקר], and to read with LXX : וַיִּמָּלֵט : ויהי בלילה ההוא וישלח וג'.' So Kp. Klo. Weir, etc.

11. לשמרו ולהמיתו בבקר] The messengers, it would seem, were not commissioned to *kill* David (see *vv.* 14. 15), but only to watch the house where he was: hence doubtless ו must be omitted with LXX, and the words rendered, 'to watch it (cf. *ψ*. 59, 1), that he might slay him in the morning.' So Th. We. Klo. etc.

אם אינך . . . מחר אתה מומת] The use of the ptcp., especially in the protasis, is very idiomatic: *Tenses*, § 137; GK. § 159[v]. Cf. Ex. 8, 17; 9, 2 f. (where, as here, the apodosis also is expressed by a ptcp.).

13. התרפים] See on 15, 23.

כביר העזים] The exact sense is uncertain. כְּבָרָה is a *sieve;* מַכְבֵּר is the *coverlet* with which Benhadad was smothered by Ḥazael, 2 Ki. 8, 15. The phrase appears thus to denote something made of goats'-hair in the manner of net-work,—probably a quilt. Ew. *Hist.* iii. 107 (E.T. 77) and Keil suggest a *fly-net* (κωνωπεῖον), such as might be spread over the face whilst a person was asleep. (The κωνωπεῖον of Judith 10, 21. 13, 9 was, however, suspended on στῦλοι—the posts of the bed.) מראשתיו does not define whether the כביר העזים was placed *above* or *under* or *round* the head: it merely expresses *proximity* to the head, see 26, 7.

בַבגד] So בַחבל Jos. 2, 15; בַדּוּדִים 2 Ki. 10, 7. To be explained on the analogy of what was said on 1, 4, and 6, 8: the garment, the cord, the pots, are each not determined by some antecedent reference or allusion, but are fixed in the writer's mind, and defined accordingly by the article, *by the purpose to which it is, or is to be, put.* Comp. Gen. 50, 26 בָארון; Ex. 21, 20 בַשֵּׁבט with *a* rod: Nu. 17, 11 את־המחתה; 21, 9 and he put it על־הַנֵּס on *a* pole: Jud. 4, 18 בַשְּׂמִיכָה; 7, 13 האהל to *a* tent; 20, 16 every one able to sling בָאבן אל־השערה with *a* stone at *a* hair, and not miss it; *ch.* 9, 9 האיש *a* man; 10, 25 (where see note); 21, 10 בַשמלה; II 17, 13 הנחל. 17 השפחה *a* girl; 23, 21 בַשבט: in compound expressions, Ex. 16, 32 מלא הָעמר; Jud. 6, 38 מלא הַסֵּפֶל; *ch.* 10, 1 את־פך־השמן. 25, 38 (see note), etc. The principle alluded to on 6, 8 might possibly account for the art. in *some* of the passages cited, but it will not account for all: and a difference between Hebrew and English idiom must here be recognised. Comp. GK. § 126[q–s].

17. ‏למה ככה רמיתני‎] The position of ‏ככה‎ as 1 Ki. 1, 6 : cf. II 13, 4. Notice afterwards the emph. ‏הוא‎.

‏למה אמיתך‎] The use of ‏למה‎ is thoroughly idiomatic; and it is by no means to be corrected (Th.) after the paraphrase of LXX to ‏אם לא‎ : see Gen. 27, 45. 2 Ch. 25, 16 (quoted by Ges. *Thes.*, p. 770). II 2, 22—each time in deprecation : similarly Qoh. 5, 5. Introducing, however, as it does, the *ground* upon which the deprecation rests, it is virtually equivalent to *lest*, and is so rendered by LXX in the passages cited (μή ποτε, ἵνα μή)[1]. And in dialectical or late Hebrew, as in Aramaic, it actually assumes this meaning, ‏שׁ‎ (‏‬) being prefixed for the purpose of connecting it more distinctly with the principal clause. See, in OT., Cant. 1, 7, and (with ‏אשר‎) Dan. 1, 10. In Aram. ܠܡܐ is thus the ordinary word for *lest*, ‏פ‎ being not in use[2]. The punct. ‏לְמָה‎ (instead of the usual ‏לָמָּה‎), on account of the gutt. (other than ‏ח‎) : cf. 28, 9. Jud. 15, 10 etc., and before ‏יְהוָֹה‎ (i. e. ‏אֲדֹנָי‎) ψ. 10, 1 etc. See *Lex.* 554[a]; GK. § 102[n].

18. ‏בנוית‎] Qrê ‏בְּנָיוֹת‎. The origin and meaning of this word, which occurs six times in the present context, are alike obscure.

Mühlau-Volck[3] derive it as follows : نَوَى in Arabic is *to intend, propose, conceive a design, make an aim for oneself,* hence the subst. نَوًى is not merely *intention, project,* but also *the goal of a journey.* Upon this basis, M.-V. *conjecture* that the root may have come to signify *to reach the goal of a journey, to rest there, bleiben, bestehen ;* hence ‏לא ינוה‎ in Hab. 2, 5 shall not *abide,* and ‏נָוֶה‎ *place of rest after a journey* (Ort der Niederlassung, spec. für den Nomaden), and in a different application ‏נָוִית‎ *dwellings,* of the Coenobium of the prophets. The explanation is in the last degree precarious, the process by which a secondary and subordinate sense in Arabic is made the origin of the primary sense in Hebrew being an incredible one, and the number of stages—all hypothetical—assumed to have been passed through before the age of Samuel being most improbable. All

[1] And so elsewhere in LXX, as Gen. 47, 19 ; Ex. 32, 12 ; Joel 2, 17 (ὅπως μή) ; ψ. 79, 10; 115, 2.

[2] In OT. ‏די־למה‎ Ezr. 7, 23. In Phoenician ‏לם‎ (i. e. ‏לְם‎) by itself has the force of *lest* (*CIS.* 2 [= Cooke, *NSI.* 5], 21 ‏לם יסגרינם אלנם‎ = *ne tradant eos Dei*) : in Hebrew it is not clear that ‏למה‎ alone has acquired this force, for Qoh. 7, 17. 18. Neh. 6, 3 are sentences in which the sense of *why? wherefore?* appears to be distinctly present to the writers.

[3] In the 11th ed. of Ges. *Handwörterbuch* (1890). In Buhl's editions (1895–1910) of the same work the explanation is not repeated.

that can be said is that, if the text of Hab. 2, 5. ψ. 68, 13 be sound, Hebrew must have possessed a verb נוה with some such sense as *to sit quiet* (which does not, however, appear in the cognate languages); and that נָוֶה may perhaps be connected with it. נָוֶה, however, does not signify 'habitation' in general, it denotes in particular a *pastoral abode* (see especially II 7, 8), and is only applied figuratively to other kinds of *abode* in poetry Ex. 15, 13, or the higher prose II 15, 25. The application is so different that it seems doubtful whether a word closely allied to this would have been chosen to denote a residence of prophets. Ewald, *Hist.* iii. 70 (E. T. 49 f.), starting from the same root follows a different track, and reaches accordingly a different goal. نَوَى is *to intend, propose, direct the mind upon* a thing; hence — here begins the process of conjecture — *to study* ('for what is study but the direction of the mind upon an object?'), and the subst. a *place of study*, a *college*, a *school!* Again, not merely is a hypothetical change of meaning postulated: but a very special sense, unsupported by analogy, and unheard of afterwards, is assumed to have been acquired by the word at a relatively early period in the history of the Hebrew language.

The Kt. should probably be pointed בְּנָיַת (cf. LXX ἐν Αὐαθ[1]) with the original fem. termination, preserved in many old proper names (*Tenses*, § 181 n.: comp. e. g. צָרְפַת, רִבְבַת, בִּצְקַת). The form נָוִית is rare (נוית, עמית, צפית: Ol. p. 412). It is just possible (on the ground of the masc. נָוֶה) that the word in itself might have signified *dwelling* (although, as Dr. Weir remarks, *the absence of the art.* is an objection to its being supposed to have any such appellative sense here): more probably it is the name of some locality in Ramah, the signification of which is lost to us.

20. עמד נצב] 'standing as one appointed over (1 Ki. 4, 7. Ruth 2, 5. 6) them.' Both ptcpp. are represented in LXX, but the combination is peculiar and suspicious, שֹׁכֵב יָשֵׁן 26, 7 being not quite parallel. Omit prob. עמד (Sm.). For וירא read ויראו (Versions).

22. עד בור הגדול אשר בשכו] LXX ἕως τοῦ φρέατος τοῦ ἅλω τοῦ ἐν τῷ Σεφει = עַד בּוֹר הַגֹּרֶן אֲשֶׁר בַּשֶּׁפִי, no doubt rightly. The article in הגדול is irregular (on 6, 18); and a שפי or *bare height* (often in Jeremiah) is a natural site for a גרן.

22b. ויאמר] sc. האומר, as 16, 4. The more usual ויאמרו is a סביר (cf. 12, 5, with the note).

23. שם] LXX ἐκεῖθεν = מִשָּׁם. So Th. Klo. Weir, Bu. etc.

---

[1] ν having dropped out in transcription; comp. Jud. 16, 4 ἐν Αλσωρηχ for בנחל שרק. Am. 1, 1 ἐν Ακκαρειμ for בנקדים.

וַיֵּלֶךְ הָלוֹךְ ויתנבא] Irregular: comp. II 16, 13 הֹלֵךְ הָלַךְ וַיְקַלֵּל; and with the pf. (as a freq.) 13, 19 וַתֵּלֶךְ הָלוֹךְ וְזָעֵקָה. Jos. 6, 13ᵃ הֹלְכִים הָלוֹךְ וְתָקְעוּ בַּשּׁוֹפָרוֹת. These four are the only irregular cases. The normal type would be וַיֵּלֶךְ הָלוֹךְ והתנבא (on 6, 12ᵃ); and this should doubtless be restored in each (so Ehrl.): notice the regular type in Jos. 6, 13ᵇ (הוֹלֵךְ . . . הָלוֹךְ ותקוע).

24. עָרֹם] i.e. as Is. 20, 2. Mic. 1, 8 without the upper garment, and wearing only the long linen tunic, which was worn next the skin. The passage records another explanation of the origin of the proverb הֲגַם שָׁאוּל בַּנְּבִיאִים, which refers it to a different occasion from the one described in 10, 10 f.

20, 1–10. David entreats Jonathan to let him know if he can discover that it is really Saul's purpose to kill him, and suggests to him a plan by which he may do this (*vv.* 5–7).

1. כִּי מבקש] with no subj. expressed: cf. on 17, 25.

2. לוֹ עשׂה] The Kt. can only be pointed לוֹ עָשָׂה i.e. '*If* my father *had* done . . . ,' which, however, yields a sense unsuited to the context. The Qrê לֹא is therefore to be preferred. As for the verb, עָשָׂה would be grammatical (*hath not done* = doth not do: *Tenses*, § 12): but the impf., which is expressed by the Versions, is preferable (Am. 3, 7): 'My father doth not anything great or small, without revealing it to me' (lit. uncovering my ear: 9, 15).

3. וישבע] עוֹד is no doubt an accidental dittograph of ע and ר: but וישבע seems sufficiently justified by the חי יהוה which follows: David strongly protests that there *is* ground for his suspicion of Saul's intentions. There is thus no occasion to follow We. al. in reading with LXX (καὶ ἀπεκρίθη) וַיָּשֶׁב for וישבע: השיב alone for השיב פ' דבר (II 3, 11) is found only in poetry, and *late* Heb. (see on 12, 3).

ואולם] a strong adversative: *but indeed*, as Ex. 9, 16 (*Lex.* 19ᵇ).

כִּי] introducing the fact asserted in the oath, as 14, 44 etc.

כפשׂע] '*the like of* a footstep, etc.' כְּ is properly an undeveloped subst., *the like of*[1]: for instances of a subst. compounded with it forming the subj. of a sentence, see Lev. 14, 35 כְּנֶגַע נראה לי בבית. Lam. 1, 20 כַּבַּיִת כַּמָּוֶת.

---

[1] See *Lex.* 453ᵃ; and especially Fleischer, *Kleinere Schriften*, i. 2 (1885), pp. 376–381.

פשׂע] only here : the meaning is clear from the Aram. פיסעא, ڣمُخَ. Comp. the cognate verb in Is. 27, 4.

4. Jonathan offers to test his father's state of mind, in any way that David may suggest.

מה תאמר וג׳] lit. 'what doth thy soul say? and I will do it for thee :' = *whatsoever* thy soul saith, I will do it for thee : similarly Est. 5, 3. 6 : *Tenses*, § 62. Cf. on 11, 12.

נפשׁך] The נפשׁ in Hebrew psychology is the usual seat of the emotional impulses : hence נפשׁך (נפשׁי, נפשׁו) is used as a *pathetic* periphrasis for the simple pronoun : Gen. 27, 4. 19. 25. 31 ; Nu. 23, 10 and Jud. 16, 30 (obliterated in AV., on account of the difference in the Hebrew and English conception of the 'soul') ; *ch.* 2, 16 (comp. note) : in poetry (often in parallelism with the pronoun), ψ. 3, 3. 11, 1. 34, 3. 35, 9 ; Is. 1, 14. 42, 1. 55, 2 ; Jer. 5, 9. 29 al. Its use, in a passage like the present, is a mark of grace and courtesy.

תאמר] 'LXX ἐπιθυμεῖ, reading perhaps תְּאַוֶּה [cf. on 2, 16], which is usually the Hebrew of ἐπιθυμέω, or תִּשְׁאַל, as in Dt. 14, 26, where also it is connected with נפשׁך. Only here is ἐπιθ. the translation of אמר' (Dr. Weir). Bu. Sm. Now. all read תאוה : cf. II 3, 21.

5. ישׁב אשׁב] 'David, as appears from *v.* 25 ff., was, together with Abner and Jonathan, Saul's daily and regular companion at table : thus the sentence ואנכי ישׁב וג׳ cannot be so related to the preceding one, as though the new-moon were the occasion of his being a guest at the king's table : on the contrary, the new-moon is rather alleged as the excuse for his absence. Consequently, the rendering, "To-morrow is new-moon, and I must sit with the king at meat" is excluded ; and the only course remaining open is to read with LXX ישׁב לא אשׁב "To-morrow is the new-moon, and I will *not* sit with the king at meat ; but thou shalt let me go " etc.' (We.). So Löhr, Sm. Now. : Bu. dissents. For the new-moon, as a festival and popular holiday, see 2 Ki. 4, 23. Am. 8, 5.

השׁלשׁית] cannot be construed grammatically with הערב, and is omitted by LXX. Targ. '(Or) on the third day.' 'But *on the third day* is always בַּיּוֹם הַשְּׁלִישִׁי ; and שְׁלִישִׁית, when without a noun, is always *a third part*' (Dr. Weir). Probably the word is a gloss due to a scribe who observed that in point of fact David remained in concealment till the third day (*v.* 35).

6. In this verse we have two idiomatic uses of the inf. abs. combined: (*a*) to emphasize the terms of a condition expressed by אִם, which has been briefly noticed before (1, 11): add Ex. 15, 26. 19, 5. 21, 5. 22, 3. 11. 12. 16. 22. 23, 22; *ch.* 12, 25. 14, 30, below *vv.* 7ᵇ. 9. 21: (*b*) at the beginning of a speech, where a slight emphasis is often required: so *v.* 3. Gen. 43, 3. 7. 20. Jud. 9, 8. *ch.* 10, 16. 14, 28. 43. 23, 10; II 1, 6; 20, 18.

נִשְׁאַל] on the force of the *Nif.* (*asked for himself, asked leave;* so Neh. 13, 6), see Ew. § 123ᵇ; Stade, § 167ᵇ; GK. § 51ᵉ.

זֶבַח הַיָּמִים] as 1, 21: cf. on 1, 3.

7. אִם כֹּה יֹאמַר] See on 14, 9.

כָּלְתָה . . . . מֵעִמּוֹ] *v.* 9. 25, 17. Est. 7, 7: *is accomplished* (= determined) *of him* or *on his part.* מֵעִם expresses origination (= Greek παρὰ with gen.): 1 Ki. 2, 33. 12, 15. Is. 8, 18. 28, 29.

8. עַל עַבְדְּךָ] Everywhere else עָשָׂה חֶסֶד עִם, or, occasionally (*Lex.* 794ᵃ), אֶת or לְ. There occur indeed נָטָה חֶסֶד אֶל Gen. 39, 21, and נָטָה חֶסֶד עַל Ezr. 7, 28. 9, 9: but עַל suits as naturally with נָטָה as it is alien to עָשָׂה. Doubtless, therefore, עִם should be restored, which is expressed also by LXX, Pesh. Targ. For the 'covenant,' see 18, 3.

הֲמִיתֵנִי אַתָּה] For the emphatic position of אַתָּה, cf. on 17, 56.

וְעַד אָבִיךָ לָמָּה זֶּה תְבִיאֵנִי] 'but to thy father wherefore shouldest thou bring me?' Notice the emphatic position of עַד אָבִיךָ, *before* the adv.: cf. before הֲ and הֲלֹא Jer. 22, 15. Neh. 13, 17. Job 34, 31 כִּי אֶל אֵל הֶאָמַר for unto God did one ever say? before כִּי Gen. 18, 20. 1 Ki. 8, 37. Mic. 5, 4. Ez. 14, 9. 13 al.; before אִם ψ. 66, 18; before מָה Est. 1, 15. 9, 12ᵃ; before עַד ψ. 141, 10.

9. חָלִילָה לָּךְ] in answer to the remark in the previous verse; so *v.* 2.

כִּי אִם וְג'] 'for if I *know* that the evil is determined of my father to come upon thee, shall I not tell thee *that?*' וְלֹא as Ex. 8, 22 (GK. § 150ᵃ; cf. on 11, 12. 16, 4): but very probably הֲלֹא should be read (so Bu.). Ke. We. construe affirmatively, assuming an aposiopesis: '. . . and I do not tell thee *that*' (*sc.* so and so may God do to me!)[1].

אתה]ולא אתה וג' is very emphatic: cf. on 15, 1 (*d*); and 21, 10.

10. או מה־יענך אביך קשה] '*if perchance* (?) thy father answer thee with something harsh.' If the text is correct, או must have here the unusual sense of *if perchance* (RV.). There is no difficulty in the indef. מה (19, 3), or in the position of קשה in apposition to it at the end (see on 26, 18): but או means as a rule *or* or *or if* (Ex. 21, 31 al.); and *if perchance* is so different from *or* or *or if*, that it is very doubtful if it is sufficiently supported by this passage and Lev. 26, 41. Most probably we should read here אם for או מה, and in Lev. וְאָם for אוֹ־אָם (Bu. Sm. Now.).

11–17. Jonathan renews his promise to let David know, if he finds his father's evil intentions towards him confirmed (*vv.* 12–13. 17). In view of David's future accession to the throne, he implores David's kindness for himself, or, in case he should not survive, for his children (*vv.* 14–16 : cf. 2 S. 9). It will be noticed that whereas in *vv.* 1–10 David entreats the help of Jonathan, the *rôles* are here reversed, and Jonathan entreats the favour of David.

12–13. This difficult passage is best rendered: 'Yahweh, God of Israel [be witness]! when I shall sound my father to-morrow [(or) the third (day)], and behold there is good toward David, shall I not (ולא, as *v.* 9, though again הֲלֹא would be better) then send unto thee, and disclose it to thee? Yahweh do so to me and more also: if one make evil towards thee pleasing to my father[2], I will disclose it to thee' etc. (so RV., the sentence being merely somewhat more closely accommodated to English idiom). It is true that commonly a more emphatic particle follows כה יעשה וג', and that the analogy of other passages might have led us to expect כי אם ייטיב . . . ., כי אגלה וג' (II 3, 9) or אם לא כי ייטיב . . . ., אגלה וג' (cf. II 19, 14); but the types of sentences with כה יעשה וג' are not perfectly uniform, and there

---

[1] It is difficult to think that Haupt is right in identifying לֹא (*la*) here with the *Arabic* asseverative particle ل (*AJSL.* xxii, 1906, p. 201, cf. p. 206).

[2] Or, with Klo. (see p. 164, note on ייטב), inserting להביא after אבי, 'if one make it pleasing to my father to bring evil upon thee.'

seems to be no *necessity* for such a particle to be used, if the sense is sufficiently plain without it. At the beginning, if יהוה is a *vocative*, it agrees badly with the speech following, in which the second person is throughout Jonathan, and in this case עַד has probably fallen out after דוד (so Pesh. RV.)[1]. On כעת מחר see on 9, 16; and on נלה אזן, 9, 15. השלשית is as perplexing and intrusive as in *v.* 5, and is no doubt, as there, 'a correction *ex eventu.*'

והנה] lit. *and behold*, used similarly in the enunciation of a particular hypothetical alternative, Dt. 13, 15; 17, 4; 19, 18; and in Lev. 13—14 frequently. Comp. above, on 9, 7.

ייטב] The punctuation (*make good* or *pleasing* to) implies as subject המיטיב (on 16, 4). Perhaps, however, the word ought to be read as *Qal* יִיטַב (*be pleasing* to), construed with את as יֵרַע II 11, 25, where see note (though Klo.'s להביא after אבי would remove even this irregularity). But the Heb. idiom for *seem good to* is not ייטב אל but יִיטַב בְּעֵינֵי; so יִיטַב after all may be right.

14—15[a]. Another difficult passage. 'And wilt thou not, if I am still alive (*sc.* when thou comest to the throne), wilt thou not shew toward me the kindness of Yahweh, that I die not?' The second ולא must be treated as merely resumptive of the first: cf. כי 1 Ki. 20, 31; ויהי Gen. 27, 30; והיה Dt. 20, 11. But most moderns prefer to point וְלֻא (II 18, 12) for וְלֹא twice: 'And *oh that*, if I am still alive, *oh that thou wouldest* shew toward me the kindness of Yahweh!' (on ולא אמות see the next note). Resumption, however, of either וְלֻא or וְלֹא would be very unusual (see on 25, 26); and what we should *expect* is simply חסד אלהים, as חסד י"י, וְאִם עודני חי הֲלֹא תעשה וג' II 9, 3.

ולא אמות] This clause does not in itself cause difficulty: nevertheless LXX, Vulg. both render as if it expressed the opposite alternative to אם עודני חי (καὶ ἐὰν θανάτῳ ἀποθάνω, *si vero mortuus fuero*). Accepting this view, we must either (Sm.) read וְלֹא מוֹת אמות for וְלֹא אמות (though לֹא would be unusual in such a connexion), or (Bu. Now.) read וְאִם מוֹת אמות, supposing ולא to have come into the text by some

<hr>

[1] Ehrlich, however, regards יהוה א' י' as an accus. expressing an oath (= By ....!): cf. in the Talm. הָאֱלֹהִים = *By God!* הזה המעון = *By the Temple!* (*Randglossen*, i. 216).

error—אם מות‎, for instance, having dropped out, אמות‎ being connected with *v.* 14, and ולא‎ being needed to complete the sense. Render then (connecting with *v.* 15), 'And, *if I should die*, thou wilt not cut off thy mercy from my house for ever[1].' Or, with a slighter change in MT., but at the cost of another 'resumption,' we might read ולא אם מות אמות ולא תכרית וג'‎ 'And thou wilt not, if I should die, thou wilt not cut off,' etc. But again, what we should *expect* is ואם מות אמות לא תכרית חסדך וג'‎.

15[b]–16. ולא בהכרת וג'‎] A third difficult passage. *V.* 15 will just admit of the rendering, 'And thou wilt not cut off thy kindness from my house for ever, *and not* (= yea, not) when Yahweh cuts off the enemies of David,' etc. But the repetition of ולא‎ is very awkward; and in *v.* 16 not merely is the covenant concluded with the *house* of David strange, but clause *b* is anacoluthic, and what is expected is not that Yahweh should require it from the hand of David's enemies, but from the hand of David himself, in case he should fail to fulfil the conditions of the covenant. LXX points to another and preferable reading, uniting 15[b] and 16, and treating the whole as a continuation of Jonathan's speech in 15[a] (as rendered in the last note): καὶ εἰ μή, ἐν τῷ ἐξαίρειν Κύριον τοὺς ἐχθροὺς Δαυειδ ἕκαστον ἀπὸ προσώπου τῆς γῆς, εὑρεθῆναι [cod. A ἐξαρθῆναι] τὸ ὄνομα τοῦ Ἰωναθαν ἀπὸ τοῦ οἴκου Δαυειδ i. e. ולא[2] בהכרת יהוה את איבי דוד איש מעל פני האדמה יכָּרֵת‎ שֵׁם יהונתן מעם בית דוד‎ = 'And when Yahweh cutteth off the enemies of David, each one from the face of the ground, *the name of* Jonathan *shall* not be cut off *from* the house of David.' The clause ובקש וג'‎, which was incongruous in MT., is now in its appropriate place, in Jonathan's speech, as a final wish expressed by him on behalf of his friend: 'and may Yahweh require [Gen. 31, 39. 43, 9. Jos. 22, 23; cf. II 4, 11] it at the hand of David's enemies!' (viz. if they presume to attack or calumniate him). The reading is also supported by 24, 22, where Jonathan says to David, 'Swear to me now by Yahweh that thou wilt not cut off my seed after me, nor destroy my name out

---

[1] We.'s ולא אם מות אמות לא תכרית‎ is a form of sentence against analogy.

[2] We. Bu. ולאלא‎ *and may not* . . . ! (LXX, representing ולא‎ by καὶ εἰ μή, vocalized wrongly ולא‎: see below, on II 13, 26; and comp. Jer. 11, 21 LXX).

of my father's house.' Jonathan, being David's brother-in-law, and prescient that David will succeed Saul upon the throne, prays that when his enemies are destroyed—especially, in accordance with the usual Oriental custom (cf. 1 Ki. 15, 29. 16, 11. 2 Ki. 10, 6. 11, 1), the family of his predecessor—his own relationship with David's house may not be forgotten or disowned. David's acknowledgement of the obligation is recorded II 9, 1 : cf. 21, 7. The expression נכרת שֵׁם מעם .... recurs Ruth 4, 10.

The passage is very difficult ; and other suggestions have been made about it. Thus Smith reads : 'And if (וְלֹא), when Yahweh cutteth off the enemies of David, etc., the name of Jonathan should be cut off with the house of *Saul* (so Luc.), then will [or may] Yahweh require it at the hand of *David ;*' i. e. should David forget the covenant, God will be the avenger. Upon this view אֹיְבֵי will be a scribe's insertion to avoid the imprecation on David (cf. 25, 22. II 12, 14). For the constr. of לֹא, see *Lex.* 530, לֹו 1 b, וְלֹא 1 b : it occurs once (Mic. 2, 11) with a pf. and *waw* consec. in the apodosis. But with regard to all these restorations, it must be remembered that the separation of either וְלֹא or וְלֹא from its verb by a long intervening clause is very un-Hebraic : in ordinary Hebrew we should expect either וּבהכרית . . . . . . , לֹא אִם (or אם) יִכָּרֵת וג', or (with וְלֹא בהכרית) the *resumption* of וְלֹא (or וְלֹא) before יִכָּרֵת (cf. on *v.* 14-15ª ; and see more fully on 25, 26 ; *Tenses,* § 118 *n.*), though it may be doubted if there are any cases of this quite parallel to that of וְלֹא (or וְלֹא) here or in *v.* 14-15ª.

17. ויוסף יהונתן להשביע את דוד] 'And Jonathan *made* David *swear* again.' But this does not agree with the context. 'The impassioned entreaties addressed by Jonathan, *vv.* 14-16, to David might with some show of plausibility be termed an *adjuration* of David : as, however, they are entreaties *on behalf of himself,* they cannot be regarded as any special token of his love *towards* David. It follows that באהבתו אתו in *v.* 17 agrees only with the reading of LXX [1] ויוסף יהונתן לְהַשָּׁבֵע לדוד "And Jonathan *sware to David* again,"—i. e. repeated the oath of *v.* 13, that he would inform David if his father still meditated evil against him,—which also has the advantage of admitting of a strict interpretation : for *v.* 12 f. (to which the reference will now be) express an actual oath, whereas *vv.* 14-16 do not properly express an adjuration' (We.). With 17ᵇ cf. 18, 3ᵇ.

---

[1] Or (Bu. Sm.) אל דוד (Jer. 38, 16).

18–23. The sequel to *v.* 10. Jonathan unfolds to David his plan for acquainting him with Saul's intentions towards him.

19. ושלשת תרד מאד] For תרד LXX has ἐπισκέψῃ, i.e. תִּפָּקֵד, in-correctly vocalized for תִּפָּקֵד *thou shalt be missed* (so Targ. תתבעי, Pesh. ܐ̇ܬܒܥܐ), which agrees as it should do with מאד *greatly*, and is evidently right. To *go down* is an idea which, as used here (Jud. 19, 11 is different), would not be qualified by *greatly:* RV. *quickly* takes an unwarrantable liberty with the Hebrew.

שִׁלֵּשׁ is a denom., *to do a thing the third time* (1 Ki. 18, 34), or, as here, *on the third day*[1]. Lit. 'and thou shalt act on the third day, thou shalt be missed greatly' = and thou shalt *on the third day be missed* greatly; cf. Is. 29, 4 ושפלת מארץ תדברי lit. 'and thou shalt be humbled, thou shalt speak from the earth' = and thou shalt *speak humbly* from the earth, the second verb, in each case, defining the application of the first. The principle is the same as that which underlies the idiom explained on 2, 3 אל תרבו תדברו, though as a rule the two verbs are in the same tense (GK. § 120ᵍ *end*[2]).

האבן האזל] LXX τὸ ἐργαβ ἐκεῖνο: cf. *v.* 41, where מאצל הנגב is rendered ἀπὸ τοῦ ἀργαβ. Clearly, in both passages, the translators found before them the same word, which they did not understand, and therefore, as in similar cases (e. g. *v.* 20 Αρματταρει; 14, 1 al. Μεσσαβ), simply transliterated. And in both passages their reading, as compared with the present Hebrew text, has the presumption of originality in its favour. Here האזל is a *vox nihili;* in *v.* 41 'beside *the south*' is a position which does not admit of being fixed, and from which, therefore, no one can be conceived as arising; at the same

---

[1] Expressions not quite identical, but analogous, are cited by Roed. from Arabic in the *Thes.*, p. 1427ᵇ.

[2] Better here (by the side of Is. 29, 4) than in § 120ᶜ, where the second verb is *subordinate* to the first (*Tenses*, § 163 *Obs.*, second paragraph). Lagarde (*Bildung der Nom.*, p. 212) illustrates the combination of *different* tenses from analogous constructions in other Semitic languages: thus in Arabic بَقِىَ يَنْظُرُ = *he continued looking*, كَرَبَ يَذُوبُ = *he was nearly melting;* لاَ يَكُونُ بَقِىَ *there shall not have been left* (Wright, *Ar. Gramm.* ii. § 10); and in Ethiopic ለመጽእ፡ ህሎ፡ *he is about to come*, ወድእ፡ ይሰክብ፡ *it hath finished to lie = it is already laid*, Mt. 3, 10 (Dillm. *Eth. Gr.* § 89. 2, *Eth. Lex.* col. 932 f.).

time, there is the presumption that אצל was in both passages followed
by some similar word. Restore, therefore, here (הַלָּז or הָאֶרְגָּב הַלָּז[1])
and in *v.* 41 הלו :מאצל הָאֶרְגָּב has occurred before in 14, 1, and is
expressed here also by Pesh. (ܐܪܓܒ): ארגב is a word which (cf. רֶגֶב)
would naturally signify a *mound of earth.*

20. וָאני] Notice the emphatic pronoun.

ואני . . . אורה] LXX אורה [צדה] בחצים אֲשַׁלֵּשׁ אני, the claims of
which are well stated by We. אֲשַׁלֵּשׁ will be construed as in *v.* 19,
to which Jonathan's promise now forms the counterpart, 'And I on
the third day will shoot to its side with arrows.' It is true, of course,
that Jonathan in fact shoots but one arrow, and the boy at once runs
to fetch it; but in the first *general* description of what Jonathan will
do, the expressions 'shoot with arrows,' 'find the arrows that I shoot'
are naturally used. As a מוֹעֵד, however, must evidently be carried
out in accordance with the terms arranged, the fact that in *v.* 35 ff.
no mention is made of the *three* arrows of MT. is an indication that
they were not originally part of *v.* 20. צדה, though omitted in LXX,
may be retained, but must be pointed צִדּ֫ה (i.e. צִדּוֹ, referring to הארגב:
see on II 21, 1). In MT. צִדָּה (not צדה, with ה *loc.*) is for צִדָּהּ
(referring to האבן), the *mappiq* being omitted, as occasionally happens
(about 30 times), e.g. Ex. 9, 18; 2 Ki. 8, 6; Is. 23, 17. 18: Ew.
§ 247ᵈ (2); Stade, § 347ᶜ; GK. §§ 91ᵉ (under '3*rd fem.*'), 103ᵍ.

לשלח לי] *so as to send it for me* etc. The reflexive ל, implying that
the שלח is done *with reference to* the speaker, or for his pleasure,
cannot be properly reproduced in our idiom. Comp. on II 18, 5.

21–22. החצים] LXX throughout have the sing., i.e. הַחֵצִי, an
unusual form (see on *v.* 36ᵇ), which might readily be changed errone-
ously into a pl., as in MT.

21. לך מצא] Either prefix לאמר (which is required in prose), or
(Sm. Ehrl.) read למצא.

קחנו ובאה] As the text stands, קחנו is addressed to *David,* the suffix
relating to the lad: 'Fetch him and come.' We. reading with LXX
החצי (sg.) makes קחנו the end of the words addressed to the boy,
'fetch it,' and treats ובאה as beginning the apodosis. But though

---

[1] Like the sporadic קָאם דָּאן, רָאשׁ לָאם (II 12, 1): GK. §§ 7ᵇ, 23ᵍ, 72ᵖ.

הַחֵצִי may be right, for the apodosis to be introduced by ו and the *imperative* is most unusual, if indeed it occurs at all in the OT. ; if, therefore, this view of קְחֶנּוּ be adopted, it will be necessary to read either וּבָאתָ or (Bu. Sm.) בֹּאָה, for וְבֹאָה; the latter is favoured by the corresponding לְךָ in *v.* 22. With אֵין דבר, cf. Nu. 20, 19.

22. שְׁלַחֲךָ] 'will have sent thee away' (*sc.* in the case supposed). The pf. as 14, 10; Lev. 19, 8; II 5, 24 (*Tenses*, § 17; GK. § 106°).

23. וְהַדָּבָר אֲשֶׁר . . .] the *casus pendens:* GK. § 143ᵃ. The reference is to David's promise to shew kindness to Jonathan and his descendants in the future (*vv.* 14–16).

24–34. Jonathan, adopting the plan suggested by David (*vv.* 5–7), discovers what his father's intentions towards him are.

25. וַיָּקָם יְהוֹנָתָן] LXX καὶ προέφθασεν τὸν Ἰωναθαν (Luc. more correctly αὐτὸν Ἰωναθαν), implying וַיִּקְדַּם. *Rose up* is out of place : the relative position of those at the table is described, and Jonathan *was in front*, opposite to Saul : the seat opposite to Abner was vacant. True, קָדַם commonly denotes *to come* or *go in front ;* but not perhaps necessarily, and the use of the word here would closely resemble that in ψ. 68, 26 קִדְּמוּ שָׁרִים the singers *were in front*.

26. בִּלְתִּי טָהוֹר] The only passage in which בלתי is used to negative an adj. (as elsewhere—at least in poetry—בְּלִי, e. g. Hos. 7, 8). It negatives a subst. once, Is. 14, 6. See *Lex.* 116ᵇ.

כִּי־לֹא טָהוֹר] LXX ὅτι οὐ κεκαθάρισται = כִּי־לֹא טֹהַר, which relieves the tautology of MT.: 'he is not clean; for he hath not been cleansed.' As thus read, the clause will state the ground why Saul supposed David to be still בִּלְתִּי טָהוֹר.

27. וַיְהִי מִמָּחֳרַת הַחֹדֶשׁ הַשֵּׁנִי] Keil: 'And on the morrow of the new-moon there was the second (day),'—a fact so patent as hardly to be worth recording. Better with LXX (and substantially RV., for the word cannot be *understood*) insert בַּיּוֹם before הַשֵּׁנִי, 'on the morrow . . . ., even on the second day.' A slight redundancy of expression is not out of harmony with Hebrew style, especially when, as here, the 'second day' will suggest to the reader a repetition of the scene described, *v.* 24 f. On מִמָּחֳרַת, see GK. § 80ᵍ *n.*

29. וְהוּא צִוָּה־לִי אָחִי] Cf. ψ. 87, 5 וְהוּא יְכוֹנְנֶהָ עֶלְיוֹן 'and *He* will establish it, even the Most High.' The unusual form of expression

may have been intended to suggest that David had received the command from one whom he would not willingly disobey. But it does not read naturally. We. Bu. would read וְהֵא *and lo* (Gen. 47, 23. Ez. 16, 43†; cf. Aram. הָא). For the words quoted LXX express וַיְצַוּ לִי אַחַי. This, or וְהֵא צִוָּה לִי אַחַי, is most probable (note 'my *brethren*' just below).

אֶחָי] in pause for אָחַי: see GK. § 29ᵛ. So הַחֲרֵב, but הֶחֱרַב.

30. בֶּן נַעֲוַת הַמַּרְדוּת] Commonly rendered 'son of a perverse[1] woman (נַעֲוַת being ptcp. Nif. fem.) in respect of rebelliousness.' The expression is, however, peculiar, and excites suspicion. The genitive is attached commonly to a descriptive adj. for the purpose of defining it (Ew. § 288ᶜ; GK. § 128ˣ,ʸ): thus (a) בַּר לֵב pure *of heart,* נְקִי כַפַּיִם clean *of hands ;* (b) אֹבֵד עֵצוֹת perishing *in regard to* counsels ; נְשׂוּי פֶּשַׁע forgiven *in respect of* transgression ; (c) סָרַת טָעַם (Pr. 11, 22) a woman turned aside *in respect of* discretion (= turned aside from discretion); שָׁבֵי פֶשַׁע (Is. 59, 22) = those turned back from transgression ; שׁוּבֵי מִלְחָמָה (Mic. 2, 8) = averse from battle. מַרְדוּת, however, does not *define* נַעֲוַת, but repeats the same idea under a different form. Further, מַרְדוּת, if derived from מָרַד *to rebel,* ought by analogy (cf. מַלְכוּת, עַבְדוּת, יַלְדוּת: Ol. § 219ᵃ; GK. § 86ᵏ) to be pointed מְרָדוּת (with aspirated ד). On these grounds, Lagarde, in a note on the expression (*Mittheilungen,* i, 1884, p. 236 f.) contends that מַרְדוּת is not derived from מָרַד, but corresponds to the Syr. ܡܰܪܕܽܘܬܳܐ *discipline* (from ܪܕܳܐ to *discipline*); and connecting נעוה with غَوَى to go *astray, leave the right path,* he renders the phrase 'son of a woman *gone astray from discipline,*' comparing the Arabic expression (Lane, p. 2305ᵇ) وَلَدُ غَيَّةٍ son *of a woman gone astray,* i.e. son of a whore. But though Lagarde's argument is philologically just, the distinctively Syriac sense which it postulates for מרדות is not probable[2].

[1] Used (N. B.) in EVV. not in its modern sense, of *contrary,* but in the etym. sense of *perversus,* διεστραμμένος (Prov. 11, 20 βδέλυγμα Κυρίῳ διεστραμμέναι ὁδοί), i.e. *twisted, crooked ;* of one pursuing crooked and questionable courses (cf. the writer's *Deuteronomy,* on 32, 5, p. 353).

[2] But Lagarde is unquestionably right in maintaining that in עוה and its derivatives *two* roots, distinct in Arabic, have, as in many other cases (see *Tenses³,* § 178 (pp. 230-232); and cf. on 15, 29), been confused in Hebrew, viz. غَوَى *to bend* (e.g. in Is. 21, 3 נַעֲוֵיתִי מִשְּׁמֹעַ ; ψ. 38, 7); and غَوَى *to err, go astray*

The text must be at fault. It is best, with We., to follow LXX
(υἱὲ κορασίων αὐτομολούντων = בֶן נַעֲרֹת (הַ)מֹּרְדוֹת), at least as far as
the ר in נערת goes, and to read בֶן נַעֲרַת הַמַּרְדּוּת *son of a rebellious girl*,
i. e. of a girl who has contumaciously rebelled against her master, and
left him,—in other words, of a runaway slave-girl. We. compares
Judith 16, 12 υἱοὶ κορασίων κατεκέντησαν αὐτούς, καὶ ὡς παῖδας αὐτομολούντων ἐτίτρωσκον αὐτούς, in the Syriac version ܡܪܘ ܕܚܠܩܬ
ܐܢܘ ܡܠܟܐ ܘܐܩܬܘܐ ܘܐܚܕܘ ܘܐܡܘ ܐܢܘ ܐܡܗ ܘ[1].

בחר] LXX μέτοχος, i. e. חָבֵר art *a companion of*, which agrees with
the following לְ (see Pr. 28, 24). בחר is construed with בּ, not with לְ.
'LXX good' (Dr. Weir). So Bu. Sm. etc.

31. בֶּן מוּת] 26, 16. II 12, 5. Cf. the poet. בְּנֵי תְמוּתָה (ψ. 79, 11.
102, 21†) ; and אַנְשֵׁי מוּת II 19, 29 ; אִישׁ מוּת 1 Ki. 2, 26.

33. וַיָּטֶל] Read probably וַיִּטֹּל, as in 18, 11.

לְהָמִית . . . כִּי כַלֵּה הִיא] For this use of הִיא (which is uncommon),
cf. 2 Ki. 18, 36. Jer. 50, 15. 25. 51, 6. 11. כָּלָה is, however, else-

---

(Qor. 2, 257. 7, 143. 19, 60 and often : especially, as Lagarde abundantly shews,
opp. to شَذَّ *to go straight, to keep on the right path*), which is found in הֶעֱוָה
to act erringly, II 24, 17 al., and in the common subst. עָוֹן *iniquity*, properly *error*.
The idea expressed by עָוָה (= غَوَى) and its derivatives is thus not that of *crooked-
ness*, '*perverseness*' (= עָקַשׁ), but *deviation from the right track, error*: and this
sense is still sometimes expressed by the ancient versions : as Is. 19, 14 (though
here probably wrongly) רוּחַ עִוְעִים πνεῦμα πλανήσεως, ܪܘܚܐ ܕܛܘܥܝܝ ; Pr. 12, 8
ܘܡܣܟܢܐ ܘܚܣܝܪ נַעֲוֵה לֵב = one deficient in understanding, Vulg. *vanus et excors*
(as though *lit.* one *gone astray from* understanding). The conventional rendering
of the frequent עָוֹן by words of general import, such as ἀδικία, ἁμαρτία, *iniquitas*,
iniquity, tends to conceal from those to whom the Hebrew term is thus familiarly
represented, the metaphor which originally underlay both עָוֹן itself, and the cognate verb.

[1] In Lucian's recension of the LXX there is a second rendering of the phrase in
question, viz. γυναικοτραφῆ, i. e. (as it seems) *woman-nourished*, effeminate. Symm.
has ἀπαιδεύτων ἀποστατούντων, Theod. . . . . μετακινουμένων. Vulg. substitutes
another disparaging comparison, based upon an old Jewish Haggadah (see Rashi ;
and Aptow. *ZAW*. 1909, p. 245), Fili mulieris *virum ultro rapientis*, which seems
to stand in some relation to the first part of the paraphrase of Chrysostom (X. 301 D,
quoted by Field), as the second does to the rendering of Lucian : υἱὲ πορνιδίων
ἐπιμαινομένων ἀνδράσιν, ἐπιτρεχόντων τοῖς παριοῦσιν, ἐκνενευρισμένε καὶ μαλακὲ καὶ
μηδὲν ἔχων ἀνδρός.—Pesh. ܘܡܣܠܝ ܣܢܝ (comp. the rendering of Pr. 12, 8
cited in the last note : hardly נֶעֱדֶרֶת).

where confined to poetry, and expresses the idea of *consumption, destruction* (usually with עשה, as Is. 10, 23), not that of *complete determination.* כְלָתָה (LXX, We. etc.) for כלה היא is certainly a more idiomatic expression (cf. *vv.* 7. 9), and is to be preferred.

34. מעם השלחן] Cf. 2, 33 (*Lex.* 769ᵃ).

35–39. Jonathan acquaints David with Saul's intentions.

36. . . . הנער רץ ו] See on 9, 5. For the idiomatic *fut. instans,* מורה, cf. 10, 8. 24, 5. 1 Ki. 2, 2 ; and on 3, 11.

החצי] So 37 *bis*, 38 Kt., 21 f. (LXX), and 2 Ki. 9, 24 MT. Probably a genuine alternative form of חץ (Ew. § 186ᵉ). Though the pl. in Hebrew is חִצִּים, the form in Arabic (خِطاً) and the plural in Eth. (አሕጻ፡ አሕጻኢት፡ Dillm. col. 134) shew that there is a parallel form, the root of which is a ל"ה verb.

38. מהרה חושה] מהרה *before* the verb which it qualifies, as 2 Ki. 1, 11 מהרה רדה, ψ. 31, 3 מהרה הצילני; and (for the sake of the rhythm) 37, 2. Is. 58, 8. Ehrlich's note is arbitrary.

ויבא] LXX, Pesh. Vulg. וַיָּבֹא, which is preferable.

40–42. The final parting between Jonathan and David.

40. אשר ל'] 17, 40. 21, 8. 24, 5. 25, 7. II 3, 8. 1 Ki. 1, 8. 33. 49. 4, 2. 10, 28. 15, 20. 22, 31. 2 Ki. 11, 10. 16, 13ᵇ. Not always with a *compound* expression. Cf. GK. § 129ʰ.

41. מאצל הנגב] See on *v.* 19.

עד דוד הגדיל] There seems no occasion to alter this; and עַד הַגְדֵּל (with the inf. *abs.*) is unparalleled Hebrew.

42. אשר] = *in that, forasmuch as,* Gen. 30, 18 etc. : cf. on 15, 15.

נשבענו] Though an oath is not expressly mentioned, an agreement such as that of *vv.* 14–16 would be naturally sealed with one (cf. 24, 22). For לאמר ונ', see *v.* 23.

21, 2. נֹבֶה] So 22, 9: cf. דְּרָנָה Ez. 25, 13 ; also the anomalous punctuation ה‍ַ in the imper. רְעֵה Pr. 24, 14, and 1 and 3 pers. impf. *ch.* 28, 15 ואקראֶה (but see note), and ψ. 20, 4 יְדַשְּׁנֶה. See GK. § 90ⁱ (*end*); Ew. § 216ᶜ; Stade, § 132.

Nob, as Is. 10, 32 shews, was a place between 'Anathoth (now *'Anâta,* 2½ miles NE. of Jerusalem) and Jerusalem, whence the Temple hill could be seen; perhaps a spot on the *Râs el-Meshârif,* 1 mile N. of Jerusalem, a ridge from the brow of which (2685 ft.) the pilgrim along the north road still catches his first view of the holy city (2593 ft.). See Nob in *DB.*

אֲחִימֶלֶךְ] 'LXX Αβειμελεχ, as also in *ch.* 22. 23, 6. 26, 6. ψ. 52, 1:
on the contrary, Αχειμελεχ 30, 7. II 8, 17. The same mistranscription
occurs in 1 Ch. 18, 16 MT., where LXX has rightly Αχειμελεχ,'
We. (the readings of LXX as given by Swete).

וַיֵּחָרֵד . . . לִקְרַאת] as 16, 4.

וְאִישׁ אֵין אִתָּךְ] Cf. Gen. 40, 8 אֹתוֹ אֵין פֹּתֵר. Jud. 13, 9. 16, 15
וְלִבְּךָ אֵין אִתִּי (but Nu. 20, 5 לִשְׁתּוֹת אֵין וּמַיִם: [p. 71]). See *Lex.* 34ᵇ *top.*

3. אִישׁ אַל יֵדַע] The same expression, Jer. 36, 19. 38, 24. מְאוּמָה
as regards anything = at all.

יוֹדַעְתִּי] Po'el from יֵדַע, according to Ew. § 125ᵃ, 'to make a person
know a thing in order to determine him to act accordingly' = *to direct.*
But this explanation requires more to be supplied than is probable.
LXX διαμεμαρτύρημαι, which points to a reading יוֹעַדְתִּי, Po'el from
יָעַד (see p. 77 *bottom*), in Qal to *designate* or *appoint* (a place,
II 20, 5 ; a person, Ex. 21, 8. 9) : hence in Po'el with a sense in
which it is difficult to perceive the characteristic force of the 3rd
Arabic conjugation (Wright, *Arab. Gr.* i. § 43 : comp. above, p. 152 *n.*),
but which is at least that of the corresponding form (from وَعَدَ to
promise) in Arabic, as وَاعَدَ Arnold, *Chrestom. Arab.*, p. 197, 10 ;
Qor. 7, 138 ; 20, 82 وواعدناكم جانب الطّور الأيمن and *we appointed
you* to the right side of the mountain. So here, 'the young men *I* have
appointed to the place of such and such a one.' The Hif. הוֹעִיד is used
in a similar, but specially *forensic,* sense Jer. 49, 19 = 50, 44 ; Job 9, 19.
Dr. Weir however writes : 'Is it not rather יָעַדְתִּי ? comp. Jer. 47, 7
אֶל חוּף הַיָּם שָׁם יְעָדָהּ.' The Qal would certainly seem to express all
that is required.

פְּלֹנִי אַלְמֹנִי] So Ru. 4, 1†: in Dan. 8, 13 פַּלְמֹנִי—the *one* example
of a real contraction which the Hebrew language affords. فُلَان
(Qor. 25, 30) and فلٰن are used in the same sense, perhaps derived
from the root of פָּלָה, and meaning properly a *separate, particular*
one. אַלְמֹנִי perhaps signifies *one whose name is withheld* (from אלם
to be dumb). Ew. § 106ᶜ renders, ' ein gewisser verschwiegener.'

4. וְעַתָּה מַה וג'] Keil, RV. and others: 'And now what is under
thine hand? Five loaves of bread give into my hand, or whatsoever
there is present.' But this leaves the emphatic position of חֲמִשָּׁה לֶחֶם

unaccounted for: and how could David ask specifically for five loaves, when his previous words had just implied that he did not know whether Aḥimelech possessed them? Read, with LXX (A, Luc.) εἰ εἰσίν (in B the first εἰ has dropped out), אִם for מה ('And now, *if* there are under thy hand five loaves of bread, give them into my hand, or whatsoever there is present'); or else (Ehrlich), מַה־יֵּשׁ תחת ידך אם יֵשׁ לחם תנה בידי וג׳. הנמצא lit. *that which is found,* i. e. that which is here present, as 13, 16. Gen. 19, 15. Jud. 20, 48. An idiomatic use of the *Nif.* of מצא.

5. אל תחת ידי] The use of אל here is destitute of analogy. In Jer. 3, 6. Zech. 3, 10. Ez. 10, 2 תחת אל of course expresses *motion* under. Here it is simply a corrupt repetition of חל.

לחם קדש יש] The position of יש after לחם קדש is partly for variety (after the preceding clause with אין), partly for emphasis: comp. Is. 43, 8 וְעֵינַיִם יֵשׁ; and אַיִן similarly, Lev. 26, 37. Mic. 7, 2 וישר באדם אָיִן. Pr. 17, 16. 25, 14 (cf. Gen. 2, 5. Is. 37, 3 al.).

6. כי אם] apparently, as Jud. 15, 7, with the force of an oath: see Ges. *s.v.* who renders *hercle.*

אשה] a good example of a sing. term used collectively. For other rather noticeable instances see Gen. 30, 37 מקל (note the following בהן). Jud. 19, 12 עיר (followed by הִנֵּה). 21, 16 (אשה as here). Jer. 4, 29[b] עיר (note בהן). Cf. GK. § 123[b]. Also in איש ישראל, etc. (14, 24, and often); and with certain numerals (as שלשים איש), GK. § 134[e-h].

עצרה־לנו] kept away (viz. by a religious *taboo,* on account of war being a sacred work) *in reference to* us, i. e. (Anglice) *from* us: cf. ל construed with verbs of removing or withholding in ψ. 40, 11; 84, 12; Job 12, 20; and in the Syr. ܟ݂ܪ݂ܝ. War was regarded as sacred; and the prohibition of women to men engaged in it is wide-spread (*DB.* iv. 827[b]; W. R. Smith, *Rel. Sem.*[2] 455).

כתמול שלשם וג׳] 'as heretofore (i. e. on previous occasions), when I have gone forth (viz. on a military expedition), so that the gear (clothes, arms, etc.) of the young men is holy, even though it is a common (i. e. not a sacred) journey; how much more so [*Lex.* אף 2], when to-day they will be consecrated with (their) gear?'— a distinction being drawn between expeditions of an ordinary kind, and campaigns opened by consecration of warriors (cf. the Heb. expression to 'consecrate' war, and warriors: Mic. 3, 5. Jer. 6, 4. 22, 7. 51, 27. 28. Is. 13, 3. Joel 4, 9), and David hinting that his present excursion is of the latter kind, and that the ceremony of consecration will take place as soon as he joins his men (so W. R. Smith, *Rel. Sem.*² 456; Now.). כתמל שלשם always means *as heretofore* (e. g. Gen. 31, 2. 5. Ex. 5, 7), not (as EVV.) 'about these three days;' and for the rend. here adopted (which places the greater break at 'gone forth'), we must move the *zāqēf qāṭōn* from שלשם to בצאתי. Read also יקדשו (LXX, Pesh. We. al.) for יקדש. Kennedy, however, renders the last clause, 'how much more to-day will they be consecrated with (their) gear?' (viz. by the consecrated bread being put into their wallets, and so, according to ancient ideas (Lev. 6, 27 [for *be* read *become*], Ez. 44, 19; see *DB.* ii. 395), conveying the contagion of 'holiness' to them): *Lex.* אף כי 3.

7. לחם הפנים] *Presence-bread*, i. e. bread set out in Yahweh's presence, and designed originally as His food. See the writer's note on Ex. 25, 30; and *DB.* s.v. SHEWBREAD.

המוסרים] The plur. might be explained as a reference to the separate loaves (cf. עשרה, חמשה לחם): but this does not accord well with הלקחו at the end of the verse. It is better, therefore, either to read there הלָּקְחָם with LXX, or to suppose that the final ם in מוסרים has arisen by error from the first מ of the word following, and for המוסרממלפני (cf. on 1, 24) to restore המוסר מלפני. Comp. Jer. 29, 9 (read חלְמִים); 36, 21 (rd. על, in accordance with idiom); Jos. 10, 21 (איש); 2 Ch. 28, 23 (rd. עֹזְרִים); Hab. 1, 16 f. (rd. בריא); Job 27, 13 (rd. מֵאֵל). See further instances in *ZAW.* 1886, 211–213 (some doubtful). On the other hand, sometimes a repeated letter has dropped out, as *ch.* 17, 17. II 3, 22. Is. 45, 11 (read תשאלוני with Hitzig, Weir, Cheyne, al.). Dt. 15, 14 (p. 133 *n.*); and probably ψ. 42, 2 (אילת), 45, 7 (כסאך כאלהים: Edghill, *Evid. Value of Prophecy*, 252).

8. נעצר] i. e., probably, *detained* in the precincts of the sanctuary, and precluded from entering it, by some ceremonial impurity. Comp. Jer. 36, 5 אני עצור לא אוכל לבוא בית יהוה; Neh. 6, 10.

אביר הרעים] אבּיר is not *chief* (RV.), but *mighty*, which, however, does not well agree with הרעים, *might* or *heroism* being hardly a quality which in a shepherd would be singled out for distinction. Read, with Grätz, הָרָצִים for הרעים, 'the mightiest of Saul's *runners,*' or royal escort (so Now.): Saul's רָצִים are mentioned afterwards, 22, 17. In a runner, strength and size, such as אביר—elsewhere, it is true, only used in poetry—connotes, would be a qualification which the narrator might naturally remark upon.

LXX has νέμων τὰς ἡμιόνους Σαουλ, whence Lagarde (*Bildung der Nomina,* p. 45 *n.*) would restore אֲבִיל הָעֲיָרִים *manager* of Saul's *young asses* (Jud. 10, 4. 12, 14): cf. אוֹבִיל, the name of an Ishmaelite, the overseer of David's camels (עַל הגמלים) 1 Ch. 27, 30. *'Ibil* in Arabic is a *herd of camels,* *'abila* (denom.) is to *be skilled in managing camels,* and *'abil* (adj.) is *skilled in the management of camels;* hence אֲבִיל, more generally, *manager* (of animals). The suggestion is ingenious : but the strong Arabism is hardly probable : and the n. pr. אוביל is not Hebrew, but *Ishmaelite.*

9. וְאֵין יֵשׁ] The combination אֵין יֵשׁ occurs ψ. 135, 17; hence אִין here is commonly regarded as an anomalous punctuation for אֵין; cf. עִירֹה Gen. 49, 11. שִׁיתוֹ Is. 10, 17. עֵינוֹת Pr. 8, 28 (for what, by analogy, would be עֵירֹה, שִׁיתוֹ, עֵינוֹת: Kö. ii. 483; GK. § 93ᵛ). So Kimchi, Ges. Ew. § 213ᵉ, 286ʰ; Stade, § 194ᶜ(2). Delitzsch, however (on ψ. *l.c.*), treats אִין as equivalent to the Aram. אִין *num ?* אִין occurs in the Palestinian Targums = *if* (ψ. 7, 4. 5 etc.), also = הֲ in *indirect* questions, and = אִם, where the answer *No* is expected, Job 6, 12 אִין חִילָא הִיךְ אֲבנִיא חילי ψ. 10, 4ᵇ. 5ᵇ. 11, 7ᵇ. 13, 9ᵇ: and אִין אִית (= Heb. יֵשׁ אִם) occurs (e. g.) simply = *if there is . . .* ψ. 7, 4ᵇ. Job 33, 23ᵃ. 32ᵃ; Job 6, 6ᵇ אִית טעם וג' *or is* there taste in the white of an egg ? in an indirect question, ψ. 14, 2 למחמי אִין אית משכיל. Lam. 1, 12. But though the *punctuators* may have thought of this, or (Kö. *ZAW.* 1898, 242 f.) of the *'in* underlying the later אֵלּוֹ, such a pronounced Aramaism is not probable in an early narrative, clearly of Judaic origin; and it is better to read simply אִם,—וְאִם having the same interrog. force as in Gen. 38, 17. וְאֵי *and where . . . ?* (Klo. Sm.) is not probable. Ehrl. וְאוּלַי *and perhaps.*

נחוץ] only here. لَكَصَ is stated to mean *institit ursitque rogando;* so *possibly* נָחוּץ may have meant *pressed on.* But the root is a doubtful one in Heb. ; and perhaps נָאוֹץ *urged on,* from אוץ to *urge* (Ex. 5, 13), should be read.

10. לוטה] Is. 25, 7. 1 Ki. 19, 13 וַיָּלֶט פָּנָיו בְּאַדַּרְתּוֹ; II 19, 5 לֹאט+.

אִם־אֹתָהּ תִּקַּח־לְךָ קַח] If thou wilt take *that* for thyself, take it. Cf. for the position of אֹתָהּ, Ex. 21, 8 Qrê לוֹ (opp. to לְבְנוֹ, *v.* 7), and p. 35; also on 15, 1.

בַּזֶּה] Elsewhere always pointed בָּזֶה.

11. נֵת] See on 6, 17.

12. מֶלֶךְ] an anachronism, generally explained now as is done by Bu. Sm. Dh. Kenn. Ehrlich, however, would read מַכֵּה (18, 27).

14. וַיְשַׁנּוֹ אֶת־טַעְמוֹ] 'And he changed it, (even) his understanding (25, 33).' The anticipation of the object of a verb by a suffix is common in Aramaic; but, though cases occur sporadically in Heb., it is not a genuine Heb. idiom; and while there are no doubt instances in which for distinctness the original writers explained the suff. by the addition of the object, there are others in which the combination is open to the suspicion of being due to a faulty or glossed text, or, in late Heb., to Aramaic influence.

Comp. Ex. 2, 6 וַתִּרְאֵהוּ אֶת־הַיֶּלֶד *and she saw him, the child*, 35, 5 (P) בָּאֵשׁ תִּשְׂרְפֻנוּ אֵת אֲשֶׁר בּוֹ הַנֶּגַע (יָבִיא rd.?), Lev. 13, 57[b] יְבִיאֶה אֵת תְּרוּמַת יְ״י, 1 Ki. 19, 21 בְּשִׁלָם הַבָּשָׂר (LXX om. הבשר). 21, 13 אֶת־נְבוֹת .... וַיְעָרְדֻהוּ, 2 Ki. 16, 15 Kt. Is. 29, 23 (render, with Hitzig, 'when his children see it, the work of my hands,' etc.; but many regard יְלָדָיו as a gloss). Jer. 9, 14 הִנְנִי מַאֲכִילָם אֶת הָעָם הַזֶּה לַעֲנָה (LXX om. את העם הזה). Ez. 3, 21 (read הַזְהַרְתּוֹ). 44, 7 שִׁתֵּמוֹ נְדִיבֵמוֹ לְחַלְּלוֹ אֶת־בֵּיתִי (om. את ביתי with LXX). Pr. 5, 22. ψ. 83, 12 'make them, (even) their nobles,' etc.[1]. Here the emphatic anticipation of an object such as טַעְמוֹ is not probable, and the form of the suffix—rare even in strong verbs (see on 18, 1)—is found only once besides with a verb ל״ה, II 14, 6, where there are *independent* grounds for questioning its correctness. No doubt וישנו is an error of transcription for וַיִּשָּׁנֶה. So Ol. p. 547; Stade, § 143[e]; Kön. i. 546.

---

[1] Comp. Ew. § 309[c]; GK. § 131[m, o]. There are also other types, as Jer. 48, 44 כי בא עליה על בבל שודד 56, 51. כי אביא אליה אל מואב שנת פקדתם in Syr., as II 11, 3. 12, 5 Pesh.; comp. above, on 5, 3); and with the suffix in the *genitive*, as Ez. 10, 3. 42, 14. Job 29, 3 (GK. § 131[n]); and in Ch., in a form recalling strongly Syriac usage, 1 Ch. 5, 26 וינלם לְ. 23, 6. 2 Ch. 25, 10. 28, 15. For the Mishnic usage, see Segal, *Mišnaic Hebrew*, p. 82 ff. Only with one word, the interrog. אַי, does the apparent pleonasm appear to be idiomatic: Is. 19, 12 אַיֵּם אֵפוֹא חֲכָמֶיךָ Where are they, then, thy wise men? 2 Ki. 19, 13 אַיּוֹ מֶלֶךְ חֲמָת ומלך ארפד ונ׳ (in the ‖, Is. 37, 13 אַיֵּה). Mic. 7, 10 אַיּוֹ יהוה אֱלֹהָיִךְ.

בעיניהם] Read לעיניהם : בעיני פ׳, as Ehrlich rightly observes, is used always idiomatically to denote *in the opinion of* (so even Pr. 1, 17).

ויתהלל] *and he behaved himself madly.* The word recurs, applied metaphorically, Nah. 2, 5. Jer. 25, 16. 51, 7.

בידם] in their hands, i. e. as they sought to restrain him (Th. Ke.).

ויתיו] Pi'el from תוה, with anomalous *qameṣ,* for ויתו, i. e. *scratched,* made meaningless marks. But LXX ἐτυμπάνιζεν i. e. ויתף *and he drummed* on the doors of the gates,—'a more suitable gesture for a raving madman' (Kp.). So moderns generally: cf. GK. § 75ᵇᵇ.

16. הסר וג׳] ' Am I in lack of mad men ? '—The question is indicated by the tone of the voice : see GK. § 150ᵇ. Cf. on 11, 12 ; and 22, 7. 15.

את־זה] See on 10, 27.

עלי] *lit.* upon me, i. e. to my trouble : Gen. 48, 7 מתה רחל עלי.

22, 1. מערת עדלם] So II 23, 13 = 1 Ch. 11, 15†. It is remarkable that the מערה is afterwards, both here, *vv.* 4. 5, and in the other passage, II 23, 14 = 1 Ch. 11, 16, spoken of as a מצודה. Can a מערה be also termed a מצודה ? A מצודה is a mountain-stronghold (ψ. 18, 3) ; and in Jud. 6, 2. Ez. 33, 27 מערות and at least מצדות (Is. 33, 16) are named side by side as *different* kinds of hiding-place. We. answers the above question in the negative ; and believes that both here and in II 23, 13 = 1 Ch. 11, 15 מערת עדלם is an old error for מצדת עדלם the *stronghold* of 'Adullam (so Bu. Now. Sm. Kitt. Kennedy ¹, Buhl, *Geogr.* 97, Ehrlich).

'Adullam is mentioned in Jos. 15, 35, next before Sochoh and 'Azēkah, among the cities of the Shephēlah. This at once shews that it cannot be *Khareitun,* about 4 miles SE. of Bethlehem, with which, since the twelfth century, tradition has identified it. Clermont-Ganneau identified it in 1871 with *'Îd el-miyeh,* 2½ miles SE. of esh-Shuweikeh (see on 17, 1), supposing the ancient name to have been transformed by a popular etymology into one of similar sound, significant in the vernacular (*PEQS.* 1877, p. 177). 'Îd el-miyeh is 'a steep hill, on which are ruins of indeterminate date, with an ancient well at the foot, and, near the top, caves of moderate size' (*EB.* s.v.). The site is suitable, but not certain (*H.G.* 229 f.).

As regards the meaning of *'Adullām,* Lagarde (*Bildung der Nomina,* 54) derives it plausibly from عَدَلَ *to turn aside* (ψ. 119, 157 ; Lane, p. 1973), with the formative

---

¹ ' The expression *cave of Adullam,* which has passed into a proverb among us, is due to a corruption of the similar Heb. word for " stronghold " in *v.* 4 ' (*Century Bible,* ad loc.).

affix דֹ__ (Ol. § 216ᵃ: Stade, § 293; Barth, *Nominalbildung*, 352 f.; cf. GK. § 85¹), found frequently in proper names (מִרְיָם, בִּלְעָם, &c.), so that the word would signify originally a *retreat*. Heb. proper names have in many cases preserved roots not otherwise found in the OT.

וירדו] 'Adullam being in the Shephēlah, and David's brethren, presumably, on the high ground of Bethlehem (2550 ft.), 12 miles to the ENE. So Gen. 38, 1. II 23, 13.

2. כל־איש אשר־לו נשא] Cf. Is. 24, 2 כאשר נשא בו ' as (one) who has a lender (creditor).'

מר נפש] Jud. 18, 25; cf. Job 3, 20; and on 1, 10.

3. מצפה מואב] There are several places in Palestine, both E. and W. of Jordan, called הַמִּצְפֶּה, or הַמִּצְפָּה, 'the *outlook-point;*' and the situation of this one is not known.

יצא . . . אתכם] If the text be sound, these words can only be rendered 'come forth (to be) with you.' But the case is not one in which such a strongly-marked pregnant construction would be expected. LXX γινέσθωσαν, Pesh. ܢܟ, Vg. *maneat*. Read probably, not יֵשֵׁב (Bu. al.), but יֻנַּח (Ehrl.), which is closer to יצא, and is used specifically of being *left behind* in a place, Gen. 33, 15. Ex. 10, 24. For אתכם LXX has παρὰ σοὶ = אִתָּךְ; so Sm. Bu. (cf. *v*. 4ᵃ).

4. וינחם] 'led them (so as to be) in the presence of the king of Moab.' Another pregnant construction, hardly less expected than the last. את פני is not used in conjunction with verbs of motion; and in Pr. 18, 16 ולפני גדלים ינחנו the prep. is different. Targ. ואשרינון, Pesh. ܣܡܟ point to the punctuation וַיַּנִּחֵם (see Jos. 6, 23 Targ.; II 16, 21 Pesh.) *and he left them*, which is altogether to be preferred. (LXX καὶ παρεκάλεσε = וַיְנַחֵם.)

במצודה] i. e. the 'hold' of 'Adullam: see on *v*. 1.

5. במצודה] Pesh. בַּמִּצְפֶּה (cf. *v*. 3), which, as the 'hold' was in the land of Judah, seems to be correct.

חרת] The site of Ḥereth is not known. LXX has ἐν πόλει Σαρικ. Conder's *Kharâs*, a village on a wooded mountain, 4 miles SE. of 'Îd el-miyeh (*Tent Work*, 243), does not agree phonetically. The suggestion that חרת is an Aramaism for חֹרֶשׁ *wood* is very precarious: in Targ. חורשא corresponds to חֹרֶשׁ (14, 27 al.); and the rare חֲרוּתָא (Levy, *ChWB*. 286ᵇ) does not mean 'wood.'

ובאת־לך] The reflexive לְ (*Lex.* 515ᵇ *bottom;* GK. § 119ˢ). Cf.

ופנית לך‏ 1 Ki. 17, 3 ; and often in the imper., as Dt. 1, 7 ‏סעו לכם‎.
‏עֲלִי לָךְ‎ : Is. 40, 9 ‏שובו לכם‎ 27, 5 ‏עברו לכם‎. 13, 2, 40.

6. ‏נודע‎] *known* = discovered : cf. Ex. 2, 14. Jud. 16, 9. II 17, 19.

‏ואנשים‎] Read with LXX ‏והאנשים‎.

‏בגבעה‎] i.e. in Gibeah of Saul : see on 9, 1.

‏אשל‎] 31, 13. Gen. 21, 33†.

‏ברמה‎] RV. 'in Ramah,' which is inconsistent with 'in Gibeah.'
RV. *m.* 'in the height :' but ‏רמה‎ is not used of a 'height' in general
(Ez. 16, 25 forms hardly an exception); and it is better to read with
LXX ἐν Βαμα (= ‏בַּבָּמָה‎) *in the high-place* (cf. 9, 12). Saul held his
court under a sacred tree (cf. Jud. 4, 5 of Deborah administering
justice under a ‏תֹּמֶר‎), and in a sacred place.

‏נצבים עליו‎] *stationed by him,* i.e. standing in attendance on him,
‏נצב על‎ (and similarly ‏עמד על‎) is said idiomatically of one standing *by*
(lit. *over : Lex.* 756ᵃ c) another (Gen. 18, 2. 28, 13), esp. of servants,
or courtiers, in attendance on their master (*vv.* 7. 17. Gen. 45, 1 ;
cf. with ‏עמד‎ Jud. 3, 19), or the people standing about Moses, as he
sat to judge them (Ex. 18, 14ᵇ : cf. ‏עֹמֵד על‎ 13ᵇ).

In clause *b* the series of ptcpp. describe the situation, as (e.g.)
1 Ki. 1, 40 ; 22, 10 ; 2 Ki. 6, 32.

7. ‏לכלכם‎ (2)] is most probably an error for ‏וכלכם‎ ; otherwise it will
be an example of ‏ל‎ marking the accus., on which see 23, 10.

8. ‏בכרת וג׳‎] 18, 3. 20, 8. 16 : without ‏ברית‎, as 20, 16.

‏חֹלֶה‎] *is sick* because of me. This can hardly be right. In the
poetical passage Am. 6, 6 the apathy of the boisterous revellers of
Samaria is well described by the words ‏ולא נֶחְלוּ על שבר יוסף‎ 'and
feel no sickness by reason of Joseph's breach :' but the passage here is
different. LXX πονῶν, which represents ‏חמל‎ in the passage of similar
import 23, 21 ‏כי חמלתם עלי‎. Hence Grätz, Klo. Bu. al. ‏חֹמֵל‎ : 'and
none of you *hath compassion* on me.' Dr. Weir makes a similar
suggestion : 'Is it ‏חָמְלָה‎? ["and there is no *compassion* on your part
upon me :" cf. Gen. 19, 16] comp. 23, 21 LXX.'

‏הקים . . . לארב‎] Cf. 13 ‏לקום אלי לארב‎ 'to rise up against me *into*
(= so as to become) one lying in wait ;' Mic. 2, 8 (reading, for
‏עַמִּי יקום לאויב‎ (‏תְּקוּמֵמוּ‎ or ‏יקום‎, ‏יקום יקומם‎. LXX (in both verses) εἰς ἐχθρόν,

which Dr. Weir prefers, remarking that 'הקים is not suitable to אֹרֵב,
but is so to אֹיֵב.' So Sm. Now. Ehrl.

9. נצב על] נצב על may mean here either merely *standing by* (Gen.
18, 2), or (*v.* 6) *standing in attendance* on Saul's עבדים (courtiers).

10. וצידה נתן לו] the variation in order is pleasing in itself, and
also gives a slight emphasis on צידה. Cf. 6, 14ᵇ. 7, 1ᵇ. Gen. 27, 16.
32, 17ᵇ. 43, 12. 13. 1 Ki. 11, 18 ולחם אמר לו, etc.

13. ושאול לו] the inf. abs., according to GK. § 113ᵉ (cf. § 113ᶻ),
Ew. § 351°, Kön. iii. § 218ᶜ. After an *inf. c.*, as 25, 26. 33 ; cf. Ex.
32, 6.

14. וסר אל משמעתך] RV. *is taken into thy council*, following Ges.
(qui *devertere solet* ad colloquium tuum, qui interioris apud te admis-
sionis est), and Keil. This, however, assumes an unusual sense for
סור, which is hardly justified by the parallels quoted, Gen. 19, 2. 3.
Jud. 4, 18. 19, 12 (to 'turn aside' to *visit* a person). Probably for
סר we should read with LXX, Targ. (ἄρχων, רב) שַׂר '*captain* over thy
body-guard' (אל for על; see on 13, 13), which would imply a position of responsibility, and close attendance upon the king. For this
sense of משמעת (lit. *obedience*, i.e. a body of men bound to obedience),
cf. II 23, 23 (= 1 Ch. 11, 25) משמעתו (Ch. על) אל דוד וישימהו: the
word is also used in a concrete sense in Is. 11, 14 ובני עמון משמעתם.
So Ew. Bertheau (on 1 Ch. *l. c.*), Then. etc.

15. החלתי] 'Have I begun?' The question is indicated by the
tone (11, 12).

שים ב' . . .] אל ישם בעבדו דבר lit. *to lay in*, i. e. to attribute to, as
Job 4, 18: so שים ל' Dt. 22, 8.

בכל בית אבי] LXX, Pesh. ובכל ו', which is required.

17. הרצים] *the runners*, or royal escort of the king: so 21, 8
(emended text). 1 Ki. 14, 27. 28 (= 2 Ch. 12, 10. 11). 2 Ki. 10, 25.
11, 4. 6. 11. 13. 19 : cf. רצים לפניו II 15, 1. 1 Ki. 1, 5; and *ch.* 8, 11
וירצו לפני מרכבתו. If the emendation on 21, 8 is correct, Doeg will
have been the most stalwart of Saul's 'runners.'

ירדם עם] 1 Ch. 4, 10: II 14, 19 (את); Jer. 26, 24 (את).

18. דוינ] Ew. § 45ᵈ. Kt. uses י in the Syriac fashion: the Qrê
warns the reader to pronounce it softly, and not differently from דואג
v. 9. 21, 8. Cf. p. 120 *n.*; and פתאים beside פְּתָיִם (GK. § 93ˣ).

סב אתה] For the emph. אָתה, cf. on 17, 56.

ויפגע הוא] Note the emphasis expressed by the pronoun : as Ex. 18, 19. 22. 26 etc. (*Tenses*, § 160 *note*).

אפוד בד] So 2, 18. II 6, 14 (= 1 Ch. 15, 27)†. LXX, however, omits בד, probably rightly : for this 'ephod' is not worn, but 'borne,' by the priests (cf. on 2, 28).

20. לאחימלך] GK. § 129ᵇ and 129ᵉ.

22. סבתי] סָבָּה in Biblical Hebrew is used somewhat peculiarly in 1 Ki. 12, 15 מעם י״י [2 Ch. 10, 15 נְסִבָּה] סִבָּה היתה כי lit. 'for there was *a turning about* (i. e. a *turn* or *change* of affairs : LXX μεταστροφή) from Yahweh that he might establish his word,' etc. : in the philosophical Hebrew of the middle ages, it acquires the sense of *cause*. Hence this passage has been rendered, 'I have been the cause in (the death of) all the persons of thy father's house.' The legitimacy of this rendering is questionable. There is no evidence that סבה possessed the sense *cause* in Biblical times; nor is it probable, if it did, that סבב (in *Qal*) would be a denominative of it; and thirdly, even though there were a verb סבב *to be the cause*, its use with ellipse of the crucial word *death* is more than is credible. It is best for סבתי to read, with Th. We., חַבְתִּי *I am guilty* in respect of all the persons, etc.: cf. Pesh. ‏ܐܠ‎. The construction with ב as חטא ב׳ 19, 5, where Targ. has the same word in the *Ethp.* with the same construction, viz. ׳אתחייב ב.

23. נפשי . . . . נפשך] The suffixes must have been accidentally transposed : נפשי . . . . נפשך (Th. We. Bu. etc.).

כי משמרת אתה עמדי] 'For thou art *a keeping* with me,' i. e. shalt be jealously guarded with me. The abstract for the concrete, according to a usage of which there are many other examples in Hebrew (*Tenses*, § 189. 2): comp. Is. 11, 14 מִשְׁמַעְתָּם עמון ובני¹. LXX ὅτι πεφύλαξαι σὺ παρ' ἐμοὶ = עמדי אַתָּה נִשְׁמַרְתָּ כי (נ for מ, the two letters being very similar in the old character),—which has nothing to recommend it.

---

¹ And the remarkable parallel in Moabitic : Mesha, line 28 מ׳שמעת דיבן כל כי *lit.* for all Dibon was *obedience.*

23—26. *David as an outlaw, in the Shephēlah, the Hill-country, and the Wilderness of Judah.*

23, 1. קְעִילָה] In the Shephēlah (Jos. 15, 44; see *v.* 33); now *Qîlâ*, a ruined village on a hill, on the E. side of W. eṣ-Ṣûr, 3 miles S. of 'Îd el-miyeh, 'the terraced sides of which are even to-day covered with corn,' so that we can understand why the Philistine raiders should have swarmed up the Vale of Elah and the Wādy eṣ-Ṣûr, past Sochoh and 'Îd el-miyeh, to rob the threshing-floors (cf. Cheyne, *EB.* s. v.; *H. G.* 230).

והמה שסים] *robbing* (without 'and they are'),—a circ. clause, like Gen. 15, 2. 18, 8 etc. (*Tenses*, § 160), and following another ptcp., as 28, 14. II 15, 30. 2 Ki. 2, 12. Jer. 38, 22.

2. והֵבֵית . . . וְהִכֵּיתִי] There is considerable irregularity in the punctuation of the 1 and 2 pers. of the conjugations (other than Qal) of ל״ה verbs: but the following points may be usefully noted :—

ִי֯ is found always in Pu. Hof. (as הָרְאֵיתָ Ex. 26, 30), and Nif. (except *once*, Gen. 24, 8 וְנִקִּיתָ); 'ִ֯ is found always in 1 pl. (נ_), and before suffixes, and in 2 sing. Pi.; and almost always in 2 pl. (as הִשְׁתַּחֲוִיתֶם), probably the only exceptions being הִרְבֵּיתֶם Ez. 11, 6, and הִתְעִיתֶם Jer. 42, 20 Qrê (Kt. התעתים).

The irregularity is greatest in 1 and 2 sing. Hif. and Hithp. and in 1 sing. Pi.; but here 'ִ֯ is very common in the first person, and 'ִ֯ in the second (as always in Pi.; see above): thus we find הֵבֵיתִי 15 times, but הֵבֵיתָ 17 times; הִשְׁתַּחֲוֵיתִי (3 times), but הִשְׁתַּחֲוֵיתָ (4 times); הֶעֱלֵיתִי (10 times), but הֶעֱלֵיתָ (6 times; also הֶעֱלֵיתָ Ex. 32, 7. 40, 4†); הִרְבֵּיתִי (12 times), but הִרְבֵּיתָ (4 times; but 2 fem. הִרְבֵּית). A notable exception is צִוֵּיתִי 5 times, but צִוִּיתָ 30 times; comp. also כִּלֵּיתִי 4 times, but כִּלִּיתָ Nu. 25, 11†: כָּסֵיתִי twice, but כָּסִיתָ 4 times. See Bö. i. pp. 410 f., 429; in GK. § 75², ᶜᵉ the usage might have been stated more clearly.

3. וְאַף כִּי] = *and how much more, when,* as 2 Ki. 5, 13.

מַעַרְכוֹת] Cf. 4, 2. 12. 16; 10 times in *ch.* 17; and II 23, 3.

4. רֵד קְעִילָה] Not from 'Adullam,—at least if this was at 'Îd el-miyeh (1468 ft.), which is *lower* than Qe'ilah (1520 ft.),—but presumably from the 'forest of Ḥéreth' (22, 5), which will have been somewhere in the higher, central part of Judah.

נֹתֵן] the *fut. instans*: see on 3, 11.

5. וַיִּנְהַג] The word used as 30, 2. 20, like the Greek ἄγειν.

6. There is some disorder in this verse: Abiathar fled to David, *before* he reached Qeʿilah ; and clause *b* cannot be construed so as to yield an intelligible sense (as it stands it can only be rendered ʿ(the) ephod *came down in his hand*ʾ) [1]. The simplest course is to read after אל דוד either, with LXX (B), והוא עם דוד קעילה ירד ו(ה)אפוד בידו (so Bu. alt.), or (cf. Now., but *not* Luc.[2]) ירד קעילה ו(ה)אפוד בידו. Even this change does not entirely relieve the verse of difficulty ; for the sense required is *after* Abiathar fled, which is not strictly expressed by בברח אביתר. AV. RV. ʿ that he came down with an ephod in his hand.ʾ This (irrespectively of the difficulty in clause *a*) yields an excellent sense : only it should be clearly understood that *it is no rendering of the Massoretic text* (אפוד ירד בידו). AV. (and occasionally even RV.) sometimes conceals a difficulty by giving a sense that is agreeable with the context, regardless of the fact that the Hebrew words used do not actually express it : i. e. they implicitly adopt an emendation of the text. Comp. on 17, 20 : 24, 20 ; 25, 30 : and see Jer. 19, 13. Ez. 45, 21 RV. 48, 29 (בנחלה for מנחלה). Ley's proposal to read את for אל (*ZATW.* 1888, p. 222) does not touch the real difficulty of the verse.

7. נִבַּר] LXX πέπρακεν = מָכַר (comp. Jud. 4, 9). *Sold*, however, is here scarcely suitable. If the text be correct, the sense will be *to treat as strange = to alienate, reject* (cf. Jer. 19, 4 וַיְנַכְּרוּ את המקום הזה), construed here pregnantly with בִיד. But the context in Jeremiah is not parallel ; and the figure here would be rather a forced one. Ch. 26, 8, we have סָגַר, which, however, would here give rise to an inelegant alliteration with the following נסגר. Perhaps Krochmal is right in suggesting סָכַר, which is construed with בְּיַד in Is. 19, 4 in exactly the sense that is here required, and only differs from נִבַּר by one letter. The Versions, other than LXX, render only by a general term *deliver* (מסר, ܡܠܐܕܡ, *tradidit*), from which nothing can be inferred as to the reading of the text which the translators had before them.

---

[1] It is moreover out of connexion with clause *a* : for according to all but uniform usage ויהי would be resumed by either ירד אפוד or ואפוד ירד or וַיֵּרֶד אפוד, but not by אפוד ירד (*Tenses,* § 78 *end*).

[2] Luc. omits καὶ αὐτὸς μετὰ Δαυειδ, but otherwise agrees with B.

נסגר לבוא] *hath shut himself in* (Ez. 3, 24) *in* (by) *entering* etc.

דלתים ובריח] Dt. 3, 5. 2 Ch. 8, 5; cf. 14, 6.

8. לרדת] presumably from Gibeah of Saul (22, 6), 2½ miles N. of Jerusalem (on 9, 1).

9. מחריש] *was fabricating, forging.* Apparently a metaphor derived from the working of metal: cf. חֹרֵשׁ נחשׁת Gen. 4, 22. 1 Ki. 7, 14. Elsewhere in this figurative sense only in Proverbs, and only there in Qal (3, 29 אל תחרש על רעך רעה. 6, 14. 18. 12, 20. 14, 22†). The position of עליו makes it emphatic, *against him* (and not some one else): comp. Jer. 11, 19, and on II 15, 4.

10. שמע שמע] See on 20, 6.

לשחת לעיר] So, with ל, Nu. 32, 15. שחת is construed so constantly with an accus. that, though there is a tendency in Heb. for Pi'el, and especially for Hif.[1], to be construed with ל, expressing the *dativus commodi* (or *incommodi*), this is probably an instance of the use of ל to mark the accusative, such as is regular in Syriac, and occurs in Hebrew, rarely in the early and middle periods of the language, and with greater frequency in exilic and post-exilic writings. See 22, 7. II 3, 30 הרגו לאבנר (see note); Jer. 40, 2 ויקח . . . לירמיה; ψ. 69, 6 אתה ידעת לאולתי; 73, 18 תשית למו al.: Ew. § 277[e]; GK. § 117[n]; *Lex.* 512[a].

11 f. בעלי קעילה] This use of בעלים to denote the *lords* or *citizens* of a town is rare: Jos. 24, 11 (of Jericho). Jud. 9, 22 ff. (Shechem). 20, 5 (Gibeah). II 21, 12 and 2, 4 LXX (Jabesh of Gilead)[2].

13. ויתהלכו באשר יתהלכו] Cf. 2 Ki. 8, 1 וגורי באשר תגורי; II 15, 20; ואני הולך על אשר אני הולך; comp. also Ex. 3, 14. 4, 13. 16, 23. 33, 19. Ezek. 12, 25. A Semitic idiom, copiously illustrated by Lagarde, in a note at the end of his *Psalterium Hieronymi* (1874), p. 156 f., especially from Arabic authors, and employed where either

---

[1] E.g. החיה ל' *to give life to,* Gen. 45, 7; הרחיב ל' *to give width to,* ψ. 4, 2 al.; הרבה ל' Hos. 10, 1; הניח ל' II 7, 1; הצדיק ל' Is. 53, 11 *to give right to.* Comp. Ew. § 282[c]; *Lex.* 511[b] 3 a; and Giesebrecht's careful study on this preposition, *Die Hebräische Praeposition Lamed* (Halle, 1876), p. 80 f.

[2] Comp. in Phoenician *CIS.* i. 120 הרנה בעלת בזנתי 'Irene citizen of Byzantium' (in the Greek Ἐρήνη Βυζαντία); and Cooke, *NSI.* p. 50.

the means, or the desire, to be more explicit does not exist. 'And they went about where they went about:' in the present case, no doubt, the vagueness of the expression corresponds with the reality. From Lagarde's instances may be quoted: אונקלוס תִּרְגֵּם מַה־שֶׁתִּרְגֵּם (Rashi on Gen. 20, 13, and elsewhere) Onqelos renders as he does render; لكان ما كان fuit quod fuit = missa haec faciam; فاصنع ما انت صانع age quod agis = non curo quid facturus sis, et liberam agendi ut volueris potestatem tibi concedo; طلع من طلع emersit [ex undis] qui emersit = non attinet exponere qui et quot emerserint; وفد على كسرى ابرويز فيما كان يفد عليه ad regem Persarum Parwêzum profectus est eo consilio quo profectus est = nil attinet explicare quaenam itineris causa ac ratio fuit: Arnold, *Chrestomathia Arabica,* p. 143, 7 nisi forte غيّرهم ما غيّرهم mutaverit eos quod eos mutavit = nisi forte nescio quae res eos mutaverit. Sm. quotes also Qor. 53, 16.

14. במדבר] i.e. in some part of the rocky and desolate region called the 'wilderness of Judah' (Jos. 15, 61–62, where six cities belonging to it are enumerated; Jud. 1, 16 [text very doubtful]; Ps. 63 *title*), bearing down by steep and rough descents to the Dead Sea, and extending some 15 miles from W. to E., and some 35 miles from N. to S. (*H. G.* 312,—followed by a vivid description of its wild and barren scenery). It begins in about the longitude of Ma'on and Carmel (23, 24. 25, 1), but becomes wilder and more desolate as it descends towards the Dead Sea.

במצדות] (mountain-)*fastnesses;* cf. Is. 33, 16 מצדות סלעים. So *vv.* 19. 29. Jud. 6, 2; and (in the sing.) 1 Ch. 12, 9. 17 [al. 8. 16].

בהר] the elevated central 'hill-country' of Judah (Jos. 15, 48–60).

במדבר זיף] probably an intrusive anticipation of *v.* 15.

15. וירא] 'Here, in spite of 26, 3, we must with Ew. *Hist.* iii. 127 (E.T. 92) vocalize וַיִּרָא, not only in order to secure a connexion with what precedes, but especially to obtain a motive for what follows: cf. *v.* 16 "strengthened his hand," and *v.* 17 "fear not"' (We.). And so Dr. Weir: 'Rather, *was afraid;* see next verse.'

זיף] now *Tell ez-Zif,* a conspicuous mound, 2882 ft. above the sea, 4 miles S. by E. of Hebron, on a plateau of 'red rolling ground, mostly bare, partly wheat and barley, broken by limestone scalps partly covered by scrub, and honey-combed by caves,' which begins soon after Hebron is left (*H. G.* 306 *n.*). This plateau is the 'wilderness' of Ziph. Jos. 15, 55 mentions Zif as in the הר יהודה.

בחרשה] The prep. ב and the ה *locale* combined. So *v.* 19; 31, 13 ברבלְתה Jer. 52, 10 באבלה; II 20, 15 בנגבה; Jos. 15, 21 ביבשה. And even with מן, as Jud. 21, 19 מצפונה ל׳; Jos. 15, 10 מצפֹּונה; Jer. 27, 16 מבבלה. Here the ה was already read by LXX (though wrongly understood) ἐν τῇ Καινῇ = בַּחֲדָשָׁה.

The word is pretty clearly (notice חרשה, not החרשה, in *v.* 16) not an appellative ('in the wood'),—Conder (*T.W.* 243) observes that trees could never have grown on the dry porous formation of the plateau of Zif,—but the name of a *place*, *Ḥōresh* or *Ḥôreshah* [on ה *loc.* in names of places, see *Tenses*, § 132 *Obs.*],—perhaps the ruin *Ḥurêsa* (or *Khoreisa*), 1½ miles S. of Tell ez-Zif (Conder; Buhl, 97; *H.G.* 307 *n.*).

16. ויחזק את ידו] fig. for *encouraged;* so Jud. 9, 24. Jer. 23, 14. Is. 35, 3. Ezr. 6, 22. Neh. 2, 18. 6, 9 al., always with the pl. *hands* (so LXX here) : cf. with the Qal II 2, 7 al.

17. תמצאך] Cf. with יד Is. 10, 10. ψ. 21, 9. But מצא does not correspond phonetically with Aramaic מְטָא, with which Mühlau-Volck, in the 10th edition of Gesenius' *Lexicon*, compare it : מצא = مَسَّ = مَسَّהُ: *advenire :* מְטָא = مسّהُ:—in conj. I 2 (= *Pi'el*) *porrigere, praebere.* See Nöldeke, *ZDMG.* 1886, p. 736.

כן] *so*, in accordance with what has just been stated. Cf. ψ. 90, 12 '*so*—i.e. in accordance with *v.* 11—teach us,' etc.

18. Cf. 18, 3.

19—24, 22. A doublet to *ch.* 26, beginning with almost the same words, and containing a different version of the same occurrences.

19. ויעלו] Tell el-Fûl (2754 ft.) = Gibeah (see on 9, 1) is lower than Ziph (2882 ft.) ; but the road from Ziph to the N. would ascend considerably (Hebron, 3040 ft., Ḥalḥul, N. of Hebron, 3270 ft.); and though it descends again to Jerusalem (2593 ft.), it rises again to Gibeah (2754 ft.), so that there would be considerable ascents between Ziph and Gibeah. The parallel, 26, 1, has, however, ויבאו for ויעלו.

זפים] Read הזפים, as 26, 1.

בחרשה . . . הישימון] These definite localities are inconsistent both with the preceding indefinite מצדות, and with the need of searching for David, expressed in the verses which follow. The words from בגבעת seem to have been inserted here from 26, 1, and בחרשה added to agree with *vv.* 15. 16. 18 (Sm.). On Ḥachîlah and Jeshimon, see on 26, 1.

20. לכל אות וג׳] ל = *in accordance with* (*Lex.* 516ᵇ): elsewhere (Dt. 12, 15. 20. 21. 18, 6†; comp. Jer. 2, 24) the phrase is used with ב: comp. on 2, 16. With the rhythm or run of clause *a*, cf. Qoh. 9, 10 (accents and RV. *margin*).

ולנו הסגירו] 'and *ours* (will it be) to deliver him,' etc. Not a common use of ל. Cf. Jer. 10, 23 (reading הָלֹךְ וְהָכֵן); and (with ל before the inf.) Mic. 3, 1; and, in late Hebrew, 2 Ch. 13, 5. 20, 17. 26, 18. Comp. עלי in II 18, 11.

22. הכינו עוד] certainly not 'make yet more sure' (RV.), but most probably, if the text is correct, '*Prepare* further;' cf., in a military sense, Nah. 2, 4. Jer. 46, 14. Ez. 7, 14. 38, 7. '*Give attention* still,' with ellipse of לב, is a very doubtful rend.: not only is the ellipse uncertain elsewhere (see Moore on Jud. 12, 6), but הכין לב elsewhere has only the sense of fixing the heart firmly in a given direction, esp. towards Yahweh (*ch.* 7, 3), or to seek Him (2 Ch. 12, 14 al.), cf. (absol.) ψ. 78, 8. Job 11, 13 (*Lex.* 466ᵇ).

מי ראהו שם] The Hebrew is abrupt (comp. on 2, 35). LXX for מי ראהו has ἐν τάχει, whence Th. We. al. restore הַמְּהֵרָה—'know and consider his place where his *fleeting* foot may be.' מָהֵר as an *adj.*, however, is a doubtful form: it occurs only Zeph. 1, 14, where it is explained questionably (see esp. Schwally, *ZAW.* 1890, p. 176) as a Pi. ptcp. (מְמַהֵר) with aphaeresis of מ (GK. § 52ˢ); and it is better to read in Zeph. מְמַהֵר, and here, with Ehrl., הַמְּהִרָה (from מָהִיר).

האומר] sc. אמר (16, 4).

ערם יערם הוא] Ex. 4, 14 דבר ידבר הוא; *ch.* 22, 18ᵇ: cf. also 27, 2; 28, 8; Qoh. 9, 15. For the inf. *Qal*, see GK. § 113ʷ.

23. ראו ודעו] In this order, only here and Jer. 5, 1. Elsewhere regularly דעו וראו (*v.* 22. 12, 17. 14, 38. 1 Ki. 20, 7. 2 Ki. 5, 7), דעי וראי (25, 17. Jer. 2, 19), דע וראה (24, 12. II 24, 13. 1 Ki. 20, 22). 25 MSS. have here ודעו וראו.

מכל] Very hard. . . . מכל may mean *any of* (Lev. 11, 24), esp. with a neg. or אם (*Lex.* 580b); but this does not suit here : it cannot mean *everyone* (Now.) ; and 'take knowledge *of*' (EVV., Dh.) gives to מן a sense which it does not possess. ידע ב' does, however, occur with the meaning *know about* (Jer. 38, 24. Job 37, 16, perhaps ψ. 31, 8; cf. *ch.* 22, 15); and as ם and ב are often confused in the old characters (Introd. p. lxvii), we may, in default of anything better, read בכל, and then we may rightly render 'take knowledge *of.*'

וישבתם] *and return.* Neither this (We.) nor וַהֲשֵׁבֹתֶם (Bu. Now. Kit.) can mean *bring back word:* see on 12, 3.

אל נכון] אל must here be used as the equivalent of עַל, which is joined sometimes with substantives to express an adverbial relation ; ψ. 31, 24 עַל יֶתֶר *upon* (the basis of) abundance = abundantly ; Jer. 6, 14 עַל נְקַלָּה = lightly; Is. 60, 7 עַל רצון = acceptably. Here *on a certainly = assuredly (Lex.* 754b).

אלפי יהודה] not 'thousands' (EVV.), but *clans* of Judah ; see on 10, 19.

24. מדבר מעון] Ma'on, in the 'hill-country' of Judah (Jos. 15, 55,— mentioned beside Carmel and Ziph), was identified by Robinson with *Tell Ma'in* (2887 ft.), on a 'great hump of rock' (Conder, *Tent Work,* 244), 4½ miles S. of Ziph. The 'wilderness of Ma'on' is an extensive steppe, E. of the Tell, consisting of 'waste pasture-land, rough rocks with that dry vegetation on which goats and even sheep seem to thrive' (*EB.* s. v.).

בערבה] The 'Arābāh (or Steppe) is the alluvial floor of the deep depression through which the Jordan runs, and in which the Dead Sea lies. It is difficult to understand how any part of the wilderness of Ma'on (2887 ft.) could be described as being 'in' the 'Arābāh (in which the Dead Sea is 1292 ft. *below* the Medit. Sea). If the text is in order, we must suppose that the wilderness of Ma'on extended sufficiently far in the E. to reach a point which could be reckoned as 'in' the 'Arābāh.

אל ימין הישימון] 'on the South of the Desolation' (AV. *Jeshimon ;* RV. *the desert* is too vague). הישימון (notice the *article*), though it is used as a general term (Dt. 32, 10; Is. 43, 19 al.), is here and *v.* 19, 26, 1. 3 (cf. Nu. 21, 20. 23, 28) used specifically of some part of the wild and desolate 'wilderness of Judah' (see on *v.* 14),—if אל ימין

is correct (26, 1 has עַל פְּנֵי), of the part *South* of about the latitude of Maʿon.

25. לבקש] 'Read לבקשו with LXX' (We.). ו has dropped out before the וי following. So Klo. Bu. Sm. etc.

וירד הסלע] In illustration of the fact, Dr. Weir refers appositely to Jud. 15, 8 וישבו בסלע רמון ארבעה; וישב בסעיף סלע עיטם 20, 45. 47 חרשים: סלעים are also mentioned as hiding-places in *ch.* 13, 6. The 'crag' here meant cannot be identified; but it must have been in some part of the מדבר מעון lower than that meant in *v.* 24.

וישב] LXX אֲשֶׁר: 'and came down to the crag *which is* in,' etc. This is probably right, הסלע not being a proper name (We.).

מדבר מעון] *into* the wilderness, etc.; not *in*, as EVV.

26. שאול] LXX שאול ואנשיו: probably rightly.

About 4 miles SE. of Tell ez-Zif there begins a deep and narrow gorge, with rocky sides, called first *W. el-Waʿr* and then *W. el-Malāqy*, which runs to the E. for a distance of some 6 miles; and it is a plausible suggestion of Conder's (*Tent Work*, 245) that this may have been the scene of the incident here recorded : there is, Conder says, no other place near Maʿon, where cliffs, or crags (*Selaʿ, v.* 28), can be found. But it is precarious to support the identification by the phonetically imperfect resemblance of ' Malāqy ' to מחלקות (*v.* 28).

ויהי דוד נחפז] 'And David came to be (on 18, 9) *hurrying in alarm*, . . . and Saul and his men were *surrounding* David and his men to take them,'—the ptcpp. describe the situation, into the midst of which the message, *v.* 27, came. For the idea expressed by נחפז, cf. II 4, 4 (Qal), 2 Ki. 7, 15 (Nif.). עטר is, however, a very rare word, found otherwise only once in poetry (ψ. 5, 13†, of surrounding protectingly with a shield); and Klo. proposes עָטִים (14, 32. 15, 19) were *flying at* David (so Bu. Sm.). This, however, cannot be said to be probable. Ehrlich, more probably, suggests עברים *were crossing over* to the other side of the mountain to take David, when the message arrived.

28. מְרְדֹּף] with dag. f. implicitum (GK. § 22ᶜ *end*) in the ר, as in כִּרְגָּדֶ Is. 14, 3 Baer and Ginsb. (GK. § 22ˢ *end*). So 𝔙 and Kit. Baer and Ginsb. read מִרְדֹּף: cf. 1, 6. 10, 24 (see the *Addenda*).

המחלקות] prob. *of divisions*[1], Saul and David there parting from

---

[1] Though מחלקת is elsewhere used only in a *concrete* sense, of the divisions

the neighbourhood of one another: cf. the Nif. in 1 Ki. 16, 21. Gen. 14, 15. A popular explanation of the meaning of the name. 'Dathe, Ges., De Wette, "rock of *escapes;*" but Th. objects rightly that the sense of *escaping* is not established for חלק' (Dr. Weir)[1]. LXX πέτρα ἡ μερισθεῖσα = סֶלַע הַמַּחְלְקֺת. Targ. has the characteristic paraphrase, 'the place where the heart of the king was divided to go this way and that.'

24, 1. ויעל] Very surprising, in the present context. 'En-gedi, in the 'wilderness' of Judah (Jos. 15, 62), the modern *'Ain-jidi*, is a spring, bursting out from under a great boulder on the rocky precipitous descent to the W. shore of the Dead Sea, and 612 ft. above it (cf. G. A. Smith, *EB.* s.v.; and the writer's note on Gen. 14, 7): it is 680 ft. below the Medit. Sea, and consequently some 3560 ft. *below* Ziph (2882 ft.), and considerably below any place which could reasonably be included in the 'wilderness of Ma'on' (*v.* 25); David could not therefore have 'come up' to 'En-gedi from any of the places mentioned before. Either something has been omitted (so that משם does not refer to סלע המחלקות in the 'wilderness of Ma'on,' *v.* 35), or the verse is due to some redactional confusion.

3. על פני] The expression is ambiguous. על פני may denote either (1) *on the surface of,* Gen. 11, 8. Ex. 32, 20. II 18, 8; or (2) *on the front of* (usually in the sense of *on the East of;* see on 15, 7). In sense (1) על פני is commonly used with words of *scattering* or *casting:* nor does it appear why here the *surface* of the rocks of the chamois-goats should be so particularly specified. Probably, therefore, (2) is preferable: though, as Ges. remarks, there is nothing here to guide us as to whether the 'front' definitely means the East. Wild goats still abound in the neighbourhood of 'En-gedi; and the צורי היעלים must have designated some locality in which they were particularly apt to congregate.

4. גדרות הצאן] Cf. Nu. 32, 16. 24. 36. Zeph. 2, 6. Low stone-walls ('build,' Nu. 32, 16), forming enclosures for sheep.

ישבים] 'were in the recesses (Am. 6, 10. Is. 14, 15. 37, 24 al.) of the cave, sitting down.'

---

of a people (Jos. 11, 23. 12, 7. 18, 10), or (especially in Ch.) of the divisions (i.e. 'courses') of priests and Levites.

[1] It is assumed (though very questionably) by the Rabbis, and even favoured by Gesenius, for the Hif. in Jer. 37, 12.

5. אשר אמר] Do these words mean *of which he said*—the allusion being to some previous assurance of deliverance from Saul, which David's followers *apply* to the present occasion (Kp.); or *on which he says,—the occasion itself* being interpreted by them as an indication of Yahweh's purpose to deliver Saul into his hands (Th. Ke. We.)? In order to answer this question properly, the nature of אשר and its use in parallel cases must be considered in some detail.

אשר is properly not a relative *pronoun,* but a relative *sign,* indicating generally and indeterminately the idea of relation = *as to which :* it is followed in strictness by a pronominal or adverbial (שָׁם) supplement, defining more closely the nature of the relation which it is used to express—האיש אשר דבר עליו the man *as to whom* he spake concerning him = the man *concerning* whom he spake. There are, however, certain cases—besides the familiar one, in which the pronominal supplement is the direct object of the verb—in which the pron. or adv. supplement is dispensed with. (*a*) with אֲשֶׁר אָמַר, followed by the words used, where, however, its place is really taken by a pronoun in the speech which follows, as Gen. 3, 17 the tree *as to which* I commanded thee, saying, Thou shalt not eat *from it,* Dt. 28, 68. 1 Ki. 8, 29. Jer. 32, 43; *ch.* 9, 23^b: *ib.* 17 the man *as to whom* I said unto thee, *This one* (זה) shall rule my people Israel; Jud. 7, 4 (exactly similar) and (where the noun repeated takes the place of the pronoun) Jud. 8, 15 Behold Zebaḥ and Ẕalmunnaʿ, *as to whom* ye reproached me, saying, Is the hand of *Zebaḥ and Ẕalmunnaʿ* now in thine hand? etc. In 2 Ki. 17, 12. 21, 4 a term nearly equivalent to the antecedent of אשר follows similarly in the speech. The pron. or adv. supplement is dispensed with (*b*) when a word denoting *time* or *place* or *manner* has immediately preceded אשר: thus (*a*) Dt. 4, 10 יום אשר עמדת the day *on which* thou stoodest, Gen. 45, 6. 1 Ki. 9, 10. 22, 25 and frequently : (*β*) Gen. 39, 20. Dt. 8, 15. Is. 64, 10 al.[1]: (*γ*) in . . . . זה הדבר אשר this is the matter *as to which* (or, account *how*) . . . Jos. 5, 4; 1 Ki. 11, 27[2]. It is dispensed with (*c*) in a few extreme instances, in which it is left to the reader's intelligence to define the relation intended : as Nu. 21, 16; Dt. 7, 19; Is. 8, 12 לא תאמרון קשר לכל אשר יאמר העם הזה קשר, where יאמר would normally be followed by לו; 31, 6 שובו לאשר העמיקו סרה Turn ye to (him, as to) whom they have deeply rebelled.

Applying the principles that have been thus determined to the passage before us, we shall see that presumption favours its being regarded as analogous to *b* (*a*). Had the sense intended by the

---

[1] And regularly after בכל אשר, באשר (*ch.* 14, 47) = *wherever,* מאשר (Ex. 5, 11. Ru. 2, 9) *from* the place *where* = *whencesoever,* אשר (אל) על *whithersoever,* II 15, 20 al.

[2] Comp. the use of דבר in the phrase . . . וזה דְּבַר Dt. 15, 2. 19, 4. 1 Ki. 9, 15; and in the first line of the Siloam Inscription.

narrator been, 'Behold the day, as to which Yahweh said to thee, I will etc.,' we should have expected (on the analogy of *a*) הנה היום אשר אמר יהוה אליך ביום ההוא אנכי אתן וג'. As it is, אשר has the presumption of being determined by the preceding היום: 'Behold the day *on which* Yahweh saith unto thee, Behold, I am about to deliver etc.' Compare the very similar passage, Jud. 4, 14.

אויביך] The Qrê is right (notice לו). Cf. on II 24, 13.

5^b. 6. To produce a logical sequence in the narrative 5^b. 6 should be transposed so as to follow 8^a.

6. את כנף] 'After כנף eight MSS., and LXX, Pesh. Vulg. insert הַמְּעִיל,—necessarily, as the art. is wanting' (Dr. Weir). So We.

7. חלילה לי מיהוה] 'Ad profanum sit mihi *a Domino*'—the usual חלילה לי (12, 23) being strengthened by the act being represented as deprecated on Yahweh's part: cf. 1 Ki. 21, 3; and see on II 23, 17.

אם] After חלילה with the force of an oath, as II 20, 20: more impassioned than the more ordinary constr. of חלילה with מן of the act deprecated (e. g. 26, 11). See GK. § 149; *Lex.* 321^a.

במשׁיחַ יְהוָֹה (אדני)] See GK. § 16^h. So *v.* 11. 26, 9 al.

8. וישׁסע . . . בדברים] 'And David *tare* his men with words.' שׁסע is *to cleave*: in Qal only ptcp., of the cloven hoof, Lev. 11, 3. 7. 26. Dt. 14, 6. 7; in Pi'el, Lev. 1, 17. Jud. 14, 6 וישׁסעהו כשׁסע הגדי and *he rent* it (the lion) as one would *rend* a kid. It follows that the Heb. text here yields no sense' (Dr. Weir). We. defends MT. on the ground that the addition בדברים (cf. Job 32, 4) implies that the verb is a *figurative* one; but if MT. be correct, David—to judge from such knowledge of the Heb. word used as we possess—must have expressed himself with singular violence, and in terms which would be suitable rather to an abusive and malicious attack by words (comp. the Lat. *proscindere* = to satirize, defame), than to a simple rebuke or 'check' (so RV., but not fully representing שׁסע). None of the emendations that have been proposed is, however, satisfactory (Th. וַיִּשְׁבֵּת; Dr. Weir, 'Perhaps וַיִּמְנַע or וַיִּשְׁקֵט;' Klo. וַיֶּאְסֹר). Bu. agrees. וַיַּחְשֹׁךְ is a word that would be appropriate to the context (cf. II 18, 16); but וישׁסע could scarcely have arisen out of this by the ordinary processes of transcriptional corruption. The renderings of the Versions are: LXX ἔπεισε, Pesh. ـةل *made to repent*, Targ.

פֵּס] *persuaded, pacified*, Aq. συνέκλασεν (hence Vulg. *confregit*), Symm. περιέσπασεν, Theod. ἠπάτησεν.

10. מבקש] *is seeking*,—much more expressive than 'seeketh' (EVV.).

11. ואמר] The tense is irregular: the pf. with simple *waw* is improbable: the pf. with *waw* conv. is out of place, the idea of reiteration being evidently not what is here intended to be expressed. Jerome's וָאֹמַר (*et cogitavi* ut occiderem te), of course, cannot be right. Either ויאמר *and one said* must be restored, or we must follow LXX καὶ οὐκ ἠβουλήθην and read וָאֵמָאֵן *and I refused* (We. etc.).

להרגך] -*og*-: cf. on 15, 1.

ותחם] Elsewhere followed always by עין (Dt. 7, 16 and frequently). The ellipse, considering the standing usage of the word, is not probable. Sept. Targ. Pesh. express the first person וָאָחֹם: ותחם may have been 'written in error by a scribe, who expected עיני to follow' (We. Sm. Now.). Or (Bu.) עיני may have dropped out after ותחם: it is expressed by Vulg.

12. רְאֵה גַּם רְאֵה] The repetition of the imper. after גם is certainly very un-Hebraic: and Ehrl. would read—as Hupfeld did long ago (*Comm. in quosdam Iobeidos locos*, 1853, p. vi)— רְאֵה גַּם רָאֹה,—the inf. abs. (see on 1, 6).

ולא הרגתיך] carrying on בְּכָרְתִי: GK. § 114ʳ; *Tenses*, § 118.

צֹדֶה] *liest in wait* (not *huntest*, צוּד): see Ex. 21, 13; also Nu. 35, 20. 22. 'LXX δεσμεύεις (= צֹרֵר), translating from an indistinct text' (Dr. Weir).

13ᵃ. Cf. Gen. 16, 5ᵇ. 31, 53. For ונקמני, see GK. § 112ꟑ.

16. . . . , והיה] The pf. and *waw* conv. with the force of a wish: cf. *Tenses*, § 119 δ.

וישפטני מידך] *and judge me* (and free me) *from thy hand:* see on 25, 39.

19ᵃ. הגדת] viz. by thy action in sparing me. But Klo.'s הגדלת '*hast magnified* (cf. Gen. 19, 19) that which thou hast done to me (as) good' yields a better sense; so Sm. Bu. Now. Kitt. Ehrlich.

אֹתִי] after עשה, as II 2, 6ᵇ; cf. with חסד, Gen. 24, 49 al.

19ᵇ. את אשר] אשר alone =*forasmuch as* (15, 15): the את is out of place, and is doubtless a scribal error, due to את אשר just before.

20. וְשִׁלְּחוֹ] will he send him away? For the question thus introduced, cf. Ez. 15, 5ᵇ: *Tenses*, § 123 β; GK. § 150ᵃ. Klo.'s וּמִי (GK. § 112ʰʰ *n.*), with 'the general subject limited afterwards to the specific אִישׁ,' is highly improbable,—though of course without אִישׁ it would have been quite suitable.

תחת וג׳] '*in return for this day*—the sense being explained by what follows—*wherein* (on *v.* 5) *thou hast wrought for me.*' But as Klo. remarks, such a use of היום is un-Hebraic. Klo. reads הַטּוֹב *this good* (Nu. 10, 32) for היום; and we must either do the same, or adopt the transposition followed tacitly (cf. on 23, 6) by EVV., and read תחת אשר עשיתה לי היום הזה. Against LXX (ἀποτίσει αὐτῷ, and ἐν θλίψει) and Th. see We.

21. וְקָמָה] = *and be confirmed*, as 13, 14; Gen. 23, 30. Nu. 30, 5.

23. עָלוּ עַל הַמְצוּדָה] from 'En-gedi (23, 29), 680 ft. *below* the Medit. Sea, up past Hebron (3040 ft.) and Ḥalḥul (3270 ft.) over the high backbone of central Judah, and then down into the Shephēlah to the 'hold' (22, 4) of 'Adullam (if = 'Îd el-miyeh, 1160 ft.).

25, 1. וַיֵּרֶד] The place from which David 'came down' does not appear. The intention of the note seems to be to state that David, on hearing of Samuel's death, came down from some unnamed higher spot in the הר יהודה to the wilderness of Ma'on (*c.* 2500 ft.).

פָּארָן] Read מָעוֹן (23, 24. 25. 26), with LXX, as the context (*vv.* 2. 4) requires. The wilderness of Paran (Nu. 12, 16) is much too far to the south.

2. וְאִישׁ] without a verb: see on 17, 12; and cf. 1 Ki. 11, 26.

וּמַעֲשֵׂהוּ] of work in the fields: cf. Ex. 23, 16 בְּפֻּרֵי מַעֲשֶׂיךָ.

בַכַּרְמֶל] now *el-Kurmul*, 1 mile N. of Ma'on, 'on the edge of the wilderness of Judah, but to the west the land is broad and fertile, not unlike scenes of upland agriculture in Scotland. The name Carmel ("garden-land") is therefore suitable' (G. A. Smith, *EB.* s.v.; cf. on *ch.* 15, 12).

גָדוֹל] So II 19, 33 of Barzillai; 2 Ki. 4, 8 of the Shunammite woman.

וַיְהִי בִגְזֹז] apparently = *and he was* (engaged) *in* the shearing of his sheep,—a most unusual type of sentence. וַיְהִי גֹזֵז, or rather וְהוּא גֹזֵז,

is what would be expected in that sense. For the unusual form of the inf. (in ע״ע verbs), נְזֹז (so Gen. 31, 19 : 38, 13 לְנֹז), see GK. § 67ᶜᶜ.

3. שׂכל] *insight, shrewdness:* Pr. 16, 22 מקור חיים שׂכל בעליו.

מעללים] elsewhere only in poetry, and in prose written in the elevated style of Dt. (Jud. 2, 19. Neh. 9, 35). רֹעַ מעלליכם(הם) occurs in Is. 1, 16, Dt. 28, 20, and often in Jer. (as 4, 4).

כלבו] Qrê כְּלִבִּי, a Calebite, the י being the usual patronymic termination. So Targ. (מדבית כלב) Vulg. (*de genere Caleb*), Rashi, Kimchi (היו״ר לְיַחֵס. לפי שהיה ממשפחת כלב קְרָאוֹ כן).

> Nabal belonged to the Caleb-clan, a clan originally distinct from Judah, but afterwards incorporated in it, which had settlements in the country about Hebron (see 1 Ch. 2, 42–49, where Ziph, Hebron, Tappuaḥ, Joqde'am [so read for *Jorqo'am*], Ma'on, Beth-zur [4½ miles N. of Hebron], are specified as some of its settlements), and also in the Negeb (see *ch.* 30, 14 the נגב כלב). See further *DB.* and *EB.* s.v. CALEB ; and Kittel's *Die Bücher der Chronik,* pp. 13 f., 19 f.

5. עלו] Carmel (2887 ft.) is considerably above most of the surrounding plateau.

כרמֶלה] Cf. Ew. § 216ᶜ; GK. § 90ⁱ.

ושׁאֶלתם] GK. §§ 44ᵈ, 64ᶠ.

6. לֶחִי] A most perplexing and uncertain word. (*a*) The text can only be the pausal form of לַחֵי = *to him that liveth* (GK. § 29ᵛ). But the rendering, ' And ye shall say thus to him that liveth, Both thou,' etc., affords a poor sense ; hence it is thought by some to be a form of salutation, of which no other instance occurs, ' And ye shall say thus, To him that liveth! Both thou,' etc. So substantially Ges.[1] Ke., the former comparing the common Arabic formula of salutation حَيَّاكَ ٱللّٰهُ *God keep you in life* = grant you good health. (*b*) Vulg. renders *fratribus meis* (לְאֶחָי), following which We., admitting the difficulty of the passage, thinks that *relatively* the best explanation of it is to punctuate לֶחִי[2], and to render 'And ye shall say thus *to my brother*' (cf. II 20, 9 השׁלום אתה אחי, where Joab uses the same term

---

[1] *Thes.* 469 f. The rendering *In vitam* is, however, doubtful, the sing. חַי *life* occurring otherwise, at most, in a particular form of oath (p. 148).

[2] In this case, however, it is almost necessary to *read* לְאָחִי (so Bu.). It is true, cases of the elision of א occur (GK. § 23ᶠ), but none after a prep. with ֶ .

in addressing Amasa, and 1 Ki. 9, 13 Ḥiram addressing Solomon) [1].
This seems the most probable (so Bu.). (*c*) Sm. would read ואמרתם
לו וּלְחָיו אתה וג׳ ' And ye shall say *to him and to his clan*, Be thou (at)
peace,' etc. (so Now.); but a reference to Nabal's clan does not seem
called for. The other Versions evidently presuppose nothing different
from the MT. LXX εἰς ὥρας [2] (= כעת חיה Gen. 18, 14); Targ. לחיך;
Pesh. ܠܟܡ ܘܢܣܒ. For חי = *clan*, see on 18, 18.

ואתה שלום] Lit. *Both thou* (be) *peace*: cf. II 20, 9 השלום אתה; and
see on *ch.* 16, 4. On ‍ׇ = *both* (rare), see *Lex.* 253ᵃ h.

7. כי נזזים לך] Cf. II 13, 23. 24.

לא הכלמנום] So *v.* 15; cf. Ruth 2, 15 *end*. For the irregular הֶ,
cf. הֶרְאָה Gen. 41, 28 al., הֶגְלָה 2 Ki. 17, 11: GK. § 53ᵖ.

לָהם ל after the pass. verb, as Ex. 12, 16 al.: *Lex.* 514ᵃ.

8. על יום טוב] על of time is most unusual. יום טוב recurs in Esther
(8, 17. 9, 19. 22).

את אשר תמצא ידך] Cf. (though in different connexions) *ch.* 10, 7.
Lev. 12, 8. Jud. 9, 33. Qoh. 9, 10.

10. רבו] irregular: see GK. § 67ᵉᵉ.

עבדים המתפרצים] The combination of a ptcp. with the art. and
a subst. without it occurs sporadically in OT., often (but not invariably)
where the subst. is definite in itself or defined by the context. Thus
Gen. 1, 21. 28. 7, 21 (with כל־חיה and כל־בשר): Dt. 2, 23. Jud. 14, 3
(with a n. pr.): 16, 27. Jer. 27, 3. 46, 16. Ez. 2, 3 [3]. 14, 22 [4]. Pr.
26, 18. ψ. 62, 4 (read גְּדֵרָה דְחוּיָה). 119, 21 (accents) [5]. Here the

---

[1] Dr. Weir: 'Or is it לְאָחִי to my brother? But see *v.* 8 thy *son* David. כה
may follow the verb, as Ex. 5, 15, though rarely.' Against the view that treats
לחי as commencing the speech is the extreme abruptness which attaches then to
ואמרתם כה: what is regularly said is (תאמרו (תאמרון), e. g. *ch.* 11, 9. The
objection derived from *v.* 8 against ' my brother' is not conclusive: for both *brother*
and *son* being used metaphorically, the terms may be interchanged (especially when
not addressed to the same person).

[2] I. e. *next year*: comp. Theocr. 15. 74 (quoted by Liddell & Scott, and also by
Field here) κῆς ὥρας κήπειτα, φίλ' ἀνδρῶν, ἐν καλῷ εἴης.

[3] Where, however, אל נוים should probably be omitted with LXX.

[4] Where Cornill is probably right in vocalizing with LXX, Pesh. Symm. Vulg.
הַמּוֹצָאִים.

[5] Some other instances are noted in *Tenses*, § 209 (2).

idea 'slaves' is virtually limited by the words הַיּוֹם רַבּוּ, which shew
that the speaker has only a particular class of them in view.

מִפְּנֵי] מִפְּנֵי is more than מִן, and usually suggests *on account of, for
fear of:* cf. Jud. 9, 21ᵇ. *ch.* 18, 11. 19, 10. 23, 26: *Lex.* 818ᵃ. It
is used especially with verbs of fleeing.

11. וְלָקַחְתִּי] *and shall I take?* cf. Nu. 16, 10. Is. 66, 9ᵇ (tone *mil'el*
on account of Tifḥa, *Tenses,* § 104): GK. § 112ᶜᶜ.

מִימֵי] LXX יֵינִי, which is generally preferred by moderns. מִימֵי is
probably, as Abu'lwalid (*Riqmah*, ed. Goldberg, p. 175) suggested
long ago, due to a *lapsus calami*. It is true, in a district (Jos. 15, 19)
in which it was scarce, water might have been a commodity which
would not readily be given away ; still, among the viands provided for
the גּוֹזְזִים, some more special beverage than water might not unnaturally
find a place (cf. *v.* 18), and the change to מִימֵי is readily explained as
a consequence of the frequent collocation of לֶחֶם וּמַיִם. For other
instances of error due to *lapsus calami,* see *ch.* 12, 15. II 21, 8. Jer.
27, 1 ; and no doubt also 1 Ki. 2, 28.

13. וַיַּעֲלוּ] See on *v.* 5.

14. וַיַּעַט] from עוט (14, 32 Qrê. 15, 19), here pointed regularly.
The Versions mostly guess. LXX ἐξέκλινεν (but with ἀπ' αὐτῶν :
מֵהֶם for בָּהֶם), as 14, 32 ἐκλίθη; Aq. ὠτρύνθη; Symm. ἀπεστράφη;
Theod. ἐξουδένωσεν; Targ. וְקִץ בְּהוֹן; Pesh. ܘܣܟ ܗܘܐ ܠܗܘܢ;
Vulg. (after Symm.) *aversatus est eos.* Th. considers that these
renderings point to וַיָּקָט (cf. ψ. 95, 10); on which We. remarks :
'ויקט, even if Pesh. etc. read it, would be of no help : all turns here
on the *expression* of Nabal's feeling.' But וַיַּבְעַט (We. al.) is hardly
probable.

15. כָּל־יְמֵי הִתְהַלַּכְנוּ] So (in the *st. cstr.*) with a finite verb Lev.
14, 46 [1]. ψ. 90, 15 (יְמוֹת): with אֲשֶׁר, Lev. 13, 46. Nu. 9, 18 (GK.
§ 130ᵈ). Elsewhere the inf., as *vv.* 7. 16. 22, 4.

17. כָלְתָה] 20, 7. עַל and אֶל here interchange in one and the
same clause : for other remarkable instances of the same variation,
see *v.* 25. II 2, 9 ; 3, 29 : Jer. 26, 15. 28, 8.

---

[1] But some treat הַסְגִּיר here as an *inf.* (GK. § 53ˡ), though in that case it
should no doubt be pointed הַסְגִּיר (see Driver on Dt. 3, 3. 4, 15. 7, 24. 28, 55).

מִדַּבֵּר] GK. § 133ᶜ. The implicit subj. is הַמְדַבֵּר: see on 16, 4.

18. נבלי] *skins* (so RV. *m.*), as 10, 4 etc. : the ἀσκοὶ of the NT.

עֲשֻׂוֹת] i. e. *'ăsŭwōth*. So Kt. On the form, see Ew. § 189ᵈ ; Stade, §§ 119ᵇ, 319ᶜ ; GK. §§ 24ᵇ, 75ᵛ : and comp. נְטֻוֹת Is. 3, 16. The Qrê substitutes the normal עֲשֻׂיוֹת *'ăsŭyōth*.

סאים] the סְאָה (= σάτον, Mt. 13, 33) was ⅓ of an ephah, or 2⅔ gallons. On קלי, see on II 17, 28.

צמקים] *dried grapes*, or *clusters of raisins* (30, 12. II 16, 1. 1 Ch. 12, 41†). The root signifies to be *dry* or *shrivelled:* in OT. only Hos. 9, 14 (שָׁדַיִם צֹמְקִים) ; in the Talm. (v. Levy) of dried figs, grapes, etc. In Ps.-Jon. עֲנָבִים לַחִים וִיבֵשִׁים (Nu. 6, 3) is rendered by עִינְבִין רְטִיבִין וְצַמְקִין. Cf. Kennedy, *EB.* ii. 1568.

דבלים] *pressed fig-cakes* (*EB.* ii. 1570): 30, 12. 1 Ch. 12, 41 (with צמוקים, as a present to David's warriors). 2 Ki. 20, 7 = Is. 38, 21†.

20. והיה] The tense is incorrect (on 1, 12). Either read ויהי (constr. as 2 Ki. 2, 11), or (though καὶ ἐγενήθη stands in the LXX) delete it as an early corrupt anticipation of the following היא (comp. then, for the form of the sentence, 9, 14 : *Tenses*, § 169).

ירדת] to meet David, on his way up (*vv.* 6. 13).

21. ודוד אמר] Note the *plupf.* (on 9, 15). The clause expresses David's thoughts as he went along before he met Abigail.

אך] as Jer. 5, 4 ; see on 16, 6.

22. לאיבי דוד] LXX τῷ Δαυειδ = לְדָוִד, certainly rightly. Analogy (cf. e. g. 20, 13) requires the imprecation to be uttered by the speaker against himself. The insertion of איבי is probably intentional, to avoid the appearance, as the threat in *b* was not carried out, of the imprecation recoiling upon David himself[1].

23. לאפי דוד על פניה] We have the types, (1) וישתחו אפים ארצה Gen. 19, 1 and often ; (2) ל' לאפיו א' Gen. 48, 12. 2 S. 18, 28†, and לאפיו alone, Nu. 22, 31† ; (3) א' על אפיו ל' 2 S. 14, 4. 33. 1 Ki. 1, 23† ; (4) א' אפיו ל' 2 S. 24, 20† ; also (5) ויפל על(אל) פניו (ארצה) Jos. 5, 14. 2 S. 9, 6. 14, 22. Ru. 2, 10 ; (6) ויפל לאפיו ארצה 1 S. 20, 41† : but never לאפי another. לפני דוד על אפיה would therefore here be more in accordance with usage (We. al.).

---

[1] Comp. similar instances in the Talm., Dalman, *Gramm. des Jüd.-Pal. Aramäisch* (1894), p. 78 ; ed. 2 (1905), p. 109.

אָרֶץ] 7 MSS. have the more usual אַרְצָה, which is also a סְבִיר (on 12, 5).

24. וַתִּפֹּל עַל רַגְלָיו] Cf. 2 Ki. 4, 37 (Bu.).

בִּי אֲנִי] Cf. 1 Ki. 1, 26 ; and see GK. § 135ᵍ; Ew. § 311ᵃ.

25. נָבָל] 'Fool' is an inadequate rendering. The word in Hebrew suggested one who was insensible to the claims of either God or man, and who was consequently at once irreligious and churlish : see esp. Is. 32, 5 f. (where *v.* 6 unfolds the *character* of the נבל in terms which recall at once the conduct of Nabal described in this chapter ¹). See further *Lex.* s. v.; *Parallel Psalter*, Glossary, p. 457. Here the best rendering would be *churl*—' Churl is his name, and *churlishness* is with him,'—or, as we might say, 'is his nature.'

26. וְעַתָּה . . . וְעַתָּה] The word repeated after the long intervening clause.

Resumption is a frequent characteristic of Heb. prose style. The case of כִּי...כִּי has been noticed on 14, 39 (cf. *Lex.* 472ᵃ) : see also on 17, 13. The following are other examples, derived partly from my own observation, partly from Kön. *Stilistik* (1900), p. 129 f. : Ex. 1, 15–16 (וַיֹּאמֶר . . . וַיֹּאמֶר). 4, 9ᵇ. 12, 41 (וַיְהִי . . . וַיְהִי). Lev. 13, 3 (וְרָאָה...וְרָאָהוּ). 17, 5 (וֶהֱבִיאוּ . . . יָבִיאוּ לְמַעַן). 27, 3. Nu. 5, 19–21. 10, 32 (וְהָיָה: so Dt. 20, 11. Jud. 11, 31). 14, 36–37 (הָאֲנָשִׁים). Dt. 4, 42 (וָנָס . . . לָנוּס). 18, 6 (וּבָא . . . יָבֹא). Jud. 9, 16ᵃ–19ᵃ (אִם בֶּאֱמֶת וְג'). ch. 29, 10 (וְהִשְׁכַּמְתֶּם בַּבֹּקֶר). II 1, 1–2 (וַיְהִי). 1 Ki. 8, 41–42 (וּבָא). 12, 10 (כֹּה...כֹּה תֹאמַר). Is. 7, 22 (יִהְיֶה). 49, 5–6 (אָמַר . . . וַיֹּאמֶר). Jer. 3, 7ᵇ–8 (reading in 8 וַתֵּרֶא, with most moderns). 20, 5 (אָתַן). 29, 25ᵇ–31ᵇ (אֲשֶׁר יַעַן). 34, 2. 10. 18–20. Ez. 21, 29 (יַעַן). 24, 25–26ᵃ (בְּיוֹם הַהוּא . . . בְּיוֹם). 28, 2ᵃ–6ᵇ (יַעַן). Hag. 2, 13ᵃ–15ᵃ. Zech. 8, 23. For some examples from later books, see Kön. *l. c.* Comp. also the cases of the resumption of a noun by הוּא, הִיא, etc. (*Tenses*, §§ 123 *Obs.*, 199; 198), and of a *casus pendens* by a suffix (§§ 123 *a*, 197, with *Obs.* 2).

אֲשֶׁר מְנָעֲךָ יְי'] The antecedent יְי' is repeated in the relative clause, because it is separated from אֲשֶׁר by the addition וְחִי נַפְשְׁךָ: contrast *v.* 34.

וְהוֹשַׁע יָדְךָ לְךָ] The inf. abs., in continuation of an inf. c., as 22, 13ᵇ (see the note); and followed by a subst. standing to it in the relation

¹ In EVV. נבל is here rendered unfortunately *vile person*, and (כְּלַי) כִּילַי *churl*. Render : (5) 'The churl will be no more called noble, nor the knave said to be gentle (i.e., in modern English, a gentleman). (6) For the churl speaketh churlishness, and his heart worketh naughtiness, to do profaneness, and to utter defection (*lit.* going astray) against Yahweh, to make empty the soul of the hungry, and to cause the drink of the thirsty to fail;' and *knave* for *churl* in *v.* 7.

of subject (rare), as *v.* 33, Lev. 6, 7. ψ. 17, 5 (Ew. § 328ᶜ towards
the end; GK. § 113ᵍᵍ). The phrase itself, implying an exploit or
success, achieved against opposing obstacles by *force*, recurs *vv.* 31.
33. Jud. 7, 2. Job 40, 14 (ימינך), and with reference to Yahweh,
Is. 59, 16. 63, 5. ψ. 98, 1 ; cf., with זרוע, 44, 4.

27. ברכה] i. e. *a present*, called a *blessing* from the feelings of good
will, of which it is the expression : 30, 26. Gen. 33, 11. Jud. 1, 14.
2 Ki. 5, 15.

הביא] An error for הביאה, as *v.* 35. So 26 MSS.

ונתנה] As in II 14, 10. Is. 9, 4, the *waw* conv. with the pf. introduces the direct predicate (*Tenses*, § 123 ; GK. § 143ᵈ): here, as
20, 5. Jud. 11, 8, with a precative force, 'And now this present, ...,
let it be given,' etc.

ברגלי אדני] *at the feet of* my lord = following him, Ex. 11, 8. Dt.
11, 6. Jud. 4, 10. II 15, 16. 17 al.

28. בית נאמן] Cf. 2, 25. II 7, 16. 1 Ki. 11, 38.

מלחמות יהוה] As 18, 17. Cf. Nu. 21, 14.

מימיך] An idiomatic expression = *all the days that thou hast lived*,
since thy birth : 1 Ki. 1, 6 מימיו אביו עצבו לא ; Job 38, 12 המימיך¹
בקר צויתה. מימיך having this sense, the pf. נמצאה לא would be the
tense naturally used with it : probably תמצא לא is chosen with the
view of generalising the statement as much as possible, so as to allow
it to include a possible future,—' *is not to be* found in thee,' etc.

29. ויקם . . . והיתה] 'And man has (as a fact) risen up, etc. . . . :
but the soul of my lord shall be,' etc. If it be thought that the sense,
' and *should a man* rise up . . . then may the soul of my lord be,' etc.
is required, וְקָם must be read (Is. 21, 7 ; *Tenses*, § 149 ; GK. § 159ᵍ):
so Sm. Bu. Now. Dh.

צרורה וג'] *bound up* for safe custody *in the bundle of life*.

את] *with* = in the care and custody of, as Lev. 5, 23 ; Dt. 15, 3 ;
Is. 49, 4.

ואת . . . יקלענה] The object resumed, and connected directly with
the verb by the suffix ; a frequent elegance of Hebrew style, as
Gen. 13, 15. 21, 13 : *Tenses*, § 197. 1, 6 ; GK. § 143ᶜ.

---

¹ Cf. ܥܡ ܡܩܒ̈ܝܣܘܢ, Wright, *Apocr. Acts of the Apostles*, p. 88, ll. 15-16.

30. ‫וג׳‬ ‫‬‫כבל‬] EVV. 'according to all the good that he hath spoken concerning thee,' which in Hebrew[1] would be ‫אשר דבר‬ ‫הטובה‬ ‫כבל‬ ‫עליך‬. 24, 19 ‫טובה‬ ‫אתי‬ ‫עשיתה‬ ‫אשר‬ ‫את‬, cited by Bu., is not parallel. The text is evidently in some disorder, though it is not certain how it is to be corrected. Either this or ‫עליך‬ ‫דבר‬ ‫אשר‬ ‫הטובה‬ ‫כל‬ ‫את‬ might be the original reading : but in either case it is not apparent how ‫הטובה‬ ‫את‬ would assume its present place. Perhaps ‫הטובה‬ ‫את‬ was originally a marginal gloss.

31. 'Then let not this be to thee a (cause of) tottering (*or* staggering), or a stumbling of heart, (viz.) to have shed innocent blood,' etc. Both expressions are peculiar : but the meaning appears to be, ' Let David avoid the difficulties which shedding innocent blood might hereafter involve him in, and the qualms of conscience which will inevitably follow it.' The kind of 'tottering' expressed by the root ‫פוק‬ may be learnt from a comparison of Is. 28, 7 ; Jer. 10, 4 ; and Nah. 2, 11 (‫ברכים‬ ‫פיק‬). The ancient translations seem merely to have conjectured for ‫פוקה‬ a meaning more or less agreeable with the context: LXX βδελυγμός[2]; Aq. Symm. λυγμός, whence Vulg. in *singultum* et scrupulum cordis: Targ. ‫יצפא‬ (solicitude), Pesh. ‫וס‬‫‬‫‬ (terror). A curious Midrashic exposition of ‫לפוקה‬ may be seen in the *Midrash Tillin* on ψ. 53 (quoted by Levy, *NHWB.*, s. v. ‫פקפק‬).

‫ולשפך‬] . . . ‫ולהושיע‬ *et* . . . *et* = *both* . . . *and.* But no stress seems to rest here upon the combination ; and no doubt the first ‫ו‬ is to be omitted, with LXX, Vulg. Pesh. After ‫ולהושיע‬ LXX express ‫יר‬ (which the translators are most unlikely to have done, had not the word stood in their text); and the insertion, as We. remarks, is a necessary one : for it just gives to the expression used the sense of *force* (*v.* 26) which is required.

33. ‫טעמך‬] *discretion, tact.* ‫טעם‬ as Pr. 11, 22.

‫כלתני‬] from ‫כלא‬: GK. § 75�q�q. Cf. 6, 10.

‫והושׁע‬] See on *v.* 26.

34. ‫כי‬ . . . ‫לולי‬ ‫כי‬] as 14, 39 : the first ‫כי‬ introduces the assertion

---

[1] In Ethiopic a different construction is possible, the antecedent being there frequently introduced into the relative clause : Dillmann, *Aeth. Gr.* § 201. 1 (*b*).

[2] Possibly (but not certainly) a corruption of the unusual λυγμός.

sworn to, the second is resumptive. Thenius, following LXX literally,
gravely proposes, for the second כי, to read אז אמרתי !

ותבאתי] By error for וַתָּבֹאִי, through the influence of the following
לקראתי (so Dr. Weir). Otherwise GK. § 76ʰ. For the tense, cf. Jos.
7, 7 : and *Tenses*, § 140.

אם נותר] if there *had* been left . . . ! = surely there had not been
left. The pf., after the oath, as II 3, 27 (though not there introduced by אם).

35. ולה אמר] The pron. is emphatic : cf. 1 Ki. 17, 13ᵇ. Jud. 12, 1.
14, 16.

עלי] She had ' come down ' (*v.* 20) to meet David.

36. והנה לו משתה] For the position of לו, cf. . . . ולו *v.* 2 ; 1 Ki. 4,
10. 13 ; and on *ch.* 1, 2. Comp. also Jud. 17, 5. Job 22, 8 ואיש
זרוע לו הארץ.

כמשתה המלך] Cf. II 13, 27 LXX.

טוב] טוב of the heart=*glad, merry:* II 13, 28 : Pr. 15, 15 וטוב
לב משתה תמיד. So the subst. טוב לֵב Dt. 28, 47. Is. 65, 14 ; and
טוֹבֵי לֵב 1 Ki. 8, 66.

עליו] lit. *upon him*, in accordance with Hebrew idiom : see on 17, 32.
' Within ' (EVV.) is a paraphrase.

37. וימת לבו] opp. is יחי לבבכם ' may your heart *live* ' = take courage,
ψ. 22, 27.

והוא] ' and he himself' (opp. to לבו).

38. כעשרת הימים] ויהי כעשרת הימים is subject : ' And there was *the
like of* ten days, and,' etc., כְּ *the like of* being an undeveloped substantive (*Lex.* 453ª). For the art., Dr. Weir compares 9, 20. Is. 30, 26.
1 Ch. 9, 25. Ezr. 10, 8. But ימים is certainly better in accordance with
analogy (so GK. § 134ᵐ). ' And it came to pass *after* ten days,' would,
of course, be ויהי מקץ עשרת ימים (Jer. 42, 7). Comp. 1 Ki. 18, 1 ויהי ימים
רבים, where ימים is similarly the *subject* of ויהי (for the *sing.*, see on 1, 2).

39. רב. . . מיד נבל] pregnantly : cf. ψ. 43, 1 ריבה ריבי מגּוֹי לא חסיד ;
and . . . שפט מיד 24, 16. II 18, 19. 31.

השיב י"י] The subj. repeated, the אשר at the beginning of the
sentence having been forgotten.

השיב . . . בראשו] as Jud. 9, 57. 1 Ki. 2, 44 : cf. דמו בראשו Jos. 2,
19 al., and the phrase in 1 Ki. 8, 32 and often in Ez. לתת דרכו בראשו.

וידבר באביגיל] 'and spake *concerning* Abigail,' i.e. (as the phrase was understood to mean) asked her in marriage. Cf. Cant. 8, 8.

42. ‏ההלכת‎] Read ‏הֹלֶכֶת‎ (the ה dittographed from ‏נערתיה‎): the word must be the predicate—she rode, and they walked in attendance behind her.

‏לרגלה‎] is not quite the same as ‏ברגלי‎ *v.* 27: the ‏ל‎ is the so-called ‏ל‎ of *norm*, 'going *according to* her *foot*,' i.e. *guided by* her foot=attending upon her. Comp. for this sense of ‏לרגל‎ Gen. 30, 30 hath blessed thee ‏לרגלי‎ *at my foot*=whithersoever I turned (RV.); 33, 14 and I will lead on softly ‏לרגל המלאכה‎ *according to the pace* of the cattle (*Lex.* 516ᵇ).

43. Aḥino'am is mentioned before Abigail in 27, 3. 30, 5; she was also the mother of David's firstborn, Amnon (II 3, 2); so probably he married her shortly before Abigail, as the Heb. here permits (not ‏ויקח ד'‎, but ‏ואת אחינעם לקח ...‎). *V.* 44 hints at the reason why David took now these two wives; he had been deprived of Michal (18, 27).

יזרעאל] Not the ‏יזרעאל‎ in the N. of Palestine, but one in the hill-country of Judah, Jos. 15, 56, evidently not far from Ma'on and Carmel (mentioned there in *v.* 55, as in *v.* 2 here).

גם שתיהן] The ‏גם‎ is idiomatic in this phrase,='both *alike:*' Dt. 22, 22. 23, 13. Ru. 1, 5. Pr. 17, 15. 20, 10. 12.

44. ‏ושאול נתן‎] '*had* given:' see on 9, 15.

פלטי] abridged from ‏פלטיאל‎, II 3, 15.

גלים] The situation of Gallim is not known; but it was plainly (Is. 10, 30†) a little N. of Jerusalem.

26. 1. The *v.* is largely identical with 23, 19 (where see the note); and the narrative following in *ch.* 24 exhibits such numerous points of resemblance with *ch.* 26 that the two have been held by many scholars to be in reality different versions of the same incident. If this opinion be correct, the more original version will be that contained in the present chapter.

הגבעתה] Gibeah of Saul, 2½ miles N. of Jerusalem (see on 9, 1).

בגבעת החכילה] Perhaps the long ridge called *Ḍahr el-Kôlâ*, 5½ miles E. of Ziph, 10 miles W. of 'En-gedi, and 1 mile N. of Wâdy Malâky (on 23, 26), 'running out of the Ziph plateau (see on 23, 14) towards the Dead Sea desert, or Jeshimon' (Conder, *T.W.* 244; Buhl, 97).

על פני הישׁימן] '*in front of* the Desolation' (see on 23, 24), i.e. over-looking it, which, if the 'hill of Ḥachilah' is rightly identified, it would do. The passage is one which shews that על פני does not always mean *East of* (comp. on 15, 7): cf. *Lex.* 818ᵇ.

2. וירד] Cf. 23, 20. Ziph is actually higher than Tell el-Fûl (see on 23, 19); but there is a descent from Tell el-Fûl (2754 ft.) to Jerusalem (2593 ft.), and from Hebron (3040 ft.) to Ziph (2882 ft.); so no doubt 'came down' is used with reference to one of these.

On the מדבר זיף, see on 23, 15.

3. Saul encamped, near the ordinary route, on the particular hill of Ḥachilah; David remained somewhere in the wilderness around it.

יושׁב] not 'abode' (EVV.) but '*was* abiding.' So *v.* 5ᵇ '*was* lying,' and '*were* encamping;' *v.* 7 '*was lying* asleep,' and '*were* lying.' The reader of the English versions, till he refers to the Hebrew, does not realize how much is lost by the frequent rendering of the participle by a finite verb.

4. אל־נכון] The same somewhat singular expression in 23, 23. Here, however, immediately following בא, the name of a *place* is expected,—and the more so, since the text, as it stands, adds nothing to what has been already stated in 3ᵇ,—unless indeed it can be argued that וידע marks any more certain knowledge than וירא. It is probable therefore that נכון here is the corruption of the name of some locality, though what that may have been it is impossible to conjecture. LXX ἐκ Κεıλα, as We. points out, is too vague.

5. במעגל] See on 17, 20.

6. אחימלך החתי] *This* Aḥimelech is not mentioned elsewhere. For his nationality, cf. אוריה החתי.

מי ירד] David must therefore have been in some part of the wilderness that was *higher* than החכילה.

אני] For the pron. in such a sentence, cf. on II 21, 6 (p. 352).

7. מראשׁתו] prop. *the parts at* or *about the head*, hence construed in the accus. adverbially (GK. § 118ᵍ), like סביבות and the corresponding מרגלותיו, Ru. 3, 8. 14. So Gen. 28, 11 וישׂם מראשׁתיו *lit.* and placed (it) *at the parts about his head.*

8. We have had before 18, 11 להכות בחנית; 19, 10 אכה בדוד ובקיר בדוד ובקיר to smite with the spear *into David and into the wall,* i.e. *to pin him* with the spear *to the wall.* The analogy of these passages shews that here ובארץ' is co-ordinate not with בחנית, but with the suff. in אכנו' (We.). בארץ and the suffix are, however, very unequally coupled; and it is better to read with Krenkel (*ZAW.* 1882, 310) בחניתו בארץ 'with *his* spear (*v.* 7) to the earth' (so Sm. Now. Dh. Ehrl.). With ולא אשנה לו cf. II 20, 10.

9. ונקה . . . מי שלח] ונקה is the pf. with *waw* conv., and שלח has a modal force (cf. the pf. in Gen. 21, 7. ψ. 11, 3. 60, 11=108, 11): 'who *is to have* put forth his hand, etc., *and be* guiltless?' The sentence is of a type that must be carefully distinguished from that of Job 9, 4 מי הקשה אליו וַיִּשְׁלָם Who (ever) hardened himself [as a fact] against Him, and escaped sound? Dt. 5, 23 (it is cited wrongly in GK. § 112ᵇ). Comp. *Tenses,* §§ 19. 2; 115 (p. 115). Still, in spite of the parallels, it is probable that a י has fallen out after מי, and that we should read מי ישלח.

10. כי אם] כי here cannot, as often, introduce the terms of the oath; for this (with אם following) would yield a sense the very opposite of what is required, viz. Surely Y. will *not* smite him! כי אם must therefore be construed together, though not in the manner adopted by Th. Ke. (*'Except* Y. smite him, or his day come, etc., far be it from me to put forth my hand against him'); for this both implies an un-Hebraic inversion of principal and subordinate clause, and yields an improbable sense: David cannot have meant to imply that if one of these contingencies happened to Saul, he would then be ready to put forth his hand against him. Either כי אם must be understood to have the force of *surely* (as above, 21, 6), or (Ges. Dr. Weir) the negative (such as usually precedes it) may be supposed to be suppressed: (minime ego Saulum caedam,) *sed* Deus caedat eum: cf. II 13, 33 Kt. (minime,) *sed* solus Amnon mortuus est.

יגפנו] by some sudden stroke, cutting him off prematurely (25, 38. II 12, 15. 2 Ch. 13, 20 al.), יומו denoting what would be considered a natural close to his life.

נספה] not 'perish' (EVV.), but *be swept away;* see on 12, 25, and cf. 27, 1.

במלחמה ירד] The position of במלחמה gives freshness of expression, and force, to the new alternative. In ירד David has in his mind a combat with the Philistines.

11. For מיהוה, see on 24, 7; and for מְשֻׁלָּח, on 12, 23.

מראשתו] The accus. of place (*v.* 7), after אשר, as Dt. 17, 14 אשר סביבותי: cf. Qor. 42, 5 مَنْ حَوْلَهَا *whoever is round about it*, 19, 5. ונלכה־לנו] 'and let us *get us away:*' so 12 וילכו להם (*Lex.* 515ᵇ).

12. מֵרַאֲשֹׁתָי] Read מִמְּרַאֲשֹׁתָי: a מ has fallen out between the two others. The י at the end, if correct, would be the one instance in OT., parallel to בָּמוֹתֵי, of that letter attached to the *st. c.* of the *fem. pl.* before an independent word (otherwise only before *suffixes*): Stade, § 330ᵇ; GK. § 87ˢ. But LXX has αὐτοῦ: so We. may be right in arguing that 'the י at the end confirms the reading ממראשתיו of LXX, instead of ממראשתי שאול' (so Sm. Bu. Dh.). In this case, of course, the anomaly will disappear.

תרדמת י″] a slumber so profound and unusual that it was regarded as sent directly from Yahweh. Cf. חרדת אלהים in 14, 15.

13. העבר] to *the side across* (cf. 14, 1. 4. 40); i.e. to the opposite side of the valley at the foot of the hill (*v.* 3).

רב וג′] a circ. clause (*Tenses*, § 161; GK. § 156ᶜ). Cf. Gen. 12, 8.

14. מי אתה קראת] In the *third* ps. comp. Is. 50, 9 מי־הוא ירשיעני; Job 13, 19 מי־הוא יריב עמדי (*Tenses*, § 201. 2): unless I am mistaken, no parallel in the *second* ps. occurs in the OT. (the sentence Is. 51, 12 is framed differently).

15. שמרת אל] In *v.* 16 עַל. An unusual construction: yet see Pr. 6, 22 בשכבך תשמר עליך, and (of *watching* in a hostile sense) II 11, 16. (In ψ. 59, 10 עזי אליך אזמרה, as in *v.* 18, must certainly be read.)

16. אשר לא וג′] See on II 2, 5.

אדניכם] the plur. of 'excellence' (GK. § 124ⁱ); cf. Gen. 42, 30.

ואת צפחת] If the text is correct, את must be explained either as marking the fresh subject (see on 17, 34), or (Sm.) as an accus. under the governing force of אי: but the last expl. especially is unsatisfactory. We expect either ואת . . . את or ואי . . . אי. As the time is night, את is improbable (We.) after ראה; it seems best, therefore, to regard ואת as an error for וַיַּ, due to a scribe influenced involuntarily by the recollection of ראה at the beginning of the sentence.

So GK. § 117ᵐ *n.* (the citation of the verse in § 117ˡ must be due to an oversight).

17. קוֹלִי] In Hebrew, the repetition of a word is a mode of signifying assent (1 Ki. 21, 20): LXX, for קוֹלִי, express עבדך, which is used for the same purpose, as II 9, 2, cf. *v.* 6 הנה עבדיך. 15, 15. The one is thus just a synonym of the other : 'the more courtly'—that of LXX [cf. 27, 5 in lieu of the pron.]—'is the less original' (We.).

18. וּמַה־בְּיָדִי רָעָה] The *order* is idiomatic : cf. 20, 10. II 19, 29. 24, 13; 1 Ki. 12, 16. Jer. 2, 5. Qoh. 11, 2. Est. 6, 3 (*Lex.* 552ᵇ).

19. יְרַח מנחה] Cf. Gen. 8, 21 יﬧﬨ, followed however by את ריח הניחח. Dr. Weir writes: 'יָרַח, perhaps יָרֵךְ as Am. 5, 22. Jer. 14, 12. Mal. 1, 10.' On הסתחף, cf. on 2, 36.

לֵאמֹר לֵךְ וג׳] For the god of the country, according to ancient ideas, could be properly worshipped only in his own land : hence banishment was equivalent to being told to go and serve foreign gods. Cf. Hos. 9, 3.

אלהים אחרים] With the possible exception of Ex. 23, 13, probably the earliest occurrence of this afterwards common Deuteronomic expression (see *LOT.* p. 92, edd. 6–8, p. 99 ; or *Deut.* p. lxxviii).

20. מִנֶּגֶד פְּנֵי יﬞי] Cf. מנגד עיניך Am. 9, 3. ψ. 31, 23.

אֶת פַּרְעֹשׁ אֶחָד] For את, cf. on 9, 3. פַּרְעֹשׁ אֶחָד appears, however, to be derived here from 24, 15 : LXX express נַפְשִׁי,—no doubt rightly : for (1) the comparison *within* a comparison (to seek a *flea*, as when one hunts a *partridge*) is not probable ; and (2) MT. agrees but imperfectly with clause *a*,—the *ground* (כי) for אל יפל דמי ארצה being only fully expressed in the reading of LXX, ' for the king of Israel is come out to seek *my life.*'

יִרְדֹּף] sc. הָרֹדֵף (on 16, 4). The art. in הקֹרֵא is *generic*, such as is often found in comparisons, where a class, not a particular individual, is naturally referred to (GK. § 126ˡˑᵒ): so II 17, 10 כלב האריה : Jud. 8, 18ᵇ כתאר בני המלך; 14, 6 כְּשַׁסַּע הַגְּדִי; 1 Ki. 14, 15 כאשר ינוד הקנה במים; Nu. 11, 12 כאשר ישא האמן את הינק, etc.

Klo. for כאשר would read כנשר,—'like a griffon-vulture (see on II 1, 23), (which) pursues a partridge on the mountains,'—which is adopted by Sm. Bu. The construction is common in poetry (e. g. Dt. 32, 11. ψ. 42, 2 : *Lex.* 454ᵃ); but in prose comparisons are expressed either by בְּ with the inf. (as Jud. 14, 6, cited above), or by באשר (see _ib._),—i.e. in the present case, כאשר ירדף הנשר את־הקרא בהרים. LXX καθὼς καταδιώκει ὁ νυκτικόραξ ἐν τοῖς ὄρεσιν, cited by Klo., is not evidence that LXX read כנשר : νυκτικόραξ corresponds here to הקרא, and represents כּוֹם (_owl_) in Lev. 11, 17. ψ. 107, 6; and in Dt. 14, 17† some other bird, but not the נשר. It is also a question, though it must be left to a naturalist to answer it, whether the נשר, or griffon-vulture, being a carrion-feeding bird, would ' pursue a partridge on the mountains :' Tristram, _Nat. Hist. of the Bible_, p. 172 ff., speaks of its keen sight, and of its swooping down from afar upon a carcase (Job 39, 29 f.), but says nothing of its pursuit of the living animal.

21. ויקרה וג'] Cf. 2 Ki. 1, 13. 14 ; also ψ. 72, 14. 116, 15.

ואשנה] Cf. 14, 24 LXX. Lev. 4, 13. Ez. 45, 20 al.

הסכלתי ואשגה הרבה מאד:] The accents treat הרבה as qualifying _both_ the preceding words.

22. הנה החנית המלך] Kt. 'behold the spear, O king !' Qrê 'behold the spear of the king,' which is better adapted to the context, ה being repeated accidentally from הנה.

23. לָאִישׁ] The art. has a distributive force : 1 Ki. 8, 39. 18, 4. Gen. 41, 48ᵇ.

בְּיָדִי] בְּיָד would be more agreeable with general custom (comp. on 19, 9) : for the cases in which בְּיָד occurs without a suffix are mostly those in which the reference is _general_ (II 23, 6. Is. 28, 2. Job 34, 20 : similarly מִיָד Pr. 6, 5), not, as here, specific. However, it is possible that ביד may have been here written intentionally, for the purpose of avoiding the assonance (which is here an awkward one) with the following ידי. 1 Ki. 20, 42 ; Ez. 12, 7 (though here LXX, Pesh. omit ביד) ; 2 Ch. 25, 20 would support the text. But some 50 MSS. have ידי ; and it is better, with Weir and most moderns, to read this.

25. עשה] used with a pregnant force, such as is more common in poetry : Is. 10, 13. ψ. 22, 32. 37, 5. Ez. 20, 9. 14. 22 (_Lex._ 794ᵃ 4).

וגם יכל תוכל] Cf. 1 Ki. 22, 22 תוכל וגם.

27—31. _David seeks refuge in the country of the Philistines with Achish. The Philistines resolve to attack Israel ; their army advances to Apheq. David is released from the necessity of fighting against his countrymen through the opportune suspicions of the Philistine lords : his vengeance on the Amalekites who had_

*smitten Ẓiḳlag. Saul consults the witch of 'En-dor. Death of
Saul and Jonathan on Mount Gilboa'.*

27, 1. אֶל לְבוּ] Gen. 8, 21. 24, 45; and with עַל = אֶל *ch.* 1, 13.
אספה] 12, 25 (see note); 26, 10.

יוֹם אחד] אחד unemphatic as Gen. 33, 13; and (of the past)
ch. 9, 15. (Not as Is. 9, 13 al. a *single* day.)

אֵין לִי טוב כי וג'] can only be rendered, 'I have no good: for
(= but) I must escape into,' etc. The first clause is, however,
harshly and abruptly expressed; LXX have οὐκ ἔστι μοι ἀγαθὸν
ἐὰν μὴ σωθῶ, i. e. 'I have no good אִפָּלֵט אִם כִּי *except* I escape,' etc.,
which is preferable.

וְנוֹאַשׁ מִמֶּנִּי] a pregnant construction, occurring with this verb only
here, but analogous to that of החריש, noticed on 7, 8.

2. גַת] If Gath was at *Tell eṣ-Ṣāfiyeh* (see on 6, 17), some 28 miles
NW. of the presumable site of Ḥachilah (see on 26, 1).

3. הכרמלית. LXX הכרמלי, in agreement with 30, 5. II 2, 2.

4. וְלֹא יוֹסַף] So Kt., the impf. having a frequentative force, as 2, 25
(see on 1, 7). The Qrê substitutes the more usual tense וְלֹא יָסַף
(15, 35; Jud. 13, 21 al.): comp. a similar case in Jos. 15, 63.

5. נא] נא belongs logically to יתנו; but it is thrown back into the
protasis and attached to אם, as regularly in this formula (Gen. 18, 3;
33, 10 al.), for the purpose of indicating as early as possible that the
speech is of the nature of an entreaty.

6. צִקְלָג] Supposed by Conder to be *Zuḥélíqeh*, 22 miles SW. of
Tell eṣ-Ṣāfiyeh: but the consonants, except ל, do not correspond
phonetically, so that the identification is very uncertain.

עַל-כֵּן [לכן is regularly used, when the origin of a name or custom
is assigned (Gen. 10, 9. 11, 9 etc.: *Lex.* 487); hence the סביר עַל כֵן
(see on 12, 5), though not supported, so far as appears, by any MS.,
is prompted by a sound literary instinct, and may be correct.

7. ימים [ימים וארבעה חדשים, by usage, suggesting *a year :* see 1, 3,
and, more distinctly, Jud. 17, 10 עשרה כסף לַיָּמִים; Lev. 25, 29.

8. וַיַּעַל] Either into the higher ground on which the tribes raided by David
lived (which would suit Gezer); or, in the uncertainty whether this ground was
higher than Ẓiqlag, in a military sense (Now.), of an attack in general, as Jud. 20, 18.
Is. 21, 2. Nah. 2, 2.

(Qrê הנשורי והגרי (והגזרי] LXX have πάντα τὸν Γεσειρι, reading, therefore, only one name (viz. הנשורי; see Jos. 13, 11. 13 LXX), so that the two are presumably doublets. As the better-known Geshur, on the *East* of the upper Jordan, is evidently out of the question, the name here and Jos. 13, 2, if the text is correct, is probably that of a small tribe between the Philistines and Egypt (Bu. Dhorme, Kenn.). We. Now., preferring the other doublet, read הַגִּזְרִי, i.e. the Canaanites who till the time of Solomon occupied *Gezer* (Jud. 1, 29 ; 1 Ki. 9, 16), 12 miles ENE. of Tell eṣ-Ṣâfiyeh: but this appears to be too far to the N.

Hommel (*Anc. Heb. Trad.* 242 f.) would read both here and Jos. 13, 2 הָאַשּׁוּרִי (cf. Gen. 25, 3 : Homm. 238–240 אֲשֻׁרִם), corresponding to the אאשור mentioned in two Minaean inscriptions as living apparently near Egypt (p. 249 f.), and Gaza (p. 252): but that א should have become corrupted into ג in *two* passages is hardly likely.

כי הנה ישבות וג׳] Very difficult. In the first place, the *fem.* is extremely anomalous. If the text be sound, this must be explained on the analogy of the usage noticed on 17, 21, by which sometimes a country, or the population of a country, is construed as a fem.: but no case occurs so extreme as the present, in which the fem. is used with immediate reference to a *gentile* name, expressed in the masc. And even the *poetical* use of יוֹשֶׁבֶת (noticed *ibid.*) is not extended to the plural. Nevertheless, as the text stands, nothing remains but to explain the passage in accordance with this poetical usage, and to render (with We.): 'For those were the populations of the land from ' etc.,—the gender of הֵנָּה being naturally determined by that of the predicate (ישבות) following. But this extension of a purely poetical usage is extremely improbable: and what we should expect is simply כי המה יושבי הארץ וג׳. In the words which follow, אשר מעולם וג׳, there is a further difficulty. בואך is used regularly to denote the *direction* in which a land or tract of country extends (15, 7 al. ; similarly in עד בואך Jud. 6, 4 al.); hence (since 'as thou comest to the land which is of old ' yields no suitable sense) it follows almost of necessity that in מעולם must lie concealed the definition of the limit in the opposite direction. LXX in Cod. B exhibits a doublet twice over (ἀπὸ ἀνηκόντων [apparently = מֵעֹלָם] ἡ ἀπὸ Γελαμψουρ

[= עלם again + שׁור] τετειχισμένων [clearly a second representative of שׁור *wall*]); but the reading Τελαμ, found in many cursives[1] in place of Γελαμ, points to מְטֵלָם for מֵעוֹלָם—'for those were the populations inhabiting the land which is *from Telam* as thou goest to Shur, even unto the land of Egypt.' From Jos. 15, 24 it appears that Telam (pointed there טֶלֶם) was a place in the Negeb of Judah (see on *v.* 10), seemingly towards the border of Edom: in ch. 15, 4 it is named as the spot where Saul assembled his forces before attacking the Amaleqites; so that it would seem to satisfy sufficiently all the conditions required of the present verse. In form, the sentence, as thus restored, will almost exactly resemble Gen. 10, 19; comp. 25, 18. Respecting שׁור, see on 15, 7.

9. והכה . . . ולקח] In a frequentative sense, describing David's *custom* whenever he engaged in one of these raids. Notice the impff. interchanging here (לא יחיה) and in *v.* 11. EVV. (*smote, saved,* etc.) fail to bring this out, either here or in *v.* 11.

ויבא] Ehrl. וַיָּבֵא: cf. להביא גת 11.

10. אל פשׁטתם] Either we must suppose that a word has dropped out, and read אֶל־מִי with LXX (ἐπὶ τίνα;), Vulg., or, which is perhaps better, we must read אָן (see 10, 14) with Targ. Pesh. (לְאָן, ܠܡܐ).
The text is untranslateable.

It is a singular fallacy to argue that because μή in Greek may ask a question, therefore אל in Hebrew may do the same: for the two words are not in the least parallel. Μή is a particle expressing generally the idea of *subjective* negation, from which its interrogative force is at once readily deduced (μὴ τέθνηκεν; = 'he is not dead, *I suppose?'*—implying that a satisfying answer is expected). אל has no such general signification, but is simply a particle of dissuasion or prohibition. In other words, the interrogative use of μή is dependent upon an element in its signification, which does not attach to the particle אל at all.

נגב] prop. the *dry* country, the root נגב (נְגִיב, ܢܓܒ) *to be dry* is in use in Aramaic (e.g. Gen. 8, 13 Onq. נגובו מיא). Hence, from the dry country κατ' ἐξοχήν being on the South of Palestine, the word acquired generally the sense of South, and geographically was applied in particular to a district in the S. of Judah (see Gen. 12, 9 RV.

---

[1] Τελαμψουρ XI. 44, 55, 71, 106, 120, 134, 144, 158, 245; Τελαψουρ 29; τε Λαμψουρ 64, 119, 244; τε Λαμψουν 74 (from Holmes and Parsons).

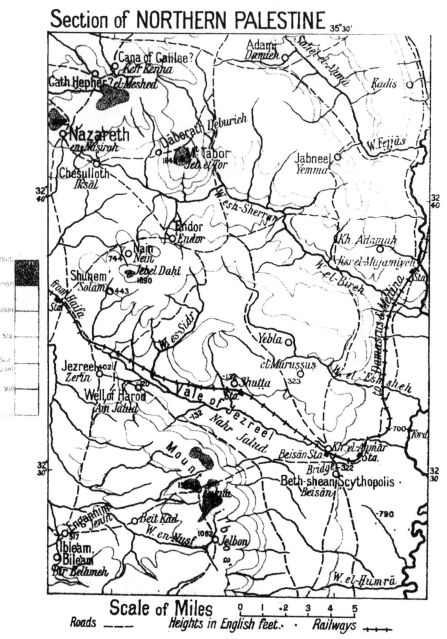

Section of NORTHERN PALESTINE

35°30'

Cana of Galilee?
Keff Kenna
Gath Hepher? el-Meshed

Nazareth
en-Nisirah

Chesulloth
Iksal

Adam
Damieh
Saiiet el-Ahmar

Kadis

Däberath Deburieh

Mt. Tabor
Jebel et Tor

W. esh-Sherrar

Endor
Endor

Jabneel
Yemma

W. Fejjas

Nain
Nein
Jebel Dahi

Shunem
Solam

from Haifa
Sta.

W. es-Sidr

Kh. Adamah
Jisr el-Mujamiyeh
W. el-Bireh

Sta.

Yebla

el-Murussus

Jezreel
Zerin

Well of Harod
Ain Jalud

Vale of Jezreel

Shutta
Sta.

Nahr Jalud

323

W. el-Eshsheh

Ford

700

Mou

Beisan Sta.

Kh. el-Ahmar
Sta.

Bridge
322

Beth-shean Scythopolis
Beisan

790

Engannim
Jenin

Beit Kad
W. en-Nusf

Jelbon

Ibleam,
Bileam
Bir Belameh

W. el-Humra

Scale of Miles

0 1 2 3 4 5

Roads ____ Heights in English feet. · Railways +++

By permission of the Palestine Exploration Fund
and of Messrs. John Bartholomew & Co.

marg.; Jos. 15, 21–32, where the cities in it are enumerated. In RV. in this special geographical sense, always with a capital S: e. g. Jos. 15, 19. Is. 21, 1). See NEGEB in *EB.*; and *H.G.* p. 278 ff. Here other districts in the same neighbourhood are called the Negeb of the Yeraḥme'ēlite, and the Negeb of the Qenite, from the names of the clans settled upon them (cf. 30, 29 'the *cities* of the Yeraḥme'ēlite and of the Qenite'): in 30, 14 also we have the Negeb of the Cherethites, and the Negeb of Caleb; and in Jud. 1, 16 (MT.) the Negeb of 'Arad (9 miles S. of Ma'on). Yeraḥme'ēl was the name of a clan allied to that of the Calebites (cf. on 25, 3): both were afterwards absorbed into the tribe of Judah; see 1 Ch. 2, 9 [read *Caleb*]. 25–33. 42. The Qenites were connected with the 'Amaleqites, 15, 6; Jud. 1, 16 (see on *ch.* 15, 6): cf. *EB.* i. 130.

11. The *athnaḥ* would be better placed at דוד, what follows (וכה משפטו וג׳) being obviously no part of the speech, but the remark of the narrator (so Now.). It must be admitted, however, that כה עשה דוד, and וכה משפטו וג׳, naturally go together: it is better, therefore, either to omit לאמר (Vulg. Sm. Dh. Ehrl.) or to read for it לאכיש (Klo. Bu.): כה עשה וג׳ will then be all the words of the narrator. כה with a subst., as Is. 20, 6. Jer. 23, 29.

12. הבאיש] lit. *put forth an ill odour* (ψ. 38, 6: GK. § 53ᵈ) against = be in ill odour with (cf. 13, 4). With a transitive force Gen. 34, 30.

לעבד עולם] Dt. 15, 17. Job 40, 28; cf. Ex. 21, 6.

28, 1. כי אתי תצא] אתי has some emphasis: cf. II 19, 39 אתי. כי אתי יאכלו האנשים בצהרים Gen. 43, 16. יעבר כמהם.

2. לכן] in answer to the remark made by another, as Gen. 4, 15. 30, 15 [where LXX, not perceiving the idiom, render οὐχ οὕτως: comp. on 3, 14]. Jud. 8, 7. 11, 8: *Lex.* 487ᵃ.

אתה] LXX, Vulg. עתה rightly. Comp. II 18, 3; 1 Ki. 1, 18. 20.

שמר לראשי] LXX ἀρχισωματοφύλαξ,—the title of the chief of the royal body-guard under the Ptolemies. See Deissmann, *Bible Studies*, s.v.

3–25. *Saul consults the witch of 'En-dor.* This section (which forms an independent narrative) appears to be out of its proper place. In 28, 4 the Philistines are at *Shunem* (3½ miles N. of Jezreel); in 29, 1 they are still at *Apheq* (in the Sharon, Jos. 12, 18), and only reach

Jezreel in 29, 11. The narrative will be in its right order, if the section be read *after ch.* 29–30. *V.* 3 is evidently introductory.

3. ויספרו] *wailed,*—with loud demonstrations of grief, in the manner of Oriental mourners. So מִסְפֵּד; cf. Mic. 1, 8 אעשה מספד כתנים, with allusion to the doleful cry of the jackal. The rend. *mourn, mourning* for ספד, מספד, is altogether inadequate: the words are never used of merely *silent* grief. See further the writer's note on Am. 5, 16 (in the *Camb. Bible*).

ובעירו] The *waw,* if correct, must be explicative (GK. § 154ᵃ *note*): 'in Ramah, *and that* in his city.' But such a construction is very unusual, and probably ו has been introduced by error (GK. *l. c.*): it is not expressed by LXX. However, בעירו ברמה rather than ברמה בעירו would be the usual order, 1, 3 LXX. II 15, 12. Jud. 8, 27 (*ib.* 20, 6 is rather different). Both the perfects in this verse have a *pluperfect* sense (see on 9, 15).

ושאול הסיר] *had* removed; see on 9, 15.

ידענים] See Lev. 20, 27 ('a man or a woman when there is *in them* אוב וידעני'), which shews that the term properly denotes not a *wizard,* but the spirit—whether the term means the *knower,* i. e. the *wise* spirit (Ew. *vielwisserisch*), or (W. R. Smith) the *acquaintance,* i.e. the 'familiar' spirit, at the beck and call of a particular person—supposed to inhabit the persons in question. See further the writer's note on Dt. 18, 11 (p. 226).

4. שונם] Now *Sōlem,* near the E. end of the Plain of Esdraelon, 448 ft. up the sloping S. side of *Jebel Nabî Daḥi* (also called Little Hermon), 3½ miles N. of Jezreel. The Philistines had thus penetrated into the heart of Northern Palestine, more than 60 miles from the northernmost of their cities, ʻEqron.

בגלבע] Gilboaʻ, now *Jebel Fuqûʻa,* is the ridge running to the SE. on the S. side of the Vale of Jezreel (see on 31, 7), 5–12 miles S. and SE. of Shunem.

7. אשת בעלת אוב] An instance of what may be termed a *suspended* construct state—אשת, not less than בעלת, being determined by אוב, but the genitive which determines it being deferred, or held in suspense, by the introduction of the parallel בעלת. So in the common phrase בתולת בת ... Is. 23, 12; 37, 22 al.; and in poetry occasionally

besides, as Dt. 33, 19 שְׁפֻנֵי טְמוּנֵי חוֹל ; Job 20, 17 נַהֲרֵי נַחֲלֵי דְּבַשׁ : Ew.
§ 289ᶜ ; GK. § 130ᵉ.

בְעֵין דוֹר] Now *Endûr*, a small village, 3½ miles NE. of Shunem.

8. קְסוֹמִי] The Kt. has the fuller form of the imperative, as Jud. 9, 8
מָלוֹכָה. ψ. 26, 2 צְרוֹפָה ; in each case the Qrê substitutes the ordinary
form, GK. § 46ᶜ. For קָסְמִי, see GK. § 10ʰ. On the probable method
of divination originally expressed by קסם, see *Lex.* s.v., or the writer's
Deut. p. 223 f.

9. הַיְּדֹעֹנִי] Twenty-three MSS. have הַיִּדְּעֹנִים ; and it is true that the
ם may have fallen out before the מ of מִן. The plural would have
the advantage of greater symmetry with הָאֹבוֹת (cf. *v.* 3. Lev. 19, 31 al.),
and is probable, though not perhaps absolutely necessary, as הַיְּדֹעֹנִי
may be taken in a collective sense.

לָמָּה] See on 19, 17.

10. יִקְּרֶךָ] With *dagesh dirimens*. It must have become the custom,
as the OT. was read, to pronounce the same word or form, in different
passages, with a slightly different articulation, which is reflected
accurately in the varying punctuation. Here the *dagesh dirimens*
has the effect of causing the ק to be pronounced with peculiar distinctness: cf. Hos. 3, 2 וָאֶכְּרֶהָ ; Ex. 2, 3 הַצְּפִינוֹ, 15, 17 מִקְּדָשׁ (in which
cases the dagesh involves the softening of the following פ and ר), etc. :
GK. § 20ʰ.

12. שְׁמוּאֵל] Six MSS. of LXX, Perles, Bu. Now. Ehrl. שָׁאוּל.

13. אֱלֹהִים וג'] The position of אֱלֹהִים before רָאִיתִי shews that it is
the emphatic word in the sentence.

עֹלִים] with the plur. partic. אֱלֹהִים seems naturally to mean *gods*
(i.e. here superhuman beings, spirits): in this case, therefore, as Saul
in *v.* 14 asks 'What is *his* form?' we must suppose that though the
woman says she saw more than one figure, Saul in his anxiety inquires
only about the one in whom he is interested. Sm. Bu. Now. Dh.,
less probably, think that אֱלֹהִים is a honorific plural (GK. § 124ᵍ⁻ⁱ),
and denotes 'a god' (so GK. § 132ʰ *note*), the pl. עֹלִים being merely
a grammatical plural, like חיים in אֱלֹהִים חיים (GK. § 132ʰ) of Yahweh
(17, 26 al.).

14. מְעִיל] such as was worn by Samuel, 15, 27. On LXX ὄρθιον
(זָקֵף for זָקֵן), see Wellh. p. 13; Aptow. *ZAW.* 1909, p. 246 f.

15. לָמֶּה] Before a guttural (other than ח) לָמָה is usual (see on 19, 17): but לָמֶּה occurs so 5 times noted by the Massorah (*Lex.* 554ᵃ).

הרגזתני] Cf. the same word, of disturbing a tomb, in the Tabnith Inscr. l. 7 (Introd. § 1): also Is. 14, 9 שָׁאוֹל מִתַּחַת רָגְזָה לְךָ לִקְרַאת בּוֹאֶךָ.

סר מעלי] Cf. *v.* 16. מעם is, however, more natural in this connexion (16, 14. 18, 12): for in Jud. 16, 19. 20 the use of מעל is evidently determined by the fact that Samson's strength was regarded as resting *upon* him in his hair, in Nu. 14, 19 (cf. Neh. 9, 19) it is determined similarly by the figure of the shade, and in *ch.* 16, 23 by the common thought of a spirit coming *on* a person (see *v.* 16). Here probably על denotes the idea of *protecting accompaniment* (cf. ψ. 110, 5 עַל יְמִינֶךָ; 121, 5 עַל יַד יְמִינֶךָ); and סר מעל expresses the cessation of this.

מעל is used in several idiomatic applications; not only as signifying *from attendance on* (comp. on 13, 8. 17, 15), but also *from attachment to* (Jer. 2, 5 רָחֲקוּ מֵעָלָי; 32, 40; לְבִלְתִּי סוּר מֵעָלָי; Ez. 6, 9 מֵעָלָי; לָהֶם סָר; 8, 6; 14, 5; 44, 10); *from companionship with* (Job 19, 13); *from adhesion to* (2 Ki. 17, 21; Is. 7, 17; 56, 3; Hos. 9, 1; and twice, for the more usual מִן, in the phrase סָר מֵעַל הַטָּאות 2 Ki. 10, 31. 15, 18); *from standing over* or *beside* (Gen. 17, 22. 35, 13: cf. 18, 3. 42, 24); *from being a burden upon* (see on 6, 5. 20), esp. of an army retiring from a country, or raising a siege (see the passages from 2 Sam. 1–2 Ki. cited on *ch.* 6, 20; and add II 10, 14. Jer. 21, 2. 37, 5. 9. 11).

וָאקראה] Very anomalous: Ew. § 228ᶜ; Stade, § 132; GK. § 48ᵈ; König, i. 608, who suggests that the — may be due to dissimilation, after the preceding unusual —; cf. on 21, 2. Read וָאֶקְרָאֶה[1].

16. וַיְהִי עֵרְ] Is there a Hebrew word עָר with the signification *adversary* or *enemy*? The common Heb. צָר (root צָרַר) corresponds to Arabic ضَرَّ *to harm* (Qor. 2, 96. 3, 107, etc.): and this (according to rule [2]) corresponds to the (isolated) Aramaic עָר Dan. 4, 16. The same word may also possibly be found in ψ. 139, 20—the Psalm is a late one, and is marked by several other Aramaisms—but this cannot be affirmed with certainty, the verse being a difficult one, and

---

[1] The supposition that the form is 'conflate,' from וָאֶקְרָא, and וָאֶקְרֶה, is not probable: 'and I met' does not suit the context, nor does קרא in *Qal* mean to 'meet.'

[2] See on 1, 6 (p. 9 *footnote*).

probably corrupt. At any rate, philology forbids imperatively the assumption of a *Hebrew* word עַר *adversary*, the equivalent of צָר [1].

Can, however, a sense, suitable to the context, be rendered probable for עַר, from any other source? (*a*) Symm. renders ἀντίζηλός σου, and in Arabic غار (*med.* i) means actually *to be jealous* or *a rival* (غَيُّور = קַנָּא Ex. 20, 5 Saad.; تَغايِروا = ζηλοῦτε I Cor. 12, 31 Erpen.). Still there is no other trace of this root in Hebrew: nor would the idea of Yahweh's becoming Saul's *rival* be probable or suitable. (*b*) Ges. Keil seek to explain עַר by a reference to Arabic غار (*med.* u) *ferbuit* (one of many meanings), *impetum fecit*, spec. excursione hostili adortus fuit (aliquem), IV (Lane) اَغَارَ عَلَى *to make a raid* or *predatory incursion* upon (comp. 13, 17 *note*): غَارَة *a raid* or *hostile incursion:* hence, the cognate subst., it is supposed, would properly have the sense of *aestus* (sc. doloris, curae, sollicitudinis), whence in Hebrew עִיר Hos. 11, 9 aestus *irae ;* Jer. 15, 8 aestus *doloris* [this explanation of עִיר is, however, very uncertain : see *Lex.* 735ᵇ; and my *Jeremiah*, p. 360 f.]. But the sense of *hostility* expressed by the Arabic root is, it will be observed, a special and derived one : is it likely, or indeed credible, that from a root meaning *ferbuit* a simple participial formation should have acquired the definite sense of *enemy ?* The etymology proposed is well intended : but it cannot be said to have probability in its favour.

It follows that if עָרְךָ has here the sense of *thy enemy*, it must be an example of a strong and pronounced Aramaism, such as, in presumably early Hebrew, is in the highest degree improbable. Only two alternatives are open to us. Either עָרְךָ is an error of *transcription* for צָרֶךָ [2] (cf. in that case, for the thought, Lam. 2, 4 ; Is. 63, 10), or, with LXX and Pesh., וִיהִי עִם־רֵעֶךָ ׃ ' and is become *on the side of thy neighbour* ' must be read (cf. רֵעַ with reference to David, *v.* 17, and 15, 28, and for the thought 18, 12 סר שאול ומעם עמו יהוה היה כי). עם רעך is accepted by most moderns (Th. Hitzig, Nöldeke, Grätz, Reinke, Kp., Dr. Weir ['LXX seems to be right']), Now. Dh.: Klo. Sm. Bu. prefer צרך.

17. ויעש י׳׳ לו] ' And Y. hath wrought *for himself*, according as' etc. Or, if עם רעך be adopted in *v.* 16, the suffix may be referred naturally to רעך (*for him*). However, the point of the

---

[1] Nor can this be the meaning of עַר in Mic. 5, 13 (AV.) or Is. 14, 21.

[2] It is possible that this was read by Symmachus. At least ἀντίζηλος as used elsewhere in the Greek Versions expresses the root צרר : Lev. 18, 18 LXX ; *ch.* 1, 6 LXX (Luc.). 2, 32 Aq. (but ψ. 139, 20 Aq. for עָרֶיךָ).

sentence lies in what is done to *Saul*, rather than what is done to David: so, in all probability, לְךָ *to thee*, expressed by 5 MSS., LXX, Vulg., is the original reading (so Sm. Bu. Now. Dh.). With 17ᵇ comp. 15, 28.

18ᵇ. For the *order* of words, see *Tenses*, § 208 (1). So *v.* 19ᵇ.

19. In MT. clauses *a* and *c* are almost identical; and the verse is decidedly improved by the omission of one of them, and by the adoption in *b* of the reading of LXX, viz. מָחָר אַתָּה וּבָנֶיךָ עָמְּךָ נֹפְלִים נֹם וג׳, i. e. (immediately after *v.* 18) 'To-morrow thou and thy sons *with thee will be fallen ;* yea, also, the camp of Israel will Yahweh give into the hand of the Philistines.' As We. remarks, *a* is out of place where it stands, neither נם nor עמך being properly understood, until *after* it has been said that Saul himself has fallen.

20. וימהר] LXX ἔσπευσεν, not only here, but also in *v.* 21 for נבהל ; so doubtless they read the same in both verses. A man would not (actively) 'hasten' to fall down : וַיִּבָּהֵל is thus more suitable than וַיְמַהֵר. וַיִּמָּהֵר (Klo. Sm. Dh.) does not seem to express the right *nuance.*

21. ואשים נפשי בכפי] 19, 5.

23. ויפרצו] 'פרץ is translated *pressed* in II 13, 25. 27 and *urged* in 2 Ki. 5, 23, but elsewhere *break forth, burst forth*, etc. Ought we not to read פצר ?' (Dr. Weir). So 20 MSS. (de Rossi, App. p. 39), Sm. Now. Dh. ; Bu. (either so, or פרץ a 'Nebenstamm' to פצר).

24. . . . ולאשה] Cf. on II 3, 7.

מרבק] 'four times, always connected with עגל : Jer. 46, 21. Am. 6, 4. עגלים מתוך מרבק . Mal. 3, 20. The root is not found elsewhere in Hebrew, but in Arabic رَبَقَ *firmiter alligavit*' (Dr. Weir).

ותפהו] for ותאפהו : cf. on 15, 5 ; and GK. § 68ʰ.

29, 1. אפק] Probably (see on 4, 1) some place in the Plain of Sharon, commanding the entrance to the Plain of Dothan (*c.* 32° 24′ N.), and so the route up to Jezreel and Shunem (28, 4).

חנים] '*were* encamping ;' not 'pitched' (EVV.), which would be וַיַּחֲנוּ . Contrast 4, 1 (חָנוּ).

בעין אשר ביזרעאל] Generally supposed to be '*Ain Jālūd*, at the foot of Mt. Gilboaʿ, on the N., 1¾ miles ESE. of Jezreel, and looking across the Vale of Jezreel to Solam, the Philistine position (28, 4), 4 miles N. by W., and 568 ft. above it. 'Jezreel' will denote here, not the town, but the Vale (31, 7). As Ehrl. remarks, however, if עַיִן means a *spring*, Heb. idiom requires עַל (Gen. 16, 7. Jud. 7, 1 al.), not בְ, so that a genitive would seem to have fallen out (cf. בְּעֵין רֹגֵל II 17, 17). 'En-dor, however (LXX, cod. A and other MSS.), on the NW. slope of J. Nabî Daḥî, and 4 miles *behind* the Philistine position, is too far off to be probable.

2. עברים (twice)] *were* passing by. The participles suggest the picture of a muster or review of troops taking place.

למֵאות] *according to, by* hundreds: לְ as II 18, 4. 1 Ki. 20, 10 לשׁעלים. Jos. 7, 14 לנברים.

3. זה ימים] not '*these* days' (EVV.), except as a paraphrase: זֶה is here, as in many similar phrases, זֶה פַעֲמַיִם, זֶה עֶשֶׂר פְּעָמִים, etc. an *adverb*, meaning properly *here* (cf. בְּזֶה): see *Lex.* 261ᵇ. So in זֶה שָׁנִים. שָׁנִים is, however, strangely indefinite; and as ימים suggests a *year* (on 1, 3), it is probable that שְׁנָתַיִם *two years* should be read, with LXX (δεύτερον ἔτος), Bu. Sm. Now. Kitt. Ehrl.

נפלו] LXX adds πρός με = אֵלָי or עָלַי, which is needed. *Falling* gives no sense: *falling to me* agrees with the usage of נפל אל (על) elsewhere (Jer. 21, 9. 37, 13 al.) *to fall over to = to desert to.* The nearer definition cannot, as Keil supposes, be supplied from the context. (Dr. Weir agrees.)

4. ירד] It is remarkable that in *v.* 9 יעלה is used for exactly the same movement. It seems that the narrator must here allow the Philistines to speak from the *Israelite* point of view (cf. *v.* 6, where Achish is represented as swearing by *Yahweh*), who would 'go down' from the mountainous country of Judah to fight against the Philistines in their plains, and so might say ירד במלחמה quite generally (cf. 30, 24).

לשׂטן] 'as a *thwarter* or *opposer*,' viz. of another man's purposes; cf. the same word in II 19, 23; 1 Ki. 11, 14. 23. 25; also Nu. 22, 22. 32. 1 Ki. 5, 18. So השׂטן is in the OT. the name of the angel, whose function it is to *oppose* men in their pretensions to a right standing with God (see A. B. Davidson's note on Job 1, 6 in the *Camb. Bible;* and the writer's note on Zech. 3, 1 in the *Century Bible*).

5. See 18, 7; and cf. 21, 11.

6. כי] after the oath, as 14, 39.

7. לך בשלום] as II 15, 27. The usual expression is לשלום.

8. כי מה עשיתי כי] states the reason for a suppressed (Why do you say this?): it recurs in a similarly worded expostulation, 1 Ki. 11, 22. 2 Ki. 8, 13.

מיום אשר הייתי] As We. remarks, we should expect naturally either מִיּוֹם הָיִיתִי (Jer. 36, 2 : cf. II 22, 1. Dt. 4, 15), or, as would be more usual, מִיּוֹם הֱיוֹתִי (v. 6, ch. 7, 2. 8, 8. II 13, 32 etc.), or (מִן־הַיּוֹם) מֵהַיּוֹם אֲשֶׁר הָיִיתִי (II 19, 25. 1 Ki. 8, 16. 2 Ki. 21, 15). However, יום may have been conceived as being in the construct state before אשר (GK. § 130ᵈ), and so defined. At least יום אשר recurs similarly, Jer. 38, 28, and (in late Hebrew) Neh. 5, 14. But מהיום would certainly be better.

ונלחמתי] The *waw* being consecutive, the tone should properly be *milra'* וְנִלְחַמְתִּי : but it is held back by the distinctive accent *zāqēf,* as happens occasionally (Dt. 2, 28: Ez. 3, 26: *Tenses,* § 104). As a rule, only *athnaḥ* and *soph-pasuq* imply a sufficient pause thus to hold back the tone of 1 and 2 sing. pf. with *waw* consec.

9. כמלאך אלהים] The same comparison, in popular speech, II 14, 17. 19, 27.

יעלה] Here (contrast *v.* 4) the Philistines speak from the point of view which would be natural to them, when they were invading the high central ground of Canaan (e. g. Jud. 15, 9. 10), cf. *v.* 11ᵇ.

10. ועתה השכם בבקר ועבדי וג'] 'And now, rise up early in the morning, *and also* the servants,' etc. The text may in a measure be defended by 25, 42. Gen. 41, 27. Nu. 16, 2ᵃ. 18ᵇ; but the sentence halts considerably, and the omission of the *pronoun* before ועבדי is contrary to standing Hebrew usage, when the verb is in the *imperative* (e. g. Gen. 7, 1. Ex. 11, 8. 24, 1). LXX, Vulg. express rightly אַתָּה before ועבדי. The only parallel to the present passage would be Jer. 19, 1 ; but there also it can scarcely be doubted that the reading of LXX is what Hebrew idiom requires, viz. וְלָקַחְתָּ מִזִּקְנֵי העם וג'. In this verse, further, clauses *a* and *b* are nearly identical : but, as We. observes, the repetition of the same thought would become perfectly natural, if only words of different import separated the two similar clauses. Such words are expressed in LXX (after

אֹתְךָ), viz. καὶ πορεύεσθε εἰς τὸν τόπον οὗ κατέστησα ὑμᾶς ἐκεῖ· καὶ λόγον λοιμὸν μὴ θῇς ἐν καρδίᾳ σου, ὅτι ἀγαθὸς σὺ ἐνώπιόν μου = וַהֲלַכְתֶּם אֶל־הַמָּקוֹם אֲשֶׁר הִפְקַדְתִּי אֶתְכֶם שָׁם וּדְבַר בְּלִיַּעַל אַל־תָּשֵׂם בִּלְבָבְךָ כִּי טוֹב אַתָּה לְפָנָי. The sentence is in style and form thoroughly Hebraic, and may well be assumed to have fallen out accidentally in MT. Λοιμὸς is often the rendering of בליעל (e. g. 25, 25): for the combination of דבר and בליעל see Dt. 15, 9 (where they occur in apposition). Ehrlich proposes שֵׁב עַד הַבֹּקֶר (followed by אתה) for השכם בבקר (keeping otherwise MT.).

ולכו] Unusual. The normal construction would be וַהֲלַכְתֶּם לכם ואור (on the analogy of Gen. 33, 13 ומתו, 44, 22 ורפקום יום אחד ומתו אביו ומת, etc.: *Tenses*, § 149); but cf. 2 Ki. 9, 2. אוֹר is, of course, the verb: Gen. 44, 3 הבקר אור; and, of the eyes, *ch.* 14, 29.

11. עלו] Viz. from Apheq in the Sharon (*v.* 11). 'Jezreel' is here, not the town, but the Vale (as *v.* 1).

30, 1. צקלג] David goes back to the city which Achish had given him ; see 27, 6.

ועמלקי] Read with LXX עמלק: cf. *v.* 18 ; and the note on 15, 6.

נגב] Unless (Now.) הכרתי or (Ehrl.) כלב has fallen out (*v.* 14), we must read הנגב (Bu.), in conformity with usage, except when נגב denotes merely the southern quarter of the compass.

2. את הנשים אשר בה] Read with LXX (cf. RV.) את־הנשים ואת־ כל־אשר בה : we thus obtain a suitable idea to which to refer the following מקטן ועד־גדול ; see also *v.* 3 (ובניהם ובנתיהם).

לא המיתו איש] A circumstantial clause, connected ἀσυνδέτως with the clause preceding, and defining *how* וישבו was effected, viz. (Anglice) '*without* slaying any.' Cf. Gen. 44, 4 יצאו את העיר לא הרחיקו ; Jer. 7, 26ᵇ; 20, 15ᵇ (see RV.): *Tenses*, § 162; GK. § 156f.

וינהגו] of leading captives, as Is. 20, 4.

3. והנה] without suffix (*Tenses*, § 135. 6, 2), as *v.* 16 : cf. on 10, 11.

נשבו] *were taken captive.* שבה is to take *captive*, נשבה to be taken captive : נלה is to go into *exile*, הגלה to carry into exile. The distinction between the two words should be noticed. Though they may be often applied to the same transaction, they denote different aspects of it : נלה migration from one's own country, *exile*, שבה capture by another, *captivity.* The rendering of נלות in Jud. 18, 30 by 'captivity' (EVV.), instead of 'exile,' has led to strange misunderstandings of the meaning,—as though, for instance, the word referred to the Philistine *domination!*

6. ותצר לדוד] The *fem.* as Jud. 10, 9 : cf. Jer. 7, 31 ולא עלתה על לבי; Mic. 3, 6 חשכה; Am. 4, 7 (unusual) תמטיר; ψ. 50, 3 נשערה מאד: Ew. § 295ᵃ; GK. § 144ᵇ. This use of the fem., especially with words denoting a mental condition, is particularly common in Syriac : ‎ܒ‎ ‎ܐܢܠܒܐ‎, ‎ܒ‎ ‎ܐܟܦܐ‎, ‎ܒ‎ ‎ܐܪܙ‎‎ (Nöldeke, *Syr. Gr.* § 254).

אמרו . . . לסקלו] *'spake of* (AV.) stoning him:' or with the sense of 'thought' (25, 21), as Ex. 2, 14. II 21, 16 ויאמר דוד להכות; 1 Ki. 5, 19. 8, 12 : comp. Ez. 20, 8. 13. 21. ψ. 106, 23. אמר ל in the sense of *command* occurs II 1, 18. 2, 26 : but more frequently in later books, especially in Chronicles, as I 13, 4 ; 15, 16 ; Est. 1, 17, etc. (comp. Ew. § 338ᵃ).

מרה] *mil'el* (GK. § 15ᶠ *n.*, p. 60), and consequently perf. from מרר, not fem. of the adj. מר. For the use of the root with נפש, cf. on 1, 10; and add II 17, 8. Job 7, 11. 10, 1. 21, 25.

ויתחזק] i. e. *took courage:* cf. 4, 9. II 10, 12 ; and similarly in Qal (Jos. 1, 6. 7 al.), and Pi'el, 23, 16 (see note).

8. ארדף] Though ה can be dispensed with (11, 12), the parallel האשיגנו supports the reading הארדף (so many MSS.) : cf. 14, 37. 23, 11.

גדוד] of a marauding or plundering band: see 2 Ki. 6, 23. Hos. 6, 9. LXX here (mis-reading) γεδδουρ: elsewhere rightly πειρατήριον (Gen. 49, 19 ; ψ. 18, 32), or μονόζωνοι (2 Ki. 5, 2. 6, 23 al.).

9. נחל הבשור] The name has not been preserved : and as the site of Ẓiqlag is uncertain, and we do not know what the point was which David desired to reach, any identification is very precarious. *If* Ẓiqlag was at Zuḥêlîqeh (on 27, 6), *W. esh-Sherî'a,* 4 or 5 miles to the S., would no doubt suit: but that is all that we can say.

10. פגרו] only here and *v.* 21.

12. דבלה . . . צמקים] See on 25, 18.

ותשב רוחו] The spirit (of life), which seemed to have left him, returned, i. e. he revived. So Jud. 15, 19.

13. עבד ל'] See on 16, 18.

היום שלשה] See on 9, 20. Here ימים must be understood, or read.

14. פשטנו נגב] על, which is expressed by LXX, must have acci-

dentally dropped out. פשט, when an object follows, is always construed with על (or the alternative אל); and here the restoration is still more commended by the two על following.

נגב הכרתי] A district in the south of Palestine (see on 27, 10) inhabited by the כרתי, who, from a comparison of *v.* 16ᵇ, appear to have been closely connected with, if not a sub-tribe of, the Philistines. In poetry the name is used synonymously with Philistine: Ez. 25, 16. Zeph. 2, 5. A contingent of הכרתי formed afterwards part of David's body-guard, II 8, 18. 15, 18. 20, 7 (cf. *OTJC.*² p. 262). It is quite possible that the name may be connected with *Crete:* the Philistines themselves are expressly stated to have been immigrants from Caphtor, i. e. Crete, Am. 9, 7 (see also Gen. 10, 14, where in accordance with this passage ואת כפתרים should no doubt be transposed so as to *precede* אשר יצאו משם פלשתים).

אשר ליהודה] i. e. the נגב יהודה of 27, 10.

נגב כלב] mentioned only here. A district of the Negeb, occupied by a detachment of the Caleb-clan (see on 25, 3).

15. התורדני] So *v.* 16.

16. וחגגים] Ki. כלומר מרקדין ומפזזין ומכרכרין בשמחה. Whether, however, the sense of *dancing* is really expressed by the word is very doubtful. Modern lexicographers only defend it by means of the questionable assumption that חגג may have had a similar signification to חוג, which, however, by no means itself expresses the sense of *to dance*, but *to make a circle* Job 26, 10: in Syriac (PS. col. 1217) *circumivit*, especially, and commonly, with ـ, *circumivit ut vitaret* = reveritus est, cavit. The Aram. חגג *to dance* is of course an altogether different word. It is best to acquiesce in the cautious judgement of Nöldeke (*ZDMG.* 1887, p. 719), who declares that he cannot with certainty get behind the idea of a *festal gathering* for the common Semitic חָג. Here then the meaning will be 'behaving as at a חג or gathering of pilgrims,' i. e. enjoying themselves merrily.

17. למחרתם] *of their following day.* The expression is unexampled. Read probably לְהַחֲרִמָם (We. Bu. Now. etc.), or (Ehrl.) וַיַּחֲרִמֵם, which is better (after ויכם, as Jud. 1, 17), though it does not explain the ל.

איש נער] used collectively—after the numeral. So נערה בתולה Jud. 21, 12; מֶלֶךְ עָזֵר 1 Ki. 20, 16; Jud. 18, 11. 17ᵇ. Cf. on 21, 6.

19. וּמִשָּׁלֵל] The *zāqēf* should stand rather on וּבֹנוֹת. But probably the word is displaced, and should follow הַגְּדוּל, as in LXX.

לָקְחוּ לָהֶם] The reflexive לְ, as Gen. 15, 10. Lev. 23, 40. Am. 6, 13; and often in the imper. קַח־לְךָ Gen. 6, 21. 14, 21 etc. (*Lex.* 515ᵇ).

20. נֹהֲגוּ וג׳] The text is evidently in disorder. The least change that will suffice for the requirements of style and sense is to read for נֹהֲגוּ לִפְנֵי with Vulg. וַיִּנְהֲגוּ לְפָנָיו 'and they drave *before him* that cattle (the cattle viz. named in clause *a*), and said, This is David's spoil.' But LXX, Vulg. do not express דוד after וַיִּקַּח, and for הַמִּקְנֶה הַהוּא LXX have τῶν σκύλων i.e. הַשָּׁלָל, the variation seeming to shew that both are alternative (false) *explicita*, added after לְפָנָיו had been corrupted into לִפְנֵי. It is quite possible, therefore, that we should go further, and with We. Now. Dh. read the entire verse thus: וַיִּקְחוּ אֶת־כָּל־הַצֹּאן וְהַבָּקָר וַיִּנְהֲגוּ לְפָנָיו וַיֹּאמְרוּ זֶה שְׁלַל דוד. This text states undoubtedly all that the verse is intended to express, and states it at the same time more naturally and simply than the reading pre-supposed by the Vulg.

21. מָאתַיִם הָאֲנָשִׁים] '*the* 200 men;' cf. Jud. 18, 17ᵇ: GK. § 134ˡ.

וַיֹּשִׁיבֵם] It is better to vocalize, with 6 MSS., LXX, Pesh. Vulg. Bu. Sm. Now. Dh. וַיֹּשִׁיבֵם (the subject being David).

וַיִּגַּשׁ וג׳] אֶת can only mean *with* (on 9, 18), and הָעָם can be only the 'people' just mentioned (cl.ᵃ) as being with David. On the other hand, the men left behind would be the ones to ask for the welfare of those who had gone into the battle (We. Sm.); and this agrees with 22, where the men who reply are those with David. The context requires imperatively וַיִּגְּשׁוּ אֶל הָעָם וַיִּשְׁאֲלוּ לָהֶם לְשָׁלוֹם (Ehrl., with We. Bu. al.). דוד is the false 'explicitum' of an original וַיִּגְּשׁוּ = וַיִּגַּשׁ (Introd. § 5. 1): וַיִּגְּשׁוּ is the natural sequel of 21ᵇ וַיֵּצְאוּ לִקְרַאת דוד: for אֶת LXX have ἕως, and 7 MSS. אֶל: LXX have also ἠρώτησαν for וַיִּשְׁאַל.

22. רַע וּבְלִיַּעַל] For the adj. + subst. (GK. § 131ᶜ), cf. Dt. 25, 15.

עִמִּי] The group regarded as a unity, and spoken of accordingly in 1 ps. sing. The usage is thoroughly idiomatic; and there is no occasion, with Grätz, *Die Psalmen*, p. 134, to substitute עִמָּנוּ. See on 5, 10: and add Gen. 34, 30 וַאֲנִי מְתֵי מִסְפָּר; Jud. 18, 23 כִּי מַה־לְּךָ נִזְעָקְתָּ (of Micah and his neighbours).

23. אֶת־אֲשֶׁר] Ewald (§ 329ᵃ: comp. *Hist.* iii. 145 [E. T. 105])
would treat the words introduced by אֶת as an exclamation, explaining
אֶת as an accus. with reference to a suppressed verb,—(Think of) that
which . . . ! and comparing Hag. 2, 5, where, however, as also in
Zech. 7, 7, the text is very uncertain. LXX for אֲשֶׁר אֶת אֹתִי express
אַחֲרֵי אֲשֶׁר, which is no doubt right (We. Bu.): 'ye shall not do so,
after what Yahweh hath given unto us, and (*Tenses*, § 76a) preserved
us,' etc.

24. לַדָּבָר הַזֶּה] Cf. on 8, 7ᵃ.

כְּ . . . וּכְ . . .] A variation for the more common type, כְּ . . . כְּ:
Jos. 14, 11. Ez. 18, 4. Dan. 11, 29. Ez. 42, 11 f. (Smend)†.

25. וּמַעֲלָה] as 16, 13.

לְחֹק וּלְמִשְׁפָּט] Cf. Ex. 15, 25. Jos. 24, 25; and חֹק alone, Gen. 47, 26.
Jud. 11, 39.

26. לְרֵעֵהוּ] 'to his *friends.*' ‑הוּ‑ (for ‑יְהוּ‑: GK. § 91ᵏ) attached
to a *plur.* as 14, 48 שָׂדֵהוּ (Stade, p. 355; GK. § 91ˡ). In this order,
however, the double לְ is scarcely Hebrew, though לְרֵעֵהוּ לְזִקְנֵי יְהוּדָה,
with the more *general* category first, would be possible. LXX וּלְרֵעֵהוּ,
followed by Sm. Klo. conjectured לְעָרֵיהֶם *by their cities* (see *v.* 27 ff.);
so Bu. Dh.: but the correction is rather violent.

בְּרָכָה] = a *present*; see on 25, 27.

27. בֵּית־אֵל] i.e. not the better known Beth'el, 10 miles N. of Jerusalem, but
the place in the Negeb of Judah, called Βαιθηλ in Jos. 15, 30 LXX (MT. corruptly
כְּסִיל), in Jos. 19, 4 MT., and בְּתוּאֵל Βαθουηλ in 1 Ch. 4, 30, in a list of
cities belonging originally to Simeon (Jos. 19, 2–8, 1 Ch. 4, 28–33), but afterwards
incorporated in Judah (Jos. 15, 26–32). The name has not been preserved; and
the approximate site can only be inferred from the known places with which it is
associated in this list, Beersheba, Molādah (very possibly—see *EB.* s.v.—the
Malatha of Euseb. *Onom.*, 4 miles from 'Arad, now *Tell 'Arad*, 17 miles S. of
Hebron, and 20 miles E. of Beersheba), Ḥormah (also near 'Arad; see on *v.* 30),
Ziqlag, and 'En-Rimmon (now, probably, *Umm er-Rumāmīn*, 10 miles NNE. of
Beersheba). LXX have here Βαιθσυρ; but the situation of בֵּית־צוּר (Jos. 15, 58 al.),
4½ miles N. of Hebron, is less suitable than that of בֵּית־אֵל (We.).

רָמוֹת נֶגֶב] *Ramoth of the South*: see Jos. 19, 8, in the list of Simeonite cities
(רָמַת נֶגֶב). LXX here also read the sing.: Ραμα νότου = רָמַת נֶגֶב. The site is
unknown (*DB.* iv. 198ᵃ; Buhl, 184).

יַתִּר] in the hill-country of Judah (Jos. 15, 48), mentioned also by P as a priestly
city (Jos. 21, 14 = 1 Ch. 6, 58 [EVV. 73])†. According to Euseb. *Onom.* 266, 43,
a large village 20 miles from Eleutheropolis. It is now generally identified with

'*Attir*, a village situated on two knolls, 11 miles SW. of Ziph. The change from ו to y is explicable (Kampffmeyer, *ZDPV.* xvi. 45, cited by Cheyne, *EB.* s.v.): LXX have remarkably here (but not elsewhere) Γεθθορ (=עתר; see p. 136 *n.*).

28. בערער] LXX have here a double rendering: καὶ τοῖς ἐν 'Αροηρ καὶ τοῖς 'Αμμαδει. 'It is clear that LXX after ערער (='Αμμαδ) read still another letter, viz. ה. The form ערערה, now, is confirmed not only by Jos. 15, 22 [1]—where, to be sure, LXX conversely omit the ה—but also by the present pronunciation '*Ar'ārah*' (We.), the name of a place in the Negeb of Judah (Jos. *l. c.*), 11 miles SE. of Beersheba: see Robinson, *Bibl. Res.*, ii. 199 [2].

שפמות] Only mentioned here. Site unknown.

אשתמע] In the hill-country of Judah (Jos. 15, 50 [MT. here אשתמה†]), mentioned by P as a priestly city (Jos. 21, 14=1 Ch. 6, 42 [EVV. 57]), mentioned also 1 Ch. 4, 17. 19†. Now probably the large village *es-Semu'*, 10 miles S. by W. of Hebron, and 4 miles W. by S. of Ma'on. The form of the name is noticeable; it is the inf. of the Arabic 8th conjug.; and it seems therefore to shew that the place must have been originally an Arab settlement. Eshtā'ōl is another name of the same form. See further Burney in the *Journ. of Theol. Studies*, 1911, p. 83 f., who supposes plausibly that the names suggested originally the ideas of *being heard*, and *asking for oneself*, and that they marked the seats of ancient oracles.

29. בכרבל] LXX בכרמל; no doubt, rightly. Carmel, now *el-Kurmul*, was in the hill-country of Judah (Jos. 15, 55), 4 miles NE. of es-Semu', and 3 miles S. of Ziph. See further on 25, 2.

ערי הירחמאלי] cities belonging to the Yerahme'elites settled in the Negeb: see on 27, 10.

ערי הקיני] See on 27, 10.

30. חרמה] In the Negeb of Judah (Jos. 15, 30), but originally Simeonite (19, 4. 1 Ch. 4, 30): mentioned also in Nu. 14, 45=Dt. 1, 44; Nu. 21, 3. Jud. 1, 17 (two divergent traditions of the origin of the name); Jos. 12, 14†. In Jud. 1, 17 the original name of Hormah is said to have been Zĕphath. The site is unknown; but Nu. 21, 1. 3 appear to shew that it was not far from 'Arad (see on *v.* 27). The identification of Zĕphath with *Sebaita*, 27 miles SSW. of Beersheba, is precarious, the names not agreeing phonetically.

בבור־עשן] This, not בכור־עשן, found in many edd., is the Mass. reading: the ב is recognised both in the Βηρσαβεε of Cod. B, and the Βωρασαν of Cod. A. The

---

[1] MT. ערעדה. But ד and ר in the old Phoenician characters are seldom distinguishable, and the context alone decides which is to be read. In proper names, unless the orthography is certain upon independent grounds, either letter may often be read indiscriminately.

[2] The identifications given here in the RV. with marginal references (taken over from edd. of AV. with marginal references) are extraordinary. Beth-el in *v.* 27 is identified with the Beth-el N. of Jerusalem; and 'Aro'er with the 'Aro'er N. of the Arnon, on the E. of the Dead Sea! Those responsible for these 'references' might have learnt better from the *Speaker's Commentary* on Samuel, published as long ago as 1872.

place may be the same as עֵיטָם of Jos. 15, 42 (in the Shephēlah). 19, 7 (Simeonite). If this is the case, it will have been situated approximately in the same region as עֶתֶר (see the next note).

עֶתֶר] In the Shephēlah (Jos. 15, 42); and mentioned in the same group with Libnah (site unknown), 'Ashan (see the last note), Neẓîb, now *Beit Naẓîb*, 2 miles SW. of Qe'ilah (see on 23, 1), Qe'ilah, Achzîb (perhaps '*Ain el-Kezbeh*, 2 miles NE. of esh-Shuweikeh = Sochoh ; see on 17, 1), and Marē'shah (*Merāsh*, 6 miles W. of Neẓîb). Its site cannot be more closely determined. It ' is called in Jos. 15, 42 MT. עֶתֶר, but in LXX עתך ('Ιθακ). In 19, 7 on the contrary both have עֶתֶר. A decision between the two variants is not possible ' (We.). LXX (B) Νοο, other MSS. Νομβε (Luc. Ναγεβ); hence Klo. would read עָנָב (Jos. 11, 21), still the name of a place 14 miles SW. of Hebron, while Guérin thinks of *Nūbā*, 8 miles NW. of Hebron, near Qe'ilah (I 23, 1). See Cheyne's art. ATHACH in *EB*.

31. חברון] In the hill-country (Jos. 15, 54). The most important town of the entire district, where David, shortly afterwards, was first proclaimed king (II 5, 3).

31. The chapter is excerpted, with slight variations, by the compiler of the Chronicles (1 Ch. 10). The variations are partly, it seems, due to accident, partly they are to be attributed to an intentional change on the part of the compiler of Chronicles, partly they have preserved the original text of the passage in a purer form than it has been transmitted to us in Samuel.

1. נלחמים] C. נלחמו.

וינס איש] C. וינסו אנשי.

הגלבע] C. גלבע.

2. וַיַּדְבְּקוּ] See on 14, 22.

הדביק sq. accus. אחרי שאול ואחרי בניו] C. אֵת שאול ואת בניו occurs here, II 1, 6. Gen. 31, 23. Jud. 18, 22. 20, 42†; הדביק אחרי occurs in the parallel, 1 Ch. 10, 2. *ch.* 14, 22. Jud. 20, 45†. הדביק sq. accus. means undoubtedly *to overtake* (so אדביק often in Targ. for both הדביק and הִשִּׂיג, as Gen. 44, 4. 6) : but ' overtake ' is a relative term ; and in II 1, 6, *vv.* 7–10 shew that the archers had not actually come up to Saul. We can hardly therefore say (Bu.) that אחרי must be here the original reading.

יהונתן] C. יונ.

אבינדב] wrongly identified in RV. *m.* here, and on 1 Ch. 8, 33, with ישוי, 14, 49 : in 1 Ch. 8, 33=9, 39 Saul's four sons are given as Jonathan, Malchishua', Abinadab, and Eshba'al ; and there can be no doubt (see on 14, 49) that ישוי corresponds to Eshba'al. Eshba'al (cf. II 2, 8) was pretty clearly not present at the battle.

3. וְלֹכֵד׃ Is. 21, 15; והמלחמה כָּבְדָה Cf. Jud. 20, 34 [ותכבד המלחמה. המלחמה.

על שאול. C. אל שאול]

וימצאהו] not 'overtook' (EVV.), but *found him* in the fight (Now.; Bu., comparing 1 Ki. 22, 30–34). מצא to *find* = to *hit* (Ehrl.), might be said of the *weapon* (Dt. 19, 5), but hardly of the archers.

המורים בקשת. C. [המורים אנשים בקשת. The rendering of LXX, however (οἱ ἀκοντισταί, ἄνδρες τοξόται), appears to presuppose אנשים; though, as it is difficult to construe אנשים בקשת together—'men with the bow' being hardly a Hebrew construction—the word must be misplaced. Probably the order אנשים המורים (מורים) (Bu.) בקשת 'men, shooters with the bow' = *some* shooters with the bow, should be restored. Comp. אנשים מִדְיָנִים Gen. 37, 28; אנשים בני־בליעל Dt. 13, 14; and for the art. 25, 10. Sm. Now. Dh. would omit אנשים בקשת, as a gloss explanatory of המורים: Bu. (alt.) would read as C.

ויחל מן־היורים. C. [ויחל מאד מהמורים.

ויחל] from חיל(חול), 'was in anguish from (Ru. 1, 13. Is. 6, 4. 28, 7 : *Lex.* 580ᵃ) the archers.' But חיל is confined elsewhere to poetry or elevated prose; מפני for מן would be the regular construction: and the sense does not seem strong enough. Read probably, with LXX (ἐτραυματίσθη), וַיָּחֶל and *was wounded by the archers* (מן with the passive verb, as Gen. 9, 11. Nah. 1, 6. Job 24, 1 : *Lex.* 580ᵃ). What LXX εἰς τὰ ὑποχόνδρια presupposes is uncertain: חֹמֶשׁ is rendered in LXX (II 2, 23. 3, 27. 20, 10) ψόα.

4. אל־נשא. C. [לנשא.

וּדְקָרָנִי] C. omits,—as it seems, rightly (We. Bu. Ehrl. etc.). What Saul dreads is mockery while alive, not mutilation after death, which, indeed, would not be prevented by his armour-bearer killing him.

והתעללו בי] and *wreak their caprice* upon me = *mock* or *abuse* me. See on this word Fleischer *ap.* Delitzsch on Is. 3, 4, who compares in particular the Arab. تَعَلَّلَ ب prop. *to engage oneself with*, then *to entertain, divert, amuse oneself with*, in Heb. in a bad sense, *to make a toy of, to abuse* or *mock.* See Nu. 22, 29; Jud. 19, 25 : and (where it is applied anthropomorphically to Yahweh's treatment of the Egyptians) Ex. 10, 2, and above 6, 6.

5. על־החרב. C. [על־חרבו.　　　עמו] C. omits.

6. וכל־ביתו יחדו מתו .C [ונשא כליו גם כל־אנשיו ביום ההוא יחדו a generalizing abridgment of the text of Samuel. LXX in Samuel do not express גם כל אנשיו . אנשיו will mean the men specially about Saul (23, 25. 26), not the whole army (the אנשי ישראל, v. 7 second time).

7. אנשי] C. כל־איש .

אשר בָּעֵמֶק .C [אשר בעבר העמק ואשר בעבר הירדן (for the six words). The עמק—a wide avenue running up between hills (see on 6, 13)— is the עמק יזרעאל (Hos. 1, 5), i.e. the broad vale running down from Jezreel, on the N. of Mt. Gilboa, in a SE. direction, past Bethshe'an (12 miles from Jezreel), into the Jordan valley (*H. G.* 384 f., 357 f.; *EB.* s.v. JEZREEL). The sense of the text appears therefore to be that the Israelites dwelling *on the other side of* the עמק (i.e. on the N. of it), and (more than this, even) *on the other side of* Jordan, fled through the panic. בעבר הירדן is used regularly to denote the territory east of Jordan. The statement respecting אשר בעבר הירדן may be exaggerated: but we are hardly in a position to question the correctness of the text; and בְּעָרֵי (twice) for בעבר (Klo. al.) is a somewhat violent emendation.

וכי . . . כי] So, whether in the sense of *that* or *because*, Gen. 29, 12. 33, 11. Ex. 3, 11. 4, 31. Jos. 2, 9. 7, 15. 8, 21. 10, 1. Jud. 6, 30. *ch.* 19, 4. 22, 17. II 5, 12. 1 Ki. 2, 26. 11, 21. 18, 27 al.; and even (though this can hardly be reputed an elegancy) לאמר . . . וכי Gen. 45, 26. Jud. 10, 10. The remark of Stade, p. 14, that וכי is 'unhebräisch,' can be due only to an oversight.

בהם .C בהם] בהן. עריהם .C [את־הערים. אנשי ישראל] C. omits.

8. ואת־בניו .C [ואת־שלשת בניו.

הגלבע] C. גלבע (as *v.* 1). Except in these two passages of Ch., always with the article.

9. ויפשיטהו וישאו את־ראשו .C [ויכרתו את־ראשו ויפשטו את־כליו ואת־כליו.

וַיְשַׁלְּחוּ] The object can be only the head and armour of Saul (cf., for the sense of the *Pi'el*, 11, 7. Jud. 19, 29). It is a question whether the word should not be pointed *Qal* וַיִּשְׁלְחוּ, in which case the meaning would be that they sent *messengers* throughout the land of the Philistines. And this would agree with the aim of וישלחו, viz. *to tell the tidings* (לבשר) to their gods and people.

בית עצביהם [C. את־עצביהם. את ('to *acquaint their idols* with the news') is (We.) much more original than בית ('to announce the tidings *in the house of* their idols'), is supported by LXX here, and agrees with the וְאֶת following. So Bu. Sm. Now.

10. בית עשתרות [C. בית אלהיהם.—בית עַשְׁתָּרוֹת will hardly be the pl. of בִּית־עַשְׁתֹּרֶת, as Keil suggests, on the analogy of בית אבות (Ew. § 270ᶜ; GK. § 124ʳ): in all probability the frequency of the plural in other connexions (e. g. 7, 3. 4. 12, 10) led to the sing. עשתרת here being incorrectly read as עֲשתרות. LXX εἰς τὸ Ἀσταρ-τεῖον. It is, no doubt, this temple of the Phoenician goddess 'Ashtart (see on 7, 3) in Ashqelon, which Herodotus (i. 105) mentions as τῆς οὐρανίης Ἀφροδίτης τὸ ἱερόν, and which, as he tells us, his inquiries shewed him to be the most ancient foundation of the goddess: the one in Cyprus (probably at Kition), he adds, was reported by the Cyprians themselves to have been founded from Ashqelon, and that in Cythēra [Paus. iii. 23. 1] was built by the Phoenicians. The proper name of a native of Ashqelon, compounded with עשתרת, occurs in an Inscription (*CIS.* I. i. 115): שם בן עבדעשתרת אשקלני : in the Greek parallel text Ἀντίπατρος Ἀφροδισίου Ἀσκαλ[ωνίτης]. The head of Astarte also appears on certain coins of Ashqelon (*DB.* i. 169, *n.*†). Here, 'Ashtart seems to have had the character of a martial goddess, of which there are other indications; see Ashtart in *Encycl. of Rel. and Eth.* ii. 116; Ashtoreth in *DB.* i. p. 170ᵃ.

ואת־גלנלתו תקעו בית דגן [C. ואת־גויתו תקעו בחומת בית שן. On the originality of the text of Samuel, and against the view of Ew. and Bertheau that the original text embraced *both* readings, see the convincing note of We. תקע ב' is *to strike* or *fix in*, as a tent-peg or nail, Jud. 4, 21. Is. 22, 25, a dart, II 18, 14: it may also have denoted to *fasten to*, even though the object fastened was not itself actually 'struck' in. We. Grätz (i. 439), Bu. and most follow Lagarde[1] in reading הקעו; but as it is uncertain what exactly this

---

[1] In his instructive *Anmerkungen zur Griech. Uebersetzung der Proverbien* (1863), page iv.

denotes (see on II 21, 6), and as on the only two other occasions on
which it is used, it refers to the *living* body (Ehrl.), it may be doubted
whether it is safe to restore it here.

בית־שן] So *v.* 12. II 21, 12: elsewhere בית־שְׁאָן ; in the Greek
period called *Scythopolis* (Σκυθῶν πόλις; Jud. i, 27 LXX, 2 Macc.
12, 29), now *Beisān*. An important fortress, standing on a natural
mound, artificially strengthened by scarping the side, and commanding
the entrance from the E. up the Vale of Jezreel, and so into N.
Palestine generally (*H. G.* 357 f.; *EB.* i. 566 f.). For long after the
entry of the Israelites into Canaan, and no doubt even at this time,
it was held by the Canaanites (cf. Jud. i, 27. Jos. 17, 11).

11. אליו ישבי יביש גלעד] C. כל יביש גלעד. אליו is very intrusive.
את כל־אשר] C. את אשר.

12. וילכו כל־הלילה] C. omits.   ויקחו] C. וישאו.

גופת . . . גוּפַת C. גוּיַת . . . גוּיַת. (נופה only here in OT. A word
belonging to Aramaic and the later Hebrew.)

מחומת בית שן] C. omits.

ויביאום.—Probably ויבאו here should be
vocalized וַיָּבֵא (so LXX, Pesh.): the suffix, though added by the
Chronicler, is not needed (see e. g. 16, 17).

וישרפו אתם שם] C. omits.

13. ויקברו את־עצמותיהם] C. ויקחו את־עצמתיהם ויקברו.

האלה ביבש] C. האשל ביבשה. On ביבשה, see on I 23, 15.

ויצמו] C. ויצומו. (*Vv.* 13–14 in Chronicles are an addition, made
by the compiler of Chronicles himself, and exhibiting throughout the
marks of his style: cf. *LOT.*⁸ pp. 526, 535 ff., Nos. 3, 40.)

II 1—5, 16. *Lament of David over Saul and Jonathan. David made
king at Ḥebron over Judah, and subsequently, after the murder
of Ishbosheth, over all Israel. Capture by Joab of the stronghold
of Jebus, which David henceforth makes his residence.*

1, 1. ודוד שב . . . וישב] a circ. clause, = 'when David *had*' etc. (as
RV.); cf. 1 Ki. 1, 41 (*Tenses*, § 160; cf. GK. § 141⁹, though here
the cases quoted are of a ptcp.). ויהי is resumed (see on I 25, 26) by
v. 2 ויהי, and the main sentence is continued by והנה ונ'.

הָעֲמָלֵק] is altogether isolated, the *art.* being used only with the *gentile* name. According to usage elsewhere, either עֲמָלֵק (LXX, Vulg.; cf. 30, 1 *note.* 18) or הָעֲמָלֵקִי (6 MSS. Pesh.) should be restored (We.). So Dr. Weir: ‘Is it not הָעֲמָלֵקִי?’

2. מֵעִם [מֵעִם שָׁאוּל as I 14, 17. וָאֶדְמָה עַל רֹאשׁו as I 4, 12ᵇ.

4. מַה־הָיָה הַדָּבָר] I 4, 16ᵇ. On אֲשֶׁר, see on I 15, 20.

הַרְבֵּה] Almost = רַבִּים. Strictly, of course, הַרְבֵּה is an inf. abs. in the accus., qualifying נֹפֵל, *lit.* ‘with a much-making there fell.’

6. נִקְרָא נִקְרֵיתִי] The inf. abs. as I 20, 6. נִקְרָא is for נִקְרֹה, verbs ל״ה and ל״א being not unfrequently confused (GK. § 75ʳʳ).

נִשְׁעָן] ptcp.: was *in the condition of one leaning* = was leaning.

בַּעַל [בַּעֲלֵי הַפָּרָשִׁים means *owner, possessor* (as בַּעַל הַשּׁוֹר, בַּעַל הַבַּיִת): so בַּעֲלֵי הַפָּרָשִׁים would mean *owners of the horsemen* (but not *captains,* or *generals,* of the horsemen [= LXX ἱππάρχαι], which would be שָׂרֵי הַפָּרָשִׁים); and בַּעֲלֵי הַפָּרָשִׁים would mean *owners of the (war-)horses* (on the confusion in MT. between פָּרָשׁ *horse* [pl. פָּרָשִׁים], and פָּרָשׁ (for פַּרָּשׁ [GK. § 84 *b*ᵇ]) *horseman,* pl. פָּרָשִׁים, see *Lex.* s. v.). If the text is correct (see on *v.* 18), we must point בַּעֲלֵי הַפָּרָשִׁים, and suppose it to be an unusual expression for *horsemen.*

8ᵇ. וַיֹּאמֶר] Qrê וָאֹמַר, evidently rightly. So Zech. 4, 2. Neh. 5, 9. 7, 3 (*Ochlah weOchlah,* No. 133).

אָנֹכִי] *mil'el* in pause; see on I 1, 15.

9. וּמֹתְתֵנִי] and *despatch me* (I 14, 13. 17, 51).

הַשָּׁבָץ] Only here. What exactly is denoted cannot be ascertained. The root denotes some kind of *interweaving* (Ex. 28, 39): تَشَبَّصَ is quoted by Freytag, apparently as a rare word, in the sense of ‘perplexus fuit (*de arboribus*).’ It is not apparent what meaning, suitable to the present passage, a derivative from such a root might express. The Versions afford no real help. LXX σκότος δεινὸν (perh. a corruption of σκοτόδινος, *dizziness;* Trendelenburg, *ap.* Schleusner, cited by Sm.); Targ. רְתִיתָא *terror;* Pesh. ܠܘܿ݁ܝ *dizziness* (PS. *s. v.*); Aq. (who renders the root Ex. *l. c.* by συσφίγγω, cf. 28, 13 מִשְׁבְּצֹת σφιγκτῆρας) ὁ σφίγκτηρ; Vulg. *angustiae.* Moderns generally suppose the word to denote either *the cramp* (Ew. Th. Ke.) or *giddiness* (as though properly a *confusion* of the senses), so Ges. Klo. RV. *marg.;* the exact meaning cannot be determined.

כי כל־עוד נפשי בי] A singular expression, an inversion, as it would seem, for the normal עוד כל נפשי, which, to judge from its recurrence in almost exactly the same form Job 27, 3 כי־כל־עוד נשמתי בי, was in use in Hebrew in this particular expression, being intended probably to emphasize the כל. Hos. 14, 3 כָּל־תִּשָּׂא עָוֹן, if the text be sound, must be similarly explained : but the separation of a word in the *constr. st.* from its genitive by a *verb* must be admitted to be wholly without analogy in Hebrew, and to be less defensible than its separation by a word like עוד.

10. וָאֲמִתְתֵהוּ] The 1 ps. impf. Pi'el. with *waw* conv., pointed anomalously with *pathaḥ :* so Jud. 6, 9. 20, 6 (see *Tenses,* § 66 *note ;* GK. § 49ᶜ).

נפלו] Elsewhere נָפְלוּ. The peculiar punctuation is attested and secured by the Massoretic note נון בחירק; cf. GK. § 61ᵇ.

ואצעדה] אצעדה, as Nu. 31, 50. The omission of the art. in such a case as the present is, however, very unusual, and hardly to be tolerated (I 24, 6). No doubt, substituting the other form of the word (Is. 3, 20), we should read with We. וְהַצְּעָדָה.

12. על עם יהוה ועל בית ישראל] Tautologous. Either read with LXX יהודה for יהוה, or (We. Bu. Now. Ehrl.) omit ועל בית י׳, supposing this to have been added, as necessary for the sense, after יהוה had been corrupted to יהודה.

13. איש גר עמלקי] 'an Amalekite *gér* (or protected foreigner) :' איש גר like איש נביא, איש כהן, etc. (*Lex.* 36ᵃ *top;* GK. § 131ᵇ). On the *gér*, see *DB.* s. v., or the writer's note on Dt. 10, 19, or Ex. 12, 48 : 'stranger' is both an insufficient and a misleading rendering. See also STRANGE, STRANGER, in *DB.*

14. מָשִׁיחַ] See on I 24, 7.

16. דָּמֶיךָ] Qrê דָּמְךָ in accordance with predominant usage (1 Ki. 2, 32. 37). However, the correction seems a needless one ; for the plural also occurs, as Hos. 12, 15 ; Lev. 20, 9.

אנכי] Notice the emph. pronoun.

18. קשת] was formerly supposed to be the name given to the following Song, from the fact that the word occurs in it somewhat prominently in *v.* 22 : 'and he bade them teach the children of Judah *the Bow.*' But there is no analogy or parallel for such a usage in

Hebrew; and קשת standing nakedly—not שירת הקשת, or even את־הקשת—is not a probable designation of a song. Ew. supposed קשת to stand as in Aram. for קשט (Prov. 22, 21 ; cf. Dan. 4, 34), and to be used adverbially = *correctly, accurately.* But the word is rare in Hebrew, and—however written—appears to be an Aramaism, such as would not probably have been used here : moreover, the word in Aramaic means always *truth, truthfully,* not *accurately.* We. holds the word to be an intruder ; and offers an ingenious theory to account for it : 'Perhaps, as a correction on פרשים in *v.* 6, there may have been attached to the text, in agreement with I 31, 3, the words בעלי קשת, of which, as *v.* 6 and *v.* 18 may have stood opposite to one another in two parallel columns, בעלי may have found its way into *v.* 6 before פרשים, and קשת into *v.* 18. By the adoption of this explanation, both verses at once would be relieved of an encumbrance' (so Now.).—With ללמד cf. Dt. 31, 22 ; ψ. 60 *title* מכתם לדוד ללמד.

הישר] Cf. Jos. 10, 13 (הלא היא כתובה על ספר הישר); and the original text of 1 Ki. 8, 13 (see LXX of *v.* 53, and recent Commentators).

The text of *v.* 18, however, excites suspicion. Not only is קשת intrusive, but, as Klo. remarks, ויאמר ought to be immediately followed by *v.* 19 (cf. 3, 33; 22, 2), and 18^b הנה כתובה וג' (on הנה without a pron. suff., see on I 16, 11) would form the natural sequel to 17. Upon the assumption that 18^b is misplaced, and was intended originally to follow 17, בני יהודה קשת will immediately precede *v.* 19 ; and it has been supposed that these words really conceal the first words of the dirge. Thus Klo. Bu. would read for them בְּנֵי יהודה קָשֹׁת (the *fem.,* Judah being personified as a *woman,* Jer. 3, 11 al., called to lament, Jer. 9, 16. 19 al.) 'Vernimm, O Juda, Grausames,' 'Hear (or *Learn*), O Judah, cruel tidings :' but, though קָשֹׁת is good Heb. for *hard things* (Gen. 43, 7. 30), בִּין does not mean *hear* or *learn,* but *consider* (Dt. 32, 7. ψ. 50, 22. 94, 8), and the thought itself is prosaic. Sm., better, omitting קשת, proposes בְּכִי יהודה 'Weep, O Judah' (for the sequel, in either case, see the next note). ללמד remains, however, as an awkward and inexplicable residuum.

19. הצבי] Ew. and Stade, following Pesh., Le Clerc, Mich. Dathe, De Wette, 'The gazelle,' supposing this to be a name by which Jonathan was popularly known among the warriors, on account of his fleetness (cf. 2, 18 ; 1 Ch. 12, 8 כצבאים על ההרים למהר). But there is no trace of such a name in connection with Jonathan: and

throughout the poem the *two* heroes are consistently spoken of (גבורים five times),—only in *vv.* 25ᵇ. 26 the singer's thoughts turning more particularly to Jonathan,—so that it is unlikely that he would begin with a word that was applicable to only one of them. The text must therefore be rendered, 'The beauty, O Israel, upon thy high-places is slain.' Saul and Jonathan, the two heroes who formed the crown and glory of the nation, are called its *beauty.* The expression *The beauty* (not *Thy beauty*) is singular, and Ehrlich hardly goes too far when he says it is not possible: but LXX must have already found the same consonantal text. By their rendering στήλωσον (= הַצֵּבִי), which agrees with the reading מתיך (see the next note but one), they appear to have understood the passage as an injunction to erect a *pillar* in commemoration of the two departed heroes: cf. 18, 18 (where ויצב is rendered καὶ ἐστήλωσεν)[1].

הַצְּבִי being thus unsatisfactory, Klo., followed by Bu. Sm. Now., conjectures הֵעָצְבִי ' *Be grieved* (I 20, 3. 34; and esp. II 19, 3), O Israel,' to which בְּכִי יהודה (above) would form an excellent parallel: the fem. (though not elsewhere used in poetry of *Israel*), as in בְּכִי יהודה. If this conjecture be accepted, 'ב must of course be pointed בְּמוֹתָיִךְ; and the clause must be rendered, *Upon thy high places* (*lie*) *the slain,*—חלל being construed collectively (Klo. Bu. Sm.). It reads, however, somewhat abruptly: and חלל as a predicate, as *v.* 25, would be more natural. Now., following the genuine rendering of LXX (see the next note), and omitting חלל, would read, 'Be grieved, O Israel, *for thy dead:*' but על ב' חלל is strongly supported by *v.* 25ᵇ (as indeed Now. owns).

On the whole, though, *in themselves,* בכי יהודה and העצבי ישראל would both be suitable, it is impossible to feel satisfied that they really express the original text. Some corruption seems to underlie הצבי: for the rest, it seems best, with our present knowledge, to leave *vv.* 18–19 substantially as they are, merely, with LXX, omitting קשת in *v.* 18, and, with Luc., prefixing ויאמר to *v.* 19.

על במותיך חלל] LXX has a doublet: ὑπὲρ τῶν τεθνηκότων (= על מתיך) ἐπὶ τὰ ὕψη σου (= MT.) τραυματιῶν : ' the first is shewn by the following *genitive* τραυματιῶν, and by the divergence from MT., to be their genuine rendering ' (We.).

21. הרי בגלבע] הגלבע was the name of the *range*, extending in the

---

[1] Aq. and MSS. of LXX ἀκρίβασαι (whence Vulg. *considera*) presupposes the same text : cf. ἀκρίβεια for יַצִּיבָא Dan. 7, 16 LXX Theod., and ἐξακριβώσασθαι for לְיַצָּבָה Dan. 7, 19 LXX, cited by Field.

arc of a circle for some 8 miles, and containing several independent peaks and heights (*EB.* 1723 ; cf. *DB.* s. v.) : hence the pl. הָרֵי, and the בַּג׳, which there is no reason to change (Bu. Sm. Now.) to הַגּ׳. Klo., cleverly, but needlessly, חָרְבִי גִלְבֹּעַ (Is. 44, 27 in pause) '*Dry up,* O Gilboa*' '* (Is. 42, 15). So far as the *form* goes, הרי בגלבע is a fusion of two constructions הרים בגלבע and הרי הגלבע, combining the greater definiteness of the former with the superior compactness and elegancy of the latter. In such an expression as הרים בגלבע, הרים is virtually qualified by בגלבע in the same degree as if it were an actual genitive, and is expressed accordingly in the construct state (cf. Is. 9, 2 כְּשִׂמְחַת בַּקָּצִיר : GK. § 130ᵃ).

וּשְׂדֵי תְרוּמֹת] תְּרוּמָה is lit. something *taken off* from a larger mass, and set apart for sacred purposes ; and it seems to have been first used (Dt. 12, 6. 11. 17) of gifts taken from the produce of the soil, esp. first-fruits (see more fully the writer's note on Dt. 12, 6, or his art. OFFER, OFFERING, in *DB.*, p. 588ᵃ) ; and *fields of offerings* is commonly interpreted to mean, fields bearing produce from which first-fruits are offered. But the expression is somewhat strange : the ridge of Gilboaʻ, except on its S. side, is bleak and bare (*EB.* ii. 1723) ; and, as the text stands, the verb, such as *come,* which we must understand with אַל טַל וְאַל מְטַר, must be carried on to *fields,* which it does not suit. It is a great improvement (with Klo. Now. al.) to insert יֵרֵד in *a,* and to omit (with Luc.) וּ before שְׂדֵי ; we then get a well-balanced distich—

הרי בגלבע אל יֵרֵד טל
ואל מטר עליכם שְׂדֵי תרומות

The principal suggestions made by those who are dissatisfied with שְׂדֵי תרומות are הָרֵי הַמָּוֶת (Now. Bu., after Luc. ὄρη θανάτου) ; שְׂדוֹת הַמָּוֶת (Sm. Bu. alt.) ; שְׂדוֹת רְמִיָּה (Klo.), or שְׂדֵי תַרְמוּת (Dh. : Jer. 14, 14†), ' ye fields of *deceit!* '—the fields on which the two heroes lost their lives being represented as having deceitfully betrayed them ; G. A. Smith (*H. G.* 404) שְׂדֵי מְהוּמֹת ' ye fields of *discomfitures !* '

נעל] נִגְעַל is *to reject with loathing,* Jer. 14, 19. Ez. 16, 5 (גֹּעַל). 45 *bis.* Lev. 26, 11. 15. 30. 43. 44†. (Job 21, 10 Hif. differently.) LXX here προσωχθίσθη (as Lev. 26, 15. 30. 43. 44 : Ez. 16, 45 ἀπωσαμένη). The meaning *defiled* is less probable : for this sense is only borne by נעל in *Aramaic*, and is not common even there (Is. 1, 6. 6, 5. 28, 8 Targ. Not in Syriac).

בלי משיח] 'not anointed with oil.' The shield of Saul is pictured by David as lying upon the mountains, no longer polished and ready to be worn in action, but cast aside as worthless, and neglected. Shields, whether made of leather or metal, were oiled in antiquity, to keep them in good condition. Cf. Is. 21, 5 מָגֵן מִשְׁחוּ i. e. prepare for action ; and Verg. *Aen.* 7. 626 Pars *laeves* clypeos et spicula lucida tergunt Arvina pingui.

בלי] Used alone (except Gen. 31, 20) exclusively in poetry ; especially to negative a subst. or adj., as Hos. 7, 8 בלי הפוכה ; Job 8, 11 בלי מים.

משיח] The form expresses a *permanent state* (GK. § 84 *a*[1]; Kön. ii. 130–133): what is required here is rather the ptcp. משוח (so 23 MSS.). An original משח (i. e. מָשֻׁחַ) has probably been read incorrectly as מָשַׁח, which ultimately became מָשִׁיחַ.

22. נשוג] Exceptionally for נָסוֹג (so some 50 MSS.). Comp. שָׂפוּן Dt. 33, 19 ; שִׂיג 1 Ki. 18, 27 ; שִׂנְשֵׂג Is. 17, 11 ; שָׂבֵךְ *ch.* 18, 9 ; שׂוּר Hos. 9, 12 (MT.); שׂוֹשָׂה (*Po'el* of שָׂעָה) Is. 10, 13 ; שָׂעַר *ib.* 28, 2 ; שַׂע always (four times) in Job for שָׂם ; שָׂתַם Lam. 3, 9 ; עָמַשׂ Neh. 4, 11 ; פרשׂ *to divide* (bread) Lam. 4, 4. Mic. 3, 3 for פרס Is. 58, 7 (= Arab. فَرَسَ *to tear*[1]), and occasionally besides. The Massorah contains a mechanical enumeration of eighteen instances (including some questionable ones) of words written *once* with שׂ for ס (Mass. on Hos. 2, 8; above, p. 52 *note*). The converse substitution is rarer (מסרף Am. 6, 10 ; נסה ψ. 4, 7 ; סכר Ezr. 4, 5).

לא תשוב ריקם] *used* not to return empty. ' The figure underlying the passage is that of the arrow drinking the blood of the slain, and of the sword devouring their flesh: cf. Dt. 32, 42. Is. 34, 5 f. Jer. 46, 10 ' (Keil).

---

[1] But פרשׂ *to spread out* = فَرَشَ (according to the rule ס = ﺱ = س ; שׁ = ﺵ = شَبِعَ = مﺣﺏﺍﻩ ; שֶׁבַע = مﺏﺍﻩ ; שָׁתַר = سَتَرَ ; שֶׁבַע = شَبِعَ ; נֶפֶשׁ = نَفْس). Cf. (on פרס, and פֶּרֶס, פֻּרְסִין Dan. 5, 25. 28) Nöld. *Z. für Assyr.* 1886, p. 414 ff.; and, on the phonetic rule, Wright, *Compar. Gramm.*, p. 59 f.

23. ‏הנאהבים והנעימם‎] (with the *art.*) are plainly in apposition with ‏שאול ויהונתן‎, and cannot (EVV.) form the predicate. The Mass. accentuation is evidently at fault: we must take back the *zāqēf* in *a* to ‏הנעימֹם‎, and render:

> Saul and Jonathan, the beloved and the pleasant,
> In their lives and in their death were not divided;
> They were swifter than eagles, stronger than lions.

‏נשר‎ is, of course, strictly not the *Eagle*, but the *Griffon-Vulture* (see Mic. 1, 16[1]; and Tristram, *Nat. Hist. of the Bible*, p. 173 f.).

24. ‏אל‎] for ‏על‎ (see on I 13, 13), as some 10 MSS. read.

‏המלבשכם‎] The suffix being conceived as the *object,* and not as the genitive (in accordance with the common construction of the ptcp.), in which case, of course, the article could not be employed: cf. ψ. 18, 33 ‏המאזרני חיל‎, where this is clear from the *form* of the suffix. See GK. § 116[f]; and on the *masc.* suff. § 135[o].

‏עם עדנים‎] 'together with *pleasures* or *luxuries*' (comp. on I 15, 32[2]), if not in particular *delightful food, dainties* (cf. Jer. 51, 34 ‏מִלָּא כְרֵשׂוֹ מֵעֲדָנָי‎. Gen. 49, 20 ‏מַעֲדַנִּים‎; also, in a fig. sense, ψ. 36, 9 ‏וְנַחַל עֲדָנֶיךָ תַשְׁקֵם‎). For ‏עם‎ cf. Cant. 1, 11. 4, 13. 14. 5, 1; and *Lex.* 767[a]. It is against the usage of this prep. to understand the phrase adverbially = *in a pleasurable manner* (Keil); and in so far as ‏עדנים‎ are not articles of dress, they must be associated with ‏שני‎ zeugmatically. The zeugma is, however, somewhat violent: hence Grätz, Klo. Sm. Dhorme, Ehrl. ‏עם סְדִנִים‎ *with fine linen garments* (Jud. 14, 12. 13 (see Moore, pp. 355, 377). Is. 3, 23. Prov. 31, 24†); G. A. Smith (*H. G.* 405) ‏עם עֲדָיִים‎ *with jewels*, to which ‏עדי זהב‎ in the following line would form an excellent climax. LXX μετὰ κόσμου ὑμῶν = ‏עם עֶדְיְכֶן‎.

‏המעלה‎] Cf. the use of ‏העלה‎ in Am. 8, 10; and the opposite ‏הורד עדיך מעליך‎ Ex. 33, 5: also ‏עלה‎ in Lev. 19, 19. Ez. 44, 17.

25[b]. 'Jonathan upon thy high places is slain!' David turns again to address Israel, as in *v.* 19.

26. ‏וְנִפְלְאַתָה‎] The normal form would be ‏נִפְלְאָה‎; but the case is

---

[1] Where the 'baldness' alluded to is the *down* (in place of feathers) on the neck and head, that is characteristic of the Griffon-Vulture, but not found on the Eagle.

one of those in which a ל״א verb follows the analogy of a verb ל״ה,
'the termination of the ל״ה being attached to it externally' (König,
i. 614: comp. pp. 610 f., 625): cf. הֶחְבֵּאתָה Jos. 6, 17; הֲנִבֵּאתוֹ
Zech. 13, 4; also קְראוֹת Jud. 8, 1; מְלֹאות Jer. 25, 12; תִּפֶּצָאֵינָה 50,
20. Comp. Stade, § 143ᵉ; GK. § 75ᵒᵒ.

אהבתך לי] 'לי alone = "thy love to me;" and לי is to be connected
with the verb' (Ehrl.), i.e. *thy love is wonderful to me.*

27. כלי מלחמה] i.e. (figuratively) Saul and Jonathan themselves,
conceived poetically as the instruments of war (Ew. Th. Ke.).

On this Lament, Ewald, *Die Dichter des alten Bundes*, i. 1 (1866),
pp. 148–151, should be compared. There breathes throughout a
spirit of generous admiration for Saul, and of deep and pure affection
for Jonathan: the bravery of both heroes, the benefits conferred by
Saul upon his people, the personal gifts possessed by Jonathan, are
commemorated by the poet in beautiful and pathetic language. It is
remarkable that no *religious* thought of any kind appears in the
poem: the feeling expressed by it is purely *human.*

2, 1. האעלה] with reference to the higher elevation of Judah, as
compared with Ziqlag (1, 1 f.): so *vv.* 2. 3.

3. ואנשיו] LXX והאנשים, agreeing better with אשר עמו.

4. אשר] Difficult. 'The men of Jabesh-Gilead are they that have
buried Saul' is an unnaturally worded sentence, besides being
questionable as Hebrew (הַקֹּבְרִים, not אשר קברו, would be the form in
which the subject should be expressed: see on I 4, 16). We cannot
be sure where the fault lies. אשר (which is not really wanted) may
have crept into the text by some error; or it may be taken as = *that,*
as in 1, 4, and, as there is no apparent reason for the emphatic
position of אנשי יביש גלעד before it (see on I 20, 8), as having been
accidentally misplaced from following לאמר (cf. LXX; and לאמר כי
1 Ki. 1, 13). Klo. would read על־אֹרת for לאמר (cf. Gen. 26, 32);
Ehrl. supposes words such as הושיעם שאול מיד נחש העמוני to have
fallen out after אשר.

5. אנשי] LXX ἡγουμένους = בעלי, as 21, 12. I 23, 11. 12; probably rightly. בעלי might easily be changed to the more usual אנשי,
especially under the influence of *v.* 4ᵇ.

ליהוה] for ל with the passive see GK. § 121ᶠ; *Lex.* 514ᵃ d.

אֲשֶׁר] *ye who* . . . implying, however, a reason (= οἵτινες), and so equivalent to *in that ye* . . . Comp. 6ᵇ. I 26, 16. Gen. 42, 21. ψ. 71, 19 *Thou who* . . .! 139, 15 *I who* . . .! (Germ. *Der du* . . . , *Der ich* . . .).

הַחֶסֶד הַזֶּה] LXX (Cod. A: B is here, for two verses, defective) τὸ ἔλεος τοῦ θεοῦ = חֶסֶד יהוה: cf. I 20, 14 MT.

אֲדֹנֵיכֶם] the plur. of 'majesty:' GK. § 124ⁱ.

6. הַזֹּאת] There is nothing in the context for this word to be referred to. The impf. אֶעֱשֶׂה, not less than the position of the clause *after* יַעַשׂ יהוה וג', postulates an allusion to something *future;* and does not permit the reference, assumed by Th. Ke., to the message of greeting sent at the time by David. The proposal of We. to read תַּחַת for הַזֹּאת removes all difficulty: 'I also will shew you good, *because* ye have done this thing.'

7. תֶּחֱזַקְנָה יְדֵיכֶם] fig. for, *Be encouraged:* so 16, 21. Jud. 7, 11. Zech. 8, 9. 13. Cf. חָזַק יַד פ' I 23, 16, with note.

וְהָיוּ לִבְנֵי חַיִל] 13, 28 *end.* I 18, 17.

וְגַם אֹתִי] For the emphatic position of אֹתִי, cf. on I 15, 1.

8. . . . . שַׂר צָבָא אֲשֶׁר] Usage requires שַׂר הַצָּבָא וג' (*ch.* I, 10; I 24, 6).

אִישׁ־בֹּשֶׁת] Cod. 93 Holmes Εισβααλ; so οἱ λοιποὶ (i. e. Aq. Symm. Theod.) in the Hexapla; comp. *Isbalem* of the Itala. See 1 Ch. 8, 33 = 9, 39 אֶשְׁבַּעַל, which leaves no doubt that this was the true name of Saul's son, changed at a later period into Ish-bosheth for the purpose of avoiding what was interpreted then as a compound of the name of the Phoenician deity *Baal.* The change, however, was not carried through consistently: the original *Ish-baal* (i. e. *man of Baal*—a title of Yahweh (see on 4, 4): comp. at Carthage אשתנת *man of Tanith* [1]) remained in the two genealogies in 1 Ch., and here in particular MSS. or recensions [2].

מַחֲנַיִם] on the border between Gad and Manasseh (Jos. 13, 26. 30):

---

[1] Euting, *Punische Steine* (1871), No. 227 = *CIS.* I. ii. 542 (אש[ת]נת).

[2] LXX has in *ch.* 3-4 the strange error Μεμφιβοσθε for אִישׁ־בֹּשֶׁת. So Lucian's recension throughout, except 4, 4, where the form Μεμφιβααλ occurs.

see also *vv.* 12. 29. 17, 24. 27. 19, 33. Gen. 32, 3. Jos. 21, 38
(= 1 Ch. 6, 65). 1 Ki. 2, 8. 4, 14†.

The site is uncertain. The narrative of Jacob's route from Ḥaran to Shechem
(Gen. 32-33) points to a site near the ford ed-Dāmiyeh, such as Deir 'allā, 7 miles
to the NE. of it (see the writer's *Genesis*, p. 301 f. ; more fully the *Exp. Times,*
July, 1902, p. 457 ff.) : the notices in 2 Sam. seem to suggest a site further to the N.
Thus Buhl (257 ' perhaps '), Budde (but admitting that the site seems too far from
the Jabbok for Gen. 32), and others, think the name is echoed in *Maḥnā*, 13 miles
N. of the Jabbok, and 6 miles E. of Jordan, at the top of W. el-Ḥimar (but comp.
on *v.* 29) ; Merrill (*East of Jordan*, 436 f.) points out objections to this, and proposes *Suleikhat*, a large ruin 7 miles SW. of Maḥnā, and 1 mile E. of the road N.
and S. through the Ghôr [not marked in G. A. Smith's Map, but just under the
figure 500 in this position] : this, though it would agree with 2 Sam. 18 (*DB.*
iii. 213ᵇ), does not suit Jacob's route (see my *Genesis*, 301). Further exploration
may discover the site of Maḥanaim : for the present, as Gen. 32 and 2 Sam. point
to different sites for it, it is better, with Dillmann, to leave it undetermined.

9. הָאֲשׁוּרִי] The name is recognised even by Keil as corrupt :
for neither the Assyrians (אַשּׁוּר) nor the Arabian tribe of אַשּׁוּרִם
(Gen. 25, 3) can be intended ; and the name of a tribe so insignificant as not to be mentioned elsewhere is not in this connexion
probable. Pesh. Vulg. express הַגְּשׁוּרִי (so Th. Ew. We.). The
situation, in agreement with the position of the name next to that
of Gilead, would suit excellently (see Jos. 12, 5. 13, 13) : but Keil
objects that Geshur at this time (see 3, 3ᵇ) possessed an independent
king, so that Ishbosheth could have exercised no jurisdiction over it.
Köhler, Kp. Klo. read הָאָשֵׁרִי (Jud. 1, 32): cf. Targ. עַל דבית אשר.
So Nöld. Bu. Sm. Now. etc.

כֻּלֹּה] The original form of the suffix of 3 sg. masc. is retained in
this word eighteen times (Is. 15, 3. 16, 7. Jer. 2, 21. 8, 6. 10 *bis.*
15, 10 MT. [but read בְּלֶּהֶם קִלְלוּנִי]. 20, 7. 48, 31. 38. Ez. 11, 15. 20,
40. 36, 10. Hos. 13, 2. Nah. 2, 1. Hab. 1, 9. 15)[1] ; and sporadically
(see on 21, 1) in other cases. For the position of כל with a suffix
after the subst. to which it refers, giving it greater independence and
emphasis, comp. 1 Ki. 22, 28 (=Mic. 1, 2). Is. 9, 8. Jer. 13, 19. Mal.

---

[1] The orthography כֻּלֹּו seventeen times : Gen. 25, 25. Ex. 14, 7. 19, 18. Nu.
23, 13. Lev. 13, 13. Is. 1, 23. 9, 8. 16. Jer. 6, 13 *bis.* Mal. 3, 9. ψ. 29, 9. 53, 4.
Pr. 24, 31. 30, 27. Job 21, 23. Cant. 5, 16.

3, 9. ψ. 8, 8. 67, 4. 6 ; and especially in Ezekiel, Ez. 11, 15. 14, 5. 20, 40. 29, 2. 32, 12. 30. 35, 15. 36, 5 (כְּפָּא) ; and in the *second* person, Is. 14, 29. 31. Mic. 2, 12.

Notice here אל thrice, followed by על thrice, in one and the same sentence : comp. 3, 29. Jer. 26, 15. 28, 8 ; and on I 13, 13.

10. היו אחרי] See on I 12, 14. As We. points out, *v.* 10ᵇ is the natural sequel of *v.* 9, and ought not to be separated from it. The chronological statements of *v.* 10ᵃ agree so indifferently with the data stated, or implied, in other parts of these books, that the entire clause is probably a late and unauthoritative insertion in the text.

12. נבענה] Now *el-Jîb*, 5 miles NNW. of Jerusalem.

13. יצאו] LXX adds מחברון : so Th. We. Klo. Bu.

יחדו] superfluous, and, indeed, hardly possible, after ויפגשום. Perhaps ויפנשו (i.e. וַיִּפָּגְשׁוּ *met each other*) was originally written ; and a scribe, not noticing the following יחדו, read it וַיִּפְגְּשׁוּ and added the suffix, which remained in spite of its inconsistency with יחדו.

אלה על הברכה מזה וג'] Cf. on I 14, 4. For the 'pool' of Gibeon, cf. Jer. 41, 12 המים הרבים אשר בגבעון. Robinson (i. 455) mentions remains of a large open reservoir, some 120 ft. in length by 100 ft. in breadth, a little below el-Jîb, which may be the ברכה referred to.

15. ויעברו במספר] 'and passed over by number,'—עבר of the individuals passing in order before the teller. Cf. Jer. 33, 13 : also Lev. 27, 32. Ez. 20, 37.

ולאיש-בשת] The ו is not represented in LXX, Pesh. : and the passage is improved by its omission.

16. וחרבו וג'] a circumstantial clause = '*with* his sword in his fellow's side.' LXX, however, after איש express ידו, in which case the two clauses will be parallel : 'And they fastened each his hand upon [Gen. 21, 18] the head of his fellow, and his sword in his fellow's side.' So Bu. Now. Sm.

ויקרא] sc. הַקּוֹרֵא (I 16, 4) : so elsewhere with this verb, as Gen. 11, 9. 16, 14. 19, 22 al.

חלקת הצרים] i.e. the *Field of Flints* (Ez. 3, 9 ; cf. חַרְבֹת צֻרִים Jos. 5, 2 : *Lex.* 866ᵃ), or, perhaps, *of* (Sword-)*edges* (ψ. 89, 44† : but Duhm מִצַּר here for צוּר). LXX Μερὶς τῶν ἐπιβούλων, i.e. (Schleusner, Ew. *Hist.* iii. 114, We.) חֶלְקַת הַצָּדִים, or rather (the root being צָדָה I 24, 12. Ex.

21, 13) הַצֹּדִים ח' the *Field of the Plotters* or *Liers in wait*, or (Now. Sm.) הַצָּרִים ח' (cf. Est. 7, 6 Heb. and LXX cod. אc.a mg.) the *Field of the Enemies.* But הַצִּדִּים *of sides*, proposed by Ehrl. in 1900, and independently by Bu. in 1902, seems evidently right : the place was so called on account of אִישׁ חרבו בצד רעהו.

18. אחד [כאחד הצבים in a comparison as 6, 20. 13, 13. Jud. 16, 7. 11. Job 2, 10. ψ. 82, 7.

20. זה] imparting directness and force, in the question, to אתה : so Gen. 27, 21. 1 Ki. 17, 7. 17. See *Lex.* 261ᵇ.

21. נטה לך] *v.* 22 סור לך: Gen. 22, 5 שְׁבוּ לכם. 27, 43 ברח־לך; Dt. 1, 7 סעו לכם. 40 פנו לכם. 2, 13 עברו לכם. Cf. on I 22, 5.

22. למה] LXX explicitly ἵνα μή. See on I 19, 17.

ואיך וג'] As both We. and Dr. Weir remark, the text of LXX (καὶ πῶς ἀρῶ τὸ πρόσωπόν μου πρὸς Ιωαβ; καὶ ποῦ ἐστιν ταῦτα; ἐπίστρεφε πρὸς Ιωαβ) contains a double rendering of these words, the second for אשא פני expressing אֶלָּה פְּנֵה, and being evidently the original LXX rendering, though made from a corrupt text.

23. באחרי החנית] It is doubtful both whether אחרי (everywhere else a *prep.* or *conj.*) can mean the *hinder part* of a spear, and also whether the butt end of a spear would be sharp enough to pierce through a man : hence Klo. conjectured אֲחֹרַנִּית (Gen. 9, 23 al.) *backwards* (i.e. driving the reversed spear backwards as he ran) : so Sm. Now. Bu. Ehrlich sees the difficulty ; but objects that adverbs of this form in Heb. (קדרנית, אחרנית, and perhaps מעדנית ; see on 15, 32) describe elsewhere only the manner or direction of *movement*, and therefore conjectures בחנית *with the spear*, supposing אחרי to be a dittograph. However, we have in Gen. 9, 23ᵇ ופניהם אחרנית ; and the smiting would imply here a backward movement with the arm (cf. I 4, 18 ויפל אחרנית) ; so that the objection seems hypercritical.

החמש] 3, 27. 4, 6 (but see note). 20, 10†.

תחתיו] idiomatically = *in his place, where he stood* (on I 14, 9).

ויעמדו . . . כל הבא [ויהי כל הבא is a ptcp. absol., exactly as I 10, 11ᵃ : cf. GK. § 116ʷ.

וַיָּמֹת] The pausal form, in accordance with the sense ; cf. p. 306.

24. . . . והשמש באה והמה] A sentence of the same type as Gen. 19, 23. 44, 3 הבקר אור והאנשים שֻׁלְּחוּ : *Tenses*, §§ 166, 169 ; cf. on

I 9, 5. Theod. for אַמָּה, from a sense acquired by it in post-Bibl. Hebr. (as in Syr.), has ὑδραγωγὸς (hence Vulg. *aquaeductus :* cf. Aq. on 8, 1): but were the word used as an appellative we should expect the art. (האמה).

אמה] Neither this place nor נִיח is mentioned elsewhere. The ' wilderness of Gibeon ' will presumably have been the country E. of Gibeon : but it is remarkable that, though there was a hot pursuit, neither pursued nor pursuers had by sunset got beyond land named after Gibeon,—or, indeed, if דרך sq. gen. is to be taken in its normal sense (Gen. 3, 24. Ex. 13, 17. I 6, 9. 12 etc.), ' the road *to* ' it,—though very soon after (*v.* 29) Abner began his all-night march through the Ghôr. The distance from Gibeon to Jericho, in a straight line, is 17 miles. *Geba'* for *Gibeon* (see the opposite error in 5, 25) would be much more probable (so Bu.): Geba' (see on I 13, 2) is 5 miles E. of Gibeon, and a route leads from it through W. Fārah (p. 103) directly down to Jericho. It is very possible that there is some further error in the text ; though it cannot be restored with certainty. נִיח is a place as unknown as אמה, though from its being used to define the position of אמה, one expects it to be better known. We. supposes it to have arisen out of גֵי הַ (LXX Γαι), and גי in its turn to be a dittograph of נִי in פְּנִי ; supplying a ב he thus gets על פְּנִי הדרך במדבר גבעון (נבע) ' in front of (= East of ? ; see on I 15, 7) the road in the wilderness of Gibeon (or, better, Geba').' So Now.

25ᵇ. אחת] hardly more than *a* : cf. 1 Ki. 19, 4 ; and see on I 1, 1. We. Sm. Bu. al. read, however, נבעת אַמָּה (as *v.* 24). Is it, however, certain that the hill was the same one ? notice ויקרא, implying some distance, in *v.* 26.

26. לנצח] LXX εἰς νῖκος : see p. 129 *n.*

עד מתי לא] So Hos. 8, 5. Zech. 1, 12†.

27. חי האלהים] LXX יהוה (as always elsewhere, in this oath). ' As God liveth, (I say) that, unless thou hadst spoken, that then only after the morning had the people gotten themselves up, each from after his brother,' i.e. if thou hadst not suggested to them *v.* 26 to cease from arms, they would have continued the pursuit till to-morrow morning. RV. interprets the passage falsely. For the repetition of כי, see on I 14, 39. או as 19, 7. מהבקר lit. *after* the morning : מן as in מיּוֹמַים, etc.

נעלה] The *Nif.* is used idiomatically, of getting away from so as to abandon (Nu. 16, 24. 27), especially of an army raising a siege, Jer. 37, 5. 11. Cf. *Lex.* 749ᵃ 1 b 2.

28. ולא ירדפו] See on I 1, 7 ולא תאכל : cf. I 2, 25 ולא ישמעו.

29. בערבה] the broad, and relatively barren Steppe, or floor of the deep depression (*el-Ghôr*), through which the Jordan flows (cf. on

I 23, 24). It would be reached from Gibeon by going down to Jericho.

כל הבתרון] accus. after וילכו (unusual): Dt. 1, 19. 2, 7 (Sm.).

הבתרון] Only here. The verb בתר is *to divide in parts*, Gen. 15, 10 (twice) †; and בֶּ֫תֶר is *a divided part* (Gen. 15, 10. Jer. 34, 18. 19 †), each time, of halves of animals cut in two in making covenants. Ges. and other moderns have accordingly generally taken בתרון to mean properly a *division* or *cleft;* and הבתרון (with the art.) to have been in particular *the* ' Gorge' leading up to Maḥanaim, as (Buhl, 121) *W. 'Ajlūn* (6 miles N. of the Jabbok), or (Budde) *W. el-Ḥimār* (12 miles N. of the Jabbok), by either of which Maḥanaim, *if* Maḥnā, could apparently be reached ; or (*H. G.* 586) the 'narrow central portion of the Jordan valley itself.' It is not, however, stated whether any of these routes traverses a pass or valley of a character in some way or other so marked as to be distinctively called הבתרון. W. R. Arnold (*Essays . . . published as a Testimonial to C. A. Briggs*, 1911, p. 13 ff.) argues, on the contrary, that, as כל הבתרון cannot be the direct object of וילכו (for the accus., as a direct obj. is very rare after הלך, Dt. 1, 19. 2, 7, and, כל בתרון being definite, the absence of את shews that it is not a direct obj.), it must be an *adverbial* accus., and that, not of place, but like *v.* 32 וילכו כל הלילה, of *time* (GK. § 118ᵏ), and denote *all the half* (sc. of the day); he then by a careful examination of *vv.* 24–32, and comparison with 4, 5–8, makes it probable that Abner would reach Maḥanaim at about noon, so that the half of the day denoted by בתרון would be the *fore-noon*. The case is ably argued; but it cannot be said to be established. Dt. 1, 19. 2, 7 shew that הלך may be construed with a direct accus.; and את is often omitted before a direct determined object. (Arnold's paper is reprinted in *AJSL*. 1912, 274 ff.)

31. ובאנשי] Read באנשי or (with LXX) מֵאַנְשֵׁי: cf. *v.* 15. מתו at the end of the verse is superfluous: שלש . . . איש being evidently the obj. (which is required) to הכו. The insertion in RV. of *so that* in italics is a sufficient indication how anomalous the verse is in the Hebrew. Th. Ke. would understand אשר before מתו: but the omission of the relative pronoun in Hebrew *prose* is almost confined to the late and unclassical style of the Chronicler; see on I 14, 21. LXX παρ' αὐτοῦ=מֵאִתּוֹ. Ehrlich שלש מאות איש ושׁשׁים איש מתו, taking הכו to mean only *wounded*. But Heb. historians rarely draw such distinctions; and in accounts of battles הכה practically means always to *smite fatally* (*Lex.* 646ᵃ), exceptions being very rare (2 Ki. 8, 28= 9, 15: *ib.* 645ᵇ e).

32. בית־לחם] 9 MSS. בבית־לחם: but see p. 37 *footnote* 2.

וַיָּאֹר להם]] The expression seems a natural one; but it occurs only here. Cf. וְאָוֹר לכם (the *verb*) I 29, 10†; הבקר אוֹר Gen. 44, 3†.

3, 1. ארכה] 'Job 11, 9 (מִדָּה). Jer. 29, 28. The masc. (which would be אָרֹךְ; GK. § 93kk) does not occur. LXX ἐπὶ πολύ, reading הַרְבֵּה (ארבה),' Dr. Weir.

הלך וחזק . . . הלכים ודלים] See on I 2, 26.

2–5] = 1 Ch. 3, 1–3. List of David's wives and sons.

2. וילדו] The Kt., as We. suggests, might be pointed וַיִּלְדוּ (for וַיִּיָּלְדוּ), on the analogy of the contracted forms which now and then occur in *Piʿel* (Nah. 1, 4 וַיַּבְּשֵׁהוּ. Lam. 3, 33 וַיַּגֶּה. 53 וַיִּדּוּ. 2 Ch. 32, 30. Qrê וַיְשָׁרוּ: GK. § 69u). However, the contraction is in all cases against analogy, and therefore probably nothing more than a clerical error; nor, in *Puʿal*, is there any instance of it at all. No doubt, the Qrê וַיִּוָּלְדוּ is here right.

לאחינעם] *belonging to,* the dat. of reference: cf. 1 Ki. 14, 13 (*Lex.* 512b 5 c). On Ahinoʿam, see on I 25, 43.

3. כלאב] Ch. דָּנִיֵּאל; LXX here Δαλουια, Aq. Symm. Theod. Αβια; in 1 Ch. 3, 1 B Δαμνιηλ, A and Luc. Δαλουια. Klo. al. regard ΔΑΛΟΥΙΑ as a corruption of ΔΑΔΟΥΙΑ=דֹּדִיָּה, and דניאל of דֹּדִיֵּאל,— two alternative forms of the same name. It is impossible to say what the original form of the name was: but לאב in כלאב is open to the suspicion of being a dittograph of לאב in לאביגל.

הכרמלי] See on I 25, 2.

נשור] A petty Aramaean kingdom on the E. of Jordan, N. of Gilead; cf. on I 27, 8.

5. אשת דוד] By analogy (see v. 3a) the name of 'Eglah's first husband would be expected: doubtless, therefore, דוד is due either to a *lapsus calami* or to some transcriptional corruption.

6. 'V. 6b is the continuation of v. 1. Vv. 2–5 have been inserted subsequently, and v. 6a conceals the juncture' (We.).

היה מתחזק ב'] '*was making* or *shewing* himself strong in' [not *for*] etc., i.e. was gaining power and importance in connexion with the house of Saul. The verb is not used elsewhere in a bad sense (cf. 2 Ch. 1, 1. 12, 13 etc.), except sq. עַל (*ib.* 17, 1); but in the light of v. 8 ff. it is probable that it is used here to suggest the idea of acquiring undue power, and presuming too much.

7. ולשאול פלגש] For the form of sentence, cf. 4, 4. 13, 3. 14, 6 ולשפחתך שני בנים. I 28, 24 etc.; cf. on I 1, 2.

ויאמר] As Ishbosheth has not been hitherto named in the present connexion, the insertion (אשבעל) איש בשת בן־שאול is necessary : cf. LXX καὶ εἶπεν Μεμφιβοσθε (p. 240 *n.* 2) υἱὸς Σαουλ.

8. אשר ליהודה] '*belonging to* Judah.' The point lies in the reference to the *Judaean* ראש כָּלֶב (cf. Ewald, iii. 116 *n.*). LXX, however, do not express the words ; and many moderns omit them, on the doubtful supposition that they are a gloss added by a scribe who vocalized כָּלֵב, in order to explain that this was the name of the Judahite clan (see on I 25, 3).

היום] with emphasis, *to-day, at this time.* Abner protests that at the very time at which Ishbosheth is bringing his charge against him, he is doing his best for the house of Saul.

אעשה] *I do,*—the impf. expressing present habit. Klo. Bu. הָעֹשֶׂה, putting the *segolta* on הֵיוֹם.

מֵרֵעֵהוּ] A *plural* form : cf. on I 30, 26.

המציתך] So, sq. ביד, Zech. 11, 6. מצא or מצה *to arrive, come to,* המצה *to cause to come to,* with ביד *place into the hand* of, *hand over* to.

ותפקד] = *and* (yet) *thou visitest,* etc. For the adversative sense, sometimes implied in ו׳, cf. 19, 28. Gen. 32, 31 : *Tenses,* § 74 β.

עון האשה] LXX עון אשה 'a fault concerning a woman' (and nothing more). So We. Klo. Bu. etc.

9. כי ... כי] The second כי is resumptive of the first (I 14, 39).

11. להשיב את אבנר דבר] דבר פ׳ השיב is properly to *turn one back with* (GK. § 117 ff) *a word;* hence, in a weakened sense, *reply to, answer :* so I 17, 30 and often. If the lit. meaning were 'bring back word *to,*' we should, by all analogy, require אל or ל for את (cf. the Arab. idiom, cited in *Thes.* 1374 b).

12. תחתו] Generally explained as=*where he was* (2, 23). But the use is singular : for the suffix would refer naturally not to דוד but to the subject of וישלח (see 2, 23 ; and on I 14, 9). Lucian has εἰς Χεβρων (= חֶבְרֹן), of which תחתו is prob. a corruption ; see below.

לאמר למי־ארץ] At least לְמִי־הָאָרֶץ would be required, if the words were meant to express *Whose is the land?* but even so, they are incompatible as they stand with what follows, לאמר כרתה בריתך אתי, which is also the purport of the message, and which according to

Hebrew usage ought to follow תחתו *immediately.* The least change that will suffice to produce an intelligible sentence, is to read לְמִי־הָאָרֶץ, and to omit the following לאמר. At the same time, it must be admitted that the proposal כרתה בריתך אתי וג׳ is complete without any prefatory introduction; and probably למי ארץ לאמר is merely a double dittograph of the preceding לאמר. LXX πρὸς Δαυειδ εἰς Θαιλαμ οὗ ἦν παραχρῆμα λέγων Διάθου κτλ., where παραχρῆμα=תחתו, so that εἰς Θαιλαμ οὗ ἦν (εἰς Θηλαμου γην Cod. A) must be a subsequent insertion, in the *wrong* place, representing תחתו again (=εἰς Θαι) and לאמר למי ארץ [ארץ] למי\(למו\) = λαμου γην, hence λαμ οὗ ἦν]. Παραχρῆμα λέγων Διάθου appears to shew that in the Hebrew text used by LXX תחתו לאמר כרתה stood together: if with Luc. חברן be read for תחתו, this would yield an excellent sense (so Now.). Bu., simplifying a suggestion of Klo.'s, would read (after דוד) לאמר תַּחְתַּי הָאָרֶץ לָתֵת לְמִי אֶרְצֶה כרתה וג׳ ' saying, The land is under me (at my disposal) to give to whom I please :' but the Heb. idiom for under a person's authority or control is not תחת פ׳ (except of a *wife*, Nu. 5, 19 al.), but תחת יד פ׳ (I 21, 4. 5. 9. Jud. 3, 30. Is. 3, 6 : *Lex.* 1065 *b*; notice also מִתַּחַת יַד פ׳ 2 Ki. 8, 20. 13, 5 al., *ib.* 1066ᵃ).

ידי עמך] Cf. Jer. 26, 24 (את); rather differently, *ch.* 14, 19.

13. טוב] i.e. *Good!* (=*I agree*): cf. I 20, 7. 1 Ki. 2, 18. Note the אני (see on I 26, 6).

כי אם לפני הביאך] ' *except before* thy bringing '—an unintelligible construction. כי אם and לפני exclude one another; and we must read either לפני הביאך *before* thy bringing, or (cf. Gen. 32, 27) כי אם הֲבֵאתָ *except* thou bring. The latter is expressed by LXX (ἐὰν μὴ ἀγάγῃς).

14. See I 18, 27.

15. מעם איש] ' from a man !' Read, of course, with LXX אִשָּׁה. For מעם, cf. I 10, 9. 18, 13.

ליש (Qrê)] See I 25, 44.

16. בחרים] On the way between Jerusalem and Jericho (16, 5. 17, 18), not improbably (Buhl, 175; *EB.* s. v.), at either *Bukē'dān* 1½ miles, or *Rās ez-Zambi* 2½ miles, ENE. of Jerusalem, near the old Roman road, leading down to Jericho. Targ. עלמת (עֲלֶמֶת) 1 Ch.

6, 45 = עַלְמוֹן Jos. 21, 18, now '*Almît* 3½ miles NE. of Jerusalem),—
no doubt from עלמת having apparently a similar meaning to בחרים
(cf. עֶלֶם *youth ;* and עֲלָמִים, בְּחֻרִים, both *youthful age*).

17. ...הֹיה ודבר] '*had* been,' a plup.: for דבר עם cf. Jud. 18, 7.
1 Ki. 1, 7.

גם תמול גם שלשם] Cf. Ex. 4, 10. *ch.* 5, 2.

הייתם מבקשים] '*have been* (continuously) *seeking.*' Cf. Dt. 9, 7.
22. 24: *Tenses*, § 135. 5 ; GK. § 116ʳ.

18. הושיע] ' Evidently a clerical error for אושיע, which many MSS.
have, and which is expressed by all versions ' (Keil).

19. טוב] טוב, after אשר, will be the *verb* (*Lex.* 373ᵃ).

20. עשרים אנשים] Ehrlich would read עֲשָׂרָה א' (Jud. 20, 10).
עשרים איש is correct (GK. § 134ᵉ) ; but the type עשרים אנשים is very
rare and anomalous : 2 Ki. 2, 16 (perhaps due to the following בני חיל :
Herner, *Syntax der Zahlw.* 106). Jer. 38, 10 (Ew. al. שְׁלֹשֶׁת)†.

ולאנשים] The men being *definite* (20ᵃ), לָאֲנָשִׁים is certainly what
would be expected: comp. 1, 11. 17, 12.

משתה] For the position, see on 14, 12.

21. וְאֵלְכָה] Notice the pausal form with the small distinctive accent,
pazer (*Tenses*, § 103 with *n.* 2). On תאוה נפשך, see on I 2, 16.

22. בא] No doubt, ' Joab is the principal person for the narrator '
(Keil) : but, with עבדי דוד ויואב preceding, בא by Hebrew idiom
ought to be plural. Read בָּאִים (i. e. in the older orthography באמ) :
a מ has dropped out before מהנדוד. סביר באו (see on I 12, 5).

24. וילך הלוך] ' and he is gone (with) a going ' = ' and he is gone
off,'—very idiomatic and forcible, not to be abandoned in favour of
the more ordinary expression here offered by LXX וַיֵּלֶךְ: הֲלֹא יָדַעְתָּ
וג' (ἐν εἰρήνῃ is manifestly derived merely from *vv.* 21ᵇ. 22ᵇ. 23ᵇ :
but while the narrator, and reporters, use the common וילך בשלום,
Joab characteristically expresses himself with greater energy וילך
הלוך). At the same time, *v.* 25 would doubtless be more forcible
as an interrogative ; and it is very probable that הלוא has *fallen out*
after הלוך.

25. כי לפתותך בא] The regular order in such constructions : cf.
Gen. 42, 9. 47, 4. Jos. 2, 3. Jud. 15, 10. 12. I 16, 2. 5.

מבואך] Why the abnormal (and incorrect) form מוּבָאֶךָ should be substituted as Qrê, unless for the sake of the assonance with מוֹצָאֲךָ, is not apparent.

26. בּוֹר הַסִּרָה] The 'cistern of Sirah.' There is an *'Ain Sārah*, about a mile N. of Hebron, on the road to Jerusalem, which may be the place meant (*DB.* and *EB.* s. v.).

27. אֶל תּוֹךְ הַשַּׁעַר] The *middle* of the gate would scarcely be the place in which Joab could converse with Abner quietly. LXX ἐκ πλαγίων τῆς πύλης = אֶל יֶרֶךְ הַשַּׁעַר (see Lev. 1, 11. Nu. 3, 29. 35 Hebrew and LXX) 'to the *side* of the gate,' which is favoured also by the verb וַיַּטֵּהוּ 'led *aside*.'

בַּשֶּׁלִי] A usage approximating curiously to the Aramaic: comp. ܒܫܶܠܝܳܐ *in quietude, quietly,* in the Pesh. I 12, 11 al. (= בְּפֶתַח). Is. 8, 6 (= לְאַט). Job 4, 13 (of the quiet of night). Ehrlich, however, for בַּשֶּׁלִי וַיַּכֵּהוּ conjectures וַאֲבִישַׁי הִכָּהוּ; cf. *v.* 30.

וַיַּכֵּהוּ שָׁם הַחֹמֶשׁ] Probably אֶל should be restored before הַחֹמֶשׁ, in conformity with the construction elsewhere (2, 23. 4, 6. 20, 10).

28. מֵאַחֲרֵי בֵן] 15, 1. 2 Ch. 32, 23†.

מֵעִם י״י] מֵעִם, the acquittal being conceived as *proceeding from* Yahweh: comp. Nu. 32, 22 וִהְיִיתֶם נְקִיִּים מֵיהוָה וּמִיִּשְׂרָאֵל.

29. יָחֻלוּ] Comp. Jer. 23, 19 = 30, 23 (of a tempest) עַל רֹאשׁ רְשָׁעִים יָחוּל; Hos. 11, 6.

וָאֵל וְעַל] סביר (see on I 12, 5); so 10 MSS.

וָאֵל יִכָּרֵת מִן] Cf. Jos. 9, 23.

فَلَسَ מַחֲזִיק בַּפֶּלֶךְ] is *to be globular* or *round* (especially of a woman's breasts): hence فَلَكٌ is *the sphere* in which a star moves (Qor. 21, 34. 36, 40), and فِلْكَةٌ *the whorl* of a spindle, Lat. *verticillus,* as פֶּלֶךְ in Hebrew, Prov. 31, 19 (see *EB.* iv. 5277 f.). Here פֶלֶךְ was formerly (LXX σκυτάλη; Rabb.; EVV.) commonly supposed to denote a *staff:* but (*a*) other words are elsewhere used in Hebrew to express this idea (see 2 Ki. 4, 29. 31, and especially Zech. 8, 4 וְאִישׁ מִשְׁעַנְתּוֹ בְּיָדוֹ מֵרֹב יָמִים), (*b*) there is no trace of such a meaning in the cognate languages (see Levy, Freytag, Lane), (*c*) the transference of the term to denote an object lacking the characteristic feature (the *whorl*) which it properly denotes, is improbable, and (*d*), even if it were so transferred, as the 'spindle' was not more than some 12 inches long, it is not likely to have been applied to a walking-stick. Aq. Symm.

(ἄτρακτον), Jer. (*fusum*), Pesh. (ܡܓܙܠܐ) render *spindle ;* and philology and usage agree in supporting this rendering: the word, meaning properly ' whorl,' will have come naturally to suggest the spindle as a whole. David's words are an imprecation that Joab may always count among his descendants—not brave warriors, but—men fit only for the occupations of women. Comp. how ' Hercules with the distaff ' was the type of unmanly feebleness among the Greeks.

30. הרגו לאבנר] ל as I 23, 10 (see note), and with הרג itself (in *later* Hebrew) Job 5, 2. The verse interrupts the narrative; and the ל may be due to its being in fact (We. Bu. Now. Sm.) a late gloss. Ew. Klo., on the ground of LXX διαπαρετηροῦντο, prefer to read אָרְבוּ *laid ambush for :* but this would scarcely be a just description of the manner in which Joab actually slew Abner: nor does the preceding narrative imply that Joab and Abishai had done previously anything that could be so described.

31. ספדו] *wail ;* see on I 28, 3.

לפני אבנר] i. e. *preceding* the bier in the funeral procession.

33. הכמות] not ' *Did* Abner die ? ' (הֲמֵת), but ' *Was* Abner on the *way to die ?* ' was this the end reserved for him? For the impf. cf. 2 Ki. 3, 27 his firstborn אשר ימלך who *was to reign* after him : 13, 14 the illness אשר ימות בו which he *was to die* of: *Tenses,* § 39 β; GK. § 107ᵏˑᵗ. For the dagesh in כ, see GK. § 100ˡ.

34. לא־אסרות] לא with the ptcp. is unusual, and to be imitated with caution: comp. Jer. 4, 22. ψ. 38, 15. Job 12, 3 (Ew. § 320ᵇ). Ez. 22, 24. Dt. 28, 61 : *Tenses,* § 162 *n.*; *Lex.* 519ᵃ b *c.*

נחשתים] a *pair* of bronze fetters : Jud. 16, 21† (GK. § 88ᵉ).

כנפול] sc. הנופל; comp. I 2, 13 (כבשל). On נבל, see on I 25, 25. Abner, David laments, has experienced a death that was undeserved: he has died the death of a נבל, a reprobate, godless person, whom an untimely end might be expected to overtake. There was nothing to prevent Abner from defending himself, had he suspected Joab's treachery (34ᵃ); as it was (34ᵇ), he had succumbed to the treacherous blow of an assassin.

35. להברות] The verb is confined to this book (12, 17. 13, 5. 6. 10): so בריה *food* 13, 5. 7. 10†. בָּרוֹת occurs Lam. 4, 10; and בָּרוּת ψ. 69, 22†.

כִּי אִם] not = *except*, as *v.* 13 : the two particles are to be separated, כִּי introducing the oath, as I 14, 44, and אִם expressing it (*if . . .! = surely not*). כֹל מְאוּמָה : Gen. 39, 23†.

36. וּכְכֹל וג׳] '*as* whatsoever the king did pleased all the people' (EVV.) would require כֹל כַּאֲשֶׁר for כְּכֹל (כ never having the force of a conjunction). The text can only be rendered, 'Like all that the king did, *it* (viz. his conduct on the present occasion) pleased all the people' (טוב being the *verb*, as *v.* 19). בֹּל for כְּכֹל (LXX, Bu. Now.) yields a very abrupt sentence, not in accordance with Heb. style.

37. מֵהַמֶּלֶךְ] So מֵיהוה הָיְתָה לּוֹ 1 Ki. 2, 15 : cf. Jud. 14, 4 כִּי מִי"ּ הִיא (*Lex.* 579ᵇ d); and מֵאֵת, as מֵאֵת יהוה הָיְתָה זֹאת Jos. 11, 20 al. (*Lex.* 86ᵇ 4 b).

39. רַךְ] *tender, weak,* opp. to קָשִׁים.

וּמָשׁוּחַ מֶלֶךְ] The contrast which, in virtue of the contrasted ideas connected by it, is implicit in the copula וְ, would be expressed in English distinctly by *and at the same time, and yet,* or *though* (cf. Cant. 1, 5). Ew. rendered, 'And I this day live delicately and am anointed as king,' etc. The sense thus attached to רַךְ is defensible (Dt. 28, 54 הָרַךְ בְּךָ וְהֶעָנֹג. Is. 47, 1) : but the rendering labours under the disadvantage of obliterating the antithesis, which, nevertheless, seems to be designed, between רַךְ and קָשִׁים. MT. (so far as the consonants go) is presupposed by LXX (συγγενὴς = רַךְ misread as רֹד, see Lev. 18, 14. 20, 20 : καὶ καθεσταμένος ὑπὸ βασίλεως = וּמָשׁוּחַ מֶלֶךְ).

4, 1. בֶּן־שָׁאוּל] 'LXX rightly inserts אִישׁ־בֹּשֶׁת before בֶּן שָׁאוּל : the omission in the Hebrew may perhaps be explained by the resemblance between אִישׁבֹּשֶׁת (אֶשְׁבַּעַל) and וַיִּשְׁמַע' (Dr. Weir).

וַיִּרְפּוּ יָדָיו] as Jer. 6, 24. Is. 13, 7 al., fig. for *lost heart:* the masc. as Zeph. 3, 16. 2 Ch. 15, 7 by GK. § 145ᴾ.

נִבְהָלוּ] a strong word, more than 'were troubled,' *were alarmed,* ψ. 48, 6. Jer. 51, 32 al. : elsewhere in early prose only I 28, 21. Gen. 45, 3. Jud. 20, 41.

2. גְדוּדִים] *guerilla bands;* cf. 2 Ki. 5, 2 ; also I 30, 8. 1 Ki. 11, 24 ; and Gen. 49, 19 'As for Gad, a *troop* may *troop* upon him ; But he will *troop* upon their heel.'

הָיוּ בֶן־שָׁאוּל] The text, as it stands, is not translateable. Read with LXX הָיוּ לְאִישׁ־בֹּשֶׁת (לְאֶשְׁבַּעַל) בֶּן־שָׁאוּל.

בְּאֵרוֹת] i.e. *Wells;* mentioned as closely associated with Gibeon, Chephîrah, and Qiryath-ye'arim in Jos. 9, 17, as Canaanite towns which long maintained their independence in Israel, and with Qiryath-ye'arim and Chephîrah in Ezr. 2, 25 (=Neh. 7, 29); and after Gibeon and Ramah, and before Miẓpeh (Nebi Samwîl) and Chephîrah, in the list of Benjaminite cities in Jos. 18, 25 f.†. It is generally identified with *el-Bireh*, a village with several springs or ' wells,' 4 miles NNE. of Gibeon, and 9 miles N. of Jerusalem, on the great northern road : Buhl (*Geogr.* 173), however, and Now., on the strength of Eusebius' statement (*Onom.* 233, 83 f.) that it was 7 miles from Jerusalem on the road to Nicopolis (*Amwâs*),—which, if this were the present Jaffa road, would be at a point about 3 miles SW. of Gibeon, —prefer this site (which would also bring Bĕ'ēroth nearer to the cities with which it is associated in Jos. 9, 17. Ezr. 2, 25). Robinson (i. 452), however, placing the ' road to Nicopolis ' more to the north, thinks el-Bireh compatible with Eusebius' description.

תַּחְשֹׁב עַל] Cf. Lev. 25, 31 עַל שׂדה הארץ יֵחָשֵׁב; and with לְ, Jos. 13, 3 לַכְּנַעֲנִי תֵּחָשֵׁב.

3. וַיִּהְיוּ שָׁם גֵּרִים] גֵּרִים is the ptcp. : ' and they *continued* (on I 18, 9) *sojourning there,*' viz. as גֵּרִים, or protected foreigners (on 1, 13). The Gibeonites, with no doubt the inhabitants of their dependent towns (Jos. 9, 17), Chephîrah, Bĕ'ēroth, and Qiryath-ye'arim, were not Israelite, but *Amorite* (*ch.* 21, 2); and the Beerothites had, for some reason, fled to Gittaim,—presumably the Gittaim mentioned Neh. 11, 33† in a list of Benjaminite cities, next after Ramah,—where they sought and obtained protection as *gêrim.*

4. וְהוּא בֶן חָמֵשׁ שָׁנִים הָיָה בְבֹא וְגֹ' [בֶּן חָמֵשׁ שׁנה] (without הָיָה) would be excellent Hebrew ; but it is not supported by LXX, as Bu. claims : LXX connects בֶּן חָמֵשׁ שָׁנִים with what *precedes,* and then for וְהָיָה has καὶ οὗτος. With MT. cf. 2 Ki. 8, 17. 14, 2. 15, 2. 33.

בְחָפְזוֹ] Ehrlich would point בְּהֶחָפְזָה=בֶּהָחֶפְזֹה (see p. 37 *n.*), remarking that the Qal (Dt. 20, 3. ψ. 31, 23. 116, 11. Job 40, 23†) is used of hurry and alarm in general, but the Nif. (I 23, 26. 2 Ki. 7, 15 Kt. ψ. 104, 7†) of hurry and alarm in *flight.*

מְפִיבֹשֶׁת] In 1 Ch. 8, 34 (*bis*). 9, 40ᵃ מְרִיב בַּעַל, in 9, 40ᵇ מְרִי־בַּעַל. One of these forms is certainly the original name. There was a time when the name בַּעַל *owner* or *master* (of the place or district)[1] was

---

[1] See art. BAAL in *DB., EB.,* and (most fully) in Hastings' *Encycl. of Rel. and Ethics,* ii. 283 ff. Cf. also above, p. 63 f.

applied innocently to Yahweh[1], as *Owner* of the soil of Canaan : but, in consequence no doubt of the confusion which arose on the part of the unspiritual Israelites between Yahweh and the Phoenician *god* ' Baal,' the habit was discountenanced by the prophets, especially by Hosea (2, 18), and ultimately fell out of use. Proper names, therefore, in which בעל originally formed part had to be disguised, or otherwise rendered harmless. This was generally done by substituting בשת *shame*[2] for בעל, as in the case of Ishbaal (above, on 2, 8), and of Meribbaal the name of Saul's grandson here, and of one of his sons by Rizpah in 21, 8. In the case of the latter name the change to מריבשת (or מריבשת) appears not to have been thought sufficient ; and the name was further disguised by being altered to מפיבשת, which was probably taken to mean ' One who *scatters* or *disperses* (cf. Dt. 32, 26 אפאיהם,—though this word is certainly corrupt) Shame[3].' Jerubbaal (Gideon), ' the Master *contends*,' being interpreted to mean ' One that contends *with* Baal ' (Jud. 6, 32), was suffered to remain, except in *ch.* 11, 21, where it was altered to Jerub*besheth.* In less read books, however, the names remained sometimes unchanged : thus אשבעל and מריבבעל are preserved in Ch., as also בעלידע, ' the Master *knows*,' the name of a son of David, called in *ch.* 5, 16 אלידע ' *God* knows[4],' and the name of David's hero בעליה 1 Ch. 12, 5, and of his officer בעלחנן 27, 28[5]. It will be observed that these names are particularly frequent

---

[1] See *DB.* i. 210[b]; *EB.* i. 403 ; *Encycl. of Rel. and Ethics*, ii. 291 f.

[2] For בשת *shame* as a designation of Baal, see Jer. 3, 24. 11, 13. Hos. 9, 10; comp. in LXX 1 Ki. 18, 19. 25 οἱ προφῆται τῆς αἰσχύνης. Dillmann, in an elaborate essay devoted to the subject in the *Monatsberichte der Kön.-Preuss. Academie der Wissenschaften zu Berlin*, 1881, June 16, observing the strong tendency shewn not only in LXX, but in other ancient versions as well, to obscure or remove the name of Baal, thinks that the habit of substituting αἰσχύνη for it is the explanation of the strange ἡ Βααλ of certain parts of LXX (e. g. Jeremiah constantly,—2, 23. 7, 9. 11, 13. 17. 19, 5 al. Hos. 2, 10. 13, 1 : so Rom. 11, 4) : Βααλ was left in the text, but the *fem.* of the art. was an indication that αἰσχύνη was intended to be read. No traces of an *androgynous* Baal have been found in Phoenician Inscriptions.

[3] Lucian has throughout (except 21, 8) the intermediate form Μεμφιβααλ. Perhaps this is a survival of the first stage in the transforming process.

[4] Comp. Jud. 9, 46 אל ברית for בעל ברית 8, 33. 9, 4.

[5] Comp. also בעל itself, as a pr. n., 1 Ch. 5, 5. 8, 30 (=9, 36).

in the families of Saul and David, both zealous worshippers of Yahweh (comp. among other things in the case of Saul the name of his son יהונתן). מריבבעל will be a name of the same form (a rare one in Hebrew: above on I 1, 20) as the Nabataean מקימאל (Cooke, *NSI.* 78, 2), and מהיטבאל, משיזבאל (above, p. 18 *note*).

5. כחם היום] Gen. 18, 1; I 11, 9 Qrê†.

את משכב הצהרים] The cogn. accus. משכב is here not the *place* of reclining (=*couch*), but the *act* of reclining (as in the expression משכב זכר Jud. 21, 11 al., and *ch.* 17, 28 [see note]), in the present context=*siesta:* 'was taking his noon-tide rest.'

6. הֵנָּה [והנה באו עד־תוך הבית לקחי חטים ויכהו אל־החמש *thither* is redundant: באו and ויכהו both anticipate prematurely 7ᵃ; לקחי חטים is inappropriate, and the rendering '*as though* fetching wheat' illegitimate. Read with We. after LXX וְהִנֵּה שֹׁעֶרֶת הַבַּיִת סֹקְלָה חִטִּים וַתָּנָם וַתִּישָׁן 'and behold the portress of the house was cleaning wheat from stones (LXX ἐκάθαιρεν: cf. Is. 57, 14 καθαρίσατε for סֹלּוּ, read as סַקְּלוּ), and she slumbered and slept, and Rechab and Ba'anah slipt in,' etc. The words explain how it happened that Rechab and Ba'anah obtained entrance to Ishbosheth's house.

נמלטו] *slipt in* or *through* (LXX διέλαθον, joining the word closely with *v.* 7 'slipt through, and entered into the house,' etc.), in accordance with the primary meaning of the root (cf. מִלֵּט Is. 34, 15; הַלְ 66, 7 הִמְלִיט and not in the special sense of slipping through or away from pursuers, i.e. of escaping.

7. הערבה] See on 2, 29.

8. חברון] *to* Hebron: see p. 37 *n.* 2.

האל הנותן (=ψ. 18, 48) So 22, 48 [ויתן ... נקמות ... משאול ומזרעו נקמות לי :comp. אחרי אשר עשה לך יהוה נקמות מאויביך Jud. 11, 36. For מן *from* (in Old Engl. *of*), cf. also Jer. 20, 10. 12; I 14, 24. 24, 13.

9. אשר פדה וג'] So 1 Ki. 1, 29. On פדה, see the writer's note on Dt. 6, 8.

10. והוא היה וג'] a circumst. clause.

ואחזה בו] after המגיד לי treated as a *casus pendens;* so 1 Ki. 9, 20 f. 12, 17. 15, 13: *Tenses*, § 127 a; GK. § 111ʰ.

---

[1] Of *laying* eggs, properly (as it seems) *elabi fecit* (Ges.). Cf. the Nif. in I 20, 29 'let me *get away*' (without the idea of escaping).

אֲשֶׁר לְתִתִּי־לוֹ בְּשֹׂרָה] 'to whom I ought, forsooth, to have given a reward for his good tidings' (so Bu. Dh.). לְתִתִּי ('to whom it was *for my giving*') must be explained on the analogy of 2 Ki. 13, 19 לְהַכּוֹת *percutiendum erat* quinquies aut sexies,—an extension of a usage more common in present time, Hos. 9, 13 etc. (*Tenses*, § 204). The clause can hardly express *David's* view of the transaction : he could not think that the Amaleqite really deserved a reward for his tidings: it must express what David ought to have done in the judgment of the Amaleqite himself, or of men in general unable to appreciate David's regard for Saul (hence 'forsooth'). Keil: 'that I might give him a reward for his good tidings' (ironically), treating אֲשֶׁר as=*namely* (Ew. 338ᵇ) : so substantially RV. But such a sense of אשר cannot be substantiated: so that, if this be felt to be the meaning of the passage, we must follow the suggestion of We. to 'omit אשר, as due to a false interpretation of לְתִתִּי לוֹ, which in its turn arose from a mistaking of the ironical sense of בְּשֹׂרָה.' So Now. Sm.; cf. GK. § 114¹ *n.* Ehrl. נתתי for לְתִתִּי: 'which I gave him as a reward for his good tidings!' This, remarkably enough, is the exact sense expressed by RV. (=AV. *marg.*), 'which was the reward I gave him for his tidings,' presumably *without* emendation !

11. אַף כִּי] *how much more* (should I do so), *when . . .*; as Ez. 15, 5. Job 9, 14 ; and וְאַף כִּי I 23, 3. 2 Ki. 5, 13.

אֶת אִישׁ צַדִּיק] אֶת followed by an *undefined* subst.; comp. on I 9, 3.

אֲבַקֵּשׁ . . . מִיֶּדְכֶם] The same idiomatic use of מִיַּד in I 20, 16. Gen. 31, 39. 43, 9. Is. 1, 12. Ez. 3, 18. 20 (דמו). 33, 8 (דמו); and with דרש Gen. 9, 5 (דם). Ez. 34, 10.

וּבִעַרְתִּי] Cf. 1 Ki. 22, 47 בִּעֵר מִן־הָאָרֶץ; 2 Ki. 23, 24 ; בְּעֵר אַחֲרֵי 1 Ki. 14, 10. 21, 21 ; and the frequent Deuteronomic phrase וּבִעַרְתָּ הָרָע מִקִּרְבְּךָ (מִיִּשְׂרָאֵל) Dt. 13, 6. 17, 7. 12 al. Jud. 20, 13.

12. וַיְקַצְּצוּ] The word is used similarly in Jud. 1, 6. 7.

5, 1–3. 6–10=1 Ch. 11, 1–9. The parallel passages in Chronicles should be compared, and the variations noted, in the manner exhibited above, on I 31. The reader who will be at the pains of doing this consistently (especially in the parts of Chronicles which are parallel to 1–2 Kings), will, when he has eliminated the variations which seem to be due to accident, understand better than from any description in books the *method* followed by the Chronicler in the compilation of his work, and the manner in which he dealt with his sources in the process.

5, 1. וַיֹּאמְרוּ לֵאמֹר] 'Thus, immediately together, rarely, 20, 18. Ex. 15, 1. Nu. 20, 3 [add Jer. 29, 24. Ez. 12, 27 LXX, Cornill. 33, 10. Zech. 2, 4 [1]]; Ges. *Thes.*, p. 119ᵇ: on the contrary, very frequently as in *v.* 6. Jud. 15, 13, separated by a pronoun or other word' (We.). Geiger in an article on this idiom [2] regards it as a mark of the later period of the language, and seeks to shew that most of the passages in which it occurs—even those of the second class noticed by We.—are redactional additions. But לֵאמֹר was in such frequent use for the purpose of introducing a speech, that its proper force must have been early forgotten ; and the habit must soon have grown up of using it instinctively, irrespectively of the fact that the same verb might have been already employed in the sentence.

הִנְנוּ . . . אֲנַחְנוּ] 'Behold us ! we are,' &c. 1 Ch. 11, 1 has הִנֵּה alone. עַצְמְךָ וּבְשָׂרְךָ אֲנַחְנוּ] So in the ‖, 1 Ch. 11, 1 ; and similarly *ch.* 19, 13 עַצְמִי וּבְשָׂרִי אַתֶּם. 14. Gen. 29, 14. Jud. 9, 2.

2. אַתָּה] Notice (thrice) the emph. pronoun.

וְהֵמְבִי [הָיִיתָה מוֹצִיא (with the *art.*) following shews that the words are wrongly divided, and that the Massorah is right in correcting הָיִיתָ הַמּוֹצִיא וְהֵמְבִי.

וְהֵמְבִי] א dropped as 1 Ki. 21, 21 הִנְנִי מֵבִי אֵלֶיךָ. Jer. 19, 15. 39, 16 : 1 Ki. 21, 29. Mic. 1, 15 (both אבי): 1 Ki. 12, 12 וַיָּבֹאוּ יָרָבְעָם al., sometimes (but not always) before another א (as though the omission were due to the juxtaposition of the two identical letters): see Ol. p. 69 ; GK. § 74ᵏ.

אַתָּה] Note the emphatic pron. (twice).

תִּרְעֶה] Here first in the metaph. sense. So 7, 7. Mic. 5, 3 ; and, with the figure usually developed explicitly, often in Jeremiah, as 2, 8. 3, 15. 10, 21. 22, 22. 23, 1–4 ; Ez. 34 (throughout), al.

לְנָגִיד] See on I 9, 16.

---

[1] Cf. Cornill, *ZATW.* 1891, p. 22.
[2] *Jüdische Zeitschrift*, iv. 1866, pp. 27–35 ; comp. v. p. 188 ; vi. p. 159.

3. וַיִּכְרֹת לָהֶם] On the force of לְ, see on I 18, 3. For the position of בְּרִית, see on *ch.* 14, 12.

4. אַרְבָּעִים] Read, with 14 MSS., and Versions, and parallel passages (as 1 Ki. 14, 21), וְאַרְבָּעִים.

6. יוֹשֵׁב הָאָרֶץ] i.e. the native inhabitants of the land: Gen. 34, 30. Ex. 34, 12. Jud. 11, 21 al.

וַיֹּאמֶר] sc. הָאֹמֵר,—of course, among the Jebusites. LXX ἐρρέθη, either a paraphrase, or, if lit., presupposing וַיֵּאָמֵר, which, standing alone, is not idiomatic (only Jos. 2, 2, sq. לִמְלֹךְ יְרִיחוֹ). In Chr. (I 11, 4ᵇ. 5) the whole sentence is altered (וְשָׁם הַיְבוּסִי יֹשְׁבֵי הָאָרֶץ: אֶל הַיְבֻסִי יוֹשֵׁב הָאָרֶץ וַיֹּאמֶר לְדָוִד for וַיֹּאמְרוּ יֹשְׁבֵי יְבוּס לְדָוִיד).

כִּי אִם הֱסִירְךָ וג'] 'but (on I 8, 19: *Lex.* 475ᵃ) the blind and the lame will turn thee aside,' substantially as RV. *m.*: the sing. by Ew. § 316ᵃ; GK. § 145ᵒ; and the pf. by GK. § 106ᵐ, though the impf. would be better (We. al.). But it is better to read יְסִירְךָ. Their fortress, they mean to say, is so strong that even the blind and the lame in it are sufficient to keep David from entering it. 'Except thou take away' (AV. RV.) would require (בַּהֲסִירְךָ or) כִּי אִם הֲסִירֹתָ. The Chronicler (I 11, 5) omits everything from כִּי אִם to the end of the verse.

הָעִוְרִים] GK. § 35ᵍ. On the forms עִוֵּר, פִּסֵּחַ, see GK. § 84 *b*ᵈ.

7. On the site of the old Jebusite stronghold, Ẓion = the 'City of David,' see Stade, *Gesch. Isr.*, i. 315 f.; *DB.* Ẓɪᴏɴ; *EB.* ii. 2417–20; most fully G. A. Smith, *Jerusalem* (1908), i. 154–169. The part of Jerusalem which is now called Ẓion, and is so marked on many maps, is the South-*West* Hill; but the tradition identifying this hill with the Biblical Zion does not reach back beyond the 4th century A. D.; and there are the strongest reasons, based on the usage of the OT. itself, for believing that the 'Ẓion' of ancient times was the South-*East* Hill of Jerusalem, on the North, and highest, part of which stood the Temple, and on the South (contiguous to the Temple) the Royal Palace, built by Solomon. The author of 1 Macc. expressly identifies 'Ẓion' with the hill on which the Temple was situate (1 Macc. 4, 37 f. 7, 33). The site of the old stronghold, Ẓion, was entirely outside the modern city, on a narrow elongated hill, stretching out to the south of the present Ḥarām esh-Sherîf: see the Map facing

EB. 2419–20 ('Ophel'), or, still better, the Maps in G. A. Smith, *op. cit.* ii., facing pp. 39, 51.

8. '‎וג‎ ‎מכה‎ ‎כל‎] The passage is very difficult, and the text certainly to some extent corrupt. ‎צנור‎ in the Mishnah means a *pipe, spout,* or *water-channel;* and in ψ. 42, 8† it denotes the *channels* (cf. ‎תְּעָלָה‎ Job 38, 25), by which the Hebrews conceived rain to pour down from heaven.

In other respects the renderings that have been generally adopted, both implying, however, a deviation from the existing MT., besides being highly questionable philologically, are (*a*) ' Whosoever smiteth the Jebusites, let him (the ‎ן‎ by *Tenses,* § 125 ; GK. § 143ᵈ) get up to the watercourse, and (smite) the blind and the lame,' etc. (so RV.). Upon this interpretation, ‎הכה‎ is supposed to have fallen out in clause *b* (‎אֶת‎ ‎וְהִכָּה‎ for ‎ואת‎). ‎ב‎ ‎נגע‎, however, elsewhere means simply *to touch :* where it may be represented by the English word *reach* it is applied not to a person arriving at a spot, but to some object *extending to it,* so as to touch it, as I Ki. 6, 27 the wing of the one cherub *touched* the wall, Hos. 4, 2 and blood *toucheth, reacheth to* blood (forming a continuous stream): more often with ‎עד‎, ‎אֶל‎, or ‎עַל‎, metaphorically of misfortune, the sword, etc., Jud. 20, 34. 41. Mic. 1, 9. Jer. 4, 10 al. *Touch,* the legitimate rendering of '‎ב‎ ‎נגע‎, is weak : *get up to* is an unjustifiable paraphrase. (*b*) The words are rendered, with ‎וְיַגַּע‎ for ‎וְיִגַּע‎, ' Whosoever smiteth the Jebusites, let him hurl down the water-channel both the blind and the lame,' etc. (so Ew. Ke.). But '‎בּ‎ ‎הִגִּיעַ‎ means merely to *make to touch* = *to join* (Is. 5, 8) : even with ‎לׁ‎, ‎אֶל‎, or ‎עַד‎, it is only used of a building (or collection of buildings) *made to touch* the ground (viz. by being levelled to it), Is. 25, 12. 26, 5. Ez. 13, 14. Lam. 2, 2 (comp. ‎עַל‎ ‎הִגִּיעַ‎ *to make to touch* (and rest) *upon* = to apply to, Is. 6, 7. Jer. 1, 9 ; with ‎אֶל‎ Ex. 12, 22 : with '‎לׁ‎ Ex. 4, 25 = *to cast to* the foot) ; or (intransitively) simply to *reach, arrive at* (I 14, 9 al.). Thus though ‎אֶל‎ ‎וְיַגַּע‎ ‎הצנור‎ (or ‎עַד‎) might mean ' level *to* the water-channel ' (so as to rest upon it), there is no analogy for interpreting ‎בצנור‎ ‎יַגַּע‎ to mean ' hurl *down* the water-channel.'

Both these renderings of ‎יגע‎ must therefore be abandoned. Of ‎צנור‎, recent excavation in Jerusalem has given an attractive and, as it seems, probable explanation. From the 'Virgin's Spring' ('Ain Sitti [i. e. *Sidti*, My Lady] Mariam, also called *'Ain Umm el-Deräj*, from the steps leading down to it), the ancient Gihon (1 Ki. 1, 33. 38. 45. 2 Ch. 30, 30. 33, 14†), the one natural spring which Jerusalem possesses, on the E. of Ophel, and just opposite to the village of Siloam (*Silwān*), there are carried through the rock two tunnels, one (1757 ft. long) leading down to the Pool of Siloam (see the Introd. § 1), the other running W. of the Spring for 50 ft., where the rock is cut out so as to form a pool : above this there is a perpendicular shaft, 6 ft. by 4 ft.,—called, from Sir C. Warren, who discovered it in 1867, 'Warren's shaft,'—which runs straight up through the rock for 44 ft., then there follows for 45 ft. a sloping ascent, rising at an angle of 45°, the tunnel then becomes horizontal for 40 ft., till finally after another ascent of 50 ft. it ends at the top of the hill, on which the original fortress of Zion must have been situated. At the top of the 'shaft' there is an iron ring, through which a rope might have been passed for hauling up water from the pool below. The purpose of this tunnel is clear : it was to enable the garrison to draw upon the Spring from within the fortress, especially in the event of a siege (G. A. Smith, *Jerusalem,* i. 92 f.; more fully Warren in the *Survey of West Pal.,* Jerusalem volume, p. 367 f. with section of tunnel facing p. 368). Could this tunnel have been the צִנּוֹר? It was certainly a 'water-channel' from the spring to the pool at the bottom of the shaft; and it is possible, at least with the help of a rough wooden scaffolding, to get up the perpendicular shaft, as Warren did, and so to pass on to the mouth of the tunnel at the top. Did some adventurous Israelites make their way up thus into the fortress of Zion, and surprise the garrison? Père Vincent thinks so (*Underground Jerusalem,* 1911, p. 34); and it seems very probable. As however has been shewn, no sense suitable to צִנּוֹר can be extracted out of וִיגַּע; and we must, if we accept this view, write bravely וְיַעַל (cf. 1 Ch. 11, 6 יואב . . . וַיַּעַל) 'let him *go up* in (or by) the water-channel:' this is at least both more scholarly, and more honest, than, with AV. RV., to force upon יגע the impossible meaning 'get up.'

The following words, וְאֵת הַפִּסְחִים וג', as they do not make a sentence, must in some way be emended : and we may either, with AV., read וְהִכָּה 'and smite the lame and the blind who are hated (Qrê) of David's soul' (on account viz. of what is said of them in *v.* 6), or (though the connexion is then poor) read שְׂנֵאָה for שֽׂנְאוּ, i.e. 'and (= for) the lame and the blind David's soul hateth.' The last words of the *v.* can only mean (RV. *m.*) 'The blind and the lame (i.e. mendicants) shall not [*or* do not] come into the house,' i.e. into the Temple (so LXX): the origin of a common saying (cf. Gen. 22, 14; I 19, 24) about mendicants being excluded from the Temple is thus explained. But the saying is unrelated to *v.* 6 in its natural and obvious sense ; and in fact *v.* 8ᵇ seems to be an old gloss, added by one who supposed 6ᵇ to mean 'Except thou remove the blind and the lame (in the *Israelite* army) who say, David will not enter in here : ' comp. the Targ., which paraphrases : ' Thou wilt not enter in here except thou remove the *sinners* and the *guilty, who say*, David will not enter in here ; ' and in 8, ' And the sinners and the guilty David's soul abhorreth : therefore they say, The sinners and the guilty enter not into the house.'

Dhorme takes the same view of צָנוֹר, though he restores the text differently : 'And David said in that day, Whoso smiteth the Jebusites, and reacheth ... [And the son of Zeruiah went up (cf. 1 Ch. 11, 6ᵇ)] by the water-channel ... (Gloss on *v.* 6 : As for [GK. § 117¹] the lame and the blind, they are hated of David's soul : therefore they say, The blind and the lame shall not enter into the Temple).'

Budde, regarding the words in *v.* 8 as spoken *after* the capture of Zion, and observing that we have a right to expect some thought worthy of a king (which hatred of enemies is not), and that David actually (24, 18) spared some of the Jebusites, conjectures : ' Whoso smiteth a Jebusite, toucheth *his own neck* (i.e. brings his own life into danger) ; the lame and the blind David's soul hateth *not* ' (בְּצַוָּ(א)רוֹ אֵת) for בצנור ואת ; and לֹא שְׂנֵאָה for (שְׂנֵאוּ) : cf. G. A. Smith, *Jerusalem*, ii. 32. The conjecture is clever : it gives נגע ב׳ its proper sense ; and it attributes to David a fine and chivalrous thought ; but it is too bold to command acceptance.

The Chronicler (I 11, 6) for the whole of *v.* 8 has ויאמר דויד כל מכה יבוסי בראשונה יהיה לראש ולשר וַיַּעַל בראשונה יואב בן צרויה ויהי לראש : Whether, however, this interpretation is correct, and words such as יהיה לראש ולשר have fallen out in Sam., is very doubtful. כל מכה is '*every one* who smites ' (cf. 2, 23. Nu. 21, 8. Jud. 19, 30. I 2, 13. 36. 10, 11), not, as would be needed if such a reward as יהיה לראש ולשר were promised, ' *any one* who smites : ' Gen. 4, 16 hardly proves the contrary ; and where, in such sentences, an *individual* is in view, the wording is different (as Jud. 1, 12 . . . אשר יכה את קרית־ספר. 11, 31. I 17, 25 והיה האיש אשר יכנו יעשרנו המלך. Nu. 16, 6. 17, 20).

9. ויבן דוד] 1 Ch. 11, 8 ויבן העיר, which is supported by LXX here (καὶ ᾠκοδόμησεν αὐτὴν πόλιν = עיר וַיִּבְנֶהָ, Bu.,—the words being differently divided), and may be the original reading.

המלוא] So in the ||, 1 Ch. 11, 8. 1 Ki. 9, 15. 24. 11, 27. 2 Ch. 32, 5†: בית מלוא near Shechem, Jud. 9, 6. 20 ; and also 2 Ki. 12, 21†. Targ. for *this* Millo has always מליתא, the word which also represents

262 *The Second Book of Samuel,*

סֹלְלָה, the *mound* of earth cast up by the besiegers of a town. The word מלוא means apparently *Filling ;* and probably denotes a *mound* or *rampart* of earth. Cf. G. A. Smith, *Jerusalem,* ii. 40 f.

וביתה] בֵּיתָה *housewards* = *inwards,* as Ex. 28, 26 al.

10. וגדול] for the construction, see on I 14, 19.

11. חֲרָשׁ] the form being for חָרָשׁ: GK. § 84 *b* b.

11–25 = I Ch. 14, 1–16.

13. מירושלם] I Ch. 14, 3 בירושלם, the more probable reading.

14. וְהַיְלָדִים] יִלּוֹד 12, 14. Ex. 1, 22. Jos. 5, 5. Jer. 16, 3†. The punctuation in all these cases is irregular: by analogy the *ptcp.* הַיִּלּוֹד, הַיְלָדִים is what would be required by the syntax. On the form, cf. Ew. § 155ᵈ; Stade, § 224; Kön. ii. 148 f.; GK. § 84 *b* e. 24: the parallels have all a substantival force (גִּבּוֹר, שִׁכּוֹר, כִּנּוֹר, etc.). It is not clear with what right Hitzig (on Jer. *l. c.*) says that 'in virtue of passages such as 2 S. 12, 14 the punctuation יִלּוֹד is correct;' and the explanation adopted (apparently) by Dillmann on Jos. *l. c.* that the form is meant to express 'in contradistinction to יְלָדִים the idea of succession' ('soll 'das "fort und fort, nach und nach" ausdrücken') is incompatible with *ch.* 12, 14 (of a *single* child). In I Ki. 3, 26. 27, and even in the parallel I Ch. 14, 4, in each of which passages (notice in Ch. the following אשר היו לו) the substantival form would have been in place, the word is pointed as a ptcp. (הַיְלָדִים, הַיִּלּוֹד). The explanation in GK. *l. c.* is artificial.

14ᵇ–16. The list of David's sons, born in Jerusalem, is repeated, I Ch. 3, 5–8, and also 14, 4–7, with the following variations :—

2 Sam. 5.	I *Ch.* 3.	I *Ch.* 14.
1. שמוע ¹⁴ᵇ	שמעא ⁵ᵇ	שמוע ⁴ᵇ
2–5 (שובב, נתן, שלמה, יבחר) without variation.		
6. אלישוע ¹⁵ᵇ	אלישמע ⁶	אלישוע ⁵
7.	אליפלט	אלפלט
8.	נגה ⁷	נגה ⁶
9–11. (נפג, יפיע, אלישמע) without variation.		
12. אלידע ¹⁶	אלידע ⁸	בעלידע ⁷
13. אליפלט	אליפלט	אליפלט

שמוע is perhaps an abbreviated, 'caritative' form, for שמעיה (Lidzbarski, *Ephemeris,* ii. 21 ; Prätorius, *ZDMG.* lvii. (1903), p. 774).

Cf. above, p. 19. In No. 12 בעלידע is evidently the true name, changed for the sake of avoiding בעל to אלידע (comp. on 4, 4). LXX in 1 Ch. 14, 7 read with MT. בעלידע (Swete, i.e. Codd. B and Sin., Βαλεγδαε; Cod. A Βαλλιαδα; Lucian Βααλιαδα; other MSS. Βαλιαδα). In the existing LXX text of 2 Sam. there are *two* renderings of the list; and in the second, which appears to be derived from Ch., the form with בעל is likewise expressed (Βααλειμαθ: so Luc. Βααλιλαθ).

5, 17. *David and the Philistines.*

17. ויעלו] from the low-lying Philistine plain; cf. on I 29, 9.

וירד אל המצודה] The verb ירד shews that the מצודה referred to cannot be identified with the מצודה of Ẓion, *v.* 9: for that lay on an elevation, and the phrase used in connexion with it is always עלה. This מצודה is no doubt the one in the wilderness of Judah, which David held (I 22, 4),—probably, in fact (see on I 22, 1) the 'hold' of 'Adullam (cf. II 23, 14, comparing 13). The natural position of 5, 17–6, 1 is immediately after the account of David's being anointed king at Hebron (*v.* 3); and here, or before *v.* 6, it no doubt originally stood (Kennedy, pp. 215, 218). David would of course both 'go down' from Hebron to 'Adullam, and also (*v.* 19) 'go up' from 'Adullam to the Vale of Rephaim, close to Jerusalem on the SW.

18. ופלשתים באו] 'Now the Philistines *had* come' (cf. on I 9, 15). וינטשו] *were let go, spread abroad*, as Jud. 15, 9. Cf. נטשים I 30, 16. עמק רפאים] Probably the broad upland plain, *el-Baq'a*, rich in cornfields and olive-gardens (Is. 17, 5 f.), with low hills on each side, which extended from a hill at the west end of the valley of Hinnom (Jos. 15, 8) for some 3 miles SW. of Jerusalem.

19. האעלה] from the מצודה of *v.* 17.

20. בעל פרצים] Perhaps *originally* (Paton, *Encycl. of Rel. and Ethics*, ii. 286[a]) 'Ba'al of the breakings forth,' the name of a fountain *bursting forth* out of the hill-side, so called from the local 'Ba'al,' who was supposed to inhabit it (see on the local Ba'als supposed to inhabit trees, mountains, springs, etc., *DB.* or *EB.* s.v., and esp. Paton's learned art. just referred to; cf. also above, p. 63 f.; many names of places embody this belief, as Baal-Hermon, Baal-Meon, Baal-Tamar, etc.). As the name of the place is explained here, however, Ba'al

does not denote the Canaanite or Phoenician god of that name, but is a title of Yahweh (cf. on 4, 4); and בעל פרצים, in the sense of 'Master of breakings forth' (upon the foe), is understood as commemorating the victory (comp. יהוה נסי Ex. 17, 15; יהוה שלום Jud. 6, 24). The explanation, '*Place* of breaches' (Keil; RV. *marg.*), is not probable: not only are the analogies quoted against it, but בעל in the sense of *owner, possessor,* though often used of human beings (e.g. בעל שֵׂעָר 2 Ki. 1, 8) is very rarely applied to inanimate objects (Is. 41, 15: *Lex.* 127ᵇ).

פרץ וג'] 'hath *broken down* my enemies before me, like the *breaking* of waters' through a dam. Cf. of breaking down a wall, ψ. 80, 13 למה פרצת גדריה; and פרץ ב' ('make a breach *in*'), Ex. 19, 22. 24; פָּרַץ פֶּרֶץ ב' *ch.* 6, 8.

21. עצביהם] LXX τοὺς θεοὺς αὐτῶν, and Ch. (I 14, 12) אלהיהם,— doubtless the original reading.

וישאם דוד ואנשיו] See *EB.* ii. 1918 an illustration of an Ass. warrior bearing in his hand a captured idol. The Chronicler, in order to leave no doubt as to what David did with the idols, substitutes ויאמר דויד וישרפו באש.

23. לא תעלה] Add לקראתם LXX, which is required by the sequel.

הָסֵב] The *Hif.* is anomalous. Either ה has arisen by dittography from תעלה, and the Qal סֹב (cf. LXX ἀποστρέφου) should be restored; or (Bu.) the word is used in a military sense, *Lead round* (thy men): cf. the seemingly intrans. שׂים and שׁית (on I 15, 2), and משׁך Jud. 4, 6. 20, 37, and perhaps 5, 14.

אל אחריהם] So 2 Ki. 9, 18. 19. Cf. אל מבית 2 Ki. 11, 15: אל מחוץ Dt. 23, 11 al.; אל תחת 1 Ki. 8, 6. Zech. 3, 10.

ובאת וג'] and come to them *off the front of* (in our idiom: *in front of*) . . . : cf. Nu. 22, 5 והוא ישב ממלי.

בכאים] Read, with LXX and 1 Ch. 14, 14 הבכאים.

24. ויהי] and *let it* be . . . : a permissive command: *Tenses,* § 121 *Obs.*; and I 10, 5 *note.*

את קול צעדה] 'the sound of a stepping.' קול may be sufficiently defined by the gen. צעדה (cf. Lev. 7, 8): but 1 Ch. 14, 15 has הצעדה (cf. GK. § 117ᵈ).

אז תחרץ] '*look sharp* is our colloquial equivalent' (Sm.). In

Ch. paraphrased, with much loss of originality and vigour, by אז תצא
במלחמה.

יֵצֵא] *will have gone* forth (GK. § 106⁰).

להכות ב'] The ב is partitive, 'to make a smiting *in*' (*Lex.* 88ᵇ).

25. מגבע] LXX ἀπὸ Γαβαων, Ch. מגבעון. This is better than גבע (on I 13, 2),
which, being 5 miles NN*E.* of Jerusalem, is in the wrong direction altogether; but
Gibeon (*el-Jib*, 5 miles NN*W.* of Jerusalem: on 2, 12) is not much better: as Sm.
remarks, ' Both Geba' and Gibeon are too far from the Vale of Rephaim for the
pursuit to begin at either one.' To judge from the large maps, also, there is no
natural route down from el-Jib to Gezer. If, however, Geba' were the name
of a place, not otherwise mentioned, near Jerusalem, on the road to Qaryet el-'Enab
(Qiryath-ye'arim), the site would suit excellently; for this road leads straight down
to Gezer. The allusion in the second clause of Is. 28, 21ᵃ (כי כהר פרצים יקום
יהוה כעמק בגבעון ירגז) may be not to this event, but to Jos. 10.

גזר] Now *Tell Jezer*, 19 miles WNW. of Jerusalem, and 12 miles
below Qaryet el-'Enab. The site, as is now well known, has been
recently most successfully excavated: see, for some account of the
principal results, the writer's 'Schweich Lectures' on *Modern Research
as illustrating the Bible* (1909), pp. 46–80, 88–98.

6. *Removal of the Ark to the 'City of David.'*

6, 1. ויסף] for ויאסף, as תֹסֶף *ψ.* 104, 29 (GK. § 68ᵇ): cf. on I 15, 5.
Whether this verse (with the omission of עוד, which may have been
added by a scribe, who inadvertently supposed ויסף to come from יסף)
is really the introduction to *v.* 2 ff., is uncertain. It may form the
sequel to 5, 17–24 (in its original position: see on 5, 17), and perhaps
at the same time (without עוד) the introduction to 5, 6–10. See
Kennedy, p. 218.

2–12ᵃ=1 Ch. 13, 5–14; between 12ᵃ and 12ᵇ the Chronicler
inserts 14, 1—15, 24; 12ᵇ–14 is expanded and varied in 1 Ch. 15,
25–27; 15–19ᵃ=1 Ch. 15, 28—16, 3 (with variations); 1 Ch. 16,
4–42 is another insertion; 19ᵇ–20ᵃ=1 Ch. 16, 43 (*vv.* 20ᵇ–23 being
omitted in Ch.). The variations between the two narratives are here
remarkably striking and instructive. In particular the earlier narrative
makes no mention of the *Levites;* the later authority is careful to
supply the omission.

2. מבעלי יהודה] In 1 Ch. 13, 6 בַּעֲלָתָה אל קרית יערים אשר ליהודה:
and this is the sense which is required: Qiryath Ye'arim is called

בַּעֲלָה Jos. 15, 9. 10, and קרית־בעל *ib.* 60. 18, 14 (and 15 LXX): doubtless, therefore, בעל יהודה *to Ba'al of Judah* must here be restored, the description 'of Judah' being added to distinguish this Ba'al from other places of the same name (in Simeon, Jos. 19, 8, in Dan, *ib.* 44 : cf. בית־לחם יהודה). בעל יהודה seems first to have been miswritten בעלי יהודה; and then, this being interpreted as= '*citizens* of Judah,' the partitive מְ was prefixed, in order to produce some sort of connexion with the preceding clause. The place must have been originally sacred to Ba'al. On its site, see on I 6, 21.

אֲשֶׁר . . . עָלָיו] 'over which is called a name, (even) the name of' etc. The phrase used betokens *ownership:* see on 12, 28. Omit one שם with LXX. The distance of עָלָיו from אשר suggests that the clause is glossed : read probably אשר נקרא שם י׳ צ׳ עליו. In 1 Ch. 13, 6 שם נקרא אשר is misplaced strangely to the end of the verse.

3ᵇ–4. The words *v.* 3 *end*–4ᵃ אשר אבינדב מבית וישאהו : חדשה בגבעה (which are not expressed in LXX) have been accidentally repeated from *v.* 3ᵃ : hence the questionable חדשה (p. 125 *note*) with אֶת־הָעֲגָלָה. Probably עם ארון האלהים was preceded originally by וְעֻזָּא הֹלֵךְ : as thus corrected the verse will explain how 'Uzzah and Aḥio 'led' the cart : Uzzah going *beside* the ark, and his brother *before* it. The pr. n. אַחְיוֹ (=אֲחִיָּהוּ : cf. אִישְׁיוֹ), in both 3ᵃ and 4, seems more probable than אָחִיו (We.), or אֶחָיו (LXX, with הלכים in *v.* 4). So Sm. Bu. Now.

5. מְשַׂחֲקִים] *were playing* or *making merry.* See on I 18, 7.

בכל עצי ברושים] The true reading of these words has been preserved in 1 Ch. 13, 8, viz. בְּכָל־עֹז וּבְשִׁירִים. So LXX here, ἐν ὀργάνοις ἡρμοσμένοις (see *v.* 14) and ἐν ἰσχύι being a double rendering of בכל (פִּלִי) עז, and καὶ ἐν ᾠδαῖς evidently representing ובשירים.

ובמנענעים ובצלצלים] Ch. ובמצלתים ובחצצרות; LXX here καὶ ἐν κυμβάλοις καὶ ἐν αὐλοῖς=ובמצלתים ובחלילים. MT. is doubtless original. For מנענעים Aq. Symm. have appropriately σεῖστρα (hence Vg. *sistra*) from σείω : see *Lex.* 631ᵇ; *EB.* iii. 3227–8 (illustr.). צלצלים recurs ψ. 150, 5†: elsewhere (but only in Chr. Ezr. Neh.) always מצלתים.

6. נרן נכון] '"*A* fixed threshing-floor"' does not satisfy the requirements of the sense: "*the* fixed threshing-floor" is not expressed in the Hebrew—to say nothing of the questionable use of the epithet

נכון ; hence נכון, as LXX and the Chronicler have rightly seen, must conceal a pr. name' (We.), or, at least some designation which, attached to נרן, would constitute a pr. name (cf. Gen. 50, 16. 17 נרן האטד ; and I 19, 22). What this name or designation was must, however, remain uncertain. LXX here have Νωδαβ, Ch. כידן.

וישלח] Versions and 1 Ch. 13, 9 add rightly את־ידו. The ellipse is not according to usage.

שמטו] Of uncertain meaning. שמט is *to let fall*, 2 Ki. 9, 33 (of Jezebel, שמטוה וישמטוה). ψ. 141, 6 ; fig. *to remit*, hence שְׁנַת הַשְּׁמִטָּה the year of the *remittance* (or rather *intermittence*) of claims for debt, Dt. 15, 1. 2 : in Aram. *to pull away* or *loosen*, Lev. 14, 40. 43 Pesh. and Ps.-Jon. (=Heb. חלץ) ; *to pull out* or *draw* a sword, in Syr. also often in other connexions for ἐκσπᾶν ; in Ethpa'el *to be pulled out* Ezr. 6, 11 (=Aram. יתנסח) ; in Ethpe'al *avelli* (PS.), as Dt. 19, 5 Pesh. (=Heb. נשל). *Let* it *fall* (so Th.) is the rendering best supported by *Hebrew* usage : but many have given the word an intransitive sense,—either, after Pesh. (ܐܬܡܠܟܘ ܗܘܘ ܐ̈, i.e. [see PS. 4207] *se* a iugo *extraxerunt*: in 1 Ch. 13, 9 ܐܘܪܨ ܗܘܘ ܗܘܘܨ), *ran away* (Maurer, Roed. in *Thes.*), or (by conjecture) *slipped* (Keil, Klo. : RV. *stumbled*) ; these renderings are, however, philologically questionable. LXX ὅτι περιέσπασεν αὐτὴν (שְׁמָטוֹ) ὁ μόσχος (in 1 Ch. 13 ἐξέκλινεν αὐτήν) ; Targ. both here and 1 Ch. מרנוהי (? *threw it down* : מנרוהי ? as 2 Ki. 9, 33) ; Vulg. *calcitrabant*[1] (probably based on Aq. or Symm., whose renderings here have not been preserved) : in 1 Ch. *bos quippe lasciviens paullulum inclinaverat eam*.

7. על השל] שלה is a very rare root in Hebrew : in Aramaic it has the sense of *to act in error* or *neglect* Job 19, 4 Targ.=Heb. שנה (cf. the *Nif.* in 2 Ch. 29, 11) ; in Af'el, *to cause to act in error, mislead* Job 12, 16 משלי=Heb. מַשְׁגֶּה (cf. 2 Ki. 4, 28 Heb. do not *mislead* me) : the subst. שְׁלוּ means *error, neglect* Ezr. 4, 22. 6, 9. Dan. 3, 29. 6, 5 : in the Targ.=מִשְׁגֶּה or שְׁגָגָה Gen. 43, 12 ; Lev. 4, 2. 5, 18. Nu. 15, 24. 25 al. השל here is commonly (since Targ. על דאשתלי) explained from this root ' because of *the error* :' but (1) שלה is scarcely a pure

---

[1] The Clementine text adds ' et declinaverunt eam ;' but this is not found in the best MSS. of the Vulgate.

Hebrew word : where it occurs, it is either dialectical (2 Ki. 4) or late (2 Ch.); so that its appearance in early Hebrew is unexpected; (2) the unusual apocopated form (שֶׁל for שְׁלִי) excites suspicion [1]. Ewald explained עַל־הֵשֶׁל in the sense of the Syriac ܩܶܢ ܡܶܟܶܠ *suddenly* (e.g. Nu. 6, 9. 8, 19 Pesh.); but this is open in even a greater degree to the same objection as the explanation *error;* and though עַל is used in Hebrew in the expression of certain adverbial ideas (as עַל שֶׁקֶר, עַל רָצוֹן: on I 23, 23), the word associated with it is expressed generally, and is not provided with the article. Ch. has עַל אֲשֶׁר שָׁלַח יָדוֹ עַל הָאָרוֹן; and when the strangeness of the Hebrew expression here used is considered, it will hardly be deemed too venturesome to regard it as a mutilated fragment of the words cited from Ch., which were either still read here in their integrity by the Chronicler, or (as the sense is sufficiently plain without them) were introduced here as a gloss from the parallel text of Ch., and afterwards became corrupted.

עִם אֲרוֹן הָאֱלֹהִים [עִם as Jud. 19, 11 etc. LXX add ἐνώπιον τοῦ θεοῦ=לִפְנֵי אֱלֹהִים which in 1 Ch. 13, 10 (Heb. and LXX) stands *in place of* עִם אֲרוֹן הָאֱלֹהִים. Perhaps that was the original reading.

8. וַיִּקְרָא] As 2, 16. LXX καὶ ἐκλήθη, reading וַיִּקָּרֵא (or paraphrasing).

10. לְהָסִיר] Cf. סוּר of *turning aside* into a house in Jud. 4, 18. 18, 3. 19, 11. 12. 15.

עַל] Read אֶל, as 1 Ch. 13, 13; cf. on I 13, 13.

וַיַּטֵּהוּ בֵית] and turned it aside *to the house,* etc. Exactly so, Nu. 22, 23 וַיֵּט בִּלְעָם אֶת־הָאָתוֹן לְהַטֹּתָהּ הַדֶּרֶךְ.

עֶבֶד אֲדֹם] The analogy of עַבְדְּאֵל, עַבְדִּיאֵל, עֹבַדְיָה, עֹבַדְיָהוּ (cf. *EB.* iii. 3284), and of the numerous Phoenician, Aramaic, and Arabic names compounded with עבד and عبد and the name of a deity [2], create

---

[1] LXX (Cod. B) omits the word: Cod. A and Luc. have ἐπὶ τῇ προπετείᾳ, whence Jerome ' super temeritate.' But *rashness* is not the idea expressed by the root.

[2] Cf. the Phoen. עבדעשתרת, עבדמלקרת, עבדאשמן, עבראשמן, עבדבעל (see further instances in *CIS.* I. p. 365; Lidzbarski, *Nordsem. Epigraphik,* 332–5; Cooke, *NSI.* 373). For Aram. names, see Lidzb. and Cooke, as cited: for Arabic names, Wellh., *Reste Arab. Heidentums²,* pp. 2–4. The pr. n. עבראדם occurs at Carthage (*CIS.* I. 295. 4); but without any further clues to its meaning than we possess for

a somewhat strong presumption that, though nothing more is at present known definitely about a god bearing this name, אדם in עבד אדם is the name of a *deity*[1]: Obed-edom, it will also be remembered, was not an Israelite, but a *Philistine*. It is true, there are some names of this form, in which עבד, عبد is compounded into the name of a king[2] (as עבדחרתת 'servant of Aretas,' Cooke, *NSI.* 82. 5, cf. p. 224): אדם does not, however, seem to be a likely name for a king; and 'servant of *men*' is not a likely explanation of the name. In a few cases the second element in such names is perhaps the name of a tribe[3]; so there remains the *possibility* that this is the case with עבד אדם.

11. בית] סביר בבית (see on I 12, 5); and so II 13, 20; but in each case unnecessarily: see p. 37 *n.* 2.

13. As both We. and Keil rightly observe, the Hebrew states only that a sacrifice was offered, when those bearing the ark had advanced six steps: as soon, namely, as it appeared that it could be moved from the resting-place with impunity, the sacrifice was offered, partly as a thanksgiving that God's anger had been appeased, and partly as an inauguration of the ceremony that was to follow. In order to express that a sacrifice was offered at *every* six steps, the Hebrew would have read וזבח . . . , (צעדו or (יעדו אם יעדו והיה (Gen. 31, 8; Nu. 21, 9: *Tenses*, § 136 δ *Obs.*).

14. מכרכר] Only here and *v.* 16: *was circling about*.

אפור בד] See on I 2, 18.

15. מעלים] *were bringing up*: note the ptcp.

בתרועה ובקול שופר] Cf. Amos 2, 2 בתרועה בקול שופר (of the shout of victory): also Jos. 6, 5 for a similar combination. ψ. 47, 6 (though the Psalm itself belongs to a much later date) appears to be based on this verse: עלה אלהים בתרועה יהוה בקול שופר. The שופר was not a metal 'trumpet,' but a *horn:* see the writer's *Joel and Amos* (in the *Cambr. Bible*), pp. 144–6.

---

the Heb. עבד אדם. The title מלך אדם, applied to a *king* (*CIS.* I. p. 365), does not throw any light upon it.

1 Comp. W. R. Smith, *Rel. Sem.*[2] 42 f.; *EB.* iii. 3462 *n.*
2 Nöldeke, in Euting's *Nabat. Inschriften* (1885), p. 32 f.; Wellh. *l. c.* p. 4.
3 Wellh. *l. c.*; cf. Cooke, p. 224.

16. והיה] 1 Ch. 15, 29, correctly, ויהי. Cf. on I 1, 12.

עיר] Prefix עַד with LXX (ἕως), and 1 Ch. 15, 29.

מפזז ומכרכר] *leaping* (lit. *shewing agility*) *and circling about.* Both uncommon words: פּוּז Gen. 49, 24† in Qal; as Arabic shews, to *be active* or *agile.* 1 Ch. 15, 30 substitutes more ordinary words, מרקד ומשחק: *skipping* (ψ. 114, 4. 6 ; Job 21, 11) and *playing* (*v.* 5).

18. העולה] Collectively (comp. הפליט Ez. 33, 21 ; הָרֶכֶב often, etc.): cf. the plural, *v.* 17.

19. . . . , למאיש] In the ‖ 1 Ch. 16, 3 the more ordinary מאיש ועד אשה (I 22, 19 al.) is substituted. The idiom לְמִן is, however, fully justified, not only by Ex. 11, 7. 2 Ch. 15, 13, but also by its use in other analogous expressions, for the purpose of denoting the *terminus a quo* in space or time (7, 6) ; see *Thes.* s. v. מִן ; *Lex.* 583ᵇ.

חלת] Elsewhere only in P, Ex. 29, 2 etc. (13 times).

אשפר] The meaning of this word, which occurs besides only in the ‖ 1 Ch. 16, 3, is quite unknown. As Lagarde points out [1], so-called 'tradition' is here remarkably at variance with itself—(*a*) LXX in Sam. ἐσχαρίτην [2], in Ch. (ἄρτον ἕνα) ἀρτοκοπικὸν (Lucian κολλυρίτην [3]); (*b*) Aq. Symm. ἀμυρίτην [4]; (*c*) Vulg. Sam. assaturam bubulae carnis unam, Ch. partem assae carnis bubulae ; (*d*) Pesh. Sam. ܠܚܡܐ (*frustum carnis* [5]), Ch. ܡܢܐ ܚܕܐ (*portio una*); (*e*) Targ. Sam. פלוג חד ; Ch. (late) פלג חד מן אשתא בתורא (= a sixth part of a bullock) [6]; (*f*) Abu'l Walid, col. 742 (Rouen gloss) قطعة لحم (*segmentum carnis*); (*g*) Rashi (in agreement with Targ. Ch.) אחד משׁשׁה בפר ; (*h*) Kimchi חלק אחד מבשׁר, but mentioning also as a possible explanation the view of the Rabbis (*Pesaḥim* 36ᵇ), also found in Targ. Ch. and Rashi, that it is a compound word (מִלָּה מוּרְכֶּבֶת) signifying אחד בשׁשׁה בפר. It is evident that these renderings are either conjectures based upon

---

[1] *Mittheilungen,* i. (1884), p. 214.

[2] אשפר probably read as אשכר : cf. δρέπανον for דרבן I 13, 21 ; τόκος for תֹּךְ ψ. 72, 14 al., etc. (comp. p. 78 *n.*).

[3] Or λάγανον τηγάνου. But the renderings of אשפר and אשׁישׁה have apparently been transposed : for λάγανον ἀπὸ τηγάνου = אשׁישׁה in Samuel.

[4] 'Vox aliunde incognita, cuius loco ἀμορίτης (= אשׁישׁה 1 Ch. LXX) ex ἀμόρα (quod Hesychio est σεμίδαλις ἐφθὴ σὺν μέλιτι, Athenaeo autem μελίτωμα πεπεμμένον) fortasse reponendum' (Dr. Field).

[5] = נתח Ez. 24, 4 (Payne Smith, *Thes.* s.v.).

[6] Cf. the marg. of the Reuchl. Cod. (Lagarde, p. xix, 3) חד מן שׁיתא בתורא.

the context, or depend upon an absurd etymology, as though אשפר
were in some way compounded of שש and פר and meant the sixth
part of a bullock! Upon Kimchi's explanation are based the renderings of Seb. Münster (1534–5), 'frustum carnis unum;' of the
Geneva Bible (1560), 'a piece of flesh;' and of RV. AV. 'a good
piece (of flesh)' depends evidently on a combination of אשפר with
שָׁפַר[1]; but the application of the root, in such a connexion, is questionable; granting that אשפר='something fair,' its employment to
denote in particular 'a fair piece *of flesh*' is not a probable specialization of its meaning. Lud. de Dieu, perceiving the impossibility of the
Rabbinical etymology, endeavoured to reach the same general sense
by a derivation from the Ethiopic ሰፈረ: *safara, to measure*, መስፈርት:
masfart, measure (Matth. 7, 2 al.), supposing אשפר to have thus
denoted '*dimensam* sacrificii *partem unam*, quantum nempe unius
sextae partis, in quas sacrificium aequaliter dividi solebat, mensura
continebat.' Ges. and Roed. (in *Thes.*) adopt the same derivation,
though not limiting the 'measure,' as was done by De Dieu, to
a particular fraction of the sacrifice. But irrespectively of the fact
pointed out by Lagarde that Eth. ሰፈረ=Heb. ספר (not שָׁפַר), the
sense obtained is insufficient and lame: between two words denoting
distinctly two kinds of food, the narrator would have placed a word
denoting simply 'a measure'—'a cake of bread, *a measure*, and a cake
of raisins'—both the amount, and the nature, of the substance
measured being left undefined. Under such circumstances, it is
wisest to acknowledge that we do not know what the word means,
and cannot propose for it a plausible etymology[2].

אשישה] ‖, Hos. 3, 1. Cant. 2, 5†. Either *raisin-cakes* (*Thes.*), or
(Kennedy, *EB*. ii. 1569) *cakes of dough kneaded with grapes*.

20. מה נכבד] *How* the king *hath got him honour* to-day...! (Not
'How *honourable* was ...,' which would be the ptcp. נִכְבָּר. 'Glorious'
of EVV. destroys the point of David's reply at the end of *v.* 23, where
the same verb is rendered 'had in *honour*.') For the medial sense of

---

[1] Cf. in the *Michlol Yophi* (Dan. 4, 24) אז ר״ל חלק יפה מן מלכי ישפר עליך.

[2] Ewald's *roast meat* (*Hist.* iii. 127), from שרף=שָׁפַר, is very improbable,
both on account of the שׁ=שׂ, and because שׂרף is not to *roast*, but to *burn up*.

נכבר, to *get oneself honour* (GK. § 51ᵉ), cf. Ex. 14, 4. 17. 18. Ez. 28, 22 al.

אֲמָהוֹת] אָמָה is the one noun in Heb., in which the plur. is enlarged by the addition of ה (אֲמָהוֹת).

In the cognate languages we have [1]—

اِبَهَاتْ², ܐܒ݂ܳܗ̈ܬܐ ,(ܐܒ݂ܐ)ܙ *fathers.*

ܐܡܳܗ̈ܬܐ(ܐܡ݂ܐ), أَمَهَاتْ ,אֲמָהָתָה *mothers.*

(ܐܡ݂ܐ)ܐܡܳܗ̈ܬܐ אֲמָהָתָה (but Arab. أَمْوَاتْ) *bondmaids.*

ܡܟܘܳ̈ܬܐ *husbands' mothers.*

ܐܝ̈ܕܝܳܐ *hands* (in fig. sense, *supports*).

ܡܟܘܳ̈ܬܐ, שְׁמָהָתָא *names.*

עקהן (and עֵקֵן) *beams* (from עַץ = אֵץ = עֵץ : p. 9), Sachau, *Aram. Papyrus aus* ..... *Elephantine* (1911), I, 11. 3, 10.

Mand. עספיהאתה (from sing. סיפתא = ܣܦܬ̈ܐ) *lips* [3].

سَنَهَاتْ (and سَنَوَاتْ) *years.*

عَمَهَاتْ (and عَمَوَاتْ), عَمَاهْ *thorn-trees* (from عَمَهَة).

Phoen. דלהת (*NSI.* 9, 3; from דל 20, A, 5, cf. ψ. 141, 3) *doors.*

נגלות] Upon analogy of the construction with the finite verb, this would be the *inf. abs.*, which is written four times with ה—probably, *if* the forms are correct, for the sake of the assonance (Kön. i. 536; GK. § 75ⁿ; cf. Maurer, *ap.* Th. here) שָׁתוֹת Is. 22, 13 ; רָאוֹת 42, 20 Qrê (Kt. רָאִיתָ) ; אָלוֹת Hos. 10, 4 ; עָרוֹת Hab. 3, 13 (? עָרִיתָ) : for the form of the *inf. abs.* with נ, cf. נִקְרֹא (1, 6), נִשְׁאֹל (I 20, 6), נוּף, etc. Ewald, however, § 240ᶜ, supposes the *inf. abs.* to have passed into the *inf. c.* by a species of attraction, under the influence of the preceding כ ; and this is not, perhaps, impossible. No other case of the *inf. c.* being strengthened by the *inf. abs.* seems to occur : so we are not in a position to say whether כְּהִגָּלוֹת נִגְלֹה or כְּהִגָּלוֹת נִגְלוֹת is more in accordance with usage. GK. § 75ʸ treats נגלות as a faulty repetition of הגלות.

הרקים] So Jud. 9, 4. 11, 3. (LXX τῶν ὀρχουμένων=הָרֹקְדִם.) For אחד, see on 2, 18.

---

[1] Cf. Nöldeke, *SBAk.* 1882, p. 1178 f.
[2] Comp. אבהי *my fathers*, Cooke, *NSI.* 63, 16 (from Zenjirli).
[3] Cf. Nöldeke, *Mändäische Gramm.*, pp. 171, 172.

21. אֲרַבֵּר בָּרוּךְ יהוה expresses יהוה after LXX [לפני יהוה. (Luc. חַי יהוה). The words will have fallen out of MT. by ὁμοιοτέλευτον (Th. We. etc.). ארקד is needed for the sense; and the whole *may* be genuine: but neither ברוך 'י nor חי 'י seems required; and the variation between them rather suggests (Klo. Bu. Kit. *ap.* Kautzsch) that each was a later addition, made in different MSS.: the scribe of the archetype of MT. and the other versions passed from 'י to 'י, and omitted both the genuine ארקד and the addition ברוך (חי) 'י.

נגיד] Some 30 MSS. and LXX (εἰς) לנגיד, which is better; cf. I 25, 30.

22. The verse is difficult. It is best to begin it with 21ᵇ ושחקתי. (*a*) Ew. We. Now.: 'And if (Jer. 20, 9 : *Tenses*, § 148 ; cf. on 19, 3) I play before Yahweh, 22 I count myself still too small for this (to play before Him), and am abased in mine own eyes ; and with the bondmaids (slave-girls) whom thou hast spoken of, with *them* should I seek (?) to get me honour?' David says that he is unworthy to play and dance before Yahweh, and the opinion which the slave-girls entertain of him is of no consequence. (*b*) Th. Sm. Bu. Dh., and substantially EVV.: 'And I will play before Yahweh, 22 and will be yet more looked down upon than this (more than I have been to-day), and will be abased in mine eyes (LXX, Th. Sm. Bu. Dh., more pointedly, "in *thine* eyes "); but with the bondmaids of whom thou hast spoken, with *them* I shall be had in honour.' Michal's taunt that he had degraded himself in the eyes of the bondmaids, David says, is unfounded: he might be still *more* despised by her, and they would nevertheless, he feels sure, continue to honour him. (*b*) is preferable. Both renderings require אִבָּבֵר for אכברה: the *cohortative* is out of place ; in (*a*), though retained by Ew. We. Now., it is inconsistent (in spite of Now.) with the *question*, in (*b*) it is inconsistent with the fact that not a wish, but a *conviction*, is what the context requires. For נקלתי, cf. קלל in Qal to *be looked down upon* (Gen. 16, 4. 5 ; I 2, 30, opp. אֲכַבֵּר, cf. here אכברה), and in Hif. to *contemn* (Is. 23, 9 לְהָקֵל כָּל־נִכְבַּדֵּי הָאָרֶץ). שָׁפָל is *abased, brought low ;* cf. Job 5, 11, and the verb in Ez. 21, 31 (36). עם *with*= before, in the sight of, almost=in the judgement of (I 2, 26). אשר אמרת, cf. on I 24, 5. עם . . . עָמָם, the resumption for the sake of

emphasis, exactly as with את Dt. 13, 1. Is. 8, 13; מן Lev. 25, 44ᵇ; ב Ez. 18, 24 al. (*Tenses*, § 123 *Obs.*).

N.B. EVV. by *vile* in this verse do not mean *morally detestable*, but simply *common, looked down upon:* see on 15, 9 (p. 125 *n.*). In the same way *base* does not mean *ignoble in character*, but merely *low in position*, as often in Old English : so e.g. in Ez. 17, 14. 29, 14. Mal. 2, 9. 2 Cor. 10, 1 AV. (RV. *lowly*). See further BASE and VILE in *DB*.

23. לא היה לה . . .ולמיכל] לה resumes ולמיכל, as עמם resumes עם in *v.* 22, but in an *un*emphatic position, and merely for the purpose of lightening the sentence : see on I 9, 20 ; and cf. Lev. 25, 46ᵇ.

ילד] The Oriental text has וָלָד, which is also found in some Western MSS. and edd., and is the general reading in Gen. 11, 30†. If in either of these passages it is correct, the primitive form with ו (וָלַד, ܘ̈ܠܕܐ) will have not entirely fallen out of use in Hebrew.

7. *Nathan's prophecy to David.   David's thanksgiving and prayer.*

Ch. 7 = 1 *Ch.* 17.

7, 1. הניח־לו מסביב מכל איביו] A Deuteronomic expression : Dt. 12, 10. 25, 19. Jos. 23, 1 (in a section of Joshua belonging to the Deuteronomic editor): cf. הניח ל׳ מסביב Jos. 21, 42. 1 Ki. 5, 18.

2. היריעה] collectively, as העולה 6, 18 : in 1 Ch. 17, 1 יריעות (We.).

3. כל אשר בלבבך] I 9, 19. 14, 7 (MT.; see note) : cf. also 2, 35 (כאשר בלבבי), and 2 Ki. 10, 30.

5. . . . .האתה] *shouldest thou* . . .? Chron., explicitly, לא אתה ; so LXX, Pesh. here.

6. למיום] So, with infin., Jud. 19, 30. Is. 7, 17†. . . . למן היום אשר *v.* 11. Dt. 4, 32. 9, 7. Jer. 7, 25. 32, 31. Hag. 2, 18†. Comp. on 19, 25 ; and see *Lex.* 583ᵇ **9 b.**

ואהיה מתהלך באהל ובמשכן] 1 Ch. 17, 5 ואהיה מאהל אל אהל וממשכן. But LXX in Ch. has only καὶ ἤμην ἐν σκηνῇ καὶ ἐν καλύμματι.   ואהיה מתהלך expresses forcibly the idea of continuance.

7. שבטי] Read, with 1 Ch. 17, 6, שֹׁפְטֵי. There is no indication of any *tribe* having been commissioned to govern Israel.   Keil, objecting that, had שפטי stood originally in this passage, the substitution of שבטי would be inexplicable, does not sufficiently allow for the

accidental confusion of letters,—a confusion against which even the best-preserved text is not invariably proof: I 14, 18 Keil himself is not unwilling to accept לפני instead of MT. ובני.

8. הנוה] See on 15, 25. Notice the separate pron. אני.

מאחר] 'The very rare מֵאַחַר (instead of מאחרי, cf. 1 Ch. 17, 7 [מן־אחרי]) is remarkably confirmed, just for the present passage, by ψ. 78, 71 מאחר עלות הביאו לרעות ביעקב עמו ובישראל נחלתו' (We.).

9ᵇ. ועשתי] The prophet here turns to the future.

'נדול after שם is absent rightly in LXX, and 1 Ch. 17, 8; for it weakens the force of the following words, out of which it might easily have arisen' (We.).

10. תחתיו]=*in its place:* see on I 14, 9; and cf. Is. 25, 10. 46, 7; Zech. 12, 6 (Klo.).

ירגז] *be disquieted.* *Be moved* (RV.) suggests a wrong sense, which has misled the author of the note in the RV. with marginal references to refer to 2 Ki. 21, 8 (where the verb is הֵנִיר).

בני עולה] 3, 34, and in the citation ψ. 89, 23 (ובן עולה לא יעננו).

11. ולמן] ו is not expressed in LXX; both the sentence and the sense are improved by its omission: 'shall no more afflict it as aforetime from the day when I appointed judges,' etc. As the text stands, the reference in 10ᵇ will be to the sufferings of Egypt; but this is a thought alien to the context, in which rather the blessings secured by the settled government of David are contrasted with the attacks to which Israel was exposed during the period of the Judges.

והניחתי לך מכל־איביך] Ew. We. etc. לו מכל־איביו, 'and I will give it rest from all its enemies,' in better agreement with the context.

11ᵇ. Here Nathan comes to the main subject of his prophecy—the promise relating not to David himself, but to his *posterity*, and the declaration that it is not David who will build a house for Yahweh, but Yahweh who will *build a house* (i.e. a family) *for David.*

והגיד לך יהוה] The pf. with simple *waw* is not what would be expected. 1 Ch. 17, 10 has וָאַגִּד לך; a slighter change would be (Kit.) ומגיד לך יהוה.

12. כי ימלאו ימיך] Prefix והיה, reading either (LXX) והיה : יעשה לך, or (1 Ch. 17, 11) והיה : יהוה לך יעשה.

אשר יצא ממעיך] 16, 11. Gen. 15, 4†.

13–15. Though *v.* 13 was fulfilled by Solomon, the terms are general—even in this verse הוא points back not to בנך but to זרעך —and the reference is to the *line* of David's descendants, of which it is said that if, in the person of any of its individual members, it commits iniquity it will be punished, as men in general are punished, but Yahweh's favour will not be withdrawn from it permanently, as it was withdrawn from Saul. Hence *v.* 16 the promise of perpetuity is conferred upon it. Comp. 1 Ki. 2, 4. ψ. 89, 31–38. 132, 12, where the terms of Nathan's prophecy are expressly interpreted of David's *sons* [1].

14. בשבט אנשים וג׳] i.e. with punishments such as all men incur when they sin, and from which the seed of David will not be exempted. Comp. the poetical paraphrase, ψ. 89, 31–34.

15. לא יסור] LXX and 1 Ch. 17, 13, more pointedly : לא אסיר.

כאשר הסירתי LXX here [כאשר הסרתי מעם שאול אשר הסירתי מלפניך

Ch. מאשר הסירתי מאשר היה לפניך : מאשר הסירתי מלפני. The *repetition* of הסירתי is not an elegancy, and the non-mention of Saul's name would seem certainly to be original : on these grounds Berth. We. Bu. etc. prefer the reading of Chronicles.

16. לפניך] LXX, better, לְפָנַי; cf. *vv.* 26. 29 ; and ψ. 89, 37[b].

19. אל] *with reference to,* as I 3, 12.

למרחוק] *from afar,* i.e. long before the history of בית עבדך was completed : comp. 2 Ki. 19, 25 (=Is. 37, 26). 'It was not enough in Thine eyes to honour me : Thy regard extends also to my house, and even in view of the distant future.' למן as *v.* 6.

וזאת תורת האדם] As the text stands, the best explanation is that of Hengstenberg and Keil : 'and this is the law for men,' i.e. to evince such regard for me is in accordance with the law prescribed

---

[1] *V.* 13 is in any case parenthetic, even if it be not, as We. supposes (*Comp. des Hex.*[2] 257), a subsequent insertion in the prophecy. Elsewhere in the promise *house* has the sense of 'family' (*vv.* 11. 16 : and on *vv.* 18. 19. 25. 26. 27. 29), and the point of the whole prophecy is not that Solomon rather than David is to be the builder of the house for Yahweh, but (as stated above) that it is not David who is to build a house for Yahweh, but Yahweh who will build a house for David. *V.* 14 ff. describe how David's descendants will be dealt with in such a manner as to give effect to this promise ; and the reference to the *material* temple in *v.* 13 interferes with the just sequence of the thought.

by God to regulate men's dealings with one another (not as Kp.);
displayed by *God*, therefore, it argues unwonted condescension and
affection. ('This is the *manner*—mos, consuetudo—of men,' Ges.
Th., gives to תורה a sense which it never has, and which would rather
be expressed by משפט.) But Hengst.'s explanation is artificial:
and there is no doubt that the text is incorrect. Ch. has וראיתני כתור
האדם המעלה, which is more obscure than the text here, and indeed
cannot be intelligibly construed. We., following a suggestion of
Ewald's, *Hist.* iii. 180 (E. T. 132), would read וַתַּרְאֵנִי דֹרֹת הָאָדָם 'and
hast let me see the generations of men,' i.e. given me a glimpse into
the fortunes of my descendants. But if descendants had been meant,
would not the idea have been expressed distinctly? No satisfactory
emendation of the passage has been proposed.

21. בעבור דברך וכלבך] The combination of two such disparate
ideas is very un-Hebraic. LXX here, and 1 Ch. 17, 19 have עַבְדְּךָ
for דברך. This is certainly an improvement. We. would also drop
וכלבך, remarking that the fact that in LXX (διὰ τὸν δοῦλόν σου
πεποίηκας [καὶ κατὰ τὴν καρδίαν σου ἐποίησας] κτλ.) πεποίηκας has no
obj., is an indication that the bracketed words are a later addition,
so that the original LXX did not read וכלבך. Nestle (*Marg.* p. 16),
retaining וכלבך, points out that in 1 Ch. 17, 18 (=*v.* 20 here) there
are found between אליך and ואת the words לְכָבוֹד אֶת־עַבְדְךָ (which,
as thus read, cannot be construed: RV. is a resort of desperation);
and, supposing them to be misplaced in Ch., utilizes them as a
beginning for *v.* 21, viz. לְכַבֵּד אֶת־עַבְדֶךָ דִּבַּרְתָּ וְכִלְבָּךְ עָשִׂיתָ—בעבור דברך
being a corruption of עבדך דברת: so Sm. Bu. This reads excellently;
and *may* well have been the original text: we can hardly say more.

גדולה] The word does not occur besides except in late Hebrew
(1 Ch. 29, Esther, ψ. 71. 145). The meaning of the expression
'done *all this greatness*' is here (unlike *v.* 23) obscure; and the verse
is greatly improved by the transposition proposed by Reifmann:
עשה) להודיע את עבדך את כל־הגדולה הזאת absol., as Is. 48, 11 al.).

22. יהוה אלהים] 'This stands in Ch. everywhere for אדני יהוה of
our text: here and *v.* 25 it has found its way into this as well, as
in I 6, 11. 17 טחרים' (We.).

23. Geiger (*Urschrift*, p. 288) and We., partly following LXX

and 1 Ch. 17, 21, suppose the original text to have been: ומי כעמך

ישראל גוי אחר בארץ אשר הָלַךְ אלהים (or) אלהין) לפדות לו לעם ולשום לו

שם ולעשות לָהֶם גְּדוֹלת ונוראות לְגָרֵשׁ מפני עמּוֹ גוי ואלהיו¹ . 'On the one

hand, the reference being to heathen gods, the sing. הלך was changed

to the pl. הלכו; on the other hand, a difficulty was found even in

supposing that another god had chosen and done great things for

a nation, and all was referred back again to the true God, hence

לשום לך in Ch. while Sam. has preserved לו, hence also לכם and

לארצך in Sam., עמך with the addition ממצרים (לך) אשר פדית [based

on לפדות לו just above] in both, and finally, as not one nation merely

but several were driven out before Israel, גוים for גוי, which, however,

is not certain in the case of Sam. [on account of the suff. in אלהיו]'

(Geig.). Bu. Sm. Now. agree. It will be observed that while the

question itself implies a reference to false gods, the terms in which

it is put allude covertly to what has been done by the true God:

hence the endeavour to accommodate them to it, if possible, explicitly.

As regards the changes in detail, הלך for הלכו is strongly supported

by the לו following²: להם and לגרש are both imperative—the former,

because a word addressed to *Israel* is here out of place, the latter

(as Chr.) in order to restore מפני to its right [*before* in AV. RV. gives

to מפני³ the sense of לפני or לעיני,[!], הנדולה ונוראות is a combination

as indifferent in style as לשור והמחלת in I 18, 6 (in support of the

restored text see Dt. 10, 21: also ψ. 71, 19. 106, 21), and the

enallage of numbers in גוים ואלהיו is alien to the practice of Hebrew

prose. As regards the other expressions in the verse, with the

opening question, comp. Dt. 4, 7. 34; with לשום לו שם Jer. 32, 20;

Is. 63, 12ᵇ. 14ᵇ; Neh. 9, 10; Dan. 9, 15 (all with עשה: for שום cf.

ch. 14, 7); and with נרש מפני Ex. 34, 11. Jos. 24, 18. ψ. 78, 55.

---

¹ Or גוים ואלהים, after LXX ἔθνη καὶ σκηνώματα (i.e. אלהים, misread

אֹהָלִים).

² LXX ὡδήγησεν αὐτὸν=הלכו has nothing to recommend it, and does not

harmonize with the following לפדות.

³ In מפני the sense of מן is never lost: Lev. 19, 32 מפני שיבה תקום not merely

to rise up *in the presence of* (לפני) the hoary head, but to rise up *from before*

it, out of respect for it; Is. 26, 17 כן היינו מפניך so were we—not *in*, but—*through*

Thy presence.

27. אֵת לבו . . . מצא] *found his heart*, i.e. took courage (RV. *m.*):
cf. *Lex.* לב and לבב 10, and phrases in Jer. 30, 21. Est. 7, 5; and
for מצא ψ. 76, 6.

28. . . . אתה הוא] Is. 37, 16. 43, 25. ψ. 44, 5 al. (*Tenses*, § 200).
יהיו] *are habitually :* but a verb is not here needed; and Ehrl. may
be right in reading יהוה.

אמת] *truthfulness,*—the abstract subst. instead of the adj.: so
הדבר (*was*) אמת היה Dt. 22, 20. 1 Ki. 10, 6; without היה, 1 Ki. 17,
24; also ψ. 19, 10. 119, 142. 151 al. (*ib.* § 189. 2; GK. § 141ᶜ).

29. הואל] *be willing.* הואיל is to *will* (I 12, 22),—with different
nuances, as to *be willing, agree* (Ex. 2, 21), to *resolve, undertake* (Gen.
18, 27. Dt. 1, 5), to *be determined* (Jud. 1, 27. 35. Hos. 5, 11). Comp.
Moore, *Judges*, p. 47; *Lex.* 384ᵃ.

מברכתך] מן=*through, from, in consequence of :* Ges. *Thes.* 803ᵇ;
Lex. 580ᵃ. Cf. Is. 28, 7 נבלעו מן־היין.

8. *Summary of David's wars; and list of his ministers.* (Close of
the history of David's *public* doings; comp. I 14, 47–51 of Saul.)
Ch. 8 = 1 Ch. 18.

8, 1. אֵת מתג האמה] The expression is peculiar: but apparently,
if the text is correct, the meaning is, 'the bridle of the *mother-city*'
(so Ges. Ke. Stade), i.e. the authority of the metropolis or capital.
אם in Phoenician has the sense of *mother-city* or *capital ;* see the coin
figured in Ges. *Jesaia*, i. p. 755 (=*Monum. Phoen.*, Tab. 34 N; p. 262)
לצר אם צדנם¹; Cooke, *NSI.* pp. 350, 352 B 15; Lidzbarski, *Nordsem. Epigr.* p. 219. ܐܡ has the same meaning in Syriac (PS. 222).
אֵם in *ch.* 20, 19 may also be compared: and it may be remembered
how בנות is often used in the sense of dependent cities or villages
(Nu. 21, 25 al.). Comp. also Jos. 14, 15 LXX μητρόπολις τῶν
Ενακειμ (similarly 15, 13. 21, 11), i.e. הָעֲנָק אֵם (regarded by some
as the original reading: Moore, *Judges*, p. 25). אַמָּה appears here
to be the fem. of אֵם, and to be used in the same metaph. sense.
מתג *bridle*, metaph. of authority, jurisdiction; cf. in Arabic the use

¹ In ללאדכא אם בכנען (*Mon. Phoen.*, Tab. 35), also cited in the first edition,
the true reading appears to be אש ('which ') for אם : Cooke, *op. cit.* pp. 46 *n.*,
349, 350.

of ‏זְמָם‎ a *nose-rein, bridle:* Schultens, on Job 30, 11 (quoted by Ges.
s.v. ‏אמה‎), cites from *Hist. Tam.* [II 228 Manger] ‏זִמָמָהָ قَابِضِين‎
holding the bridle of those (countries), with other exx. ; see also Lane,
Arab. Lex. p. 1249.   1 Ch. 18, 1 for ‏מתג האמה‎ has ‏גת ובנותיה‎,
‘Gath and her daughters’ (dependent villages), apparently reading,
or interpreting, ‏מתג‎ as ‏גת‎, and supposing ‘Gath the mother’ to include
her dependencies.   The Versions render no help.   LXX τὴν ἀφωρι-
σμένην (? ‏מִתְגֻּרְשָׁה‎; τὰ ἀφωρισμένα=‏מִגְרָשִׁים‎ Jos. 14, 4 al.) ; Aq. τὸν
χαλινὸν τοῦ ὑδραγωγίου (from the Syr. sense of ‏אמה‎ Sir. 24, 30: cf.
Theod. ὑδραγωγοῦ in *ch.* 2, 24); Symm. τὴν ἐξουσίαν τοῦ φόρου,
whence Vulg. *frenum tributi;* Targ. ‏תקון אמתא‎ ; Pesh. ‏ܐܦܟ ܚܡܐ‎.

2. ‏בַּחֶבֶל‎] On the art., see on I 19, 13; and on the *fem.* ‏ותהי‎ (cf.
vv. 5. 6), on I 17, 21.

‏השכב‎] The inf. abs., defining *how* David ‘measured’ them, as
I 3, 12 : Ew. § 280ᵃ; GK. § 113ʰ.

‏מנחה‎] Cf. 1 Ki. 5, 1.   The word denotes properly a *complimentary
present,*—in different applications.   As a sacrificial term, of the particular gift known as the ‘meal-offering:’ in a connexion such as the
present, of gifts offered to a prince or other person, whose good-will
it is desired to secure, whether voluntarily (Gen. 32, 14. 43, 15. 2 Ki.
8, 8), or as something expected or exacted (as here), so that it nearly
= *tribute.*

3. ‏הדדעזר‎] Some 50 MSS., many edd., LXX (Αδρααζαρ), Pesh.,
Vulg., read ‏הדרעזר‎.   That ‏הדדעזר‎ is right ‘appears from a recently
found Aramaic seal with the inscription ‏להדדעזר‎, in which ‏ד‎ and ‏ר‎ are
clearly distinguished[1].’   Comp. also the Assyrian equivalent (Schrader,
*KAT.*² p. 201 ; cf.³ p. 446) *Dad'idri,* ‏הדדרמן‎ Zech. 12, 11, and the
n. pr. ‏בן־הדד‎.   Hadad was the name of the chief deity of the
Aramaeans, identified by the Assyrians with Rammān, and hence
probably the god of storm and thunder (Cooke, *NSI.* pp. 164, 360).
This name, therefore, as pointed, will signify *Hadad is help:* cf. ‏יֹעֶזֶר‎
Yah is help, and ‏אֶלְיֶעֶזֶר‎.   The vocalization of LXX would suggest
the form ‏הֲדַדְעֶזֶר‎ (like ‏יְהוֹשָׁפָט‎, etc.) *Hadad helpeth.*

---

[1] Baethgen, *Beiträge* etc., p. 67 ; Euting, *Berichte der Berl. Akad.* 1885, p. 679
(= *Epigr. Miscellen,* p. 11). See *CIS.* II. i. No. 124. Cf. *PRE.*³ vii. 288–291.

צוּבה] here and *v.* 5 [=1 Ch. 18, 3. 5]. 12. 10, 6 and 8 (צוֹבָא).
23, 36. I 14, 47. 1 Ki. 11, 23 (הדדעזר מלך צובה). 1 Ch. 18, 9. 19, 6
[=צובא *ch.* 10, 6]. 2 Ch. 8, 3 (חֲמָת צוֹבָה). *ψ.* 60, 2 (from *ch.* 8, 12)†.

להשיב ידו ב'] The phrase is difficult, and affords no satisfactory
sense. השיב יד על means to turn one hand *against* (Am. 1, 8. *ψ.* 81,
15 ; Ez. 38, 12), and though השיב יד ב' might have a similar sense,
this would not suit with the object בנהר. And though יד in itself
might be used metaph. = *dominion*, השיב ידו certainly could not express
the idea '*recover* his dominion :' for השיב with יד would suggest not
the idea of *regaining*, *restoring*, but simply of *bringing back*, with
which the *metaphorical* sense of יד would not harmonize. Hence it is
best to read with 1 Ch. 18, 3 להציב ידו, i. e. either *to stablish* his hand,
fig. for his *dominion*, or, perhaps (cf. I 15, 12 מציב לו יד ; *ch.* 18, 18),
to set up his *monument* of victory (Symm. τρόπαιον): so Gottheil,
ZAW. 1906, 277 ff. (where numerous examples are cited of such
stelae set up by the Assyrian kings). The subject will be Hadad'ezer.

בנהר] (Kt. בַּנָּהָר) 'by the River,' sc. κατ' ἐξοχήν, i.e. the Euphrates
(see 10, 16; so e.g. Gen. 31, 31. *ψ.* 72, 8—always in this sense with
a capital R in RV.). The Qrê בִּנְהַר פְּרָת agrees with LXX here and
with 1 Ch. 18, 3.

4. הרכב] A collective,—here, unusually, denoting the *chariot-horses*.

5. לעזר ל'] ל' as 21, 17 ; and frequently with the same verb in late
books (especially Chronicles).

6. נציבים] See on I 13, 3.

7. שלטי הזהב] On שלט, see esp. W. E. Barnes, *Exp. Times*, x.
42–5 (Oct. 1898), cf. p. 188.

על=אל] (on I 13, 13); for היה על, of things *worn*, cf. Ex. 28, 43.
Not *that belonged to:* אל is not used in the sense of ל.

7ᵇ. 8ᵇ. On the additions here in LXX, see We.

8. ומבטח] 1 Ch. 18, 8 ומטבחת—and this order of consonants is
supported by LXX here ἐκ τῆς Μασβακ. Cf. Gen. 22, 24 (טֶבַח).

ומברתי] 1 Ch., strangely, וּמִכּוּן.

9. 10. תעי] 1 Ch. 18, 9. 10 תעו, as also LXX (Θοου), the more
probable form philologically. The termination וּ- characterizes many
Semitic proper names, especially of the tribes bordering on Canaan

(e.g. in Nabataean, בענו, נרו, נלהמו, מלכו, etc.; Cooke, *NSI.* p. 214):
cf. in OT. נשמו the 'Arabian.' It is the Arabic nominative termination (cf. p. 18).

9. חמת] a large and important town in ancient times, and also now (*Ḥamā*), on the Orontes, some 120 miles N. of Damascus.

10. יורם] 1 Ch. 18, 10 הדורם, supported, at least in part, by LXX here ('Ιεδδουραν). Originally, no doubt, הֲדַדְרָם.

ולברכו] i.e. to *congratulate* him : I 25, 14. 1 Ki. 1, 47 (*Lex.* 139ᵃ).

איש מלחמות תעי] 'a man-of-battles of Toi' = a man engaged often in conflict with Toi: for the construction, comp. Gen. 14, 13 בעלי ברית אברם; Dt. 1, 41 כלי מלחמתו; Is. 41, 12 אנשי מלחמתך; 56, 7 בית תפלתי; *ch.* 23, 1 נעים זמירות ישראל; and see Ew. § 291ᵃ; GK. § 135ⁿ. LXX appears to express כי איש מלחמות היה להדרעזר; but איש מלחמות (Is. 42, 13. 1 Ch. 28, 3) is merely a *warrior*, not an *antagonist*.

12. מארם] 9 MSS., LXX, Pesh. Ch. מֵאֱדֹם, probably rightly.

13. ויעש ... שם] Cf. Gen. 11, 4 ונעשה לנו שם, where Delitzsch argues that שם, from the context, requires a more concrete sense than 'name,' and would render—in accordance with the supposed primary meaning of שם, something *lofty, conspicuous*—'monument,' comparing the present passage (as also Is. 56, 5. 55, 13) for a similar sense. But whatever the *primitive* meaning of שם, it is in actual usage so largely and constantly 'name,' even in conjunction with עשה (see the references on 7, 23), that it is difficult to think that it can have a different sense here. It is safest, therefore, to render ' gat him a name,' comparing the similar phrase ויעש חיל used of Saul, I 14, 48. It will be observed that in the text as emended (see the following note) ויעש שם is connected with David's *victory* (either over Edom, or over Syria), not as in MT. with his *return* after the victory, when his ' fame' would have been already made, and the erection of a monument to commemorate it might have been rather supposed to be referred to.

ואבשי בן צרויה הכה] 1 Ch. 18, 12 בשבו מהכותו את־ארם בגיא מלח אדם. וישב יואב ויך את־אדום בגיא מלח בניא; ψ. 60 *title* את־אדום בגיא מלח המלח (supported also by LXX, Pesh. here) is unquestionably the true reading before גיא המלח : for this valley was near Edom (see 2 Ki. 14, 7), and far from the scene of the Syrians' defeat. Even, however, with אדם for ארם, the text is still defective: for *v.* 14 presupposes a *positive* statement of the victory over Edom in *v.* 13, and not merely a notice of what David did when he *returned* from smiting it. Keil would read בשבו מהכותו את־ארם ויך את־אדם בגיא מלח, supposing the three words added to have dropped out through the (virtual) homoioteleuton: Bu. Now. ובשבו מהכות את־ארם הכה את־אדם; We., with LXX (ἐν τῷ ἀνακάμπτειν αὐτὸν ἐπάταξεν), ובשבו הכה את־אדם בגיא המלח, which does not, however, account so well for the existing text (מהכותו for הכה); Sm., deviating least from MT., בשבו בהכותו את־אדם בגיא מלח (' on his returning, in that he smote,' etc.). In any case, as We. observes, דוד here is more original than either Joab (ψ.) or Abishai (Ch.); for throughout the summary which this chapter contains everything is ascribed to David *personally*, and ויעש דוד שם immediately precedes. For שמנה, here and Ch., ψ. 60, 2 has שנים.

15–18. *List of David's ministers.*

15. ויהי . . . עשה] Cf. 1 Ki. 5, 1. 24, and on I 2, 11ᵇ. 18, 9.

16. מזכיר] Probably not the *recorder*, but the king's *remembrancer* (cf. the verb in Is. 62, 6), who brought state-business to the king's notice, and advised him upon it. Cf. RECORDER in *DB.* or *EB.*

17. אחימלך בן־אביתר] Read with Pesh. אביתר בן־אחימלך. Abiathar is mentioned *before* David's accession as priest: he is mentioned also *during* David's reign and at the beginning of Solomon's reign as priest; and though it is no doubt possible, as Keil suggests, that for some temporary cause, such as sickness, his place might have been taken by his son, it is not likely that in a formal and official list of David's ministers, his name should be superseded by that of his son. It is, indeed, not impossible that the transposition in the text was made intentionally: see We.'s note. 1 Ch. 24, 3. 6. 31 (where *Ahimelech* is named by the side of Zadoq) are probably dependent upon this passage, *after* the original reading had become corrupted. Most modern scholars accept the correction.

שריה] LXX Ασα. In 20, 25 Kt. שיא, Qrê שׁוָא (LXX 'Ιησοῦς, Σους, Σουσα), 1 Ch. 18, 16 שׁוְשָׁא (LXX 'Ιησους), 1 Ki. 4, 3 שִׁישָׁא (LXX Σαβα). שריה is the form least attested of all: some such word as שׁשׁא

seems to be the most original. The vocalization must remain uncertain ; but *shu* is best attested.

ספר] *scribe,* i.e., as we should say, *secretary ;* so RV. *m.*

18. והכרתי] For ו, read as in Ch. and the parallel passage *ch.*
20, 23 על. The body-guard of הכרתי והפלתי (who are mentioned,
under this title, only during the reign of David : *ch.* 15, 18. 20, 7. 23
Qrê [see note], 1 Ki. 1, 38. 44) must have been composed of
foreigners. הכרתי is in form a *gentile* noun, and occurs as such in
I 30, 14 (see note), so that even on this ground alone a connexion
with הכרית *to cut off* would be doubtful. פלתי can only be another
gentile name ; it does not, however, occur except in this phrase, so
that what nationality is denoted by it must remain uncertain. The
supposition that it is contracted from פלשתי, though it has found
some support from modern scholars, is not in accordance with
philological analogy.

כהנים] The Chronicler, unable to understand how any could be
priests except sons of Aaron, paraphrases (1 Ch. 18, 17) הראשנים
ליד המלך ; but the sense of כהן is so uniform in Hebrew, that it is
impossible to think that it can have expressed, to those who heard it,
any idea but that which *priest* would convey to us. There is no trace
of the word having connoted any merely *secular* office : in Phoenician,
Aramaic, and Ethiopic it has the same meaning as in Hebrew : in
Arabic the corresponding word means a *soothsayer.* The etymology
of כֹּהֵן is uncertain. To say that it is derived ' from a root meaning
to serve or *minister* ' (Kp.) suggests an incorrect idea : in Heb. the root
does not occur at all [1] ; in Arabic *kāhin* (=כֹּהֵן) is a *soothsayer,* and
the verb means *to give oracles* [2]. It has been thought possible that
כֹּהֵן is derived from a by-form of כּוּן (cf. מָהַל beside מוּל ; Aram. בְּהֵת
beside בּוּשׁ), and hence may mean properly one who *stands up* with an

---

[1] The Pi'el כִּהֵן is a denominative from כֹּהֵן.

[2] The Arab. and Heb. senses of כהן have a meeting-point in the early function
of the Hebrew 'priest' to *give answers* by the אורים ותמים, or the אפוד (I 30,
7 f. etc.; also Jud. 18, 4–6), as well as to *pronounce authoritative decisions* (הוֹרָה)
on cases submitted to him. Comp. Kuenen, *Hibbert Lectures,* 1882, pp. 67, 81–87 ;
Wellhausen, *Reste Arab. Heidentums,* 130–134, 167 ([2]131–138, 143) ; art. PRIEST
in *EB.,* and *Encycl. Brit.*[10] xxii. 319b–320b.

affair, *manages, administers it* (Fleischer, *ap.* Delitzsch on Is. 61, 10), or one who *stands* before Yahweh in serving Him (Stade, *Gesch.* i. 471 ; *DB*. iv. 67ᵇ). But there is no evidence that כּוּן ever meant to 'stand¹.' Whatever be the ultimate etymology of כֹּהֵן, it was so limited by usage as to denote one who exercised certain *sacred* offices, whom we should term a '*priest.*' The word recurs, in the same application, 20, 26. 1 Ki. 4, 5.

What relation, however, did these כהנים bear to the כהנים of *v.* 17 ? From 20, 26 (היה כהן לדוד), 1 Ki. 4, 5 (כהן רעה המלך), it may be inferred that they stood in some special relation to the king. It seems not improbable that they were 'domestic priests'(Ew. *Hist.* iii. 367 [E.T. 268]), appointed specially to perform religious offices for the king.

In Egypt, we are told (Diod. Sic. i. 73), the king's responsible advisers were chosen from among the priests; and Delitzsch² supposed that the office here referred to was one to which members of the priesthood had the first claim, but which was sometimes conferred upon others, of good family, but not of priestly descent. But in Egypt the king's advisers *were* priests : is it likely that David, in establishing his court, would have adopted a title denoting a minister by a qualification which he did not possess? It has also been supposed (*DB.* iv. 73ᵇ) that the title was adopted in imitation of the Phoenicians, among whom members of the royal family often filled priestly offices (cf. Introd. § 1, the Inscription of Tabnith). But these members of the royal house, so far as appears, *were* priests. Neither the Egyptian nor the Phoenician parallel thus makes it probable that the Heb. כהן should have been used to denote persons who were not really ' priests ³.'

9—20 [with the sequel in 1 Ki. 1—2]. *History of events in David's court life, shewing how Amnon, Absalom, and Adonijah failed in turn to secure the succession : viz.* 9 *Mephibosheth (see* 16, 1–5 ; 19, 25–31); 10—12 *the war with Ammon (shewing how David became acquainted with Bathsheba, and narrating the birth of*

---

¹ To judge from its derivatives, כּוּן must have meant *to be established firmly, to subsist:* in Phoen. Arab. Ethiop., in a weaker sense, *to exist, be* (for which in these languages it is the term in ordinary use, as היה, הוא are in Heb. and Aram.). In Syr. the adj. ܟܺܝܢ and subst. ܟܝܳܢܐ have the sense of *prosperous, prosperity, opulence*, etc. (= εὐθηνῶν, κατευθύνων Jer. 15, 11 ; εὐθηνία, εὐημερία, εὐπραγία): which Fleischer seeks, with questionable success, to connect with the supposed root-meaning *to stand* (as though properly ' wolbestellt,' ' Wolstand ').

² *Zeitschr. für kirchl. Wissenschaft und kirchl. Leben*, 1880, p. 63.

³ Notice in 20, 26 the words 'and *also*,' which likewise imply that Ira, as ' priest,' stood on no different footing from the כהנים of *v.* 25.

Solomon); **13** *circumstances which led to the murder of Amnon ;* **14—19** *rebellion and death of Absalom ;* **20** *revolt of Sheba* (*an incident springing out of the revolt of Absalom*) [1].

9, 1. הכי] Gen. 29, 15. Comp. on *ch.* 23, 19.

2. ולבית שאול וג'] 'And the house of Saul *had* a servant,' etc. : not as EVV.

עבדך] See on I 26, 17.

3. האפס] except in the sense of *save that only* (*Lex.* 67ᵃ), אפס occurs in prose only here, 2 Ki. 14, 26. Am. 6, 10. Dn. 8, 25.

חסד אלהים] Cf. י״י I 20, 14.

4. בית מכיר] 'in the house of M. :' see p. 37 *n.*

לו דבר] 17, 27 (לא דבר), Jos. 13, 26 (לדבר), on the E. of Jordan, probably not far from Maḥanaim, Ish-bosheth's capital.

7. שאול אביך] Cf. בן אדניך *v.* 9 f., מפיבשת בן שאול 19, 25. Πατρὸς πατρός σου of LXX here has the same value as their υἱὸς υἱοῦ Σαουλ 19, 25. אֲבִי אֲבִי פלוני does not occur, though naturally it would be no impossible combination' (We.).

8. מה עבדך כי . . . ,] 2 Ki. 8, 13.

הכלב המת] I 24, 15. II 16, 9†.

אשר כמוני] אשר in a phrase of this sort is idiomatic : Gen. 44, 15 ; Jer. 5, 9 (=5, 29. 9, 8). כמוני alone would read badly.

10. והבאת] 'and thou shalt *bring in* (the produce) :' cf. Hag. 1, 6, and תבואה, of crops, properly *what is brought in.*

והיה לבן אדניך לחם וַאֲכָלוֹ] Read prob. with Luc. Bu. Sm. Ehrl. וְהָיָה לְבֵית אֲדֹנֶיךָ לֶחֶם וַאֲכָלֻ.

11ᵇ. The words are unsuited to the mouth of Ẓiba : and the ptcp. will not permit the rendering of EVV., 'As for M., *said the king,* he shall eat,' etc.—to say nothing of the awkward and improbabie position for such a remark on the part of David, after Ẓiba in 11ᵃ has signified his assent. LXX for שלחני express שֻׁלְּחַן דָּוִד, and render אֹכֵל ἤσθιεν. With this reading, which is adopted by Keil, We. Bu. Sm.

---

[1] The sequel to this group of chapters is 1 Ki. 1—2, which has every appearance —except in the verses 2. 3–4 which must have been added by the Deuteronomic compiler of the Book of Kings—of being by the same hand, and which narrates the failure of David's *third* son Adonijah to secure the throne, and the confirmation of Solomon as his father's successor.

Now., the words are a remark of the narrator : 'And M. *ate at the king's table,* as one of the sons of the king.' We. indeed observes that they are even then out of place, anticipating *v.* 13 : however, *v.* 13 states the new fact that Mephibosheth dwelt at Jerusalem, his eating at the king's table being merely referred to as the ground of his residence there.

12. מיכה] See 1 Ch. 8, 34 ff., where his descendants through many generations are enumerated.

Ch. 10 = 1 Ch. 19.

10, 1. מלך בני עמון] i.e. Nahash (*v.* 2): see I 11, 1.

3. . . . המכבד דוד] Gen. 18, 17 . . . המכפה אני מאברהם; Nu. 11, 29 הַמְקַנֵּא אתה לִי : *Tenses,* § 135. 4.

העיר] i.e. עמון בני רבת (12, 26 al.), or רַבָּה (11, 1); called by the Greeks (from Ptolemy Philadelphus, 285–247 B.C.) Philadelphia, now '*Ammān*, with extensive Roman remains of the age of the Antonines, on the left (N.) bank of the Jabbok, 25 miles E. of the fords of the Jordan near Jericho. See the description in the *Survey of East Pal.*, p. 19 ff.

4. מדויהם] So 1 Ch. 19, 4 : but the form (in the sing. [מָדוֹ], from a √מָדָה, GK. § 93ˣ) is very unusual, and the only root otherwise known is מדד. Read probably מַדֵּיהֶם; and see on I 17, 38.

בַּחֲצִי] חֵצִי is in pause for חֲצִי (GK. § 93ʸ), on account of the *Ṭifḥa ;* cf. Ex. 25, 10 וְחָצִי . . . וְחֵצִי . . . וְחֵצִי; and see on I 1, 15. 18. The 'half' is not half in length, but half in breadth, one entire side, to make them look ridiculous.

עד שתותיהם] Cf. Is. 20, 4 שֵׁת (rd. חֲשׂוּפֵי) חֲשׂוּפַי.

5. יְרֵחוֹ] So always, according to the Massorah, in Nu. Dt. Sam. Ezr. Neh. Chr. and once in Kings (2 Ki. 25, 5; but in the ‖, Jer. 52, 8, יְרֵחוֹ !); יְרִי or יְרֵ in Jos. Jer. and six times in Kings (+ once יְרֵחֹה).

עד וג'] See on I 1, 22.

יצמח] In *Qal* of plants growing; in *Piʿel* only of *hair* (Jud. 16, 22. Ez. 16, 7; and the ‖, 1 Ch. 19, 7†).

6. נבאשו בדוד] See on I 13, 4. 1 Ch. 19, 6 substitutes התבאשו עם דויד.

בית רחוב] Jud. 18, 28†; cf. רחוב *v.* 8. Nu. 13, 21†.

צובא] See on 8, 3.

מֵעָכָה] *v.* 8. 1 Ch. 19, 6 (אֲרַם מַעֲכָה). 7 [‖ to this *v.*]. Gen. 22, 14†; מֵעֲכָת Jos. 13, 13†; הַמַּעֲכָתִי Dt. 3, 14. Jos. 12, 5. 13, 11. 13. *ch.* 23, 34. 2 Ki. 25, 23. 1 Ch. 4, 19. Jer. 40, 8†. On מַעֲכָה אָבֵל בֵּית, see on 20, 14.

אִישׁ אֶלֶף] These words are out of construction: they cannot be rendered legitimately (EVV.) '*with* 1,000 men.' Read וְאִישׁ אֶלֶף (the וְ of 'concomitance:' p. 29). The 32,000 of 1 Ch. 19, 6 have been supposed to shew (We. al.) that the Chr. did not read אֶלֶף אִישׁ here, and they have hence been regarded as coming in by error from the end of the verse; but their omission leads to fresh difficulties and improbabilities in connexion with אִישׁ טוֹב. For טוֹב, see Jud. 11, 3. 5; and cf. Τούβιον 1 Macc. 5, 13.

7. הַצָּבָא הַגִּבּוֹרִים] EVV. 'the host *of* (!) the mighty men.' Read וְהַצְּ. The צָבָא was the army in general, the גִּבּוֹרִים a corps of select warriors (16, 6. 20, 7. 23, 8 ff.).

8. פֶּתַח הַשַּׁעַר] *at* the opening of the gate (p. 37 *n.*).

9. הַיְתָה] פְּנֵי הַמִּלְחָמָה being treated as a *collective* (GK. § 145^k): comp. Job 16, 16 Kt. פָּנַי חֳמַרְמָרָה; and see on I 4, 15.

בַּחוּרֵי בְיִשְׂרָאֵל (Kt.)] See on 1, 21. The combination is, however, unusual in *prose:* Jud. 8, 11 הַשְּׁכוּנִי בָּאֹהָלִים is very strange. True, as Th. remarks, it is *more* admissible here than it would be in I 26, 2: but no doubt 1 Ch. 19, 10 preserves the original reading מִכָּל בָּחוּר בְּיִשְׂרָאֵל. The Qrê is מִכָּל בְּחוּרֵי יִשְׂרָאֵל, which is read also by some 50 MSS.; but the בְּ is supported by the text of Ch.: see also *ch.* 6, 1.

11. תֶּחֱזַק] Cf. I 17, 21. לִישׁוּעָה *for deliverance* (I 14, 45).

12. וְנִתְחַזַּק] GK. § 54^k. וַיִּהְוֶה וג'; cf. I 3, 18.

14. מֵעַל] *from attacking:* 2 Ki. 3, 27 וַיִּסְעוּ מֵעָלָיו; 18, 14 שׁוּב מֵעָלַי. See on I 28, 15.

16. הֲדַרְעֶזֶר] Both here and in *ch.* 8 there is much variation in MSS. between הֲדַרְעֶזֶר and הֲדַדְעֶזֶר. Here MS. authority preponderates in favour of הֲדַרְעֶזֶר, as in *ch.* 8 it preponderated in favour of הֲדַדְעֶזֶר. The name must evidently be the same throughout. Both in Inscriptions (Phoen. and Hebrew) and in MSS. ד and ר are often not distinguishable, and only the context enables the reader to know which is intended. For the reason stated on 8, 3, the correct form is הֲדַרְעֶזֶר.

חֵלָם] *v.* 17 חֵלְאָם. Taken rightly by LXX, Pesh. Targ. as a pr. n. Perhaps to be read in Ez. 47, 16 after סַבְרַיִם (where LXX add Ηλιαμ).

18. פרשים] Probably a *lapsus calami* for איש: cf. 1 Ch. 19, 18 איש רגלי. The number of *horsemen* is disproportionately large.

Ch. 11, 1 = 1 Ch. 20, 1ᵃ (*ch.* 11, 2—12, 25 is passed by in Ch.).

11, 1. המלאכים] = המלכים, as is read by some 40 MSS., Qrê, Versions, and 1 Ch. 20, 1: comp. 10, 17 beside 16; and p. 168 *footnote*.

3. בת־שבע] 1 Ch. 3, 5 בת־שוע, no doubt to be pronounced בַּת־שֶׁוַּע, and probably merely an error for בת־שבע. LXX has everywhere the strange corruption Βηρσαβεε.

אליעם] in 1 Ch. 3, 5 עמיאל, which (We.) supports MT. against LXX Ἐλιαβ.—ויאמר sc. האומר (on I 16, 4).

אוריה החתי] one of David's famous גבורים (23, 39).

4. והיא מתקדשת וג׳] A circumstantial clause, defining the state of Bath-sheba at the time of וישכב עמה = '*as she* purified herself from her uncleanness' (cf. 13, 8). This is the only rendering of the words consistent with grammar. To express, 'and when she was purified etc., she returned . . .,' the Hebrew would have been וַתָּשָׁב . . . וַתִּתְקַדֵּשׁ, or (Jud. 18, 3 etc.) הִיא הִתְקַדְּשָׁה . . . וְהִיא שָׁבָה; in other words, to express anything *subsequent* to וַיִּשְׁכַּב עִמָּהּ, a finite verb, not the ptcp., would have been employed. The *athnaḥ* is thus in its right place (against Th. We.)[1]. Comp. *Tenses*, § 169 *note*.

6. שלח יואב. ... אל יואב שלח] ‘Without לאמר, as 19, 15, cf. Nu. 23, 7 before לכה' (We.).

8. משאת המלך] Comp. Gen. 43, 34.

10. הלוא מדרך אתה בא] Notice the position of מדרך: cf. Gen. 16, 8.

11. ואני אבוא אל ביתי] = 'and shall *I* enter into my house?' etc., the juxtaposition of two incongruous ideas, aided by the tone in which the words are pronounced, betokening surprise, and so suggesting a question. So not unfrequently, as Jer. 25, 29 ואתם הנקה תנקו. 45, 5. 49, 12 ואתה הוא נקה תנקה. Jon. 4, 11 ואני לא אחום. Ez. 20, 31 ואני אדרש לכם. 35, 25ᵇ. Jud. 14, 16ᵇ וְלָךְ אַגִּיד. Zech. 8, 6. *ch.* 15, 20. Comp. on I 11, 12 and *ch.* 18, 29. לִשַׁבַּב by GK. § 45ᶜ.

---

[1] מטמאתה is explained rightly by Lucian ἐξ ἀφέδρου αὐτῆς, Pesh. ܡܢ ܟܐܦܗ (see Lev. 15, 19. 20. 25 LXX and Pesh.): Rashi מנדתה. The remark is added to shew why conception followed: the time indicated was favourable for it. Cf. W. R. Smith, *Marriage and Kinship in Early Arabia*, p. 276, ed. 2, p. 133.

חֵיך וחי נפשך] This form of the oath does not occur elsewhere, and the tautology implied makes it improbable. LXX for חֵיך πῶς=אֵיךְ. 'But thus absolutely, as it seems, אֵיךְ could at most stand—at least that is the case in Arabic—when what here is placed before at the beginning of the verse *followed* as a circumstantial clause with ו. Either, therefore, read for חֵיך, חי יהוה [followed by וחי נפשך, as I 20, 3. 25, 26 al.], or omit וחי נפשך as an explanatory gloss on the un-common חֵיך' (We.). For וְחֵי נפשך, see on I 17, 55.

12. וממחרת] 'and *on* the morrow' (not as Th.: see Lev. 7, 16). A specification of time is, however, desiderated in *v.* 13 for ויקרא לו; and as even in MT. the promise ומחר אשלחך is not carried out by David, it is better to end *v.* 12 at ביום ההוא: ויקרא וממחרת will then begin *v.* 13 (ו as I 4, 20). So We. Bu. Now.: also LXX (Luc.) and Pesh. ויהי ממחרת (Ehrlich) would, however, be better; יהי might easily have been lost after ו ההוא.

15. הבו] if correct, הבו *give,*=*set* (like נתן): but the case goes beyond other usages of הבו, הב (*Lex.* 396ᵇ); and perhaps הָבֵא (LXX εἰσάγαγε) should be read (Klo. Bu. al.).

16. בשמור . . . אל] Comp. (in a *friendly* sense) I 26, 15.

17. מן העם וג׳] *from* the people *some of* (*v.* 24. Ex. 16, 27), etc.

19. לְדַבֵּר] *preceded* by its object: comp. Dt. 28, 56. Lev. 19, 9, and the Aramaic examples cited in *Tenses,* § 208. 3 *Obs.*

21. ירבשת] For ירבעל (Jud. 7, 1 al.). Unlike Ishbosheth and Mephibosheth, however, the alteration in this case has been made only in a single passage.

22. את כל־דברי המלחמה] LXX continues: את כל־אשר שלחו יואב ויחר לדוד על יואב אל המלאך ויאמר למה נגשתם אל העיר להלחם הלוא ידעתם את אשר תֵּפּוּ מעל החומה: מי הכה את אבימלך בן ירבעל הלוא אשה השליכה עליו פלח רכב מעל החומה וימת בתבץ למה נגשתם אל החומה: ויאמר וג׳ (*v.* 23): in other words, the text of LXX describes in detail how what Joab anticipated *vv.* 21-2 took place. The addition is a necessary one: for as the text stands, the terms in which the messenger speaks in *v.* 23ᵃ are unexplained (notice especially his opening words, *Because* etc., which presuppose a question to have been asked).

23. כי נברו] as the text stands, כי is the כִּי *recitativum* (on I 2, 16);

with the insertion from LXX (see on *v.* 22), it will be 'Because,' introducing the answer to David's question.

‏וְנִהְיָה עֲלֵיהֶם‎] 'appears to be correct. Comp. e.g. the use of ‏הָיָה‎ with ‏אַחֲרֵי‎ I 12, 14. Ex. 23, 2: the stress rests upon the preposition, the idea of which it is simply the purpose of ‏הָיָה‎ to render verbal' (We.).

24. ‏וַיִּרְאוּ הַמּוֹרְאִים‎ (Kt.)] as if from ‏יָרָא‎ (cf. ‏לִירוֹא‎ for ‏לִירוֹת‎ 2 Ch. 26, 15); Qrê ‏הַיֹּרִים‎ ‏וַיֹּרוּ‎, the regular form, from ‏יָרָה‎: GK. § 75ʳʳ.

25. ‏אֶת הַדָּבָר הַזֶּה‎ ... ‏אַל־יֵרַע‎] ‏הַדָּבָר הַזֶּה‎, though grammatically a nominative, is construed κατὰ σύνεσιν as an accusative. Comp. I 20, 13 (if ‏יִיטַב‎ be read); Jos. 22, 17; Neh. 9, 32: Ew. § 277ᵈ *end;* GK. § 117¹; *Lex.* 85ᵃ c.

‏בָּזֹה וְכָזֶה‎] So Jud. 18, 4. 1 Ki. 14, 5†.

‏וְחַזְּקֵהוּ‎] 'strengthen—i.e. encourage (Dt. 1, 38 al.)—him (Joab).'

27. ‏וַיַּאַסְפָה‎ ‏אסף‎] as Jos. 2, 18 ‏תַּאַסְפִי אֵלַיִךְ הַבַּיְתָה‎, Dt. 22, 2; Jud. 19, 15 (Pi.).

12, 1. ‏רָאשׁ‎] for ‏רָשׁ‎ (as *v.* 3); see GK. §§ 23ᵍ, 72ᵖ.

2. ‏לְעָשִׁיר‎] ‏לֶעָשִׁיר‎ would be expected, and should prob. be read.

3. ‏וַיְחַיֶּה‎] *and kept alive:* Ex. 1, 17. 18. 1 Ki. 18, 5.

‏תֹּאכַל וְגוֹ׳‎] The impff. expressing significantly its *habit*.

4. ‏לְאִישׁ הֶעָשִׁיר‎] The punctuation (for ‏לְאִישׁ‎) is anomalous. Comp. on I 6, 18; and Ew. § 293ᵃ; GK. § 126ˣ (read ‏לָאִישׁ‎).

5. ‏בֶן מֽוֹת‎] See on I 20, 31.

6. ‏אַרְבַּעְתָּיִם‎] LXX ἑπταπλασίονα=‏שִׁבְעָתַיִם‎, in all probability the original reading. As Th. remarks, David speaking impulsively is more likely to have used the proverbial 'sevenfold' (cf. Prov. 6, 31), than to have thought of the law Ex. 21, 37: ‏אַרְבַּעְתָּיִם‎ will be due to a corrector who noticed the discrepancy.

‏וְעַל אֲשֶׁר לֹא חָמַל‎] Schill (*ZAW.* 1891, p. 318), Ehrlich, Bu., attractively, though not necessarily, ‏לוֹ‎ for ‏לֹא‎ 'and spared *that which was his own.*'

7ᵇ. Observe the emphatic ‏אָנֹכִי‎: compare—likewise in a reproach—Amos 2, 9. 10.

8. ‏אֶת בֵית אֲדֹנֶיךָ‎] Possibly ‏אֶת בַּת אֲדֹנֶיךָ‎ (Pesh. ‏בנות א׳‎) ‏אֶת‎ should be read (Sm. Bu.), with allusion to Michal: ‏אֶת בֵית א׳‎ certainly does not harmonize with the following ‏בְחֵיקֶךָ‎.

ואת נשי אדניך] Not elsewhere recorded of David, though it would be in accordance with Oriental custom (16, 22. 1 Ki. 2, 17; cf. *ch.* 3, 7).

את בית ישראל ויהודה] Pesh. את בְּנוֹת י׳ וי׳, perhaps rightly (Sm. Bu.): the meaning of course would be not that they were given to him actually, but that he could choose his wives from them as he pleased (3, 2–5).

ואספה] 'then would I add' (not 'would *have added*,' AV.). There is a similar mistake in AV. of ψ. 81, 15. 16.

The ְ, as thus used, is rare: but see Gen. 13, 9 (*Tenses*, § 136 β*).

כהנה וכהנה] i.e. other similar marks of favour: cf. כָּזֹה וְכָזֶה (11, 25). כזאת וכזאת (17, 15), said where details need not be specified.

9. דבר] Probably to be omitted with Luc. and Theod.: cf. esp. *v.* 10b. Notice the emph. position of את אוריה, ואת אשתו, and אתו.

11. לרעיך] The *yod* is not the *yod* of the plural, but is due to the fact that רֵעַ is properly רֵעֶה *rē'ay* (cf. רֵעֵהוּ: comp. מְפַתֶּיהָ *alluring her* Hos. 2, 16: עֹשֶׂיהָ Is. 22, 11 (Ew. § 256b; Ol. p. 250; GK. § 93ss).

12. נגד] *in front of*, expressing more strongly than לפני the idea of being *conspicuous before*: comp. Nu. 25, 4; 1 Ki. 21, 13.

13. גם יהוה] Yahweh, also, on His part: the גם *correlativum;* cf. on I 1, 28a.

העביר] The same figure, lit. to *make to pass away*, in 24, 10: comp. Zech. 3, 4 העברתי מעליך עונך. Job 7, 21 ותעביר את עוני.

14. את איבי י״י] נאץ does not elsewhere mean *to cause to blaspheme:* so doubtless Geiger is right (*Urschrift*, p. 267) in supposing the original reading here to have been את י״י: cf. the insertion of איבי in I 25, 22. For הַיִּלּוֹד, see on 5, 14.

15. ויאנַשׁ] for this pausal form of -נַשׁ, see GK. §§ 29q, 51m; and cf. on I 15, 23.

16. ובא וג׳] A series of perfects with *waw* conv., indicating that David acted as here described repeatedly.

ולן ושכב] LXX (B) omits ושכב; Luc. omits ולן, and expresses ושכב בַּשָּׂק (1 Ki. 21, 27),—not (Sm. Bu. Now.) ולן בשק, for καὶ ἐκάθευδεν represents ושכב, not ולן.

17. ברא] Read, with many MSS. and edd. ברה; see on 3, 35.

18. איך נאמר . . . ועשה רעה] The two verbs are coupled together

under the government of אֵיךְ, exactly as Gen. 39, 9 (*Tenses*, § 115
s.v. אֵיךְ), though the change of *subject* makes a literal rendering hardly
intelligible in English. RV. text and margin are merely two different
paraphrases, designed to meet the exigencies of English idiom.

20. וַיָּ֫סֶךְ] The *Hif.* only here; cf. GK. § 73ᶠ. Read וַיָּ֫סָךְ (Ehrl.).

21. בעבור הילד חי] for the sake of the child (when) alive: LXX
rightly ἕνεκα τοῦ παιδαρίου ἔτι ζῶντος. But בעד (as *v.* 22) for בעבר
(ד=ר, and ב repeated by error), as We. conjectured in 1871, and
as is confirmed by Luc. Pesh. Targ., is much more probable (so Sm.
Bu. Ehrl. etc.). (In Jer. 14, 4 read, with Duhm, עֹבְדֵי האדמה חַתּוּ for
בעבר האדמה חתה.)

22. מי יודע יְחָנֵּנִי Kt.; מי יודע וְחַנַּנִי Qrê] *who knows ?*=peradventure.
The correction of the Qrê is unnecessary: the Kt. is exactly like Joel
2, 14. Jon. 3, 9. In Esther 4, 14 we have . . . מִי יודע אם.

23. זה] למה זה אני צם adds point to למה (on I 10, 11): cf. Gen.
25, 22 למה זה אנכי to what purpose should I yet be ?

25. וישלח] We. Bu. וַיִּשְׁלְמֵהוּ (Now. וַיְשַׁלַּם) *and he* (David) *delivered
him into*, etc., viz. for his education. But to *make wholly over* to,
to *deliver up*, is an Aram. sense of השלים (e.g. Dt. 32, 30 Onk.
אשלימנן for הִסְגִּירָם; and ܐܫܠܡ constantly for παραδοῦναι), in Heb.
found at most in late poetry (Is. 38, 12. 13 LXX, Duhm, al.; Is. 42, 19
מְשֻׁלָּם by conjecture for מְשֻׁלָּם); so it is not a very likely word to have
been used here. With וישלח, it is an improvement to begin the
verse with ויהוה אהבו.

בעבור י״] Luc. י״בדבר,—perhaps rightly (Sm. Now. Dh.).

12, 26=1 Ch. 20, 1ᵇ (abridged); 12, 30–31=1 Ch. 20, 2–3.

26. עיר המלוכה] The 'royal city' would be Rabbah itself, whereas
(27) Joab had taken only what was called the *Water-city*, and (28)
invited David to take Rabbah itself. Read therefore, probably, as
v. 27, עיר המים (Bu. Sm. Now. Dh.).

27. עיר המים] No doubt a fortification, or part of the city, which protected
the water-supply. Polybius (v. 71) relates that when Rabbah was besieged by
Antiochus III in B.C. 218, he was unable to enter the city till a prisoner revealed
the underground passage by which the besieged used to descend to fetch water.
The remains of a citadel are on a hill about ½ mile N. of the Jabbok, 200–300 ft.
above the valley, and connecting by a saddle with hills further to N.; on this
saddle there is a fine rock-cut tank, 20 ft. by 90 ft.; and just inside the entrance

to this tank there begins an underground passage leading in the direction of the citadel, which it has been supposed was the one mentioned by Polybius (see G. A. Barton, *JBL.* xxvii. (1908), p. 147 ff., esp. 149 f. ; and Conder, *Survey of E. Palestine,* p. 34, with the Plan facing p. 34). The fortification surrounding either this or some other water-supply was doubtless the ' Water-city ' mentioned here.

28. פֶן אלכד אני] ' Lest *I* (emph.) take the city,' etc.: comp. Ex. 18, 19. Jud. 8, 23. 2 Ki. 10, 4. Is. 20, 6. Jer. 17, 18. ψ. 109, 28 al. *ch.* 17, 15 יעצתי אני ; and comp. on I 17, 56. 23, 22.

ונקרא שמי עליה] 'And my name *be called over it'*—in token viz. of its conquest by me. The passage shews the genuine sense of the phrase, often occurring (especially in Dt. and dependent books) with reference to the nation, the city, or the Temple, ' over which Yahweh's name is called,' in token viz. of the right of possession or ownership by Him (generally paraphrased obscurely in AV. ' called by My name [1]'). See Am. 9, 12 אשר נקרא שמי עליהם (in allusion to the nations embraced by David in the dominion of Israel). Dt. 28, 10 וראו כל עמי הארץ כי שם י"י נקרא עליך. 1 Ki. 8, 43 (על הבית). Jer. 7, 10. 11. 14, 9. 15, 16 (of the prophet). 25, 29 al. Is. 63, 19 we are become as those *over whom Thy name has not been called* (i. e. whom Thou hast never owned).

30. מלכם] LXX מִלְכֹּם (1 Ki. 11, 5 al.)—probably rightly. In the whole context, no allusion is made to the *king* of Rabbah ; nor has there been any mention of the people, but only of the city, so that, with the Massoretic punctuation, the suffix ם— is without an antecedent.

ואבן יקרה] Read, with Pesh. Targ. here, and 1 Ch. 20, 2 : וּבָהּ אבן יקרה. A ' talent' of gold weighed 65, if not 130, lbs. av. (Kennedy, *DB.* iv. 903ᵇ).

31. חרצי הברזל] Cf. Am. 1, 3 חרצות הברזל.

במלבן] So Kt., which Th. following Kimchi defends, supposing the meaning to be the place in which victims were sacrificed to Molech (punctuating either בְּמָלְכֶּם in their ' Molech,' or בַּמֹּלְבֹּם in the Molech-image). But such a sense for either מֹלֶךְ or מלבם is highly improbable ; and the Qrê בַּמַּלְבֵּן must be adopted. The meaning of מלבן, however, has only recently been cleared up. From its form

---

[1] Which really expresses a *different* phrase, נקרא בשמי Is. 43, 7 : cf. 48, 1.

(with מ prefixed), it would naturally be supposed to denote either a *place* (like מַכְתֵּשׁ) or *instrument* (like מַפְתֵּחַ) of making bricks, but not the one rather than the other. It has, indeed, been commonly rendered as though it meant the former, viz. *brickkiln:* but this rendering lacks support either in the use of the word elsewhere or in the renderings of the ancient Versions. In an elaborate study on the word[1], Georg Hoffmann has shewn that in post-Biblical Hebrew, it is used firstly of a brick*mould*, and then metaphorically of different objects of the same *rectangular* shape, such as the *frame* of a door, sofa, window, or again, of a garden-bed, but not of a brick*kiln*. In Arabic and Syriac the corresponding words are used similarly : مَلْبَن denotes a *brickmould* (Freytag), and occurs also in Saadyah's version of Is. 6, 4 of the *framework* of a door ; ܡܠܒܢܐ signifies a *brickmould* (PS. col. 1887), as also a *quadrangle* or *square* (Hoffmann, p. 65) : but for neither language is the meaning *brickkiln* quoted. Nor is this meaning required for either of the two other passages in the OT. in which מלבן occurs. In Nah. 3, 14 הַחֲזִיקִי מַלְבֵּן the rendering 'lay hold of the brickmould' (in preparation for a siege, immediately following 'go into the clay, and tread the mortar ') is as suitable as 'make strong the brickkiln ; ' and in Jer. 43, 9 a 'brickkiln ' in front of Pharaoh's palace would be by no means so suitable a spot for the prophet to deposit in it his symbolical stones, as a *square*, or open quadrangle, in the same position, especially if, as appears from *v.* 10, the stones were to mark the site *upon which* Nebuchadrezzar's throne was to be erected. Nor again, is the meaning *brickkiln* recognized by any of the ancient Versions. Here, LXX have διήγαγεν αὐτοὺς διὰ τοῦ πλινθίου[2], Luc. περιήγαγεν αὐτοὺς ἐν Μαδεββα, Pesh. [3] ܐܘܒܠ ܐܢܘܢ ܒܡܣܩܬܐ, Targ. וְנַגֵּר יַתְהוֹן בְּשׁוּקַיָּא

---

[1] *ZATW.* 1882, pp. 53–72. See also Levy, *Neuhebr. Wörterbuch*, s. v.

[2] 'Led them through the brickmould,' the sense being, at least, not worse than that of Jerome's 'traduxit in typo laterum,' or of countless other passages in the LXX Version. Πλινθίον has been supposed to mean 'brick*kiln* :' but no such sense is recognized in the last edition of Liddell and Scott's Lexicon.

[3] *Made them pass through the measure*,—meaning, perhaps (PS. 2237), some arrangement for allotting them to different forms of punishment (*ch.* 8, 2) ; cf. Nestle, *Margin.* 17. Comp. also ܐܠܨ ܡܣܩܬܐ ܠܒܢܬܐ in 2 Macc. 4, 12 (cited PS. *ib.*).

and he dragged them *through the streets,* Vulg. *et traduxit in typo laterum :* in Nah. 3, 14 LXX κατακράτησον ὑπὲρ πλίνθον, Pesh. ܘܐܠܒܟ ܣܟܠܒܐ (brickmould), Targ. אתקיפי ביניניך (thy building), Vulg. *tene laterem :* in Jer. 43, 9 במלבן במלט LXX probably omit [1], οἱ λοιποί· ἐν τῷ κρυφίῳ ἐν τῷ πλινθίῳ, Pesh. ܟܣܐܠܟܐ ܐܟ ܟܣܐܠܟܐ (in the *quadrangle*), Targ. בטפל בניינא in the mortar of the building, Vulg. *in crypta quae est sub muro latericio.* Thus usage, whether of Hebrew or of the cognate languages, or as interpreted by ancient authority, offers no support to the meaning *brickkiln* for מלבן. Hence Hoffmann, in the article referred to, holds the common interpretation of this passage to be incorrect, and reading הֶעֱבִיד for העביר would render, ' And he brought forth the people that were therein, and set them *to* saws, and *to* harrows of iron, and *to* axes of iron, and *made them labour at the brickmould :*' in other words, instead of torturing them, employed them in different public works [2]. This view of the passage is accepted by Stade (*Gesch. Isr.* i. 278), We. Bu. Now. Sm. König, *NKZ.* 1891, p. 667, Nestle, al., and is represented on the margin of the Revised Version. שם ב' in the sense of *to set among*=*to employ about* [3] may be illustrated from I 8, 11 וישם לו במרכבתו. 1 Ch. 20, 3 has indeed וַיָּשַׂר *and sawed* for וישם : but this may be either a textual *corruption,* or a mistaken interpretation of the compiler. Certainly, if we could honestly relieve David of the act of cruelty, which the Hebrew text here appears to attribute to him, we should be glad to do so : no doubt, it may be shewn to be in harmony with the manners of the age (Am. 1, 3 of the Syrians of Damascus), but it is alien to all that we know of the personal character and temper of David. Hoffmann's view is unquestionably an attractive one ; and the only ground which may occasion hesitation in accepting it, is the circumstantiality in the mention of three separate kinds of instruments, ' saws ' and ' harrows ' and ' axes,' and the character of the instruments themselves,

---

[1] Or express by ἐν προθύροις. But ἐν προθύροις ἐν πύλῃ are more probably a double rendering of בפתח,—the former in accordance with the rendering elsewhere in Jer. of פתח (1, 15. 19, 2. 26, 10. 36, 10), and ἐν πύλῃ a correction.

[2] Cf. how Mesha' employed his Israelite prisoners (Inscr. ll. 25-6).

[3] *Under* (AV.) is a paraphrase of ב' in no way necessitated by the Hebrew.

both of which might have been expected to be somewhat more general, had the narrator merely intended to state that the Ammonites were put to forced work by David. On the other hand, it is true that the sense *brickkiln* cannot be shewn to be expressed by מלבן in any other passage where it occurs in either Biblical or post-Biblical Hebrew, or even in the cognate languages. The correction of העביר into העביד is, of course, no source of difficulty. The terms employed in the first part of the verse favour the common interpretation of the passage: the term מלבן—so far as our knowledge of it goes—favours as decidedly—not to say more so—Hoffmann's view. The state of our knowledge is not sufficient to enable us to arrive at a decision with entire confidence. But those who refuse to allow the meaning *brickkiln* for מלבן may at least claim to have a sound philological basis for their opinion.

יעשה] Luc. rightly ἐποίει. Comp. the same tense in the description of the behaviour of an invading army, 2 Ki. 3, 25.

13, 2. ויצר לאמנון להתחלות] 'And Amnon was distressed (Josephus χαλεπῶς διέκειτο: cf. I 13, 6. 28, 15), so that he made himself sick,' etc. The *athnaḥ* would stand better at אחתו (Th. Ke. We. al.), what follows stating the reason why Amnon felt such distress: 'Because she was a virgin, and (this being so) it was hard,' etc.

3. שמעה] See on I 16, 9. Jonadab was cousin both to Absalom and Tamar and to Amnon.

חכם] 'subtil' (AV. RV.) is scarcely a fair paraphrase: the text says that Jonadab was *wise*. (*Subtil*=ערום Gen. 3, 1.)

4. את תמר . . . אני אהב] The regular order with the ptcp. and pronoun: Gen. 37, 16. 41, 9 etc. (*Tenses*, § 208. 3; GK. § 142f (d) *note*).

5. והתחל] 'and *make thyself sick*'—here and v. 6 in pretence (GK. § 54e), v. 2 in reality.—On ובא אביך . . . ואמרת see on I 19, 3.

9. משרת] Only here. The etymology is not apparent: but the meaning appears to be established by the Aram. מסרית, which clearly signifies *plate* or *pan* (Lev. 2, 5; Ez. 4, 3 al. Targ.: for מחבת). LXX τήγανον, as always for מחבת. Kön. ii. 184 thinks it may be an old corruption of מחבת, and, as such, the source of the Targ. מסרית. For ותצק, see GK. § 71.

הוציאו כל איש מעלי] So Gen. 45, 1. מעל=*from attendance on.*

10. הֶחָדְרָה] The lengthening of the ה of הַחַדְרָה in pause involves the change of the preceding ַ to ֶ, the collocation הַחַ being avoided. So אַחִי becomes in pause not אֶחָי, but אֶחָי; see GK. § 29ᵛ.

12. כי לא־יעשה כן] The impf. as Gen. 34, 7; cf. 20, 9.

אל־תעשׂה] GK. § 75ʰʰ; Ew. § 224ᶜ; Stade, § 143ᵈ (3); Delitzsch on Is. 64, 3; König, i. p. 531.

נבלה] Jud. 19, 23 את הנבלה הזאת תעשו אל; and comp. the phrase עשה נבלה בישראל Gen. 34, 7; Dt. 22, 21 (נעשׂתה); Jer. 29, 23 (each time of a sexual offence); Jos. 7, 15 (of Achan's impiety). The word expresses more than 'folly.' Just as נבל (2, 33: see more fully on I 25, 25) denotes one who lacks all regard for God or man, so נבלה means *godlessness, impiety.* It is *applied,* both here and elsewhere, to immorality, but it does not specifically *denote* immorality. The ideas which the Hebrews associated with the word appear with especial distinctness in Isaiah's description of the נבל (32, 6); see on I 25, 25.

13. כאחד הנבלים] For the form of the comparison, comp. 2, 18.

14. ויחזק ממנה] 'and overpowered her.' Cf. I 17, 50.

וישכב אתה] When שכב is used of illicit intercourse, the pronoun with את is regularly pointed by the Massorites as though it were the *object* of the verb in the accus. (Gen. 34, 2. Lev. 15, 18. 24. Nu. 5, 13. 19. Ez. 23, 8). It is doubtful whether this is not an arbitrary distinction on the part of the punctuators, and whether in all cases the word was not originally intended to be the prep. אִתָּה [1]. (1) There is no other indication of שכב being construed with an accus.—the *Qré* in Dt. 28, 30 ישכבנה obviously proving nothing as to the usage of the living language; (2) שכב עם is used constantly in the same sense (11, 4; Lev. 15, 33; Dt. 22, 22–29, etc.), and if so, עם and את being closely synonymous, there is a strong presumption that שכב את was understood in a similar sense.

15. וישנאה . . . שנאה גדולה] GK. § 117ᑫ.

מאהבה] Read מֵהָאַהֲבָה, which is needed.

16. אל־אדות וג'] The text is untranslateable: neither RV. nor

---

[1] In Ez. the form is indeed אוֹתָה; but in this book (as in Jer.) the *prep.* is constantly written אֹתָ- instead of אָתָ- (e.g. 3, 22): see on *ch.* 24, 24.

RV. *m*. is a rendering of it. The text of LXX has been corrected to agree with the Hebrew: but what is evidently the fragment of a genuine rendering has been preserved out of its place in *v*. 15, viz. μείζων ἡ κακία ἡ ἐσχάτη ἢ ἡ πρώτη=גְדוֹלָה הרעה הָאַחֲרֶת מֵהָרִאשֹׁנָה. Lucian's recension of LXX has Μή, ἀδελφέ· ὅτι μεγάλη ἡ κακία ἡ ἐσχάτη ὑπὲρ τὴν πρώτην ἣν πεποίηκας μετ᾽ ἐμοῦ, τοῦ ἐξαποστεῖλαί με; and similarly the Old Latin, 'Noli frater expellere me, quoniam maior erit haec malitia novissima quam prior quam fecisti mecum, ut dimittas me,' i.e. אַל אָחִי כִּי גְדוֹלה הרעה הזאת מֵהָאַחֶרֶת אשר עשית עמי לְשַׁלְּחֵנִי. This substantially must be adopted, the only question being whether in the middle clause we accept הזאת מהאחרת (Luc.) or האחרת מהראשנה (as in Cod. B). The former deviates least from MT., and is adopted by Sm.: but We. Now. prefer the latter, arguing that MT. מֵאַחֶרֶת (without the art.) attests indirectly the reading of Cod. B האחרת, and considering that the corruption of האחרת into מאחרת necessitated its transposition, and the alteration of מהראשנה to הזאת. Bu. expresses no preference. Either form, it is evident, expresses substantially the same sense. For אל in deprecation, comp. Jud. 19, 23.

17. אֶת־זֹאת] See on I 10, 27.

מֵעָלַי] not מֵאִתִּי, but מֵעָלַי, the word used of dismissing a menial (*v*. 9), or one whose presence was obnoxious, Ex. 10, 28 לֵךְ מֵעָלָי.

18. 19. כְּתֹנֶת פַּסִּים] Elsewhere only Gen. 37, 3. 23. 32. As to the meaning, the earliest authorities are divided; and it cannot be said to be established beyond reach of doubt. LXX in Gen. χιτὼν ποικίλος (so Pesh. here), here χιτὼν καρπωτός (i.e. with sleeves *reaching to the wrist:* so Pesh. in Gen.); Luc. here χιτὼν ἀστραγαλωτὸς (i.e. *reaching to the ankles*); Aq. in Gen. χ. ἀστραγάλων, here χ. καρπωτός; Symm. in both places χ. χειριδωτὸς (i.e. *sleeved:* Hdt. 7. 61); Jerome in Gen. (following LXX) tunica *polymita*, here (as Aq. in Gen.) tunica *talaris*. Targ. Onk. and Jon.[1] כִּיתוּנָא דְפַסֵּי, transliterating. פַּס in Aram. means the *palm* of the hand (Dan. 5, 5. 24; cf. the *fem.* I 5, 4 al. Targ.), or *sole* of the foot (Dt. 2, 5 Pesh.). Thus both alternative renderings have ancient authority in their favour. On the whole, however, as the explanation '*parti-coloured* tunic' implies a sense of

---

[1] Targ. Jerus. and Ps.-Jon. on Gen. פַּרְגוֹד מְצַיֵּיר (or מְצַיֵּיר) *a variegated tunic*.

פסים (*patches*), which has no sufficient philological basis, the other explanation 'a tunic reaching to the hands and feet' ('a long-sleeved tunic,' Sm.; 'a long garment with sleeves,' RV. *marg.*)—notwithstanding that *wrists* or *ankles* might have been expected to be named, rather than פסים (if the word be rightly explained as=Aram. פס)— is the more probable.

18. כי בן תלבשנה] Cf. Gen. 50, 3 כי כן ימלאו ימי החנטים.

מעילים] We. Bu. Now. Sm. Ehrl. מְעוֹלָם. The מעיל was *distinct* from the כתנת (*DB.* i. 625ᵇ, 3 *a* ; *EB.* Mantle : cf. Ex. 28, 4).

ונעל] so Jud. 3, 23. Cf. on I 1, 12 ; and GK. § 112ᵗᵗ.

19. ידה] Read יָדֶיהָ with LXX ; and see Jer. 2, 37 (Ehrl.).

ותלך הלוך וזעקה] The *waw* conv. and the pf. indicating reiteration, Jos. 6, 13. But read probably וְזָעֹק [so Stade, *Akad. Reden u. Abhandl.* 1899, p. 199][1], the normal construction : see on I 19, 23.

20. אמנון] אמינון is not a *compound* pr. n., and hence אמינון can be no alternative form (as אבנר and אבינר, אבשי and אבישי, אבשלום and אבישלום). In Arabic, the י is used to form *diminutives* (as *kalb* dog, *kulaib* little dog: Wright, i. § 269), even in pr. names ; and it has accordingly been supposed (Ew. § 167ᵃ, Bö.) that the form *Aminon* here is a diminutive used intentionally by Absalom, for the purpose of expressing his contempt for Amnon[2]. It is true, as We. remarks, that 'the Arabic inner diminutive-formation is akin to tendencies in that language which are foreign to Hebrew:' nevertheless, there are examples of forms and constructions occurring in *isolation* in Hebrew, which are idiomatic only in Arabic ; so that this explanation of אמינון must not be pronounced altogether impossible. The alternative is to treat י as a clerical error.—היה עם, as Gen. 39, 10. 14 (Th. Ke.).

---

[1] Not (Bu.) וְזָעֲקָה, which would require a preceding הֹלְכָה (I 17, 41): καὶ κράζουσα is no proof that LXX *read* וְזָעֲקָה: see 15, 30. Jud. 14, 9.

[2] So also Wright, *l. c.*, who adds, with Ew., as another example from Hebrew שְׁפִיפוֹן, remarking that the י‑ֽ in these two words must be regarded as a weakening of י‑ֽ (orig. י‑ֽ), as in גְּלִית. וְעַיִר in Heb., and ܟ̈ܠܝܐ *a youth*, in Syr., are almost certainly diminutives; perhaps יְמִימָה Job 42, 14 (for יְמִימָה a *little dove*, from Arab. *yemāmāh*, a dove) is another. See further GK. (Engl. transl.) § 86ᵉ *footnote* ; Lagarde, *Bildung der Nom.* 87–89; and on diminutives in the Mishnah, Segal, *Mišnaic Hebrew*, p. 64.

שׁת לב לֹ'] See on I 4, 20.

וִשְׁמֵמָה] 'and that desolate.' The ו is peculiar, though just defensible (GK. § 154ᵃ note (*b*); *Lex.* 252ᵇ): but probably it should be deleted. Or an adj. *may* have fallen out before it; but not יָשֵׁב (Bu.), for an *adj.* only follows הָלַךְ (see on I 14, 19). In form שְׁמֵמָה is a ptcp., either Qal (Siegfr.-Stade, *Heb. WB.*; *Lex.* 1030ᵇ), or Po'el (Kön. ii. 106) with the מ dropped, as happens sometimes, esp. 'where the ptcp. becomes a mere adj. or subst.' (Ew. § 160ᵃ: cf. עֹנֵן (beside מְעוֹנֵן), עוֹלֵל (beside מְעוֹלֵל), שׁוֹרְרִים (from שׁוּר) *insidious eyers*, often in the Psalms; and Kön. *l. c.*). The fem. with pre-tonic *ṣērē* is found both in an ordinary ptcp. in pause, even with a minor disj. accent, as here and Is. 33, 14 אֵשׁ אֹכֵלָה, and in a ptcp. used as a subst., as סֹחֵרָה, יֹלֵדָה a *buckler*, ψ. 91, 4 (Stade, § 214ᶜ; GK. § 84 *a*ᵃ). The forms שׁוֹמֵמָה, שׁוֹמֵמִים etc. recur Is. 49, 8 נַחֲלוֹת שֹׁמֵמוֹת 54, 1 רַבִּים. בְּנֵי שׁוֹמֵמָה. Lam. 1, 4. 13 נְתָנַנִי שֹׁמֵמָה. 16. Dan. 9, 26 (all with disj. accents).

סביר בבית [בית אבשלום (see on I 12, 5), quite needlessly: see p. 37 *note*.

21. וַיֵּחֶר לֹו מְאֹד] LXX after these words express וְלֹא עָצַב אֶת־רוּחַ אַמְנוֹן בְּנוֹ כִּי אֲהֵבוֹ כִּי בְכוֹרוֹ הוּא: which are accepted by Ew. Th. We. Bu. etc. as part of the original text. For עָצַב see 1 Ki. 1, 6; and Is. 54, 6 עֲצוּבַת רוּחַ (Th.). The words, if a gloss, are at any rate an instructive one.

22. לֹא דבר . . . למרע ועד טוב] i.e. anything at all. Cf. Gen. 31, 24. 29; and also לֹא יֵרַע י' ולֹא יֵיטִיב Zeph. 1, 12; similarly Is. 41, 23. Jer. 10, 5. למן in למרע, as 6, 19 (*Lex.* 583ᵇ).

עַל דְּבַר אֲשֶׁר] Dt. 22, 24. 23, 5: GK. § 130ᶜ *n.*

23. שנתים ימים] 'two years, days.' So 14, 28. Gen. 41, 1. Jer. 28, 3. 11†: for the pleonastic ימים, cf. חדש ימים, ירח ימים, and (in late Hebrew, Dan. 10, 2. 3) שָׁבֻעִים ימים: and see Ges. *Thes.* p. 585ᵇ; *Tenses,* § 192. 1; GK. § 131ᵈ. The לְ, to denote the *end* of a period, as Gen. 7, 4. 10. Ex. 19, 15 (rare): *Lex.* 517ᵃ b.

נוזים] Gen. 38, 12. Ba'al Ḥaẓor is probably *Tell 'Aṣur*, on an elevated height 4½ miles NE. of Bethel (Buhl, 177; *EB.* ii. 1979). For *Ba'al*, see on 5, 20.

עם אפרים] עם=*beside* is used to denote proximity to a town or other spot, as הם עם יבום Jud. 19, 11. 1 Ki. 1, 9, but not to a large area such as 'Ephraim :' were the tribe intended, as Th. rightly observes, the phrase used would be אשר לאפרים (I 17, 1 etc.), not אשר עם אפרים. Either אפרים is the name of some place not otherwise named, or the text is false. The supposition (Bö. Th. Ke.) that the place meant is עֶפְרוֹן 2 Ch. 13, 19 (עֶפְרַיִן Qrê) derives support from LXX (Luc.) Γοφραιμ (Klo.), though it is true that the ע in 2 Ch. is not represented by Γ.

'Ephron is mentioned close after Bethel and Yeshanah (cf. on I 7, 12) ; and has been thought to be the same as 'Ophrah (I 13, 17 ; LXX Γοφρα), prob. (see note) *eṭ-Ṭaiyibeh*, 4 miles NE. of Bethel, and 2½ miles SE. of Tell 'Aṣur, in the valley below it. Whether this distance is too great to be denoted by עם, will depend on whether Ba'al-Ḥaẓor was so much less important than 'Ephron that it was necessary for its position to be thus defined. But it is odd that the site of a conspicuous hill, such as that on which Ba'al-Ḥaẓor was (3318 ft.), should have to be defined by its nearness to a place (2850 ft.) nearly 500 ft. in the valley below it.

25. ויפרץ] Read ויפצר : see on I 28, 23. So *v.* 27.

ויברכהו] = bade him 'fare-well,' as Gen. 24, 60. 47, 10. *ch.* 19, 40 al.

26. וְלֹא יֵלֶךְ־נא] 'Precisely analogous examples of the same construction are Jud. 6, 13. 2 Ki. 5, 17. 10, 15 : the latter demonstrates incontrovertibly the correctness of the punctuation, and obliges us to render : *And if not,* let Amnon go with us,' We., excellently. Observe the disjunctive accent at וְלֹא[1]. Cf. *Tenses,* § 149 *end.*

27. כל־בני המלך] LXX adds משתה כמשתה המלך . ויעש אבשלום . The words may, indeed, be an addition, suggested by a reminiscence of I 25, 36 : at the same time an express notice of the feast prepared by Absalom is quite suitable, and their omission may be due to *homoioteleuton.*

28. טוב [כטוב . . . . ואמרתי] טוב with כ is of course the infin. of the *verb* טוב (I 16, 16. 23 etc. ; Est. 1, 10, as here). The tense ואמרתי as I 10, 8. 1 Ki. 2, 37 etc. (*Tenses,* § 118 ; GK. § 114ʳ). טוב, applied to the heart, as in Jud. 16, 25 כי טוב לבם (Qrê כְּטוֹב לבם); 19, 22 הם מיטיבים את לבם ; and comp. on I 25, 36.

---

[1] And so in 2 Ki. 5. In 2 Ki. 10, however, the accentuation expresses a false interpretation and is misleading. Render, ' And Jehonadab said, It is. *And if it is,* give thine hand.'

הלא כי] Cf. הכי 9, 1. Observe that *I* is emphatic.

חזקו וג'] Cf. 2, 7.

30. המה בדרך ו] See on I 9, 5.

31^b. Read with LXX וכל עבדיו הנצבים עליו קרעו בגדיהם.

32. שימה . . . כי־על־פי] . . . על פי may denote *according to the mouth*
(i.e. *the appointment, commandment*) *of* (AV.: see Ex. 17, 1 etc.), or
upon the mouth of (Ges.: cf. Ex. 23, 13. ψ. 50, 16): שִׂימָה (Kt.) will
here be the ptcp. pass. of שָׂם (cf. Nu. 24, 21), with the sense of
settled. The sense thus obtained is not unsuitable, though על פי is
not, perhaps, quite the phrase that might have been expected to be
used with שימה, and some clearer statement of the nature of the
intention then harboured by Absalom is certainly desiderated (cf. the
addition להמית 3, 37). Ewald's suggestion respecting the word, *Hist.*
iii. 234 (E.T. 172), deserves mention. Comparing the Arabic شَأَمَ
sinister et infaustus fuit alicui, شُؤْم *inauspiciousness, ill-luck,* he supposes it to signify *an inauspicious expression,* an expression boding
misfortune (Anglice, *a scowl*),—'For upon the mouth of Absalom
there hath been *a scowl* since the day when Amnon humbled his
sister Tamar.' The suggestion is an exceedingly clever one: the
only doubt is whether a word meaning in itself simply *unluckiness*
(Lane, p. 1490) could be used absolutely to signify *a token of unluckiness* (ein Unglückszeichen) for others. It is accepted by We.,
W. R. Smith (*Encycl. Brit.,* ed. 9, art. DAVID, p. 840^b *note,* cf. ed. 10,
p. 858^b), Now. Sm. Bu. does not decide between this and Ewald's
alternative suggestion שְׂטֵמָה (Ezr. 4, 6†).

33. ואל ישם . . . אל לבו דבר] 'let not my lord the king take aught
(דבר, not הדבר) to heart, saying' etc.: שם אל לב as 19, 20. In
form, as well as in the use of דבר, the sentence resembles I 22, 15
אל ישם המלך בעבדו דבר בכל בית אבי.

כי אם] So Kt.: כי Qrê. כי is sufficient (cf. 32); and אם may have
arisen by dittography from the following word: but כי אם is defensible,
the context suggesting the negative to be understood: Ges. (minime,)
sed solus Amnon mortuus est. Comp. on I 26, 10.

34. ויברח אבשלום] The words interrupt the narrative, and are an
awkward anticipation of 37^a. We. Bu. Now., unable to suggest
anything better, excise them: Ehrlich, very cleverly, suggests בחרב

אַבְשָׁלוֹם (forming the end of v. 33). No doubt, the narrator *might*
have written the words there; but they seem somewhat superfluous.
Klo. וְיֶתֶר אֶחָיו שָׁלוֹם (constr. as I 16, 4), which Bu. accepts.

מדרך אחריו] The text cannot be right. דרך cannot be in the
st. c.: and 'from *the* way' would need the art. EVV. 'by the way
of the hill-side behind him' is no translation of the Heb. LXX has
an insertion (καὶ παρεγένετο ὁ σκοπὸς καὶ ἀπήγγειλεν τῷ βασιλεῖ καὶ
εἶπεν Ἄνδρας ἑώρακα ἐκ τῆς ὁδοῦ τῆς Ωρωνην ἐκ μέρους τοῦ ὄρους), which
enables We. both to restore a text satisfactory in itself, and at the
same time to remove the difficulties attaching to MT. The text
as thus restored reads as follows : והנה עם רב הלכים בְּדֶרֶךְ חֹרֹנִים בַּמּוֹרָד

מדרך. וַיָּבֹא הַצֹּפֶה וַיַּגֵּד לַמֶּלֶךְ וַיֹּאמַר אֲנָשִׁים רָאִיתִי מִדֶּרֶךְ חֹרֹנַיִם מִצַּד הָהָר
is now provided with the desiderated genitive; and אחריו is seen
to be a corruption of חרנים[1]. The omission in MT. arose from
a copyist's eye passing from בדרך חרנים to מדרך חרנים. The *dual*
form חרנים does not occur elsewhere in MT.: but from the fact of
an Upper and Lower Beth-ḥoron being spoken of, it is probable
in itself, and it actually occurs in LXX of Josh. 10, 10. 11 (Ωρωνειν
for בית־חורן).

On the two Beth-ḥorons, see on I 13, 18. Upper Beth-ḥoron is
just 10 miles NW. of Jerusalem, as the crow flies. The road from
it would pass Gibeon, and enter the great North road 4½ miles N.
of Jerusalem. What particular 'descent' and 'hill' are meant, can
hardly, however, be determined. Notice הלכים *coming*.

35. באים] באים *are arriving* would be an improvement; באו *are
arrived* follows in 36 (Ehrl., who compares aptly Gen. 29, 6 בָּאָה,
and 9 בָּאָה).

37. Absalom takes refuge with his mother's father (3, 3).
עמיחור] Qrê עמיהוד, which is supported by the Versions.

37–38ᵃ. 38ᵃ is tautologous after 37ᵃ: at the same time, 37ᵇ—

---

[1] We.'s restoration was based on Codd. BA, which do not express the first חרנים,
but have for it ὄπισθεν αὐτοῦ (= אחריו); but he found afterwards (p. 222) that Luc.
had (τὴν ὁδὸν) τῆς Ωραιμ [so We. quotes; but Lag., with MSS. *ap.* Holmes and
Parsons, has τὴν Σωραιμ]; and other MSS. *ap.* H. and P., after ἐν τῇ ὁδῷ, have
the doublet τῇ Ωραμ (Ωραν, Οραμ) ὄπισθεν αὐτοῦ,—all with the same forms in *b*,
and all evidently representing חרנים.

as the *subject* of ויתאבל shews—connects closely with *v.* 36. In all probability a transposition has taken place, and the original order was 37ᵇ, 37ᵃ, 38ᵇ, 39 :—38ᵃ being no part of the original text, but due to a scribe who, having accidentally in the first instance passed over 37ᵇ, discovered his mistake, inserted it after 37ᵃ, and then repeated as much of 37ᵃ as was necessary in order to render 38ᵇ ויהי שם שלש שנים intelligible.

37ᵇ. ויתאבל] Insert after this word המלך דוד, with LXX.

39. ותכל דוד המלך] Untranslateable. The connexion with 14, 1 shews that the verse must describe the preparatory or initial stage in the desire which Joab soon afterwards perceived to be stirring in David's mind towards his absent son. Ewald, *Hist.* iii. 234 (E.T. 173), conjectured וַתֵּכֶל חֲמַת דוד המלך 'and David's anger *ceased* to manifest itself towards Absalom.' On this conjecture, We. observed : 'Though it satisfies the conditions imposed by the context, it is open to the objection that the sense assumed for צאת is not substantiated, and that חמת דוד ought not to be combined. For the unusual *order* דוד המלך (1 Ki. 2, 17. 12, 2. 2 Ki. 8, 29 = 9, 15 [1]) shews that it must be in דוד that the feminine required as the subject of ותכל lies concealed. It follows that instead of combining חמת דוד, דוד should have been changed into חמת, if no other feminine subst. is to be found which more closely resembles דוד graphically.' The acuteness and justice of this criticism were brilliantly confirmed, when We. discovered subsequently (p. 223) that Codd. 19, 82, 93, 108 (i.e. the recension of Lucian), as well as many others, actually expressed the substantive רוח ! Read, therefore, וַתֵּכֶל רוּחַ המלך וג' 'And *the spirit of the king longed* [2] to go forth unto Absalom.'

14, 1. וידע] *came to know* = perceived : I 18, 28. Jer. 32, 8.

2. תקועה] Teqoaʽ (תְּקוֹעַ), the home of Amos (Am. 1, 1), now *Teḳuʽa*, was in the hill-country of Judah, just 10 miles S. of Jerusalem.

התאבלי] '*feign thyself to be* a mourner :' cf. הִתְחַלָּה 13, 5.

זה ימים רבים] The זה is very idiomatic : I 29, 3 (*Lex.* 261ᵇ).

---

[1] And in *late* Hebrew, as 1 Ch. 24, 31. 29, 1. 9. 24. 29. 2 Ch. 26, 18. 21, etc., as regularly in Aramaic (דריוש מַלְכָּא, etc.).

[2] Lit. *failed* with longing to . . . : comp. ψ. 84, 3. 119, 81. 82. 123.

3. וישם יואב את־הדברים בפיה] Ex. 4, 15. Nu. 22, 38. Ezr. 8, 17 al.

4ᵃ. ותאמר] Clearly וַתָּבֹא must be read, with LXX, Pesh. Targ. Vulg., as well as many MSS.

המלך] LXX express הושעה a second time, after המלך,—perhaps rightly. The repetition would be 'in thorough harmony with the affected emotion which the woman displays in speaking to the king' (Th.).

5. אֲבָל] *verily, of a truth:* Gen. 42, 21. 1 Ki. 1, 43. 2 Ki. 4, 14. (In *late* Heb. with an adversative force: *Lex.* 6ᵃ.)

אשה אלמנה] So 1 Ki. 7, 14. 17, 9: comp. *ch.* 15, 16 נשים פלנשים. 1 Ki. 3, 16 נשים זנות; שתי נשים נביא, איש כהן, איש etc.

אֲנִי] Observe the pausal form with *Tifḥa,* where a pause in the voice is appropriate to the sense. So 18, 22: cf. Gen. 15, 14 יעבֹדו; Dt. 13, 5 תלְכו; Hos. 8, 7 יורְעו; *v.* 7 below שפחתֶך, and נשארה (perf.), etc.; and regularly in חַי־אָנִי. Cf. *Tenses,* § 103.

6. וַיכּו האחר את־האחד] 'And he smote him—the one (namely) the other.' Such an anticipation of the object by the pronoun, rare altogether[1] (see on I 21, 14), produces here, however, an intolerable sentence. Read, with Luc. (καὶ ἐπάταξεν ὁ εἷς τὸν ἀδελφὸν αὐτοῦ), וַיַּךְ הָאֶחָד אֶת־אָחִיו: probably ויכו was meant to be read וַיַּכּוּ, and arose from a false interpretation of האחד וג' (as though this meant *one another*[2]).

7. בנפש] the ב *pretii:* cf. Dt. 19, 21 נפש בנפש. Lam. 1, 11; and see GK. § 119ᵖ; *Lex.* 90ᵃ 3 b.

נחלתי] Ges. compares ζώπυρον 'de spe generis ad paucos redacta, v. c. de iis qui diluvio erepti erant, Lucian, *Timon,* § 3' (ζώπυρόν τι τοῦ ἀνθρωπίνου σπέρματος,—from Plato, *Legg.* 677 B).

שם ושארית] Cf. שם ושאר Is. 14, 22.

8. ואני] Note the emphatic pronoun.

10. המדבר אליך והבאתו] As a *woman* is addressed, וַהֲבֵאתִי should be read (We. Bu. etc.). The construction is exactly as Ex. 4, 21. 12,

---

[1] From Gen. to 2 Sam. the only examples are the few quoted in the note on I 21, 14. The usage is somewhat more frequent in later books; in genuine Hebrew it was never idiomatic except in the one expression אִישׁ, אָיִם (see *ib.*).

[2] Cod. B has the doublet τὸν ἕνα τὸν ἀδελφὸν αὐτοῦ,—τὸν ἀδελφὸν αὐτοῦ being the original rendering, τὸν ἕνα a correction after MT.

44. Is. 56, 6-7, etc. (*Tenses*, § 123 *a*; GK. § 116ʷ). Against מי המדבר (LXX, Pesh. Th. Bu.) there is (in addition to the ground urged by We., that the king thinks of a definite מְדֻבָּר, viz. the *Go'el*, *v.* 11) the syntactical objection that . . . מִי would not be followed by והבאתו (Zech. 4, 10 is doubtful), but by הָבִיאִי (or יָבִיאוּ): comp. on I 11, 12, and *Lex.* 567ª. GK. § 137ᶜ, cited by Bu., does not shew that this objection is unfounded.

11. מהרבית] Qrê מֵהַרְבַּת: the punctuators apparently treating the word as the cstr. form of the abs. inf. הַרְבָּה Gen. 3, 16. 16, 10. 22, 17† (Ew. § 240ᵉ *note*). In fact, however, the Kt. מהרבית is merely an error for the normal מֵהֲרֻבּוֹת (so Ol. § 258ᵇ; Keil; König, i. 537; GK. § 75ᶠᶠ). For the construction of הרבות לשחת, see on I 1, 12. The מן in מהרבות has its frequent negative force (*Lex.* 583ª).

'Destroy *any more*' (EVV.), however, is certainly wrong; for the גאל הדם had not as yet destroyed at all. The meaning is *destroy greatly* (2 Ki. 21, 6. Is. 55, 7). Klo. Sm. Bu. לְהַרְפּוֹת 'so as not to *let* him destroy:' but this seems hardly in line with the ordinary uses of הִרְפָּה—sq. acc. to *let go*, Cant. 3, 4, *abandon*, Dt. 4, 31 al., sq. לְ to *let alone*, as I 11, 3 (הֶרֶף לָנוּ), sq. מן to *desist from*. The idiomatic Hebrew for to *allow* is נתן לְ, Gen. 20, 6 etc. (*Lex.* 679ª).

משערת בנך] See on I 14, 45.

12. תדבר־נא שפחתך אל־אדני המלך דבר] 'Let thy handmaid, I pray thee, speak a word unto my lord, the king.' Observe the difference between the Hebrew and English order of words: the Hebrew order would, in English, be stiff and artificial; the order which in English is idiomatic would give rise to a weak and feeble sentence in Hebrew (דבר אל־אדני המלך). The object at the end, to the Hebrew ear, completes and rounds off the sentence. So regularly, as Gen. 42, 30 דבר האיש אדני הארץ אתנו קשות (not קשות אתנו as in Engl.); 43, 16 לא תכרת; Ex. 23, 32 לאכל את־העברים לחם; וירא יוסף אתם את־בנימין; 8, 15 ועשינו עמך חסד; Jud. 1, 24 להם ולאלהיהם ברית; Lev. 26, 16ᵇ; end; I 16, 1 *end;* 20, 34ᵇ; *ch.* 3, 20ᵇ; 10, 2; 12, 17ᵇ; 13, 33ª; 17, 13. 14ᵇ; ψ. 15, 3; 24, 4; 25, 15ᵇ; 26, 6. 9; 33, 7ᵇ; 105, 14; Mic. 2, 3 (not 'abnormal,' J. M. P. Smith), etc. Comp. on I 1, 4.

13. וּמְתַדֵּבֵּר] = וּמִדַּבֵּר (GK. § 54ᶜ), as Nu. 7, 89. Ez. 2, 2. 43, 6†, according to the punctuators.

כאשם] 'as one guilty'—in thus speaking the king condemns himself.

לבלתי] not '*in* not bringing back' (Keil), but *in order not* to . . .
The clause is epexegetical, not of כאשם, but of כזאת—the explanatory
inf. at the *end*, as 13, 16. 19, 20 (We.).

נדּחו] See GK. § 92^b *n.*

14. The application of the truth is to Absalom. Life may end
at any moment: when it is past it cannot be recalled: thou mayest
find this to be too true in the case of thy son, if thou leavest him in
banishment. 'And God doth not take away life, but deviseth plans
in order not to banish (further) from him one that is banished,' *i.e.*
and even God acts more mercifully than thou art acting. But the
text of clause *b* is doubtful. The antithesis is imperfect (doth not
take away life, but *recalls from banishment*); and the expression
thinketh thoughts (in this connexion[1]) is of doubtful propriety (We.),
as applied to God. Ewald's emendation (iii. 174) is easy (חׁשֵׁב for
וְחָשַׁב[2]), and yields a decidedly better sense: 'but God will not take
away the life of him that deviseth plans not to banish from him one
that is banished,'—the words being understood as an encouragement
to David to take steps for recalling Absalom. So We. Now. Bu.
Kennedy,—the last two, however, understanding 'from him' to refer
to Yahweh, who will visit with His favour the man who exerts himself
to restore to Yahweh and His worship one who, while in exile,
is banished from it (see I 26, 19).

לבלתי ידח] לבלתי with the impf. (virtually, of course, a *relative*
clause), instead of the usual *inf. c.*, as once besides, Ex. 20, 20[3].
Cf. מִן־יָקוּמוּן once, Dt. 33, 11, in place of the normal מקום[4].

15. ועתה אשר] 'and now (it is) that I am come,' etc. The construction is very unusual, אשר being in fact superfluous. See,
however, Zech. 8, 20 . . . עד אשר. 23 . . . בימים ההמה אשר.

---

[1] Jer. 18, 11 is evidently different: so also are Mic. 4, 12 ; Is. 55, 8. 9.

[2] For the misplacement of ו, cf. Jer. 2, 25 Kt. 17, 23 Kt. 32, 23 Kt. al.

[3] Either יבאו ישובו, or בוא שוב, must also be read in Jer. 23, 14. 27, 18, for
באו שבו, after לבלתי.

[4] כמים, Targ. הא כמיא, which illustrates Dan. 4, 43 הא כדי פרזלא. The
pleonastic use of הא *behold* in comparisons is frequent in the Targums : Gen. 49, 4
הא כמיא. Dt. 32, 33 הא כמרת תנינא. *ch.* 23, 4. Is. 5, 28. 9, 4. 18, 1. 21, 3.
10. 29, 16. 32, 6. 35, 6. 59, 5. 6. 60, 8. Nah. 2, 12 etc.

16ᵇ. להשמיד] The Heb. cannot be rendered '*that would* destroy me' (EVV.): restore הַמְבַקֵּשׁ (LXX) before 'לה.

17. כמלאך האלהים] The comparison as *v.* 20. 19, 28. I 29, 9.

לשמע] to *understand*, or *discern* ; cf. 1 Ki. 3, 9 לֵב שֹׁמֵעַ. 11 : cf. *Lex.* 1033ᵇ g, h. The ל=*in regard to :* see on I 12, 17 ; and cf. *v.* 25.

19. היד יואב אתך] Cf. Jer. 26, 24. 2 Ki. 15, 19 ; and with עֵ, 1 Ch. 4, 10.

אִשׁ [אם אש להמין softened from יֵשׁ: comp. Mic. 6, 10 הַאִשׁ † (text dub.: הַאִשֶּׁה ?) for הֲיֵשׁ. There are analogies for the softening in the *middle* of a word in Hebrew (e.g. צְבָאִים, טְלָאִים for טְלָיִים, צְבָיִים ; Stade, § 122; GK. § 93ˣ): but the softening at the beginning is very anomalous, and has really no analogy[1] except in Syriac (as ܐܝܬ itself = יֵשׁ: ܐܝܬܝܟ, ܐܝܬܘܗܝ; Nöld. *Syr. Gr.* § 40 C). Ew. § 53ᶜ cites as a parallel אִישַׁי 1 Ch. 2, 13 for יִשַׁי (as the name is written in *v.* 12). Probably both there and here the א is not original, but due to a late transcriber[2]. Cf. p. 120 *n.* The *construction* of ל ('ישׁ) אשׁ, as 2 Ki. 4, 13 (*Tenses*, § 202).

להמין] for לְהֵימִין : cf. Gen. 13, 9 ; and see GK. § 70ᵇ,ᵉ.

להשמיל] for לְהַשְׂמִאִיל : GK. §§ 53ᵍ, 23ᶠ.

והוא . . . הוא] emph. : cf. 23, 18. 20. Dt. 3, 28. 9, 3.

20. לבעבור] 17, 14. Ex. 20, 20†.

21. עשיתי] *I have done*=I do (GK. § 106ᵐ).

25. להלל מאד] lit. '*in respect of* praising greatly :' the clause defines the *tertium comparationis :* Gen. 3, 22 ye shall be as one of us לָדַעַת *in respect of* knowing, etc. Is. 21, 1 as whirlwinds in the South לַחֲלוֹף *in respect of* sweeping up, 1 Ch. 12, 8 כצבאים על ההרים לְמַהֵר (*Tenses*, § 205; *Lex.* 514ᵃ e *b*). הלל, as Gen. 12, 15 (Ehrl.).

26. ובגלחו וג'] The constr. is involved : 'And when he shaved his head—now it used to be from time to time when he shaved it, because it was heavy upon him, that he shaved it—he would weigh,' etc. והיה after an intervening temporal or other clause, is always resumed

---

[1] According to Ḳimchi, however, יְקֹטֹל was pronounced *iktol* (and therefore, to avoid confusion, the 1st pers. was vocalized אֶקְטֹל): GK. §§ 24ᵉ *end,* 47ᵇ *end.* But the examples (including אֵשׁ) cited § 47ᵇ *n.* are in all probability textual errors.

[2] The Massorah has here the note סביר יֵשׁ : above, p. 90.

either by the bare impf., or by the pf. and *waw* conv., so that . . . והיה
אשר יגלח cannot be rendered 'And it used to be from time to time
that he shaved it:' והיה can only be resumed by וגלחו. It is true,
either אשר יגלח *or* וגלחו is logically superfluous; but the case is one in
which the tautology would not be un-Hebraic: cf. Lev. 16, 1.

ימים לימים] = *every year*. So only here: cf. מימים ימימה I 1, 3 al.

מאתים שקלים] = c. $3\frac{5}{7}$ lbs. av. (*EB.* iv. 904ᵃ).

באבן המלך] For the standard, cf. the Ass. *manu sha-sharri;* מנין
בזי מלך (so many) *minas by that of the king* on the lion-weights from
Nineveh (8–7 cent. b.c.), Cooke, *NSI.* 66; *CIS.* II i. 1–14; and
almost the actual corresponding words in Aramaic (באבני מלכא) found
often in the Jewish Papyri from Elephantine (Sayce and Cowley,
Aram. Papyri from Assuan, A 7. B 14, 15. C 15 al.), with reference
to the Persian king. אבן=*weight*, as Dt. 15, 13. Pr. 16, 11 al.

27. היא היתה] as Gen. 4, 20. 10, 8: cf. p. 108 *n.*

28. שנתים ימים] as Gen. 41, 1 al.   See on 13, 23.

30. אל ידי] See on I 4, 13.

ולו שם שערים] See on I 1, 2; and cf. 17, 18.

31. החלקה אשר לי] See on I 20, 40: GK. § 129ʰ.

32. טוב לי עד אני־שם] 'it were well for me (that) I were still
there.' עד אני שם defines that in respect of which Absalom says
טוב לי.   Comp. Ew. § 338ᶜ. But עֹדֶנִּי would be better than עַד אֲנִי
in *early* Hebrew (*Lex.* 728ᵇ). Kön. (iii. 558) would read עַד אני.

ואם יש בי עון] Cf. I 14, 41 LXX. 20, 8.

33. לו] insert with LXX ויפל.

15, 1. ויעש וג'] Cf., of Adonijah, 1 Ki. 1, 5ᵇ. See on I 12, 6;
22, 17.

2. והשכים . . . ועמד] Notice the pff. with *waw* conv., indicating
what Absalom *used* to do. From 2ᵇ to 4, however, the narrator
lapses into the tense of simple description, only again bringing the
custom into prominence in *v.* 5, and 6ᵃ (יבאו).

ויהי כל האיש אשר . . . ויקרא] Exactly as 2, 23ᵇ, except that a subst.
and rel. clause takes here the place of the ptcp. and article.

כל האיש] The collective singular, as Dt. 4, 3; כל הבן Ex. 1, 22;
כל הבא 20, 24; ch. 2, 23. 20, 12; כל הראה Jud. 19, 30.
כל המקום 20.

3. דבריך] i.e. thy *statements, arguments*=thy *case:* Jos. 20, 4.

מאת המלך] 'thou hast none to hear *on the part of* the king.' AV.
excellently, '*deputed of* the king.' Comp. מאת of a grant *from*, or due
rendered by, a person; Gen. 47, 22. Lev. 7, 34. Nu. 3, 9. 8, 11.

4. מי ישמני] *Who* will make me ...?=O that one would make
me ...! so 23, 15 מי ישקני מים=O that one would give me to drink
water, etc.! and constantly in the phrase מי יתן: GK. § 151ᵃ⁻ᵈ.

ועלי יבא] 'that *to me* might come' etc. Note the position of עלי:
1 Ki. 2, 15; 2 Ki. 5, 11 behold, I thought אלי יצא יצוא ועמד that
he would come out to *me*, and stand, etc.; Gen. 30, 16. 43, 16.

והצדקתיו] The pf. and *waw* conv. in continuation of an impf. with
the force of a Latin imperf. subjunctive; exactly so Amos 9, 3.

5. החזיק לו] Read החזיק בו with some 30 MSS.

6. ויגנב ... את לב] 'stole the *understanding* (Jer. 5, 21. Hos. 4, 11.
7, 11 etc.) of,' i.e. *duped:* so Gen. 31, 20 ויגנב יעקב את לב לבן.

7. ארבעים] LXX (Luc.), Pesh. (שׁנים) ארבע,—*forty* years evidently
cannot be right.—The accentuation in 7ᵇ, placing the greatest break
after המלך at ליהוה rather than at נדרי, connects בחברון rightly with
אלכה נא ואשלם, not with נדרתי (see *v.* 8).

8. אם ישיב ישבני] Kt. ישׁיב 'if he brings back, brings me back,'—
an utterly un-Hebraic sentence. Qrê ישׁוב, from ישׁב *to dwell*, unsuitable beside ישבני will *bring back*. LXX ἐὰν ἐπιστρέφων ἐπιστρέψῃ με,
Targ. אם אתבא יתיבינני, Pesh. ܡܗܦܟܘ ܢܗܦܟܢܝ, i.e. אם הָשֵׁב ישבני in
entire accordance with idiom (e.g. I 1, 11).

ועבדתי את יהוה] add probably with LXX (Luc.) בחברון (see *v.* 7).

10. וישלח] 'The sending out of the spies is to be regarded as
taking place simultaneously with the departure of Absalom for Ḥebron,
so that וישלח is used quite regularly, and there is no ground for
rendering it [as Th. had proposed to do] as a pluperfect,' Keil,
rightly. To render by a plup. would be indeed contrary to grammar:
the plup. (see on I 9, 15) would have been expressed by ואבשלום שָׁלַח.

11. קראים] as guests to the sacrificial feast at Ḥebron: cf. I 9, 13.
22. 24. 16, 3. 5. 1 Ki. 1, 9.

לתמם] The same idiom in 1 Ki. 22, 34 משך בקשת לתמו. The ל
is expressive of norm or standard (Ew. § 217ᵈ; *Lex.* 516 i): comp.
לפי חרב etc.

ולא ידעו כל־דבר]='and knew nothing at all.'

12. וישלח וג׳] It is clear that Absalom did not, as he would do according to MT., send Ahitophel *out of* Giloh, but that he sent *for* him *from* Giloh. שלח את, however, cannot be rendered 'sent *for* ' (EVV.); and a word must have dropped out after אבשלום,—either וַיָּבֵא (cf. I 16, 12 Bö.) or, better, וַיִּקְרָא (We. with LXX (Luc.) καὶ ἐκάλεσε). ויקרא ל׳ is more common than ויקרא את: but את is perfectly admissible: see the similar passage I 22, 11. Ahitophel was Bathsheba's grandfather (cf. 23, 24 with 11, 3), which no doubt explains his hostility to David.

הגילני . . . מנלה] The form of the gentile adj. shews that גִּלֹה stands for an original גִּלֹּ, and that the root, therefore, is גיל or גול, not גלה (from which גִּלְיֹן, גִּלְיֹ, or גָּלֹן might be formed, but not גִּלֹה). So שילני from שִׁילֹה, root שול or שיל, not שלה. Giloh is mentioned in Jos. 15, 51 among the cities of the hill-country of Judah,—perhaps *Jâla*, 5 miles NNW. of Hebron.

הולך ורב] See on I 2, 26.

13. היה . . . אחרי] *is come to be* (Jud. 17, 13 : here = *is gone*) *after* . . .; cf. on I 12, 14.

14. מהרו ללכת] GK. § 114^{m,n}.

והדיח] *set in motion, drive, impel* evil upon us: comp. the *Nif.* in Dt. 19, 5 ונדחה ידו בגרזן. Usually the Hif. signifies to *ex*pel (especially of Israel expelled from their country).

16. ברגליו] as I 25, 27.

את] out of place before an indef. obj., and no doubt introduced by some error (cf. GK. § 117^d).

17 f. We. points out how here the genuine LXX rendering of 17^b–18 stands 'wedged in' between the two halves of another Greek translation agreeing closely with MT., the concluding words of the first half being repeated at the beginning of the second: [καὶ ἔστησαν ἐν οἴκῳ τῷ Μακράν. 18. καὶ πάντες οἱ παῖδες αὐτοῦ ἀνὰ χεῖρα αὐτοῦ παρῆγον καὶ πᾶς Χεττει καὶ πᾶς ὁ Φελετθει,] καὶ ἔστησαν ἐπὶ τῆς ἐλαίας ἐν τῇ ἐρήμῳ. 18. καὶ πᾶς ὁ λαὸς παρεπορεύετο ἐχόμενος αὐτοῦ, καὶ πάντες οἱ περὶ αὐτὸν καὶ πάντες οἱ ἁδροὶ καὶ πάντες οἱ μαχηταί, ἑξακόσιοι ἄνδρες, καὶ παρῆσαν ἐπὶ χεῖρα αὐτοῦ. [καὶ πᾶς ὁ Χερεθθει καὶ πᾶς ὁ Φελεθθει καὶ πάντες οἱ Γεθθαῖοι, οἱ ἑξακόσιοι ἄνδρες οἱ ἐλθόντες τοῖς ποσὶν αὐτῶν εἰς Γεθ, καὶ πορευόμενοι ἐπὶ πρόσωπον τοῦ βασιλέως]. The unbracketed

words in the middle are the genuine version of LXX, in which,
however, the close of *v.* 18 has dropped out, for καὶ παρῆσαν ἐπὶ χεῖρα
αὐτοῦ is merely a doublet to παρεπορεύετο ἐχόμενος αὐτοῦ. The only
variation, however, with a claim to be preferred to MT., is עבדיו for
העם in 17ᵃ, and העם for עבדיו in 18ᵃ. The עבדי המלך are influential
persons, in immediate attendance upon the king, and distinguished
from 'the people' generally (cf. e.g. 16, 6). Hence 'the reading of
LXX is right. The king and his attendants (כל עבדיו) remain at the
last house of Jerusalem, in order to let the people (כל העם) and the
body-guard pass. Only in *v.* 23 does David with his attendants
resume his progress.'

17. בית המרחק] the *Far House* (RV. *m.*),—probably the last house
of Jerusalem in the direction of the Mt. of Olives.

18. Notice the ptcp. עברים (twice).

וכל הגתים] prefix (Ehrl.) וְאִתַּי. As We. pointed out, 'after *him*
from Gath,' as the text stands, can refer only to David, which can
scarcely be right, whereas a notice of Ittai is needed here, as an
introduction to 19. With ואתי, the sf. in ברגלו (rd. ברגליו as 16. 17)
will naturally apply to Ittai.

19. נכרי] a *foreigner*, as always, e.g. Jud. 19, 12. Of course
'stranger' (from Lat. *extraneus*) meant this formerly: but it is a great
pity that this now misleading archaism has been retained so often
in RV. Similarly בן נכר (22, 45. 46), אלהי נכר (1 7, 3), etc., should
be always rendered 'foreigner,' '*foreign* gods.' See STRANGE,
STRANGER in *DB.*; or my *Nah.–Mal.* in the *Century Bible*, pp. 313,
314. The archaism is particularly obscuring in '*strange* gods,' the
point being that they are *foreign* gods.

וגם גלה אתה למקומך] 'going in exile *to* thy place,' explained by
Keil as meaning *in search of* a resting-place,—an improbable idea,
and also unnaturally expressed. AV. renders as if למקומך followed
שוב (!); RV. supplies 'return' in italics. In fact למקומך is simply
a copyist's error for ממקומך (LXX, Vulg.).

20. והיום אניעך] 'and to-day shall I make thee wander with us in
going?' For נוע in the sense of wandering up and down (properly,
with an unsteady, uncertain gait: see my note on Am. 4, 8) with no
settled home, cf. Nu. 32, 13 וינעם במדבר. Am. 8, 12. ψ. 59, 12 הניעמו

314 The Second Book of Samuel,

בחילך והורידמו (where Gen. 4, 12 נע ונד makes Lagarde's והנידמו for
והורידמו (*Proph. Chald.*, 1872, p. xlviii) highly plausible).

ואני הולך על אשר אני הולך] = am going whither I know not. See
on I 23, 13.

חסד ואמת] Explicable grammatically as an adverbial accusative,
'and take back thy brethren *in* mercy and faithfulness:' but such
a use of the accus., except in two or three familiar expressions (as
בֶּטַח, מְעַט, מְאֹד: Ew. § 279ᶜ; GK. § 118ᑫ), scarcely occurs in prose.
Keil and RV. (neglecting the *Tifḥa* at עִמָּךְ) render: 'with thee be mercy
and faithfulness.' Though not impossible, however, the construction
which this rendering implies is harsh: עמך is almost demanded by
את אחיך as its complement, and יהי is desiderated with חסד ואמת.
The difficulty of the verse is at once solved by LXX: שוב והשב את
אחיך עמך וְיִהְוָה יַעֲשֶׂה עִמְּךְ חסד ואמת 'Return, and take back thy
brethren with thee; *and Yahweh shew toward thee* mercy and faithfulness:' comp. 2, 6. The three words supplied have simply dropped
out of MT. by homoioteleuton.

21. כי אם ונ'] The Qrê is here right: כי has been changed into
כי אם by a scribe, who omitted to notice how the sentence ended.
Without אם, the sentence following the oath is in form (כי במקום...
כי שם ונ') exactly like 3, 9.

23. בוכים] κατὰ σύνεσιν, as Dt. 9, 28 (*land*, as here): cf. on I 17,
46 (*earth*). For the syntax of קול נדול, see GK. § 117ᶠ.

דרך את המדבר [על פני דרך את המדבר is an unparalleled and untranslateable expression; על פני, also, does not mean 'toward' (EVV.).
We. in his note on the passage suggested על פניו דרך המדבר, but
added 'It is probable that between the *st. c.* דרך and the genitive
המדבר another word once stood, of which את is a fragment.' Again,
his conjecture was found afterwards to be confirmed by Lucian's
recension, which reads πρὸ προσώπου αὐτοῦ κατὰ τὴν ὁδὸν τῆς ἐλαίας
τῆς ἐν τῇ ἐρήμῳ=עַל־פָּנָיו דֶּרֶךְ הַזַּיִת אֲשֶׁר בּמדבר, or, with less deviation
from MT., זֵית המדבר (Sm. Bu.). This reading may be unreservedly
accepted. The route must have lain across the Qidron valley, up
the N. part of the Mt. of Olives, by the then usual road to the Jordan
(cf. on 2, 24); and the זֵית המדבר must have been some conspicuous
tree near the spot where the uncultivated land began. והמלך עבר just

before, should, however, in all probability be וְהִמְלַךְ עֹמֵד. This is required, not merely by the restoration עַל פָּנָיו, but by the *context*, especially *vv.* 24–29. David *stood* in the valley of Qidron, while the people passed on before him: amongst them came Ẓadoq and Abiathar, who *set down* the ark while the rest of the people passed on; there followed the conversation with David, *vv.* 25–28. All this presupposes that David was *stationary* at the time. (On the interchange of ב and מ, see the Introduction, p. lxvii.)

24. Ẓadoq is mentioned here (except in the list 8, 17) for the first time.

וכל הלוים אתו] A mention of Abiathar is greatly desiderated the first time that Ẓadoq is mentioned; 'Ẓadoq and Abiathar' in *v.* 29 suggest strongly that ואביתר originally stood here, but that וכל הלוים אתו was substituted by a later scribe, whose point of view was that of the Chronicler (Bu. Sm. Now. Kit. Dh.).

ברית] Prob. a later insertion: notice ארון אלהים just afterwards, and also in 25. 29; and comp. on I 4, 3–5. So Bu. Kit. (*ap.* Kautzsch), Dh. etc.

ויצקו] 'and *poured out*' (!). Read וַיַּצִּ֫גוּ, and *set down* (6, 17. I 5, 2). In Jos. 7, 23 וַיַּצִּקֻם may be correct; cf. הִתִּיךְ 2 Ki. 22, 9.

ויעל אביתר] The words are obscure ('went up' whither?), and where they stand interrupt the connexion ('they set down the ark until all the people,' etc.): Luc. does not express them. Unless it might be supposed that עֹלוֹת (6, 17. 1 Ki. 3, 15) had fallen out after אביתר, the text would seem to be imperfect: perhaps the name of Abiathar was once more prominent than it now is, and the words quoted are a misplaced fragment. We. and others suppose its present imperfection to be due to an attempt, made in post-exilic times, to eliminate the name of Abiathar from it.

25. אם אמצא . . . והשבני] *Tenses*, § 136 *a.* So Gen. 18, 26. Ex. 23, 22. Nu. 21, 2 etc.

ואת נוהו] נָוֶה, as 7, 8 shews, properly denotes an *abode of flocks;* comp. Is. 65, 10 וְהָיָה הַשָּׁרוֹן לִנְוֵה צֹאן: Ez. 34, 14 תרבצנה בְּנָוֶה טוֹב. It is, however, of frequent use in poetry in the sense of *abode* generally: thus Ex. 15, 13 נְוֵה קָדְשֶׁךָ of Canaan, Is. 33, 20 נָוֶה שַׁאֲנָן of Jerusalem, Job 5, 3 of the abode of an individual person. In prose, the word

occurs only in 7, 8 (= 1 Ch. 17, 7) and in the present passage, where it
is used in the same general sense that is otherwise confined to poetry.

26. וְאִם כֹּה יֹאמַר] See on I 14, 9.   For הִנְנִי, cf. on I 14, 43.

27. הֲרוֹאֶה אַתָּה] 'Seest thou?' (Ez. 8, 6) i.e. dost thou see how
matters are? But the text excites suspicion; and many attempts
have been made to correct it. Keil would read הָרֹאֶה, and render
O seer: but the priest is never identified with the prophet; nor is
the term *seer* ever applied to him. LXX has ἴδετε, which may either
represent רְאוּ, or be a misreading of רְאֵה (15, 3. Gen. 41, 41 etc.);
and as the plural pronouns at the end of the verse and in *v.* 28, shew
that Abiathar and Zadoq are both present, either רְאֵה (Bu.) or רְאוּ
(Now. Dh. Kit.) may have been used here, according as David began
by addressing Zadoq in particular, or both together. With the text
otherwise as it stands, אַתָּה must go with what follows, 'return
thou:' but in view of the plural following and esp. of *v.* 29[a], it is
highly probable that for אַתָּה שֻׁבָה we should read אַתָּה וְאֶבְיָתָר שֻׁבוּ
(Bu. Now. Ehrl. Kit. Dh.).

28. בְּעַבְרֹת] *at the fords of.* So Kt., which *ch.* 17, 16 shews to be
more probable than בְּעַרְבוֹת *in the steppes* (Jos. 4, 13) *of* (Qrê and Verss.),
and which is preferred, after Böttcher, by most moderns (Th. Ke.
We., etc.). The word occurs only here, 17, 16, and 19, 19 (see note),
the usual term being מַעְבָּרָה, מַעְבַּר. The fords meant are probably
Machādat (the 'ford') *el-Ḥajlah,* and *Machādat el-Ḥenû,* 4 and 3 miles
respectively from the mouth of the Jordan (Kennedy).

29. וַיֵּשְׁבוּ] LXX, Bu. Now. Sm. וַיֵּשֶׁב, referring to the ark.

30. David here commences the ascent of the Mount of Olives.
The *ptcpp.* serve to represent the scene vividly, as well as state what
was happening at the time when David received the intelligence
related in *v.* 31.

עֹלֶה . . . עֹלֶה וּבֹכֶה] Cf. I 17, 41.

חָפוּי . . . חָפוּ] The word is an uncommon one. It recurs, joined
with רֹאשׁ, Jer. 14, 3. 4. Est. 6, 12.

וְעָלוּ עָלֹה וּבָכֹה] GK. § 113[s]; and on I 6, 12[a].

31. וְדָוִד הִגִּיד] Read וּלְדָוִד הִגִּיד (sc. הַמַּגִּיד), or, following LXX,
וּלְדָוִד הֻגַּד: הִגִּיד is never construed with an accus. of the person *to*
whom a thing is told.

32. וַיְהִי דוד בא] Cf. on I 7, 10; and add 1 Ki. 20, 39. 40.

אשר ישתחוה שם] The subj. may be either המשתחוה or דוד—'to the place where *men were wont* (or *he was wont*) to worship God:' the former is more probable. The reference is to some spot at the top of the Mount of Olives, which was frequented as a sanctuary, or place of worship. והנה לקראתו as I 10, 10; *ch.* 16, 1.

הארכי] LXX ὁ ἀρχιεταῖρος Δαυειδ = הארכי רעה דוד (cf. *v.* 37; 16, 16), no doubt rightly, the title being added naturally on the *first* occurrence of the name. In LXX the gentile name has been strangely Graecized —either by the original translators, or by a scribe, too anxious to improve his author's text (cf. p. 78 *n.*)—and combined with ἑταῖρος, so as to produce the compound '*Chief* companion.' The נבול הארכי was a little W. of Bethel (Jos. 16, 2).

קָרוּעַ כתנתו] 'torn *as to* his tunic;' GK. §§ 116ᵏ, 121ᵈ (*d*).

33. והית עלי למשא] Is. 1, 14 למרח עלי היו. Job 7, 20.

34. ואם העיר תשוב] For the position of העיר, cf. on *ch.* 17, 13.

עבדך וג'] The accents must be disregarded. 'If thou returnest to the city, and sayest to Absalom, "Thy servant, my lord, O king [see below], will I be: I was thy father's servant formerly, and now I will be thy servant," thou wilt defeat for me the counsel of Aḥitophel.' Read for ואני (1), introducing the *subj.*, אני (Bu. on Job 4, 6ᵇ), and probably also, in spite of Gen. 40, 9. 16 (*Tenses*, § 125 *Obs.*; GK. § 143ᵈ), for ואני (2). The construction of Ew. § 348ᵃ, adopted in *Tenses*, l.c., and ed. 1, is hard.

עבדך אני המלך אהיה] The separation of אני from its verb makes a very awkward sentence; and Ehrlich's אדני for אני is highly probable.

35. והיה כל ... תגיד] Similarly I 2, 36. 17, 25. 1 Ki. 20, 6ᵇ. See *Tenses*, § 121 *Obs.* 1.

37. רֵעֶה דוד] The same anomalous punctuation (for רֵעֶה in *st. c.*), according to Norzi, is found also in the best MSS. 16, 16 (where Hahn has רֵעֶה) and 1 Ki. 4, 5: cf. *ch.* 24, 11 חֹזֵה דוד; and GK. § 93ˡˡ. Elsewhere the form in use is always רֵעַ, except in Prov. 27, 10 Kt. (Qrê רֵעַ), the form רֵעֶה being only presupposed in רֵעֵהוּ (cf. לרעיך 12, 11). The term—of Ḥushai also 16, 16. 1 Ch. 27, 33 (רֵעַ)—was probably a court-title (cf. 1 Ki. 4, 5), as it was also in Egypt from an early period, and at the courts of the Ptolemies and Seleucidae (cf.

1 Macc. 2, 18. 10, 16. 19. 20. 65. 2 Macc. 1, 14. 7, 14. 8, 9. 10, 13. 14, 11) : see *EB.* s.v., and Kennedy, p. 272.

ואבשלום יבוא] *went on to enter: Tenses,* § 27 γ; Davidson, p. 69.

16, 1. מעט] only here of *space.* צמוקים, as I 25, 18.

קיץ] *summer-fruits,*—but fruits belonging to the *late* summer, the time of vintage (Is. 16, 9. Mic. 7, 1 : cf. Jer. 40, 10. 12), probably figs.

2. מה אלה לך] 'what are these *to thee, with reference to thee ?'* AV., idiomatically and excellently, 'What *meanest thou by* these ?' So Ez. 37, 18 *end.* Gen. 33, 5. מי לך כל המחנה הזה 8; and similarly Ex. 12, מה האבנים האלה לכם 6 ,4 .Jos. מה העבדה הזאת לכם 26.

ולהלחם] The ל affords an example of the accidental repetition of a letter from a preceding word, such as has taken place—though it is not there corrected by the Massorah—in Is. 32, 1ᵇ.

לעבר נאולים 10 ,51 .Is : לשתות העם 1 ,17 .Ex .Cf [לאכול הנערים (GK. § 115ᶠ).

3. הנה ישב] without הוא; cf. on I 16, 11.

ממלכות] See on I 15, 28. Read probably מַמְלֶכֶת.

5. ובא] Irregular. Restore וַיָּבֹא; cf. on I 1, 12.

בחרים] See on 3, 16.

גרא] Probably the Benj. clan of this name (Gen. 46, 21); cf. Jud. 3, 15 אהוד בן גרא.

יֹצֵא יָצוֹא וּמְקַלֵּל] Comp. Jer. 41, 6 הָלֹךְ הָלוֹך וּבָכֹה. The type is unusual: יָצֹא יָצוֹא וְקַלֵּל would be the ordinary one : see on I 6, 12. For the inf. abs. after the *ptcp.,* see also *v.* 13. Jos. 6, 13ᵃ,ᵇ. Is. 22, 17ᵇ אמרים אמור Jer. 23, 17 וְעֹטְךָ עֲטֹה. (GK. § 113ʳ *end ;* Kön. iii. § 220ᵃ).

8. והנך ברעתך] 'and behold, thou art in thy calamity.'

9. הכלב המת הזה] Cf. I 24, 15 כלב מת; II 9, 8.

10. Kt. כִּי יְקַלֵּל; Qrê כֹּה יְקַלֵּל פִי] The Qrê gives the best sense : *So let him curse, for,* etc. The Kt. is, 'If he curseth, and if Yahweh hath said to him, Curse David, who, then (*Tenses,* § 124), shall say . . . ?' so We. Now. But this is not very natural. LXX have καὶ ἄφετε αὐτὸν καὶ οὕτως (cf. Qrê) καταράσθω ὅτι κύριος . . . ; Luc. καὶ ἄφετε αὐτόν, διότι (Kt.) καταρᾶταί μοι, ὅτι κύριος . . . , whence Klo. Sm. Bu. . . . , פי יהוה אמר (as 11ᵇ) הַנִּחוּ לוֹ וִיקַלֵּל. Ehrl. פִי יְקַלְלֵנִי יהוה וג' 'If he curseth me, Yahweh hath said to him,' etc.

12. Kt. בעוני] i.e. בַּעֲוֹנִי *on mine iniquity,* i.e. the iniquity done to me.

But this would be rather חָמָסִי; and the sense expressed by LXX,
Pesh. Vulg. *upon my affliction*, i.e. בְּעָנְיִי, is altogether preferable. The
expression ראה בְּעָנִי (אֶת־עָנִי) פ' is a common one: I 1, 11. Gen.
29, 32. (Qrê בְּעֵינִי upon mine *eye*, which is interpreted by the Jews—
see A V. marg.—to mean my *tears!*)

קללתי] i.e. *the curse* uttered upon me: cf. (Ehrl.) Gen. 27, 13 קללתך.
According to Baer, however (p. 113), the Qrê קללתו is the true Mass.
reading.

13. הלך . . . הלוך ויקלל] Another irregular type. The normal וַיְקַלֵּל
should doubtless be restored. See on I 19, 23; and *ch.* 13, 19. For
the inf. abs. after the ptcp., see on *v.* 5.

לעמתו] 'over against him' AV. RV.: more exactly, *parallel with*
him: *alongside* him: Ez. 1, 20. 21.

ועפר] frequentative (I 1, 3). Either וְסָקַל for ויסקל, or וְעִפֵּר . . . וְסִקֵּל
(Ehrl.), carrying on קִלֵּל, would make the sequence more regular, and
be an improvement.

14. עיפים] The name of a *place* is imperatively demanded in
clause *a* (on account of both ויבא and שם in clause *b*). Either עיפים
is this place—though it has not the appearance of a prop. name, and
would naturally signify *weary* (LXX ἐκλελυμένοι)—or the name has
disappeared from the text, having either been corrupted into עיפים, or
fallen out beside it, owing to its graphical similarity with it. Lucian
after עיפים has παρὰ τὸν Ἰορδάνην=הַיַּרְדֵּן. Klo., ingeniously, suggests
עַד־עָפְנִי (Jos. 18, 24); but though 'Ophni was a Benjaminite town, we
do not *know* that it was in a suitable position.

וינפש] Ex. 23, 12. 31, 17†.

15. וכל העם איש ישראל] 'and all the people, even the men of
Israel.' But העם is superfluous and is not expressed in LXX. It is
further to be observed that throughout the narrative כל העם are
regularly with David: כל איש ישראל are with Absalom. No doubt
the word has come into the text by error from the line above.

18. לא] Here, of course, the Qrê לו is necessarily right (cf. on
I 2, 3). Notice the emphatic position of both לו and אתו: so e.g.
Dt. 6, 13. 13, 5. לו אהיה may mean either, '*His* will I be,' or
(Ehrl.) '*For him* will I be;' cf. Gen. 31, 42. Jos. 5, 13 *end.* ψ.
118, 6 al.

19. עבר ל' [לְמִי, as I 4, 9; Jud. 2, 13.

עברתי] Perhaps עמדתי should be read (Ehrl.): cf. 1 Ki. 12, 6. 8 al.

היה לפני [כן אהיה לפניך, as 19, 14 (see note): cf. עמד לפני I 16, 22.

20. הבו לכם עצה] Jud. 20, 7 הבו לכם דבר ועצה הלם: הבו לכם also Dt. 1, 13. Jos. 18, 4. The reflexive ל (*Lex.* 515ᵇ).

21. נבאשת את־אביך] See on I 13, 4.

22. האהל] *the* bridal *tent* of the Semites, which has survived, in the canopy of the Jewish wedding ceremony, to the present day (Sm.). The חֻפָּה of Joel 2, 16. ψ. 19, 6. Cf. W. R. Smith, *Kinship and Marriage*, p. 168 f., ed. 2, p. 199; *DB.* iii. 272ᵇ.

לעיני כל ישראל] Cf. 12, 11ᵇ. 12ᵇ.

23. כאשר ישאל] sc. הַשֹּׁאֵל. The Qrê איש is not needed.

17, 1. אבחרה־נא] LXX לי אבחרה־נא. The reflexive ל is idiomatic with this verb, especially where one person's choice is opposed, expressly or by implication, to that of another: Gen. 13, 11. Jos. 24, 22. 1 Ki. 18, 23 etc.

2. והוא יגע] a circumst. clause (*Tenses,* § 160; GK. § 141ᵉ).

רפה ידים] Cf. on 4, 1. For והחרדתי, see on I 15, 18.

3. כשוב הכל וג'] 'as the return of the whole, is the man whom thou seekest; all the people shall be at peace' (Keil, and substantially RV., disregarding the accentuation, which places the greatest break in the clause at הכל). This is explained to mean that if the person of David be secured by Absalom's adherents, it will be tantamount to securing the return of the people generally. But it is unnecessary to point out how awkwardly, and inaccurately, the comparison is expressed, and how little consonant with Hebrew style is the abruptness with which the last clause is attached to the one containing the comparison. The difficulty is removed by the reading of LXX, which exhibits the full text, of which MT. has preserved only a mutilated fragment; ὃν τρόπον ἐπιστρέφει ἡ νύμφη πρὸς τὸν ἄνδρα αὐτῆς· πλὴν ψυχὴν ἑνὸς ἀνδρὸς σὺ ζητεῖς, καὶ πάντι τῷ λαῷ ἔσται ἐν εἰρήνη = כשוב הכלה אל־האיש רק נפש איש אחד אתה מבקש וכל־העם וג' 'And I will bring back all the people unto thee *as a bride returneth to her husband: thou seekest but the life of one man,* and all the people will be at peace.' A copyist's eye passed from אל איש to איש; and the letters which remained were re-grouped (הכל האיש for איש הכלה) and

altered, for the purpose of extracting from them the best sense possible under the circumstances.

שלום] a (virtual) accus., the predicate to יהיה. The substantive verb, as Arabic shews, is construed—in pointed opposition to the principles of Greek and Latin syntax—with an *accusative*[1]. Elsewhere שלום itself often constitutes the predicate: see on I 16, 4.

5. קרא] Better, with LXX, קְרָא.

בפיו גם הוא] GK. § 135ᶠ.

6. אם אין אתה דבר] 'if not, speak *thou:*' אם אֵין (for which some 30 MSS. have ואם אין) as Gen. 30, 1 ואם אֵין מתה אנכי. Ex. 32, 32. Jud. 9, 15. 20. 2 Ki. 2, 10[2].

8. אתה ידעת את . . . כי וג'] i.e. ' *Thou* knowest that thy father and his men were mighty men;' as Gen. 1, 4 וירא את האיר כי טוב= ' And he saw that the light was good,' and frequently (GK. § 117ʰ *end*).

מרי נפש] Cf. Jud. 18, 25. Rather differently from I 1, 10. 22, 2.

ולא ילין את העם] 'will not *pass the night* with the people,' but, as an experienced man of war, will place himself somewhere where he cannot be surprised.

9. באחת] Read באחד : פחת is masc. (18, 17), the ת being radical; אחת arose probably from the following הפהתים. With באחד הפחתים, cf. 12. Gen. 37, 20 באחד הברות. Jud. 19, 13. 2 Ki. 2, 16; comp. also *ch.* 2, 18 כאחד הצבים (see note).

---

[1] Strictly an accus. of limitation—'will subsist *as peace*,' the accus. defining the manner in which the subsisting takes place (Wright, *Arab. Gr.* ii. § 41 : cf. § 44ᶜ, with Rem. *c, h* ; § 74).

[2] The athnaḥ appears to be right (against We.). Had it been a disjunctive question, meaning 'Shall we do after his saying, or not? speak thou' (i. e. had a *verb* to be supplied mentally after אם), אם לא, not אם אין, would have been in accordance with usage : see Gen. 24, 21 לא ההצליח יהוה דרכו אם לא. 37, 32. Ex. התשמר 16, 4 אם לא. Nu. 11, 23 היקרך דברי אם לא. Dt. 8, 2 הילך בתורתי אם לא. Jud. 2, 22: we have also האתה זה בני 21 ,27 in Gen. מצותי אם לא. אם לא. But in a disjunctive question אם אֵין is only used where יֵשׁ אם precedes, and where, therefore, a *subst.*, not a verb, has to be mentally supplied: Ex. 17, 7 היש ישׁ"י בקרבנו אם אין, Nu. 13, 20 הי"ט בה עין אם אין (in Gen. 24, 49 ואם לא after אִם יֶשְׁכֶם עֹשִׂים). דַּבֵּר is to be taken in a pregnant sense : Absalom invites Ḥushai not merely to say *whether* he agrees with Aḥitophel's advice or not, but, *if* he disagrees, to state his views in full.

בהם כנפל] בהם has no antecedent: read with Luc. בעם, ' when there fall (some) among *the people;* ' the first reverse among Absalom's followers will create a panic (*v.* 10).

השמע וישמע] See on I 16, 4.

10. חיל בן נם והוא] Whether הוא be taken as referring to הַשֹּׁמֵעַ, *v.* 9 ('And he, even (though) a man of valour '), or (Sm.) forwards to חיל בן נם ('And he, (I mean) even the valiant man '), the sense is forced, and הוא seems superfluous. Luc. והיה for והוא yields a much more natural sentence, and is probably the original reading (Bu. Now.). והיה will then be introductory, as Ex. 4, 11. 1 Ki. 17, 4. 19, 17. 20, 6 (*Tenses,* § 121 *Obs.* 1). EVV. do not translate הוא.

ימס המם] מסס, except in the poetical passages, Is. 10, 18. ψ. 58, 8 (ימאסו). 112, 10, is always, when used figuratively, joined with לב (Jos. 2, 11. 5, 1. 7, 5. Is. 13, 7. 19, 1 al.): no doubt in the thought of the speaker, though not in grammatical construction, לבו is sufficiently near to indicate what part of the חיל בן the words ימס המם referred to.

11. יעצתי כי] 'For' does not seem in place: יעצתי cannot give the *reason* for anything that has preceded. EVV. 'But:' but כי only means 'but' after a negative. Keil, better, 'Surely;' and there are places (*Lex.* 472ᵇ e) in which כי, even standing alone, and so unlike the cases noted *ib.* d, appears to have this meaning; but they are rare, and many also are doubtful: certainly, for instance, the meaning is not needed in I 17, 25. 20, 26 EVV. If any conjunction were needed here, it would be לְכֵן, not כי: this, however, has no support from the Versions, and is not a probable corruption of כי. כי]אַל[אֶל is the best suggestion that has been made (Ehrl.); and כי]אַל לְכֵן[would be better still. יעצתי יָעַץ כֹה כִּי (We. Bu.), after LXX ὅτι οὕτως συμβουλεύων ἐγὼ συνεβούλευσα, retains the unsuitable כי, besides being rather a heavy sentence, esp. before יָאֵסֵף הֵאָסֹף.

בַּקֶּרֶב הלכים ופניך] קֶרֶב *battle* is an Aramaic word, in Hebrew mostly, if not entirely, confined to late writers (ψ. 55. 68. 78. 144. Job 38. Qoh. 9. Zech. 14†). No doubt בְּקִרְבָּם *in their midst* should be read with LXX, Pesh. Vulg.

פניך]=thy presence: comp. Ex. 33, 14. Dt. 4, 37 brought thee forth בפניו *with His presence.*

12. באחת המקומֹת] The Qrê ובאחד must be right. מקום is so constantly masc., that in the three exceptions the text can hardly be right. In Gen. 18, 24 בְּקִרְבֹּה may well be the original reading, or the suff. in בְּקִרְבָּהּ might refer to העיר: in Job 20, 9 תשורנו might easily be an error for יִשׁוּרֶנּוּ, due to the preceding תוסיף; and באחת here, and in many MSS. (v. Kitt.) in *v.* 9, is probably due to the following fem. termination of מקומֹת.

ונחנו] 'and *we will light* upon him.' Others take נחנו as=אֲנַחְנוּ (as Gen. 42, 11. Ex. 16, 7. 8. Nu. 32, 32. Lam. 3, 42†); but a *verb* is desiderated. The verb נוח is chosen on account of the comparison with *dew:* it is used also of locusts (Ex. 10, 14) and flies (Is. 7, 19). כאשר יפול the impf. in a comparison, expressing what is *usual*, as regularly, e. g. 19, 4. Dt. 1, 44. Is. 29, 8 etc.

ולֹא נוחַר־בּו] ־ֵ for ־ַ, on account of the tone leaving it (GK. § 29ᶜ⁻ʰ). The jussive form is unusual: I 14, 36 (*Tenses,* § 50 *Obs.;* GK. § 109ᵈ). Read probably נֹותַר בּו.

13. . . . אל עיר] ואם אל עיר immediately after אם for emphasis. Cf. I 2, 25 (ואם ליהוה); Ex. 21, 9. יאסף=*withdraw himself:* cf. Ex. 9, 19; and אסף of *withdrawing* or *receiving* into a house (Dt. 22, 2; Jos. 2, 18; *ch.* 11, 27).

והשיאו] The *Hif.* only Lev. 22, 16 besides, in a different application והשיאו אותם עון *cause* them *to bear* guilt. Here *cause* (men) *to bring* ropes=cause ropes to be brought.

נמצא] The fut. perf. after עד, as after עד אם Gen. 24, 19; עד אשר אם *ib.* 28, 15 al.

14. לבעבור] 14, 20. Ex. 20, 20†.

15. כזאת וכזאת] So Jos. 7, 20. 2 Ki. 5, 4. 9, 12†. Cf. 11, 25.

יעצתי אני] '*I* (emph.) counsel:' 12, 28. 2 Ki. 10, 4 ואיך נעמד אנחנו. Is. 20, 6 ואיך נמלט אנחנו. Ez. 16, 60. 62.

16. אַל־תָּלֶן] The tone is drawn back by אל: see on I 9, 20.

בעברות המדבר] See on 15, 28.

פֶּן־יְבֻלַּע למלך] 'lest *it be swallowed up to* the king'=lest the king be swallowed up (i.e. *fig.* undone, destroyed: 20, 19. 20, and often in poetry). Impersonal passives occur, though rarely, in Hebrew: Nu. 16, 29 אם פְּקֻדַּת כל האדם יִפָּקֵד עליהם if *it be visited upon* them with (cogn. accus.) . . . Dt. 21, 3 אֲשֶׁר לֹא עֻבַּד בָּהּ wherewith *it had*

not been worked. 4 אֲשֶׁר לֹא יֵעָבֵד בּוֹ. Is. 14, 3 the hard labour אֲשֶׁר
עֻבַּד־בָּךְ wherewith (accus.) *it was worked* with thee. 16, 10. 53, 5
נִרְפָּא לָנוּ. Ez. 16, 34 וּזְנֶה לֹא־הָיָה וְאַחֲרַיִךְ. Lam. 5, 5 יָגַעְנוּ לֹא־הוּנַח־לָנוּ we
are wearied, *it is not respited to* us=we are not respited. יִבָּלַע לֹ׳
would be the passive of בִּלַּע לֹ׳ (as הוּנַח לֹ׳ in Lam. of הֵנִיחַ לֹ׳), the
לֹ being the *nota accusativi*, as I 23, 10.

17. עֹמְדִים ... וְהָלְכָה וְגֹ׳] 'were staying at 'En-rogel, and a maid
used to go and tell them, and *they* (emph.) *would* go and tell the king;
for they could not, etc.' The tenses are all frequentative, and express
how communication was *regularly* maintained between David and his
friends in the city. הַשִּׁפְחָה *the* maid—defined in the narrator's mind
by her being chosen for this office: from our point of view, *a* maid
(comp. on I 19, 13).

עֵין־רֹגֵל] mentioned in Jos. 15, 7. 18, 16† as on the boundary line
between Benjamin and Judah, and evidently at the foot of the valley
of Ben-Hinnom. In all probability the present *Bîr 'Eyyûb*, the 'Well
of Job' (? for 'Joab'), S. of Jerusalem, at the junction of the Valley
(נחל) of Kidron from the N., and the Valley (גיא) of Ben-Hinnom
from the W. See G. A. Smith, *Jerusalem* (1907), i. 108 ff.

18. וַיֵּרָא] On this particular occasion, however, a lad saw them
and told Absalom. The tense used, unlike those in *v.* 17, describes
a *single* act. Comp. the similar change to וַתֶּבְכֶּה in I 1, 7 b.

וּלְאַ בְאֵר בַּחֲצֵרוֹ] Cf. on I 1, 2.

19. הַמָּסָךְ] GK. § 126r: cf. on I 19, 13.

הָרִיפוֹת] Prov. 27, 22 אִם תִּכְתּוֹשׁ אֶת־הָאֱוִיל בַּמַּכְתֵּשׁ בְּתוֹךְ הָרִיפוֹת בַּעֲלִי
אָוַלְתּוֹ מֵעָלָיו תָסוּר.† The meaning is uncertain. No √רוּף or רִיף with
a suitable meaning is known. LXX αραφωθ; Luc. Theod. παλάθας
(cakes of compressed fruit); Aq. Symm. πτισάνας (peeled or pearl-
barley); Aq. Theod. in Prov. ἐν μέσῳ ἐμπτισσομένων (things *peeled*
or *brayed:* see πτίσσω in Liddell and Scott); Vulg. (both times)
ptisanas ; Pesh. ܩܘ̈ܛܐ (*hordeum decorticatum*, PS.); Targ. דִּקְלִין *dates :*
in Prov. LXX oddly ἐν μέσῳ συνεδρίου (cf. Tg. Pesh.). Something
that could both be pounded (or be the result of pounding) in a mortar,
and be dried in the sun, must be intended: but that is about all that
can be said. Kimchi *bruised corn:* so RV. Pointed רְפוֹת, the word
might=رُفَات (from رَفَتَ) *broken* or *crumbled pieces* (Lane, 1118):

but the sense *Abfälle* (Schulthess, *ZAW.* 1905, p. 357 f.) does not seem probable.

מפי החירת (so on I 12, 5), as Nu. 33, 8 מפי החירת (so Sam. Onq. Pesh. Vulg.) for מפני החירת. So Tg. Vg. and 10 MSS.: several other MSS. also have פי on the margin.

20. מיכל] The word is doubtful. مَكَلَ, even supposing that מיכל were a legitimate formation from it, is a word used of a well, meaning *to contain black and muddy water:* not only, however, is מיכל not a legitimate formation from a root מָכֵל, but the sense obtained would be questionable and unsatisfactory: Ges. rivulus *parum aquae* continens is arbitrary. Friedrich Delitzsch (*Ass. HWB.* 718ᵃ) compares the Assyrian *mêkaltu*, a word not hitherto found in a connected text, but explained in a syllabary as meaning a *water-trough* or *water-channel:* but such a derivation is precarious. The Versions render no help. LXX παρῆλθαν μικρὸν τοῦ ὕδατος; Luc. διεληλύθασι σπεύδοντες; Targ. כבר עברו ירדנא; Pesh. ܐܚܒܕܘ ܠܡܘܢ ܟܒ ('they have passed on hence,' continuing 'because they sought water and found none'); Vulg. (cf. Luc.) *Transierunt festinanter, gustata paululum aqua.* If the word be not corrupt, it is one of which the meaning is unknown. מִזֶּה אֶל *from here to* (Ehrlich) is a plausible emendation. Bu. suggests מֵהֵרָה.

22. עד אחד] Anomalously for אֶחָד: so Gen. 48, 22. Is. 27, 12. Zech. 11, 7. Obviously the form, though in appearance that of the *st. c.,* cannot be so really; though why in these four instances the vowel of the ultima should remain against custom unlengthened in the *st. abs.* (and so the *pathaḥ* of the penultima be preserved) it is impossible to say: the passages do not resemble each other in any other common feature; and the form אֶחָד occurs elsewhere too frequently in 'the flow of speech' (Ew. § 267ᵇ; cf. GK. §§ 96 Rem. on אחד, 130ᵍ), for it to be reasonably attributed to that cause, as Ew. suggests, in these four passages. As in many other cases, the anomalous form is due in all probability to an accidental corruption in the tradition which the punctuation represents.

לא נֶעְדָּר] the pf. in pause. The case is not one in which לא might, exceptionally, be construed with a ptcp. (*Tenses,* § 162 *n.*).

23. ויצו אל ביתו] i.e. gave his last directions to his family: cf.

2 Ki. 20, 1 (= Is. 38, 1) צו לביתך. In New Heb. צַוָּאָה is a *will.* It is a pity that the obscure 'set his house in order' has been retained in RV.

וַיֵּחָנֶק] In pause for וַיֵּחָנֵק: cf. on I 15, 23. The word exemplifies well the reflexive sense often expressed by the Nif'al.

24. מחנימה] On Maḥanaim, see pp. 241, 245.

25. ואת עמשא] Notice the order: עמשא is put first for emphasis.

יתרא] In 1 Ki. 2, 5. 32. 1 Ch. 2, 17 יֶתֶר.

הישראלי] The *Israelite!* הַיִּשְׁמְעֵאלִי *the Ishmaelite* must be read, with 1 Ch. 2, 17 and LXX (Cod. A) here; for a notice of another Ishmaelite among David's subjects, see 1 Ch. 27, 30.

נחש] In 1 Ch. 2, 16 Abigail is said to be the daughter of *Jesse,* and sister of Zeruiah (mother of Joab) and David. It is uncertain how the two statements are to be reconciled. Luc. and other MSS. of LXX have Ιεσσαι here (so Now.); but that may be a harmonizing alteration. According to We. (formerly), and Bu. בת נחש came in here by error from בן נחש just below. Now, however (*Isr. u. Jüd. Gesch.*[3] 56 *n.*), We. considers that greater weight should be attached to this passage than to Ch.: perhaps, if the word is correct, Naḥash was either the first husband of David's mother, or (if we were sure that Naḥash was a woman's name) a second wife of Jesse.

26. ארץ הגלעד] '*in* the land of Gilead:' cf. p. 37 *n.*

27. שבי] son of Naḥash, and consequently brother of Ḥanun (10, 1), whom David, after his capture of Rabbah (12, 29–31), had presumably made governor of the Ammonites.

לא דבר] See on 9, 4, where also מכיר בן עמיאל is mentioned as the protector of Mephibosheth.

ברזלי] no doubt, Nestle is right (*AJSL.* 1897, p. 173) in regarding this name not as connected with בַּרְזֶל, but as a compound of the Aram. בַּר *son* with זלי, the 'pr. n. of some person, place, or God.' Another ברזלי comes from Meḥolah (21, 8); this ברזלי has a son כמהם, a name presumably derived from ڪمه to *be blind,* and the other has a son עדריאל, who married Merab (I 18, 19), i.e. (from حبى) 'Help of God,' or 'My help is God' (=Heb. עֲזַרְיאֵל),—both likewise suggesting Aramaean surroundings (Nestle).

רגלים] 19, 32†. The site is unknown.

27^b–29^a. הביאו . . . משכב . . . ושבי] (1) for משכב LXX have δέκα
κοίτας καὶ ἀμφιτάπους, i.e. (δέκα, as Klo. acutely saw, being עֲרֻשֹׂת
miswritten, or misread, עֲרֶשֶׂת) עֲרֻשֹׂת מִשְׁכָּב וּמַרְבַדִּים 'couches for lying
down and rugs' (Pr. 7, 16. 31, 32†: cf. רבד, restored in I 9, 25).
(2) For the *order*, which is unusual, but adds emph. to the subj.
(*Tenses*, § 208. 3; GK. § 142^f *d*), comp. 2 Ch. 31, 6. There is,
however, an incongruity in the text, as among the things brought
to David לאכול those at the beginning are obviously unsuitable.
Insert הֵבִיאוּ after וכלי יוצר (Sm. Now. Bu.), and the difficulty disappears: we then get viz. '. . . brought couches for lying down, and
rugs, and basons, and earthen vessels; and offered wheat, and barley,
etc., to David and to his people to eat.' הגיש is rightly used of offering
food: Gen. 27, 25. Jud. 6, 19. I 28, 25.

28. סַפּוֹת] *bowls* or *basons:* סַף Ex. 12, 22. Zech. 12, 2. Hab. 2, 15
(read מִסַּף חֲמָתְךָ); סַפּוֹת 1 Ki. 7, 50. 2 Ki. 12, 14; סִפִּים Jer. 52, 19†.

וקלי (1)] *parched corn,*—a common food in the East (*DB*. ii. 27^b):
I 17, 17. 25, 18. Lev. 23, 14. Ru. 2, 14†; cf. Lev. 2, 14 אביב קלוי באש.
Jos. 5, 11 (קָלוּי).

פול] *beans* (Ez. 4, 9†); and עדשים *lentils* (23, 11. Gen. 25, 34. Ez.
4, 9†): see *DB*. iii. 28.

וקלי (2)] not expressed in LXX, Pesh.; and evidently repeated
by error.

29. שְׁפוֹת בקר] *שׁ'* only here: LXX σαφφωθ βοῶν, Luc. γαλαθηνὰ
μοσχάρια *sucking calves;* Targ. גובנין דחלב תורין *cheeses of kine's milk;*
Pesh. ܓ̈ܒܢܐ ܕܬܘܪܐ *cheeses of kine* (so EVV.). 'Cheeses' would be not
unsuitable: but how שפות would come to mean this, is not apparent.
Wetzstein (*ZAW.* 1883, p. 276), upon doubtful grounds, would render
cream; Kennedy (*EB*. iii. 3091) emends שָׁאֲפוֹת (from שאף = שׁוף to
crush), which he conjectures to have meant *dried curds*, which, 'rubbed
down' and mixed with water, form a refreshing beverage.

18, 2. וישלח] Luc. ἐτρίσσευσε=וַיְשַׁלֵּשׁ: which, as the less common
word, is the more likely to be original (Sm.). So Klo. Bu. Ehrl., etc.

3. לא ישימו אלינו לב] Cf. on 19, 20.

כי עתה וג'] 'for now there are ten thousand such as we,'—which
yields no sense agreeable to the context. Read with LXX, Symm.
Vulg. אַתָּה for עַתָּה: 'for *thou art* the like of us (being) ten thousand'

= for thou art worth ten thousand of us. עתה and אתה are elsewhere confused, cf. 1 Ki. 1, 18. 20 MT. and Versions.

מעיר] the art. is needed. Read either מֵהָעִיר, or בָּעִיר (LXX), followed by either לְעֶזֶר or לַעֲנָר.

לעזיר Kt.] i.e. לְהַעֲזִיר=לַעֲזִיר (as I 2, 28). But a *Hif.* of עזר is doubtful (on 2 Ch. 28, 23, cf. on I 21, 7), and the yod may have readily found its way into the word through the influence of the preceding עיר. Read with the Qrê the *Qal* לַעְזוֹר.

4. למאות] Cf. I 29, 2.

5. לאט־לי] ל in לאט=*gently,* as in לבטח (on *ch.* 15, 11). לי lit. *for me*=I pray: comp. 2 Ki. 4, 24 אל תעצר־לי לרכב slacken *me* not the riding, except I tell thee; and above, on I 20, 20.

6. אפרים] Luc. Μααιναν=מַחֲנַיִם, which Klo. adopts. However, a יער, even on the E. of Jordan, might, from some circumstance unknown to us, have been called the יער אפרים (cf. *H. G.* 335 *n.*).

7. ותהי שם ....] 'And the slaughter was there great on that day,' etc. (not, as RV., 'And there was a great slaughter there that day:' notice the art.; and cf. I 4, 10). The שם, however (*together with* ביום ההוא), overweights the clause, and is not expressed by LXX. Probably it was introduced here by error from the line below where it is in place.—After עשרים אלף add, with LXX, איש.

8. נפצות] The punctuation נַפְצוּת is hardly probable: it is better to follow the Qrê נָפוֹצֶת, and to suppose that ו has become misplaced: cf. on *ch.* 14, 14.

9. ויקרא .... לפני] 'And Absalom happened by chance (1, 6: with לפני, Dt. 22, 6) before ...,' i.e. came in front of them accidentally.

ואבשלום רכב] a circumst. clause: cf. on I 19, 9.

ויתן] and he *was set* or *put.* LXX καὶ ἐκρεμάσθη, Pesh. Targ. ﺍﻟﺗﻟﻭ=וַיִּתָּל (cf. 10), perhaps rightly (so Bu. Sm. Now. Dh.). At least הַתָּן does not occur elsewhere in a similar connexion.

10. איש אחד] I 1, 1.

11. והנה ראית ומדוע] 'and lo, thou sawest ...,' a more vivid way of expressing 'and if thou sawest:' comp. on I 9, 7 והנה נלך ומה נביא לאיש; and וְהֵן Ex. 4, 1.

ועלי לתת] 'and it would have been *incumbent on* me, would have *devolved upon* me to give:' על as Neh. 13, 13 ועליהם לחלק לאחיהם; היה על 1 Ki. 4, 7ᵇ; cf. ψ. 56, 13 עָלַי נדריך, etc. (*Lex.* 753 c).

חגורה‎] a girdle would be a welcome present; for it was a necessary part of a soldier's accoutrement. Comp. 1 Ki. 2, 5; and notice the phrase for doing military service, 2 Ki. 3, 21 מכל חֹגֵר חֲגֹרָה ומעלה‎, and 1 Ki. 20, 11 אל יתהלל חֹגֵר כִּמְפַתֵּחַ‎.

12. וְלֹא אנכי שֹׁקֵל ... לֹא אשלח‎] 'And though *I were weighing*' etc. The sequence of tenses exactly as ψ. 81, 14–17; 2 Ki. 3, 14 (with לולי‎): *Tenses*, § 145. We. Bu. Now., on the ground that the payer, not the receiver, 'weighs' the money, would read שֹׁקֵל (אלף כסף‎ the subj., and אנכי‎ *casus pendens*, GK. § 145ᵃ): but the construction is forced, and (Sm.) the meaning seems to be, 'If I were to *feel the weight* of the money paid into my hand.' LXX ἵστημι (=שָׁקֵל‎). וְ is used as in *v.* 11, to subjoin an emphatic exclamation: see on 24, 3.

באזנינו‎] immediately follows כי‎, as the emph. word in the sentence.

שמרו־מי בנער‎] 'Have a care, *whosoever ye be*, of the young man.' Such, if the text be correct, must be the sense of מי‎, on the analogy of מה‎ *v.* 22. I 19, 3, though no example occurs even of מה‎ entirely parallel. LXX φυλάξατέ μοι, Pesh. ܘܰܛܰܪܘ ܠܺܝ‎, i.e. שמרו־לי‎: לי‎ as *v.* 5, probably rightly (so Bu. Now. Sm.).

13. אוֹ עשיתי בנפשו שקר‎] 'Or if (GK. § 159ᶜᶜ) I had dealt against his life falsely (lit. had wrought falsehood against his soul)—and nothing is hid from the king—then (*Tenses*, § 124) thou wouldst stand aloof' (i.e. wouldst do nothing to shield me). LXX joins the first three words to *v.* 12ᵇ, reading μὴ ποιῆσαι κτλ. i.e. מֵעֲשׂוֹת בנפשו שקר‎— 'Have a care, I pray you, of the young man, even of Absalom, so as not to deal against his life falsely.' But this does not agree with what follows: for ואתה תתיצב מנגד(ו)‎ cannot mean 'and thou wouldst have to stand *before him* (the king): ' מנגד‎ never means simply *in the presence of*, but either '*from* the presence of' (Is. 1, 16) or (absolutely) *at a distance* (Gen. 21, 16. 2 Ki. 3, 22. 4, 25), *aloof*.

14. לֹא־כֵן אחילה לפניך‎] 'Not so would I fain wait (I 10, 8) before thee,' i.e. I will not delay here in your presence—while you are making up your mind—on any such pretexts as you allege. לא‎ must be regarded as negativing כן‎, not joined with the cohort. (which would require אל‎). The sense thus obtained is not, however, very good. LXX, in the first of its two renderings (διὰ τοῦτο ἐγὼ ἄρξομαι—the second being οὐχ οὕτως μενῶ), which is the only one in Luc., and Targ. express לָכֵן אָנֹכִי אָחֵלָּה‎ 'Therefore (see on I 28, 2) *I* will

begin before thee;' so Bu. Now. Kit. Dh. Ehrlich's conjecture yields a thought more in accordance with Joab's sturdy independence : לֹא כֵן אֲחִלָּה פָנָיו 'Not so will I court his (the king's) favour!'

שבטים] *rods* or *clubs* (II 23, 21 ; ψ. 23, 4), which, however, would not be thrust into the heart. Read, with LXX βέλη, שְׁלָחִים *darts* (so Th. We. Bu. Now. etc.).

עודנו חי] Cf. 12, 21; 1 Ch. 12, 1 : *Tenses,* § 161 *Obs.* 2 ; GK. § 156ᶜ. Bu. rightly objects to beginning *v.* 15 with עודנו חי (Th. Now. al.). To express the sense 'While he was yet alive, ten young men surrounded him,' Heb. idiom would require (though in the examples we have of the construction, עוד is usually followed by a *ptcp.*) (וַיָּסֹבּוּ) : עודנו חי (not וְהוּא עוד חי (Sm.) וַעֲשָׂרָה נערים ... סָבְבוּ וג'. see Nu. 11, 33 הבשר עודנו בין שניהם ... וְאַף י"י חרה בעם. ψ. 78, 30 f. : cf. on I 14, 19 ; and see *Lex.* 729ᵃ ; *Tenses,* § 169.

בלב האלה] לב as in the phrases בלב־ים Ex. 15, 8 al. in the *heart* of the sea; בלב ימים ψ. 46, 3 al.: עד־לב השמים Dt. 4, 11.

16. מִרְדֹּף] See on I 23, 28.

17. ויציבו] ויקימו would be better (Bu.): see Jos. 7, 26. 8, 29.

18. לקח] For this use of לקח, cf. 17, 19. (In Nu. 16, 1 וַיָּקֶם must be read: so Bö. We. Dillm. etc.)

את מצבת] Elsewhere, except Is. 6, 13 (in a different sense), the abs. form is always מַצֵּבָה. The absence of the art. is irregular (on I 24, 6; *ch.* 1, 10); and no doubt המצבת should be read. מצבה in the sense of a sepulchral stele occurs Gen. 35, 20 ; and the corresponding Phoen. form מצבת occurs often in this sense, as Cooke, *NSI.* 15, 1 (see the note). 16, 1. 18, 1 (=*CIS.* i. 58) מצבת בחים אש יטנא עבדאסר לאבי לארכתא 'The pillar among the living (the *cippus inter vivos,* also, in *CIS.* i. 59) which 'Abd-osir set up to his father, to Archetha,' 19, 1 (all from Kition in Cyprus). No. 16 is an instance of a pillar, like Absalom's, set up by the person himself whose grave it marks. 'I 'Abd-osir ... set up (this) pillar in my life-time over my resting-couch for ever.'

בעמק המלך] Gen. 14, 17†.

על שמו] *according to* his name : Ex. 28, 21 al. (*Lex.* 754ᵃ).

יד אבשלום] יד as I 15, 12 in the sense of *sign, monument.* Ct. Is. 56, 5 יָד וָשֵׁם.

19. כי שפטו יהוה מיד איביו] Cf. *v.* 31, and on I 24, 16.

20. כִּי עַל בֵן [כי על כן (Gen. 18, 5 al.: *Lex.* 475[b]) must be read with
the Qrê: כן has fallen out before the following בן.

21[b]. כושי] No doubt הכושי should be read, as *vv.* 21[a]. 22. 23. 31.
32. The reference is to some particular Cushite (i.e. Nubian) slave,
or negro (Jer. 13, 23), among David's attendants.

22. ויסף ... ויאמר] GK. § 121[d].

מה [ויהי מה as Job 13, 13 החרישו ממני ואדברה אני ויעבר עלי מה=
and let come upon me *what will* (*Lex.* 553[b] c).

למה זה אני צם 12, 23 [למה זה אתה רץ.

ולכה] Merely an orthographic variation for וּלֵךְ: see on I 1, 26.

אין בשרה מצאת] Probably 'no message *finding* or *attaining* (aught),'
i.e. no message that will secure you a reward (cf. LXX εἰς ὠφελίαν).
But the expression is peculiar: and other suggestions have been made
with regard to it. RV. *m.*, Ehrl. 'no *sufficient* message:' but it is
doubtful whether מצא itself *means* to 'suffice,' and whether in the
three passages (Nu. 11, 22 *bis*. Jud. 21, 14) in which מצא(ו)להם is so
rendered, the rend. is not a paraphrase, the lit. rend. being '*one*
(or *they*) *found* for them' (cf. the Nif., lit. *be found*, Jos. 17, 16. Zech.
10, 10: the emend. אֶמְצָאָה לְיֹשְׁבֵי יְרוּשָׁלִם *ib.* 12, 5 is very doubtful).
We. Bu. Now. punctuate מָצֵאת (Hof.) 'no reward for good tidings
(as 4, 10) will be *brought forth* (= *paid out*) to thee:' cf. הוֹצִיא, יָצָא
2 Ki. 12, 13. 12, and فَصَّ, لَفَّصَ, frequently.

23. ויהי מה] Prefix, with LXX, ויאמר, as Hebrew idiom requires.

דרך הככר] *by the way of* (i.e. here *through*) *the Oval*, viz. of Jordan.
The word bears a specific geographical sense, and denotes the broad,
and somewhat elongated plain into which the Jordan-valley expands
N. of the Dead Sea[1]: Gen. 13, 12 ערי הככר. 19, 17. 25. 29. Dt.
34, 3; ארץ הככר Gen. 19, 28; ככר הירדן Gen. 13, 10. 11. 1 Ki. 7, 46.
ככר means properly a *round;* but as this plain is not circular, perhaps
we might represent the word by the term *Oval*. The meaning of the
passage will be that, while the Cushite went straight across the mountains from the 'wood of Ephraim' to Maḥanaim, Aḥima'az made
a *détour*, coming down into the Jordan-valley, and then following
the high road through it, and up whatever wādy it might be (see

---

[1] In Genesis it seems indeed to include more: see my note on 13, 10; and cf.
DB. iii. s.v. PLAIN, 4; iv. s.v. VALE OF SIDDIM, and ZOAR (pp. 986[b]-987[a]).

pp. 241, 245), which led to Maḥanaim.   The route, though longer, was easier and quicker than the one taken by the negro.

24. בֵּין שְׁנֵי הַשְּׁעָרִים] i.e. in the space between the outer and inner gates of the city gateway.

25. וַיֵּלֶךְ הָלוֹךְ וְקָרֵב] See on I 14, 19.

26. אֶל הַשֹּׁעֵר] 'to the *porter.*'   LXX, Pesh. Vulg. vocalized אֶל הַשַּׁעַר, which is accepted even by Keil as preferable to MT.: the king was sitting *within* the gateway, *v.* 24, the watchman called out directly to him, *v.* 25, and here, *v.* 26ᵇ, receives from him an immediate reply : he called, therefore, not to the porter, but *into the gate,* addressing himself directly to David.

וַיֹּאמֶר הִנֵּה אִישׁ] Add, with LXX, אַחֵר.

28. וַיִּקְרָא] We. cleverly וַיִּקְרַב,—evidently unaware that his conjecture was supported by Lucian καὶ προσῆλθεν 'Αχιμαας.   In 27, Aḥima'az is still at a distance : his *drawing near* is just a point which a Hebrew narrator would mention, before stating that he addressed the king.

לְאַפְּיו] In spite of Gen. 48, 12. Nu. 22, 31. I 20, 41 (see on I 25, 23), אַפּיו should probably be read, the לְ being repeated by error from the preceding לַמֶּלֶךְ (cf. Is. 32, 1ᵇ).

29. שָׁלוֹם] The Massorah (see Norzi, *Minḥath Shai,* ad loc.) has a note ג׳ סבירין הֲשָׁלוֹם (above, on I 12, 5), viz. here, I 16, 4, and 2 Ki. 9, 19.   So 16 MSS. (see de Rossi).   And we have הֲשָׁלוֹם in *v.* 32.   But see note on I 16, 4.

רָאִיתִי וְג׳] Keil: 'I saw the great commotion at Joab's sending the servant of the king and thy servant.'   But the position of יוֹאב makes this rendering impossible.   In all probability אֶת עֶבֶד הַמֶּלֶךְ is a correction, intended as a substitute for the less courtly *second* person אֶת עַבְדְךָ.   The correction found its way into the text, in a wrong place, by the side of the original reading, and the conjunction ו was added, for the purpose of producing the semblance of a coherent sentence.   Read, therefore, רָאִיתִי הֶהָמוֹן הַגָּדוֹל לִשְׁלֹחַ (פִּשְׁלֹחַ) יוֹאָב אֶת עַבְדְךָ.   So We. Kp. Stade, Klo. etc.—For מָה, cf. Pr. 9, 13. I 19, 3.   Bu. Sm., however, suggest לֹא יָדַעְתִּי מַה־הוּא.

לִשְׁלֹחַ] Though לְ with the inf. is used in certain phrases, as לִפְנוֹת

ערב, to denote time (GK. § 114^f *n.*; *Lex.* 517^a 6 a *end*), in a case like this analogy strongly requires 'כ or 'ב. So Bu. etc.

19, 1. וירגז] רגז is to *shake* or *be agitated* with some force, e.g. of mountains, Is. 5, 25: it is also often used of strong *mental* agitation, sometimes in anger (Is. 28, 21), more often fear (Is. 32, 10. 11: comp. the לב רַגָּז of Dt. 28, 65). Here, not so much definitely in grief, as through the shock which paralysed and unnerved the king.

עלית השער] The עליה, or *roof-chamber*, was a chamber built on the flat roof of an Oriental house (see illustr. in Moore, *Judges, SBOT.* Engl. ed., p. 59), Jud. 3, 20. 1 Ki. 17, 19. 2 Ki. 1, 2 al. Here of a similar chamber on the top of the gateway.

וכה אמר בלכתו וג'] The entire narrative is remarkable for both its minuteness and its vividness; but especially so just here. We. (*Compos. des Hex.*, p. 262) calls attention to the graphic בלכתו. Luc. and other MSS. of LXX, read, however, בְּבֹכתו, which Bu. Sm. Ehrl. prefer. Observe in what follows the feeling which David throws into the expression of his sorrow by the addition of the pronoun מי יתן מותי אני תחתיך אבשלום בני בני (GK. § 135^f). On מי יתן מותי, see GK. § 151^b; *Lex.* 678^b f.

2. בָּכֹה וַיִּתְאַבֵּל] *Tenses*, § 80.

4. ויתגנב . . . לבוא] Very idiomatic: see GK. § 114^n (with *n.*); and cf. Gen. 31, 27.

העם הנכלמים] The art. is generic, as constantly after כ and כאשר (GK. § 126°).

5. לָּאט] Only here: comp. הֵלִיט, לוּט I 21, 10. 1 Ki. 19, 13. Is. 25, 7†. Prob. לָאט should be pointed (We.): cf. p. 168 *n.*

6. הובשת] from בוש: GK. § 78^b.

7. כִּי לֹא . . . כִּי] The second כי is resumptive of the first (on I 14, 39). For יֵשֵׁר the *verb* יָשַׁר must certainly be read (Ehrlich).

8. דבר על לב] as Is. 40, 2 al.

כי] as the text stands, כי will=*if* (*Lex.* 473^a; cf. I 20, 13): but the סביר (on I 12, 5) כִּי אִם *that, if* is more in accordance with analogy: אם and the ptcp. in the protasis, as I 19, 11. Gen. 20, 7. 24, 49. Ex. 8, 17 al. (*Tenses*, § 137).

ורעה] the 3 pf. fem. of the *verb* רעע (as Dt. 15, 9): ל, as ψ. 106, 32.

9. לפני המלך] The verse should end here. With the following words the scene changes, and a different subject is introduced.

10. ויהי . . . נדון] 'And all the people were *in a state of mutual strife.*' The *Nif.* of דין is not found elsewhere: but such would be its force (GK. § 51ᵈ): comp. נוֹכָח Job 23, 7, and נִשְׁפָּט Pr. 29, 9. Luc. γογγύζοντες=נְלֹון: so Klo. and Sm. ('perhaps'), but only because the Nif. נדון does not occur elsewhere. ויהי and the ptcp., as explained on I 23, 26.

מעל אבשלום] The people picture David as having fled from Absalom, as from one whom his presence encumbered: cf. מעל in Gen. 13, 9. 11; 25, 6; Ex. 10, 28; Neh. 13, 28 ואבריחהו מעלי. It is a strange remark of Bu. that מעל before the personal name 'schlecht passt.'

11. At the end of this verse, LXX, Pesh. express the clause which stands now in MT. (with the addition of אל ביתו) as *v.* 12ᵇ, viz. ודבר כל ישראל בא אל המלך. Evidently *v.* 11 is its right place; it is required here to explain David's action described in 12ᵃ: on the contrary, as 12ᵇ, it interrupts the close connexion which subsists between 12ᵃ and 13ᵃ. (It is followed in 12ᵇ by the words אל ביתו repeated by error from the middle of the verse: observe, המלך precedes each time.)

14. הֶּמְרוּ] See on I 15, 5. For 'Amasa, see 17, 25.

היה לפני] חתיה לפני suggests the idea of being in a person's service: cf. עמד לפני; and 2 Ki. 5, 2ᵇ ותהי לפני נעמן אשת; and *ch.* 16, 19 *end.*

15. וַיֵּט את לבב] So Kit.: but Gi. Baer וַיַּט, with many MSS., LXX, Pesh. (ﻭﺃﻤﺎﻝ'), Vulg.; and this with את is obviously right (cf. 1 Ki. 11, 3). Targ. אתחפני, as Jud. 9, 3, which, if an *exact* translation, implies the omission of את.

16. הגלגלה] See on I 10, 8.

17. וירד] viz. from the hill-country of Judah to the depression through which the Jordan runs, *v.* 25. Cf. Luke 10, 30.

18. The first four words of this verse, describing who accompanied Shimei, belong to *v.* 17: the rest of *v.* 18 relates to *Ziba,* forming with 19ᵃ (which ought to belong to 18) a sort of parenthesis: the purport of the allusion to Shimei appears in 19ᵇ ff.

חמשת עשר] GK. § 97ᵉ.

וצלחו‎] Of uncertain meaning. The word does not otherwise occur in a sense appropriate here; elsewhere, it means in *Qal* to *come forcibly* (of a spirit, I 10, 6 al.), sometimes (though the *Hif.* is more common in this sense) *to advance unchecked*, to prosper (ψ. 45, 5. Is. 53, 10 al.). Here, the rendering in closest accordance with the general meaning of the root is *to rush down to, dash into* (comp. LXX κατεύθυναν *came straight down to :* Vulg. *irrumpentes* Jordanem). The word excites suspicion : but if correct, it must be intended to indicate the zeal with which Ẓiba and his men exerted themselves to reach the Jordan in time to conduct the king across[1]. The first four words of *v.* 18 being joined to *v.* 17, וציבא וג'‎ is left without a predicate : and as the pred. introduced by *simple* ו‎ is barely defensible (2 Ki. 11, 1 Kt. : *Tenses,* § 129), it is better to suppose the ו‎ to have arisen by dittography from אתו‎, and to read simply צלחו‎. Render, therefore, ' And Ẓiba etc. *sped down* to Jordan before the king, and *crossed over the ford* (see on *v.* 19) in order to bring the king's household over,' etc.

19. ועברה העברה‎] ' And the ferry-boat[2] *kept passing over,*' i.e. crossed to and fro. But העברה‎ is not found elsewhere with the meaning *ferry-boat ;* and probably we should restore with We., after LXX (which here has a doublet, the first rend. being καὶ ἐλειτούργησαν τὴν λειτουργίαν=ויעברו העבדה‎ (וַיַּעֲבְרוּ הָעֲבָרָה‎, or better וְעָבְרוּ הָע'‎ (freq.), ' and they passed to and fro over the ford (15, 28) in order to bring the king's household over, and to do what he thought good.' The words will then describe the purpose with which Ẓiba and his attendants, *v.* 18ᵇ, came down to the Jordan.—On לעביר‎, for להעביר‎, see I 2, 28.

וישמעי‎] *V.* 19 should begin here (see above).

בעברו בירדן‎] = ' as he was *about to* pass over Jordan ' (so RV. *marg.*): cf. on I 18, 19. It is plain from *vv.* 34, 39 (Kimham *shall* pass over with me), 40 that David did not cross until *after* the conversation with Shimei. עבר ב'‎ as Is. 43, 2. ψ. 66, 6.

---

[1] In Arab. צלח‎ is *recte se habuit :* in Aram. *to cleave* (I 6, 14 Targ. Pesh. ; ψ. 136, 13 Targ.); whence Ges. (after Abu-'lWalid) *fiderunt transeundo* (RV. *went through*). But such a sense would be isolated in Heb., and imply a rather violent metaphor.

[2] *Had gone over* (Keil) would have been והעברה עברה‎.

20. אל יחשב וג׳] Cf. ψ. 32, 2. For הֶעָוֹה, see p. 170 *n.*, and cf. 7, 14. 24, 17.

לשׂום ... אל לבו] Cf. 18, 3. I 9, 20 (sq. לֹ). 25, 25 (אל): *Lex.* 524ᵇ 3 c, 523ᵇ 3 c.

21. אני] Note the emphatic pronoun.

לרדת] to the Jordan.

23. היום יומת איש בישראל] Comp. Saul's reply, I 11, 13 לא יומת איש ביום הזה. The question indicated by the voice: I 16, 4.

ידעתי] Luc. Bu. Sm. Dh. יָדַעְתֶּם.

25. בן שאול] a good case of בן=*grandson :* cf. יהוא בן נמשי.

ירד] from Jerusalem, *c.* 3760 ft. above the ford el-Ḥajlah.

עשה] as Dt. 21, 12ᵇ.

שפמו] 'his *moustache :*' Lev. 13, 45. Ez. 24, 17. 22. Mic. 3, 7†.

למן־היום לכת המלך] 'from the day, the going of the king,' לכת being in apposition with היום. An unusual construction: but another instance, exactly similar, occurs Ex. 9, 18 (where, however, the Samaritan text has לְמִיוֹם): cf. also 2 Ch. 8, 16 ; and see GK. § 127ᶠ.

26. ירושלם] מירושלם (LXX) must obviously be read. Not only is RV.*m.* 'when Jerusalem was come' very forced and unnatural, but after 25ᵃ, some statement about *Mephibosheth* is desiderated in 26ᵃ.

27. רמני] רמה here=*betray :* cf. 1 Ch. 12, 18.

כי אמר עבדך אחבשה לי] LXX, Pesh. Vulg. כי אמר עבדך לֹ חָבְשָׁה־לִי. The text might express merely what Mephibosheth *thought :* the reading of the Versions makes it clear that the command was actually given to Ẓiba, and affords a more substantial ground for וירגל בעבדך in *v.* 28.

חמור] עליה is here used exceptionally of the female ass, which is properly אתון : cf. GK. § 122ᶠ.

28. כמלאך האלהים] Cf. 14, 17. 20. I 29, 9.

29. ומה ... צדקה] See on I 26, 18.

30. תדבר ... דבריך] *speakest thy words,* with a touch of contempt,— go on talking (not, as EVV., 'speakest any more *of thy matters*'): otherwise, of course, in the *first* person, Gen. 24, 33, and in Jud. 11, 11. Luc. for תדבר expresses תֻּרְבֶּה, which Klo. Bu. Dh. adopt, and which, though not exactly a necessary change, may well be original.

אמרתי] I have said (viz. this moment)=*I say* (GK. § 106i): this is my decision.

32–41. The interpretation of this passage is uncertain on account of the ambiguity in the force of עבר: does it mean *pass over* (the river), or only *pass on*? and the uncertainty is increased by a various reading in *v.* 40, which leaves a doubt as to whether David took leave of Barzillai before, or after, crossing the Jordan.

32. הירדן] *passed on to* Jordan (Jos. 16, 7),—not (EVV.) 'went *over* Jordan.' Sm. Bu. Dh., however, thinking (see on *v.* 40) that the sequel will not permit B. to have yet reached the Jordan, delete הירדן.

לשלחו] to *escort* him (προπέμπειν), as Gen. 12, 20. 18, 16 al.

את־בירדן] A mixture of two readings את־הירדן (as *vv.* 37. 40) and בירדן (*v.* 19). Probably the less common ב is original. The Kt. is destitute of all philological analogy, and, in fact, meaningless.

33. בשיבתו] Obviously an error for בְּשִׁבְתּוֹ. שִׂיבָה implies a most anomalous aphaeresis from יְשִׁיבָה, a form, in an abstract sense, itself most improbable in early Hebrew; and the י may have been introduced accidentally into the word through the influence of שֵׁיבָתְךָ, while it still stood in *v.* 34 (We.). On גדול, see on I 25, 2.

34. אתה עבר] The emph. pron., as 20. 6. Ex. 5, 11. Gen. 24, 60. More commonly *after* the imper.: see on I 17, 56.

אתך] LXX, Ew. We. Bu. Now. Dh. אֶת־שֵׁיבָתְךָ: see Ru. 4, 15.

35. אעלה] from the deep Jordan-valley.

36. בקול . . . אשמע] *listen to* the voice, with satisfaction or enjoyment; more than קול שמע '*hear* the voice.' Cf. ראה ב'.

אל] = על: see 15, 33; and cf. 8, 7.

37. כמעט וג'] כמעט, lit. *like a little*, often occurs with the sense of *within a little of, almost*, but not elsewhere with the sense of *with but a little more, just* (RV.). If this rend. is legitimate, the verse occasions no difficulty. Modern scholars, however, generally suppose מעט to be intended, either reading מעט (the כ dittographed from המלך), or (Luc.) כִּי מעט, or (Kimchi, AV.) treating כ as pleonastic (cf. Is. 1, 9. ψ. 105, כמעט ונרים בה 12). The sense in this case, however, cannot, it seems, be (AV.) *go a little way over* (i.e. beyond) *Jordan*, for this, by the analogy of 16, 1, would be מעט מן הירדן: those, accordingly, who take this view, delete את הירדן as a gloss, due to the supposition that

יעבר meant 'pass *over*,' whereas, if כמעט means *a little way*, it must mean, 'will pass *on* a little way with the king,' i.e., as B., *v.* 32, is already *at* Jordan, *across it*,—or, if הירדן in 32 be omitted (Sm. Bu. Dh.), so that B. is not yet at the Jordan, *towards* it, or (retaining הירדן, with אל for את) *to* it.

יגמלני וג'] 'recompense me with this reward,' i.e. reward me for my former hospitality to him (17, 27–9; not, as EVV. '*it*,' the crossing over Jordan), with this invitation (*v.* 34).

38. עם] *near* or *by :* cf. I 10, 2.

את אשר טוב] טוב is the *verb ;* see on 3, 19.

39. אתי . . . ואני] Both words are emph.: for אתי cf. on 15, 4.

תבחר עלי] *choose* (and lay) *upon me :* cf. Gen. 30, 28 נקבה שכרך עלי. הרבו עלי מאד מהר ומתן 12, 34.

40. עבר וישק] implying clearly that David took leave of Barzillai *after* crossing the river.

Luc. here expresses עמד for עבר (cf. 15, 23), implying that David *halted* while the people passed over Jordan, and that he took leave of Barzillai *before* crossing himself. This, with the omission of הירדן in 32, and of את הירדן in 37 (to enable B. to go some way (37) with David, before parting from him (40) *at* the Jordan), is adopted by Sm. Bu. Dh., on the ground that the king's crossing is first narrated in *v.* 41; and certainly 16ᵇ. 42ᵇ do support the view that וכל עם יהודה העבירו את המלך in 41ᵇ refer not, as they must do, if the king crosses in 40, to the people escorting him *from* the Jordan to Gilgal, but to their escorting him *across* the Jordan. This argument, however, can hardly be termed decisive ; and, as just explained, the adoption of עמד in 40 involves the rejection of words in 3² and 37, though, it is true, these are glosses which might readily have arisen from a misinterpretation of ויעבר and יעבר. It seems that, to judge from the data we possess, each view of the passage must be allowed to be possible.

41. ויעבר וג'] If עבר in 40 is right, 'And *passed on* (from the Jordan) to Gilgal.' Or, with עמד in 40, 'And *passed over* (the Jordan) to Gilgal.'

ויעבירו] Kt. 'יַ, defensible in the abstract (I 14, 19), but improbable: read either Qrê הֶעֱבִירוּ, or, better (LXX), עֹבְרִים '*were passing on* with the king' (viz. from Jordan to Gilgal). Or, as before, with עמד in 40, '*were passing over* (the Jordan) with the king.'

43. אלי] Cf. *v.* 44, and on I 5, 10.

האכול וג'] i.e. have we obtained any advantage from our tribal connexion with David? A side-glance at the Benjaminites, who, it may be inferred from I 22, 7, had been benefited by their connexion with Saul (Th. from Michaelis).

אם נשאת נשא לנו] Difficult. *Three* main views have been suggested. (1) 'Or has anything been carried away by us?' i.e. gained, acquired by us (Th. Keil). נִשָּׂאת is then regarded as an inf. abs., formed on the analogy of the inf. abs. in ת, which occurs occasionally in verbs ל"ה (on 6, 20): but the form is unparalleled in verbs ל"א (Kön. i. 632 f.); and if an inf. abs. is thought to be needed we must simply correct to נָשֹׁא (so GK. § 76b). (2) Bu. Now. render (reading נִשָּׂא), 'Or has he been carried away by us?' (appropriated by us), Bu. also suggesting, as 'perhaps better,' Klo.'s נְשָׂאֻהוּ, or simply נָשָׂא אֹא, 'Or are we at all taking him away for ourselves?' (3) Kön. (i. 633 f.; cf. ii. 578 n., iii. p. 116 n.), following Kimchi, treats נִשָּׂאת as a ptcp. Nif. (which it might be: Zech. 5, 7. 1 Ch. 14, 2), with the force of a subst. (cf. נֶחֱרָצָה Is. 10, 23 al.; נִבְהָלָה Zeph. 1, 18†), 'Or has anything been carried away by us as a *portion?*'—נָשָׂא being used of *carrying away* a *portion* of food (מַשְׂאֵת, lit. *something carried*) from the table of a superior as a compliment to a guest or other person: see Gen. 43, 34 וַיִּשָּׂא מַשְׂאֹת מֵאֵת פָּנָיו אֲלֵהֶם 'And *one carried* (= *There were carried;* see on I 16, 4: LXX ἦραν) *portions* ('messes') from Joseph's presence to his brethren;' 2 Sam. 11, 8. This idea suits the parallel האכול אכלנו מן המלך excellently: but, if it is adopted, it is far better to *read* מַשְׂאֵת or מַשְׂאֹת (Grätz, Dh.) than to have recourse to the precarious expl. of נִשָּׂאת as a subst. נָשָׂא, as pf. Nif., might then be construed with מַשְׂאֵת by GK. § 121a, or, better, נָשָׂא (sc. הַנִּשָּׂא, = *there hath been brought:* cf. Gen. 43, 34) might be read: 'Or hath any *portion* (from his table) *been brought* to us?'—like the preceding clause, fig. for, Have we derived any advantage from what we have done for the king?

The Versions mostly paraphrase. LXX has a double rend., the first being free, the second literal: ἢ δόμα ἔδωκεν ἢ ἄρσιν ἦρεν ἡμῖν ; (cf. ἄρσις for מַשְׂאֵת in *ch.* 11, 8); Pesh. 'Or has a gift been given us from him?' Targ. אִם מַתְּנָא מַנִּי לָנָא 'Or has he apportioned us a gift?' Vulg. *Aut munera nobis data sunt?* Cf. AV. RV. 'Or hath he given us any gift?' which must be understood also as a paraphrase, not as a lit. rendering; for נָשָׂא (Pi'el), though it means to *lift up, support, assist* a person (with wood, money, etc.), 1 Ki. 9, 11. Ezr. 1, 4 al., never means to *give*, nor does נִשָּׂאת ever mean a *gift*.

z 2

44. ידות] Metaph. (note the *fem.* pl.)=*parts:* so Gen. 43, 34.

וגם בדוד אני ממך] 'and also in David I am (more) than thou.'
וגם, however, points to something *additional ;* whereas the sentence as
thus understood adds nothing to what has been just said עשר ידות לי
במלך: for it is evidently impossible to draw a distinction between
המלך and דוד, as though 'David' expressed or meant more than 'the
king.' LXX καὶ πρωτότοκος ἐγὼ ἢ σύ (the following words καί γε ἐν τῷ
Δαυείδ εἰμι ὑπὲρ σὲ are a doublet representing the existing MT.), i.e.
בְּכוֹר for בדוד 'and I am also *the firstborn* rather than thou:' see 1 Ch.
5, 2. So Th. Ew. We. Stade, Klo. It is not true that בכור מן is
'a phrase incompatible with the meaning of בכור' (Keil); for it does
not imply that Judah was in some measure a firstborn: מן may be
used to express the idea of *rather than, and not:* ψ. 52, 5 אהבת רע
מטוב; Hab. 2, 16 שבעת קלון מכבוד thou art filled with disgrace *rather
than* glory.

ולא היה] Either read הֲלֹא, or render, 'And was not . . .?' (on
I 16, 4). AV. RV. (text), 'should not be,' would require imperatively
ולא יהיה.

לי] After דברי this seems superfluous. It may have arisen by error
from the following 'לה.

20, 1. בכרי] perhaps=בֶּכֶר, the name of the Benj. clan, Gen.
46, 21. 1 Ch. 7, 6. 8, 8. Cf. נרא שמעי בן גרא (16, 5).

איש לאהליו ו'] i.e. Resume your old tribal independence ; cf. 1 Ki.
12, 16.

This is one of the 18 passages in which, according to the Jews, there has been
a תִּקּוּן סֹפְרִים, or 'correction of the scribes,' intended to remove some expression
derogatory to Yahweh, alleged to have been the original reading. Here לאהליו
is stated to have been altered for this reason from לֵאלֹהָיו *to his gods.* The other
passages (the alleged original reading, where not stated here, is given by Kittel)
are Gen. 18, 22. Nu. 11, 15. 12, 12. 1 S. 3, 13 (לוֹ). 2 S. 16, 12 (originally, it is
alleged, בְּעֵינוֹ). 1 Ki. 12, 16 = 2 Ch. 10, 16 (as here). Jer. 2, 11. Ez. 8, 17. Hos.
4, 7 (orig. כבודי בקלון הֵמִירוּ). Hab. 1, 12. Zech. 2, 12. Mal. 1, 13. ψ. 106, 20.
Job 7, 20. 32, 3. Lam. 3, 20 (orig. נפשׁך). The probability of the alleged original
reading must be decided in each case on its own merits : in some it may be considerable, here it is quite out of the question. See more fully Ginsburg, *Introd. to
the Heb. Bible,* p. 347 ff. ; Geiger, *Urschrift,* p. 308 ff.

2. ויעל] Idiom. = *withdrew:* cf. 23, 9 ; and esp. from a siege,
1 Ki. 15, 19 al. (*Lex.* 748ᵇ e). Cf. on 2, 27 נַעֲלָה מֵאַחֲרֵי.

3. בֵּית מִשְׁמֶרֶת] מ׳ in this sense only here: elsewhere מִשְׁמָר, Gen. 40, 3. 4 al.; 42, 19 בֵּית מִשְׁמַרְכֶם.

אַלְמְנוּת חַיּוּת] '(*in*) *widowhood of livingness*'—the English is not more singular than the Hebrew. The punctuation can hardly express the sense intended by the writer. The application of the adverbial accus., which it implies, is unusually harsh; and the idea which the entire expression is supposed to convey is difficult, if not impossible, to seize[1]. We. Bu. Now. al. point אַלְמְנוֹת חַיּוֹת, supposing that being treated as widows, although their husbands were alive, they are called by a figure of speech, not without parallels in other languages, 'living widows' (so LXX χῆραι ζῶσαι).

4. שְׁלֹשֶׁת יָמִים] As the text stands, this can only mean *for three days;* and there is nothing to shew, or suggest, that וְאַתָּה פֹה עָמָד is only to come at the *end* of the three days. As We. observes, שְׁלֹשֶׁת יָמִים and וְאַתָּה פֹה עָמָד belong together, and fix the מוֹעֵד of *v.* 5. The athnaḥ must thus be transposed to יְהוָֹה; we then get, spoken in the tone of a command, 'Three days, and then stand thou (present thyself) here!' For וְ cf. Ex. 16, 6 עֶרֶב וִידַעְתֶּם 'At even, *then* ye shall know,' etc. וּבֹקֶר וּרְאִיתֶם וג׳ (*Tenses*, §§ 123 β, 124). (The transposition (Kit. *Bibl.*) to the end of the *v.* would yield a wrong sense, and must be an oversight: it is not followed in the transl. in Kautzsch.)

5. וַיֵּחַר] Qrê וַיֹּחַר, which may be either *Qal* (so Ol. § 241ᶜ: cf. וַתֵּחֶז *v.* 9 from אחז) from אָחַר[2], or *Hif.* (not elsewhere) lit. *shewed,* *exhibited* delay (so Ges. *Lg.* p. 377; Stade, § 498ᶜ; König, i. 397[3]). The Kt., unless (Kön.) the י is a mere error for ו, is probably to be read וַיִּיחַר, for וַיֵּאחַר (cf. וַיֵּתָא for וַיֵּאתָא Dt. 33, 21): Stade, § 112ᶜ, cf. GK. § 68ⁱ.

מִן הַמּוֹעֵד] מִן before a noun with the art. is much commoner in all books than מֵה׳: before other words it is most frequent in Chr. (Kön. ii. 292; *Lex.* 577ᵇ; GK. § 102ᵇ *n.*).

6. רַע לִי] רַע לִ is not used in the sense of '*be harmful* to:' read

---

[1] EVV. *living in widowhood* yields an excellent sense; but unfortunately is neither a rendering, nor a legitimate paraphrase, of the Hebrew.

[2] This is indeed וְאָחַר in Gen. 32, 5, but both וְאָהַב and אֲהֵב occur from אָהַב.

[3] In Aram. the *Afel* אוֹחַר, ܐܘܚܪ is in use, which might support this view.

with EVV. (though the change of text is not admitted by them openly) יֵרַע.

פֶּן מָצָא] ' lest he *have found* . . . :' cf. 2 Ki. 2, 16, and *Tenses,* § 41 *Obs.* But the following והציל (perf. with *waw* conv., which regularly follows פֶּן with the *impf.,* e.g. 12, 28. Ex. 34, 15 f.) suggests that מָצָא is simply a clerical error for יִמְצָא (GK. § 107ᵠ *n.*). In 2 Ki. 2, 16 the past tense is defended by the following וַיַּשְׁלִיכֻהוּ.

והציל עינגו] Difficult. LXX καὶ σκιάσει τοὺς ὀφθαλμοὺς ἡμῶν : Pesh. ܘܢܣܚܘܠ and pluck (*lit.* dig) out our eyes : Targ. (paraphrasing) ויעיק לנא and distress us : Vulg. *et effugiat nos.* הציל is properly to *pull* or *take away* (see Ges. : نَصَلَ *exemit, eduxit* rem, v.c. festucam ex oculo, dentem), Gen. 31, 9. 10, *Hithp.* Ex. 33, 6 to *pull* or *strip off* oneself, though it is mostly used in the sense of *pulling away,* i.e. *rescuing, delivering,* from an enemy. Hence the text can only be rendered either *and deliver our eye,* which here yields no sense ; or *pull out our eye,* either lit. (Bö. Th. ; cf. Pesh.), as an expression meaning *harm us irretrievably,* or metaphorically, as Ges. ' Singulare est עיני פ' הציל *auferre oculum alicuius,* i.e. *eum fallere,* subtrahere se oculis eius ' (cf. RV.). AV. *escape us,* with marg., ' Heb. deliver himself from our eyes ' (cf. Rashi להציל עצמו מעינינו) ; but to ' understand ' a couple of words in this way is of course quite illegitimate. Ewald, *Hist.* iii. 262 (E. T. 193), Keil, We. Bu. Dh. follow LXX, deriving הציל,—or rather הֵצֵל,—from צלל to *be shadowy* or *dark* (Neh. 13, 19), i.e. '*be-shadow* or *becloud* our eye,' metaph. for 'occasion us anxiety.' For the *eye,* as the organ in which the Hebrew saw changes of emotion, or mental states, expressed, comp. I 14, 27. ψ. 6, 8. 88, 10. Job 11, 20. 17, 7 etc. Sm., following Luc. (σκεπασθῇ ἀφ' ἡμῶν), reads וְנִצַּל מִמֶּנּוּ *and escape* (Nif. : Dt. 23, 16 al.) *from us,* obtaining thus, by legitimate means, exactly the sense which AV. obtained by illegitimate means. Now., retaining הַצִּיל, *and take them* (הַצִּיל, as Gen. 31, 9. 16) *from us.* Bu., though adopting הֵצֵל, makes a clever suggestion, to read viz. וְנִצַּל לְעֵינֵינוּ *and escape before our eyes,* defiantly (Dt. 28, 31).

7. אחריו אנשי יואב] Read אחריו אבישי יואב.

8. הם עם . . . , ועמשא בא] exactly as Jud. 19, 11 ; cf. on I 9, 5.

בא לפניהם] came (=appeared) *in front of* them (accidentally).
'Came to meet them' (RV.) would be בא לקראתם.

וּיוֹאָב חָגוּר מִדּוֹ לְבֻשׁוֹ וג׳] 'and Joab was girt with his warrior's
dress, his clothing, and upon it was the girdle of a sword fastened
(i.e. the sword) upon his loins in its sheath.' The sentence is involved
and obscure: though the fact is effectually concealed in the free
rendering of RV. מדו לבושו is a strange combination; לבש, not חגר,
would be the verb naturally used with מדו (read prob., in the sense
warrior's dress, מַדָּו; see on I 17, 38); חָגוּר also (the *fem.* מצמרת
referring only to the *sword*) appears to be superfluous. The text
must be in some disorder. Löhr, Now. (improving on We.): ויאב
מַדָּו לְבֻשׁ וְעָלָיו (cf. I 17, 38. 39) חָגוּר (LXX περιεζωσμένος) חרב
מצמרת על מתניו בתערה; this deviates but little from MT. Dhorme:
מעל לבושו: (Dh. writes ויאב חָגוּר מֵעַל לְלְבֻשׁוֹ וְעָלָיו חרב מצמרת וג׳
but see I 17, 39). According to the view expressed in these restorations, Joab had *one* sword only, which afterwards (*v.* 8 *end*) fell to the
ground, and was then (though this is not mentioned) picked up by
Joab with his left hand, in such a way as not to arouse 'Amasa's
suspicions. Klo. Bu. Sm. Kitt., on the other hand, think that Joab
had *two* swords, an outside one in its usual place, which fell to the
ground, and was left there, and another concealed under his dress on
his left, the existence of which 'Amasa had no reason to suspect.
Klo., accordingly, supposing two words to have become corrupted,
and one omitted, reads (insert הוא) ויאב חרב בְּיָדוֹ מִתַּחת ללבושו ועליו
חָגוּר חרב מצמרת וג׳ 'and as for Joab, a sword was in his hand
underneath his dress (cf. Jud. 3, 16), and upon it (i.e. outside) he was
girt,' etc. (so Sm. Kit.). Bu., thinking that Joab would hardly have
kept his left hand, holding the concealed sword, under his dress,
as he approached 'Amasa, would read ויואב חָגוּר חרב מתחת לְמַדָּיו
ועל לבשו חרב מצמרת וג׳ (Jud. 3, 16). As Joab's right hand was
otherwise employed (*v.* 9), the יד יואב of 10 must have been his left
hand: and Klo.'s בידו for מדו explains, as MT. does not explain,
how the sword came to be in this hand. On the other hand, Klo.'s
emend.,—and still more Bu.'s,—differs considerably from MT.: *v.* 10,
also, in saying not that 'Amasa did not *see* the sword in Joab's hand:
but that he did not *guard himself* against it, rather implies that he saw

it; and if so, this will have been the one sword which he had, which had fallen to the ground, and been picked up by him. It seems best, on the whole, to follow Löhr and Now.

והוא יצא ותפל] Read, with LXX, וְהִיא יָצְאָה וַתִּפֹּל *and it* (the sword) *came out, and fell.* The text is contrary to idiom. With the emph. הוא, the form of the sentence would be (וְהִיא or) וְהַחֶרֶב יצא יצא נָפָלָה: (see on I 9, 5).

10. נשמר ב׳] reflexively, *guarded himself:* so 2 Ki. 6, 10.

ולא שנה לו] I 26, 8.

11. עליו] *over* or *by* him, i.e. by 'Amasa.

מי אשר . . . לדוד אחרי יואב:] in form as Ex. 32, 26: cf. on I 11, 12. For the exclam., cf. also 2 Ki. 3, 23 לשלל מאב; Jud. 7, 18.

12. ויסב . . . השדה] *into* the field: cf. on 6, 10.

כאשר ראה כל הבא עליו ועמד] 'when he saw every one *who came by him, and stopped.*' ועמד is the pf. with *waw* conv., carrying on (GK. § 116ˣ), as a frequentative, the ptcp. כל־הבא (=whosoever came) in *past* time, just as it does in *present* time (e.g.) Jer. 21, 9 היוצא וְנָפַל whoso goeth out and falleth to the Chaldaeans. etc. (*Tenses,* § 117). But עָמֵד for ועמד (Now.) would be an improvement: 'When he saw every one who came to him *stopping.*' 'When he saw *that* every one . . . stood still' (EVV.) would require כִּי עָמַד (Gen. 1, 4). The clause stating the reason for the man's acting as he did, would, however, stand naturally *before* וירא; and perhaps, with והיה (freq.) prefixed, it should be transposed there: 'And it came to pass, when every one who came by him saw him ('Amasa), that he stood still' (cf. Jud. 19, 30).

13. הֻגַּה] Hof., for הֻגְּנָה: GK. § 69ʷ. But the root (Syr. ܘܢܓ̈ to *drive away, remove*) occurs in Heb. only here; read prob. either הִפָּה (Bu.), as 3, 27, or הַגֵּה (in Qal, Pr. 25, 4. 5; Isa. 27, 8†).

14. אבלה ובית מעכה] Read אָבֵלָה בִּית מעכה 'to Abel *of* Beth-Ma'achah' with Ew. Th. We. Klo. etc., as *vv.* 15. 18. 1 Ki. 15, 20. 2 Ki. 15, 29. Now *Abil,* a village on a hill (1074 ft.), overlooking the Jordan-valley, 2½ miles W. of the river, and 4 miles W. of Tell el-Ḳāḍi (Dan). For מעכה, cf. on 10, 6.

וכל־הברים] No place or people named הברים is known: and after the mention of Abel of Beth-Ma'achah as the goal of Sheba's movements,

the words *and all the Berites*, if treated as coupled to them, yield no
intelligible sense. The athnaḥ, then, must be moved back to מעבה.
The sense of what follows turns upon the meaning of ויבאו אף אחריו.
בא אחרי is not a mere synonym of either הלך אחרי (to *follow*), or
רדף אחרי (to *pursue*): it means *to enter after some one* into a place, as
Ex. 14, 17 ויבאו אחריהם viz. into the sea (as *vv.* 23. 28, explicitly);
I 26, 3 Saul *came in* after him into the wilderness; 2 Ki. 11, 15;
2 Ch. 26, 17; so בא אחר Nu. 25, 8. Hence ויבאו וג' will mean, 'and
went in after him,' viz. as is required by the context, into Abel of
Beth-Ma'achah. This shews that the subject of ויעבר, as well as the
object in אחריו, is Sheba; and lends at the same time plausibility
to Klo.'s proposal to read, instead of the obscure כל הברים, after
LXX καὶ πάντες ἐν Χαρρει, וכל־הַבִּכְרִים *and all the Bichrites* (the
following ·ו as I 14, 19)[1]. Sheba is described in *v.* 1 as בן־בכרי; and
the meaning of the verse will then be that the members of his family
or clan took part with him and *went in after him* into the city in which
he had taken refuge[2]. The narrative reverts to Sheba's *pursuers*
in *v.* 15.

אף] אף simply=גם (not as=*how much more*: on I 14, 30) is very
unusual in plain narrative, being confined chiefly to poetry, and
where it occurs in prose having generally some rhetorical force[3].
Here it does not in fact appear to be required, and perhaps arose
by error out of the first two letters of אחריו: it is not expressed by
LXX. Bu., followed by Kenn. Dh., supposes that a transposition has
taken place, and suggests, very cleverly and plausibly: והוא עבר בכל
שבטי ישראל וַיְקַלְּהוּ (Kt.) ויבא אבלה בית מעכה וכל הַבִּכְרִים באו אחריו.
וַיְקַלְהוּ = *treated him with contempt* (see 6, 22. 19, 44).

15. אָבֵל [אָבֵלָה בית מעכה meadow, unlike אָבֵל (adj.) *mourning*

---

[1] Though it does not usually follow the subject *immediately* (Jer. 44, 25).

[2] The reading (Th. al., after Vulg. *omnesque viri electi*) וכל־הַבַּחֻרִים *and all the
young men* (viz. followed after him [Joab]; or pursued after him [Sheba]) is
inconsistent with the meaning of בא אחרי.

[3] האף Gen. 18, 13. 23. 24: with a pron. אף אני Gen. 40, 16 and with singular
frequency in Lev. 26 (*vv.* 16. 24. 28. 41, and ואף *vv.* 39. 40. 42. 44); אף היא, אף הם
Dt. 2, 11. 20, אף הוא 2 Ki. 2, 14: alone, Nu. 16, 14. Dt. 15, 17 and here. These
are all the occurrences of אף alone (i.e. not in the combination אף כי) in prose
from Gen. to 2 Kings.

(ψ. 35, 14), does not change its form in *st. c.* (Kön. ii. 438; iii. § 285ʰ): so אָבֵל מצרים Gen. 50, 11, אָבֵל מְחוֹלָה 1 Ki. 4, 12: cf. יָבֵשׁ גלעד. The ה- *loc.* in *st. c.*: GK. § 90ᶜ.

וישפכו] alluding to the earth, 'poured' out of baskets, of which the סללה was constructed. So regularly, as 2 Ki. 19, 32. Anglice, 'threw up.'

ותעמד בחל] The ב is difficult. חל is explained to mean the smaller outer wall—בן חומה or בַּר שׁוּרָא, as the Jews define it—or 'outwork,'— 'rampart' (RV.) is not sufficiently distinctive,—surrounding a city, between which and the principal wall there would be a space, consisting, at least partly, of a moat. It has been supposed (Ges. Keil) that the word included this space; and so Keil renders, 'And it (the סללה) stood in the moat.' But this is hardly likely. ותעמד בחל must belong, somehow or other, to אשה חכמה in *v.* 16. ותעמד בחל ותקרא אשה חכמה מן העיר might suffice: but ותצא אשה חכמה מן העיר ותעמד בחל ותקרא is more what we should expect, though it is not apparent how the present text would be derived from it.

משחיתם להפיל החומה] '*were destroying*, to cause the wall to fall,' i.e. were battering it. Cf. Ez. 26, 4 צר חומות ושחתו: the ptcp. here of course implying that the action was only in *process*, and not completed. The expression is, however, a little peculiar; and Ew. Bö. Th. Dh. treat the word as a denom. of שׁחת *pit—were making a pit* to cause the wall to fall, i.e. were *undermining* it (RV. marg.). LXX have ἐνοοῦσαν, and Targ. מתעשׁתין, which no doubt represent מַחֲשָׁבִים Prov. 24, 8 (We.)—'*were devising* to bring the wall down.' Perhaps this is the true reading: it is adopted by Klo. Bu. Sm. Now.

18–19. דבר ידברו וג'] 'They were wont to speak aforetime, saying, Let them but enquire at Abel, and so they finished (a matter). I (consist of) the peaceable (and) faithful ones of Israel,' etc.; i.e. Abel was famed from of old for the wisdom of its inhabitants, hence a proverb arose advising people to consult them in any difficult undertaking. In 19ᵃ the woman, in saying אנכי, speaks in the name of the community: hence she uses 1 ps. sg. (as I 5, 10), though the predicate is in the plural (referring to the individual members of it: comp. Gen. 34, 30 ואני מתי מספר). שלמי אמני is a 'suspended' *st. c.*, to be explained on the principle of אשת בעלת אוב I 28, 7 where see the note. LXX have ἠρωτημένος ἠρωτήθη ἐν τῇ Ἀβελ καὶ ἐν Δαν εἰ ἐξέλιπον ἃ ἔθεντο οἱ πιστοὶ τοῦ Ἰσραηλ [ἐρῶντες ἐπερωτήσουσιν ἕνα ἐν Ἀβελ καὶ οὕτως, εἰ ἐξέλιπον. ἐγώ εἰμι εἰρηνικὰ τῶν στηριγμάτων Ἰσραηλ], σὺ δὲ ζητεῖς, κτλ. Here the bracketed words are evidently a correction made to express a text resembling the existing MT. and introduced already into Cod. B by the side of the original LXX version, which precedes. The text presupposed by the original LXX would read as follows:—שָׁאוֹל יִשְׁאֲלוּ בְּאָבֵל וּבְדָן הֲתַמּוּ אֲשֶׁר שָׂמוּ ¹ אֱמוּנֵי יִשְׂרָאֵל ' Let them ask in Abel and in Dan whether that had ever come to an end which the faithful of Israel had established!' which is adopted by Ew. *Hist.* iii. 264 (E. T. 195), We. Bu. Now.; i.e. if one desired to find a place in which old Israelitish institutions were most strictly preserved, he was told to apply to Abel and to Dan: why should Joab seek to destroy a city that was thus true to its hereditary character and nationality?

18. יִשְׁאֲלוּ שָׁאוֹל] The inf. abs. in *Qal*, while the principal verb is in a derived conjugation, as happens sometimes: with Pi'el, as here, Jos. 24, 10²; with Hif. I 23, 22. Gen. 46, 4. Is. 31, 5; with Hithpo'lel and Hithpo'el Is. 24, 19; most frequently with Nif., *ch.* 23, 7. Ex. 19, 13. 21, 20. 22, 11. 12. Is. 40, 30. Jer. 10, 5. 34, 3. 49, 12 (contrast 25, 29). Mic. 2, 4. Nah. 3, 13. Zech. 12, 3. Job 6, 2, and with Hof. in מוֹת יוּמַת Ex. 19, 12 (and often). Cf. GK. § 113ʷ.

19. לְהָמִית] Unsuitable to a 'city.' Read לְשַׁחֵת (cf. 20 אם אשחית), Nestle, Sm. Now. המית cannot be rendered 'destroy' (EVV.).

אם] 'an important and venerable city with dependent villages, called in Heb. idiom its "daughters," Nu. 21, 25 al.' (Kenn.). Cf. on 8, 1.

21. הנה . . . , משלך] The fut. instans. with a *passive* ptcp.: cf. I 19, 11.—On מעל, here and *v.* 22, see on I 28, 15.

22. ותבוא . . . העם] 'In LXX there is a doublet: καὶ εἰσῆλθε πρὸς πάντα τὸν λαὸν and καὶ ἐλάλησε πρὸς πᾶσαν τὴν πόλιν; the latter is

---

¹ We. הֵשִׁימוּ. But a Hif. הֵשִׂים is so rare and doubtful (Ez. 14, 8. 21, 21), except at most in the *participle* (Is. 41, 20. Job 4, 20†), that forms of it cannot legitimately be introduced by conjecture into the MT. (Nöldeke, *ZDMG.*, 1883, p. 530 = *Beiträge zur Sem. Sprachwissenschaft*, 1904, p. 37).

² ברוך might indeed be inf. abs. Pi'el (as רַפֹּא); but this is elsewhere בָּרֵךְ.

genuine, and the Hebrew text to which it points (וַיִּתְדַּבֵּר אֶל־כָּל־הָעִיר) is preferable to MT. Cf. the interchange of וַתָּבֹא and וַתֹּאמֶר 14, 4' (We.). So Now. Kit. Klo. Bu. Dh. prefer וַתָּבֹא הָאִשָּׁה] אֶל הָעִיר וַתְּדַבֵּר] אֶל כָּל הָעָם.

23–26. See 8, 16–18.

23. אֶל] a strong case of עַל=אֶל: contrast 23ᵇ and 8, 16.

כָּל־הַצָּבָא יִשְׂרָאֵל] Of course יִשְׂרָאֵל cannot be *a genitive* after הַצָּבָא: it must therefore be in apposition with it. This appositional construction, however, 'all the host, Israel' is harsh, and, since no relation of *identity* subsists between *the host* and *Israel,* unsuitable. Grammar will only admit one of two alternatives: כָּל־צְבָא יִשְׂרָאֵל, or simply כָּל־הַצָּבָא: the latter is preferable (cf. 8, 16 וְיוֹאָב בֶּן צְרוּיָה עַל הַצָּבָא. 17, 25. 1 Ki. 2, 35 al.).

הַכָּרִי] (Kt.) recurs 2 Ki. 11, 4. 19 (הכרי והרצים), where it probably signifies *Carians.* The king's body-guard appears to have consisted of foreigners. But here no doubt the Qrê is right in reading הַכְּרֵתִי, as 8, 18, where see the note.

24. אֲדֹרָם] LXX Αδωνειραμ, as 1 Ki. 4, 6. 5, 28 אֲדֹנִירָם. The form אֲדֹרָם occurs also 1 Ki. 12, 18 where LXX Cod. B ᾽Αραμ, Cod. A ᾽Αδωνιραμ; in the parallel passage 2 Ch. 10, 18 הֲדֹרָם (LXX Αδωνιραμ). The variation is not greater than attaches to many less familiar names, when they occur in parallel texts: see e.g. Nu. 26, or Ezra 2 *passim* (RV. *marg.*). The true name here is probably אֲדֹנִירָם (cf. מַלְכִּירָם, יוֹרָם); הֲדֹרָם is a *Ḥamathite* name (see on 8, 10).

עַל הַמַּס] over the *labour-gangs* (or the *corvée*),—gangs of men doing forced labour, such as an Eastern monarch is wont to exact from his subjects. The מַס appears first as an institution in Israel at the end of David's reign: it was more fully organized by Solomon, who needed it for the purpose of carrying on his buildings: Adoniram was the officer who superintended it: how unpopular it was, may be inferred from the fact that the populace, disappointed at Rehoboam's refusal to relax his father's imposts, wreaked their vengeance on Adoniram and stoned him (1 Ki. 12, 18). Phrases used in connexion with it are הֶעֱלָה מַס מִיִּשְׂרָאֵל to bring up (=to levy) a מַס out of Israel 1 Ki. 5, 27 (cf. 9, 15); הֶעֱלָה לְמַס עֹבֵד to levy (them) for a toiling labour-band 1 Ki. 9, 21: הָיָה לְמַס Dt. 20, 11 al. to become a labour-band; היה לְמַס עֹבֵד Gen. 49, 15. Jos. 16, 10 to become a toiling labour-band. In Jud. 1, 28. 30. 33. 35 certain Canaanites are described as reduced to 'labour-gangs' by their Israelitish conquerors. Ex. 1, 11 שָׂרֵי מִסִּים *overseers of labour-gangs* (or *gang-masters*). See *Lex.* 586 f. The rend. *tribute* depends on a baseless Rabb. derivation from מֶכֶס (*Lex.* 493ᵇ): it suggests a totally incorrect idea; and it is greatly to be regretted that it should have been retained in RV.

26. היארי] i.e. of Jair, a Gileadite family, Nu. 32, 41 al. But Pesh. ܝܥܝܪ (cf. Luc. ὁ Ἰεθερ), whence Th. Now. Dh. would restore הַיַּתְּרִי *of Yattir*, in the hill-country of Judah (see on I 30, 27). It is observed that in notices of this kind the *home*, not the *family*, is usually mentioned; and I 30, 27 shews that David had friends in Yattir. Yattir *may* also have been an old priestly settlement (cf. Jos. 21, 14). In any case this 'Ira will not be 'Ira the *warrior* of 23, 38. Klo. Bu. Sm. retain הַיָּאִירִי.

21–24. *An Appendix to the main narrative of the Book, of miscellaneous contents: (a)* **21,** 1–14 *the famine in Israel stopped through the sacrifice of the sons of Saul by the Gibeonites; (b)* **21,** 15–22 *exploits against the Philistines; (c)* **22** *David's Hymn of Triumph (=ψ. 18); (d)* **23,** 1–7 *David's 'Last Words;' (e)* **23,** 8–39 *further exploits against the Philistines, and list of David's heroes; (f)* **24** *David's census of the people* [1].

(a) **21,** 1–14. *Saul's sons sacrificed by the Gibeonites.*

1. ויבקש וג'] Vulg., interpreting rightly, 'Et consuluit David *oraculum* Domini.' Cf. Ex. 33, 7. The technical expression is שאל בי' (I 22, 10 al.).

ואל בית הדמים] 'and for *his* bloody house' would require imperatively ואל בית הדמים אשר לו: the pron. could not in a case like the present be dispensed with. LXX καὶ ἐπὶ τὸν οἶκον αὐτοῦ ἀδικία διὰ τὸ

---

[1] In this Appendix, *a* and *f* in style and manner are closely related, as also *b* and *e*. Further, as the Appendix interrupts the *continuous* narrative *ch.* 9–20. 1 Ki. 1–2 (p. 286 *note*), it may be inferred that it was placed where it now stands *after the separation had been effected between the Books of Samuel and Kings.* Its compiler, presumably, thus lived at a later date than the compiler of the main narrative of Samuel.

αὐτὸν θανάτῳ αἱμάτων=‎ וְאֶל־בֵּיתֹה דָּמִים‎ [1] 'upon Saul and *upon his house* (rests) *blood* (cf. 16, 8. Dt. 19, 10), because he slew the Gibeonites.' The words in MT. have simply been wrongly divided (cf. *v.* 12 ; 5, 2): ‎ ביתה‎ is the old orthography for ‎ ביתו‎, no doubt once written uniformly in Hebrew (as in Moabitic), but afterwards, except in a few sporadic instances, modernized. See the Introd., p. xxxii f.

2. ‎ הַמֵה . . . לֹא‎] *Lex.* 216ª **3 b**, 241ᵇ **3 b** ; *Tenses*, § 198.

3. ‎ בַמֵה‎] Cf. Mic. 6, 6 ‎ בַּמָּה אֲקַדֵּם יהוה‎.—In ‎ וברכו‎, the imper. is used instead of the more normal voluntative, for the purpose of expressing with somewhat greater force the intention of the previous verb: cf. I Ki. 1, 12 ; Ew. § 347ª ; *Tenses*, § 65 ; GK. § 110ⁱ.

4. Kt. ‎ לִי‎] Qrê, assimilating to the next clause, ‎ לָנוּ‎. But see on I 5, 10. 30, 22.

‎ וְאֵין־לָנוּ וג׳‎] (against the accents) 'and it is not open to us to put any man to death in Israel.' ‎ אֵין לְ‎, as more frequently in the later language, Ezra 9, 15. 2 Ch. 22, 9 al.: *Tenses*, § 202. 1. Cf. ‎ אֵשׁ (יֵשׁ) לְ‎ *ch.* 14, 19.

‎ מַה אַתֶּם אֹמְרִים אֶעֱשֶׂה לָכֶם‎] 'What say (think) ye (that) I should do for you?' So Ew. (§ 336ᵇ; cf. GK. § 120ᶜ), Keil, ‎ כִּי‎ being (unusually) omitted. The constr. 'What do ye say? I will do it for you'=whatsoever ye say I will do for you (so in effect EVV.) yields a better sense: but ‎ וְאֶעֱשֶׂה‎ (which is actually expressed by LXX) would in that case be more in accordance with usage (cf. on I 20, 4). See, however, Jud. 9, 48 ‎ מָה רְאִיתֶם עֲשִׂיתִי מַהֲרוּ עֲשׂוּ כָמֹנִי‎ (lit.) 'What have ye seen (that) I have done? hasten and do like me.' (‎ מַה‎ must not be treated as if it were equivalent to the late ‎ מַה־שֶׁ‎ *that which.*)

5. ‎ נִשְׁמַדְנוּ‎] 'that we *should* be destroyed' (EVV.) is no rendering of a *perfect* tense: '(so that) we have been destroyed' (RV. *marg.*) would require ‎ עַד אֲשֶׁר‎ to be expressed: moreover ‎ דִּמָּה לָנוּ‎ does not mean 'devised against us.' Read with Ew. We. ‎ וַאֲשֶׁר דִּמָּה לְהַשְׁמִידֵנוּ‎ 'and who meditated *to destroy us* that we should not,' etc. So LXX (one rendering) ὃς παρελογίσατο ἐξολεθρεῦσαι ἡμᾶς. (What follows, viz. ἀφανίσωμεν αὐτόν, merely expresses MT. differently vocalized, viz. ‎ נַשְׁמִדֶנּוּ‎,—contrary to the sense.) ‎ דִּמָּה לְ‎ as Jud. 20, 5.

---

[1] ἀδικία αἱμάτων is a paraphrase of ‎ דמים‎ : διὰ τὸ αὐτὸν θανάτῳ is a partial doublet to περὶ οὗ ἐθανάτωσεν in the following clause.

6. ‏וְיִנְתֶן־לָנוּ‏] Kt. ‏יֻתַּן־לָנוּ‏: Qrê ‏יִתֶּן־לָנוּ‏. Both conjugations are in use : the Hof. is perhaps somewhat more elegant (1 Ki. 2, 21. 2 Ki. 5, 17). The construction as below, *v.* 11.

‏וְהוּקַעֲנוּם לַיהוה‏] ‏הוּקִיעַ‏ only here, *vv.* 9. 13. Nu. 25, 4 ‏הוֹקַע אוֹתָם‏ ‏לַיהוה נֶגֶד הַשֶּׁמֶשׁ‏ (cf. on I 31, 10). The exact sense is uncertain. ‏وَقع‏ is to *fall* (Qor. 15, 29. 22, 64): hence W. R. Smith, *Rel. Sem.* 398 (² 419), comparing ‏הוּקִיעַ‏ with ‏أَوْقَعَ‏, thought that *precipitation* from a rock was intended : this would suit ‏וַיִּפְּלוּ‏ *v.* 9, but hardly ‏בָּהָר‏ *ib.*; and 2 Ch. 25, 12, where that form of punishment is mentioned, the expressions used are different. **ⲱⲫⲟ:** (rare) is to *beat* (Dillm., *Lex.* 913). Elsewhere in Heb. ‏יקע‏ means to *be separated, dislocated,* of a joint (Gen. 32, 26†), fig. to *be severed, alienated* (Jer. 6, 8. Ez. 23, 17. 18†); hence Ges. to *impale* (cf. Aq. ἀναπηγνύναι), 'because in this form of punishment the limbs were dislocated.' Other versions express the idea of *expose* (LXX here ἐξηλιάζειν, in Nu. παραδειγματίζειν; Pesh. in Nu. ‏ܦܩܥ‏); or render *crucify* (Targ. here ‏צלב‏; Vulg. *crucifigere, affigere;* Saad. in Nu. ‏صلب‏), or *hang* (Symm. κρεμάζειν; Vulg. in Nu. *suspendere*). Targ. in Nu. has merely ‏קטל‏ *kill;* and Pesh. here ‏ܘܕܒܚ‏ *sacrifice.* Perhaps *crucify* (in *late* Heb. ‏צלב‏), implying at least an unnatural extension of the limbs (cf. ‏יקע‏ Gen. 32, 26), is as probable a rend. as any : in this case, however, it would be better, for ‏יפלו‏ *v.* 9, to read with Klo. ‏וַיִּתָּלוּ‏ *and they were hung* (and ‏שָׁם‏ *there,* with Luc.). 'Expose,' though a natural *consequence* of either impalement or crucifixion, can hardly be the actual *meaning* of ‏הוּקִיעַ‏ : it is weak, and has no philological justification. Cheyne remarks justly (*Exp. Times,* x, Aug. 1899, p. 522) that the word 'seems to be a religious synonym of ‏תלה‏ :' but it must also, it seems, have denoted some special form, or method, of hanging.

‏בְּגִבְעַת שָׁאוּל בְּחִיר י״י‏] 'The hill (‏הָהָר‏) on which according to *v.* 9 the sons of Saul were hung can hardly be any other than the hill *by Gibeon itself.* If however ‏בגבעון‏ (LXX ἐν Γαβαων) is thus to be restored for ‏בגבעת‏ (cf. 5, 25), ‏שָׁאוּל בְּחִיר י״י‏ falls through of itself. ‏בהר י״י‏ (cf. *v.* 9) became corrupted into ‏בחר י״י‏ (E. Castle *ap.* Then.), and ‏בגבעון בחר י״י‏ was understood in the sense of ‏בחיר שאול י״י‏ ' (We.). Read accordingly ‏בְּגִבְעוֹן בְּהַר יהוה‏ (so Bu. Now. Dh. etc.).

The הר יהוה will have been the sacred hill on which the ' great high-place of Gibeon' (1 Ki. 3, 4) lay.

אני אתן] With the pron. expressed, as in a reply a slight emphasis is not unsuitable: cf. *ch.* 3, 13. I 26, 6. Jud. 6, 18. 11, 9. 1 Ki. 2, 18. 2 Ki. 6, 3. Comp. *Tenses,* § 160 *Obs. n.*

7. שבעת י"י] See I 20, 42. 23, 18. The expression as Ex. 22, 10. 1 Ki. 2, 43.

8. רצפה בת איה] Saul's concubine, *ch.* 3, 7.

מיכל] a *lapsus calami* for מרב (so Luc., as well as other MSS. of LXX, and Pesh. [ب, which, however, stands regularly in Pesh. for מרב]): see I 18, 19 [1].

9. לפני יהוה] Cf. I 15, 33.

Kt. שְׁבַעְתִּים] 'they fell seven times together,' which is defended by Bö. Keil, and interpreted to mean 'they fell by seven similarly.' But the thought would be expressed most illogically: for though seven men fell together, this is by no means tantamount to *a group of seven falling seven times,* which is what the Hebrew would signify, the subject of ויפלו being the seven men. Read with Qrê שְׁבַעְתָּם 'and the seven of them fell together:' and cf. שְׁלָשְׁתָּם 'the three of them' Nu. 12, 4 al.; אַרְבַּעְתָּם 'the four of them' Ez. 1, 8 al.

בראשנים] So already LXX ἐν πρώτοις, but הראשנים is what would be expected. No doubt the ב is a *lapsus calami.* On the sing. נתך, see on I 1, 2.

11. ויער . . . את] So Gen. 27, 42. See GK. § 121ᵃ; Ew. § 295ᵇ; and the *Journal of Philology,* xi. 227–229.

12. חלום] Kt. תְּלוּם the regular form: Qrê תְּלָאֻם, as though from תְּלָא (GK. § 75ʳʳ; König, i. 539, 544): cf. תְּלוּאִים Dt. 28, 66. Hos. 11, 7; also עֲשָׂאֻן *Yōmā* 3, 9, *Pē'āh* 2, 6; בְּנָאוֹ *'Abōdāh zarah* 3, 7.

שֵׁם הפלשתים Kt.] שָׁמָּה פלשתים Qrê. פלשתים occurs much more frequently than הפלשתים: but the latter is found (e.g. I 4, 7. 7, 13).

13. ויאספו] In the same connexion, Jer. 8, 2. 25, 33 al.

14. בנו] add with LXX וְאֶת־עַצְמוֹת הַמּוּקָעִים.

צֶלַע] presumably = צֶלַע הָאֶלֶף, mentioned in Jos. 18, 28 among the

---

[1] But Targ. explains characteristically מיכל (*brought up*) דְּרַבִּיאַת בְּנֵי מרב: so [Jer.] *Quaestiones,* ad loc.; *Sanh.* 19ᵇ (see Aptow. *ZAW.* 1909, p. 251).

cities of Benjamin, next before Jerusalem, Gibeah, and Kiriath-ye'arim. Its site is unknown.

ויעתר] 'and *let himself be* entreated' (sc. successfully): the *Nifal tolerativum* (GK. § 51c). So Gen. 25, 21 al. The Arab. عَتَرَ is to *slaughter for sacrifice* (Wellh. *Heid.*[2] 118 n., cf. 142 n.; *Rel. Sem.* 227 f.): so (ל) אל (העתיר) עתר (Gen. *l.c.*; Ex. 8, 4. 5 al.) will apparently have meant originally to *sacrifice to*, weakened afterwards to *make entreaty to*.

(b) 15–22. *Exploits against the Philistines.*

15 f. 'From *vv.* 18, 19 [ותהי עוד המלחמה בגב] it is probable that *v.* 15 also speaks of a battle in Gob: observe in those two verses the article המלחמה, which is absent, so soon as the scene changes, in *v.* 20. No one, now, would read the words וישבו בנב *v.* 16, regarded by themselves, otherwise than as וַיֵּשְׁבוּ בְּנֹב; and it will be granted that נב and נב are readily interchangeable. As, however, a notice of the place at which the contest occurred is here required, the reading וישבו בנב *and abode in Gob* is in fact the correct one; the words are misplaced, and stood originally after עמו *v.* 15. By their removal ויעף דוד אשר בילידי ונ' stand in juxtaposition: in ויעף דוד is concealed the name of the Philistine, and perhaps a verb as well, such as ויקם, of which ויאמר 16b would be the sequel. It is no loss to be rid of the name *Yishbo-benob*, and of the statement that David *grew wearied*; and, as has been remarked, the scene of the battle can least of all at the beginning remain unmentioned' (We.). Read, therefore (after פלשתים): וַיָּקָם . . . אשר בילידי הרפה, the name of the Philistine being no longer recoverable. The site of 'Gob' is unknown.

16. בילידי הרפה] So *v.* 18 (in 1 Ch. 20, 4 מילידי הרפאים). הָרָפָה, not of an individual, but, as the *article* shews, collectively, of the race (cf. the *plur.* in 1 Ch. 20, 4): so *vv.* 20. 22 (=הָרָפָא 1 Ch. 20, 6. 8). The sing. is found only in these passages. The pl. רפאים occurs in the names of certain parts of Palestine reputed to have been the abode of a pre-historic giant population: Dt. 2, 11. 20. 3, 13; 3, 11 ('Og מיתר הרפאים : so in the Deuteronomizing sections of Joshua, Jos. 12, 4. 13, 12); Jos. 15, 8 al. (see on 5, 18) the עמק רפאים SW. of

Jerusalem; 17, 15; Gen. 14, 5 (E. of Jordan). 15, 20.—With·the unusual ילידי cf. the ילידי הענק Nu. 13, 22. 28. Jos. 15, 14.

קינו] from קַיִן, only here, explained as meaning *spear* (so LXX), from Arab. قَانَ to *forge iron*, قَيْن an *iron-smith* (but *not* a 'spear'). Klo. conjectured קובעו *his helmet* (I 17, 38; in *v.* 5 כובע): so Bu. Sm. Now. (not Dh.).   300 shekels of bronze would weigh about 13 lbs. av. (cf. on I 17, 5).

משקל נחשת] Read שֶׁקֶל נחשת. (AV. RV. are obliged to supply *shekels* in italics!)

חדשה] 'a new . . .:' either a subst. with which חדשה would agree has dropped out, or, which is more probable, חדשה is a corruption of the name of some rare weapon, which the Philistine wore.   LXX κορύνην *a club*.

17. את־נר ישראל] The lamp burning in a tent or house being a figure of the continued prosperity of its owner (ψ. 18, 29. Pr. 13, 9. Job 18, 6) or of his family (cf. the נר promised to the house of David, 1 Ki. 11, 36. 15, 4. 2 Ki. 8, 19=2 Ch. 21, 7†).

18–22 = 1 Ch. 20, 4–8.

18. בנב] Ch. בגזר.

סף] In 1 Ch. 20, 4 ספי.   On the varying terminations of one and the same pr. n. in parallel texts, comp. p. 4, and Wellh. *De Gentibus*, etc. (cited *ib.*), pp. 37–39.

‎19] ויך אלחנן בן יערי ארגים בית הלחמי את גלית הגתי.

Ch.   ויך אלחנן בן יעור ¹   את לחמי אחי גלית הגתי.

It is evident that ארגים has found its way into the text here by accident from the line below, though the error must be older than LXX²; and that יעיר must be read for יערי, with LXX, Pesh. and 1 Ch. 20, 5 Qrê. But what of the other variants? Is בית הלחמי את the original reading, and את לחמי אחי a corruption of this, or correction made for the purpose of harmonizing with I 17 (where it is

---

¹ Qrê יעיר as LXX, Pesh. (Jerome 'filius *saltus*' [cf. Aptowitzer, *ZAW*. 1909, p. 252], i.e. יער, without the *plena scriptio*).

² Or, at least, than Codd. BA (Αριωργειμ). Some twenty others, however, have Αρωρι; and Lucian reads καὶ ἐπάταξεν Ελλαναν υἱὸς Ιαδδειν υἱοῦ τοῦ Ελεμι τὸν Γολιαθ.

David who slays Goliath), or is את לחמי אחי the original text, and בית הלחמי את a corruption? When the character of the two alternative readings is considered, it is difficult to resist the conclusion that the former is the more probable. It is scarcely credible that a scribe having before him a text identical with that of Ch., even supposing that some letters in it had become obliterated or obscure, could, with the knowledge of I 17 that he must have possessed, have so altered or emended it as to make it state that 'Elḥanan the son of Ya'ir *the Beth-leḥemite* slew Goliath of Gath!' It is not merely the case of a word אחי 'brother of' having *dropped out* of the original text (which could readily be imagined), which the latter supposition involves, but the *substitution* of את for אחי, and the still more remarkable one of בית־הלחמי 'the Beth-leḥemite' for את־לחמי 'Laḥmi.' On the other hand, a motive for the correction of the text of Samuel by the Chronicler—or even by a copyist of the Chronicles—is obvious. So even Bertheau (on Ch.), as well as Ewald (*Hist.* iii. 70), Thenius, Wellh. (*Hist. of Israel*, p. 266), Kuenen (*Onderzoek*, §§ 21. 10; 23. 4)[1]. Upon the historical question involved, if the reading of Samuel be accepted as original, this is not the place to enter. See Kennedy, p. 122.

ועץ חניתו כמנור ארגים] See on I 17, 7.

20. Kt. מדין] i.e. probably מְדִין *vir mensurarum :* cf. אנשי מִדּוֹת Nu. 13, 32 : the ן of the pl. might be defended by צדנין I Ki. 11, 33. This ן, however, is rare (25 times, including מִלִּין 13 times in Job), and chiefly late (GK. § 87e) ; and the *masc.* form of the pl. does not occur elsewhere. Qrê מָדוֹן, so read already by LXX (καὶ ἦν ἀνὴρ Μαδων), but of uncertain signification. It is best to read מִדָּה with I Ch. 20, 6; cf. אנשי מִדָּה Is. 45, 14.—Observe that here מלחמה, unlike *vv.* 18. 19, is without the art., in agreement with the fresh scene of battle גת (We.).

מספר] adv. accus. '*in* number :' cf. on I 6, 4.

להרפה] So *v.* 22, and in I Ch. 20, 6. 8 (להרפא). The unusual

[1] Grätz (*Gesch.* i. 427) would explain the divergent readings by assuming as the original text ויך אלחנן בן יעיר בית הלחמי את לחמי אחי גלית הגתי.

retention of the art. after the prep.¹ may arise from הרפה being treated as a proper name.

21ᵃ. וַיֶּחֱרַף] Cf. I 17, 25, of Goliath.

21ᵇ Kt. שמעי] So LXX (Σεμεει): Qrê שִׁמְעָא. See on I 16, 9.

22. אֶת... יֻלְּדוּ] Ew. § 277ᵈ compares Jud. 20, 44. 46. Jer. 45, 4 : את having nearly, as it seems, the force of *as regards* ('*as regards* these four, they were,' etc.), and being used sometimes 'in the transition to something new,' sometimes, as here, 'in the brief repetition of a thought:' comp. *Lex.* 85ᵃ 3 a; and see also Kön. iii. §§ 108–110. But probably יֻלַּד (GK. § 121ᵇ) should be restored; cf. *v.* 11, above.

(c) 22. *David's Hymn of Triumph.*

This recurs (with textual variations) as ψ. 18, and has been so adequately dealt with in Commentaries on the Psalms accessible to the English student, that a fresh series of explanatory notes does not appear to the writer to be required.

(d) 23, 1–7. *David's 'Last Words.'*

1. נאם] The genitive which follows is usually יהוה (occasionally a synonym, as הָאָדוֹן Is. 1, 24. 19, 4): except here, נאם is joined with the name of a human speaker only Nu. 24, 3. 15 (with הגבר in the parallel clause, as here). 4. 16 (of Balaam). Pr. 30, 1 (הגבר): ψ. 36, 2 the gen. is פשׁע personified.

הֻקַם] The tone is thrown back from the ultima on account of the tone-syllable immediately following: the retrocession, however, takes place, as a rule, only when the penultima is an open syllable, as here (GK. § 29ᵉ; for exceptions, see § 29ᵍ; Kön. i. 475). The פ, found in many edd., is contrary to the Massorah.

עָל] על is here a substantive (as in מֵעַל Gen. 27, 39 al.), construed in the accus. after הֻקַם 'raised up *on high*,' as Hos. 7, 16 ישׁובו לא על they return, (but) not *up*wards; 11, 7 אֶל־עַל יִקְרָאֻהוּ they call it *up*wards, if the text of these two passages is correct.

---

¹ Elsewhere (except in כהיום) rare, and mostly late : *ch.* 16, 2 Kt. (the ל an error) ; I 13, 21 וּלְהַקַּרְדֻּמּוֹת (also probably an error : notice the following וּלְה') ; 2 Ki. 7, 12 Kt. ; Ez. 40, 25 ; 47, 22 ; ψ. 36, 6 ; Qoh. 8, 1 ; Neh. 9, 19 ; 12, 38 ; 2 Ch. 10, 7 ; 25, 10 ; 29, 27 being all the examples that occur. Cf. GK. § 35ⁿ.

נעים זמירות ישראל] Lit. *the pleasant one of* (the) *songs of Israel.*
נעים is *pleasant, agreeable* (cf. 1, 23 (of Saul and J.), Cant. 1, 16,
and the verb *ch.* 1, 26 (נעמת לי מאד); and זמירות means *songs* (not
necessarily ' psalms '), Is. 24, 16. 25, 5 (זמיר עריצים יענה). ψ. 95, 2.
119, 54. Job 35, 10†. Does, now, the whole expression mean (*a*),
The pleasant one of songs (= *The pleasant singer*) *of Israel* (so Ew.
§ 291ᵃ)—נעים זמירות, like I 25, 3 רַע מַעֲלָלִים, Jer. 32, 19 גְּדוֹל הָעֵצָה,
ψ. 119, 1 תמימי דרך etc. (GK. § 128ˣ; Kön. iii. § 336ᵇ), and ישראל
limiting, not זמירות alone, but the compound idea נעים זמירות, like
Dt. 1, 41 כְּלֵי מִלְחַמְתּוֹ, not ' the weapons of his war,' but *his weapons-of-
war ;* Is. 50, 8 בעל משפטי; 28, 1 עֲטֶרֶת גֵּאוּת שִׁכּוֹרֵי אפרים *the crown of
pride* (= *the proud crown*) *of the drunkards of Ephraim ;* and the
parallels cited on *ch.* 8, 10 (איש מלחמות תעי), and GK. § 135ⁿ? Or
does it mean (*b*), ' The pleasant *object* of the songs of Israel, the " joy "
(Sm.) or the " darling " (Klo. Bu. Kenn. Kit.) of the songs of Israel? '
If (*a*) be right, David will be alluded to as the writer of graceful and
attractive poetry (cf. Am. 6, 5ᵇ),—not necessarily either including,
or excluding, religious poetry, though the rend. ' the sweet *psalmist* of
Israel' suggests much too strongly the unhistorical David of the
Chronicles and the titles of the Psalms; if (*b*) be right, it will allude
to him as a popular favourite, whose achievements in war were
celebrated by the poets of his people (cf. I 18, 7 = 21, 12 = 29, 5).
König (iii. § 281ʰ; *Stilistik*, 284) supports (*a*), and it is, grammatically,
a perfectly legitimate rendering : but most moderns prefer (*b*). The
explanation of נעים from نَغَم, as meaning *singer* (Now. Dh.; *Lex.* 654ᵃ
' perhaps '), is precarious.

2. דבר בי] דבר ב' is used similarly, of God (never of men [1])
speaking with a person, Nu. 12, 2. 6. 8ᵃ. 1 Ki. 22, 28. Hos. 1, 2ᵃ.
Hab. 2, 1 ; and in the phrase הַמַּלְאָךְ הַדֹּבֵר בִּי Zech. 1, 9. 13. 2, 2. 7.
4, 1. 4. 5. 5, 5. 10. 6, 4. The usual expression, even when the
subject is God, is דבר אל (e.g. Ex. 33, 11. Nu. 12, 4. Hos. 1, 2ᵇ) [2];
and it is a question what is the exact force of דבר ב'. In some
of the passages the meaning *in* or *through* [3] would be admissible ;

---

[1] Except in other senses, as *against, about* (I 19, 3 ; 25, 39).
[2] Or sometimes דבר את, as Gen. 17, 3. 22. 23. Ex. 25, 22. Ez. 2, 1. 3, 22. 24.
[3] Though *through* would be more properly בְיַד : Is. 20, 2. Hos. 12, 11ᵇ al.

but these will not suit the phrase in Zech. Ew. (§ 217[f]) understood the phrase on the analogy of שחק ב׳ to play *with*, עבד ב׳ to labour *with* (=to use as a labourer, Ex. 1, 14 al.), in the sense of *to speak with*, but with the collateral idea of a superior speaking *with* an inferior as his minister (Now. *Hosea* (1880), p. 3; cf. C. H. H. Wright on Zech. 1, 9). Others regard the ב׳ as having the force of a strengthened *to* (cf. ראה ב׳, הביט ב׳ to look *at*: שמע ב׳)[1]: others, again, suppose it to express the idea of speaking *into* a person (*hinein*reden)[2]. On the whole, the explanation of Ewald appears to be the most probable. But, however it be explained, the phrase certainly appears to imply closer and more intimate converse than the ordinary דבר אל.

ומלתו] מלה is properly an Aramaic word, in Heb. used only in poetry, *ψ*. 19, 5. 139, 4. Pr. 23, 9 and thirty-four times in Job.

3. אלהי ישראל] Luc. Sm. Bu. Now. Dh. אלהי יעקב. The variation, as compared with 3[b], is an improvement: cf. *v*. 1.

צור ישראל] Is. 30, 29: cf. *ch.* 22, 3. 32. 47; Dt. 32, 4. 15. 18. 31. 37.

מושל וג׳] 'When one ruleth over men, as a just one,
When one ruleth (in) the fear of God,
(*v*. 4) Then is it as the light,' etc.

מושל is a ptcp. absolute; cf. on I 2, 13; and Jud. 7, 17. 9, 33 (*Tenses*, §§ 126; 135. 6; GK. § 116[w]): for ו, marking the pred., comp. Job 4, 6 (Delitzsch); Pr. 10, 25; *ch.* 15, 34 (*Tenses*, § 125 *Obs.*; GK. § 143[d]). The accents must be disregarded: the chief break in clause *b* should be at צדּיק. For יראת as adv. accus., GK. § 118[q]. 20 MSS., however, read בְּיראת י׳.

4. 'Then is it as the light of morning, when the sun ariseth,
A morning without clouds,
That maketh the young grass to shoot after rain out of the earth.'

The beneficent operation of a just and gracious rule is compared to the influence of the sun, on a cloudless morning after rain, in refreshing and invigorating the growing verdure of the earth.

---

1 König, *Offenbarungsbegriff des A T.s*, ii. (1882), p. 179.
2 Riehm, *Messianic Prophecy* (ed. 2), 1891, p. 41.

ובאור בקר] LXX καὶ ἐν Θεοῦ φῶτι, which is adopted by Th. We. and Stade (*Gesch.* i. 297): 'Then is it as the light of God (of Yahweh, We.), in the morning when the sun ariseth,' etc. But אור and בקר are often conjoined in Heb.; and it is doubtful if the addition is an improvement.

לא]לא עבות and בלי in poetry, and אין in prose as well, are construed with a following subst. as a circumstantial clause, in which case they become equivalent to the English *without:* Ex. 21, 11 ויצאה חנם אין כסף she shall go out free, *without* money; Job 24, 10 naked, they walk up and down בלי לבוש *without covering;* 12, 24 בתהו לא דרך=in a *pathless* waste (*Tenses*, § 164).

מנגה ממטר וג'] 'Through brightness after rain the young grass (springeth) out of the earth.' נגה of a brightly shining light, as Is. 62, 1. Pr. 4, 18; and מן of the cause, as Job 4, 9. 14, 19 מֵרִיחַ מַיִם יַפְרִחַ (cf. on 7, 29). But there must be some error here. A verb is imperatively required; and the two nouns with מן (מנגה ממטר) are not an elegance. הָשָׁאָה אָרֶץ (cf. Joel 2, 22) *the earth springeth* might be a sufficient change: but Klo. Bu. al. may be right in thinking that a ptcp. is concealed under מנגה. Klo. suggests מַצְמִיחַ (ψ. 104, 14), מְחַיֶּה, or even מְנוֹבֵב (Zech. 9, 17); Sm. proposes מַגִּיהַּ *making to gleam* (viz. in the sunlight after the rain), מנובב, to judge from the Qal, and נִיב, suggests the idea of *fruit* too much to be suitable for דשא. מצמיח would be the best; but the *ductus litterarum* differs a good deal from that of מנגה.

5. 'For is not my house thus with God?
>   For he hath appointed for me an everlasting covenant,
>   Set forth in all things and secured.
> For all my welfare, and all my pleasure,
>   Will he not cause it to spring forth?'

In *v.* 5ᵃ, as the text stands, כי is explicative (*Lex.* 473ᵇ c), introducing an example of the general truth expressed in *v.* 3ᵇ–4: the blessings of a righteous rule, described in general terms in *v.* 3ᵇ–4, David in *v.* 5 anticipates in particular for his own dynasty, on the ground of the covenant established with him by Yahweh, and of his assurance that the welfare which he desires himself for his house and people will be promoted by God. כן points backwards to the descrip-

tion in *v.* 3ᵇ–4. In כי לא וג׳ the question is indicated by the tone
(on I 11, 12). The case is, however, an extreme one; and הֲלֹא for
כי לא (Bu.) would be an improvement. Still כי was read by LXX.
ברית עולם is an allusion to 7, 12–16. Nestle (*Marg.* 21), comparing
7, 26ᵇ (ובית עבדך דוד יהיה נכון לפניך), would indeed read נָכוֹן for לא כן
(so Now. Dh.), 'Surely (*Lex.* 472ᵇ ⊝) my house is *established* with
God,' etc. ערוכה בכל ושמרה is an expression borrowed probably
from legal terminology, and intended to describe the ברית as one
of which the terms are fully and duly set forth (comp. the forensic use
of ערך in Job 13, 18 al. *to state in order* or *set forth* pleadings), and
which is secured by proper precautions against surreptitious alteration
or injury. ישע *welfare,* as Job 5, 4. 11. Is. 17, 10, and often in the
Psalms, as 12, 6. 18, 3. 36. 20, 7 etc. For חפץ read חֶפְצִי : to *understand* the suff. from ישעי,—in spite of Ex. 15, 2=Is. 12, 2=ψ. 118, 14
(where either render זִמְרָת ' a song,' or, better, read זִמְרָתִי)),—is contrary
to idiom. For the following כי לא read probably הֲלֹא (We., GK.
§ 150ᵃ *n.*); as the text stands, כי will be resumptive of the כי just
before. צמח is used figuratively: comp. II Isaiah 45, 8. 58, 8. 61,
11ᵇ. But יַצְלִיחַ 'cause it to *prosper*' would be a good emendation.

In *vv.* 6–7 the poet contrasts the fate of the wicked, whom men
spurn and extirpate by force, with the love and honour awarded
by his people to the righteous rulers described in *vv.* 3–4.

6. ' But worthlessness—as thorns chased away are all of them :
    For not with hand do men take them.'

בליעל is a *cas. pendens* (as Is. 32, 7 וְכֵלַי כֵּלָיו רָעִים, ψ. 89, 3 and
often: *Tenses,* § 197. 2), and the suff. in כלהם refers to the *persons*
in whom the בליעל is conceived implicitly to inhere. The form
כֻּלָּהֶם (GK. § 91ᶠ) is to be explained on the analogy of שְׁרָפָתַם, וּגְנַבְתַם,
etc. (Stade, §§ 350ᵃ. 3 ; 107ᵇ. 1): this uncontracted form of the suffix
of 3 pl. does not occur elsewhere with sing. substantives in MT. (except
in the *fem.* : כֻּלָּהְנָה I Ki. 7, 37 ; בְּתוֹכְהֶנָה Ez. 16, 53 ; and in a few forms
such as לְבַדְּהֶן Gen. 21, 28. מִלְּבֶהֶן Ez. 13, 17: Stade, §§ 353ᵃ 1a, γ, 2, 353ᵇ),
but it must be assumed in Jer. 15, 10 [see p. xxviii]; cf. מִנְּהֶם once,
Job 11, 20, for מֵהֶם, also אֶתְהֶם (5 times), עֲמָהֶם often, both in and out
of pause [the sign † in Stade, § 350ᵃ. 4 ; 377ᵇ is an oversight], לָהֶם
always. מֻנַד is the passive either of הֵנַד *to chase away* (Job 18, 18

(וַיָּדֻד בחזיון לילה 8, 20: וּמִתְּבֵל יְנַדֻהוּ), or of הֵנִיד *to put to flight* (ψ. 36, 12 וַיָּד רשעים אל תְּנַדֵנִי 2 Ki. 21, 8 האדמה מן ישראל רגל להניד). But the word excites suspicion: for it is not one that would naturally be applied to *thorns*. Klo. proposes קוֹץ מִדְבָּר (cf. Jud. 8, 7. 16); so Sm. Bu. (alt.) Now. Dh. For ביד see on I 26, 23. The subj. of יקחו is, of course, הלוקחים (on I 16, 4).

    7. ' But the man (who) touches them arms himself with iron and
        a spear's shaft;
    And with fire are they burned utterly.'

יִמָּלֵא, on the analogy of מִלֵּא יָדוֹ בַקֶּשֶׁת 2 Ki. 9, 24, lit. *fills himself*, viz. in so far as the hand using the weapon is concerned. בַּשֶּׁבֶת: lit. *in the sitting*, which is interpreted to mean ' in (their) place,' or ' on the spot.' But the expression is a very singular one; and the supposed meaning is destitute of analogy, תַּחְתָּם being the idiomatic word for expressing it (Job 40, 12 וַהֲדֹךְ רשעים תחתם: cf. I 14, 9). Nor is *cessation, annihilation* (from שָׁבַת), proposed by Delitzsch on Pr. 20, 3, a more probable rendering. The word is in fact otiose after ובאש שרוף ישרפו; and, it cannot be doubted, has arisen in the text by error from בשבת in the line below.

Conjectural restorations of 5ᶜ–7 :—Now. (agreeing with Sm., except in the part left vacant) כי כל ישעי וכל חפצי בו || כי לא יצמיחו בליעל | כקוץ מדבר כלהם || כי לא ביד ילָקֵטוּ | ואיש לא יִנַּע בהם || ...... | .... || (כי לא וג') ובאש שרוף יִשָּׂרֵפוּ: *For they are not picked up by hand, neither*—Now. omits the לא, but it is needed—*doth any man labour upon them*, i.e. they are worthless). Bu., though not very confidently, suggests : || כי כל ישעי וחפצי בו כי לא יִצְמַח (יַצְלִיחַ) בליעל | כקוץ מדבר (כמוץ נִדָּח (or) כלהם || כי לא ביד יקָּחוּ | ולא איש יִגַּע יְיַע בהם || לא יְמַלֵּט (יָעַל or) ברזל ועץ חנית | כי באש שרוף יִשָּׂרֵפוּ: (כי לא וג') *For not by* (human) *hand* (Job 34, 20) *are they taken away, nor doth man touch them; iron and the shaft of a spear doth not deliver* (or *profit*) *them, but*, etc.).

On this poem, comp. Ewald, *Die Dichter des Alten Bundes*, i. 1 (1866), pp. 143–145; Orelli, *Old Testament Prophecy*, § 20. The central idea is the prophetic thought, expressed by David in the near prospect of death, that if his successors upon the throne are guided by righteous principles of government, his dynasty ('house,' as 7, 16), under the blessing of God, will be established and prosper.

This thought is developed in the three strophes (*vv.* 3ᵇ-4, 5, 6-7) which form the body of the poem. Observe the finished parallelism of the exordium (*vv.* 1-3ª, forming a strophe of eight lines).

(*e*) **23,** 8-39. *Further exploits against the Philistines* (comp. **21,** 15-22), *and list of David's heroes.*

23, 8-39 = 1 Ch. **11,** 11-41ª: twelve of the names recur also in 1 Ch. 27, 2-15, as those of the captains of the twelve divisions of David's army.

Here are the three lists, as they stand in MT.,—the names in several instances vary, nor is it always possible to determine which form is original, or whether both may not be corrupt :—

2 Sam. 23.	1 Ch. 11.	1 Ch. 27.
8. ישב בשבת תחכמני	11. ישבעם בן חכמוני	2. ישבעם בן זבדיאל
9. אלעזר בן דדי בן אחחי	12. אלעזר בן דודו האחוחי	4. דודי האחוחי
11. שמה בן אגא הררי		
18. אבישי אחי יואב	20. אבשי אחי יואב	
20. בניהו בן יהוידע	22. בניה בן יהוידע	5. בניהו בן יהוידע
24. עשהאל אחי יואב	26. עשהאל אחי יואב	7. עשהאל אחי יואב
אלחנן בן דדו	אלחנן בן דודו	
25. שמה החרדי	27. שְׁמוֹת ההרורי	8. שמהות היזרח
אליקא החרדי		
26. חלץ הפלטי	חלץ הפלוני	10. חלץ הפלוני
עירא בן עקש התקעי	28. עירא בן עקש התקועי	9. עירא בן עקש התקועי
27. אביעזר הענתתי	אביעזר הענתותי	12. אביעזר הענתותי
מבני החֻשתי	29. סבכי החֻשתי	11. סבכי החֻשתי לַזַּרְחִי
28. צלמן האחחי	עילי האחוחי	
מהרי הנטפתי	30. מהרי הנטפתי	13. מהרי הנטופתי לַזַּרְחִי
29. חלב בן בענה הנטפתי	חלד בן בענה הנטופתי	15. חלדי הנטופתי לעתניאל
אתַּי בן ריבי	31. איתי בן ריבי	
30ª. בניהו פרעתני	בניה הפרעתני	14. בניה הפרעתוני

2 Sam. 23.		1 Ch. 11.	
30b.	הדי מנחלי געש	32.	חורי מנחלי געש
31.	אבי־עלבון הערבתי		אביאל הערבתי
	עזמות הברחמי	33.	עזמות הבחרומי
32.	אליחבא השעלבני		אליחבא השעלבני
	בני ישן	34.	בני השם הגזוני
33.	יהונתן : 33 שמה ההררי		יונתן בן שנא ההררי
	אחיאם בן שרר האררי	35.	אחיאם בן שכר ההררי
34.	אליפלט בן אחסבי בן המעכתי		אליפל בן אור
		36.	חפר המכרתי
	אליעם בן אחיתפל הגלני		אחיה הפלני
35.	חצרו הכרמלי	37.	חצרו הכרמלי
	פערי הארבי		נערי בן־אֶזְבֵּי :
36.	יגאל בן נתן מצבה	38.	יואל אחי נתן
	בָּנִי הגדי		מבחר בן הַגְרִי
37.	צלק העמוני	39.	צלק העמוני
	נחרי הבארתי		נחרי הברתי
38.	עירא היתרי	40.	עירא היתרי
	גרב היתרי		גרב היתרי
39.	אוריה החתי	41a.	אוריה החתי

First come the 'Three,' Ishba'al, Eleazar son of Dodo, and Shammah (*vv.* 8–17), whose exploits are specially recorded, then two others, Abishai and Jehoiada (*vv.* 18–23), whose bravery did not place them on an equality with the 'Three,' but who ranked above the 'Thirty,' lastly the 'Thirty' (*vv.* 24–39).

8–12. Exploits of the Three.

8. ישב בשבת] LXX Ἰεβοσθε (i.e. איש־בשת, as 2, 8 etc.); Luc. Ἰεσβααλ (i.e. אשבעל; cf. on I 14, 49); LXX 1 Ch. 11 ἸεσεβαΔα, (no doubt for ἸεσεβαΛα), Luc. Ἰεσσεβααλ [1]; 1 Ch. 27 Σοβαλ. The original name was thus evidently אֶשְׁבַּעַל (so first Geiger, *ZDMG.* 1862, p. 730; and then We. Klo. Bu. etc.); אשבעל will then have been first altered to אשבשת (on 4, 2), whence LXX Ἰεβοσθε; this

---

[1] Also Codd. 44, 74, 120, 134, 144, 236, 243, Ἰεσεβααλ ; 56, 119, 121, Ἰσβααλ.

next became יֵשְׁבֶשֶׁת (cf. יֵשׁוּי p. 120), which in its turn was corrupted into יֵשֵׁב בְּשֶׁבֶת. In 1 Ch. 11, 27 בְּעַל was got rid of by a different change : but in each of the three passages the original name still existed uncorrected in the MSS. by which some texts of the LXX were revised.

תחבמני] Read הַחַכְמֹנִי with We. Kp. etc.: cf. 1 Ch. 11, 11. 27, 32.

הִשְׁלִשִׁי] Explained to mean *knights* שָׁלִישִׁים (Ex. 14, 7. 1 Ki. 9, 22. 2 Ki. 10, 25 al.): but this leaves the gentile or patronymic '—- unaccounted for. From the sequel, it is tolerably clear that we must read either (with 1 Ch. 11, 11 Kt.) ראש השלושים, or (with Lucian, both here and 1 Ch.) ראש הַשְּׁלֹשָׁה (so We.). The latter is probably better (Bu. Now. Dh.): Ishba'al is styled *Chief* of the 'Three.'

הוא עדינו העצנו] The words are meaningless[1]. Most moderns read, with 1 Ch. 11, 11, הוּא עוֹרֵר אֶת־חֲנִיתוֹ he *brandished* (Is. 10, 26) *his spear:* cf. *v.* 18. But this is rather an easy emendation; and it is not supported by the LXX ; for ἐξήγειρε τὸ δόρυ αὐτοῦ, *v.* 18, shews that ἐσπάσατο τὴν ῥομφαίαν αὐτοῦ here is derived from the LXX translation of *Chronicles* (We.). Luc. οὗτος διεκόσμει τὴν διασκευήν, which Klo. thinks points to עוֹרֵר מַעַרָכָם (cf. 1 Ch. 12, 38), improved by Marquart into עֹרֵר מַעֲצָדוֹ *brandished his axe* (Jer. 10, 3. Is. 44, 12†): so Bu. Dh. עוֹרֵר חֲצִינוֹ, also *brandished his axe* (Ass. *ḥaṣinnu, axe;* Eth. חצין *iron* (the common word for it: Dillm. *Lex.* 623); Targ. חֲצִינָא= מעצד Jer. 10, 3. Is. 44, 12, and in Talm.: Syr. ܡܥܨܐ *axe* (rare): cf. Fränkel, *Die Aram. Fremdwörter im Arab.*, 1886, p. 86 f.). Either מעצדו or חצינו resembles העצנו more than חניתו does ; and it is possible that one of these corrections is right.

עַל שְׁמֹנֶה מֵאוֹת] '*over* 800 slain ones,' i.e. in triumph, after he had slain them. For שמנה 1 Ch. 11, 11 has שלש. But 'the text here is attested by all Versions [except Luc., who has ἐννακοσίους]; and is also more probable independently, as otherwise ' Ishba'al ' would have no superiority over Abishai, *v.* 18 ' (Thenius).

9. דֹּדִי] so Kt. and 1 Ch. 27, 4 : דֹּדוֹ Qrê, LXX (τοῦ πατραδέλφου

---

[1] On the curious rend. of the Vulg. ('ipse est quasi *tenerrimus ligni vermiculus*'), based on a Haggádic interpretation of עדינו and העצנו, see Aptowitzer, *ZAW.* 1909, p. 252) כשהיה יושב ועוסק בתורה היה מְעַדֵּן עצמו כתולעת וּבַשָּׁעָה שיוצא (למלחמה היה מַקְשֶׁה עצמו כעץ).

αὐτοῦ), and 1 Ch. 11, 12. דֹּדִי seems best: probably short for דֹּדִיָּה 'Yah is my uncle (or friend):' cf. אֲחִיָה, אֲבִיָה etc.; *EB.* 3289 f., and § 52 *end;* Gray, *Heb. Prop. Names,* 60 ff.; and also above, p. xc (on דודה).

בן־אחחי] No doubt an error for האחחי, as in 1 Ch. 11 and 27: in 1 Ch. 8, 4 אחוח is the name of a Benjaminite clan. In 1 Ch. 27 the words אלעזר בן appear to have accidentally fallen out before דודי.

הוא היה עם דוד בפס דמים] Read after Ch. עם דוד בחרפם בפלשתים ופלשתים (cf. I 17, 1 אפס דמים): the mention of the *place,* as Th. remarks, is required by the following שם. That the text of Samuel is imperfect appears independently (1) from the construction of חרף with ב, which is not found elsewhere, and not substantiated by חרף ל 2 Ch. 32, 17; (2) by the omission of אשר (implied in MT.) before נאספו, which is suspicious in prose (on I 14, 21).

ויעלו] *were gone up,* i.e. had retreated (cf., from a siege, 1 Ki. 15, 19. Jer. 21, 2; and on *ch.* 20, 2): in 10ᵇ they *return.*

10. הוא] Read, after the preceding הוא היה עם דוד דוד (see the last note but one), והוא (Luc. Pesh. Sm. Bu. etc.).

ותדבק וג'] The muscles became so stiff that he could not relax them. Cf. the parallel cited by Sm. from Doughty, *Arabia Deserta,* ii. 28: 'The Kusman perished before me until the evening, when my fingers could not be loosed from the handle of the sword.'

ישבו] More picturesque than שָׁבוּ: *ch.* 2, 28.

אך] Position as I 21, 5. Ex. 10, 17 al. אך הפעם.

11. אנא] Luc. Ηλα, whence Klo. Dh. אֶלָא (1 Ki. 4, 18).

הררי] Read הַהֲרָרִי, as *v.* 33 and 1 Ch. 11, 34.

לחיה] חיה (*v.* 13) yields here no suitable sense. Read with Bochart, Kennicott, Ew. (iii. 141), Th. Bö. We. Keil, Kp. Bu. etc. לֶחְיָה *to Lehi* (Jud. 15, 9: Luc. ἐπὶ σιαγόνα); and note the following שם.

11–12. ותהי שם ... תשועה גדולה] In 1 Ch. 11, 13–14 these words (slightly varied) are referred to the exploit of *Eleazar,* the words from 9ᵇ ויעלו to 11ᵃ לחיה (incl.) having been accidentally omitted. For עדשים *lentiles* Ch. has שעֹרים *barley.*

12. ויתיצב] 'and took his stand:' similarly I 17, 16.

13–17. An exploit of three of the Thirty.

13. Kt. שלשים] An evident error: read with Qrê שְׁלֹשָׁה for שְׁלֹשִׁם. These 'three of the Thirty chief' are not those just mentioned (Ishba'al,

Eleazar, and Shammah), but three others, belonging to the 'Thirty' named *v.* 24 ff. (Keil). The 'Thirty' have not, however, yet been mentioned; so perhaps We. is right in treating *vv.* 13-17ᵃ as not standing here in their original connexion, and regarding 17ᵇ as the original close of *vv.* 8–12 (notice 17ᵇ אלה, which suits 8–12 much better than 14–17ᵃ).

מהשלשים ראש] ראש is not expressed by LXX, Pesh. (though 1 Ch. 11, 15 has it), and it seems out of place: the standing expression is the 'Thirty,' and ראש, where it is used, denotes their *leader* (*v.* 18 ; cf. 8). The Heb. also is peculiar : we should expect משלשים הראשים (GK. § 134ᵉ, ¹; for the place of the art., see Gen. 18, 28. Jos. 6, 8. 22. I 17, 14)); but, as exceptions occur (Jud. 11, 33. 1 Ki. 9, 11 ; Nu. 16, 35. Jos. 4, 4 שנים הֶעָשֹׂר אִישׁ: Kön. iii. § 313ⁱ, and esp. his luminous synopsis of constructions of numerals in *AJSL.* xviii. (1902), p. 138 ff. ; Herner, *Syntax der Zahlwörter,* 1893, pp. 93–119), this ought not perhaps to be pressed. See the next note.

אל קציר] cannot mean *in* or *during* harvest—for אל is not used thus of time. Luc. has εἰς τὴν πέτραν ; and so 1 Ch. 11, 15 עַל־הַצֻּר *to the rock* (omitting ויבאו): but the fact that the place to which the three heroes went is stated *after* אל דוד is an objection both to this reading, and also to the supposition that any place-name (LXX εἰς Καδων) is concealed under קציר. Perhaps Bu. is right in the suggestion that ראש קציר 'at the *beginning* of harvest' should be read (before ויבאו),—ראש as Jud. 7, 19. Nu. 10, 10.

מערת עדלם] Read probably מְצֻדַת עדלם: see *v.* 13 ; and on I 22, 1. With וירדו cf. 5, 17ᵇ.

חית] the fem. of חַי I 18, 18 according to Nöldeke, *ZDMG.* 1886, 176, i.e. a *clan,* or *company of related families,* making a raid together (*Lex.* 312ᵇ). Explained in Ch. by מחנה.

בעמק רפאים] in 5, 18. 22 also the scene of a Philistine attack. No doubt the occasion also was the same.

14. המצודה] במצודה I 22, 4. 5. 24, 23. II 5, 17.

בית לחם] *in* or *at* Bethlehem : p. 37 *note.*

15. מבאר] Kt. מִבְּאֵר from the *well ;* Qrê מִבֹּאר (Ch. מִבּוֹר) from the *cistern.* The Qrê may be due to the fact that there was no 'well' known at Bethlehem in later times: there seems to be none there

now (Rob. i. 470, 473). If 'Adullam was at 'Îd el-mîyeh (on I 22, 1),
Bethlehem would be about 13 miles from it.

17. יהוה] Read, with many MSS., Lucian (παρὰ Κυρίου), Pesh.
Targ. and Ch., מיהוה, in accordance with usage (e.g. I 26, 11).

. . . הרם] On the aposiopesis, cf. Ew. § 303ᵃ; GK. § 167ᵃ. The
aposiopesis is, however, extreme : and it is better to insert אשתה (LXX)
after בנפשתם. Bu. objects indeed to the position : but though it is true
that הֲ, like אם, יען, למען, etc., is, as a rule, followed immediately by the
verb, the object, or some other word, may quite correctly follow it for
emphasis (pp. 35, 323): cf. Nu. 16, 14 הֲנַקֵּר האנשים ההם תְּנַקֵּר. 2 Ki.
6, 22 הֲאֲשֶׁר שבית בחרבך ובקשתך אתה מַכֶּה. Am. 5, 25; with other
words, Gen. 3, 11. Nu. 20, 10. Dt. 32, 6. *ch.* 3, 33. 2 Ki. 1, 6. Job
15, 8. Is. 36, 12. Jer. 5, 9. Ez. 20, 30. Cf. after הֲלֹא, Nu. 23, 12.
Jud. 11, 24. Dt. 31, 17. Jer. 44, 21. Ez. 34, 2 הלוא הצאן ירעו הרעים.

בנפשותם] The ב is the *Beth pretii : at the cost* or *risk of* their lives :
cf. 1 Ki. 2, 23.

18–23. The Thirty.

18. Kt. השלשי] The sense requires that we should read, with
Pesh. We. Grätz[1], Berth. (on 1 Ch. 11, 20 f.) הַשָּׁלִשָׁם *the Thirty*, with
מִן־הַשָּׁלִשָׁם in 19ᵃ (see 23ᵃ). Abishai was chief of the 'Thirty,' and
distinguished beyond the rest of the 'Thirty : ' but he was not equal
to the 'Three.' ולו שם בשלשה (similarly of Benaiah, in *v.* 22ᵇ)
occasions difficulty. In spite of 1 Ch. 11, 21 (RV. *marg.*) it does
not appear that a *second* triad of worthies, to which Abishai and
Benaiah might have belonged, is here really indicated; and yet, as
it seems, the reference cannot be to the 'Three' (Ishba'al, Eleazar,
Shammah): for it is expressly said of these two that they did not
equal them. The majority of modern Commentators read (both
here and, *mutatis mutandis*, in 22ᵇ) either (Bu. Sm.) בַּשְּׁלשָׁה *like the
Three*—they had a name *like* that of the Three, though they did not
actually belong to them; or, with Pesh. We. Berth. Now. Kit. (in 22,
ap. Kautzsch), Dh. בַּשְּׁלִשִׁים—in spite of the tautology (Bu.) with 19ᵃ
and 23ᵃ—*among the Thirty*,—Abishai and Benaiah attained *fame*

---

[1] In a note on the lists of David's heroes, *Gesch. der Juden*, i. (1874), pp.
419–428.

(emph.) among the Thirty, and were more distinguished than the others ; but they did not equal the Three. J. T. S. Stopford, however, suggests very plausibly (*Hermathena,* viii. 223) וְלֹא שֵׁם לוֹ בַּשְּׁלֹשָׁה. For Abishai, see I 26, 6–9. *ch.* 2, 18. 24. 3, 30. 10, 10. 14. 16, 9. 11, etc. ; 21, 17.

19. הכי] הכי=*Is it that* ...? 9, 1 (in a simple interrogation). Gen. 27, 36 (expressing surprise[1]). 29, 15. Job 6, 22 (expecting a negative answer)†: for כי, comp. on I 8, 9. Here, however, an *affirmative* answer is required, which does not seem to be compatible with the usage of הֲכִי (AV. RV. *interpolate* ' not '). The word does not stand in 1 Ch. 11, 21, or in the similarly worded sentence below, *v.* 23ᵃ (though there 1 Ch. 11, 25 has מִן הַשְּׁלוֹשִׁים הִנּוֹ נִכְבָּד הוּא); and can scarcely be right. It is easiest to suppose it a corruption of הִנּוֹ, preserved in 1 Ch. 11, 25. For the position of מִן־הַשְּׁלשָׁה, comp. on I 20, 8.

20. בניהו בן יהוידע] 8, 18. 1 Ki. 1, 8—2, 46. 4, 4.

(Qrê) בן] בן איש חיל is not expressed in LXX. Read either איש חיל, בן having been accidentally repeated from בן יהוידע ; or איש בן חיל (the sing. of אנשים בני חיל Jud. 18, 2 : cf. איש גבור חיל Ru. 2, 1, איש נביא etc.): the former is preferable.

רב־פעלים] The expression has a poetical tinge. פֹּעַל, except in the ‖, 1 Ch. 11, 22, and Ru. 2, 12 (פֶּעֳלֵךְ י׳ יְשַׁלֵּם), occurs only in poetry. Cf. I 25, 3 רַע מַעֲלָלִים.

קבצאל] 1 Ch. 11, 22. Jos. 15, 21 (in the Negeb, in the direction of Edom.)†; יקבצאל Neh. 11, 25†. Not identified.

את שני אראל] Read אֶת שְׁנֵי בְנֵי אֲרִיאֵל with LXX ; and then either מִמּוֹאָב (cf. above מִקַּבְצְאֵל), or, as מִן is not usual with the name of a country, הַמּוֹאָבִי, for מוֹאָב. Klo., however, observing that an exploit against a lion follows, which, as the text stands, is wedged in between two exploits against warriors, conjectures, very cleverly, and almost convincingly, אֶת־שְׁנֵי בְנֵי הָאֲרִי אֶל־מַחֲבֹאָם, which Bu. accepts : ' smote (and pursued) the two young lions (the cubs of the lion mentioned in *v.* 20ᵇ : בְּנֵי, as in בְּנֵי לָבִיא Job 4, 11) into their hiding-place (I 23, 23).' אֲרִאֵל (except Is. 29, 1, as apparently a cryptic name of Zion) does not occur elsewhere as a pr. n.: but this is not a fatal objection to

---

[1] ' *Can it be that* he is called Jacob, and has hence overreached me twice ? '

its being a pr. n. : we might also punctuate אַרְאֵל. For another view
of the meaning of אראל, see W. R. Smith, *Rel. Sem.* 469 (² 488).

ירד והכה] the sequence is unusual, though instances occur (*Tenses,*
§˙133; GK. § 112ᵖᵖ⁻ᵘᵘ). יֵרֵד וְהִכָּה here would be unsuitable: for
obviously a *single* exploit is referred to.

הבאר] here הַבְּאֵר (=הַבּוֹר), the *cistern,* is evidently better than הַבְּאֵר
the *well* (cf. 15).

21. את איש מצרי] Cf. 4, 11 את איש צדיק; and GK. § 117ᵈ. Read,
with Bu., either איש מצרי, or (1 Ch. 11, 23) את האיש המצרי : the
former is better.

Kt. אשר מראה] LXX ἄνδρα ὁρατὸν=Qrê איש מראה. But, as We.
remarks, איש מראה would mean a *handsome* man (Is. 53, 2 : cf. Gen.
39, 6 etc.), not, like the German 'ein ansehnlicher Mann' (Th. Keil),
a *considerable* or *large* man : so that the true reading is no doubt
preserved in 1 Ch. 11, 23 איש מִדָּה (see on *ch.* 21, 20). Klo., cleverly,
and at the same time retaining the Kt. אשר, אשר חֵרְפָה *who had defied
him* (21, 21).

22. ולו שם בשלשה הגברים] Read (see on *v.* 18) either בַּשְּׁלשָׁה הגבורים,
or בִּשְׁלֹשִׁים הגברים (cf. for the plur. noun Cant. 3, 7. *ch.* 9, 10; and
see on *v.* 13), or (see p. 368 *top*) ולא שם לו בשלשה הגברים.

23. ונכבד] Read either נִכְבָּד (pf.), or נִכְבָּד הוא. 1 Ch. 11, 25 הִנּוֹ
נכבד הוא,—a mixture of הִנּוֹ נכבד and נכבד הוא.

אל משמעתו] *over his body-guard.* See on I 22, 14.

24. עשהאל] 2, 18 ff.; 3, 27. 30.

בן דודו] LXX υἱὸς Δουδει (=דֹּדִי; cf. *v.* 9) τοῦ πατραδέλφου αὐτοῦ
(=דּוֹדוֹ; cf. *v.* 9, Jud. 10, 1),—a doublet. Cf. on *v.* 9, and 3, 3.

בית לחם] Luc. (ἐκ), and 1 Ch. 11, 26, מבית לחם, rightly.

25ᵃ. החרדי] LXX 'Ρουδαῖος : perhaps *of Ḥarod,* Jud. 7, 1.

25ᵇ. אליקא החרדי] Not in LXX. Omitted, probably through
ὁμοιοτέλευτον, in 1 Ch. 11, and not recognized in 1 Ch. 27.

26. הפלטי] From Beth-peleṭ, in the Negeb of Judah, Jos. 15, 27.
Neh. 11, 26†.

התקעי] Teqoaʿ was 10 miles S. of Jerusalem : see on 14, 2. 27.

27. הענתתי] 'Anāthoth, now 'Anātā, was 2 miles N. of Jerusalem
(cf. Is. 10, 30).

סִבְּכַי [מבני] (Ch.) is probably correct : so *ch.* 21, 18. BA have ἐκ τῶν υἱῶν (=MT.) ; but many MSS. Σαβουχαι, Luc. Σαβενι.

28. צלמון] LXX Ελλων, Luc. Αλιμαν : cf. Ch. עילי.

האחחי] See on *v.* 9.

הנטפתי] Netōphah (Ezr. 2, 22=Neh. 7, 26†) was probably the present *Beit Nettif,* 12 miles W. of Bethlehem, and 1¾ miles NE. of Sochoh (on I 17, 1).

29. חלב] Probably חלד or חלדי (cf. Zech. 6, 10) is correct. In Cod. B this name is omitted : Luc. has Αλλαν, other MSS. Ελα.

מנבעת בני בנימין] See on I 9, 1.

30ª. בניהו פרעתני] Read, with Ch., הפרעתני. LXX corruptly, מבנימן האפרתי. On Pir'athon, in Ephraim (near Shechem), cf. Jud. 12, 15. Not improbably the modern *Far'atā,* 6 miles NNW. of Nablous (Shechem).

30ᵇ–31ª. Transposed in LXX to the end of the chapter.

30ᵇ. נעש] מנחלי נעש] נעש is the name of a mountain in Ephraim, a little S. of Timnath-séraḥ (Jos. 19, 50. 24, 30=Jud. 2, 9 [תמנת־חרס],—probably (Buhl, 101, 170) *Tibneh,* 10 miles NW. of Bethel).

31ª. אבי־עלבון] Ch. אביאל, supported here by LXX Cod. B (Γαδαβιηλ υἱὸς (τοῦ Αραβωθαίου)= נעש אביאל בן)[1], and Luc. (Ταλσαβιης (ὁ Σαραιβαθι), for נעש אבי עלבון : ΤΑΛϹ prob. an error for ΓΑΑϹ),—perhaps originally (We. Bu. Now. Dh.) אביבעל. Klo. would restore אביאל בית־הָעֲרָבָתִי, supposing אבי־עלבון to be a corruption of בית אביאל, due to a copyist's eye catching השעלבני in *v.* 32. This is very plausible. Either בית־הערבתי or הערבתי will be the gentile adj. ot בֵּית־הָעֲרָבָה, a place near the Jordan, in the 'wilderness of Judah' (Jos. 15, 5. 61, called הערבה (but בית הערבה in LXX; *v.* Kittel) *ib.* 18, 18).

31ᵇ. הברחמי] Ch. הבחרומי. Probably הַבַּחֲרִמִי of *Baḥurim* (3, 16) is meant.

32ª. השעלבני] 'of שעלבים' (1 Ki. 4, 9), in Dan (Jos. 19, 42, where it is called שַׁעֲלַבִּים),—a Canaanite city, the inhabitants of which were reduced to forced labour by the 'House of Joseph' (Jud. 1, 35)†. See on I 9, 4.

---

[1] Twelve Codd., also, have actually (for Γαδαβιηλ) Αβιηλ, eleven others Αριηλ.

32ᵇ–33ᵃ. If 32ᵇ be compared with 1 Ch. 11, 34, it will become evident (as shewn in the Table) that יהונתן belongs to *v.* 33ᵃ, that ישׁי corresponds to השׁם, and that the gentile name has fallen out after it in the text of Samuel. Either בני ישׁי and בני השׁם are both corruptions of one and the same name, now lost, or, as Luc. has here Ἰεσσαι ὁ Γουνι[1], and in Ch. Εἰρασαι ὁ Γουνι, it may be supposed with some plausibility that בני (in both texts) has arisen by dittography from the preceding שׁעלבני. The name *Gizon* (Ch.) is not otherwise known: Lucian's ὁ Γουνι points to הַגּוּנִי, which, as Klo. observes, was the name of a Naphtalite family (Gen. 46, 24. Nu. 26, 48). Read, then, in 32ᵇ יָשֵׁן הַגּוּנִי. The name in 33ᵃ will now be יהונתן בן שׁמה ההררי: Ch. has שׁנא for שׁמה, but Luc. there has Σαμαια, and here LXX and MT. agree: שׁמה has thus the presumption of being correct. The Jonathan mentioned was a son of 'Shammah the Hararite' of *v.* 11.

34ᵃ. אליפל בן אחסבי בן־המעכתי]=1 Ch. 11, 35ᵇ–36ᵃ בן־המעכתי is the gentile adj. of מעכה (*ch.* 10, 6. 8) or בית־מעכה (20, 14. 15. 1 Ki. 15, 20. 2 Ki. 15, 29), as 2 Ki. 25, 23 (=Jer. 40, 8); perhaps, however, בית־המעכתי (like בית־הלחמי) should be read (Klo. Sm. Dh.). אור חפר=אחסבי (Ch.) are probably both corruptions of the name of Eliphelet's father: אחסבי is a suspicious form.

34ᵇ. אליעם בן־אחיתפל הגלני] Evidently mutilated in 1 Ch. 11, 36ᵇ אחיתפל הגילני. אחיה הפלני is mentioned in 15, 12.

35ᵃ. חצרו] Qrê חֶצְרַי (but not in Ch.); so LXX Ασαραι, Luc. Εσσερι.

הכרמלי] See on 1 25, 1.

35ᵇ. פערי הארבי] LXX corruptly τοῦ Οὐραιοερχει. ὁ ερχει here would point to הָאַרְכִּי (Klo.): cf. Jos. 16, 2; and חושׁי הארכי. A place אֶרָב in the Negeb of Judah,—possibly *er-Rabíyeh*, 6 miles W. of Carmel,—is, however, named Jos. 15, 52. Some twenty MSS. have τοῦ Οὐραι (Οὐρε) υἱὸς τοῦ Ἀσβι: cf. Ch.

36ᵃ. מצבה] Attested substantially by LXX ἀπὸ δυνάμεως (as though מִצָּבָא). צֹבָה as 8, 3. If this be original, מבחר (which corresponds

---

[1] Twenty-one other Codd. Βασαι ὁ Γωννι (Γωνι, Γουνι).

in position in Ch.) will be a corruption of it, and בְּנֵי הַגְּרִי here will deserve the preference above בֶן־הַגְרִי in Ch.[1]

37. הבארתי] See on 4, 2.

38. היתרי] A family of Qiryath-ye'arim 1 Ch. 2, 53,—unless indeed we should read הַיַּתְרִי (Th. Klo. Bu. Now. Dh.: LXX ὁ Αἰθειραῖος) *of Yattir,* in the hill-country of Judah, Jos. 15, 48. 21, 14; see on I 30, 27; also the note on II 20, 26.

39. כֹּל שְׁלֹשִׁים וְשִׁבְעָה:] '(The) whole, thirty-seven.' הַכֹּל would be better (2 Ki. 24, 16. 25, 17. Ezr. 2, 42. 8, 35[b]. 2 Ch. 28, 6); but cf. Nu. 13, 2 : כֹּל נְשִׂיא בָהֶם. 1 Ch. 11, 41[b]–47 adds sixteen other names. —How is the number thirty-seven to be computed? The actual numbers are—the 'Three' (*vv.* 8–12), and, for the 'Thirty,' 2 (*vv.* 18–23) + 31 (*vv.* 24–39)=33. 'That the names are more than 30 need occasion no surprise, as we may suppose the corps to have been kept full after losses in war' (Sm.): we know that Asahel, for instance, died early in David's reign (2, 23).

(*f*) 24. David's Census of the People.

Ch. 24=1 Ch. 21, 1–27.

24, 1. The narrative is evidently the sequel of 21, 1–14 (comp. especially the opening words ויסף אף י"י וג' with the representation implied in 21, 1. 14[b]), with which also it has linguistically points of contact: cf. *v.* 25[b] with 21, 14[b] (ויעתר אלהים לארץ).

ויסת] *moved, incited.* The meaning of the word may be illustrated from Jos. 15, 8. I 26, 19 (of Yahweh). 1 Ki. 21, 25 (of Jezebel influencing or inciting Ahab): Job 2, 3.

לאמר לך מנה] 1 Ch. 21, 1[b], accommodating to the later historiographical style (which is apt to state the fact, instead of narrating the words), למנות. Cf. *ib.* 17, 25 as compared with *ch.* 7, 27; and Ew. § 338[a].

2. אל יואב שר החיל אשר אתו] For שר read with Luc. and Ch. וְאֶל־שָׂרֵי 'to Joab *and to the captains of* the force, that were with him;' with which *v.* 4 agrees: Joab's natural title would be not שר החיל אשר אתו but שר הצבא (1 Ki. 1, 19).

---

[1] Some twenty Codd., however, have here Μαβααν (al. Μαβλαν, Μααβαν, Μανααν, etc.) υἱὸς Ἀγαρι(ν, μ).

שׁוֹט] Rare in prose: but see Nu. 11, 8; also Job 1, 7. With the emended text שׁוֹטוֹ must be read; so Luc.

3. וְיֹסֵף] ׀ is used sometimes in Heb. (like *et* in Latin) to subjoin an impassioned question or exclamation: cf. *ch.* 18, 11. Nu. 12, 14. 20, 3. 2 Ki. 1, 10. 7, 13. 19. Comp. *Tenses*, § 119 γ *note;* GK. § 154ᵇ; *Lex.* 254ᵇ d.

יסף עליכם כהם אלף פעמים [Dt. 1, 11 כהם וכהם מאה פעמים.

וְעֵינַי . . . רָאוֹת] The same idiomatic usage as וְעֵינֶיךָ רָאוֹת Dt. 28, 32. 1 Ki. 1, 48. Jer. 20, 4 (a circumstantial clause).

וַאַרְנִי הַמֶּלֶךְ לְמָה . . .] On the position of the subj., see on I 20, 8.

4. לִפְנֵי הַמֶּלֶךְ] 'Vulg. Pesh. [and Lucian ἐκ προσώπου] מפני המלך [rather, מִלִּפְנֵי הַמֶּלֶךְ]: for according to MT. David himself would have gone forth as well' (Bö.). לְפְנֵי=before (*ch.* 5, 24): מלפני= *from* before (Gen. 41, 46 ויצא יוסף מלפני פרעה; 2 Ki. 5, 27. 6, 32).

5. וַיָּחֵלּוּ מֵעֲרוֹעֵר וּמִן הֶעָרִי וּג' 'Read וג' [ויחנו בערוער ימין העיר וג' in agreement with Dt. 2, 36. 3, 12. 16. 4, 48. Jos. 12, 2. 13, 9. 16. 2 Ki. 10, 33. The starting-point must here be named, from which they *began* to number the people. As such, the southern border (Nu. 22, 36) was the most natural, as it lay nearest to Jerusalem' (We.). This acute and felicitous conjecture was found afterwards to be confirmed by the same four MSS. of Holmes, 19, 82, 93, 108— i.e. Lucian's recension[1]—which had so remarkably supported the emendations in 13, 34. 39. 15, 23. 18, 28. In the passages cited, 'the city that is in the midst of the wādy' (perhaps 'Ar; see the writer's note on Dt. 2, 36) is repeatedly named side by side with 'Aro'er. 'Aro'er, now *'Ara'ir*, was on the N. edge of the deep gorge through which the Arnon flows from the E. into the Dead Sea.

הגד] In MT. this word is out of construction: הנחל הגד cannot be rendered 'the wādy of Gad,' and the case is not one in which apposition would be admissible (cf. *Tenses*,³ p. 254). Read with Lucian (τὸν Γαδδει) הַגָּדִי (Bu.), which, with the text as emended, will be construed as an accus. of direction, 'And they began from 'Aro'er

---

[1] Καὶ διέβησαν τὸν Ἰορδάνην καὶ ἤρξαντο ἀπὸ Ἀροηρ καὶ ἀπὸ τῆς πόλεως τῆς ἐν μέσῳ τοῦ χειμάρρου κτλ.

and from the city that is in the midst of the wâdy, *towards the Gadites* and *on* unto Ja'zer.' Cf. *v.* 6ᵃ 'And they came to Gil'ad, *and on unto* the land,' etc. Ja'zer was a border-town of Gad (Nu. 21, 24 LXX [יַעְזֵר for עַ], Jos. 13, 25 [read מֵיַעְזֵר], cf. *vv.* 16. 30), in the direction of Rabbath-'Ammon : Ṣâr, 7 miles W. of 'Ammān, would suit Eusebius' description (*Onom.* 264, 98 ff.), though of course there is no philological connexion between *Ṣâr* and יעזר. See the writer's art. in the *Expos. Times*, xxi. (Sept. 1910), p. 562 f. (the second of two articles, criticizing the many doubtful identifications of ancient sites to be found in modern maps of Palestine).

6. אֶרֶץ תַּחְתִּים חׇדְשִׁי] Evidently corrupt. For תחתים Hitzig (*Gesch. d. Volkes Isr.* p. 29) suggested הַתַּחְתִּים; and for חדשי Th. suggested קֶרְשָׁה,—both strikingly confirmed subsequently by Lucian's recension (εἰς γῆν Χεττιειμ Καδης) : 'to the land of *the Hittites, towards Qedesh.*' The Qedesh or Qadesh—in which case the word would be more correctly vocalized קָרֵשָׁה—meant, is the important Hittite city of that name on the Orontes, a little S. of the Lake of Höms (Maspero, *Struggle of the Nations*, pp. 137, 141 f.), and 100 miles N. of Dan. החתים may be confidently accepted ; but קרשה, attractive as it is, occasions difficulty. A place 100 miles N. of Dan is very remote to be mentioned as the N. limit of Isr. territory,—it is, for instance, much further N. than the region probably meant by the ' entering in of Hamath,' mentioned Am. 6, 14 and elsewhere as marking the same point (see *H. G.* 177 ; my note on Am. 6, 2 ; RIBLAH in *DB.*); hence, if accepted, *to Kedesh* must be understood as embodying a highly idealistic conception of the N. limit of Isr. territory. Ewald (*Hist.* iii. 162) conjectured חֶרְמֹן for חדשי ; and this, whether we read (*EB.* iv. 4889) אֶל אֶרֶץ הַחִתִּים תַּחַת חֶרְמֹן (see Jos. 11, 3, cited below), or (Sm.) אֶל אֶרֶץ הַחִתִּים חֶרְמֹנָה, certainly yields a more probable locality,—viz. a little E. of Dan : for the Hittites bordering here on the Israelites, see Jud. 3, 3 (where הַחִתִּי must evidently be read for הַחִוִּי), and esp. Jos. 11, 3 (where read with LXX in *a* הַחִוִּי for הַחִתִּי, and in *b* וְהַחִתִּי for וְהַחִוִּי,—תַּחַת חֶרְמֹן (וְהַחִתִּי). Buhl (94) also prefers חרמן to קרשה. Klo. and Guthe (*Gesch.* 94) would read אֶרֶץ נפתלי קָרֵשָׁה: this would be quite suitable topographically, the קרש meant

being the Kedesh of Naphtali, 4 miles NW. of Lake Ḥuleh: but,
as an emendation of תחתים, נפתלי cannot come into competition with
החתים.

ויבאו] דנה יען וסביב אל צידון No place *Dan of Ya'an* is known.
LXX καὶ παρεγένοντο εἰς Δαν Ειδαν καὶ Ουδαν, καὶ ἐκύκλωσαν εἰς Σιδῶνα :
Luc. καὶ ἔρχονται ἕως Δαν, καὶ ἐκύκλωσαν τὴν Σιδῶνα τὴν μεγάλην. As
We. remarks, what the sense requires is וּמִדָּן סָבְבוּ אל צידון : and from
the text of LXX, corrupt as the proper names in it are, it at least
appears that the translators found דן *twice*, and had a verb in place
of וסביב. Read accordingly ויבאו דָן וּמִדָּן סָבְבוּ אל צידון (We. Now.
Dh.). Klo. emends differently : . . . . ויבאו דָּנָה וְעִיּוֹן וַיִּסֹבּוּ (so Bu.):
for עיון, see 1 Ki. 15, 20 (mentioned immediately before Dan and Abel
of Beth-ma'achah). 2 Ki. 15, 29. For Dan, see on 20, 18. עיון was
doubtless some place in the *Merj 'Ayun* ('Meadow of 'Ayun'),
a fertile oval plain, stretching out immediately to the N. of Abel
of Beth-ma'achah.

צידון] LXX (A, Luc., and many other MSS.)+רַבָּה: so Jos. 11, 8.
19, 28.

7. מבצר צר] The *fortress* of Tyre, on the mainland. So Jos. 19, 29†.
Cf. Harper on Am. 1, 9. Tyre would be just 27 miles W. of Dan.

החוי] The original inhabitants of Shechem (Gen. 34, 2), and Gibeon
(Jos. 9, 7, cf. *v.* 3), in Central Canaan.

9. ותהי] See on I 17, 21.

שֶׁלֵף] For the retarding *metheg*, producing an 'incomplete retrocession' of the tone, see GK. § 29ᶠ.

10. ויך לב דוד אתו] I 24, 6.

אחרי כן ספר את־העם] Read אחרי סָפַר את העם (cf. LXX μετὰ τὸ
ἀριθμῆσαι): construction as in I 5, 9 (so Now. Dh.). אחרי כן must have
been written in error by a scribe who did not notice the sentence that
was following. Klo. Bu. Sm. prefer, with Luc. (μετὰ ταῦτα, ὅτι),
to insert כי after כן.—העבר as 12, 13.

11. היה] *had been*,—before David arose in the morning.

חֹזֶה דוד] The — in *st. c.* (so Ginsb. Kit.) is most anomalous
(GK. § 93ʳʳ); no doubt Ew. § 213ᵉ *note* is right in treating it as
merely an error for חֹזֵה (so Baer, p. 117, with Kimchi). Comp.
ch. 15, 37 רֵעֶה דוד.

12. אנכי נוטל עליך] do I *lift up* (LXX αἴρω), or *hold*, over thee. The root is rare (Is. 40, 15. Lam. 3, 28); and Ch. נטה is more probable.

13. התבוא] The *fem.*, the subject being conceived *collectively :* see on I 4, 15.

שבע] LXX here, and Ch., שָׁלֹשׁ—probably the original number : notice the *three* months and the *three* days following.

והוא רדפך] The words form a circ. clause, as *v.* 3. With regard to the *sing.* הוא immediately after צָרֶיךָ, no doubt a group or body of men may be spoken of in Heb. in either the sing.[1] or the pl. (cf. Is. 17, 13ᵇ בו וג׳ (after 12–13ᵃ) : in Is. 5, 26 לְגוֹי should probably be read) : but in a passage like the present, in which the sing. follows the pl. so closely, the incongruity is inelegant, and it is better to read צָרֶךָ [notice before בְּאַרְצֶךָ], as in Dt. 21, 10 אֹיְבֶךָ. 28, 48 אֹיְבֶךָ. Jer. 6, 23 הוא [in the ‖ 50, 42 הֵמָּה] and עָרוּךְ; cf. I 24, 5 Qrê. Ch. וחרב רדפיך, which We. Bu. prefer.

This case differs from the one noticed on I 2, 10, in which the sing., interchanging with the plural, denotes—not, as here, the class as a whole, but—an *individual* of the class. To the examples of the latter class there noted, add :—Lev. 21, 7 ואשה גרושה מאישה לא יקחו כי קדש הוא לאלהיו (notice here 5–7ᵃ pl., 7ᵇ–8 sing.). 25, 17ᵃ. 31ᵇ. Dt. 7, 3 f. Jud. 12, 5. Jer. 8, 1 את עצמות מלכי יהודה ואת 44, 9 מלכים יושבים לדוד על כסאו . . . הוא ועבדיו ועמו. 22, 4 עצמות שריה (נשיו). Is. 30, 22 *end* כמו דוה צא תאמר לו. Am. 6, 9 f. Zech. 14, 12. Job 21, 10 (after 7–9). 24, 16–24. But in extreme cases, as when the sing. and pl. occur in *one and the same clause*, the text should no doubt be corrected : as Lev. 25, 14ᵃ (Versions תמכר). 31ᵃ (rd. יֶחְשָׁבוּ; cf. p. lxii f.[2]). Dt. 7, 10ᵃ (rd. שֹׂנְאוֹ for שֹׂנְאָיו, and note שֹׂנְאוֹ in ᵇ). Jos. 2, 4. Hos. 4, 8 (rd. נפשם). 10, 5 (rd. עָגֶל). Mic. 2, 9. Zech. 14, 12 *end* (rd. בפיהו). ψ. 5, 10 (rd. בפימו). 62, 5. 63, 11. 64, 9. Is. 5, 23 (LXX צדיק; cf. Qoh. 10, 15 LXX Codd. אA הכסיל). Cf. GK. § 145ᵐ.

ואשיבה חֹרְפִי דבר. Cf. Pr. 27, 11 מה אשיב שלחי דבר] Lit. *with what word I shall turn back* (=*reply to :* see on 3, 11) *my sender.* For דבר . . . מה, see on I 26, 18.

---

[1] Cf. the series of almost uninterrupted sing. pronouns and verbs, referring to העם הזה in Dt. 31, 16–18. 20–21.
[2] The principle of Lev. 17, 14 כל אכליו יִכָּרֵת. 19, 8 is different (GK. § 145ˡ).

14. נפלה] 'very unjustly changed by LXX and Chron. into the singular' (We.).

15ᵃ. LXX has: καὶ ἐξελέξατο Δαυειδ ἑαυτῷ τὸν θάνατον· καὶ ἡμεραὶ θερισμοῦ πυρῶν, [καὶ ἔδωκεν Κύριος ἐν Ἰσραηλ θάνατον ἀπὸ πρωίθεν ἕως ὥρας ἀρίστου·] καὶ ἤρξατο ἡ θραῦσις ἐν τῷ λαῷ, [καὶ ἀπέθανεν, κτλ.]. The bracketed words in the middle agree with MT. The unbracketed words = ויבחר לו דוד את־הדבר והימים ימי קציר חטים וַתָּחֶל המגפה¹ בעם, the circumstantiality and tragic force of which (70,000 dying, though the plague had only *begun*) constitute (see We.) a presumption in favour of their originality (so Now. Bu. Sm. Dh.), as against the more colourless and ordinary narrative in MT. (. . ,ויתן מועד): ויבחר also is the natural sequel to 12–14; and the time of wheat-harvest agrees exactly with Araunah's threshing, in *v.* 20. The meaning of עד עת מועד in MT. is altogether uncertain. *To the appointed time* cannot be right, for it appears from *v.* 16 that the plague was stopped *before* the three days had terminated. Targ. paraphrases the words מהבקר ועד עת מועד by 'from the time when the daily burnt offering was killed *until it was offered ;'* and so Rashi and Kimchi: another Jewish explanation, cited by Kimchi, is 'until midday' (cf. LXX ἕως ὥρας ἀρίστου; Pesh. 'till the sixth hour'). But neither of these explanations has any basis in usage ; and for the former sense a different expression is employed (1 Ki. 18, 29 עד לעלות המנחה. 36. 2 Ki. 3, 20). There is force in We.'s remark that the absence of the art. is an indication that the clause springs from a time when the word had acquired a technical sense, of the *season* fixed by Yahweh for interposing: cf. ψ. 76, 3. 102, 14. Ehrlich would restore boldly עד עֵ[ת]לֹ[וֹ]ה[מ]נחה[.

15ᵇ. וימת] The sing. as I 1, 2. Nevertheless it is possible that originally the Hif'il וַיָּמֶת was intended.

16. המלאך] The order verb, object, subject is unusual, and where it is employed has the effect of emphasizing the subject at the end

---

¹ So, if והימים ימי קציר חטים is merely a *parenthetical* note of time (cf. Nu. 13, 20). But if the words belong to the sequel, and are to be rendered (Now.), 'And it was the time of wheat-harvest, *when,'* etc., then, by analogy, it should be וְהמגפה הֵחֵלָּה: see 2, 24. Gen. 19, 23. 44, 3 (*Tenses,* § 169).

(*Tenses,* § 208. 4). Here there is no apparent reason why the ordinary order וישלח המלאך ידו should not have been used. We. thinks the unusual position of המלאך an indication that it was not originally part of the text, but was introduced afterwards as an 'Explicitum' (see p. lxii f.), and (as a corollary of this) that it was mentioned in some preceding part of the narrative (which must now, accordingly, be defective), and was the subject of וַיָּמָת *v.* 15 [1].

ירושלם] *towards* Jerusalem : cf. Is. 10, 32.—עַל=אֶל.

בעם] partitive, *among* the people. So 17 המכה בעם (*Lex.* 88[b]).

רב] as Gen. 45, 28. 1 Ki. 19, 4 (*Lex.* 913[a] f). To be joined with what follows, though not closely with עתה : 'Enough! now relax thy hand [2].'

עם] as I 10, 2.

האורנה Kt.] *v.* 18 Kt. ארניה, *vv.* 20. 22–24 ארונה : Ch. uniformly אָרְנָן : LXX in both texts 'Ορνα. The article with a personal name is impossible : perhaps Bö. may be right in attaching it to גרן, and reading עם גֹּרְנָה אורנה (cf. on I 23, 15). The choice between the other forms is difficult. The Qrê in Samuel is everywhere אֲרַוְנָה, which Bertheau (on Ch.) and Keil prefer, supposing that just on account of its un-Hebraic form it may represent a genuine ancient tradition.

17. העויתי] as 7, 14. 19, 20: cf. p. 170 *footnote* 2. Observe the emphatic אנכי (twice) ; and ואלה הצאן placed before מה עשו for the purpose of setting it in strong contrast to אנכי. Luc., after ואנכי expresses הָרֹעֶה,—an unnecessary explanatory gloss.

18. עלה] i.e. to the higher ground, at the *top* of the hill, on which the threshing-floor was : so *v.* 19 ויעל.

20. וישקף] *looked out* or *forth,* viz. from the גרן or the enclosure surrounding it. It is the word used of *looking out* through a window, *ch.* 6, 16 al., from heaven, ψ. 14, 2 al. : somewhat more generally Gen. 18, 16. 19, 28.

---

[1] Against Movers' proposal (adopted in the *Speaker's Comm.* on Ch. p. 200) to read for ידו (after Ch. האלהים) יהוה, it was already rightly objected by Th. that this text would represent Yahweh as repenting *directly after* sending the angel.

[2] The accentuation is not opposed to this rendering : the position of the *zāqēf* is regulated by the *speech,* the words introducing it being treated as subordinate. Cf. Gen. 19, 2 ; and see Wickes, *Hebrew Prose Accents* (1887), p. 35 f.

עברים עליו] So 2 Ki. 4, 9; על=*by*, as in נִצָּב עַל Gen. 18, 2, cf. the correlative מעל ib. 3 אל־נא תעבר מעל עבדך.

אפיו ארצה] Elsewhere always either אפים ארצה (the more usual phrase) or על אפיו ארצה or לאפיו ארצה: cf. on I 25, 23.

21. מעמך] Cf. 3, 15 (*Lex.* 769ᵃ c). Elsewhere מֵאֵת, as *v.* 24, Gen. 25, 10 al.

מעל] Cf. I 6, 5. 20.

22. הַמּוֹרִגִּים] *the threshing-boards* (or *-drags*, or *-sledges*), i.e. heavy boards with sharp stones set in the under side, which were dragged over the corn : see the description, with illustr., in the writer's *Joel and Amos*, p. 227 f. ; or *EB.* i. 82, 83 (Fig. 10). Cf. Is. 41, 15 הנה שמתיך לְמוֹרַג חָרוּץ חדש בעל פיפיות. On the plur. מוֹרִגִּים, see GK. § 93ᵖᵖ.

כלי הבקר] i.e. the wooden yoke, comp. 1 Ki. 19, 21.

23. הכל וג׳] 'the whole doth Araunah, O king, give unto the king,'—the words being the continuation of the speech in *v.* 22. But it is not in accordance with general Hebrew custom for a person, in ordinary conversation, to introduce his own name in the 3rd person : Bö. conjectured that עבד אדני had fallen out after ארונה. We., on the basis of Bö.'s suggestion, conjectures with still greater plausibility that עבד has fallen out, and that ארונה is a *corruption* of אדוני. Read therefore הכל נתן עֶבֶד אֲדוֹנִי המלך למלך 'the whole doth *the servant of my lord the king* give unto the king' (so Bu. Now. Sm. Dh.): the courtly form of expression is quite natural under the circumstances. 'That the speech of Ornan is continued in 23ᵃ might have been understood from 24ᵇ, which in agreement with Hebrew custom restates the substance of the speech in a final sentence marked by a fresh ויאמר' (We.).

נתן] It is only meant by Ornan as an offer, which is not accepted, *v.* 24. But there is no occasion with We. to point on this account נֹתֵן : נָתַן, implying that the gift is (in intention) completed, is more courteous : cf. Gen. 23, 11 נתתי.

24. מאותך] For מֵאִתְּךָ, as (except in the case noted on *ch.* 13, 14) twice before in MT., viz. אֹתָם Jos. 10, 25. אוֹתִי *ib.* 14, 12 ; and often in 1 Ki. 20—2 Ki. 8 (as 1 Ki. 20, 25. 22, 7. 8. 24), and especially in Jer. and Ez. (as Jer. 1, 16. 2, 35. 4, 12 : Ez. 2, 1. 6. 3, 22. 24. 27). Cf. *Lex.* 85ᵇ.

עלות חנם] Cf. 1 Ki. 2, 31 דמי חנם.

שקלים חמשים] The order is unusual, and generally late : Neh. 5, 15.
2 Ch. 3, 9. 50 shekels of silver, at 2*s.* 9*d.* a shekel (*DB.* iii. 420[a]),
would be worth, as bullion, £6 17*s.* 6*d.*, but would possess naturally
much greater purchasing power (*ib.* 431[b]–432[a]).

25. ויעתר . . . לארץ] Cf. 21, 14.

ותעצר המגפה] Cf. 21. So Nu. 17, 13 (cf. 15). 25, 8 (= ψ.
106, 30)†.

I. INDEX OF SUBJECTS

Abbreviations in Old Heb., p. lxviii f.
Abinadab, not = Ishui, 227.
Abstract subst. for adj., 133, 182.
Accus., cognate, strengthening verb, 8 f.
— defining state, 32, 40, 42, 94, 102, 129 (adv.); 321 (after היה); of limitation, 54, cf. XX.
Adverbial relations expressed by a verb, 13, 24, 135, 167, 333.
Alphabet, early history of the Hebrew, i-xxvi.
Amplicative plural, 25.
Apposition, 30, 45, 87, 108.
Aquila, iii *n.*, xl f., lxxxii f.
'Arāq el-Emīr, Inscriptions at, xx.
Article used idiomatically : = our 'a,' 6, 54, 85, 157; in comparisons, 208 ; with a distrib. force, 209.
— used exceptionally : as אבן הגדולה, 58, 96, 137, 197 (a *ptcp.*); after a prep. or כ, 356 with *n.*; with force of relat., 75 f. ; וכל המלאכה נמזבה (incorrect), 124.
— omitted exceptionally : with אחד, 5; in בלילה הוא, 156; incorrectly, 193, 233, 240.
'Ashtart (MT. 'Ashtōreth, plur. 'Ashtāroth), 62 f., 230.
Attraction, I 2, 4.

Ba'al, meaning of, 253 f. ; as name of a deity, 63 f. ; as applied to Yahweh, 254 f. ; in names of persons, II 2, 8, pp. 253-255, 263, II 23, 8. 31ᵃ; of places, II 5, 20. 6, 2.
' Base ' in EVV. = low in position, 274.
Be'elyada', changed to Elyada', 263.
Βηρσαβεε for Bath-sheba', 289.
Bichri, Bichrites, 340, 345.
Bridal tent, the, 320.

Caleb-clan, the, 196.
Casus pendens, 27, 96, 306 (*v.* 10), 360 ; in clause introd. by והיה, 40, by ויהי, 82.
Cherethites, 223, 284.
Circumstantial clauses, 13, 42 etc.; 81, 183.

Collectives, 174 ; after כל, 310; after numeral, 223. *See also* Fem. sing.
Compound names of deities, xc f.
Confusion of letters, lxiv-lxviii.
' Conjugation of attack ' (Po'el), 152.

Dagesh in לא ויאמרו, 68 ; dirimens, 215.
δῆλοι = אורים, 117.
Diminutives, 300.
Dittography, 36 (?), 175, 264.
Division of words, incorrect, xxviii f.
Dod, divine title, xc, II 23, 9. 24.
Doublets (in LXX), xlix, lv-lvii, lxi.
Dual names of places, 2.
Duplication of word for emphasis, 24.

ἐγώ εἰμι (with a *verb*) in LXX, lix.
Egyptian Aramaic (inscriptions and notes on the dialect), xii-xix.
Emendation, conjectural, XI f., xxxv *n.*, xxxvii *n.*, xlix.
Emphasis. *See* Order of words *and* Pronoun.
English Versions (AV. and RV.), illegitimate renderings in, I 23, 23. II 1, 23. 3, 36. 5, 8 (p. 260), p. 277, II 10, 7. 13, 34. 14, 16ᵇ. 15, 12. 23. 17, 11. 19, 44. 20, 3. 6. 8. 19. 23. 21, 5. 23, 19; emendations implicitly adopted in, I 15, 9. 23, 6. 24, 20. 25, 30. II 15, 19.
' Explicita,' lxii, lxxiii.

' Fellow-wife ' (צרה), 9 f.
Fem. sing. construed with collectives, 48, 288, 376; used of countries, and peoples, 143, 211 (ישבות,— anomalous).
Final letters, origin of, xix.
First person sing. used of a people, 53, 224.
' Fool,' bad rend. of נבל, 200.
Force of interrog. or neg. extending over two clauses, 24.
' Futurum instans,' 43, 95, 107, 183.

Γ in LXX = ע, 136 *n.*
Gezer, Inscription of, vii f.
Guilt-öffering (אָשָׁם), 53 f.

Hadad'ezer (name), 280.
Hebrew, illustrated from Phoenician, xxv–xxvi.
Hebrew Inscriptions, iv, vii, ix, xi, xx, xxi, xxiii.
Hebrew MSS., character of, xxxiv–xxxvii, lxiv–lxix.
Hexapla, Origen's, xli–xliv.
'Hypocoristic,' or 'caritative,' names, 19, 262.

'Idem per idem' constructions, 21, 185 f.
'Ιε- in LXX for -י, -א, 120 f.
Imperfect with frequent. force, I 1, 7 (*bis*). 13. 2, 22. 3, 2. 5, 5. 13, 17. II 12, 31, etc. ; = *was to*, II 3, 33.
— with *waw* consec. introducing pred., I 4, 20 (וּבְעֵת מוֹתָהּ וַתְּדַבֵּרְנָה). 6, 6. 15, 27; 14, 19 (וְהָהָמוֹן אֲשֶׁר בְּמַחֲנֶה). 17, 24 (וּפְלִשְׁתִּים וַיֵּלֶךְ); irreg. for pf. and *waw* consec., I 2, 16. 14, 52 ; continuing ptcp., I 2, 6.
Impersonal passive, 323 f.
Implicit subject, 132, 242 ; with inf., I 2, 13 (כְּבַשֵּׁל הַבָּשָׂר). 11, 2. II 3, 34.
Inf. abs., force of, 31, 36, 38, 249 ; in the protasis, 12 f., 162 ; at the beginning of a speech, 162 ; defining, 43, 280. *See also* Types of sentence.
— with וְ carrying on finite verb, 36 (*v.* 28), or inf. constr., 181.
— in Qal, emphasizing a verb in a derived conjug., 347.
Inf. constr. continued by finite verb, 26, 49.
Inf. constr. in הָ‑, 11 f.
Ishba'al, 120, 240, 363.
Ishbosheth, correction for Ishba'al, 240.
Ishui, correction for Ishba'al, 120.

Judge, the, God regarded as speaking through, 35 f. ; judgement a sacred act, 66.
Jussive with לֹא, 116, 323.

καί γε (LXX) for גָּם, lix *n.* 3.
κάρπωσις (LXX), 30 *n.* 1.

Lapsus calami, 95, 198, 289, 352 (*bis*).
Letters confused (י and ו, ד and ר, מ and כ), lxiv–lxvii ; כ and מ, lxviii *n.*
Letters wrongly transposed in MT., 80, 308 with *n.* 2.
Lucian's text of LXX, xlviii–li, lv–lvii.

Maps of Palestine, X, xcv f.
Μεμφιβοσθε for אִישׁ־בֹּשֶׁת, 240 *n.* 2.
Mephibosheth, correction for Meribba'al, 253–255.
Moabite Stone, the, lxxxiv–xciv.

Nif'al, reciprocal sense of, 92 f. ; *tolerativum*, 353.
νῖκος in LXX for נֵצַח, 129 *n.* 1.
'Nomen unitatis,' 119.
Numerals, not expressed anciently by letters, 97.

Obed-edom, meaning of name, 268 f.
Old Latin version, lii f., characteristics of, lxxvi–lxxx.
Omissions in I 17–18 (LXX), 140, 150 f., 155.
Order of words :—
Obj. at end of long sentence, 7, 307 ;
לִי לְכֹהֵן, 36 ; וּמָה בִּידִי רָעָה, 208 ; וְלֹא . . . . , 5 ; וְלִשְׁאוּל פִּלֶּגֶשׁ, 246; וְלָהּ אָמַר . . . , 203 ; וְהִנֵּה לוֹ מַשָּׂתָה I 25, 35.
— emphatic :—emph. word next to אִם לֹא, הֲ, פֶּן, etc.: 35 אִם לַיהוה (לֹא יָדוּ נִגְעָה בָנוּ), 55 (וְיֶחֱטָא אִישׁ), II 15, 34 (אָם), 17, 13 (אִם), 367 (הֲלֹא); גַּת יִפֹּב, 52 ; אֹתִי, אֹתוֹ (הֲ), etc., before verb (various cases), 121 (see also on I 8, 7. 14, 35. 18, 17. 20, 9. 21, 10); וְעַד אָבִיךְ, לְמַה־זֶּה תְבִיאֵנִי, 162, II 24, 3 ; יִשְׂרָאֵל כֻּלֹּה, 241 f.; כִּי אַתִּי תֵצֵא, 213, 311 ; . . . וְעָלִי יָבוֹא, II 19, 39; לוֹ אֶהְיֶה, 319; יֵשׁ and אַיִן *after* noun, 174; לִזְבֹּחַ לַי״י בָּאתִי, 132, 249 (II 3, 25).
— unusual : שָׁאוּל הַמֶּלֶךְ (late); 151, 305 ; שְׁקָלִים חֲמִשִּׁים, 380.
— obj. first, introducing variety, I 22, 10 (וְצֵידָה נָתַן לוֹ).
Origen, xli–xliv.
Orthography, early Hebrew, xxvii–xxxiii; lxii–lxiv (וֹ- at the end of a verb) ; lxiv–lxviii (letters confused).
ὅταν, ἡνίκα ἄν, etc. in LXX with impf. indic., 145 *n.* 2.

Palmyrene Inscription, xxii.

Participle, force of, noted, I 1, 9. 26, 3.
29, 1. II 1, 6. 6, 14. 15. 15, 30.
17, 17, etc.; with היה, I 2, 11ᵇ.
17, 34. II 3, 17, or ויהי, I 7, 10.
18, 9. 23, 26. II 4, 3. 15, 32. 19, 10;
in protasis after אם, I 19, 11; with
no subj. expressed, I 17, 25. 20, 1,
cf. 6, 3; ptcp. absolute, I 2, 13. II
23, 3; delicate use of, to denote
incipient action, I 14, 8; expressing
the *fut. instans*, I 3, 11. 12, 16.
20, 36; with art. as predicate, I 4,
16; with the art., and subst. without
it, I 25, 10.
Pausal form with minor disj. accent,
14. 15, 244, 249, 287, 306.
Pelethites, 284.
Perf. and simple *waw* used irregularly,
13, 199.
Perf. and *waw* consec. with frequent.
force, I 1, 3. 4ᵇ. 2, 15. 19. 20. 7, 16.
14, 52. 17, 34ᵇ–35. 12, 16. 15, 2ᵃ.
II 17, 17, etc.
— introducing pred. or apod., I 2, 11ᵇ.
25, 27. II 14, 10.
'Periphrastic' future, 67.
'Perverse,' sense of, in EVV., 170 *n.*
Peshiṭto, the, li f.; characteristics of, in
Sam., lxxi–lxxvi.
Phoenician Inscription (Tabnith), xxiv–
xxvi.
Pluperfect, how expressed in Heb., 73,
199, cf. 311.
Po'lel, intensive (מְמוֹתֵת), 108.
Pronominal suffix anticipating object
of verb, 177, 306, or genitive, 50,
177 *n.*
Pronoun emphatic: before verb, I 8, 5.
17. 10, 18. 12, 20. 17, 28 (אֲנִי).
II 12, 7ᵇ. 19, 34 (אַתָּה עָבֹר). 24,
17; in response to question, II 21, 7.
— after verb, I 17, 56 (שָׁאַל אתה). 22,
18 (ויפגע הוא). 23, 22 (עָרֹם יָעָרֹם)
הוא). II 12, 28 (פֶּן אלכד אני).
17, 15 (יעצתי אני).
— . . . כי הוא (in causal sentence),
110 *n.* 2, 153.
— הוא, היא, resuming subject, I 1, 13.
II 14, 19.

Question indicated by the tone of the
voice: I 11, 12 (שאול ימלך עלינו).
21, 16. 22, 15. II 19, 23; 16, 4
(שלום). 18, 29; I 20, 9 (. . . ולא).

12. 14 (?). II 19, 44; 24, 20
(. . . ולשלחו). 25, 11 (. . . ולקחתי);
II 11, 11 (. . . ואני); 15, 20.
Rephaim, the, 353 f.
Resumption, 200 (various cases).
— of object by pron., I 9, 13ᵇ. 15, 9.
25, 29 (יקלענה . . . ואת נפש);
ולאתחנות . . . אל חיים את לבך
להם, I 9, 20. II 6, 23; with emph.,
II 6, 22 (עָם . . . עַמָּם אכברה).
— of כי, I 14, 39. 25, 34.
— of other words, I 17, 13. 20, 14ᵇ (?).
15ᵇ (?; cf. p. 166), and on I 25, 26.
Revised Version, margins of, XVII.
Roof-chamber (עֲלִיָּה), 333.
'Runners,' the (the royal escort), 181.

'Scriptio plena' and 'defectiva,' xxx–
xxxii.
Sentences, unusual types of: I 5, 10
(וישימו); 6, 11 (להמיתני ואת עמי)
את ארון י"י אל העגלה ואת
(האר־גו וג׳).
Septuagint, xxxix f.; the Hexapla, xli–
xliv; original text of LXX, xliv–
xlvi, liv f.; MSS. of, xlvi f.; Lucian's recension, xlviii–li, lv–lvii;
characteristics of the translation,
lv–lxii (corruptions in the Greek,
lvii–lix; Heb. words transliterated,
lx–lxi, 78 *n.*; rend. suggested by
similarity to Heb., 51); character
and script of Heb. basis, lxiii–lxix;
breathings and accents, XVIII.
Siloam Inscription, viii–x.
Sing. nouns used collectively, 174; after
numerals, 223; after כל, 310.
Sing. and plur. interchanging, 27, different cases of, 376.
Sing. 1 ps., of nation or group of persons,
I 5. 10. 30, 22. II 20, 19; cf. p. 37.
'Strange,' 'stranger,' often = 'foreign,'
'foreigner,' in EVV., 233, 313.
Suffix, omission of, in inf., 153.
Suspended genitive, I 28, 7. II 20, 19.
Symmachus, xl f., lxxxi–lxxxiii, 96 *n.*

Targum, li, characteristics of, lxix–lxxi.
Tertium comparationis, introduced by ל,
309.
Theodotion, xl f., lx *n.*, 129 *n.* 1.
Threshing-drags (מוֹרְגִּים), 379.

Tikkūn sopherim, 340.

Τοιαύτη (Hebraism), 46.

Tone, retrocession of, 24, 356, 375.

Types of sentence with inf. abs. :—

וַיֵּלֶךְ (הֹלֵךְ) or וְהָלַךְ (or הָלֹךְ וְנָעוֹ, 56,
  cf. 45; four irregular cases, 160.

וַיֵּשׁוּבוּ הָלוֹךְ וָשֹׁב (rare), 56.

וַיֵּצֵא יָצוֹא וָשֹׁב, 56.

וְאַדַבֵּר הַשְׁכֵּם וְדַבֵּר (Jerem.), 56.

וַיֵּלֶךְ הָלוֹךְ וְרָב (adj.), 110.

יָצֹא יָצוֹא וּמְקַלֵּל (rare), 318.

Types of sentence with ptcp. :—

וְהָעָם הֹלֵךְ וְרָב (adj.), 36.

וַיֵּלֶךְ (הֹלֵךְ) or הֹלֵךְ וְקָרֵב (rare), 146.

Verb with implicit subject,—finite, 90,
  infin., 86.

Versions, ancient, value of, xxxiv–xxxix.

'Vile,' sense of, in EVV., 125 *n*. 1, 274.

Vulgate, the, liii f., characteristics of, in
  Sam., lxxx–lxxxiii.

Zākēf, the first in a half-verse the chief
  divider, 22.

Zuphite, 1.

II. INDEX OF HEBREW WORDS AND IDIOMS

Heb. words, idioms, etc. :—

א softened from י, 309, cf. 120 *n*.

א, elision of, 15.

אֶבֶן הַגְּדוֹלָה, 58, cf. 96.

אֶבֶן הַמֶּלֶךְ, 310.

אָגֵן, 127.

אוֹת- = אֵת-, 298, 379.

אֶחָד = 'a,' 54; אַחַר in *st. abs.*, 325;
  . . . בְּאַחַד, 243; . . . בְּאֶחָד, 321.

אִי = *not*, 49.

אַיִן, idiom. uses of: 70 (וָאַיִן . . .);
  . . . (אַיִן) וְחֶרֶב אַיִן, 147, 173, cf.
  71; אֵין לָנוּ לְ, II 21, 4.

אַיִן (peculiar), 176.

אִישׁ (collect.), construction of, 99.

הָאִישׁ prefixed to pr. n., 19.

אַךְ asseverative, 133, 199.

אָכְלָה (inf. c.), 11 f.

אַל not = μή ; 212.

אַל-תִּישֵׁם, 74.

אֶל = *in among*, 84, 174.

— = *with reference to*, 21, 43, 49.

— = עַל, 43, 101, 281, 348.

אֶל (אֵל) = אֵלֶּה, xxv *n*. 2, 34 *n*.

. . . אֵלֶּה הֵם, 47.

אֱלֹהִים construed as a pl., 47.

Heb. words, idioms, etc. (*cont.*) :—

אֱלֹהִים אֲחֵרִים, 208.

אֱלֹהֵי נֵכָר, 62.

אֶלֶף *clan*, 84.

אִם אַיִן and אִם לֹא, 321 with *n*. 2.

. . . אִם אֵינְךָ, 157.

. . . אִם כֹּה יֹאמַר, I 14, 9.

אֲמָהוֹת, anomalous plural of אָמָה,
  272.

אֲמִינוֹן ? dimin. form, 300.

אמר (ויאמרו) לֵאמֹר, 257.

אמר with inf. and לְ, 222.

אֲנִי emph., in answer to qu., 352.

אָנֹכִי, 14.

אַף in prose, 26, 345.

אַף כִּי, 114 f., 174, 175, 183, 256.

אפים (לְאַפּיו) אַרְצָה, 199, 332.

אַשְׁפֹּת, 26.

אֲשֶׁר, a connecting link, 126; = *in
  that, for that*, 34, 126, 172 ; =
  οἵτινες, 240; = *as*, 133; pron. or
  adv. supplement, when dispensed
  with, 192; = כִּי 'recitativum,'
  127, 232, 239; אֲשֶׁר כָּמֹנִי (idiom.),
  286; omission of, in prose (rare),
  111; . . . אֲשֶׁר אֶת, 66; אֲשֶׁר
  . . . הוּא, 84; אֲשֶׁר לְ, 138, 172.

Heb. words, idioms, etc. (*cont.*) :—
את, irregular uses of, 29, 225 ; with undefined noun, I 9, 3. 26, 20; with a gramm. nom., I 17, 34. 26, 16. II 11, 25. 21, 22.

ב and מ interchanged in LXX and MT., lxiv, lxvii.
הבאיש, נבאש [בא'ש,], 98, 213.
בזאת *on this condition*, 85.
בי אני, 200.
בית־אל '*in* Bethel,' but הבית not 'in the house,' 37 *n.* 2.
בית־השמשי, 57.
בעל in pr. names. *See* Ba'al.
בעלים = *citizens*, 185, 239.
בקרים (rare and dub.), 68.
ברזלי, 326.
ברית added to ארץ in MT., 45.

גָּלָה, 49 f. ; how different from שָׁבָה, 221.
גָּלְיָת (the termin.), 139, 159.
גַּם :—גַּם *correlativum*, 21, 292 ; in גם שתיהן, I 1, 6; כעסתה גם כעס 25, 43.
גַּעֵל, 236 f.

דִּבֶּר ב', I 19, 3. 25, 39; II 23, 2.

ה of Hif. inf. elided after prep., 37.
— of Hif. retained in impf., 147.
ה (art.), retained after prep. or כ, 356 with *n.*
— = relative, 75 f.
הֲ, emph. use of, 36, 368.
ה-, sf. of 3 sg. masc., xxxii f., 350.
הָ— for הָ— (sf. of 3 sg. fem.), 168.
הָא כ' (Aram.), 308 *n.* 4.
הדביק אחרי, הדביק את, 111, 227.
הדרעזר, 280, 288.
הוא formerly written הָא, xxx f. ; כי כלה I 1, 13; והנה היא מדברת 33 ,20 ,היא מעם אביו.
הוֹאִיל, senses of, 279.
הוקיע, 351, cf. 230 f.

Heb. words, idioms, etc. (*cont.*) :—
מעט רבש הזה : הזה, I 14, 29; incorrect, I 17, 12.
הַוִּיר, 112.
הֶחָ', 298.
הֶחֱרַמְתִּי, but וְהַחֲרַמְתִּי, 126.
היה and ptcp. *See* Participle.
היה אחרי, 94, 242, 291, 312.
הֲכִי, II 9, 1. 23, 19.
הֵכִין in military sense, 188.
הַבַּיְתָה, but הֵבִיאָ, 183.
הַלֵּן, 105.
הנה באו . . . וְשָׁאוּל אמר, etc., I 9, 5. 11. 17, 23 (והנה); cf. II 2, 24.
הַפַּשְׁחִית, 102.
הִנֵּה, expressing vividly a condition, 71, 164, 328; without suff., 72, 125, 134; והנה לקראתו, 82.
הִנְנִי expressing resignation, 119.
הַפְצַר, 127.
הַרְאִיתֶם, 84, XIX f.
הַשְׂכִּיל, meaning of, 149.
הֵשִׁיב דָּבָר פ', construction of, 144, 247, cf. 89.
התהלך לפני, 38.
התנבא, 81.
התעלל, 228.

ו and י confused, I *n.* 2, lxiv *n.* 3, lxv f.
ו = *and also*, 55.
ו apparently (not really) = *as*, 94 *n.*
ו = *both* (rare), 197.
ו of concomitance, 29, 149, 288.
וּ subjoining an emph. exclam., 373.
יּ-, old nomin. termin., 18, 282.
יּ- of 3 plur. omitted, 103, cf. 69, 91.
יּ- wrongly added in 3 sing., 91, 126.
וְהוֹשֵׁעַ ירד לך, 200 f.
והיה for ויהי, 13.
והיה כל־הנשאר ובא, 40.
וַיֶּחֱבוּ, 149.
וִהִי, sq. plur., 5.
ויהי היום, 6.

Heb. words, idioms, etc. (*cont.*) :—

וַיְהִי כָל־יוֹדְעוּ וִיִרְאוּ, 82.

וַיְשָׁרֵנָה, 55.

. . . אָמַר . . . וְכִרְאוֹת, 148.

וְלֹא = *and if not*, 302.

וּ-, in 3 pl. impf., 30 f.

וְשִׁלַּשְׁתָּ תְּפַקֵּד (construction), 167.

וַתֹּאכַל, 15.

זֶבַח הַיָּמִים, 20.

זֶה, as adv., 219 (זֶה יָמִים), 305; enclitic, 83 (מַה־זֶּה), 148 (בֶּן מִי זֶה),
(לָמָה זֶּה) 293 (אַתָּה זֶה), 243.

חָנֵג, 223.

חִי *group of related families*, 153, cf.
197, 366 (חַיָּה).

חֵי נַפְשֶׁךָ, 148.

חֲלִילָה, construction of, 96, 193.

חָלַף, 79.

חֲסִידִים, 26.

חֵצִי *arrow*, 172.

הֶחֱרִים, חֵרֶם, 130 f.

טַבַּח (meaning of form), 67.

-י, Syr. sound of, 120*n.*, 181; softened
to א, 309.

י and ו confused, I *n.* 2, lxiv *n.* 3, lxv f.

יָד = *monument*, 125, 281, 330.

יִדְעֹנִי, 214.

יוֹשֵׁב הָאָרֶץ, 258.

יֻלַּד, II 5, 14.

יָמִים = *year*, 5, 16, 210; שְׁנָתִים יָמִים,
II 13, 23.

יִ‏ֵ‏, in 2 fem. sg. impf., 14.

יִ‏ֵ‏, in masc. pl., xciii *n.* 3, 355.

יָרֵחַ, 287; יָרְחוֹ, יְרֵחוֹ, lxxxix.

יֵשׁ, 147; יֶשְׁנוֹ, 116 f.

יְשׁוּעָה, etym. meaning of, 118 f.

כ and ו confused in MSS., 33.

כְּ, properly an undeveloped subst.,
106.

. . . וכ׳, ב׳, 225.

כָּמוֹ, כְּב׳, 85, 108 *n.* 2.

Heb. words, idioms, etc. (*cont.*) :—

כֹּה יַעֲשֶׂה לִי אֱלֹהִים וְגֹ׳, 44.

כְּהַיּוֹם, I 9, 12, p. 356 *n.*

כֹּהֵן, 284 f.

כִּי :—after oath, 117, 118; (resumed)
כִּי . . . כִּי, 117, 202 f., 247; . . . כִּי
וְכִי, 229; כִּי 'recitativum,' 31 f.;
כִּי after אַךְ, אֶפֶס, etc., I 8, 9. 10, 1;
כִּי אָמַר פֶּן, . . . 206; כִּי אִם, . . .
103; . . . כִּי הוּא, 110*n.*; כִּי מֶה,
I 29, 8; כִּי עַתָּה, I 13, 13. 14, 30.

כְּיוֹם בְּיוֹם, 152.

בַּיּוֹם *first of all*, 31, 78.

הַכַּבֵּר, כִּבֵּר, 331.

כֹּל, sq. collective sing., 310.

כַּלָּה, xxxiii, 241.

כְּלָהֶם, II 23, 6.

כֻּלּוֹ *after* its subst., 241 f.

כָּלִיל, 64 f.

כַּעַס *vexation*, 8.

כְּעָסַתָּה גַם כָּעַס, 8 f.

כָּעֵת מָחָר, 73.

כְּפַעַם בְּפַעַם, 43.

כִּפֶּר, 47 f.; כֹּפֶר, 88.

כְּתֹנֶת פַּסִּים, 299 f.

לְ, as dat. of reference, I 2, 33. 9, 3.
11, 2; מַה אֵלֶּה, 21, 6; עֲצוּרָה לָנוּ,
לָךְ, II 16, 1; לָאַט לִי, 18, 3.

— = *in respect of*, I 8, 7*ᵃ*. 14, 33.
II 14, 17. 25 (defining the *tertium
comparationis*).

—reflexive, I 3, 13 MT. 8, 18
(לְשַׁלַּח לִי). 20, 20 (בְּחַרְתֶּם לָכֶם).
לְקַחְתּוֹ). 30, 19 (וּבָאתָ לָךְ), 5, 22
(לָהֶם). II 2, 21 (נָטֶה לָךְ). 16, 20
(הָבוּ לָכֶם). 17, 1.

— of norm, I 23, 20. II 15, 11.

—as 'nota accusativi,' I 22, 7. 23, 10.
II 3, 30. 17, 16.

—after pass. verb = *by*, I 25, 7.
II 2, 5.

— . . . וְלָנוּ הַסְּנִיר, I 23, 20.

Heb. words, idioms, etc. (*cont.*) :—

לְ with inf. as subj. of sentence, I 15, 22.

לֹא and לוֹ confused, 32.

לֹא with ptcp., 251.

לְבִלְתִּי, sq. impf., 308.

לָכֵן, idiom. use of, 44, 213 ; rendered οὐχ οὕτως in LXX, 44.

לָמָה used idiom. in deprecation, 158.

לְמָן, 270, 274, 276, 301.

לְהַעֲלוֹת, 37. for לַעֲלוֹת ?

הָיָה לִפְנֵי, 334.

לִשְׁכָּה, 15.

מ and ב interchanged in LXX and MT., lxiv*n.* 3, lxvii ; מ and כ, lxviii.

מֵאֵת, idiom. uses of, I 1, 17 (*c.* שְׁמַע) ; 8, 10 (*c.* שָׁאַל) ; II 15, 3 (מֵאֵת הַמֶּלֶךְ) ; 24, 24 (*c.* קָנָה).

מָדִים, 145 f.

מָה = *aught*, I 19, 3. II 18, 22. 23.

מֹהַר, 154.

מוּג, meaning of, 110 with *n.* 1.

מוֹקֵשׁ, 153.

מִזֶּה . . . מִזֶּה, 106.

מִי, how = *whoso*, 87 (cf. מָה, 161).

מִיָּד . . . , idiom., 256.

מֵיכַל (II 17, 20), ? meaning, 325.

מִיָּמִים יָמִימָה, 5.

מָכַר, fig., I 12, 9.

מַלְכֻּן, 294–297.

מִלִּפְנֵי, I 8, 18. 18, 12 ; p. 373.

מִן = *aught of*, I 3, 19, cf. on 23, 23 ; *even one of*, 14, 45 ; אַל־תַּחֲרֵשׁ וַיִּמָּאֵס מִמְּלֹךְ, 7, 8 ; מִמֶּנּוּ מִזְעָק 15, 23 ; with verb, denoting source or cause, 31, 3. II 7, 29.

מְנוֹר אֹרְגִים, 139 f.

מִנְחָה, 280.

מַס *labour-gang*, II 20, 24.

מֵעַל, idiom. uses of, 216: also on I 1, 14 (*c.* הֵסִירִי יֵינֵךְ). 6, 5 (*c.* יָקַל). 15, 28 (אַל מִי יַעֲלֶה מֵעָלֵינוּ) 20

Heb. words, idioms, etc. (*cont.*) :—

הוֹלֵךְ 15, 17 (קְרַע . . . מֵעָלֶיךָ).

הֵסִיר 26 (*c.* וְיָשַׁב מֵעַל שָׁאוּל).

שׁוּב 10, 14 (*c.* חֶרְפָּה). II 2, 27.

מֵעָלַי . . . שָׁלְחוּ 10, 19 (מֵעָלַי . . . שָׁלְחוּ) 13, 17.

ברח מעל אבשלום 20, 21. 24, 21.

ותעצר המגפה מעל ישראל).

מֵעִם after שאל I 1, 17, קָנָה II 24, 21 ; = *from beside*, I 2, 33. 20, 34 ; = *from with*, I 14, 17. 18, 13. II 3, 15 ; of origination, I 20, 7. II 3, 28.

מִפְּנֵי, force of, 278 *n.* 3.

מָצָא, not = Aram. מְטָא, 187.

מַצֵּבָה, מַצֶּבֶת, 330.

מַרְדוּת, 170.

מָרַת נֶפֶשׁ, 12.

מַשְׂאֵת, 339.

מִשְׁמַעַת, in concrete sense, 181.

מֹתַג הָאַמָּה, 279.

ן-, in impf., I 1, 14. 2, 15.

נָבָל, 200 ; נְבָלָה, 298.

נָגִיד, 73.

נָוֶה, 315 f.

נָוִית (Qrê נָיוֹת), 158 f.

נוֹעַ, 313.

נִמְצָא, idiom. for *present*, 71.

נֶפֶשׁ, in Heb. psychology, the seat of *feeling, desire*, etc., I 1, 15. 2, 16. 19, 4.

נִצָּב עַל, 180, 181.

נֵצַח יִשְׂרָאֵל, 128 f.

נָצִיב, 78.

נָשָׂא (with אֵפוֹד), to *bear* (not *wear*).

סָבַב = *sit round* a table, 134.

סְבִיר (Massoretic term), 90 f. ; סְבִירִין in Samuel, 91 f.

סָפַד to *wail*, 214.

סָפָה to *sweep away*, 96.

ע = ρ in LXX, 136 *n.*

עֶבֶד־אֲרָם, meaning, 268 f.

עַד בַּלֹּתָם, 126.

Heb. words, idioms, etc. (*cont.*) :—

עַרְדְּם (etymol.), 178 f.

עָוָה = عوى to *bend*; and غوى to *go astray, err* (cf. עָוֹן), 170 f.

עָכַר, 114.

עַל a *substantive*, 356.

עַל, idiom. uses of :—I 17, 32 אל יפל (לב ארם עליו *25, 36; 21, 16 (להשתגע עלי); II 15, 33 (וְהָיְתָ; (ועלי לתת) 18, 11 (עלי למשא; 24, 20 (עברים עליו).

— = אֵל, I 1, 10. 13. 2, 11 ; p. 101.

עַל פני, usu. = *on East of*, 123, 191; not so, 205.

עִם *near*, 78 ; = *in the opinion, judgement of*, 36, 273.

עמר לפני = to *wait upon*, 136 f.

עֵמֶק, 56 f., cf. 229.

עמק רפאים, 263.

עֲפָלִים, 51 f.

עָר, not = צָר, I 28, 16.

עשׂה, with pregnant force, 107, 209, 217.

עַשְׁתֹּרֶת, הָעַשְׁתָּרוֹת, 62-64; in Ashkelon, 230.

עָתָר, נֶעְתַּר, 353.

פדה, 119.

פוּק, I 25, 31.

פֶּלֶךְ, II 3, 29.

פלל to *mediate*, 35.

פֶּן, sq. perf., 342.

פָּרַץ for פָּצַר, 219.

פָּרָשִׁים and פְּרָשִׁים, 232.

צ - ض = Aram. ע (and ק), 9 *n*.

צאן, construed with fem. pl., I 17, 28.

צלח, 81.

צֻמְקִים, I 25, 18.

צִנּוֹר, 259.

צרה (= فَرَّة = ﺣﻨﻠ), *rival-* (or *fellow-*)*wife*, 9 f.

צריח, I 13, 6.

קָטֹן and קָטָן, 74 *n*.

הקטיר, קִטֵּר, meaning of, 31.

קֹלוֹת *voices*, of thunder, 95.

קָמָה עֵינָיו, 48.

קסם, 215.

קֶרֶב *battle* (Aram.), 322.

ר, 10, 122, 190, and esp. XIX f.

לְרַגְלִי, בְּרַגְלִי—רֶגֶל, I 25, 27. 42.

רִיפוֹת, II 17, 19.

רַע, of the heart = *be sad*, 11.

רָעָה, fig. for *rule*, 257.

רֹעֶה in *st. c.*, 317.

רֵעֵהוּ *his friends*, 225.

הרעים, רָעַם, 10.

שׂ = Aram. ס = شׂ, 237 *n*.

שׂ written for ס, 237, cf. 52 *n*. 1.

שָׂטָן, I 29, 4.

שְׂיָהוּ, 115.

שׁ = Aram. שׁ = س, 237 *n*.

שאל = *borrow*, הִשְׁאִיל = *lend*, 22.

שאל לפ' לשלום, 79.

שָׁבִין, 232.

שכב, sq. accus., II 13, 14.

נקרא שם פ' על—:שֵׁם, 294.

שמואל, etym. of, 16-19.

שָׁמֵט (II 6, 6), 267.

שְׁמָמָה (with *ṣērē*), 301.

שְׁנָתַיִם יָמִים, 301.

שֹׁאֵהוּ (for שֹׁאִיָּהוּ), 120.

שְׁפוֹת, II 17, 29.

שֹׁפֵט אָנִי, 43.

תֹּהוּ, 95.

תחתינו, idiom. = *where we are*, I 14, 9. II 2, 23. 7, 10.

תקופת הימים, 16.

תרומה, 236.

III. INDEX OF PLACES

Abel of Beth-Ma'achah, 344.
'Adullam, 178 ; cave of, prob. a textual error, *ib.*
Aijalon (Ayyalon), 115.
'Ain Jalud, 218.
Ammah, 244.
'Anāthoth, 369.
Aphek, 45 f., 218, XIX.
'Arāb, 371.
'Arābah, the, 189, 244 f.
Archite, the, 317.
'Aro'er (1) ('Ar'ārah), 226; (2), 373.
Ashdod, 50.
Asherite, 241.
'Ashkelon, 57.
'Athak, 227.
'Azēkah, 138.

Ba'al, Ba'alah, and Kiryath-Ba'al, old names of Kiryath-ye'arim, 265 f.
Ba'al-Hazor, 301.
Ba'al-Perazim, 263 f.
Bahurim, 248 f.
Bē'ērōth, 253, XX.
Be'ēr-sheba', 66.
Berites (?), the, 344 f.
Betah (? Tebah), 281.
Beth-aven, 99.
Beth-car, 65.
Bethel (1), 65, 79, 98 ; (2), 225.
Beth hā-'Arābah, 370.
Beth-horon, 102, 134.
Beth-pelet, 369.
Beth-rehob, 287.
Beth-shean, 231.
Beth-shemesh, 57.
Bezek, 86.
Bithron, the, 245.
Bor-'ashan, 226 f.

Carmel, 125, 195, cf. 226 (for רכל).

Dan-ja'an (corrupt), 375.
Desolation, the (הישימון), 189 f.

Eben-'ezer, 45, XIX.
'Ekron, 53.
Elah, vale of, 138.
'En-dor, 214.
'En-gedi, 191.
'En-rogel, 324.
Ephes-dammim, 138.

Ephraim (name of town), 301 f.
Eshtemoa', 226.

Far House, the, 313.

Ga'ash, 370.
Gai (rd. Gath), 147.
Gath, 57.
Gaza, 57.
Geba', 98, xcvi ; 265 (on II 5, 25).
Geshur (1), 211 ; (2), 246.
Gezer, 265, cf. 211.
Giah, 244.
Gibeah (הגבעה) = Gibeah of Benjamin
    = Gibeah of Saul, 69, xcvi.
Gibeah of God, 80, 82.
Gibeon, 242, 265, 351 f., xcvi n. 3.
Gilboa', 214.
Gilgal (1), 82 ; (2), 65 (I 7, 16), 70.
Giloh, 312.

Hachilah, 204.
Hamāth, 282.
Havilah, 123.
Hebron, 227.
Hēlām, 288.
Helkath haz-zurim, 242 f.
Hēreth, 179.
Horesh, 187.
Hormah, 226.

'Iyyun, 375.

Jabesh of Gilead, 85.
Jattir, 225 f., 372.
Ja'zer, 374.
Jezreel (in Judah), 204.
Jordan, the fords of, 316.
— the *Kikkar* of, 331.
Judah, the wilderness of, 186.

Kedesh, 374 (*bis*).
Ke'ilah, 183.
Kenites, the, 122.
Kiryath-ye'arim, 59.

Lo-debar, 286.

Ma'achah, 288 ; the Ma'achathite, 371.
Mahanaim, 240 f.
Ma'on, 189.
Michmas, 98 ; Pass of, 105, 106, XIX.

Millo, the, 261 f.
Miẓpah, 64.
Miẓpeh of Moab, 179.

' Naioth' (Qrê), 159.
Negeb, the, 212 f.; of Judah, 213, of the Yeraḥme'ēlite, 213, 229, of the Qenite, 213, of the Cherethite, 213, 223, of Caleb, 213, 223.
Neṭōphah, 370.
Nob, 172.

'Ophel, the, 259 f.
'Ophrah, 102.

Pir'athon, 370.

Rabbath-'Ammon, 287, 293 f. (the ' Water-city ').
Rachal (rd. Carmel), 226.
Rachel's grave, 78.
Ramah (Is. 10, 29. Jer. 31, 15), 78.
Ramah, Ramathaim, 3 f.
Ramathaim-Zophim (!), 1.
Ramath-Negeb, 225.
Rephaim,Vale of, 263.
Rogelim, 326.

Sha'alabbim, 370, cf. 70.
Sha'alim, 70.

Sha'araim (?), 147.
Shalisha, the land of, 70.
Shen (השׁן), 65; ? rd. Yeshanah, 65, XIX.
Shiloh, 5.
Shu'al, the land of, 102.
Shunem, 214.
Shur, 123.
Sirah (הסירה), 250.
' South,' the. *See* Negeb.

Teḳoa', 305, 369.
Tēlām, 122, 212.
Timnath-ḥéres (-sérah), 370.

Wilderness, the, of En-gedi, I 24, 2 ; of Gibeon (? Geba), II 2, 24 ; of Ma'on, I 23, 24. 25 ; of Paran (?), 25, 1 ; of Ziph, 23, 14. 15. 26, 2.

Yeraḥme'ēlites, 213.

Zebo'im, Ravine of the, 103.
Ẓēlā', 352 f.
Ẓelẓaḥ, 78.
Ẓiḳlag, 210.
Zion, position of, 258.
Ziph, 186 f.
Zobah, 281.
Ẓor'āh, 57.
Ẓuph, land of, 71, cf. 1.

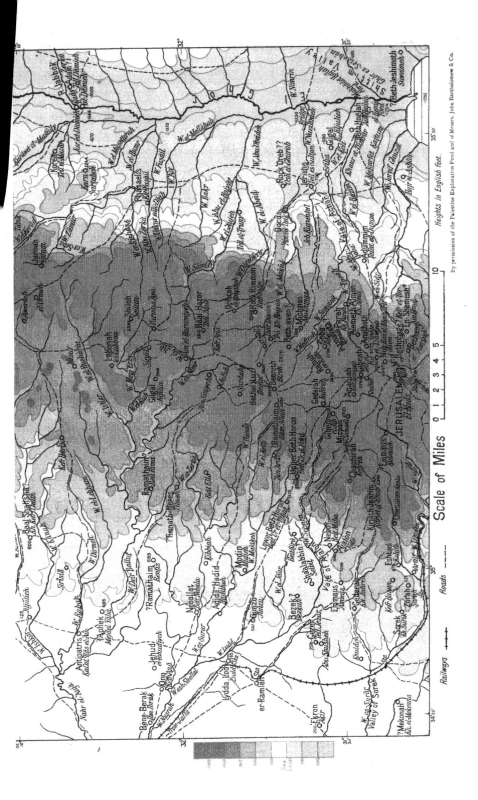

Scale of Miles

0 1 2 3 4 5   10

Heights in English Feet.

By permission of the Palestine Exploration Fund and of Messrs. John Bartholomew & Co.

Railways ▬▬▬▬▬   Roads ▬▬▬▬▬

JERUSALEM

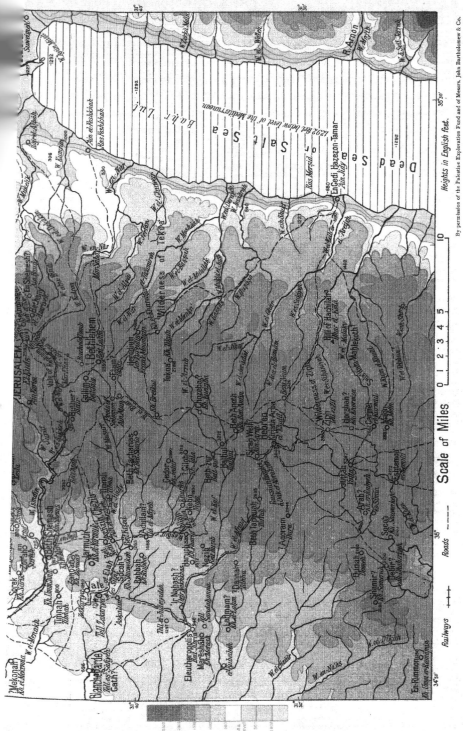

By permission of the Palestine Exploration Fund and of Messrs. John Bartholomew & Co.

Heights in English feet.

Scale of Miles

0 1 2 3 4 5 — 10

Railways ‖   Roads ---

279